LABOR
AND THE
LAW

LABOR

AND THE

LAW

BY CHARLES O. GREGORY
AND HAROLD A. KATZ

THIRD EDITION

W·W·NORTON & COMPANY

NEW YORK · LONDON

FOR

THE EDUCATION OF R. P. McK.

Copyright © 1979, 1961, 1958, 1949, 1946 by W. W. Norton & Company, Inc.
Published simultaneously in Canada by George J. McLeod Limited, Toronto.
Printed in the United States of America.

Library of Congress Cataloging in Publication Data
Gregory, Charles Oscar, 1902–
      Labor and the law.

      Includes index.
      1. Labor laws and legislation—United States.
I. Katz, Harold Ambrose, 1921–   joint author.
II. Title.
KF3369.G7   1979   344′.73′01   79–4291
ISBN 0-393-01208-5
ISBN 0-393-09995-4 pbk.

1 2 3 4 5 6 7 8 9 0

CONTENTS

5

CONTENTS

PREFACE TO THE THIRD EDITION

THE SECOND EDITION of this book came out over twenty years ago. Since then, profound and extensive developments have occurred in American labor law. These changes have been chiefly in federal legislation, court decisions, and administrative rulings. Shortly after *Labor and the Law* first appeared in 1946, Harold Katz, a student of mine who had previously worked for the NLRB, and I conceived the idea of bringing out a casebook on labor law to be used for teaching in law schools. This ambitious undertaking was completed and published in 1948 under our joint authorship.

I did a second edition of *Labor and the Law* with the valuable editorial advice of Dudley C. Lunt, who had also helped me whip the first edition into shape. It was published in 1958 and was followed shortly thereafter by another printing with the Landrum-Griffin supplement.

Labor and the Law finally went out of print because of the many new developments since 1961. Nevertheless, I was of the opinion that most of the book was and would remain contemporary, not only from the historical point of view, but also as an adequate treatment of still existing legislation and the impact of judicial and administrative output. And I continued to envision getting out a third edition in which the first thirteen or so chapters would stay virtually intact, with new chapters bringing the book up to date. Busy as Harold was, with his law practice in Chicago and increasingly responsible duties in the Illinois legislature, I persuaded him to undertake the task of filling in the gap from 1958 through 1978—a task in which I would help where I could.

Little did we realize what an undertaking this would be. It proved to be a tremendous job just isolating the labor board and court decisions—both federal and state—let alone statutory innovations including the new federal legislation concerning civil rights, old age, pensions, and safety and health. After many

11

months of hard work, several conferences and the exchange of innumerable letters, memos, and pages of manuscript (he in Chicago and I in New Hampshire), we at last had the final draft where we wanted it—ready to show to professional colleagues for their critical comments. Finally the completed manuscript was submitted in the fall of 1978, although with a book like this, there can be no finishing date. From day to day, new decisions and rulings of courts and boards keep popping up—literally to be tucked into galley proof at the last moment, well into 1979.

Labor and the Law, unlike our 1,324-page casebook of 1948, is not directed exclusively to law students. It is written also for the interested lay person who wants to know about labor law and legal institutions. For union and management officials engaged in labor relations work, it furnishes a panoramic view of our law as it affects their everyday dealings with each other.

In preparing this third edition, we are much indebted to Irving Friedman, Harold's law partner, for his penetrating, overall criticism and advice; and also to Estelle M. Wirpel for her many useful suggestions regarding the manuscript. We also acknowledge our gratitude to Lee Iverson, Jr., for his services as a legal assistant and for his suggestions concerning the sections on Title VII and public employees; to Martin H. Schneid for his critical reading of and comments on the chapters relating to the NLRA; to M. Jay Whitman and Stanley Eisenstein for suggestions in connection with the ERISA section; and to Alan M. Katz for his critical observations and suggestions regarding the section on discrimination based on handicap. We also want to acknowledge with thanks permission by Professor Archibald Cox and the *Harvard Law Review* to reprint a passage from his article, "Rights under a Labor Agreement," 69 *Harvard Law Review*, 601 (1956). We are also indebted to Barbara Lindeman Schlei and Paul Grossman for permission to reproduce material from their excellent text, *Employment Discrimination Law* (1976), and to their publisher, the Bureau of National Affairs.

JAFFREY, NEW HAMPSHIRE   CHARLES O. GREGORY
1979

CHAPTER I

EARLY ORGANIZATION AND CRIMINAL CONSPIRACY

Does this measure tend to make good workmen? No: it puts the botch incapable of doing justice to his work, on a level with the best tradesman. The master must give the same wages to each. Such a practice would take away all the excitement to excel in workmanship or industry. Consider the effect it would have upon the whole community. If the masters say they will not sell under certain prices, as the journeymen declare they will not work at certain wages, they, if persisted in, would put the whole body of the people into their power. Shoes and boots are articles of the first necessity. . . . If these evils were unprovided for by the law now existing, it would be necessary that laws should be made to restrain them.—Moses Levy, Recorder, charging the jury in *The Trial of the Journeymen Boot & Shoemakers of Philadelphia,* 1806.

THE ANCIENT struggle between capital and labor now travels under a new name—the conflict between management and organized unions. Laws governing this clash of interests are not the invention of modern times. Centuries ago in England, long before the industrial revolution, the relationship of master and servant was comprehensively defined by statute. The old craft guilds maintained strict controls over the duties of journeymen and apprentices, conceding them hardly any rights at all. Indeed, at times there were criminal statutes which placed ceilings on wages and occasionally on prices in general. And after a manpower shortage caused by the Black Death in the 1300's, it was a serious offense to entice away another's workman by offering him higher wages. These are early instances of the reflection in law of changes and developments on the labor front.

Not until after the industrial revolution did conditions arise that resulted in combinations of workingmen for the purpose of securing from their employers better conditions of work. By that time the centralization of production into the factory system had begun to herd wage earners into the towns and to reduce them to little more than one of the commodities essential to manufacture. These changes of condition incited them in desperation to collective demonstrations against their exploiters. Here was the beginning of modern unionism in England at a time when our country was still a group of colonies largely devoted to agriculture. And in those times began the body of law designed to control these revolutionary attempts at self-help and to keep the working class in its ordained place.

Economists of those times accepted the prevailing philosophy of the owners of enterprise. In their writings they made it clear that the best of all possible worlds was one in which these owners were left free to pay for wages and materials as little as they had to through direct dealings with the individuals concerned. These notions found ready supporters in the judges, who reflected them in their decisions that combinations of labor to secure higher wages were common crimes. And Parliament itself insured proper respect for this judicial development in suppressive statutes aimed at unionism.

But even while courts in this country were entrenching these judicial doctrines of England in our own states, labor organizations in England had begun their fight before Parliament to free unionism from the stigma of criminality. This fight was virtually won in 1875, although the substance of the victory was not assured until the Trades Disputes Act of 1906 was adopted. In the meantime American courts had embraced the English notion that unions were criminal and had already virtually discarded it by the middle of the nineteenth century. But this did not mean that unions in this country were given the same economic freedom that English unions had ultimately secured by political action. Far from it. For during the middle of the nineteenth century they were hemmed in by state statutes according them a narrow field of activity. Their leaders were constantly subjected to civil actions for damages. And during the latter part of that century our courts developed against unionism a control far more effective than any criminal device—the labor injunction.

The period from around 1890 to 1932 was characterized by the inception and growth of modern labor unions as well as by the last-ditch struggle through litigation in our courts to suppress union activities and to keep them from expanding. At the same time the country was undergoing what might be called a twentieth century industrial revolution—the inception and growth of the assembly line in mass production. During this period the craft unions were too busy to realize the implications of this important social development. Their chief preoccupation at this time was the extension of their organizations. Their efforts in this direction were largely aimed at getting rid of the labor injunction and in discouraging the use of the Sherman Antitrust Act against them in the federal arena. As industry grew into larger and larger units of a national character, most of the activities of unions began to take on a nationwide significance. Although early union attempts to abolish the labor injunction failed miserably, their efforts finally achieved the effective Norris-LaGuardia Anti-injunction Act in 1932.

This statute furnishes a fitting threshold to the New Deal period. The next few years saw legislation undreamed of a decade or two earlier. The National Labor Relations Act in 1935 guaranteed independent organization to employees in all large industries. The Fair Labor Standards Act of 1938 established a forty-hour week and minimum wages. Both of these measures were upheld by the Supreme Court in the teeth of long-established constitutional doctrine to the contrary. Social security legislation was adopted by Congress to insure workers against the ravages of unemployment and to assure them of a financially independent old age. And right in the midst of all this the CIO sprang into being with a program for the unionization of millions of workers theretofore not practicably organizable under the laws of earlier decades.

Then came World War II with its emergency legislation and administrative facilities for promoting labor relations and collective bargaining. The whole world then witnessed the most remarkable feats of production ever staged—all made possible by the extraordinary co-operation of management and labor during these years and by their determination to see the job through to the end together. A program of government-conducted collective bargaining was carried on by the War Labor Board in such a way that the wheels of industry kept at a tremendously high level of production with relatively little inflation ensuing. But then came the peace among nations and quick upon its heels a renewal of the struggle between our industrial Titans — organized management and organized labor. What has transpired since then is a matter of common knowledge.

Reflection over the span of years indicates pointedly how the developments in labor law, so slow in their early stages, have accelerated their pace. Mass production and the assembly line were making their imprint on the total industrial scene. These new techniques, conceived by the brilliant ingenuity of our industrialists, inevitably brought to the fore the organizational aptitude of our most able statesmen in the field of labor —and the great industrial unions sprang into being. This development, in turn, led to some of the violent clashes between union philosophies—the conflict between craft and industrial unions exemplified in some of our bitter interunion disputes. And all of these phenomena cried out for the orderly guidance of the law.

These changes, which are still going on so fast, present a challenge to American political genius. Fortunately the American people are endowed with a native political ability to find in the long run the answers to most of their troubles. And they are able to achieve settlements of most of their internal disputes by peaceful solutions. Never have they been faced with a greater need to apply this knack than they are in these days. They have in their midst organized agencies for the production of vast wealth—management and labor. But they have come to a time when the traditional laws of the market place no longer provide the final answer as to how this abundance should be divided. Now they must concentrate their political genius on the most effective schemes for solving this pressing internal problem—how to perfect the rules whereby through peaceful means the pie may be fairly divided to the real satisfaction of all at the table.

THE COMMON LAW DEVELOPMENT IN ENGLAND

Before we begin, it is necessary to understand the difference between statutes and the common law. The bulk of our law and of England's law has in the past been what is known as common law. This is the law which consists of the accumulated decisions of courts, developed by the judiciary without the aid of legislatures. The laws specifically enacted by legislatures are called statutes. They usually denote departures from, or particular developments of, certain phases of our customary or common law. Statutes usually represent changes in our law resulting from political pressures which are articulated from the people through their duly elected representatives in the legislatures. Our courts, who are the trustees of our common law, profess not to make or change the law but only to interpret and apply it as they find it to be. This they do, or profess to do, whether the law they interpret and apply be statute or common law.

In the process of applying the common law, they have undertaken during the centuries to set it forth in general and sometimes rather vague principles which, in themselves, have come to be called law. Naturally, when a bench of judges are confronted with an issue for which there is no exact precedent and which is not covered by a statute, they are compelled by tradition either to dismiss the case altogether or to deal with it on its merits in accordance with the principles of the common law. If they do the latter, the law grows and the principles themselves are modified and enriched. Thus our courts, who claim that they do not make law but only interpret it, are nevertheless able to keep abreast of the times and to dispose on its merits of almost any litigated dispute which may be presented to them.

An analysis of labor problems and of labor law may be made in terms of the institution of property. Certainly, the ownership and control of property has traditionally implied economic and political power over others. The political, constitutional, and legal departments of our social community have been devoted chiefly to insuring the integrity of property and to maintaining the complete freedom of its use. In so far as government or any substantial part of the community has attempted to modify this institution of property, it has always failed unless it could demonstrate clearly some supervening social need of recognized great importance or could overcome determined opposition through great political superiority. This leaves out of account, naturally, the recourse to violent organized revolution—a technique for the eradication of established social institutions, well known in history but fortunately still unknown for that purpose in our own country.

The traditional emphasis laid on the importance of property and its incidents in England and the United States has always in the past seemed to overshadow assertions of purely personal rights dissociated from property. This is not intended to imply that these two countries have not always cherished high ideals of personal liberty. Far from it. Personal freedom of contract has traditionally been maintained with remarkable vigor. But the practical application of this political ideal has sometimes seemed to compromise it. Thus, when English wage earners of the eighteenth century attempted through combination to effect improvements in their immediate employment conditions by direct economic action, the courts regarded them as criminals and threw their leaders in jail. Such economic action was the concerted refusal to work unless certain concessions were made—in other words, the strike. And this device consisted merely of the concerted exercise of their individual freedom of contract by all the participants in the strike acting together.

English courts were not originally acting under statutory authority when they adopted this stern position. And since they felt impelled by tradition to rest their official disapproval of strikes on some formal legal grounds, they decided to dress it up for public consumption in what they called the doctrine of criminal conspiracy. A few scholars have professed to be greatly puzzled on logical grounds concerning the inception and nature of this doctrine. They point out that there was nothing unlawful in combination itself, nothing unlawful in an individual's refusal to work, and nothing unlawful in a workingman's desire to obtain better standards of employment. How then, they asked, could the courts have put these elements together to constitute a crime, when each of the component parts was perfectly lawful according to the common law as they understood it?

The answer to this question seems fairly simple. English judges believed that the use of the economic power made possible by combination and the concerted action of working people was bad for the economy of England. Since individual refusals of wage earners to work under conditions not acceptable to them had no discernible effect on the national economy, the vice was combination and concerted action. Hence the judges found it possible to maintain the principle of freedom of contract—at least for individuals—and at the same time to declare unlawful the united efforts of workers to change the conditions under which they worked.

This result seems to have rested on the premise that the objectives of organized workers were unlawful because they interfered with the "natural" operations of basic principles of economics—the sanctions of the market. English judges took it for granted that the labor of an individual is worth only what it commands in the market. Any concerted attempts of workers to increase its value by demanding higher wages they regarded as arbitrary invasions of the employers' rights. They thought employers were compelled to resist such attempts even though the resulting strikes disrupted industry and trade. For if an employer bought peace with his organized workers by granting their demands, his competitive position in relation to other employers was jeopardized. And if all English employers were eventually compelled by strikes to concede better wages and working conditions, the consequent general rise in production costs would impair England's trade in world markets. How could English merchants hope to compete with Continental goods produced in countries officially fostering the doctrine of the utility of poverty—that workers are most productive and will work best under the constant incentive of hunger and the direst need?

These were the times when Malthus was expounding his theory that if the working people in an industrial country were allowed more than the barest means of subsistence, they would merely increase and thus provide more mouths to feed at the same marginal standard of living. And about then economists were developing the wage fund theory. This was the belief that in any national community there was available in any one year a fixed fund for wages, which ought to be distributed equitably among the working population. The first of these theories made any attempt to improve the conditions of labor seem hopeless. The second made any organized attempt by some workers to wrest from the wage fund more than their proper share seem wicked and malicious. These were the notions that led Carlyle to refer contemptuously to economics as "the dismal science."

It seems most reasonable to suppose that English judges during the eighteenth century cherished all these beliefs. How, then, could they have failed to regard the disruptive undertakings of labor combinations as anything but pernicious? And knowing, as they did, that combination and concerted action alone made possible the effectiveness of organized labor's demands, no wonder they picked upon that factor as the element of illegality involved and labeled the whole business criminal conspiracy. The idea of conspiracy as a category of illegality in other contexts was not new.

Parliament had by statute previously declared certain undertakings of business enterprisers to be unlawful conspiracies, such as combinations to buy up and hold for artificially high prices staple commodities like grain and hops. These statutes acknowledged the vice inherent in a combination of economic power sufficiently strong to do what few, if any, individual merchants could have done. And even if Parliament had not yet acted against combinations of workers, the courts found the analogies presented in these statutes aimed at merchants' combinations too apt not to use against them.

English judges of these times must seldom have been troubled by the reflection that they might be using the doctrine of criminal conspiracy to deny working people the enjoyment of their personal civil rights to combine and jointly to exercise their liberties of contract. After all, rights of any kind are relative matters. The judges were also aware that the owners and operators of industry had what might be called their personal civil rights in the ownership and administration of property. As long as the development and operation of industry was left in private hands, then it was incumbent upon government to see that industrial enterprisers remained free to prosecute their business unhampered by concerted oppression from their laborers. Industrial operators and investors of capital were providing the means of support to the nation's working class.

The fact that this new factory system of production had originally divorced wage earners from their traditional sources of livelihood, making them dependent on the system itself, hardly mattered any more. Industry must be fostered and encouraged, for it was rapidly becoming the very life blood of the nation, without which England could hardly hold her place in the world. Hence, if there was any choice to make between protecting the civil rights of the owners and operators of industry, on the one hand, and those of wage earners on the other, the courts could easily be counted on to uphold the former as against the latter. In doing so they would be supporting the interests of the dominant political class in England

and, to their way of thinking, no doubt, would be taking the obvious and only sensible course open to them. For in maintaining the law in this fashion, they were fulfilling their obligations to the group that placed them on the bench and were betraying no political obligation of any sort to the working class who did not yet enjoy the privilege of voting.

THE FIRST AMERICAN CASES

Although Parliament did eventually enact several statutes forbidding labor combinations to exercise direct economic pressure against employers, English courts had achieved this same position independently of Parliament as a matter of common law. This conclusion was important in the United States during the early nineteenth century, since it largely governed the disposition of what has been called America's first labor case. That case appears to have set the tone for the early judicial treatment of organized labor in this country.

This was the famous *Philadelphia Cordwainers'* case decided in 1806. Cordwainer is an ancient term meaning a shoemaker working particularly in cordovan leather. The journeymen cordwainers, or employees, were united in a club. They met together and presented their employers, the master cordwainers, with a schedule of sums which they claimed should be paid to them for their production of fancy tops, back straps, long boots, cossacks, and bootees—the proposed increases ranging from 25 to 75 cents the pair. The journeymen demanded adoption of this schedule—or else. The reaction of the master cordwainers was immediate. This demand was most embarrassing to them. They were trying to lower the prices of their shoes in order to compete with rival shoemakers in other cities for the expanding markets in the recently settled territories in the South and West. Their reaction took the form of an appeal to the public prosecutor.

The upshot was that the grand jury found a true bill charging the journeymen cordwainers with "contriving, and intending unjustly and oppressively, to increase and augment the prices and rates usually paid and allowed to them and other artificers" for their labor, and with preventing, "by threats, menaces, and other unlawful means," other journeymen from working at the occupation of cordwainer for wages below a fixed schedule of rates. Furthermore, they were accused of "unjustly and corruptly" conspiring not to work for a master who employed any cordwainer breaking any of their society's rules and bylaws and of preventing any other workmen and journeymen from working for such master. This indictment, of course, was a list of the charges as they were viewed by the prosecutor; but it really meant only that the workers organized, set wage rates agreeable to themselves, concertedly refused to work for less, and brought social and economic pressure on both their fellow workers and masters who ignored their schedule of rates.

At the trial of this case counsel for the defendants engaged in some wonderful flights of oratory in an endeavor to discredit the common-law doctrine of criminal conspiracy, which the prosecution insisted had been adopted intact in this country along with the rest of the English common law. He attempted to show "that the spirit of the revolution and the principle of the common law, are opposite in this case," and "that the common law, if applied in this case, would operate an attack upon the rights of man." In effect, he asked, why did we fight the revolutionary war for liberty, only to find that we are not free to combine and concertedly to refrain from work if we see fit—and that because of English law against which we had successfully conducted a revolution a few years ago?

This argument raised a square enough issue before the judge, Recorder Levy. He reflected the sentiments of property owners and businessmen of Philadelphia, the only people who could vote in the days before popular franchise was adopted. Thus he found that the views prevailing among the substantial citizens of Philadelphia were admirably reflected in the common-law doctrine of criminal conspiracy. To support his belief, he recited the principles of supply and demand economics, showing how prices and wages are regulated in the natural course of things. What the defendants were doing, he declared, was "artificial regulation . . . governed by no standard, controuled by no impartial person, but dependent on the will of the few who are interested . . . an unnatural, artificial means of raising the price of work beyond its standard, and taking an undue advantage of the public."

He said that the rule of law is not bottomed upon such principles. If it were, the commerce of the city would be ruined. He went on, "Is there any man who can calculate (if this is tolerated) at what price he may safely contract to deliver articles, for which he may receive orders, if he is to be regulated by the journeymen in an arbitrary jump from one price to another?" Concerning the workers who did not wish to join the combination or tie themselves to its fixed wage schedule, he observed that "a term of reproach is fixed upon them." The members would not work with them, and refused to board or lodge with them. The result was that everyone was compelled to join the society.

The recorder then observed that most of the answers are found in the volumes of the common law, the rules of which are the result of the wisdom of ages. As he put it, the common law says what one man may do without offense, many combined may not do with impunity.

Then he went on: "A combination of workmen to raise their wages may be considered in a two-fold point of view: one is to benefit themselves . . . the other is to injure those who do not join their society. The rule of law condemns both. If the rule be clear, we are bound to conform to it even though we do not comprehend the principle upon which it is founded. . . . It is enough, that it is the will of the majority. It is law because it is their will—if it is law, there may be good reasons for it though we cannot find them out. But the rule in this case is pregnant with sound sense and all the authorities are clear upon the subject."

The key to the practical importance of this case was revealed in the recorder's opinion. Shoe manufacturing in Philadelphia was changing from a "bespoke," or personal order, to a wholesale contract basis. With the advancing settlement of the South and West and the development of transportation facilities to these far points, shoe manufacturers on the eastern seaboard were undertaking to supply large orders of ready-made shoes to merchants in those regions. Since competition among them was already keen, and since it centered around the price contract for large future deliveries of shoes, any intervening rise of production costs in any particular locality participating in this venture might endanger the prosperity of the whole community. At any rate this is what Recorder Levy and his business friends believed.

The labor combinations were trying to force this increase of production costs in the shape of higher wage rates. Hence they were threatening with injury the welfare of the entire community. It seemed irrelevant that they were trying to defend themselves against the effects of advancing commercialism which destroyed all incentive of individual workmen to excel, in the interests of more and more quantity production at an ever decreasing price per unit. They were throwing a monkey wrench into the system and were hurting everyone, including themselves. Hence, as the recorder observed, "If these evils were unprovided for by the law now existing, it would be necessary that laws should be made to restrain them."

Within the next thirty years there followed a series of similar cases throughout the East, reflecting these sentiments. In some of them courts conceded the right to strike for higher wages but condemned strikes to compel the discharge of workmen who would not join the unions as arbitrary means "which went to deprive their fellow citizens of rights as precious as any they contended for." Shortly after that Chief Justice Gibson spoke forth in the Pennsylvania case, *Commonwealth v. Carlisle*, decided in 1821, which is chiefly significant because of what he said about combination among businessmen. Several shoe man-

ufacturers were prosecuted for using the united front technique
to depress wages. Their defense, which the court thought good,
was that they were trying to resist the concerted attempts of
their employees artificially to raise wages above their true
market worth and to decrease high rates already secured by
strikes. The court declared that a combination of employers to
lower wages, aside from such a defense, would amount to criminal conspiracy as would "a confederacy among the bakers to
extort an exorbitant price for bread, which everyone will
acknowledge to be indictable."

This was apparent, for "The labouring classes purchase their
bread with their labour, or, what is the same thing, they give
their labour for the money with which they purchase bread,
and it is evident the more labour is depreciated, the more of it
will be required to purchase any given quantity of bread."
But all combination was not unlawful, the court remarked.
"The combination of capital for purposes of commerce, or to
carry on any other branch of industry, although it may in its
consequences indirectly operate on third persons, is unaffected
by this consideration, because it is a common means in the
ordinary course of human affairs, which stimulates to competition and enables men to engage in undertakings too
weighty for an individual." In this modest statement the court
forecast the trend which culminated in our mighty corporate
enterprises, the size and economic strength of which have
given rise to most of our modern labor problems.

In 1836 the New York Supreme Court, deciding *People v.
Fisher,* read into an exceedingly vague statute a legal bar
against labor activity comparable to that of common-law conspiracy. The legislature had enacted that "If two or more persons shall conspire . . . to commit any act injurious to the
public health, to public morals, or to trade or commerce; or
for the perversion or obstruction of justice or the due administration of the laws—they shall be deemed guilty of a misdemeanor." A group of journeymen shoemakers, organized in
a club, were indicted under this statute for striking to procure

the discharge of a workman who accepted wages lower than the minimum approved by them. If they were guilty at all under this law, it was for a conspiracy to commit an act injurious to trade or commerce.

A provision of such generality was not much of a guide. But the court readily accepted the responsibility of using it to convict the defendants. It saw the issue as one of a conspiracy to raise wages. Artificially high wages meant correspondingly higher prices for boots, which prevented local manufacturers from selling as cheaply as their competitors elsewhere. Furthermore, the community was deprived of the services of the man whose discharge was effected by the union. Such results were, in the court's opinion, clearly injurious to trade and commerce, and their causes should be punished under the statute.

These and numerous other criminal convictions of workers for taking advantage of what they regarded as their ordinary civil privilege to exercise their right to work or not work, under such terms as they saw fit, bred ill-feeling throughout the East. Mobs of laborers held mock trials of judges and hung them in effigy to show their resentment at being treated as common criminals for having done what they believed they had a perfect right to do. Juries were refusing to convict in some of these prosecutions, in spite of clearly proved cases of criminal conspiracy under the prevailing law. Even the press attacked judicial statements that the unions were of foreign origin or were mainly upheld by foreigners. These were implications that were patently false. News of these events traveled fast. The owners of the newly established textile and shoe factories in Massachusetts were as much concerned over the judicial treatment of organized labor as were the unions themselves.

In the case of *Commonwealth v. Hunt* one of their lower courts had convicted seven members of The Boston Journeymen Bootmakers' Society for organizing a strike against an employer who had hired and retained one Jeremiah Horne, a journeyman, who was not a member of the society. The indictment had charged them with having unlawfully, perniciously, deceitfully, unjustly and corruptly conspired not to work for any master who employed any workman not a member of their union, after he was notified to discharge such workman; with having compelled by these means at least one master named Isaac B. Wait to discharge Horne; and with the "wicked and unlawful intent to impoverish" and to keep him from pursuing his trade. The trial judge had instructed the jury that the indictment set forth a course of conduct amounting to criminal conspiracy. This meant that if such acts were proven at the trial, a verdict of guilty should follow.

The convicted shoe workers appealed to the highest court of the state on the ground that the indictment had not charged a crime. Its decision came down in 1842, Chief Justice Shaw writing the opinion for the court. He was no lover of unions and probably believed them to be thoroughly vicious. In other connections he showed himself unsympathetic to wage earners by preventing them from recovering damages against their employers for personal injuries due to the defective conditions of premises and appliances or because of the carelessness of fellow employees. This had the effect of lessening the overhead risks of infant industry at the expense of workers who could ill afford to bear them.

Nevertheless, he realized from reading the newspapers that Massachusetts workers would react violently if courts persisted in calling them criminals for trying to advance their interests by their refusal to work. He knew that the fortunes of many a future old Boston family were tied up in the newly built mills and that a wave of strikes, on the heels of the recent depression, could easily finish them off. Such a disaster, in turn, might have political repercussions fatal to the proposed tariff believed necessary for the protection of incipient industry. Something simply had to be done to discourage the indiscriminate use of the doctrine of criminal conspiracy against the workers!

Shaw rose to the occasion in an opinion which was a masterpiece of tact and technicality. He disregarded the adverbs in the indictment as mere recital—wishful thinking by the prosecuting attorney. All the indictment really charged, he said, was the intention of the society to induce all those engaged in the same occupation to become members of it. This was a not unlawful objective designed for the purpose of securing power. Such power, he said, might be used for useful and honorable purposes as well as for dangerous and pernicious ones. If the latter were the real ends in view, and were susceptible of proof, they should have been specially charged. For all the court could tell from the indictment, the purposes of the society might be laudable, such as discouragement of the use of ardent spirits. "Such an association might be used to afford each other assistance in times of poverty, sickness and distress; or to raise their intellectual, moral and social condition; or to make improvement in their art; or for other proper purposes." If this were so, the indictment could not support a conviction. And the court refused to assume that the workers' objectives were bad.

Everyone, including the court, knew what the union's purposes really were, even if they had not been set forth in the indictment. Hence this decision issued by perhaps the most able state judge of his time gave the doctrine of criminal conspiracy a considerable setback. Shaw had not abolished the doctrine of criminal conspiracy as some wishful thinkers think he did. But by so obviously side-stepping the real issue in the case as a matter of expedience, he discouraged the use of this doctrine for many years. And, as Dean Landis of Harvard Law School, a prominent writer in this field, has remarked about Shaw's opinion . . . "he foreshadows clearly the doctrine of a later day that the legality of a strike is to be made to depend upon the end sought to be attained."

Common-law criminal conspiracy has never again played a prominent part in the control of labor unions by American courts, although it was used occasionally after the Civil War to break up strikes. Parliament by statute formally discarded this doctrine for all time in 1875, after English labor unions had achieved substantial political power. But in America it just faded away, perhaps chiefly because the courts developed a much more effective means of control in the injunction. It had served as a formal vehicle—a legal abracadabra, if you please—in the name of which English and American judges had made labor unionists conform to the principles of classical economics.

Like most legal principles, this doctrine was an arbitrary statement of a result, and depended for its existence on the economic views of the judges using it. Indeed, it is clear in retrospect that these economic views were really the law, while the doctrine of criminal conspiracy was merely the form in which it was presented for public consumption. The fact that it was relished neither in England nor this country may partially explain why it was supplanted by other doctrines. But acknowledgment of this fact does not tell why these new doctrines reflected the same economic views adapted to conditions in a somewhat changed world. That, however, is a matter which must be told. For without it there will be lacking the very basis on which rests an understanding of modern common law concerning the activities of organized labor.

CHAPTER II

FREE ENTERPRISE IN ENGLAND—THE DOUBLE STANDARD

One of the eternal conflicts out of which life is made up is that between the effort of every man to get the most he can for his services, and that of society, disguised under the name of capital, to get his services for the least possible return. Combination on the one side is patent and powerful. Combination on the other is the necessary and desirable counterpart, if the battle is to be carried on in a fair and equal way.—Holmes, J., dissenting in *Vegelahn v. Guntner*, 1896.

DURING the last third of the nineteenth century the courts in both England and this country evolved general principles to govern suits brought against those whose economic activities caused harm to others. The most conspicuous approach to a statement of general rules was made in what has come to be known as the Trilogy of the House of Lords. This Trilogy comprised three cases involving the activities of combinations, one of business and two of labor. These cases deserve careful consideration here, not only because they influenced the law of this country but also because they reveal much judicial double talk behind some of the law.

THE HOUSE OF LORDS TRILOGY—THE COMPANY CASE

In *Mogul Steamship Company v. McGregor, Gow and Company*, decided in 1892, a new transport line sued a combination of shipping lines which had secured control over the carriage of goods between England and the Far East. This combine served all ports whereas the newcomer called at but a few. At the same time most shippers of consequence had interests in all ports, with access to both the combine's and the new company's facilities. The combination had put the screws on this new company in two ways. First, it offered kickbacks to all shippers who sent goods exclusively in its ships. In addition to this bait, it had a club. It refused to accept goods from anyone out there who patronized the new company. Under this economic pressure the shippers in the Far East were forced to the use of the combination's vessels. As a result the new company went bankrupt. It sued the combine for damages and sought an injunction against future conduct of the same sort. Its case rested on the tort theories of intentional commission of harm without justification and of civil conspiracy.

For the benefit of readers who may be unfamiliar with legal terms, a tort is merely a civil wrong. One who has sustained damage as a consequence of a tort may ordinarily secure compensation therefor against the aggressor. A maxim in the law of torts says that intentionally inflicted harm is actionable, although it goes on to state that this is not necessarily so if the infliction of harm is justifiable under the circumstances presented. The complaining company in this case showed that the damage in question had been deliberately inflicted on it by the combination and argued that it was therefore actionable.

Conceding that the combination had intentionally ruined the new company, the court nevertheless thought the other companies not liable for the damage because there was justification for its infliction. Here was a conflict between two equally protected rights—that of plaintiff to protection in the legitimate exercise of trade and that of defendants to carry on business as they see fit, as long as they observe the law. The combination of defendants here, it said, "have done nothing more against the plaintiffs than pursue to the bitter end a war of competition waged in the interest of their own trade." And when the plaintiff company claimed that the ill-will of the defendant companies rebutted just cause and excuse, the court replied: "So to hold would be to convert into an illegal motive the instinct of self-advancement and self-protection."

The court dismissed that part of the plaintiff's action based on the theory of civil conspiracy because there was no proof of "the intentional doing of some act to the detriment of the plaintiff's business without just cause or excuse." Combination alone cannot imply illegality, it said. Suppose one capitalist had bought up all of the companies in the combination? Or suppose that they all belonged to one joint stock company? Such situations, the court said, would imply unity and not combination. And it would be an odd principle of law that would penalize the defendants in this case, just because of their combination with each other, but which would tolerate the same effects by an identical aggregation of economic power when it was all owned and controlled by a single person or a single joint stock company. Presumably the court did not choose to regard either of these latter "units" as the combinations of capital, managerial skill, and administrative capacity which they would have been, in spite of unitary ownership.

"The truth is," the court remarked, "that the combination of capital for purposes of trade and competition is a very different thing from such a combination of several persons against one, with a view to harm him, as falls under the head of an indictable conspiracy. There is no just cause or excuse in the latter class of cases. There is such a just cause or excuse in the former." Only legislation—some sort of antimonopoly act—could make unlawful the conduct of the combination in this case. Until such a statute were passed, the court could show its disapproval of the combination's potentiality for harm only by refusing to lend its aid to the combination or to any of its members in suits arising among them over matters of internal interest.

This decision of the House of Lords was remarkably important because it established so clearly the immunity with which a combination might impose very serious harm on another through the exertion of economic pressure, as long as it was done for self-advancement and in the pursuit of gain. Here the defendants, pooling their economic strength in a combination, had exercised ruthless compulsion on the plaintiff company, deliberately causing it great harm. But they had done this only by concertedly refusing to deal with shippers who, in turn, dealt in any way with the plaintiff. Such refusal to deal, except upon terms agreeable to the members of the combination, did not involve conduct in itself unlawful, such as beating with a club, or fraudulent misrepresentation or libel or the types of conduct employed by gangsters in "shaking down" a victim. Refusal to deal with another was not, in itself, a civil wrong, whether indulged in by an individual or by a group. It was, rather, a civil right, the exercise of which the courts confessed complete inability to control.

By this technique the combined defendants had compelled the shippers to become the unwilling instruments in bringing harmful pressure on the plaintiff. This was, in effect, a secondary boycott—a term frequently encountered in labor law. It implies the refusal by one party to deal with another unless such other will, in turn, refuse to deal with a third—the real object of the first party's animus. In telling the shippers that the combination would have all of their trade, or none, it let them know that it would not deal with them at all unless they, in turn, refused to deal with the plaintiff. It was this last effect which the combination sought—the bringing of harmful economic pressure on the plaintiff company by the shippers. For if this new enterprise could get no customers among the shippers, it would fold up. The end result was advantageous to members of the combination, since they retained a complete monopoly over the Far East to England transportation business, free from outside competition. This was a curious consequence of a legal principle based on the notion that the otherwise wrongful deliberate imposition of harm on another is privileged as competition itself.

THE FIRST LABOR UNION CASE

Labor unions in England thought the *Mogul* case was wonderful. Even though it concerned the activities of a business group, it stood for the principle that any combination, intent on promoting the interests of its members, was free to do so by using even ruthless economic coercion against others as long as it did not engage in conduct contrary to any established category of tort or crime. Yet in the second of the great Trilogy cases, *Allen v. Flood,* the application of this broad principle to the activities of labor groups was vigorously opposed.

It seems that in 1894 a ship-repair company employed 40 boilermakers who belonged to a union of that name. These men objected when the company employed two shipwrights, who belonged to a different union, and threatened to strike unless the company discharged them. Allen, the business representative of the boilermakers' union, came down from London and put the matter up to the company. Since it did not want a strike on its hands, the company fired the two shipwrights, Flood and Taylor. This it had a legal privilege to do, as they were only employees at will and not hired under contract. The fired shipwrights thereupon sued Allen for the damage they suffered when they lost their jobs as a consequence of Allen's having compelled the company to exercise its privilege of discharge.

At the trial of this case, the judge left it to the jury whether Allen could be charged with malice, whatever that might mean. The jury went ahead and found that Allen had "maliciously induced" the employer to discharge the shipwrights and not to rehire them. Judgment against Allen for 40 pounds was affirmed by the Court of Appeal. He then appealed to the House of Lords, where his case was argued four days in December, 1895 and, in the additional presence of several lower judges whose advice was being sought, for six days in March, 1897. Plainly the last guess was going to be no snap judgment, however certain the courts below had been that the activities of the union were unlawful.

In June, 1897, these invited lesser judges dragged out their opinions for the edification of the law lords through 56 dreary pages of small print, six of them recommending affirmance and two urging reversal for the defendant. At the conclusion of these opinions there appears in the report the following understatement: "The House took time for consideration." And finally, in December, 1897, the law lords screwed up their courage and, in 114 pages of opinions, set forth their vote of six to three for reversal. Of 21 judges voting on this case, 13 believed that Allen had committed a wrong. But the nine law lords had the last say, and a majority of them apparently felt that sound policy required approval of what he had done for the union in this case.

A glance at two of the final set of opinions should give some idea of how law comes into being and of how slender are the threads with which legal theories are spun. Lord Chancellor Halsbury, the equivalent of chief justice, headed up the dissent in this case. He made it plain that all men have the right to get work and pursue their calling without molestation from others, basing this on "that freedom from restraint, that liberty of action . . . found running through the principles of our law." He said that this was like the wild duck case in which English judges long ago held that a man behaved unlawfully when he deliberately scared away wild fowl from his neighbor's decoys by firing a gun into the air over his own land. One would have to be at least a lord chancellor to see the connection between these two cases. And he declared that the jury's finding of malice clearly negatived any just cause and excuse Allen might offer as a defense against a charge of intentionally caused harm.

The theory of Halsbury's dissent is not apparent from his opinion. He could hardly have been willing to permit a common jury's finding of malice to foreclose consideration by the law lords of whether or not the labor union's objectives in this case furnished just cause and excuse for the harm which occurred. If this factor was a matter for legitimate consideration in the case at all, it was a most fundamental issue for the court. And Halsbury must have known that the trial judge had no business submitting it to the jury. What had happened was perfectly clear from the evidence. It was apparent that Allen had not sought the discharge of the shipwrights either out of a devilish desire to cause them harm or just to have some fun—the presumable components of malice. He did it pursuant to the policy of the union which was to secure to union members as much of the available work, in terms of jobs, as possible. And even if the union's policy to be served had been the broader one of subjecting all employees to union membership, permitting new workers to remain on the job as long as they joined the union, in order to insure the observance of union standards throughout the plant, Halsbury still could not conscientiously have agreed with a verdict of malice. For the union would be serving some economic end of its own conception under any interpretation of the evidence.

Lord Herschell wrote the leading majority opinion. In it, he inveighed against the idea that while inducing breach of the employment relation might not be unlawful, maliciously doing so would be unlawful. He also emphasized the folly of leaving the issue of malice to a jury under the circumstances of this case. He deplored the introduction of motive as the issue upon which legality depended. Even if the defendant's motive was the pursuit of his own interest, and malice were made to depend on the means employed in accordance with the test of what an honest and fair-minded man would do, he still did not like it. "The truth is," he said, "this suggested test makes men's responsibility for their actions depend on the fluctuating opinions of the tribunal before whom the case may chance to come as to what a right-minded man ought or ought not to do in pursuing his own interests." He just could not see why motive should ever render unlawful a course of conduct, such as a refusal to work for or deal with another, which, aside from motive, does not fall within a recognized category of illegality like beating with a club or libel and slander. And he believed his position to be perfectly consistent with what the House of Lords had maintained in the ship combination decision—the *Mogul* case.

He remarked that union men "act in the interest of their class. . . . If they do not resort to unlawful acts they are entitled to further their interests in the manner which seems to them best, and most likely to be effectual." If the men believed it unfair for others to be given work that they regarded as rightly theirs, then regardless of how the law lords personally felt, they were within their rights in taking any steps not unlawful to keep such work for themselves. A man's right not to work or to determine when or where or with whom he will work "is in law a right of precisely the same nature, and entitled to just the same protection as a man's right to trade or work. They are but examples of that wider right of which I have already spoken. That wider right embraces also the right of free speech." A man may say what he pleases, as long as he does not slander or deceive or commit any of the conventional wrongs articulated through speech. Unless he thus abuses his right, "why is he to be called upon to excuse or justify himself because his words may interfere with someone else in his calling?"

Although he did not believe that Allen, the boilermakers' business agent, had to show justification for what he did, and thought that competition was neither "regarded with special favour by the law" nor "should be so regarded," Herschell nevertheless declared that if competition could be established as a special category of defense, then the present case fell within it. The object of the defendant and the workmen he represented was to assist themselves in their competition with the shipwrights. According to him a man may take steps to compete most advantageously in the use of his labor and to shut out what he regards as undesirable competition just as much as if he were conducting the business of ocean transport, like the combination in the *Mogul* case.

In concluding his 28 page opinion, Lord Herschell observed with some asperity that he was "not behind my noble and learned friend [Halsbury] in the desire to preserve individual liberty" but that he thought it "never in greater danger than when a tribunal is urged to restrict liberty of action because the manner in which it has been exercised in a particular instance may be distasteful." He then submitted "with all deference to my noble and learned friend on the woolsack that any other conclusion would run counter to principles of the common law which have been long well established," in the *Mogul* case. He apologized for the time he had taken, but justified his efforts by remarking that the position supported by his noble and learned friend Halsbury was "one absolutely novel, and which can only be supported by affirming propositions far-reaching in their consequences and in my opinion dangerous and unsound."

THE SECOND LABOR UNION CASE

So the boilermakers won the last round in the House of Lords —and this second installment of the Trilogy was most pleasing to the unions. Now they seemed to be on a par with businessmen in the use of economic pressures to promote what they conceived to be their best interests. Henceforth they could wield their collective privilege to work or not to work at their pleasure and under whatever conditions they chose, as far as the penalties of the law were concerned. But their triumph was to be short-lived. For even as the learned law lords were cudgelling their wits to do right by England in this case, the final disillusioning chapter of the famous Trilogy was being fought out in the lower courts of Ireland.

There, a rural wholesale slaughterer named Leathem was asked by the meat workers' union to hire his help only from among its members. He would not do this, but offered to pay the dues and other obligations required for the installation of his regular employees into the union. The labor folk insisted upon adherence to their union's objective of placing its existing members first on the list for jobs, in preference to all nonmembers or late comers. It was also stipulated that if Leathem's workers joined up, they must nevertheless relinquish their jobs and, as new members, await their turns for further employment. When Leathem refused to comply, the union leaders threatened to bring pressure on him by taking away his best urban customer, Munce, who ran a large retail market. This they proposed to do by calling out Munce's union employees if he would not at their request discontinue purchasing his meat from Leathem. Leathem remained adamant, so they asked Munce to cease dealing with him. Since Munce did not want a strike on his hands and since he was not under contract with Leathem, he bought his meat elsewhere. Leathem then brought this action against Quinn and other members of the union to recover damages for the loss of his trade with Munce.

This case of *Quinn v. Leathem* presented an instance of what has become a typical secondary labor boycott. It was put into effect by a refusal of the unionists to work for Munce if he, in turn, did business with Leathem, whose employment policies were contrary to their interests as they conceived such interests to be. They could not bring pressure against Leathem directly by refusing to work for him because he did not employ union men to begin with. From the *Mogul* case and *Allen v. Flood* they understood that a group of employees acting in concert might lawfully refuse to work for their employer without giving any reason or for any reason they wished to give. Hence they believed that they might get at Leathem by exerting direct pressure against Munce, on whom they had some hold, so that he in turn would be forced to become the instrument for putting pressure on Leathem. They simply placed one condition on the continuance of their members' employment with Munce—his discontinuance of business dealings with Leathem—and let his self-interest take its course.

The trial and lower appellate courts in Ireland, one judge out of nine dissenting, came up with damages in favor of

Leathem. The reason they did this is not easy to determine. At the trial the jury was asked to consider (1) did the defendants wrongfully and maliciously induce the plaintiff's customers to refuse to deal with him, and (2) did the union defendants maliciously conspire to induce the plaintiff's customers not to deal with him? On the meaning of the words "wrongfully and maliciously," the trial judge instructed the jury to consider whether the defendants had gone beyond "securing or advancing their own interests or those of their trade by *reasonable means,* including lawful combination," or whether their acts were intended to injure the plaintiff in his trade, through combination, "as distinguished from acts *legitimately done* to secure or advance their own interests." He told them that a union may do acts to better itself as long as they are not "maliciously—that is to say, intentionally—done to injure a third party." Such wrongful acts occur, he said, when there has been "a conspiracy, a common intention and a combination on the part of the defendants to injure the plaintiff in his business."

This language of the trial judge was hardly the sort of stuff a jury is equipped to handle. The court might just as well have told the jury that if it did not like what the defendant unionists were up to, then to "give them the works." He did not give the jury any idea what he meant by "legitimately done" or "reasonable means." So naturally the jury supplied its own definitions from its own background of social experience. And it is hard to see how any group of jurymen in this case, trying to discharge their duty in accordance with the judge's instructions, could have failed to find the defendants guilty of an illegal conspiracy to injure Leathem.

On appeal by the union defendants, the House of Lords affirmed the judgment against them. Lord Brampton wrote the longest and most thorough opinion. He clearly thought that the real issue concerned a conspiracy to injure Leathem in his trade. But before he finally dealt with the conspiracy issue, he had already concluded that what the defendants had done was unlawful, anyway, aside from conspiracy. He and his fellow law lords believed that this case was different from the *Mogul* case because the defendants here could not justify their conduct "as legitimate trade competition." And those law lords who believed that there had been a showing of competition in *Allen v. Flood* thought that that case did not apply here because Allen, the boilermaker union's business agent, had acted individually in warning the employer of a probable strike, and he could not in his individual capacity constitute a conspiracy.

Now, if Lord Brampton was correct in concluding that the defendants could not justify their commission of harm on Leathem, and if at the same time he coupled this conclusion with the maxim of law that the intentional commission of unjustifiable harm is illegal, then the unionists were caught both in the maxim and in the doctrine of civil conspiracy. For all civil conspiracy amounts to is a tort occurring when defendants combine to achieve a lawful end by illegal means, an unlawful end by legal means, or an unlawful end by illegal means. So Lord Brampton had the unionists coming and going.

Just how did Brampton happen to conclude that the defendants in the *Leathem* case were not prompted in what they did by the instinct of self-advancement and self-protection, to borrow a phrase from the *Mogul* case? According to him, apparently, these union folk were engaged in aimless mischief and were hurting Leathem just for the hell of it. Their acts were not done, he said, "to obtain or maintain fair hours of labour or fair wages, or to promote a good understanding between employers and employed and workman and workman, or for the settlement of any dispute, for none had existence." But anyone able to read could tell from the report of the case that the union had a very definite interest at stake—not unlike that of the boilermakers' union in *Allen v. Flood*. Its endeavor to unionize Leathem's slaughter house indicates quite clearly that it was competing directly with unorganized labor for particular jobs—that it wanted to control Leathem's employment potential in order to keep its unemployed members at work. This alone seems clearly to supply the element of self-advancement mentioned in the *Mogul* case.

Furthermore, unless this union was different from all other large unions, it had another important economic interest about which nobody was very articulate in the early 1900's. The report of the case indicates that the union included in its membership the employees not only of retail butcher shops but also of slaughter yards—the equivalent in those days of packing houses. In this respect it resembled the AF of L Amalgamated Meat Cutters and Butcher Workmen of North America as it exists today. Now, in so far as the union had slaughter yards already organized with advantageous standards of employment, it had an interest in stabilizing and maintaining employment conditions in *all* slaughter yards. For in this way alone could it prevent the undermining of its already established standards in organized units by the undercutting competition between union slaughtered meat and nonunion slaughtered meat—the competitive factor being the wage differential which made nonunion meat cheaper.

This seems clearly to supply the element of self-protection mentioned in the *Mogul* case. As long as Leathem's slaughter yard and others like it were free to undersell their unionized competitors, because of lower wage rates, the welfare of the unionized employers would be hurt and they, in turn, would try to drive the union standards of their employees down to the nonunion level. This would certainly hurt the union. So by organizing the nonunion firms, it would strive to eliminate the competition of the nonunion meat with the union slaughtered meat in order to maintain the prosperity of the unionized firms and thus stabilize the security of the union men employed in them.

It is true that this attenuated but nevertheless real example of competition between union members and unorganized workers in the industry was not clearly thought out and expressly articulated at the time of *Quinn v. Leathem*. But even if it had been, it might not have played a very important part in the case, because the union placed so much emphasis on putting old union members in Leathem's jobs and almost no emphasis on the mere unionization of Leathem and his old employees. Consequently, it looked as if the only substantial competitive factor in the case was the struggle between the union and Leathem's old employees for the opportunities to work in his slaughter yard. Nevertheless, there seemed to be considerable evidence of real union interest to prevent Brampton from concluding so forcefully that the defendants were not serving any useful purpose by their conduct but were merely inflicting aimless and unjustifiable harm on the plaintiff.

Nonetheless, as indicated above, Brampton believed the defendants in this case to have been guilty of something called civil conspiracy. His extended remarks on this matter would have been most distressing to the recently deceased Lord Herschell, had he been able to read them. "It has often been debated," Brampton said, "whether, assuming the existence of a conspiracy to do a wrongful and harmful act towards another and to carry it out by a number of overt acts, no one of which taken singly and alone would, if done by one individual acting alone and apart from any conspiracy, constitute a cause of action, such acts would become unlawful or actionable if done by the conspirators acting jointly or severally in pursuance of their conspiracy, and if by those acts substantial damage was caused to the person against whom the conspiracy was directed: my own opinion is that they would. . . .

"Much consideration of the matter has led me to be convinced that a number of actions and things not in themselves actionable or unlawful if done separately without conspiracy may, with conspiracy, become dangerous and alarming, just as a grain of gunpowder is harmless but a pound may be highly destructive, or the administration of one grain of a particular drug may be most beneficial as a medicine but administered frequently and in larger quantities with a view to harm may be fatal as a poison." And he concluded that a conspiracy is "a powerful and dangerous engine, which in this case has, I think, been employed by the defendants for the perpetration of organized and ruinous oppression."

With these words before us, we should return to a statement made in the *Mogul* case by the same Lord Chancellor Halsbury who presided over the unanimous judgment of the law lords in the *Leathem* case. There he had said: "What injury, if any, has been done? What legal right has been interfered with? Because if no legal right has been interfered with, and no legal injury inflicted, it is vain to say that the thing might have been done by an individual, but cannot be done by a combination of persons." It is true that Halsbury then said he did not deny there were "many things which might be perfectly lawfully done by an individual, which, when done by a number of persons, become unlawful," referring to an instance of organized co-ordinated hissing of an actor. But trading, he said, is different from hissing and insulting. Merchants must seek the co-operation of others without whom they cannot carry on business. Yet he could not see a labor union—a lawful enterprise under British statutes—in this light, although it could function and exercise its normal purposes only in the same way a company did.

Halsbury, who could see no wrong in the *Mogul* case where the combination of defendants ruthlessly crushed the plaintiff without offering it any alternative, stoutly declared that if Leathem could not recover against the labor union defendants "it could hardly be said that our jurisprudence was that of a civilized community." And this, when Leathem's alternative of avoiding damage by complying with the union's terms was always open. Of course, the union was determined to supplant Leathem's employees with their members of longer standing who had been out of work for some time. This no doubt was regarded as thoroughly wicked, although it is of the very essence of competition as understood by sober and conservative business folk. At any rate, Chief Justice Palles of the Irish Queen's Bench Division thought his colleagues were behaving most inconsistently in the *Leathem* case. He concluded that however much he disliked what the defendant unionists had done, he could not conscientiously read the law as declared in the *Mogul* case and *Allen v. Flood* to furnish anything other than complete support for the legality of their conduct.

THE LAW OF THE TRILOGY

Now these three cases are what is called law. Just what that law is seems to defy statement in principles which judges and scholars can agree upon and consistently apply. At first it looks as if people are free to combine and in concert to inflict serious harm on others, as long as they do not indulge in conduct falling into categories of specific torts or crimes and as long as they can justify the commission of harm by showing that it was not done wantonly but was in pursuit of advantage and gain. In other words, combination is not illegal since combination alone is not a tort or a crime. Similarly a refusal to do business with another is not illegal since it is not a tort or a crime. Finally the refusal by members of a combination to do business with others is not illegal as long as it is done to serve some selfish purpose cherished by them. This is apparently the lesson of the *Mogul* case.

In *Allen v. Flood* we learn that this is still true, although Lord Herschell, who apparently did not participate in the *Mogul* decision, clearly expressed his doubt that the conduct of the defendants in that case depended on their showing any sort of justification. He thought it obvious that motive was immaterial as long as the defendants had not engaged in activity which was unlawful under any established category of tort or crime. In his opinion appears what might be called a very broad civil rights doctrine—the unquestionable right of anyone to indulge in activity not traditionally illegal and not contrary to any statute, regardless of its harmful effect on others and regardless of the actor's motives. He did not address himself to any sort of conspiracy doctrine, except to observe in passing that it is anomalous in more than one respect.

Up to this point the law seemed clear enough. The only matter still open related to the requirement for a showing of justification or excuse. Herschell took the position that such a requirement did not exist as long as the conduct leading to harm was not comprised under some established category of tort or crime or was not unlawful under a statute. But the decision of *Quinn v. Leathem* knocked all this galley west. In so far as it depended on the civil conspiracy doctrine, it undid a great deal to which the House had committed itself in the *Mogul* case. Indeed, this was virtually the reintroduction in civil dress of the old notion of criminal conspiracy, which had presumably been laid to rest for all time by Parliament in 1875.

The position that the House of Lords adopted in the *Leathem* case was simply this. If a common jury does not approve of the conduct of a group of people acting to promote their own ends, then such conduct is illegal when it causes harm to another, even though this conduct does not fall into any established category of illegality. And it still retained this position although the evidence showed clearly that the group's conduct was carried on for the purpose of advantage and gain —clearly enough, at any rate, so that under the doctrine of the *Mogul* case if the defendants had been businessmen, a judgment against them would not be sustained. In other words, the *Leathem* case was an unwholesome and rather disgraceful exhibition by the law lords of what might accurately be called both class prejudice and skulduggery. It is to Parliament's credit that the effects of this decision were wiped out by legislation in 1906.

It is difficult in commenting on these three famous cases not to insist that the prevailing law governing the conduct of all groups trying to get ahead should be embodied in the adage "What's sauce for the goose is sauce for the gander." In other words, what is good law for the activities of businessmen is also good law for the activities of labor leaders. Of course, this position seems unassailable as far as it goes. The fault implicit in this philosophy is the assumption that what happened in the *Mogul* case was desirable or even tolerable. But here arises the crux of the whole matter.

Granting that what the defendants did in the *Mogul* case was ruthless and deliberate, resulting in no benefit to anyone but themselves and only in detriment to society as a whole, who is going to make this judgment officially? Are the judges in a position to do so as a matter of common, or unwritten, law? The answer seems clearly to be in the negative. That is essentially an issue for the legislature to handle, as Lord Bowen indicated in the *Mogul* case, implying that even Parliament would find it impossible to choose adequate standards of conduct. Like most other matters of grave social policy, that is a matter with which the peoples' representatives, politically elected and responsible to their constituents, should handle. If these representatives are inept, according to popular opinion, they can be kicked out and replaced at the next popular election.

Now, in this respect, what difference is there between the conduct of traditional business enterprise and that of the new type of co-operative business enterprise called labor unionism? The answer is: absolutely none. This is no attempt to defend labor unions in what they do. Many believe with good cause that labor unions have been up to a good deal of mischief in the past and that several of their leaders are rascals who are out for all they can get. Rather, it is an attempt to persuade people to think honestly and clearly about one of the most troublesome issues confronting us all in modern times. One way of approaching the problem is to show how thoroughly mixed up on this matter were the deliberations of one of the world's most important and influential judicial bodies. Assuredly there is nothing very complicated about the common law involved in this discussion. And the duty of judges to apply it is equally simple and forthright. If the result of its application seems shocking, society has the power under our type of government to change the law. And this conclusion applies with equal force to the law as it is brought to bear on the activities of companies and of unions alike.

Let us reflect on these three cases briefly before we dismiss them for good. The combination in the *Mogul* case put the screws on the shippers of tea so that they could not avail themselves of the plaintiff's ships. Thus it suppressed competition, and in the name of competition maintained a monopolistic control of a substantial cost item in the price of tea. The plaintiff was ruthlessly eliminated, as the combination intended it should be. It could have gone elsewhere for trade. And if the public does not like the price of tea, it can drink hot water. The House of Lords said that if society does not like this, let it think up something better and enact it in legislation.

The boilermakers' business agent in *Allen v. Flood* told the employer that the union members would not work for him at all unless they could do all of his work, which they were competent to do. The employer acquiesced by discharging the two men he had employed, who were not members of the union. This was hard on them, but they could no doubt find work elsewhere. If they could not find such work, then the result would be two shipwrights unemployed instead of two boilermakers. Such a result could increase the employer's labor bill, as he might have made a better wage bargain with the shipwrights than he had made with the union. Society, therefore, might suffer to some extent through the increased price of ships. But the House of Lords, this time in a six to three vote, again said that if society does not like this, it can change it by legislation.

The union leaders in *Quinn v. Leathem* put the screws on Munce, the urban retail butcher, so that he in turn would compel Leathem, the slaughter-house man, to deal with the union on its terms if he still wanted Munce's custom. They were much more considerate than the combination of defendants in the *Mogul* case were to the plaintiff in that case. They did not try to run Leathem out of business. Indeed they wanted him to remain in business with union employees of

long standing doing his work for him. Of course, they were
not very considerate about Leathem's present employees whom
they wanted to displace with their own unemployed members.
But as far as they were concerned, it was a choice between one
or another of the two sets of workmen remaining unemployed.
Naturally they made the choice in favor of their own lads.
Leathem's loyalty to his old employees was commendable and
touching. But it is hard to see why he should expect both to
have his cake and eat it in a world run on the principles set
forth in the *Mogul* case. Yet here the House of Lords unanimously said that it was its business, and not society's as a political matter, to intervene on behalf of Leathem—a position which
it is unthinkable Lord Herschell would have taken had he still
been in the House.

It seems apparent from the perspective of years that the
House of Lords deeply regretted its position in *Allen v. Flood*
shortly after it was taken. Certainly it indicated in the *Leathem*
case the flimsiest distinction possible between the two cases—
that Allen could not in his sole capacity have constituted a conspiracy, conveniently ignoring the fact that he was speaking
for a whole local union of boilermakers, and implying that his
conduct was actually quite as antisocial as that of the defendants in the *Leathem* case. In any event, the latter case was
an excellent chance to repair the damage done in the former,
and the House did not let it slip.

In this famous Trilogy we have a suggestion of what was
later to be termed in this country the *illegal purpose* doctrine—
a judicial device by which courts were in a position to hold unlawful any conduct of labor unionists which was outwardly
lawful but through which a union was attempting to achieve
some end not judicially approved. As long as the courts were
willing to reserve this power to declare any particular objective
unlawful—apparently in accordance with some subjective judicial standard of how business should properly be conducted—
then in the name of law they were able to crack down on any
union activity not to their liking. All laymen reading this book

must perceive quite as easily as lawyers do that this was an extraordinary way to administer the law—making it up as you go along and to suit your own notions of propriety.

There is nothing wrong with an illegal purpose doctrine as long as the proper body states what the illegal purpose is. That body is the legislature, speaking for the people who elected it. In England, the legislature's voice is final and controlling except in so far as the courts may find loopholes by interpretation. In the United States, the legislatures, both state and national, must stay within the provisions of our constitutions as the courts read them. But within these limits, the legislatures alone have any right to say what are the illegal purposes of trade groups, be they employer or labor groups. What the legislatures should conclude are illegal purposes is a large order. Society alone, expressing its social and economic aims politically, can supply the answer. But one thing seems already clear from our consideration of the famous House of Lords Trilogy—we cannot safely leave these delicate issues of policy to our courts alone when they are so prone to develop one law for industry, and another law for labor.

CHAPTER III

FREE ENTERPRISE IN AMERICA—
CONFLICTING STATE POLICIES

Scarce any man has the means of knowing a twentieth part of the laws he is bound by. Both sorts of law are kept most happily and carefully from the knowledge of the people: statute law by its shape and bulk; common law by its very essence. It is the judges (as we have seen) that make the common law. Do you know how they make it? Just as a man makes laws for his dog. When your dog does anything you want to break him of, you wait till he does it, and then beat him for it. This is the way you make laws for your dog: and this is the way the judges make law for you and me. They won't tell a man beforehand what it is he *should not do*—they won't so much as allow of his being told: they lie by till he has done something which they say he should not *have done,* and then they hang him for it. What way, then, has any man of coming at this dog-law? Only by watching their proceedings: by observing in what *cases* they have hanged a man, in what *cases* they have sent him to jail, in what *cases* they have seized his goods, and so forth. —Jeremy Bentham, *Works,* Volume 5, page 235, 1843.

No DEVELOPMENT comparable to the House of Lords Trilogy ever took place before the United States Supreme Court. These labor matters used to be local issues in this country. Our parallel to the famous English cases may be found in the reports of state supreme court decisions. In our leading industrial states there were two main lines of development. These may conveniently be termed the conservative philosophy—reflected chiefly in decisions of the Massachusetts court—and the liberal philosophy, set forth most typically in the decisions of the New York court and suggested in two of Justice Holmes' famous dissents in the Massachusetts cases.

Each of these state courts applied the common law. The fact

that they differed radically from each other should not be surprising since each court, in its own jurisdiction, was entitled to regard whatever it thought best as *the* common law. Indeed, that was its job. Hence, we shall see the Massachusetts court doing almost exactly what the House of Lords did in the Trilogy cases, employing the illegal purpose doctrine instead of resorting expressly to a notion of civil conspiracy. And we shall see the New York court finally adhering to Herschell's position in *Allen v. Flood*—the civil rights theory. Holmes on the other hand carved out a middle course that harm intentionally inflicted is actionable unless justified, taking a view of justification broad enough to include the normal objectives of labor unions.

THE MASSACHUSETTS DOCTRINE—A CONSERVATIVE APPROACH

Perhaps the most convenient point of departure is an American counterpart of the famous *Mogul* case discussed in the previous chapter. *Bowen v. Matheson*, decided in 1867 by the Massachusetts Supreme Court, was not a labor case, although it bore a curious resemblance to one in that it involved the supplying of sailors to ships sailing out of Boston harbor. John Bowen was engaged in housing and boarding seamen between voyages and in signing them up on out-going vessels. He complained that a combination of Boston shipping masters —his competitors—had agreed among themselves to secure control of all of this business locally, to the exclusion of all non-members of their combination. In short, they excluded him. To implement this purpose, he declared, each member had conspired with the others to refrain from dealing with any sea captain who hired any men from nonmembers. Since the combination controlled the great bulk of available seamen—so many, that no sea captain could man his ship without going to the combination—all shipowners and sea captains began to drop the services of nonmembers and to patronize only the members of the association. Thus the plaintiff John Bowen was faced with ruin. He asked the court to stop the association from conspiring to ruin him and to grant him damages against its members.

Judge Chapman, speaking for the Massachusetts court, ignored the allegation of conspiracy, observing that to win, the plaintiff must have set forth factually the commission of illegal acts. What the plaintiff did charge was that (1) defendants took men out of ships hiring his men, (2) they refused to ship men with his men, (3) they prevented men from shipping through him, (4) they notified the public that "they had laid him on the shelf," (5) they publicly notified his customers and friends that he could not ship men for them, and (6) they "did break up the plaintiff in his business and calling by their conspiracy, acts and doings, as aforesaid, and compel him to abandon his said business." These charges the court thought unimpressive because they did not describe any specifically illegal conduct falling within settled categories of tort or crime.

By reference to the association's charter, the court perceived that conformance to a wage schedule for seamen was the chief item of its policy. Concerning its various stipulations, as well as the matters charged by the plaintiff, the court failed to recognize anything unlawful. "If their effect is to destroy the business of shipping-masters who are not members of the association," Judge Chapman said, "it is such a result as in the competition of business often follows from a course of proceeding that the law permits. New inventions and new methods of transacting business often destroy the business of those who adhere to old methods."

Here was economic pressure on the shipowners, by cornering the market for able seamen, to compel their co-operation in eliminating Bowen. This was a secondary boycott pressure, implemented by the refusal of all association members to deal with any shipowner who dealt with the plaintiff. As in the *Mogul* case, a monopoly existed in this collective assertion of privileges not to deal with others with the object of destroying the beneficent competition of rivals offering the same commodity at a lower price. A more charitable view of the association's program might reveal an attempt to maintain a high level of seamen's wages and other working conditions, with an incidentally higher commission for shipping brokers, against the attempts of enterprisers like the plaintiff to keep both such items more nearly at the marginal level indicated by an uncontrolled market demand. This curious similarity to the normal objectives of labor unions is apparent only because the commodity in which the parties dealt was the services of men. Had that commodity been lumber, for instance, the suggestion of similarity would have been absent, although the analogy which has just been suggested would still remain in a purely economic sense.

In this case the Massachusetts court made its general position fairly clear. Since nothing the association had done fell within any established category of tort or crime, the harm it inflicted on the plaintiff in the pursuit of gain was not actionable but was justified as competition. The members of the association, individually or in concert, were free to deal with whom they wished, or even not to deal with anyone at all, if such a course promoted their interests. This seemed a fair statement of the common law, consistent with the later *Mogul* pronouncement by the House of Lords.

Hence the decision of the Massachusetts court three years later in *Carew v. Rutherford* is surprising. There a general contractor brought suit to recover $500 from a union on the ground that this sum had been illegally exacted from him. It seems that he was erecting a cathedral on contract and that he sent certain ornamental stone cuttings to be done in New York. The stonecutters' union had resolved in its bylaws that such work should not be sent out because it deprived them not only of an opportunity to earn more money but also of a chance to teach their apprentices their complete trade. Pursuant to this resolution, the union had notified the general contractor that he must not send out such work. Since he proceeded to do so, the union officials imposed a fine on him roughly equivalent to their opinion of the damages they had suffered, declaring that they would not continue work until it was paid. In order to keep his stonecutters on the job, the contractor paid the $500 fine to the union. Then he brought suit for restitution after the cathedral was completed.

The Massachusetts court, declaring the union's act to be extortion, allowed recovery of this sum on the theory of duress. This must have come as a bit of a shock to the Journeymen Freestone Cutters' Association of Boston and vicinity who in the preamble to their constitution had provided:

"Whereas in the course of human events civilization is spreading its salutary effect over the globe; and whereas societies and honorable combinations are marching hand in hand with enlightened bodies, and for their mutual support and protection certain classes of men in their respective callings do assemble and commune together, to adopt rules and regulations to govern their professions, and to develop and embrace the advantages that are derived from a thorough knowledge of business throughout this land; and whereas stonecutters heretofore, in this great and growing country, were looking on with calm indifference at the prosperity derived from such association, but have finally been awakened from their lethargy, and now behold with delight the solid advantages they may derive from a similar institution; they therefore have formed themselves unanimously into one body, to guard and cherish that trade which gives to them an honorable livelihood, and do adopt for their government the following constitution and by-laws, and to show to the world that they are alive to their moral as well as their pecuniary interest."

Although Judge Chapman for the court quoted from a criminal statute dealing with extortion, he chose to rest the civil liability of the union on the common law. From old English law, he mentioned several quaint precedents of tort liability against defendants for threatening to maim and vex one's customers and workmen so that they ceased buying and working;

against a defendant who "menaces my tenants at will of life and member, *per quod* [because of which] they depart from their tenures"; and against a defendant who frightened away wild fowl by discharging guns near a decoy pond. In order to suggest the idea of civil conspiracy, he cited the case of one who hired several to hiss and groan at an actor to persuade the manager to cease employing him. And he mentioned a line of cases wherein money was recovered from those who had exacted its payment by withholding property to which they had no right, by oppression and fraud, by abuse of legal process, by threats of a groundless prosecution and by show of force with a group of armed men. As if these precedents bound the defendants in this case from stating a condition to the continuance of their services as free workingmen, the court called their conduct "an illegal, if not a criminal, conspiracy; . . . a species of annoyance and extortion which the common law has never tolerated."

The judge went on to remark that the principle involved did not interfere with business, but protected it. "Every man has a right to determine what branch of business he will pursue," he declared, "and to make his own contracts with whom he pleases and on the best terms he can. . . . He may refuse to deal with any man or class of men. And it is no crime for any number of persons, *without an unlawful object in view,* to associate themselves together and agree that they will not work for or deal with certain men or classes of men, or work under a certain price, or without certain conditions."

In this passage the judge may seem to have talked himself out of his decision against the defendants, although if faced with this charge, he would no doubt have pointed to the phrase in italics. And this would reveal something very strange, indeed, about the state of the law. For the court's general principle is supposed to indicate what is or is not lawful. If workmen are told they may in combination lawfully refuse to deal with any man and refuse to work without certain conditions, it seems odd that when their conduct is carefully confined to such ambit, the court should still be able to find something unlawful about it.

The court here seemed to believe that the union's conduct was quite different from a strike for higher wages, which by this time it was apparently willing to condone as lawful, even if the result were an increase in wages far in excess of the $500 here involved. At first glance, this distinction may seem clear. The defendant's conduct resembled the shakedowns of the prewar racketeer days. They were using an extralegal technique to compel the payment of money which was not owed to them and which they could not have secured by suit in the courts. Furthermore a strike usually concerns future wage rates and implies an unwillingness to continue work unless the employer will pay a more advantageous scale. And such a concerted exercise of pressure obviously bears a close relationship to the exchange of something of value controlled by the strikers and which the employer is anxious to secure if a price can be determined.

But strikes are not always called to achieve only future benefits. They have been known to secure retroactive settlements as well, occasionally amounting to very substantial sums for each worker concerned. Moreover, the exaction of a money payment under circumstances similar to those in the case under discussion has in recent times been termed a reasonable exercise of economic pressure to achieve a desired economic end. In 1937 the House of Lords declared that a trade association of merchants may black-list an individual merchant who sells certain commodities at prices below an approved schedule and, by threatening to withhold their patronage from any manufacturer who sells to the proscribed merchant, may lawfully compel that merchant to pay a stipulated fine before his name is removed from the black list. The English Court of Criminal Appeal had in a similar situation affirmed the conviction of this same association's secretary for blackmail.

But the law lords took the position that, in the absence of a statute forbidding price fixing, the use of collective coercion of this sort was proper to enforce compliance with the association's schedule of prices. They then observed that the technique employed was the only way in which such coercion might be practiced. For the rebellious merchant, who was not a member of the association, had already violated the schedule. Since there was no way to insure that he and others like him would not do so again without compelling him to make amends for the past and thus really feel the penalty, the imposition of the fine was in their opinion a permissible alternative to the continuation of the black listing.

In some respects the trade association practice condoned by the House of Lords was far more questionable social conduct than that condemned by the Massachusetts court in this labor case. First, it was allowed as a device to enforce price fixing and to suppress competition in the sale of goods—a particularly reprehensible restraint of trade. And second, it depended for its success on the secondary boycott technique. The practice in the Massachusetts case, on the other hand, does not appear to have involved either of these factors. Certainly it was true there, as in the English case, that the union could hardly have insured recognition of its policy without imposing a punishment for a past offense, enforced by a concerted refusal to work.

The union's motive, then, seemed quite as reasonable as that of the English trade association in the sense that it was not just to make easy money but was to protect trade standards. And in each case the practice depended on a concerted refusal to continue trade relations—by the union to work and by the association to deal—a recourse recognized by each court concerned as lawful in itself. Hence it seems fairly clear that the Massachusetts court in this case initiated its illegal purpose doctrine under which it could declare unlawful any outwardly lawful acts of labor unions, undertaken to achieve purposes of which the court does not approve. The net result of this earlier Massachusetts litigation is no different from that in the Trilogy of English cases, although it does not expressly depend on any idea of conspiracy.

HOLMES' ATTIC SALT IN THE MASSACHUSETTS CHOWDER

In the decade commencing with 1896 the Massachusetts court went on to establish in an important series of cases its principles of modern labor relations law from which it did not recede until recently. The first of these, *Vegelahn v. Guntner,* is chiefly important because of the challenging dissent filed by Judge Holmes. It seems that a union called a strike to secure better wages and working hours and had established a picket line to back up the strike, to persuade loyal workers to join them and to discourage new employees from accepting jobs. By this time all American courts had come around to the view—possibly as a matter of political expedience—that strikes for direct objectives like higher wages and shorter work days were lawful. The Massachusetts court accepted this change by regarding these objectives as lawful, thus excluding such strikes from the operation of its illegal purpose doctrine. The issue before the court in this case was the propriety of an order forbidding peaceful picketing—a patrol posted outside the employer's premises merely to accost and speak to persons leaving and proposing to enter the plant. A majority of the court thought the order was proper. Judges Holmes and Field disagreed. Field thought it unwise to prevent a striker from trying to persuade applicants for jobs not to apply, by simply relating the truth, believing it "a dangerous principle to leave his liability to be determined by a jury upon the question of his malice or want of malice."

But Holmes raised some broad issues in stating what he called the less popular view. He denied the court's assumption that the patrol necessarily implied a threat of bodily harm to anyone. Conceding the infliction of temporal damage and the proposition that it is actionable unless justified, he observed that the law recognizes justification in numberless instances. On this issue of justification, he observed that judicial reasoning was frequently inadequate. "The true grounds of decision are considerations of policy and of social advantage," and logic built on universally accepted general propositions of law solves few problems. Propositions concerning public policy, on the other hand, are not generally accepted. Although a special training is required to form an intelligent opinion about them, judges nevertheless act upon them, he observed, rather as inarticulate instincts than as definite ideas. A new tradesman drives established rivals to ruin, but the courts do not call this unlawful.

"The reason, of course, is that the doctrine generally has been accepted that free competition is worth more to society than it costs, and that on this ground the infliction of the damage is privileged," as long as "the damage is done not for its own sake, but as an instrumentality in reaching the end of victory in the battle of trade." Of course, the methods of inflicting this damage must be carefully scrutinized. He went on to say that force or threats of force are not permissible. But it is otherwise with persuasion of free customers—the refusal or withdrawal of various pecuniary advantages within the defendant's lawful control, and the withdrawal of or threat to withdraw, such advantages from third persons who have a right to deal or not to deal with the plaintiff, as a means of inducing them not to deal with him either as customers or servants. As to threats, compulsion, annoyance and intimidation, words only too apt to suggest unlawfulness in themselves, "it depends on what you threaten" or how you compel, annoy or intimidate. In this respect, economic pressure and violence should be sharply distinguished.

Holmes deprecated the commonly heard assertion "that the conflict between employers and employed is not competition," and he declared: "If the policy on which our law is founded is too narrowly expressed in the term free competition, we may substitute free struggle for life. Certainly the policy is not limited to struggles between persons of the same class competing for the same end. It applies to all conflicts of temporal interests." At the peak of his dissent Judge Holmes used language which has been and still is widely quoted. He said:

"It is plain from the slightest consideration of practical affairs, or the most superficial reading of industrial history, that free competition means combination, and that the organization of the world, now going on so fast, means an ever increasing might and scope of combination. It seems to me futile to set our faces against this tendency. Whether beneficial on the whole, as I think it, or detrimental, it is inevitable, unless the fundamental axioms of society, and even the fundamental conditions of life, are to be changed. . . . One of the eternal conflicts out of which life is made up is that between the effort of every man to get the most he can for his services, and that of society, disguised under the name of capital, to get his services for the least possible return. Combination on the one side is patent and powerful. Combination on the other is the necessary and desirable counterpart, if the battle is to be carried on in a fair and equal way."

When it is considered that Holmes wrote this in 1896, its tolerance and its penetrating wisdom are those of a true legal prophet. The full significance of his position appears in the Massachusetts court's next outstanding labor case decided in 1900—*Plant v. Woods*. Previously, he had recalled the day when many people thought that strikes were wicked, as organized refusals to work. In supposing that intelligent economists and legislators have given up that notion today, he implied his belief that other judges had long since concluded that strikes for *any* purpose, aside from incidental violence and breach of contract, were lawful. He expressed the hope that they would shortly share his views on picketing. This next case, therefore, must have given him a terrible jolt.

It seems that a large local union of painters and decorators had split up—probably over the same difference of opinion that had broken up the national organization of which it had been a part. The two resulting locals each retained the same name and local number and practically the same bylaws and constitution, the only obvious distinguishing features about them being the headquarter cities of the two resulting national unions with which these locals were affiliated. The old national union had its headquarters in Baltimore, and the defendants adhered to the organization still housed there. The plaintiffs, however, were in the offshoot union headquartered in Lafayette, Indiana. Prior to this law suit the Baltimore unionists had been conducting a campaign to wipe out the Lafayette union and to bring its members back into the fold. To achieve this end, they had refused to work for any employer or contractor who also hired men belonging to the rival union. Because the Baltimore adherents included most of the best workers, the employers could not afford to ignore their demand, deciding under economic compulsion to hire only them and not to deal with their rivals. In the latters' suit for an injunction to forbid the continuance of this undertaking, the Massachusetts court took the view that the Baltimore outfit was threatening to strike for the closed shop—that is, to secure an agreement from the employers that they would hire only workers belonging to the Baltimore union, membership in which would be a condition of employment. The court thought this practice should be enjoined. It intimated that the threatened strike was unlawful under the illegal purpose doctrine because its objective—the closed shop—was in its opinion undesirable.

The court emphasized a statement made by the Baltimore unionists that if the employers did not cease hiring men from the rival union, they "might expect trouble in their business." Now strikes always cause trouble of some sort and are intended to do so. But trouble is an ambiguous term and in connection with a strike—unless evidence appears to the contrary —should be assumed to mean no more than the general economic inconvenience normally attendant upon loss of a steady and unrestricted supply of labor. The court nevertheless thought it meant more than merely ceasing work, which it called the "preliminary skirmish." This threat of trouble, it declared, meant organized social pressure to discourage the continued employment of others, physical injury to the employers' property, attempts to injure and ruin the employers' business, and violence toward applicants for employment.

This passage calls for two caustic remarks. First, the court's belief that a strike necessarily implies damage of the sort suggested is plainly incorrect. Its assumption that the strikers would as a matter of course behave illegally and commit acts of violence, and its approval of an injunction based on this assumption before any such violence occurred, indicate a serious abuse of judicial authority. These apprehensions of unlawfulness, concededly not yet committed but anticipated in order to justify the injunction, betrayed a display of power which all classes of men might well dread. Second, the court openly disclosed its purpose to protect the employers and their business. But the employers had not complained or asked the court's protection, the suit having been filed only by the members of the Lafayette union. The threatened strike, it is true, was to be against the employers if they continued to hire members of that union. But if they were willing to forego hiring the Lafayette unionists in order to retain peaceful relations with the Baltimore boys, why should the court have concerned itself with nonexistent harm to their interests?

The court said its chief concern was to preserve the equal rights of all workmen to dispose of their services with full freedom. The Baltimore lads, of course, had no quarrel with this aim. They claimed it to be the basic premise of their position. But the court declared that the motive behind the threatened exercise of their liberty of contract was all important. It all depended upon whether they employed this coercion to further their interests or merely to injure others. If it *was* to further their interests, then it depended upon whether they used pressure generally recognized in the business world to be legitimate, as competition, or clearly thought to be unpermissible, as extortion. While the court admitted that the Baltimore unionists were attempting to promote their interests, it nevertheless thought that the case involved the outright commission of harm for harm's sake against the employers and the Lafayette union. It thought the situation to be more like extortion than competition, and that it resembled *Carew v. Rutherford,* the "extortion" case, rather than *Bowen v. Matheson,* involving the "corner" on seamen, and the *Mogul* case. As the court observed: "The necessity that the plaintiffs [the Lafayette unionists] should join this association is not so great, nor is its relation to the rights of the defendants [the Baltimore unionists], as compared with the right of the plaintiffs to be free from molestation, such as to bring the acts of the defendants under the shelter of the principles of trade competition."

Although the court did not expressly base its decision on the "illegal purpose" of the defendants, it impliedly did so by stressing the importance of motive in judging the legality of otherwise lawful conduct. Hence this rival unions case of *Plant v. Woods* is generally taken to mean that a strike for the closed shop is unlawful. And it is clear from the opinion that the court also dealt with the case under the maxim that the intentional infliction of harm on another is actionable unless justified, choosing to regard as justification only trade competition, which it found to be absent between the parties involved.

Certainly Judge Holmes so interpreted its position, for in his dissent he was pleased that the court had made its decision depend on the presence or absence of justification. Then he inferred from this position that the difference between him and the rest of the court was simply one of degree. He perceived in the court's opinion a tacit acknowledgment of the right to strike for wage and hour adjustments as long as the strikers refrained from violence and from inducing breaches of contract.

"To come directly to the point," he said, "the issue is narrowed to the question whether, assuming that some purposes would be a justification, the purpose in this case of the threatened boycotts and strikes was such as to justify the threats. That purpose was not directly concerned with wages. It was one degree more remote. The immediate object and motive was to strengthen the defendants' society as a preliminary and means to enable it to make a better fight on questions of wages or other matters of clashing interests. I differ from my brethren in thinking that the threats were as lawful for this preliminary purpose as for the final one to which strengthening the union was a means. I think that unity of organization is necessary to make the contest of labor effectual, and that societies of laborers lawfully may employ in their preparation the means which they might use in the final contest."

He went on to add: "I cherish no illusions as to the meaning and effect of strikes. While I think the strike a lawful instrument in the universal struggle of life, I think it pure phantasy to suppose that there is a body of capital of which labor as a whole secures a larger share by that means." He declared that production is consumed "by the multitude," and that "organization and strikes" may get a "larger share" for the organized, but only at the expense of the less organized, thereby implying no belief in the old wage fund theory. His view was that wage increases won by union efforts raised the prices of commodities. Then the union men with their higher wages came to market with greater purchasing power than did the unorganized workers who remained on a relatively lower scale of wages. "They do not create something out of nothing," he declared of the unions. "But," he concluded, "I think it lawful for a body of workmen to try by combination to get more than they now are getting, . . . and to that end to strengthen their union by the boycott and the strike."

Now just because Judge Holmes declared that the difference between a strike for higher wages and a strike for the closed shop is one of degree, and not of kind, does not make that proposition true. There is a good deal of difference in kind between pressure by a group of employees to secure higher wages, and coercion exercised by the bulk of the employees in a plant to compel their employer and fellow workers to acknowledge the employment of only union members. This latter purpose is an attempt to establish overwhelming bargaining power by preventing the employer's access to an open and uncontrolled labor market and by denying nonunion labor free access to employment in his plant. Perhaps Holmes meant that there was no difference in kind between the coercive techniques used in strikes for wages and strikes for the closed shop. This, of course, is true. In each case the striking employees concertedly refuse to work. One of the chief objects of the strike for the closed shop, however, is to disable the employer from resisting future collective bargaining undertakings such as a simple strike for wages. And the court condemned it as a grab for power.

Holmes must have experienced a sardonic pleasure when he learned that the majority of his court made the legality of strikes depend on the presence or absence of justification. He knew that the only justification the court recognized was so-called trade competition. Logically he might have taken its concession that strikes for wages were lawful to imply in such strikes the presence of competition. But he probably realized that, according to the court's conception of trade competition, none could fairly be found in wage strikes, and hence the court could logically find no justification for them. Yet it declared such strikes were permissible!

It should not, of course, require the legal insight of a Holmes to perceive that the Massachusetts court was really making the lawfulness of strikes depend on its conception of legality of purpose and not upon any intelligible conception of competition at all. Even this court had finally felt obliged to concede the legality of strikes for direct benefits, like wages. This may have been because it would be politically impracticable to continue deciding otherwise. After all, it was hard to impute any illegality of purpose to a desire for higher wages or a shorter work day. However, it saw no need to extend this privilege of striking for direct benefits to any but voluntarily associated workmen. And it was determined to discourage strikes intended to spread monopolistic and pervasive unionism.

Five years later this same court again aired its views on trade competition as justification for the commission of harm, in a suit involving a closed shop contract. Such a contract requires all employees of the company in question to be members of the union as a condition of continued employment. Pursuant to the terms of this contract, an official of a local shoe workers' union required an employer to discharge the plaintiff, an employee of some years' standing who had refused to join the union after the contract was executed. In his suit for damages caused by his discharge, the union official offered as a defense this term of the contract making union membership a condition of employment. Acknowledging this defense as proper if the contract were lawful, the court made its validity the issue in the case. It concluded that the contract for the closed shop was unlawful, thus depriving the union of its defense. Thus in this case of *Berry v. Donovan* the discharged employee received substantial money damages.

The union had argued in justification of the plaintiff's dis-charge that its achievement and use of the closed shop contract was "a kind of competition." But the judges did not regard this as competition. This was like the previous rival unions case of *Plant v. Woods,* since the union was not trying to get the plaintiff's job for one of its existing members but wanted him to remain at work as a member of the union. "Indeed," they said, "the object of organizations of this kind is not to make competition of employees with one another more easy or successful. It is rather, by association, to prevent such competition, to bring all to equality, and to make them act together in a common interest." And they then remarked that the defense "rests entirely upon another kind of socalled competition, namely, competition between employers and the employed, in the attempt of each class to obtain as large a share as possible of the income from their combined efforts in the industrial field."

This, the judges thought, was not in a strict sense competition at all but was a struggle among interests of different kinds, not operating on the same plane of endeavor. It was not like the conflict between two tradesmen for the same customers or between two groups of workmen for the same jobs. The union achieved no *direct* benefit from this closed shop policy, said the court, but secured only increased bargaining power. Such an object "is too remote to be considered a benefit in business" so as to justify the intentional infliction of harm in securing it. If it were otherwise, the unions could force all workmen to join and would have "complete and absolute control of all the industries of the country." And then it added: "Employers would be forced to yield to all their demands, or give up business. The attainment of such an object in the struggle with employers would not be competition, but monopoly." Indeed, the more this court attempted to distinguish labor cases from the good old business competition cases like the "corner" on seamen in *Bowen v. Matheson* and the *Mogul* decision, the more alike they seemed in all their implications.

But the Massachusetts court's position is not complete without reference to one more case. *Pickett v. Walsh,* decided in 1906, is a case frequently contrasted to *Plant v. Woods,* the rival decorators' case. This suit was also between two sets of workers. The bricklayers' and stonemasons' unions wished to secure the work of pointing bricks and stones as well as of laying them. This extra work had always been done by pointers, who were not members of either of the unions and who had been persistently denied a charter by the AF of L. The unions told the general contractors by whom their members were employed that they would not work for them at all unless they could do the pointing, as well. In other words, they would do all of their work, or none. While the employers preferred to retain the pointers at this work, because they were more skillful and charged less, they had to have the bricklayers and stonemasons on their jobs. Hence the contractors were obliged to let the union men do all of the work and to let the pointers go. The pointers thereupon sued the masons and bricklayers to enjoin them from this commission of harm through their threatened concerted refusals to work. The Massachusetts court decided this case in favor of the masons and bricklayers.

This is the way the judges looked at it. They observed that "there is no question of the general right of a labor union to strike." But they mentioned several purposes for which it might not lawfully strike, citing *Plant v. Woods*—the rival decorators' case—to the effect that "a labor union could not force other workmen to join it by refusing to work if workmen were employed who were not members of that union." The *Pickett* case, however, "is one of competition between the defendant unions and the individual plaintiffs for the work of pointing." The situation is peculiar because the fight here is necessarily a triangular one, involving two sets of workmen and their employers. In this respect it is like the *Mogul* case, the court said, overlooking the same resemblance to *Plant v. Woods*. "The right which the defendant unions claim to exercise in carrying their point in the course of this competition is a trade advantage, namely, that they have labor which the contractors want, or, if you please, cannot get elsewhere; and they insist upon using this trade advantage to get additional work, namely, the work of pointing the bricks and stone which they lay." The opinion indicates that all that the labor unions have done is to say: You must employ us for all the work or none of it, and they have not forbidden the employment of a particular category of artisans doing their own kind of work, as the union did in the decorators' case.

Thus the masons and bricklayers left the employers free to make their choice between the pointers and their unions, with the understanding that if they chose the pointers they would have to get somebody else to lay their bricks and stones, well knowing that they could get nobody else. The pointers could not lay brick and stone, but the masons and bricklayers could point. And pointing is not so far removed from masonry and bricklaying that the court could fairly deny the defendants' right to compete for this work. The unions would not allow the pointers to join their organizations because of their inability to lay bricks and stones. This was disastrous to the pointers. They had either to move away or learn new trades. "But this is not the first case," said the judges, "where the exercise of the right of competition ends in such a result. The case at bar is an instance where the evils which are or may be incident to competition bear very harshly on those interested, but in spite of such evils competition is necessary to the welfare of the community."

In the court's opinion, the distinction between these two cases lay in the fact that while the defendant decorators' union in *Plant v. Woods* was striking to achieve power, the masons' and bricklayers' unions in *Pickett v. Walsh* were striking to get more work for their members. Another way to put this is to say that while in the former case the infliction of harm could not be justified as competition, in the latter case it could be. Now this is really amusing. One of the reasons for the decision in *Plant v. Woods,* the decorators' case, is that a union has no right by striking for the closed shop to deny a workman the opportunity of gainful occupation. Yet in that case the union wanted the plaintiffs to remain at their jobs, merely stipulating that they join the defendants' union as a condition of doing so. But in *Pickett v. Walsh,* the pointers' case, the unions would not permit the pointers to join their organizations at all nor to retain their employment and trade. They deliberately forced the general contractors to discard them and saw to it that they were ruined economically. Not only did the Massachusetts court place a considerable premium on utter ruthlessness in determining its conception of the proper significance of the concept "competition," but it also seems to have abandoned the principle of protection accorded in *Plant v. Woods,* the decorators' case, to guarantee all workers free access to employment opportunities of their own choosing. Furthermore, while forbidding the strike for the closed shop in *Plant v. Woods,* the court in *Pickett v. Walsh* condoned what is now recognized as the most wasteful of all union coercive techniques—the true jurisdictional strike—hardly justifiable on any theory of law or economics.

From the foregoing it must appear that the Massachusetts bench had a fairly rigid conception of competition. It plainly believed that competition could exist only between people or groups of people striving against each other on the same plane of endeavor for the same thing. Apparently its thinking on this subject ran somewhat like this. The usual object of competition is a market of some sort for the goods or services of the competitors. The purpose of the strife is to secure trade outlets through preferred access to customers. Presumably completely free competition occurs when prices are shaved so that potential customers choose the successful competitor's wares to serve their own self-interest. This makes efficiency and skill in production and distribution the most important factors in free competition.

But when a group of enterprisers competing for a certain market band together and pool their economic power to control the market, an entirely different situation results, although theoretically this is still supposed to be competition. In the first place, the members of the group are no longer competitors among themselves. To that extent, at least, their compact has eliminated competition. Their object may also be to prevent any outside competition, usually through intermediate economic pressures on persons other than such potential competitors, so that they may have the market in question entirely to themselves and be in a position to control supply and fix prices. Pursuit of these objectives by this group is competition between the group and the enterprisers outside of the group. The result, if successful, is always a suppression of competition. This is a paradox apparent to the courts but is dismissed by them with the hope that persistent new enterprise will eventually win out and break down the noncompetitive control of the combination.

According to this conception of competition, the Massachusetts court did not believe that workmen competed with their employers but were rather engaged in a joint productive effort with them to turn out goods which neither of them could produce alone. In its opinion, employers and their employees were not striving against each other on the same plane of endeavor and for the same thing. It did not think matters improved by saying that they were competing with each other for a different division of the profits from their joint enterprise. Believing all this, the Massachusetts bench could not justify a simple strike for higher wages as competition, especially as it could not overlook the early judicial decisions holding strikes for wages unlawful because they were the very antithesis of competition. Actually, it did not try to do so. In spite of its feeling for classical theories of competition, the Massachusetts judges knew that strikes for wages and other direct benefits—in brief, all collective bargaining strikes—had to be made lawful as a matter of political expedience. And as long as it stuck to the view that the deliberate infliction of harm on another is unlawful, unless justified, and at the same time defined justification only in terms of competition, no other explanation seems possible.

In *Pickett v. Walsh*—the pointers' case—the judges recognized the familiar pattern of conduct frequently undertaken by business enterprises. Here was an instance of economic strife between two sets of workmen competing between themselves for the same opportunity to earn money—the work of pointing stones and bricks. Success by one group meant exclusion of the other from this advantage. Hence, if the court was to remain true to its own notions, it had to excuse this commission of harm during the course of competition. But in *Plant v. Woods*—the rival decorators' case—a different situation was apparent. Instead of trying to exclude the Lafayette unionists from jobs in that case, the defendants wished to share the available work with them, simply requiring that they first join the Baltimore union. There was no competition for the exclusive opportunity to earn money. Since this situation did not have the appearance of conventional competition, the court concluded that it could not be justified as such. Finally it refused to recognize any analogy between the strike for the closed shop and a strike for higher wages because it thought that the same reasons of political expedience for conceding the legality of a strike based on already existing economic power did not apply to a strike aimed at building up even greater bargaining power.

Within its own broad principles of law, similar to those developed in the English cases, the Massachusetts court seems to have been confused. Analytically both the strike in *Plant v. Woods*—the decorators' case—and the strike in *Pickett v. Walsh*—the pointers' case—can be shown to have been competition. Neither the parties nor the judges in these two cases were then sufficiently accustomed to thinking about organized labor enterprise in terms of present-day economic analysis to recognize that this was true. If they had been, they would have realized that the defendants in *Plant v. Woods* were anxious to extend their organization in order to perfect the economic advantage of all organized labor against unorganized, or differently organized, labor in the decorating industry. They were concerned in carrying on their battle of trade, if you please, against the mass of unorganized or, in their opinion, poorly organized, workers who were satisfied with employment standards below those which they thought acceptable.

Through their organization they had established better conditions of employment than those which the rival union and unorganized labor had been able to secure. If they left employers free to hire nonmembers of their union at wages below their standard rates, their security would be undermined in the long run. Such an effect is today more easily observed in an industry consisting of several units producing the same commodity, some of which are unionized and some not. The employers in unorganized units enjoy a competitive advantage over organized units, based on the wage differential which normally exists. If the union is to retain its higher standards of employment, it must go out and organize those other units. If it does not do so, the consuming public will eventually tend to purchase only the cheaper nonunion-made goods; and the organized employers will either have to abandon the union employment standards or go out of business.

This, of course, hurts the union. Naturally the union, in striving to overcome this effect, does not attempt to put the nonunion plants out of business but undertakes to eliminate the nonunion competition by absorbing it into the union ranks. Such an undertaking seems reasonably described as competition between organized and unorganized labor. Nor does strife between two unions already established in the same industry, as in *Plant v. Woods*—the decorators' case—seem much different from this, when one of them has secured high employment standards and the other has not. For in a competitive sense the more successful union is entitled to believe that it is prevented from maintaining its high standards and from achieving even higher ones just as much by the weak bargaining of the other union, over whose affairs it has no control, as it is by the individual bargaining of completely unorganized labor, over which it likewise has no control.

In the long run, the Massachusetts court, and other courts following its lead, got no further than did the House of Lords in developing a consistent body of law to govern the activities of both business and organized labor enterprise. It first enunciated a broad principle based on the maxim that harm intentionally inflicted even without recourse to specifically illegal means is actionable unless justified, stating clearly that trade competition is an acceptable justification. This was not as broad as the justification asserted by the House of Lords in the *Mogul* case—pursuit of self-interest and gain—but it meant the same thing. Then, by construing the concept of trade competition in an exceedingly narrow fashion, it held organized labor accountable for all harm it caused others through the exercise of purely economic pressures in the pursuit of self-interest and gain. And it denied the effect of this category of justification except in one case of a ruthless fight to the death, too closely resembling business competition to be treated otherwise. The House of Lords had also perverted its original broad principle of trade competition as a justification in this same fashion. But while the law lords kept an ace under the woolsack in the shape of the doctrine of civil conspiracy—to be used when everything else failed—the Massachusetts court, and others following it, invented the illegal purpose doctrine to use as a last resort. Both courts, however, failed to state any articulate standards of lawful conduct or legal objectives against which to judge the activities and motives of organized labor. This in effect promulgated a government of men and not of law.

THE LIBERAL DEVELOPMENT IN NEW YORK STATE

A startling contrast to these views occurred in the liberal philosophy developed at about the same time by the highest court in the neighboring state of New York. How the judiciary of two adjacent, highly industrialized states could have been such poles apart in their interpretations of what were supposed to be the same common-law principles must remain a mystery. At any rate, after the New York court had begun to follow the lead of the Massachusetts judges, it suddenly switched to the opposite extreme position taken by Lord Herschell in *Allen v. Flood,* the most liberal of the three House of Lords Trilogy cases.

In 1897 the New York court had decided in *Curran v. Galen* that a union was liable in damages to a nonunion employee whose discharge it secured under a closed shop contract. This contract, the court said, was invalid, declaring that while the "social principle" of organized self-help was all right, unions could not go so far "as either to intend, or to accomplish, injury to others." And it concluded its short opinion with the remark: "While it may be true, as argued, that the contract was entered into, on the part of the [employer], with the object of avoiding disputes and conflicts with the workingmen's organization, that feature and such an intention cannot aid the defense, nor legalize a plan of compelling workingmen, not in affiliation with the organization, to join it, at the peril of being deprived of their employment and of the means of making a livelihood."

Five years later this same court completely reversed its position, after a slight shift in its personnel. Thus, in *National Protective Association v. Cumming* a majority of the court, through Chief Justice Parker, established beyond any doubt the right of a union to sponsor a strike for the closed shop. Briefly he outlined the privilege of any employee to leave his job at will without stating his reasons and his freedom to disclose that he was quitting because he did not wish to work alongside of certain other workmen. If the employer wished to discharge tl.ese other workmen as the price of retaining the employee about to quit, he was at liberty to do so. "The same rule," he said, "applies to a body of men who, having organized for purposes deemed beneficial to themselves, refuse to work. Their reasons may seem inadequate to others, but if it seems to be in their interest as members of an organization to refuse longer to work, it is their legal right to stop. *The reason may no more be demanded, as a right, of the organization than of an individual, but if they elect to state the reason their right to stop work is not cut off because the reason seems inadequate or selfish to the employer or to organized society.* And if the conduct of the members of an organization is legal in itself, it does not become illegal because the organization directs one of its members to state the reason for its conduct."

Although the chief justice declared flatly "that the defendants had the right to strike for any reason they deemed a just one, and further, had the right to notify their employer of their purpose to strike," he nevertheless went on to suggest some reasons which might justify their decision not to work with certain fellow employees. "I know it is said in another opinion in this case," he declared, "that 'workmen cannot dictate to employers how they shall carry on their business, nor whom they shall or shall not employ'; but I dissent absolutely from that proposition, and assert that, so long as workmen must assume all the risk of injury that may come to them through the carelessness of co-employees, they have the moral and legal right to say that they will not work with certain men, and the employer must accept their dictation or go without their services." He pointed out that some of the workmen's compensation acts had been held unconstitutional and asked how else the men could protect themselves from the carelessness of fellow servants unless they could refuse to work with men who did not measure up to set standards of care. He then repeated that he was saying this not to justify completely the collective refusal to work with certain men but merely to point out that some obviously reasonable purposes did exist for such action.

The chief justice then derided the proposition that motive rendered the collective exercise of economic coercion lawful or unlawful. "Within all the authorities upholding the principle of competition, if the motive be to destroy another's business in order to secure business for yourself, the motive is good; but, according to a few recent authorities, if you do not need the business, or do not wish it, then the motive is bad. . . ." This reference to narrow Massachusetts conceptions of trade competition as a justification and to scattered state court decisions promulgating as law purely judicial notions of so-called "fair" and "unfair" competition, depending on the lenience or harshness of the aggressor, he meant as a contemptuous reminder that only legislatures, and not judges, had any business to inquire into motives behind otherwise lawful conduct or to declare such conduct unlawful because they thought its purpose unworthy. But even conceding the validity of this trend as sound law, he said that it made no difference in the decision of the case at hand.

This *Cumming* case was a struggle between two rival organizations of workingmen, somewhat like that described in *Plant v. Woods*—the Massachusetts case involving the struggle between the rival decorators' unions—although in some respects different. It appeared in the report that the defendants, by refusing to work for any employers hiring members of the rival

union, wanted to drive the members of that union out of the
industrial field of steam fitting and plumbing and to fill their
places with their own unemployed fellow members. But it was
also suggested that they thought that the members of the rival
organization were not sufficiently up to the formers' standards
of skill to make them eligible for membership in their own
union—the fair implication being that they would otherwise
be welcomed as members. Apparently the defendants were most
concerned over the fact that their higher wages and other conditions of employment were being undermined by plaintiff's
members, who were willing to work for less and were frequently
chosen by employers for that reason. Hence, in so far as the defendants were attempting to take work away from the plaintiff's
members, they were behaving lawfully. And in so far as they
were trying merely to unionize such rivals as could qualify in
their union, for the ultimate protection of their established
standards, the chief justice thought that the defendants were
still acting lawfully, even under the recent judicial trend
toward standards of fair competition, the validity of which he
conceded only for sake of the argument.

Toward the end of his opinion in the *Cumming* case the
chief justice referred to the last of the trial court's findings,
which read in part as follows: "I find that the threats made by
the defendants and the acts of the said walking delegates in
causing the discharge of the members of the plaintiff association by means of threats of a general strike of other workmen,
constituted an illegal combination and conspiracy." He dismissed this as not a finding of fact, but a conclusion of law
erroneously drawn from the facts. Since the findings nowhere
even suggested that the defendants threatened an illegal or
unlawful act, they could not possibly support a judgment "that
absolutely enjoins the defendant associations and their members from striking."

This so-called finding of the trial court is of considerable interest, since it reveals in such an undisguised fashion the latent
vitality of the old conspiracy formula, which even the dis-

senting justices of the highest New York court had the political good sense not to support openly. Justice Vann, for the dissent, saw the defendants' activity as illegal threats to destroy the employers' freedom to do business as they saw fit. His inability to reconcile defendants' acts with any conception of competition is revealed by the following statements: "Public policy requires that the wages of labor should be regulated by the law of competition and of supply and demand, the same as the sale of food or clothing. . . . Competition in the labor market is lawful, but a combination to shut workmen out of the market altogether is unlawful."

This decision in the *Cumming* case committed the New York court to a liberal view quite different from the narrow position adopted by the Massachusetts court. Another decision, five years later, revealed its complete acceptance of the legality of the closed shop. There it appeared that the defendant manufacturer had voluntarily entered into a closed shop agreement with a union. The employer had guaranteed compliance with its terms by giving a note to the union, on the understanding that this note would be paid if he violated the agreement. Subsequently he did break the contract. When the union sued him on the note, he based his defense on the contention that the agreement violated was void as against public policy because of the closed shop provision.

The highest New York court in *Jacobs v. Cohen* gave the union judgment on the note, upholding the validity of the agreement. Judge Gray, for the majority of the court, spoke of the "underlying law of human society" which "moves men to unite for the better achievement of a common aim" as a "social principle" justifying organized action. The "surrender of individual liberty" involved is, he said, "but an extension of the right of freedom of action," and unless it is specifically illegal or used merely to injure others with no ultimate purpose of selfish advantage, it is perfectly proper. Justice Vann, for the dissent, thought the closed shop agreement contrary to public policy, condemning it as a device through which the union had secured a monopoly of employment in the needle industry in New York. This abrogation of their own rights by both the employers and workers co-operating with the union, he said, "was a form of slavery, even if voluntarily submitted to, for whoever controls the means by which a man lives controls the man himself." But his voice was virtually the last note of resistance against the liberal trend in New York, at least until a kind of reaction set in around the end of the 1930's.

This account of judicial developments in Massachusetts and New York reveals the radically different conceptions of labor policy which prevailed in this country around the turn of the century. One school of judges took the position that the economic activities of unions were lawful or unlawful in accordance with the illegal purpose doctrine, which in effect meant in accordance with inarticulate judicial notions of rightfulness or wrongfulness of motive. The nearest this school approached to a helpful general principle was the acknowledgment that unions, like conventional business groups, might justify their harmful economic activities under the cloak of competition, but it took an exceedingly narrow view of competition—that of a pattern seldom reproduced outside of business circles. It failed to make allowance thereunder for most of the purely economic coercion initiated by unions intent on self-protection and gain. Instead of guiding itself by the principle that sauce for the goose is sauce for the gander, leaving the legislatures to decide as a political matter what conduct and objectives are permissible and what are not, this school of judges boldly undertook to decide these issues on their own responsibility.

The more liberal courts, on the other hand, took either one or both of two quite different positions. Some judges belonging to this school of thought believed that unions causing harm to others, while in pursuit of gain, were behaving lawfully unless they engaged in conduct specifically tortious or criminal in itself, such as assault and trespass. As long as unions refrained from specific transgressions of this sort, these judges declared them to be within the law as they found it to be, leaving the creation of new controls to the proper branch of government, the legislatures. Generally, they refused to scrutinize the purposes behind union activity, holding that if the outward conduct was lawful in itself, the purposes to be served by such conduct were none of their business as judges unless, of course, such purposes themselves were illegal under established categories of tort and crime.

This position, we may, for lack of a better term, call the *civil rights* doctrine. Some of the liberal judges, however, preferred to follow the maxim that the intentional infliction of harm on others is actionable, unless justified, taking a broad view of justification and including within it a conception of competition which covered all uses of concerted economic coercion for self-advancement and self-protection. This might conveniently be called the economic interest approach. But whatever we may choose to call these various judicial developments in nineteenth and early twentieth century America, they constituted, together with the contemporary English views, the foundation on which our modern law of labor relations has been built. They serve as a fitting threshold to the remaining chapters of this book.

CHAPTER IV

THE JUDICIAL RESTRICTIONS OF UNIONS—THE LABOR INJUNCTION

> We especially object to government by injunction as a new and highly dangerous form of oppression by which Federal Judges, in contempt of the laws of the States and rights of citizens, become at once legislators, judges and executioners.—*Proceedings of the Democratic National Convention,* 1896.

THE GENERAL principles discussed in the preceding two chapters stemmed originally from litigation involving business combinations. But in the course of their adaptation to labor union cases they became somewhat confused. It is, of course, very easy to criticize the courts for applying these original principles in one way against business combinations and in another way against labor unions. But it is justifiable criticism as long as they remain on the books as accepted law. For then they should have been consistently applied. Even if they were so applied, however, the principles themselves would by no means remain beyond reproach. While courts applying these common-law principles consistently have done what they were bound to do as judges, it is not at all clear that such principles reflect a sound commercial policy in sanctioning the exercise of all kinds of economic coercion through uncontrolled combination, whether among businessmen or labor unions.

Some of these techniques have been ruthless and vicious. And it seems impossible to justify them under any conception of competition. Certainly the kinds of activities carried on by the business combinations described in the preceding two chapters are of no real service to the consuming public; and those of the unions cannot fairly be judged in any different light. Many no doubt regard such activities as the sort of competition which is the life of trade. But many more probably believe that competition of this character results in a stifling of trade and the throttling of that type of economic interplay between competing units which tends to benefit consumers in lowering prices by increased efficiency in production and marketing methods. For these activities constitute a course of conduct intended to promote the security of enterprisers through the control of production and marketing and the elimination of so-called "wasteful competition"—that is, of competition as it has been traditionally recognized in economics textbooks.

Perhaps the courts cannot fairly have been expected to hit upon a common economic theory of competition and to enforce it uniformly. Anyone who has been around must realize that there are always a variety of economic theories competing with each other in the general market place of ideas. Since many of us are addicted to one or another of such theories as the only valid one, we may find it shocking when the conclusion is suggested that the official choice of one system of economic values to prevail over all others is a political matter. No economist worth his salt would like to make this admission, any more than a priest of one church would concede that the choice of the true faith is a matter of the general consensus. Yet in so far as our legal system is concerned, the choice of our prevailing economic philosophy is inescapably a political matter. The obvious choice between economic philosophies now seems to be between substantially free enterprise, on the one hand, and a more or less controlled or planned economy on the other. Of course, these concepts are very broad verbalizations, charged in these days with a good deal of emotional content. But they do suggest attitudes and ways of thinking about our economic life. At least we may be able to agree that people subscribing to the idea of substantial free enterprise want an absolute minimum of official governmental control, while those embracing the idea of a controlled or planned economy feel otherwise, albeit these latter folk may differ radically among themselves as to the methods and degrees of control and planning.

But it does seem futile not to admit that the making of such choices is essentially a function of our political life. If it is, then such choices are not for our courts to make. They are, rather, matters for our legislatures to handle, within the framework of our state and federal constitutions. In this way alone can the choice be safely made if we are to continue as a representative government, even if the choice which actually prevails is regarded by some groups of experts as horrible and disastrous. It is theoretically possible for people in a country like the United States to become sufficiently educated to make fairly objective choices. As a matter of practical fact, most people voting on choices of this sort have only the haziest notions of what they imply, with perhaps particular convictions that the courses of action they support will best serve their own interests. And these choices at elections, as well as those made by elected representatives in response to the voting, are influenced largely by spates of rhetoric either too confusing to be intelligible or sufficiently clear to be disturbing. Nevertheless, this is the way our choices are made. Our judges should properly have no part in the matter at all.

When these policy choices have become crystallized into statutes, our courts just have to say whether or not these new laws are valid expressions of constitutional power. If they are, their job then is to interpret and apply them. Until such political changes occur, their function remains that of applying the values of the past as they are reflected in the principles of the common law. By and large, when the legislatures have not spoken, the common law leaves no room for judicial speculation about economic theories.

The inherited, unwritten common law contains categories of illegal conduct such as assault and battery, trespass, fraud and deceit, libel and slander and inducing breach of contract, as well as deeply imbedded notions about property and personal rights and their protection. Granted that it is not always easy to detect from evidence submitted in courts the absence or presence of specific illegal conduct like that just mentioned, yet it is perfectly simple to observe its complete absence in most cases of purely economic coercion. And when it is clearly absent in actions brought at common law to secure redress for harm caused by economic coercion, courts are supposed to dismiss such actions, regardless of what they may think about the implications of the coercive undertaking in question—certainly if it appears that it was initiated to promote some interest of the defendants.

Now it is true that the common law is occasionally rather vague and general, with plenty of room for judicial interpretation. Thus, a particular jurisdiction may have as part of its unwritten law the proposition that intentionally inflicted harm on another is actionable, unless justified. And a court applying this principle to a case in which economic coercion alone is shown, having found that no specific illegal act such as assault, trespass, fraud or libel has occurred, must then inquire into the crucial issue of justification. This is where it runs into difficulty about competition and economic theory in general. By and large, the only safe test the court can apply in detecting justification is whether or not the particular pressure in question was exercised to further some interest or objective of the person or group behind it.

A detail in this inquiry may well be whether or not this interest must be of *direct* pecuniary concern to the members of this group if the justification is to stand. If so, then the court's task of determining what is "direct" is a much greater problem than most people unfamiliar with our law could possibly imagine. Certainly it must be plain that the scrutiny of alleged justification in applying this principle of law gives play to the economic predilections of judges and invites them to enter upon excursions into the field of policy which is properly reserved for legislators only. Indeed, it is this danger which has no doubt led some courts to deny the principle of law under discussion and to insist that conduct harmful to others is illegal only if it falls within some clear-cut category of tort or crime such as assault and battery, et cetera, or constitutes a breach of a statute—the so-called civil rights theory.

Assuming, then, that a court should not make fundamental choices of policy in litigation involving economic coercion but should leave such matters to the legislatures, the proper judicial attitude may seem to be some kind of free enterprise philosophy. It can resemble complete laissez faire, as when the court recognizes no need for justification, or it can seem relatively limited, as when the court does require the showing of some kind of justification like self-advancement or self-protection in an economic sense—just as long, in either event, as it leaves out of consideration all theories of economics and sticks to settled categories of illegality and established rules of law as the standards to be enforced. But some people will then suggest that the courts pursuing either course have willynilly adopted the *economic philosophy* of laissez faire or free enterprise— that is, have adopted an economic value position. And the answer is that, while such a result may well be true, what the courts are really doing is to leave to the legislatures the choice of curbs, if any, to be imposed on all kinds of economic enterprise, business or labor. For whether we like it or not, the prevailing Anglo-American common-law philosophy has always been one of free enterprise.

The ideal of the common law was to build up a series of sanctions against specific types of behavior too egregiously bad to tolerate, such as assault and battery, et cetera, leaving plenty of room within which people remained free to operate at will. According to the spirit of the common law, no penalty was to be created against the use of purely economic coercion, so long as it was exercised by means which in themselves were perfectly lawful, such as buying, selling, and refusals to deal in any way with others. Perhaps the greatest confusion occurred in the common law when the courts created judicial curbs against the purely economic activities of labor combinations. Yet it must be said on behalf of the early courts that in creating these curbs, they were trying to fulfill their ideals of free enterprise by protecting business and industry—which they regarded as the life stream of society—from the most determined interferences with achievement of these ideals. Their mistake was a failure to recognize in the interests and activities of labor unions simply another type of economic enterprise—from the angle of trying to get ahead and to pursue gain, not much different from the types of enterprise they were trying to foster. It would seem, therefore, that the only way in which the courts could really be impartial, and at the same time achieve their common-law ideals, would have been to treat all purely economic activity as lawful until the legislatures declared otherwise or except in cases in which such activity did not conform to some established common-law principle requiring proof of justification.

SOME ASPECTS OF THE LAW OF TORTS IN RELATION TO LABOR UNIONS

Now it is time to examine in detail the nature of the controls which our courts have traditionally exercised over the economic activities of labor unions. From a formal point of view, these controls may be defined as convictions for the commission of crimes, adverse money judgments for the commission of torts, and injunctions restraining the continuance of injuries to property interests. Now everyone knows that in the heat of industrial conflict labor unionists frequently commit wrongful acts. If they beat up strikebreakers and representatives of management, assault them, or threaten to do so, they should be punished. And if they violate property rights by breaking windows, sabotaging a plant, damaging cars and goods and by otherwise invading tangible interests of others, they should be punished. Such conduct is obviously illegal. Society cannot compromise upon how it should be treated. But in most of our states there are more subtle categories of common-law tort liability, easily adaptable to labor cases, the desirability of which is not so clear.

Thus, some of our courts declare that conduct offensive or harmful to others, even if it is in itself absolutely lawful, becomes unlawful when done with malice. An illustration of this is the spite fence case. Two neighbors have a falling out and, just for spite, one builds a fence between their yards, anywhere from ten to thirty feet high. This sort of thing, with variations, has happened many times. Of course, the man building the fence has a perfect "right" to do it, or so several of our state courts have decided. His neighbor would have had no redress if the erection had been a building of some sort, shutting off light, air and the view in the same way. But other state courts have declared that the erection of a useless structure, just to spite one's neighbor, is tortious, the malicious motive making it unlawful. And they have made the offender remove it.

Another illustration is the man in the valley who does not like his neighbors above him on the hill. All of these people concerned are dependent on the percolating water beneath them, which they pump up for domestic use. Each has the property right, as an incident to the ownership of surface land, to pump up all of the water he wishes. The man in the valley pumps it continuously, and what he does not need, he lets run off on the surface. Since by force of gravity the percolating water constantly flows down to his pump, his neighbors on the hill soon have insufficient water for their needs. A court, holding that spite or malice makes otherwise lawful conduct unlawful, will prevent this sort of thing, although it recognizes the right of the man in the valley to take all of the percolating water if he puts it to some useful purpose. But the Wisconsin Supreme Court would not stop him when he merely wasted it to quench his spite, declaring that whatever his motive might be, it was the exercise of a property right. Indeed, it went to the questionable extent of deciding that even the legislature could not constitutionally prevent this conduct.

This sort of case may occur in the business world under

somewhat different circumstances. Thus, a rich man forecloses a mortgage on a business building in a very small town, taking the premises over himself. He fits up a place in it as a modern barber shop and then invites the town barber to leave his old stand and rent this new place. The barber refuses to do so, which is his right. Thereupon the rich man hires a couple of barbers from out of town to run his shop and enables them practically to give away haircuts and shaves until the first barber is ruined financially and has to shut down. Then the rich man leases his shop to one of the barbers he brought in and has a profitable investment. The Minnesota Supreme Court said that this was unlawful if the barber could prove that the rich man had done what he was alleged to have done. And when a small retail oil peddler refused to handle its oil on his house-to-house route, a great national oil company, which did not engage in retail sales, set up its own delivery service to undersell the peddler until he went into bankruptcy. When the company's immediate end was accomplished, it promptly sold its horses and wagons to another man who contracted to purvey its product. The Iowa Supreme Court said that this was unlawful.

Most people, no doubt, would agree that these two decisions were correct and achieved what they would call justice. They would probably justify their belief by concluding that the rich man and the oil company were rascals. But these cases are not as simple as that. They involve the lawful use of property—economic power, if you will—to advance temporal interests in a social system based on property and its free use. For surely even a rich man is free to give away haircuts and shaves. Presumably a great oil company is entitled to retail oil at as low a price as it wishes! While the defendant's motives may have been purely malicious in the spite fence and percolating water cases, in each of these last two the dominant motive was plainly commercial. The rich man wanted to lease his shop and the oil company wanted to maintain and protect retail market outlets for its product. Just as soon as the courts permit juries to speculate on the motives of these enterprisers in order to determine whether or not they were malicious, they are going to get into trouble. Indeed, there is something ironic about drawing indignant juries for this purpose from the very cross section of society which, by accepting the free haircuts and by purchasing the cheaper oil, made it possible for these instances of economic coercion to succeed.

In spite of the obvious difficulties, several of our courts believe that they can set up standards in accordance with which conduct of this sort can be judged lawful or unlawful. With the approval of some legal scholars, they are tending toward a new category of tort liability called unfair competition, under which they are trying to prevent conduct of the type just described. Some of them make recovery depend on proof of malice, although this malice frequently turns out to be simply the deliberate intention to do what was done. Other courts, recognizing this, incline toward legal controls of competitive methods which employ what they regard as the contemptible use of superior economic power. But they are taking a good deal on themselves when they try to establish reasonably clear standards of what might be considered fairness in the competitive world.

A referee of a boxing match applies a set of arbitrary rules to the fighters; but he would never think of making up such rules as he goes along or even of introducing into his decisions long-felt personal notions of what he believes is fair in the ring. Referees of sporting contests accept and conform to a set of legislated rules. They would be out of work very quickly if they did otherwise. Courts are expected traditionally to behave in much the same fashion. The rules they enforce have been long established and are well recognized. If they are to be changed, it seems best that the legislatures should make the changes. For any modifications of them strike at very fundamental social policy and should be considered and debated by our traditional policy-making branch of government. In this way such changes will become the resultant of all social opinion and will not tend merely to reflect the notions of a few judges, which vary from man to man.

Certainly courts judging the behavior of labor unionists in accordance with some standard of malice or unfair competition, which they have more or less made up for the occasion, are bound to get into trouble and produce confusion. What happened to the law lords in the meat cutters' case of *Quinn v. Leathem* may then happen to any judge. They may perceive wickedness, unfairness and malice in labor union activity no more ruthless than the conduct of the business association in the *Mogul* case, which the House of Lords thought perfectly permissible. And if courts once become well embarked on the attempt to prevent all purely economic activity which they do not believe to be fair, then all our economic life has become subject to judicial censorship and we will have slipped imperceptibly into an uncharted oligarchy.

Before examining any other categories of tort liability, we should consider one other aspect of harmful conduct which is clearly lawful aside from the motive behind it. Everyone will agree that it is lawful to spend one's own money or to withhold it, to deal freely with others or to refuse to do so. But suppose a man gives money to another to secure the murder of a third person. Here we have no trouble recognizing both crime and tort on the part of the man paying the money, for he did something more than merely pay out money. And if he had merely refused to continue a course of legitimate business advantageous to another unless such other person murdered a third, we should have an equally clear case.

Hence, we can probably afford to make the general statement that pure economic coercion, ordinarily lawful in itself when designed to secure an objective even quite harmful but not illegal in itself, becomes unlawful when exerted to secure an end which is illegal in itself. Such a principle is well established and is perfectly easy to apply as long as the court applying it is scrupulous in seeing that the objective to be secured by the economic coercion is illegal in itself when judged in strict accordance with other well-established common-law or statutory categories of tort or crime. The only possible difficulty—and it is a very real one—is that courts using this general rule may too easily slip into the habit of concluding that the objective to be secured is not to their liking and is, hence, illegal. This is the sort of thing which occurred when Anglo-American courts once used the doctrine of criminal conspiracy. It has unfortunately recurred in labor litigation as one phase of applying another very questionable category of tort liability called civil conspiracy. And it is almost exactly what happened in the development of the illegal purpose doctrine. A rule of this sort is a very dangerous toy for the courts to play with, because it enables them to conceal under the dignified cloak of legal verbiage conclusions on matters of economics and policy which only the legislatures should make.

Another tort category, adapted out of its original context to certain labor situations, is inducing breach of contract. This tort originated shortly after the middle of the nineteenth century in a case involving a once famous opera singer, Johanna Wagner. Lumley had her under contract to sing only for him in London. Gye induced her to break her contract with Lumley and sing only under his management. Now Lumley, of course, could have secured a judgment against Miss Wagner for breach of contract. But for reasons best known to him—perhaps Miss Wagner's impecuniosity—Lumley preferred to recover damages from Gye, who had started all the trouble. In a decision creating this new tort, the English courts gave him a judgment for damages against Gye. Apparently the judges believed that Gye had damaged a thing of value to Lumley, in the nature of a property right, just as obviously as if he had taken a hatchet and chopped up Lumley's coach.

Of course, the court's position might have been analogized to the rule described in a previous paragraph, except that Gye had not offered Miss Wagner money to commit a tort or crime but only to break her contract with Lumley. In any event, the tort became established for inducing the breach of any con-

tract for personal service. It has been developed in most jurisdictions to cover inducements of the breach of almost any
kind of commercial contract. Courts administering this tort
category at first required the proof of malice before recognizing
its existence in a particular case. But this has been changed,
since all that malice has finally come to mean is proof that the
inducement of the breach was deliberate and intended to further the defendant's ends. Since the inception of this tort,
however, courts have recognized justification for inducing
breaches of contract in proper instances, as when a doctor ad-
vises a patient because of the state of his health to break a
contract he has made binding him to work under precarious
conditions in the jungles of Africa.

These various categories of tort liability were not originally
used by the courts against labor unions. But when they discovered the usefulness of injunctions to control labor union
activities, the courts found that these vague and ambiguous
tort notions furnished admirable theoretical foundations on
which to rest their injunctions. In the decade preceding the
1890's American courts had followed the contemporary English
pattern of controlling the unpopular activities of labor unions
by awarding to the persons harmed money judgments in tort
actions against the unions' leaders. By this time the criminal
penalty had all but disappeared with the dwindling away of
the doctrine of criminal conspiracy, only occasional convictions
recurring at intervals under state statutes expressly prohibiting
certain defined activities of unions. Of course, neither of these
proceedings could be exercised against unions, as such, but
could be used practicably only against their leaders and members as individuals, since unions as a rule were not incorporated
and could not be sued as legal persons. But judgments for
damages and the occasional convictions under statutes were
not very effective sanctions against labor union activities harmful to others, even if they did succeed in stigmatizing so much
of what organized labor did as unlawful. Most of the time union
leaders and their constituents did not have the money to pay

judgments against them. And if they did pay, they were not in the least discouraged. Furthermore, adverse money judgments and criminal convictions usually followed the occurrence of strikes, picketing, and boycotts, and were small solace to employers for the harm which had already befallen them.

Employers and the courts needed a more adequate tool—some sort of preventive device which could be used to nip such mischief in the bud before it occurred. Criminal prosecutions and tort actions for damages were cumbersome and involved too much of the law's delay, what with lengthy procedure and jury trial. Furthermore they deprived courts of complete control over unions, because they could never be certain that juries would convict or bring in adequate verdicts against the defendants. Here was a situation crying out for a judicial technique which could insure swift and effective justice, and over which the courts might exercise a complete and exclusive control, free from the cumbersome devices of the common law and from the vagaries of common juries. The answer to this need happened along in a most fortuitous fashion.

THE LABOR INJUNCTION AND ITS ABUSE

Sometime around 1880 an equity court appointed a receiver to run a railroad which was in financial difficulties. It was the receiver's duty to manage the property in a prudent and profitable manner in order to protect the interests of investors. The railroad's employees threatened this objective by a strike for higher wages. But they did not realize that by this conduct they were interfering with the duties of an officer of a court—and of an equity court, at that.

Now the point of this story will be more clear after an interpolation explaining what an equity court is. An equity court—now usually the same judge who also sits as a court of law, except that he does not follow the same rules when exercising equity powers—is set up to do far different things from those ordinarily done by a law court. In short, it exists to "do equity," a concept which in itself requires some explanation. Equity is an historical development from the days of the early king's courts in England whereby the king's secretary, his chancellor, was ordered by the king to satisfy the royal conscience by doing justice in all cases, usually involving property, with which the king's regular courts of law were not empowered to deal under the limited common law and statutes of those days.

Eventually this duty was accorded to established equity courts which built up a body of precedent law all of their own. They were primarily concerned with litigation where money damages would not be suitable, where "the remedy at law would be inadequate," as they put it. Their judgments usually consisted of orders either to do or undo some act or to refrain from entering upon or continuing a threatened or already undertaken course of action. They did not have to use juries in reaching their judgments. They could fulfill their function of preventive justice by issuing a temporary restraining order or injunction, pending the actual trial, in order to be sure that the harm threatened could effectively be avoided if the trial ultimately revealed that the person threatening the harmful course of conduct really was in the wrong. And if the order of an equity court was not obeyed scrupulously, this disobedience was an offense which could be punished summarily as a contempt of court by the court itself, acting without a jury—such punishment being immediate imprisonment for as long as the occasion warranted.

Now to return to our story about the receiver of the railroad. He complained to the equity judge, for whom he was acting, that the strike endangered the property entrusted to him. Although he did not formally request an injunction against the strikers, he asked the court to treat the strike as a contumacious disregard of the court's order setting up the receivership. The analogy to the injunction itself was, of course, obvious. At any rate, the court proceeded against the leaders of the strike and jailed them for contempt. Then the strike was over. The whole transaction, from strike to jail, could be counted in hours rather than in the weeks and months required in actions at law.

Here was a device for the control of labor disputes that really worked. Our courts rapidly took it over, making it a well-established American institution by the 1890's. All they required to be shown to make the injunction appropriate was an actual or threatened tortious invasion of property which, if it were not stopped or forbidden, would result in irreparable damage to the property, under circumstances indicating no adequate remedy at law. The only stumbling block—not a very serious one to the American judges—was the uncertainty of whether or not strikes and boycotts were harmful to actual property. Of course it was easy to see that strikers who broke windows and damaged buildings, machinery and rolling stock, or threatened to do so, were harming or threatening to harm property. But it was not so obvious that the purely economic pressures of unions, which caused great monetary losses to employers and sometimes to nonunion labor, were harmful to property. If they were, it was certainly in a different sense. For the harm to intangible interests of employers and nonunion labor, such as loss of production, of customers and business, and of profitable relationships, did not touch anything theretofore conventionally thought of as property.

The English courts consistently refused to issue injunctions against labor unions, even when they regarded the conduct assailed as unlawful, as long as such conduct was purely economic coercion causing harm to intangible interests of this sort. They regarded the injunction as something to prevent harm to irreplaceable tangible property interests. Thus, if the defendant proposed to cut a certain grove of old trees, claiming a right to do so, at the instance of another who insisted that the trees were his, an English court would order the defendant not to proceed with his plan, pending litigation. If, during the trial, the defendant was found to have been mistaken in his claim, the court would make the injunction permanent.

But the American courts chose to go further and to assume that intangible business interests also are property, to be protected by injunction. It seems apparent, however, that they really did not care whether or not such interests were property at all but were only concerned with declaring them to be things of value which they believed should be safe-guarded in the only practicable way to do so—by the injunction. And if this use of the injunction did not conform strictly to the traditions of equity, which recognized the use of this remedy only to preserve property from irreparable harm, then so much the worse for those traditions. Furthermore, they seemed never to have had any doubts that the remedy at law in damages for the harm done would be inadequate as long as the wrongdoer was a labor union, preferring rather to assume that wage earners would be unable to pay adverse judgments. And they completely ignored the policy behind the traditions of equity, which left people free from personal interference at the hands of the court, except in very special cases of unreasonably precipitated threatened harm to tangible property. And they disregarded the traditional assumption that the personal liberty of even a potential wrongdoer is more important to society than the fact that he might not be able to pay a judgment granted against him for the harm caused by his wrong.

Many American liberals have tried to undermine the use of the injunction against labor unions by arguing that this device is appropriate only to protect tangible property interests and that doing business and maintaining profitable relationships are not property at all. They agree with Holmes, who said in another connection: "By calling a business 'property' you make it seem like land, . . . An established business no doubt may have pecuniary value and commonly is protected by law against various unjustified injuries. But you cannot give it definiteness of contour by calling it a thing. It is a course of conduct and like other conduct is subject to substantial modification according to time and circumstances both in itself and in regard to what shall justify doing it a harm." But this argument of the liberals seems futile. And it by no means strikes anywhere near the root of the real trouble in the use of the injunction against labor unions.

In spite of the ancient tradition of equity courts to the contrary, there is a great deal to be said in favor of the injunction as a device to protect anything or any person against certain types of irreparable harm. Indeed, it is sometimes a pity that our courts do not feel more free to use the injunction where it would prevent great mischief. Of course, it is an exceedingly dangerous device and should be used sparingly, since our American social philosophy is predominantly in favor of allowing freedom of action and enterprise. Rather than to prevent people from doing or saying certain things, it is our tradition to let them act or talk, holding them accountable subsequently for damages to the injured parties if they go too far as measured by our laws. But if judges are convinced that money or punishment would not compensate the complaining victim for the harm he is likely to sustain or right the wrong against him, it would seem sensible for them to do what they can to prevent its occurrence.

The case against the use of the injunction to restrain labor union activities, however, can easily be made on the basis of its past abuse. Justice Frankfurter wrote an overwhelming indictment in his book published while he was still a professor at Harvard Law School. What he has covered in a whole book can only be touched upon here, but the substance of it can be briefly suggested. As soon as the labor injunction became established in the late 1880's almost anyone with an interest in obstructing the activities of labor unions could promptly secure temporary restraining orders for the asking. Continuance of a strike or boycott, after a restraining order or injunction was issued against it, brought down on the heads of the offenders the vengeance of the court through the exercise of its contempt power, unrelieved by the tender mercies of a jury. Hence, strikes, picket lines and boycotts were easily broken up almost before they were begun.

An employer with a strike or other union pressure on his hands went to a judge, regardless of whether or not he was actually sitting on the bench at the time, submitted to him affidavits made out by his own agents to the effect that the strikers or other union folk were about to commit or were committing, and would continue to commit, alleged unlawful acts at his plant, all of which would cause irreparable damage to his property, and prayed for a restraining order pending suit for a permanent injunction. Judges usually issued such orders on request, frequently in the absence of anyone representing the persons to be enjoined. Sometimes these orders were directed at named individuals, but frequently they were not. And in any event they all purported to restrain everyone "whomsoever," in a vague but grand manner. Obviously not much care was devoted in these transactions to legal theory or even to what was actually transpiring around the plant. And by the time the matter was set for the trial which was to determine whether or not the employer was justified in securing protection of this sort, the strike was broken up, either through the obedience of the union leaders or because they were in jail for disobedience.

As a rule, judges behaved in the same casual fashion after the trial between the two parties, when they had to decide whether or not they should grant formal injunctions and, if they decided to do so, how far they should go in preventing what kind of conduct by whom. At these trials, of course, both sides were represented and the judges took testimony, affording opportunity for cross examination. These proceedings took place before judges without juries. Frequently the evidence indicated actual or imminent violence and other unlawful conduct on the part of union members. But whether it did or did not, too many judges got into the habit of making findings of actual or threatened violence and other specifically unlawful conduct where nothing of the sort had occurred or was imminent. In these injunction suits it was customary to serve a summons only upon the leaders of the unions involved, although the injunctions were issued virtually against the world in general. Consequently, anyone violating the broad and comprehensive terms of such injunctions was punished for contempt, whether or not he had been served as a party in the suit, had had the injunction called to his attention by service of its provisions on him, or had ever heard of the injunction at all. For instance, a barber, usually patronized by railroad men, was held in contempt for violation of the broad injunction issued in the 1922 railroad workers' strike because he had hung in his window a sign to the effect that no scabs or strike-breakers were wanted as customers.

Injunctions were drawn in such technical and ambiguous legal terms that one leading state supreme court scathingly compared them to the intricately worded corporate mortgage. And there was seldom any attempt to couch these injunctive prohibitions in simple language which workmen could understand, either in English or in any of the foreign languages prevailing among large sections of our labor population. Too often the judges signing these injunctions did not draft them personally but followed the prevailing custom—perfectly proper in litigation involving less contentious issues—of permitting counsel for the complaining employers to prepare them instead. Unfortunately such injunctions left little, if any, scope for even peaceful economic coercive activity on the part of unions. And the harm occasioned to unions by this summary suppression was not undone even when appellate courts, as they seldom but occasionally did, set aside or modified injunctions because they were against the weight of the evidence adduced or contrary to established law. By that time months had passed, the possible effect of the strike or boycott was long since neutralized, and the union's investment of time, effort and money to organize the pressure was lost.

Even leading conservatives of the early 1900's inveighed against the manner in which courts issued injunctions against organized labor. They were genuinely terrified by the power judges assumed and exercised in these proceedings with such a free hand. Somewhat reasonably, they compared this sweeping exercise of power with the function of legislatures. It was perceived that judges issuing broad and general injunctions against all people whomsoever, regardless of whether or not they had been served with a summons to appear and defend, were virtually promulgating little statutes which declared in advance the illegality of anything done in the premises which the judges did not wish to be done. And they condemned the fashion in which these judges used their contempt power to punish all persons failing to comply with their injunctions, regardless of whether or not such persons had ever been served with a summons originally or had ever had the injunctions brought to their attention. Indeed, they thought this practice furthered the analogy of such injunctions to little statutes, since nonobservance of statute law is always a violation, even if the offender has never heard of the law. But even one who violated a statute was better off than some of the workers hauled up for contempt proceedings, since he had a right to a trial by jury, while the workers held for contempt were tried and punished personally by the judge whose orders they had, sometimes unwittingly, disobeyed.

But perhaps the most alarming feature of the labor injunction, less obvious than the shortcomings just discussed, was the ease with which its use increasingly tempted judges to dispense with any well-founded independent theory of illegality. After all, the injunction was originally supposed to be a kind of remedy. And judicial remedies were supposed to operate as a control of some sort of illegal conduct, actual or threatened. But many courts using the injunction against the activities of labor unions fell into the bad habit of overlooking the need for proof of specific and independently unlawful conduct, either already committed or only threatened, on which to base their injunctive orders. They came to look at much of organized labor's economic coercive activity as enjoinable in itself, without bothering to find or to state in their opinions that it was also unlawful. This was an unfortunate tendency which fed on itself. It seemed to lead many courts to grant sweeping injunctions on the basis of personal or class dislike of organized labor's economic program instead of in accordance with settled standards of law. A process of this sort lent itself admirably to the use of the illegal purpose doctrine.

Instead of pondering over the law governing certain kinds of conduct in an endeavor to determine its legality or illegality, many courts simply looked at the purpose of the conduct or at the economic context in which it occurred, disregarding completely the legal significance of the conduct in itself. And since no generally recognized body of law existed, aside from that governing various specific types of conduct, by which to judge the legality of purposes and contexts, many courts asked to issue injunctions unfortunately slipped into the custom of using as standards their own notions of what they believed to be good or bad as a matter of policy. In this way too many judges began to think of labor union activity as something enjoinable in itself. And since union leaders could not anticipate the vagaries of the judicial mind, they could not define for themselves or their followers the area of permissible economic conduct within which they were legally free to act. This unwholesome state of affairs, where labor unionists never knew just where they stood under the shadow of a brooding and undefined judicial power, involved an almost certain threat of suppression to most of organized labor's bargaining and organizational program, without benefit of any legislative declaration of policy or, indeed, of any rules of the game that might be called law.

A few of the highest state courts consistently held fairly liberal views concerning the lawful ambit of union conduct. Even these courts, however, believed that the injunction was an appropriate device with which to prevent improper labor union activities. But they were relatively generous in the scope of economic action they allowed and were also careful in the way they used their power to issue injunctions whenever they exercised it. The federal courts, like most of the state courts, took a very narrow view of what unions might lawfully do. With the exception of a few individual judges, they became almost the worst offenders in the abuse of the labor injunction. Perhaps because of this, the national political forum became the scene of the most determined fight against the continuance of this abuse. The American Federation of Labor focused on Congress such political pressure as it could muster in an endeavor to secure legislative restrictions against the further misuse by federal judges of their equity powers. In 1914, Congress passed an anti-injunction act of sorts, which was shortly copied by several state legislatures. This federal act and its state prototypes eventually proved abortive. And until the fight against its abuse fell into the more skillful hands of a few outstanding liberals under the natural leadership of Professor Frankfurter, culminating in the really effective Norris-LaGuardia Anti-injunction Act of 1932, the labor injunction remained the most critical issue in the law affecting unions.

CHAPTER V

STRIKES AND BOYCOTTS—CONCERTED REFUSALS TO WORK

I do not perceive any distinction upon which a legal difference of treatment should be based between a lockout, a strike, and a boycott. They often look very unlike, but this litigation illustrates their basic identity. All are voluntary abstentions from acts which normal persons usually perform for mutual benefit; in all the reason for such abstention is a determination to conquer and attain desire by proving that the endurance of the attack will outlast the resistance of the defense.—Hough, J., in *Gill Engraving Company v. Doerr,* 1914.

AFTER ALL of this inquiry into judicial theories and practices, it is high time to make a detailed examination and analysis of the traditional organizational and collective bargaining techniques such as strikes, boycotts, and picketing. Unions naturally try to get all they can for their constituents. Labor leaders, in their relationships toward union members, in many ways resemble business management in its relationship toward stockholders and investors. They like to achieve their ends amicably and with a minimum of trouble, preferring to remain within the law if they can at the same time get what they want. But they are occasionally tempted to take short cuts and indulge in ways of getting things done which are not always proper. While they normally have insufficient wealth to achieve their objectives through the use of money, they sometimes employ the more readily available direct methods of force and threats of violence. They do not expect society to condone such conduct. Also over some generations they have taken the trouble to develop more cumbersome but ultimately just as effective techniques of coercion through the exercise of economic pressures. The most important of these devices are built on concerted refusals to work. They range from the simple strike to fairly complicated boycott situations, sufficiently varied in their nature to require considerable detailed analysis.

STRIKES—LAWFUL AND UNLAWFUL

Combination and concerted action are the very backbone of the whole union movement. While devices like picketing and refusals to patronize are important phases of concerted action, virtually the entire structure of a union's self-help program rests on one simple practice—the refusal to work. The strike is the most simple manifestation of this practice. Indeed, it is, in a manner of speaking, its only manifestation. But the strike occurs in a variety of circumstances, some of which are exceedingly complicated.

The best-known strike is that for higher wages and for other immediate conditions of labor such as a shorter work day or any other term ordinarily embraced in a collective labor agreement. A strike of this sort is initiated by a group of employees against their immediate employer as the result of a failure on their part to achieve their objectives by negotiation. It is an attempt to compel the employer to comply with the collective demands of his employees, at the risk of suffering damage through the shutdown of his plant if he refuses to do so. In short, it is a conflict or tussle, if you please, in which the group of employees on strike pit their economic lasting power against that of the employer. These employees have something their employer wants—their labor—and they proceed on the assumption that he has something within his control they want —the ability to grant such terms and conditions of employment as they are demanding in return for their labor. These striking employees have no intention of severing employment relations with their employer, except temporarily for the duration of the strike, although the employer is free to replace them, if he can. Indeed, this recourse of the employer to the available pool of unorganized labor is theoretically one of the strongest economic assets he has in combatting a strike. And one of the strikers' chief concerns is to see that he does not gain free access to this supply of labor.

Although simple strikes are all essentially the same, whatever their objectives may be, in that they are merely concerted refusals of employees to continue work until their employer complies with some demand they have made, many courts have traditionally classified strikes in terms of their purposes. And depending upon whether or not any such court has regarded the purpose of any particular strike to be lawful or unlawful, it has accordingly declared the strike itself to be legal or illegal. Theoretically this approach is indefensible, since presumably workmen are perfectly free to associate and may concertedly refuse to work, except on such terms and under such conditions as they choose. But law, like everything else, has its intensely practical side. And it was perhaps inevitable that courts should forbid the use of the strike in pursuit of objectives thought to be wholly undesirable and hence illegal. It was not inevitable, however, that they should have carried this illegal purpose doctrine to the extremes which they did. And a proper line of demarcation between lawful and unlawful strikes pointedly illustrates these abuses of judicial power.

There are two fairly obvious analytical methods of testing the legality of a simple strike. Behind each is the realization that the strike is a powerful and compelling economic force which involves the deliberate commission of damage on another. If a strike is called to secure an objective that is, in itself, unlawful under some common-law or statutory category of tort or crime, then it seems fairly apparent that a court should declare the strike illegal. In so far as this depends on the objective being unlawful under a statute, it must appear that the statute in question was constitutional.

An illustration of this test is a strike called to secure management's co-operation in practicing a fraud against the government, such as suppressing information to the proper authorities about the draft irregularities or incomes of certain employees. Since a union and its members consciously attempting by the strike to procure such an objective would virtually be participating in its achievement if they were successful—quite as much as one who paid money to a gunman to murder his enemy would be participating in the murder—it seems an obviously valid exercise of judicial power to declare the whole business unlawful. Indeed, Justice Brandeis once made it quite plain that a strike is unlawful if it is called to achieve a purpose declared unlawful by legislation, when he declared that a state court's conviction of a union official who called a strike under these circumstances was valid under the 14th amendment of the Constitution.

The second test is not so easy to apply. It has a perfectly sound traditional basis in a maxim of the common law which tells us that the deliberate commission of harm on another is unlawful unless it is justified. Justification is sometimes narrowly defined as a kind of competition, but it would be more accurate to describe it as the pursuit of self-interest and gain. Assuming, therefore, that a strike does not in itself involve any conduct illegal under any category of tort or crime and is not intended to achieve any unlawful objective, it should be declared lawful and justifiable in spite of any infliction of harm on the employer, if it is intended to promote the welfare of the strikers, as they see it. And if it is not so intended, then it may be declared unlawful.

The stock illustration of this test is the so-called sympathetic strike. Suppose a carpenters' union strikes a general contractor to secure higher wages, and the local streetcar workers' union, satisfied with their own conditions of employment, strike in sympathy with the carpenters. Many people believe such a sympathetic strike is not quite as aimless as it may appear, since they look upon all labor as a class, the various functional groups of which are in a position to scratch each others' backs at opportune times. They say that through this strike the streetcar workers may conceivably be promoting their own interests by obliging the carpenters' union to aid them in some future clash which they may have with their employer. These people attempt to justify this sympathetic strike by showing that it gives the streetcar company a reason for exerting pressure on the general contractor to make him give in to the carpenters, so that the streetcar operators will then return to work—no doubt the richer for their conviction that they have won the friendship and future backing of the carpenters' union, when, as and if they ever call upon them for like assistance.

Our courts seem perfectly reasonable when they declare such a sympathetic strike unlawful because they cannot perceive that the streetcar operators had at stake any appreciable, or even observable, economic interest, the pursuit of which could amount to a justification for their action. It would be difficult, indeed, to detect anything remotely resembling economic advantage or self-interest in such a strike. Hence, the courts seem to be correct in concluding that a sympathetic strike is an unlawful infliction of damage, aimless and unjustifiable because of the absence of any direct economic advantage to the group of workers participating in it.

But this judicial position nevertheless has its dangers, since it is not always easy to detect the absence of advantage or self-interest on the part of the strikers. After all, it must constantly be kept in mind that many regard the freedom to refrain from work as a sort of civil right, not to be questioned on the basis of its purpose or objective. Courts cannot afford lightly to cast this conceptual position aside but should, rather, retain it as the basic principle from which they may grudgingly make concessions, out of deference to the existing practical needs of the community as against the asserted economic needs and self-interest of the strikers in question.

It might occur to some, as a possible defense of sympathetic strikes, that our judges should place less emphasis on self-interest and more on altruism in providing a justification for intentionally caused harm. But they seem rightly to have made

no allowance for sentimentality in this respect. In administering this maxim, the courts have assumed that people will
mind their own business and have granted them a fairly generous scope for doing just that, realizing that the general run
of people will place their own interests first and will go to
considerable lengths to advance these interests. All they can
properly do to foster this spirit of free enterprise is to stipulate
that people must not pursue their instinct of self-advancement
by conduct in itself illegal and must not seek advantageous
objectives unlawful in themselves. As long as people obey
these strictures, however, they are and should be allowed
plenty of leeway. And though, in the absence of specific legislation, our courts should not be too free in saying what are or
are not lawful objectives, they certainly should be free in determining the nature of justification to take a fairly objective
and realistic view of what constitutes self-protection, self-
interest, and selfish gain.

Actually, the courts have gone rather far in undertaking to
pass on the legality of objectives for the purpose of deciding
whether or not strikes are lawful. For instance, they have declared generally that the removal of foremen whom the workers do not like is an illegal objective, rendering a strike for
that purpose unlawful. Yet foremen are frequently unreasonable in their demands. They sometimes play favorites and hold
grudges, and in other ways affect adversely the working conditions of the employees under them. Decisions to this effect
have been justified as preventing the unwarranted invasion of
management prerogative. But this reasoning seems questionable, because any strike for any purpose is a serious challenge
to management prerogative, whatever that concept may be.

After all, the world is not run to define and maintain the
interests of employers any more than it is to establish and enforce the interests of organized labor. By and large, such matters are either to be decided solely by management through
fiat or by individual employment contracts in the absence of
unionism, by the interplay of collective bargaining when the

employees are organized, or by the operation of political forces through legislation. There is no divine classification of employer prerogatives free from the effects of collective bargaining. As long as a union can show that it is pressing some interest of importance to its constituents not illegal in itself, then, even if its demand reflects poor judgment or bad taste on the part of the employees, no court should undertake to declare unlawful a strike called to secure that objective in the absence of legislation enabling it to do so. Some judges apparently find it very difficult to recognize self-interest on the part of unions in particular strikes. But if they are to perform their duties, they must conquer their own economic predilections in attempting to understand and to judge the matters of interest and importance to working people.

STRIKES AGAINST TECHNOLOGICAL CHANGE

More distressing examples of direct coercion to promote the immediate economic welfare of union members, as they see it, are strikes against technological changes and the old-fashioned jurisdictional strike. The former situation occurs when an employer introduces some mechanical development into his plant for the purpose of saving labor and lowering production costs. Illustrations of this are almost numberless. Suppose a coal mine operator buys machinery which enables him to produce with half as many employees the same amount of coal formerly mined by hand. Suppose a shoe manufacturer installs machines with which one relatively untrained operator can stitch in a given time the number of shoes formerly requiring the work of 80 skilled operators. The old employees can see in these changes only the disappearance of their livelihood through immediate discharge due to technological displacement or through the transformation of their art and a cheapening of the value formerly placed on their manual skill, leading to less opportunities for work and to greatly lowered rates.

Their first instinct is naturally to strike against the intro-duction of changes that affect them so drastically. Such strikes, of course, are futile, because the changes occur anyway, and are almost always of ultimate social value. Yet these displaced workers take small comfort from the assurance that as mem-bers of society they will benefit in the long run by getting cheaper shoes and cheaper coal, as well as a slightly reduced price on everything dependent for its production on coal. And the dependent children of livery stable workers and teamsters could hardly have been expected to foresee the millions of future jobs coming for them in the wake of the new horseless buggy which was putting their fathers out of work.

Courts required to pass on the legality of strikes against technological change have been puzzled about what to do. Indeed, they are still grappling with the problem in different mechanical contexts, such as the displacement of live musicians by the radio, recording devices and the theater organ. But their judicial duty seems to be clear enough. Exasperating as such strikes are, it is hard to see, under our law as it now stands, how the courts can declare them unlawful by assuming that the objective is illegal, simply because it is futile and inci-dentally harmful to society.

The real problem created by technological change is not a judicial problem at all. It is, rather, one of the most acute of our contemporary legislative problems of social security—a matter which cannot be handled adequately without all of society helping to finance, presumably through some sort of taxation, a displacement wage, a retraining period and a re-placement program. For if the consuming public benefits by technological development, as it undoubtedly does, then it should share the burden of paying for such benefits and not leave the social cost almost entirely on the shoulders of dis-placed wage earners and their families. Indeed, a perfectly valid argument justifying our courts in refusing to interfere with technological strikes of any kind is the effect such strikes might have in accelerating the type of legislation mentioned above. After our legislatures have in this way obviated the disastrous immediate effects of technological progress, then, and only then, will even they be in a position to make technological strikes unlawful.

JURISDICTIONAL STRIKES

Courts find themselves in an almost equally difficult position when they are asked to declare jurisdictional strikes unlawful. Strikes of this sort occur frequently when the same employer hires members of two different craft unions to work for him at the same time. For instance, a general building contractor puts carpenters to hanging metal doors and the metal workers, who are engaged elsewhere on the operation, strike because they are not given this work to do. They claim that the work should be theirs because they have always installed materials made of metal, although they concede that doors have not previously been made of metal. And the carpenters claim that the work is properly theirs because they have always hung doors, even if they had always been made of wood. If the general contractor gives the job to the metal workers, the carpenters will strike. If he does not, the metal workers will remain on strike. In either event the whole operation may come to a halt.

This is a difficult situation for courts to solve. Indeed, there is no way they can properly solve it at all, since such a strike is called to secure a perfectly proper economic advantage. Yet this is one of the most wasteful and distressing of all union undertakings. The employer does not really care which union hangs his doors as long as the whole operation is completed. But here again, suppression of such strikes, either by the courts under the illegal purpose doctrine or by the legislatures, does not provide a satisfactory solution. A situation of this type obviously requires legislation creating some sort of body to make jurisdictional awards. Presumably it could be handled by compulsory arbitration. At one time the AF of L established a board of jurisdictional awards within its own organization to settle these cases among its member craft unions. It did not work very well, however, since the stronger union usually got the award on the basis of its greater political influence in the organization—a result which led the weaker union to see what it could gain by striking, since it figured that it had nothing to lose.

But as far as courts are concerned, they seem compelled to declare such strikes lawful in accordance with their own principles of common law. Indeed it would be hard to find a clearer case of what might be called conventional competition as justification for the occurrence of the substantial damage accompanying such strikes. The only possible flaw in this argument is that neither of the two unions mentioned is in a position to do all of the work usually performed by the other union. In *Pickett v. Walsh,* the Massachusetts pointers' case, the bricklayers and stonemasons were able to do all of the work in question, whereas the pointers could perform only one part of it. Under such circumstances the general contractor had a clear way out of his difficulties, while in most jurisdictional strikes he has no recourse at all.

Here again, if courts consistently refuse to interfere with these strikes, our legislatures may be compelled to develop some device like arbitration or a public board of jurisdictional awards, compelling the interested parties to seek recourse to such methods of settlement by declaring these strikes unlawful. In the meantime, developments in industrial as against craft unionism may provide a practical solution of this difficulty. For if all of the building crafts ever become consolidated into one industrial union, either through a rival CIO building trades union or a modification of the present AF of L craft setup, these matters of craft jurisdiction in the building industry would automatically disappear.

STRIKES FOR THE CLOSED SHOP

Courts have perhaps most frequently questioned the legality of strikes that have had as their objective the closed shop. Whether or not such strikes may properly be declared unlawful depends, of course, upon the legality of the closed shop itself. Now the closed shop is one in which membership in a particular union is a condition of employment. Closely allied to it is the so-called union shop in which membership in a particular union becomes a condition of continued employment beyond a certain number of days after hiring or after a collective agreement to that effect becomes operative. The legality of the closed shop and of the union shop has recently become a matter of political concern in several states.

Although it is doubtful that many voters appreciate the issues involved, nevertheless if a majority of them see fit to conclude that the closed or union shop be made unlawful in their state, that is their business. And it is hard to see on what grounds such legislation could possibly be overturned as unconstitutional. But in the absence of statutes outlawing the closed shop, it is equally difficult to understand how state courts can maintain the position that the closed or union shop is unlawful. Yet there is no question that many courts have done so in the absence of legislation, simply by declaring the closed shop an illegal objective because it is monopolistic and attaches a condition to free employment. It is probably safe to guess that just prior to the war, more of our highest state courts adhered to this position than otherwise.

If the closed or union shop is not made unlawful by statute in a particular state, then the courts of that state should not condemn a strike to secure its concession from an employer as an attempt to achieve an illegal objective. Nevertheless, several courts of last resort have done so. This seems indefensible as a matter of common law, for the closed shop is simply the control by a union of all employment opportunities at a particular place of business. As such, it is no different in prin-

ciple from any of the situations where business combinations
have exercised control over certain types of markets through
the use of superior economic power—usually the concerted
refusal to deal with others who refuse in turn to deal solely
with the combination in question. These instances of economic
coercion by business combinations have usually been declared
lawful by our courts in the absence of statutes making them
expressly unlawful. The theory of courts so deciding has been
that a concerted refusal to deal with others is a common-law
privilege, as long as it is not practiced to secure an end in itself
illegal. But this concerted refusal to work is all that a union
does in its attempt by strike to secure a closed shop in a particular plant.

It is true that it strives for complete control of all jobs in
the plant, not only excluding nonunion labor from such jobs
but also preventing the employer from hiring or retaining in
his employment anyone but members of the union. Employees
or applicants for employment who are eligible for membership
in the union, but are unwilling to join, suffer no more harm
than those who are compelled by business combinations either
to abide by the rules of the association or to stay out of the
field entirely. Indeed, unreasonable as some unions have been
about entrance requirements, it is doubtful if they have ever
exercised the ruthless exclusionary pressures which many business combinations, in the name of competition, have been permitted by our courts to practice against outside entrepreneurs.

The unions at least permit applicants for employment to
secure jobs by joining their ranks. And the employer who is
no longer free to hire nonunion employees, or to retain them
as such after a certain number of days, suffers no more harm
than does any of the consumers of goods whose access to markets for such goods is controlled by an effective business combination. He is in a position to get all the labor he wants
through the union—as long as he meets the union's terms. If
the union is not able to supply his needs, he is of course free
to hire where he pleases, usually on the understanding that in-

dependently hired nonunion employees become members of the union if retained beyond a certain time. Naturally all of this deprives the employer of the advantages he might secure from being able to hire help in an unorganized labor market at whatever wage bargains he might be able to drive. But there is no particular reason why an employer should expect under our common law to have a fairly available supply of labor at advantageous terms any more than he should expect thereunder to have uncontrolled access to raw materials.

The strongest arguments against the closed or union shop have always been that it interferes both with the freedom of nonunion labor to secure employment and with the freedom of employers to secure labor. These effects, of course, are conceded. But any argument that courts should therefore declare that the closed shop and strikes to secure it are unlawful, because it leads to the enslavement of workers and to the control of industry by the unions, is sheer sentimentality. If such an argument had ever been used by the courts to break up the effective market controls created by businessmen, it would have been treated as a denial of freedom of enterprise and an invasion of the natural rights of industrial entrepreneurs. Anyone doubting this statement has only to reflect on the attitude of most businessmen toward the Sherman Act. Perhaps the trouble is that so many of us do not really believe in free enterprise at all, although we may think we do, because we are unwilling to see the courts permit the same freedom of action to organized labor as they freely accord to organized business enterprise. But we should remember that as long as the industrial world is set up to allow freedom of organization and enterprise to businessmen and investors, these same freedoms should be accorded to all. When this tolerance causes harm to consumers, the only possible remedy is by legislation.

Certainly, if our courts continue to pursue the double standard in economic life, we must inevitably expect organizations like the CIO's political action committee who will make it their business to influence the election and appointment of legislators and judges willing to place all enterprise, including labor unionism, on a common and consistent basis. And it is no answer at all to say that since big business has built the country and made it what it is today, it is therefore essentially good and should be left in a class by itself. Organized laboring people, whether rightly or wrongly, believe that they can make the country a lot better both for themselves and for others by pursuing the same techniques which big business first made popular. Even if some of us are inclined to doubt this, it is hard to see how we can retain our present form of government and deny the unions the chance to prove that they are right. Certainly the courts should not do it. For this is a legislative matter suitable for disposition only in the political arena.

The closed shop, and strikes to secure it, have objectives of value to unions more tangible than mere control of jobs. At one time, before workmen's compensation acts became generally accepted, associated workers in particular plants found it to their advantage to exclude workers who could not, or would not, measure up to their standards of safe and prudent conduct during everyday operations. Their physical safety was jeopardized by workers who did not observe certain precautions. And employers anxious to get their work done at any price had no incentive to hire or retain only prudent men, because they were not responsible in damages to their employees who were hurt either because of careless conditions on the premises or by the negligence of their fellow laborers.

The only sure way they had to protect themselves against such hazards was to see that imprudent workers stayed out of their plants. By establishing standards of work, and by insuring observance of these standards through so-called entrance requirements, members of these associations could protect themselves against incompetent workers and against their employers' tendencies to hire such labor. Furthermore, they could in this way insure maintenance at a high level of the standards of performance of their particular arts which constituted their livelihoods. These safety factors involved in the closed shop are no longer relevant, in view of modern legislation, including workmen's compensation acts.

In any event, these factors are negligible when compared to the broader economic significance of the closed shop to organized labor. Unions have always valued the closed shop as an effective bargaining climate. The success of a strike for higher wages, to take an example, would be jeopardized if substantially all of the workers in the plant did not act as a unit. Unified action of his employees can really make an employer feel the economic pinch that might compel him to concede the union's demands. If he can retain a substantial number of his employees at work during such a strike, he has a great advantage and might successfully thwart the union's collective bargaining ambitions. Naturally, this is exactly what the employer should do under the circumstances if he wishes to defeat the strike. But this possibility provides the union with a strong economic incentive to secure the unified action of all employees for collective bargaining purposes.

The Massachusetts Supreme Court did not regard the achievement of bargaining strength as a sufficiently direct interest to justify a strike for a closed shop. Indeed, it regarded the possession of such economic power as unlawful in itself, and condemned strikes directed at this objective, although it had sanctioned not only a similar economic control but an analogous technique in achieving it when the combination in question was composed of businessmen in the case involving the corner on seamen. But even if we concede for argument that a strike to achieve bargaining power is not, in itself, aimed at an economic advantage like higher wages, it still seems clear that the closed shop has always been of vital importance to unions in protecting and maintaining its already achieved gains.

Suppose a union in a particular plant has secured advantages through collective bargaining. If the employer remains free to hire nonunion workers, his normal labor turnover may eventually enable him to supplant a great many of his union employees with men willing to work under any conditions he sees fit to impose. This may so dilute the union's strength that at the expiration of the current contract the employer may successfully refuse to renew it at all. Such a result may imply a serious lowering of employment standards, to the great harm of all of the workers in the plant. In order to avoid the undermining of economic stability in this respect—a matter quite as important as securing higher wages in the first instance—the union is compelled to seek the protection afforded only in the closed shop. The situation just described indicates how an employer in an open shop may pit nonunion and union employees against each other, thus creating a kind of competition between them, which the union may effectively combat only through establishing the closed shop.

BOYCOTTS—PRIMARY AND SECONDARY

So far, the discussion has concerned only strikes called to improve the terms and conditions of employment existing between the strikers and their employers. There are also instances of collective refusals to work by employees who are apparently satisfied with their own terms of employment— even including the closed shop—but who have economic interests at stake other than those involved in their own employment relationships. Such strikes constitute the first step in what are known as secondary labor boycotts.

A boycott is usually an organized refusal to deal with someone in order to make him change some practice which he follows. Quite frequently it is a systematic refusal to buy particular products, but it may also be an organized refusal to work. For instance, any simple strike for higher wages is a direct primary labor boycott, in which the strikers refuse to deal with their employer until he modifies some aspect of their terms of employment. A secondary labor boycott occurs when a group of employees refuse to remain at work for an employer, not because of any complaint over their labor standards under him but because he persists in dealing with a third person against whom they have some grievance. Their pressure is exerted against him in the hope of forcing him to cease dealing with the third person in question, as in *Quinn v. Leathem,* the slaughter-house case. As such, it is an attempt to secure the economic assistance of their employer to compel this third person to capitulate to the union over some issue between them, at the risk of losing the unionized employer's business if he does not capitulate.

An illustration should show clearly what all of this means. Carpenters employed in woodwork shops and those in the building trades are organized in the same country-wide union. In a given metropolitan area, say around New York City, the building trades are so well organized that general contractors employ only union carpenters. Woodwork shops around this area are, however, poorly organized. It is thought necessary by the carpenters' union that all of such shops be unionized. Certain unionized general contractors customarily purchase wood trim, such as doors and window frames, from a nonunion mill. The union officials notify these contractors that henceforth their members will not handle nonunion-made products from this mill and will discontinue work altogether if the contractors persist in buying such mill's product. Faced with this ultimatum, the contractors are likely to purchase their wood trim from union shops, preferring to pay more for their materials than to have their carpenters strike. The woodwork mill can preserve its established market only by unionizing its shop, a step it has previously refused to take. If it persists in resisting the union, it will suffer great loss and probably complete ruin. And this, of course, is exactly what the union intends should happen if the mill should refuse to capitulate.

A situation of this sort raises at least two questions. First, what can the employer against whom the union threatens to strike, or actually does strike, do to prevent this economic pressure? Second, what can the employer, who is the ultimate target of the union's coercion, do to stop this practice? Most of our courts have always held that the secondary boycott in any form is unlawful when practiced by labor unions, apparently on the complaint of either of the two employers. Simply by calling it unlawful, in itself—as if it were in a separate category of tort liability—they have concluded that it's wrong because it's wrong, although they have universally upheld the legality of the secondary boycott when it is practiced by business combinations. A few of our courts, however, have concluded otherwise in the labor cases, taking some pains to show that the majority ruling on this point does not stand up under analysis. Some of these courts place their conclusion on the right of working people to refrain from work for any reasons they see fit, or for no reason at all. Others have evolved a theory of legality based upon justification, and it is this analysis which seems irrefutable.

In response to the first question above—what recourse has the employer against whom the strike is threatened or actually called—the practical answer is that an employer in this position almost never seeks the aid of the courts, usually complying with the union's demand in order to avoid trouble. But if—to use the illustration of the general contractor, the carpenters' union and the unorganized woodwork shop—the general contractor tried to prevent the strike, the union could show that his continued patronage of the nonunion producer was hurting its interests. And the analysis tending to prove the union's contention in this respect would be virtually the same as that used to answer any complaint filed against the union by the operator of the woodwork mill. In this illustrative case, the carpenters' union could show that the nonunion mill, by operating on lower than union standards of employment, presented a continuous competitive hazard to unionized woodwork mills and, thus, to the union carpenters employed in them. For the nonunion mill enjoys a competitive advantage based on the wage differential between union and nonunion employees, which would enable it over a period of time either to drive all union-made wood trim off the market, or to break down the union standards in already organized mills.

This conclusion, of course, rests on the assumption that consumers of wood trim will naturally buy the cheaper material if they are left free to do so. Hence it is a matter of union interest to eliminate this undermining competition in order to protect its already established gains in unionized units of the woodwork industry. Since the union is not in a position to bring direct pressure on the nonunion woodwork mill by strike, its members in the building industry do the next best thing by refusing to work on such mill's nonunion-made product.

Thus, according to this analysis, the general contractors who use nonunion-made wood trim, as well as the property owners for whom they are working, themselves profit by and support subunion labor standards when they purchase and use the cheaper material. Although the union is in no sense competing with such contractors and owners, it argues that it cannot be compelled to assist them to support and to profit by the nonunion enterprise, thus hurting its own members in their competition with nonunion labor in the unorganized mill. And the union might add that it can stabilize its established standards in the unionized woodwork mills only by insuring them against competition from nonunion mills.

While this explanation shows a real economic interest on the part of the unionized shop carpenters sufficient to justify any action they might have taken to protect themselves against the undermining effects of the nonunion enterprise, what justification does it show for the coercive activity of the building trade carpenters, whose standards of employment in their industry are satisfactory? The building trade carpenters do have a personal interest in the labor standards prevailing in woodwork mills because many of them seek employment in such mills after they become too old to continue active construction work. Aside from this, however, the only actual interest they can show is membership in the same craft union with the shop carpenters and a joint concern with them over the maintenance of employment standards for all members of their union. This identity of interest is, perhaps, more easily observed as the building up of a powerful bargaining device covering similar functional operations. A common interest achieved between building and shop carpenters, through membership in the same union, certainly distinguishes the building carpenters' threatened or actual strike from one called, for instance, by a streetcar operators' union out of sympathy for the economic plight of the shop carpenters, who are trying to establish union standards in all of the woodwork mills. Since the streetcar operators have no conceivable economic interest in the welfare of woodwork mill employees, any pressures they exert to help them could not possibly be justified as pursuit of self-interest and gain. But the coercion practiced by the building carpenters in the case under discussion does affect their interests as well as those of the shop carpenters, because they are all in the same union and in the same industry built around the same craft function.

From the foregoing account it will be apparent that the secondary labor boycott is essentially an organizational device and that it can be used only by a union comprised of workers performing at least two different phases of a common industrial function, for at least two different types of employers. This is true of the carpenters' case, and many instances of a similar sort come to mind.

Thus, typesetters, pressmen and lithographers may be organized under one union roof. But while most book manufacturers employ typesetters and pressmen, lithography is fairly specialized and is usually farmed out by such manufacturers. The union may have an advantageous contract with a book manufacturer covering the labor standards of typesetters and pressmen. But this manufacturer may have certain lithographing done at a nonunion plant. If the union believes that the operation of this other plant, on subunion standards, endangers the welfare of its member lithographers in unionized plants, it may notify the book manufacturer that its member typesetters and pressmen will not handle the nonunion-made lithograph in his books. The manufacturer is likely to heed this warning and give his lithograph work to a union shop in order to avoid trouble.

But whatever the factual context may be in which a secondary labor boycott occurs, it is always true, from the angle of the workers actively implementing this pressure, that it amounts only to a simple strike or threat to strike. In spite of the fact that it affects, and is intended to affect, others besides the employer against whom this pressure is aimed in the first instance, the secondary boycott, for the purpose of analytically determining its legality, should be treated exactly like a strike or concerted refusal to work. Thus, if the employees who implement the secondary boycott by their refusal to work can show an economic interest of their own at stake, then our courts should hold such boycotts justifiable and lawful as, indeed, some of our courts have already done.

One of the most interesting of secondary economic pressures in other types of cases occurred when the Allis-Chalmers foundry, in an attempt to defeat a strike by its molders, shopped out various of its molding jobs to different foundries throughout the Middle West. At all of these other plants the molders, members of the same international union to which the strikers belonged, refused to work on any of the struck foundry's patterns. It is true that these other molders would not have benefited directly and immediately by the success of the strike at the original plant. But they did have an interest in the labor standards established at that plant because it competed with their own employers. They were interested in having standards of work raised as high as possible in all competing plants so that such plants could not undercut their own employers, thus affecting them indirectly, on the basis of any competitive advantage arising from wage differentials.

In a suit brought against the national union by the struck plant, a federal court denied an injunction on the ground that members of the molders' union in these various plants were justified in refusing to work on the original plant's patterns. The court took the view that this refusal to work could not be condemned as sympathetic pressure, because the local union calling the original strike was just as free to solicit and receive aid from other locals of the same union, in its economic tussle with the employer, as the employer was to seek the aid of other plants in getting out its orders. While the court's reasoning seemed apt, the argument based upon actual interest would appear to have been preferable.

While this situation involved secondary pressure, it was not an instance of a typical secondary boycott. The national union, through the co-operation of some of its locals, was merely trying to prevent outside plants from aiding Allis-Chalmers. This was essentially a defensive course of action, inspired by the struck plant's original recourse to outside assistance. As such, it seemed quite different from the aggressive attempt to impose additional positive economic pressure on Allis-Chalmers from outside, which a typical secondary labor boycott would have implied. Most assuredly it was not an instance of a sympathetic strike because of the interest which all of the locals had in the success of the strike at the Allis-Chalmers plant. After all, the national molders' union, composed of these various locals, had a real interest in the standardization of employment conditions in all of these competing plants at as high a level as possible. This interest may seem to have been indirect. But it was sufficiently apparent to justify the members of these other locals of the same national union in refusing actively to assist the struck plant against their striking fellow members by working on its orders at these other plants.

A somewhat similar situation might occur when a large non-union printing establishment which, in the opinion of the pressmens' union, has jeopardized the position and security of the union throughout the printing industry, seeks the aid of unionized competitors in getting out weekly and monthly periodicals during rush seasons. If the union ordered its members in these other shops not to work on any of the nonunion company's jobs, their refusal to do so would no doubt cause a good deal of damage. But this pressure would seem quite justifiable under the circumstances in view of the union's interest in stabilizing employment standards throughout the industry and by unionizing the publishing house in question. Certainly it could justify its conduct as a refusal to help that company which presents to it the most serious economic threat to its standards in other plants in the industry.

LABOR UNION COUNCILS

Other common settings for a type of secondary economic pressure through refusals to work, albeit not accurately included in the category of the secondary labor boycott but in some ways resembling it, are the local labor union council and the local allied trades union council. The building trades council affords a graphic example of the latter. It is composed of all of the craft unions ordinarily engaged in the building industry, including carpenters, bricklayers and stonemasons, electricians, plumbers, hod carriers, painters and decorators, metal workers, and the like.

Suppose that one of these unions is either attempting to secure some advantage from a particular general contractor, like higher wages, or is trying to compel him to recognize the union in the first place and to employ only members of that union for the performance of the particular work in question. Such a union, for instance, the electricians' union, may call a strike of its members at a particular building site. The contractor might easily be able to break this strike by recourse to non-union electricians hired in the open market. But in accordance with the rules of the building trades council, no members of any of the associated unions may work on a building for a contractor against whom one of the associated unions has called a strike at that place. In the face of a complete shutdown of all work on the building, assuming that the other building trades unions are fairly well represented there, the general contractor has no practicable alternative to granting the electricians' demands.

This organized pressure is obviously not a conventional secondary boycott. It more closely resembles the so-called sympathetic strike. The effective pressure brought by the associated unions, other than that representing the electricians, serves no possible direct interest of these other unions, since they are not demanding anything for themselves. A court asked to prevent continuance of this complete refusal to work might naturally conclude, therefore, that the associated unions, other than the electricians, cannot justify the deliberate commission of harm which they impose on the general contractor since they have no economic interest of their own to promote.

But this position is not obviously correct. It is far more doubtful than denying the right of the streetcar operators' union to strike in sympathy with the electricians. In the latter case there is no possible community of economic interest involved, while in the case under discussion it is arguable that all of the building trades unions, being concerned with the same industry, have an interest in all employment conditions in that industry. We may still feel certain that the other associated unions support the electricians' strike out of sympathy, in the hope that when any of them is in a similar position, the electricians will support it in the same way. Yet we must confess that if all of the building trades crafts were organized into a single industrial union, instead of in several craft unions, a conflict over electricians' rates would then be *the* union's fight, which all members of *the* union might lawfully support because of the more direct interest involved as far as their union's welfare is concerned. This argument has a considerable bearing on the case in hand. For a building trades union council, while it retains the separate craft identity of the several unions for some purposes, merges them virtually into an industrial union for other purposes. This council, including only unions engaged in the same industry, *is* an industrial union for most of the practical purposes of conducting an economic enterprise.

Certainly, under the circumstances, it would be difficult for a court to rationalize granting an injunction against the strikes of the other associated unions in this case, where they retain their separate craft identities, while denying one where all of the craftsmen involved were organized directly into one common industrial union.

Quite a different result might ensue in this situation, however, if the electricians' strike was to prevent the general contractor from installing electrical fixtures manufactured in a nonunion plant. As far as the strike by the electricians alone is concerned, assuming that their craft union comprised workers not only in the building industry but also in shops manufacturing electrical equipment, it would probably be regarded by the courts as similar to the building carpenters' strike in aid of the mill carpenters, discussed above. Such a strike would be the implementation of a true secondary labor boycott. And the interest to the building trades electricians, as members of the same union to which the shop electricians belong, would probably constitute adequate justification for their exercise of economic pressure.

But if the other unions, associated with the electricans in the building trades council, also walked out to aid these electricians in their attempt to force the general contractor to desist from nonunion-made electrical equipment, they would find it difficult, indeed, to show an interest justifying their action. They might contend that it was to their interest to build up the strength of one of their associated unions and that the electricians' union, as a whole, would be stronger if the nonunion manufacturer were organized. But this alleged interest, not concerning employment conditions in the building industry in any way, would be so attenuated as to be almost nonexistent. It could hardly be accepted as justification for the commission of harm by the other associated unions through their concerted refusal to work. Here the industrial union analogy would not apply. For if the building trade crafts were all comprised in one industrial union, then all interest between the building and shop electricians would be severed, anyway. In short, their interest would be too remote.

The local labor union council is fundamentally different from the allied trades union council situation. Instead of centering the association around a common functional or industrial interest, it sets up as the bond of unity the fact that all members of the associated unions belong to the laboring class and, as such, presumably have common economic interests against the rest of the world. Such an association includes all local unions from entirely unrelated trades and industries. It is in a position to practice powerful economic pressures in the aid of member unions, if permitted to do so by the courts.

Suppose a restaurant workers' union at a particular hotel strikes for higher wages or to organize the employer in question. To assist it, other local unions in the association refuse to serve the hotel as long as this strike exists. Presumably some sort of case could be made out for the justification of pressures exerted by other hotel service unions, by analogy to the allied trades union council activities. But if other members of the association, like the butchers', the bakers' and the candlestick makers' unions, all refused to serve the hotel or to work on products or materials destined for the hotel, they would have considerable difficulty in persuading a court that their exercise of economic pressures was justified. Their only possible interests would be the enlisting of reciprocal aid in the future and the building up of a class strength, both of which are much too attenuated by common-law principles to qualify as justification for their deliberate commission of harm against the hotel.

This expression of a class community of interest among all unions—more obviously an incident of craft as against industrial union organization in light of actual developments in this country—is frequently made apparent in so-called secondary consumption boycotts and in certain types of picketing. But what we have here been concerned with is how the practices employed in the use of the strike and the labor boycott might or might not be legally justifiable in terms of the economic interests of those refusing to work in various industrial contexts. It should serve to introduce readers to the economic analysis of justification and interest, which plays such an important role in the more complicated practices, and in the provisions of the law designed both to confine and to expand their scope.

CHAPTER VI

SECONDARY CONSUMPTION BOYCOTTS AND PICKETING—ORGANIZED REFUSALS TO PATRONIZE

> We would thereby give to one labor union an advantage over another by prohibiting the use of peaceful and honest persuasion in matters of economic and social rivalry. This might strike a death blow to legitimate labor activities. It is not within the province of the courts to restrain conduct which is within the allowable area of economic conflict.—Pound, J., in *Stillwell Theatre, Inc. v. Kaplan*, 1932.

LABOR organizations and business combinations have at least one thing in common—their most effective economic pressures to secure selfish advantages consist of concerted refusals to deal with others. The best-known union version of this technique is the concerted refusal to work, variously illustrated in the previous chapter. Business combinations practice a comparable type of pressure when they refuse to sell some commodity over which they have gained control. But another effective pressure which both groups use is the systematic refusal to patronize. This practice more strictly conforms to popular notions of the boycott. It was developed originally by business combinations, and some of these groups still use it effectively. In the past, and to some extent now, the courts have permitted them under the common law to apply pressures of this sort.

For instance, an association of master plumbers in the eastern United States set up a plan to secure for its members all of the lucrative plumbing business in their several cities. All of the members agreed among themselves not to buy plumbing supplies from any manufacturer who sold his products in these cities to any plumber not a member of the association. The upshot of this plan, which the courts called lawful competition, was to force nonmember plumbers in these cities out of business, compelling them to become journeymen plumbers. For the manufacturers of plumbing supplies did not dare to risk the loss of patronage of the association's members by violating its rules. And an association of retail lumber dealers in Minnesota, resenting the loss of profits involved in direct sales of lumber from manufacturers or wholesalers to consumers, agreed among themselves not to handle the lumber of any manufacturer or wholesaler who engaged in this practice unless he paid the association a fine amounting roughly to the lost profit. The Minnesota court declared this practice permissible at common law. A similar device for making retailers observe price schedules still prevails in England, with the blessing of the House of Lords.

MORE ABOUT SECONDARY BOYCOTTS

Courts have called all of these practices permissible competition under the common law. Yet they are all quite clearly secondary consumption boycotts, the threatened refusal to buy being aimed in each case directly at a manufacturer or wholesaler in order to make him in turn bring pressure on the real object of the association's dislike. In each of these instances, the members of the particular association had an economic ax to grind—or *thought* they had, as their organized expedients to protect their trade violated current notions of prevailing economic theory. Hence the harm caused by these economic pressures was said to be justified, since the coercion was directed at self-interest and gain, even though it amounted at the same time to a drastic interference with the free enterprise and competitive undertakings of others. All that could be proved against these associations was the concerted exercise of perfectly lawful refusals to deal with others, except on certain conditions.

The combination into associations, of course, alone made this economic coercion effective. But the courts consistently maintained that this element of combination was not in itself unlawful. Indeed, in these business association cases the whole affair—combination, as well as its use to exert economic coercion—was considered by judges to be virtually a sort of natural civil right. They took this view as long as the objective was some element of gain and nobody had violated a specific category of established common or statute law, such as assault, breach of the peace, trespass, libel or fraud and deceit. Any contrary view, the courts said, would have to come from the legislatures.

In the two decades prior to the New Deal organized labor attempted to use this same type of secondary coercion, based on organized refusals to patronize, with indifferent success before the courts. In many instances courts have declared such undertakings unlawful merely because they were secondary boycotts. This was a ridiculous reason in view of the fact that they had previously conceded the legality of secondary boycotts practiced by business associations without having called them such. Under recognized principles of the common law, however, they could have distinguished many labor consumption boycotts from those of business associations, because of the attenuated interest of the participants.

At any rate, the New York Court of Appeals had no difficulty in doing so in *Auburn Draying Company v. Wardell*, a case decided around 1920. There a teamsters' union wanted a trucking company to bargain with it. But the company refused to do so. Left to its own resources, the union would have been unable to exercise effective coercion on the company. But it belonged to a local council of various labor unions which, while functionally unrelated in any way to the trucking business, were nevertheless in a position to lend the teamsters powerful assistance in the form of economic coercion. Upon the company's refusal to deal with the teamsters, all of the unions represented in the council, including electricians, butchers, iron molders and what not, agreed that none of their members would patronize any local merchant who, in turn, patronized the trucking company. This possibility of losing the trade of all organized wage earners in the locality led the retail merchants to stop using the service of the trucking company. And this, in turn, faced that company with economic annihilation as the only apparent alternative to compliance with the union's demands.

There was, of course, nothing inherent in this choice which rendered the council's action unlawful. But, according to the New York court, the vice of this plan was the lack of any direct interest on the part of any of the unions involved, with the exception of the teamsters. The council's organized pressure imposed serious damage on the trucking company. And even though it resulted from purely economic coercion involving merely the right to deal or not to deal, as the members of the council saw fit, the court thought that the parties imposing it should show that they had an economic interest of their own at stake in order to justify it. Since employment conditions at the trucking company could not conceivably affect the economic status of the electricians, butchers, or iron molders in any observable way, their organized participation in this harmful pressure on the company could not be justified. Hence it was declared unlawful as the unjustifiable infliction of temporal harm.

What the court declared unlawful in this case was the systematic action of the council in organizing the participation of its member unions, presumably by inducing all of such unions in turn to require their constituents to spend their family incomes as the council directed. Naturally the court could not undertake to prevent a particular electrician or molder from refusing to spend his income in any store for any reason. That would be too extreme an invasion of personal liberty. A court would no more go this far than it would attempt to end an unlawful strike by ordering each of the strikers back to work—an unconstitutional imposition of involuntary

servitude which it would avoid by forbidding only the continuance of organized direction of the strike on the part of the
union and its leaders, leaving the individual strikers free to
resume work or not, in accordance with their personal choices.

The court proceeded similarly in this *Auburn* consumption
boycott case. After it ordered the council to abandon its organized scheme of boycotting against any local tradesmen who
persisted in patronizing the trucking company, many of the
union folk in the locality might still choose personally to
pursue the same policy. They were at liberty under the law to
do this. But without the investigational facilities of the council, they would find it difficult to learn what merchants were
dealing with the trucking company, and most of them would
no doubt soon forget all about it.

The secondary pressure in this *Auburn* trucking boycott
case was quite evident. In two other consumption boycott
cases, this secondary effect was not so obvious. Take, for instance, the case of *Seattle Malting and Brewing Company v.
Hansen,* decided in 1905 by a federal district court in California. There a brewery workers' union demanded the closed
shop from a brewing company. When the company refused to
comply, the union enlisted the aid of the community in exerting economic pressure to achieve its objective. It had handbills printed and circulated throughout the locality in question, notifying people that the company's brand of beer was
"unfair" and should not be consumed. The effect of this campaign was to discourage saloon keepers from handling the
company's beer, both because it ceased to be a good seller and
because they feared that people who were sympathetic to the
union would not patronize their places at all if they continued
to handle it.

The court enjoined this practice because it hurt and destroyed the company's business. This was an invalid reason for
declaring the practice unlawful, since all of organized labor's
perfectly legitimate economic pressures are harmful and destructive, just as those practiced by business combinations are.

Nevertheless, this same decision might have been explained on the ground that the union's undertaking depended on the aid of outsiders who had absolutely no economic interest at stake in the working conditions prevailing at the brewery. In this respect it resembled the situation in the *Auburn* trucking case. The members of the community who made possible the boycott against the brewery had no more interest in employment conditions at the brewery than the members of the various unions in the Auburn labor union council had had in the standards of work at the trucking company. In each case there was "a conscription of neutrals," so to speak. The consumers, whose refusal to deal with others caused the harm in question, could not justify this imposition of damage by showing that it was designed to promote any economic interest of their own; and the union groups organizing these boycotts by neutrals could stand in no better position.

However, these two cases were not identical. In the *Auburn* trucking case, the union council which conducted the boycott against the merchants had no economic interest in the outcome of the pressure, except in so far as the members of the truckers' union itself were concerned. The brewery workers' union, which alone had initiated the boycott against the brewing company's beer, on the other hand, had a very real interest in the outcome of the pressure exerted. Thus, any organized refusal by the brewery workers alone to drink the beer in question or to patronize any saloon that sold it could not logically have been declared unlawful under prevailing principles of the common law. It was only their union's organization of the general public against the brewery which could logically have been enjoined under these principles.

One other phase of these two cases is highlighted by a third situation. In the *Auburn* truckers' case the refusal to patronize was not aimed at any particular consumers' commodity, while in the California brewers' case the boycott was aimed directly at the company's beer. In the truckers' case the direct pressure was aimed only *at merchants* who patronized the trucking company, while in the brewers' case, it was aimed at the brewing company's *beer*—a commodity of commerce. A case before the Supreme Court in 1911, *Gompers v. Bucks Stove and Range Company*, illustrates the operation of a consumers' boycott against a particular commodity—Bucks stoves—a boycott conducted by a nation-wide confederation of unions which, except for the stove workers' union, had no economic interest in employment conditions at the Bucks plant. This case combined the features appearing separately in the *Auburn* truckers' and the California brewers' cases.

The American Federation of Labor is a loose association of national and international unions, chiefly craft unions, most of which have no functional relationship to each other. This cover-all organization published in a paper circulated among these federated unions a blacklist of so-called unfair products. These were products manufactured by employers who refused in one way or another to deal with the appropriate craft unions or to make desired concessions to them in collective bargaining. In this "We don't patronize" list the AF of L included Bucks stoves because that company had refused to deal with the stove workers' union, one of the unions in the AF of L. This resulted in a sharp decrease in sales of the company's stoves to wage earners all over the country. The company naturally wanted union folk throughout the country to be free to make up their own minds about what kinds of stoves they wanted. It also desired to relieve retailers from the odium cast on them for carrying the company's line of stoves, thus making it possible for them to continue selling them. Upon the complaint of the Bucks Stove and Range Company a federal court enjoined this practice, ordering the AF of L to drop this company from its unfair list and to cease to promote what it held to be an unlawful boycott.

Samuel Gompers and other high AF of L officials refused to obey this injunction. They claimed that it violated their right of free speech. When they continued their efforts to boycott Bucks stoves, they were held in contempt of court, again at the instance of the company. They appealed to the Supreme Court, contending that what they had done amounted only to communication, or speech in written form, and that they could not constitutionally be muzzled in this way. Hence, they declared, the injunction was invalid to begin with and, since it did not thus merit obedience, no contempt was involved when they ignored it.

While setting aside the commitment on purely technical grounds, the Court clearly indicated its belief, concerning the merits of Gompers' contentions, that the AF of L's nation-wide boycott was unlawful. It said that the organization of the boycott itself was the unlawful element, with speech amounting only to a "verbal act" or "signal" to set in operation the boycott. Hence, it concluded at this point, the mere presence of speech in effecting this boycott did not immunize the AF of L's otherwise illegal conduct under any constitutional doctrine for the protection of free speech. Apparently the Court perceived little difference between using speech and communication for the purpose of conducting an illegal boycott and for the purpose of perpetrating libel or fraud and deceit. One who libels another may not plead in defense that he has committed this tort through the medium of speech. It is hard to see how else it could be committed. Under this view, the constitutional guaranty of free speech is reserved for the expression of opinions or statements not in themselves unlawful and not used to implement practices which are unlawful under any recognized common-law or statutory categories of tort or crime.

But why did the Supreme Court regard the AF of L's nation-wide boycott of Bucks stoves as illegal? Strictly speaking, it was not a secondary boycott, although many retailers of stoves had become reluctant to sell Bucks stoves because organized wage earners refused to buy them. The proper explanation seems to be that the AF of L had organized against the Bucks company a consumption boycott supported by a class of consumers who, with the exception of the stove workers themselves, had no recognizable economic interest at stake in employment conditions prevailing at the company's plant. In short, this was an instance of organized "sympathetic" pressure, little different from a sympathetic strike. As such, it resembled the situation which later occurred in the *Auburn* truckers' case, although that case also involved secondary pressure. But inasmuch as secondary pressure alone has repeatedly been shown both in business combination and labor union cases not to be unlawful in accordance with prevailing common-law principles, this element of sympathetic pressure remains as the determining factor of illegality in these two cases.

All three of these situations—the *Auburn* truckers' case, the California brewers' case and the AF of L's blacklist against Bucks stoves—present illustrations of conduct which courts might justifiably declare unlawful under long-established principles of the common law. Although each differs from the others, all of them reveal the imposition of damage on others through organized agencies having no economic interest to be served. In the truckers' and stove cases, to be sure, the labor union council and the AF of L were interested in seeing the truckers' and the stove workers' unions triumph, in so far as such victories would strengthen unionism as a whole. But this interest through alliance was not the kind of economic interest recognized at common law under the justification of competition and the pursuit of gain. True, the brewery workers had a direct interest to be served. But this interest justified only the harm caused by their own abstention from the company's beer. It did not justify their organization of the public against the company.

This common element of recourse to organized sympathetic pressure in these three cases distinguishes them from practically all of the consumption boycotts of business combinations in which the direct economic interest of the participants was usually obvious. Hence, it remains apparent that in so far as labor unions have sought the aid of dissociated supporters—such as other unions or the general public—to further their consumption boycott pressures, they have violated established principles of the common law. Plain as this may be in these consumption boycott cases, people tend to lose sight of it when it comes to picketing.

SOME OF THE PROBLEMS OF PICKETING

Now picketing is a well-known union technique. Normally a patrol of union folk walks back and forth in front of a place of business which is under strike or under organizational pressure, or associated in some way with an employer whose employment conditions are the ultimate concern of the picketers. Peaceful picketing has become one of organized labor's most effective techniques for implementing consumption boycotts through the participation of the general public. Until fairly recently, most courts have discouraged the use of this device, except in very restricted situations. Originally our courts thought picketing to be unlawful under all circumstances. Unions once employed this device only in connection with strikes, both to notify applicants for employment about the existence of the strike, in the hope that they would not accept employment while the strike continued, and to induce the cooperation of employees who had remained at their jobs during the strike.

Naturally this conduct was harmful to the employer. The strikers found it effective as a means of cutting off the employer from access to the labor market, so he would be sure to suffer economic embarrassment leading to his capitulation and they would thus not have their jobs filled by other men. However, workers on strike did not always exhibit restraint while picketing, frequent brawls and fist fights giving it a bad name. Indeed, most of our courts a generation ago denied that there could be any such thing as peaceful picketing. They frequently declared that all picketing, no matter how restrained, carried with it an underlying implication of force and threatened violence which influenced people approaching a picket line to react more through motives of safety and personal welfare than out of sympathy toward the strikers' cause.

Eventually, most courts modified their views about picketing by strikers, conceding that it was lawful as long as it remained peaceful—that is, nonviolent, nonlibelous and nonfraudulent. And this definition had reference not only to the number and behavior of pickets but also to the nature of their communications to others. But lawful picketing was generally confined to actual strikers who were attempting by their strike to force their employer to comply with a demand for some lawful objective. Only a few of our courts have ever recognized the legality of what may be called "stranger picketing"—that is, picketing by organized outsiders—usually initiated for the purpose of unionizing the employer. This is not surprising in view of the reluctance of most courts to concede that peaceful picketing even by strikers was lawful.

That limited concession made a certain amount of practical sense to courts as soon as they had recognized the legality of strikes themselves. They probably decided to allow a certain amount of orderly picketing, incident to lawful strikes, for much the same practical and political reasons which led them to call certain strikes lawful in the first instance. Since strikers usually had a fairly direct economic interest at stake, sufficient to justify the harm caused by their strike, then presumably they had the same interest to be served by their picket line. Picketing by others than strikers, on the other hand, did not appear to promote an interest of the picketers sufficiently direct to afford a justification for the harm they caused. Hence, most courts would not allow picketing by nonstrikers, no matter how peaceful it was, possibly for much the same obscure reasons which led them to deny the legality of strikes for the closed shop.

An analysis of economic interests involved in various contexts of stranger picketing should be preceded by some brief comments on the nature of peaceful picketing in general—that is, on the idea that all such picketing may be a form of constitutionally guaranteed freedom of speech. This notion has become generally accepted since 1940, although it is by no means completely justified, as a later chapter will show. It is a point of view that has always had a considerable appeal to most so-called liberals. Picketing has always seemed to them a method of communicating information and, as such, a type of speech, whether it involves direct verbal contacts with others, the carrying of placards or signs containing information, or merely the conveyance of ideas implicit in a picket's silently walking back and forth or just standing in front of a plant or store, without any placard or sign, whatsoever, indicating what he believes.

It is not appropriate at this time to plunge into the issue of whether or not peaceful picketing really is *merely* speech or communication or, from any sensible point of view, can be so considered in all contexts. Certainly it is a method of communication, just as the AF of L's "We don't patronize" list appeared to be. That instance of speech or communication appeared to be an integral part of an unlawful consumption boycott, according to the Supreme Court. It may be that picketing under certain circumstances will analytically appear to be something similar when used to implement an unlawful economic pressure. If so, even though it be considered a form of speech or communication, it should arguably be considered unlawful as a part of such pressure, just as much as the federation's blacklist was thought to be.

But the primary purpose of this chapter is to describe and analyze the practical and legal effects of coercive union techniques, rather than their constitutional aspects. There are hundreds of actual court decisions affording opportunities to illustrate the application of general legal principles to picketing. The most interesting and instructive of these illustrations involve what was referred to above as stranger picketing—that is, picketing of a plant by a union group not on strike against the picketed enterprise and not formerly employed by it. For instance, a nationally affiliated union, which has already established itself in several units of a particular industry, moves in on a nonunion plant in this industry and sets up a picket line. This picketing is intended to impress the employer's present and would-be employees, as well as any of his customers that happen by, with the union's existence and its economic aims, in the hope that they will exert pressure on the employer by refusing to work for or deal with him, thus leading him to organize with the union to regain their co-operation. The courts calling this unlawful have done so on the assumption that the picketers had no interest in employment conditions prevailing in a plant where none of them had been employed, declaring that they could therefore not show any valid justification for the harm they were imposing on the employer. They contrasted this situation with picketing by strikers, pointing out the obvious direct interest which such picketers had in the employment conditions at the plant under strike.

This seems to be an incorrect application of a perfectly good legal principle, since the union clearly had a very real economic interest in organizing the picketed enterprise, even if none of its members participating was or ever had been employed there. For all units in a particular industry are presumably competing with each other and selling their goods in the same markets. And assuming that employment standards are higher and constitute a larger portion of overhead costs in the unionized, as against the nonunion, units in the industry, then it becomes apparent that all nonunion units have a competitive advantage over the unionized units, due to the wage and other labor standards differentials existing between them. Under such competitive conditions, the nonunion units may in time dominate the market for the industry's products by underselling the organized units. This, of course, would hurt the unionized employers. Moreover, it would adversely affect the organized workers, since it is plain that a union can thrive in a competitive industry only if the units within which it is established also prosper.

The union in question would either have to abandon some

of its already achieved standards in order to protect the union-ized employers' competitive positions, or go out and organize the competing nonunion plants in that industry. And since the former alternative is clearly against the union's interests as it sees them, the latter is necessary from its point of view so that it can impose on such plants employment standards conform-ing to those already established in the unionized units of the industry. Stranger picketing and the secondary consumption boycott are about the only organizational techniques practically available to the union. The latter of these two is effective only when it receives already organized outside support, like that furnished in response to the AF of L's "We don't patronize" list. Therefore a union in this position usually resorts to stranger picketing as the most expedient organizational device. It is the one which *is* interested in employment conditions at the nonunion units in the industry and it is the one which does the picketing designed to bring about the organization neces-sary to standardize those employment conditions.

This, at any rate, is the line of reasoning adopted by the few courts that have declared stranger picketing lawful. As the judge speaking for New York's highest court put it in a case decided in the late 1920's: "Economic organization today is not based on the single shop," implying that the aims of or-ganized labor cannot be achieved without universal organiza-tion throughout an industry. And it is exceedingly difficult to perceive in what respect the picketers in the type of case just discussed lack the economic interest necessary for justification of the harm they themselves cause, any more than do picketers who happen merely to be on strike against their employer. One might suppose, of course, that the strikers have a real tangible dispute with their employer concerning, say, their wages, which he refuses to increase in accordance with their collective de-mand, while the stranger picketers cannot be indulging in a real dispute of any kind when they picket an employer whose workers appear to be satisfied with what he is actually paying them.

Why then, one might ask, should the courts allow a group of outsiders to descend on an employer, at peace with his employees, and create a dispute where none existed before? The answer seems clearly to be that these outsiders are affected by the state of affairs in the picketed nonunion shop, just exactly as much as they might have been affected by their own employers' refusals to raise their wages before they had succeeded in unionizing them. As the unions see it, nonunion employers in a partially organized industry are battening on nonunion labor conditions and constitute a standing offense to union folk in that industry. They do not regard the dispute involved in stranger organizational picketing as in any way imaginary. To them it is just as real as the dispute over wages between striking workers and their employers. And they can prove the grounds for their belief arithmetically in terms of dollars and cents. Indeed, they can also contend that whereas strikers are aggressively out for what they can get, the stranger picketers are out merely to protect and maintain what they have already achieved and are, therefore, behaving defensively.

No court is likely to concede that an employer refusing to grant an increase to his organized employees is less deserving of its consideration than one whose employees have not yet organized and are not on strike, although his wage and other labor standards are below those prevailing in the organized units of the industry. Yet declaring a picket line to support a wage strike lawful and in the same breath holding stranger picketing by the union concerned unlawful is practically another way of admitting that proposition to be true. The fact is that both of these employers deserve all of the consideration from the courts to which they are entitled under the law. Neither of them is any better or worse than the other from any objective standard of judging their conduct. An employer is as morally justified in denying the collective demands of his own employees as he is in refusing concessions to an outside union, under these circumstances. And there is absolutely no good reason for giving an employer more consideration by preventing stranger picketing against him under these circumstances than there is for allowing his own immediate employees to picket him peacefully. According to the only intelligible legal test, justification in either case is simply a matter of proving that the economic interests of strikers or the picketers are being served. And this can be shown quite as easily in the one case as in the other.

Another variant of picketing indicates more clearly how unions enlist the economic assistance of outsiders—members of the consuming public, who have absolutely no interest in the conditions of employment in the industry involved—under circumstances where it may appear at first glance that the picketers themselves lack any real interest in the affairs of the picketed enterprise. Suppose that a manufacturer of ready-to-eat meat products runs a nonunion shop in an industry in which a substantial number of units are organized with a union. It appears that his wage scale is as much as 40 or 50 cents per hour lower than the established union scale in some operations, while all through his shop wage rates are substantially below the approved union rates in effect elsewhere. Naturally this gives the manufacturer in question a great competitive advantage over rival unionized manufacturers. As has already been shown, this disparity in wage rates in turn has a harmful effect on the union workers, as well. For presumably the manufacturer's product is just as good as that of his competitors. And he can sell it for less, while making a greater profit, because of the wage differential. Obviously, the union has a very real economic interest in taking coercive steps to unionize this manufacturer.

The case where these facts actually occurred was *Goldfinger v. Feintuch* decided in 1937 by the highest New York court. There the union established a picket line around the plant. Since this pressure was ineffective, the union placed pickets outside of delicatessen shops purveying this manufacturer's nonunion product, in the hope of compelling them to discontinue his line. The results of this step were very gratifying to

the union, because the majority of the consuming public either
stopped buying the product in question or kept away from the
picketed shops altogether. The manufacturer immediately began to feel the economic pinch, and he presumably approved,
if he did not actually support, the action brought by a delicatessen owner to test the legality of this practice.

The delicatessen owner contended that the union had no
economic interest in picketing him, because he did not have any
employees (the shop being a family store run by him and his
wife) and because the union showed no interest in securing
employment for its members at his shop. Hence, he argued,
this was not a labor dispute at all but was a case of deliberately
imposed and unjustifiable harm. The court, however, thought
otherwise. It pointed out that the union had a very substantial
economic interest at stake in keeping the manufacturer's nonunion product off the market, where it would compete with
union-made products of the same type. This interest, it said,
would have justified the exertion of pressure at the plant itself.
And it was sufficient also to justify its exercise at points where
the nonunion product was retailed. The court did not reach
this conclusion, however, without tying the shopkeeper up with
the nonunion manufacturer sufficiently closely to show that he
was practically participating in the latter's enterprise. And even
then the court told the union that while it might picket the
nonunion product in front of the shop, it must not appear to
be picketing the proprietor himself.

Apparently the court thought that nobody should be subjected to union picketing unless he had adopted a course of action adverse to the interests of the union. Thus, it implied that
it would not tolerate picketing against an influential citizen
merely to enlist his aid in bringing pressure against a nonunion employer, where the picketed citizen had no economic
connection of any kind with the employer. Certainly, it would
seem an unmitigated affront to expose people to such pressures
when they had not identified themselves in any way with the
nonunion practices under fire. The New York court, however,

thought that the delicatessen owner was very closely identified with the nonunion manufacturer, declaring that his ability profitably to undersell competing stores which handled union-made products, on the basis of the nonunion wage differential, indicated a "unity of interest" between the manufacturer and himself in perpetuating the former's nonunion employment conditions. It regarded the delicatessen owner as virtually a distributional arm of the manufacturer, not bound to him by any legal tie, to be sure, but even more closely welded to him, in a real sense, through their common interest in manufacturing and marketing the nonunion product, to their mutual advantage. For the manufacturer could not benefit from his low overhead costs unless his product reached consumers, and the delicatessen owner could not benefit as he did without the nonunion manufacturer to supply him.

Now this picketing was intended to create pressure on the manufacturer, through decreased retail sales, by enlisting the sympathy of ultimate consumers of the nonunion-made product. The union hoped either that consumers would not cross the picket line at all or, if they did, would refrain from buying the nonunion product in question. Both of these hopes were amply fulfilled. It was apparent that systematic picketing of this sort at all retail outlets of the manufacturer's product would sooner or later ruin him or compel him to make peace with the union on its terms. How does this situation differ from the AF of L's "We don't patronize" unfair list which was circulated to all members of all unions affiliated within the federation? Publication of that list was declared unfair because it organized the assistance and support of people who had no economic interest at stake in the labor conditions prevailing at the stove company's plant. In this delicatessen shop case, the entire success of the union's pressure plan depended upon the cooperation of ultimate consumers—people who not only had no interest at all in establishing union conditions at the manufacturer's plant but who seemed to have a very real economic interest as consumers in seeing that the plant remained nonunion, so they could buy the product in question at a relatively lower price.

Any difference between these two situations is, presumably, that while the federation's pressure through its unfair list was actively initiated and implemented by union people who did not have a direct interest in the stove workers' employment conditions—people like Sam Gompers who was president of the AF of L as well as the thousands of workers in various crafts, composing the union public—in the delicatessen shop case the pressure was actively organized only by members of the meat workers' union itself. But even this difference is minimized to some extent by the fact that the stove workers directly contributed to the support of Gompers and his fellow officials, thus creating some sort of mutual interest among them to see that the stove workers' employment conditions were improved.

It is hard to escape the conclusion that in each case the real punch behind the pressure was furnished by ultimate consumers. The fact that the roster of federated union consumers, having no direct economic interest at stake, was highly organized against the stove company in one case, while the consuming public was not organized in this fashion in the meat products case, seems somewhat offset by the fact that the federated union folk certainly had more interest in achieving success for their "cousins" in other federated unions than did the consuming public in helping the meat workers' union win their fight with the nonunion manufacturer. And it seems apparent that the California brewery workers' appeal, through circulars to the general public, was not much different, if any, from either of these two situations.

One possible explanation for the different judicial views in the federation's "We don't patronize" case and the brewery workers' case, on the one hand, and this New York delicatessen shop case on the other, is that the courts in the first two believed that any secondary pressure was in itself unlawful, while the New York court had long since abandoned that view in general, retaining it only when *organized* persons creating the primary pressure, through their refusals to consume, had no interest at stake, as in the *Auburn* truckers' case. It was somewhat puzzling to see the various judges in the New York delicatessen shop case differing among themselves as to whether or not the union's picketing amounted to a secondary boycott. Why were they concerned about this? Apparently they thought that if it were a secondary boycott, it would be like the *Auburn* truckers' case, and the picketing would hence be illegal. And it looks as if they had satisfied themselves that it was not such a secondary boycott because of the "identity" of the meat manufacturer and delicatessen owner through their "unity of interest" in exploiting nonunion labor. They were convinced that picketing against the nonunion manufacturer was all right, and they apparently went to some lengths to show that there was no difference between that situation and the one before them.

Actually the delicatessen shop case was clearly an instance of secondary pressure—a secondary boycott, if you please. The union created primary pressure against the retailer with the hope that he would cease handling the nonunion product, thus in turn bringing pressure on the nonunion manufacturer. It had an economic interest at stake in doing so, because the retailer's enterprise in distributing nonunion product was harmful to the union. Hence, even in the absence of these fictions of identity and unity of interest, the union had, in plain ordinary language, an interest for bringing pressure on the delicatessen owner. Had its members been employed there, a strike by them to compel him to stop selling the nonunion product would have been accepted as routine. Also an organized refusal by members of the particular union to patronize the retailer would have been regarded as routine.

Why, then, should there have been any difficulties over the union's picketing him, as long as picketing had been accepted as lawful along with the other coercive techniques of organized labor? Certainly, the economic interest of the union was quite as potent here as it was in most instances of stranger picketing which this court had previously thought to be lawful.

Even conceding the presence of a secondary boycott pressure in this case, it was not at all like the *Auburn* truckers' case, where the primary pressure was furnished through the organized boycott of union people who had no direct interest at stake and who were, therefore, exerting sympathetic pressure. And even accepting the fiction of the identity between the manufacturer and the retailer, the delicatessen shop case is still distinguishable from the federation's "We don't patronize" case, because there the AF of L had organized the purchasing power of unions having no direct interest at stake.

Perhaps the court was worried by the fact that peaceful picketing of any sort—and particularly in this case—"organized" the purchasing power of the public to exert a sympathetic pressure, not founded on any personal economic interest, against the retailer and, through him, against the manufacturer. Maybe the court was worried by this practical similarity between the case before it and these instances of admitted sympathetic pressure, thus perceiving for the first time this fundamental difficulty of allowing immunity to peaceful picketing under the defense of justification based on interest, when this practice depended for its success on the co-operation of a sympathetic public. If this be so, it was hardly worth worrying about, since the proper time for such speculation had been before these courts had ever committed themselves so broadly in the first place to the notion that peaceful stranger picketing is permissible whenever the picketers themselves have an economic interest at stake. At this late date such courts had to shut their eyes to the "sympathetic" incidents of stranger picketing intended to influence the consuming public, in spite of the fact that they had been developing a requirement of a rigorous "economic interest" as the price of admission to the allowable area of economic conflict. Now they must concentrate on peaceful picketing as simply a form of speech or communication, ignoring any implications of "psychological coercion" and winking at the harm that follows when the consuming public responds to picketing, whether its response is influenced by "coercion" or is simply an expression of sympathy, being in either event not founded on any perceptible economic interest in the union's affairs.

A CONCLUSION OR TWO

While the preceding analysis is involved, it must be apparent that if our courts and legislatures are going to work out a body of rules to govern the peaceful self-help activities which unions employ to promote their programs, and are going to develop these rules along the lines of economic interest, then this sort of analysis is necessary in order to understand what they are doing and what they should be doing. From the previous chapter, and the foregoing account in this one, it may be seen that unions with interests at stake are given a free hand in exerting economic pressures against enterprises conducted on a basis inimical to the interests of such unions, although they are restricted from exercising purely sympathetic pressures. But in instances where unions use peaceful picketing to make bids for the co-operation of the consuming public, depending on its sympathy for the creation of effective economic pressures, it seems that many courts lose sight of the fact that this is purely sympathetic coercion, remembering only that the union itself creating this pressure has an economic interest at stake.

A recent California decision shows more clearly how courts have in this way permitted unions, through picketing, to evade the legal sanction against sympathetic support from even organized workers having no economic interest at stake. In *McKay v. Local Union No. 1067,* a salesmen's union wanted to organize the sales employees of a large garage and automobile agency. Neither the employer nor his salesmen wanted to sign up with this union, so the union threw a picket line outside of the employer's place of business. Thereupon his unionized mechanics and other craft employees, who were perfectly satisfied with their own conditions of employment, refused to come to work because "they could not cross a picket line." No union truck driver would call at the employer's place of business, either to deliver or pick up, for the same reason. These other union workers were acting in accordance with a resolution of a local council of craft unions not to cross each other's picket lines.

Now this is a plain instance of sympathetic pressure, for the other unions had no conceivable interest in the success of the salesmen's union, even conceding the fact that some of them might possibly have had a "common industrial interest" with automobile salesmen in view of their joint concern with automobiles. Of course, this was a sympathetic refusal to work, instead of to consume. The same sort of arrangement, about not crossing the picket lines of sister unions, existed among all of the unions in the council for the purpose of organizing the patronage of their members in their capacity of consumers as well as of workers. The court, however, could not very well outlaw the personal convictions of the members of other craft unions or forbid them as individuals to refuse to cross the picket line of the immediately interested union, even though it could have enjoined active support by the other unions, as organizations, through a formal council arrangement. Actually what the California court did was to uphold the picketing as "constitutionally guaranteed freedom of speech," and it did not enjoin the sympathetic pressures imposed by the other unions.

Most of us are aware of the purely sympathetic aspects of economic pressures built up through picketing by appeals to would-be patrons of picketed enterprises. This sort of thing exists when moving picture machine operators, attempting to organize their employer or to secure some immediate advantage from him, picket the front entrance to his theater, or when a retail clerks' union, for the same reasons, pickets the entrances to a store. In all cases of this sort the picketing is done to enlist the economic assistance of customers; and even if such picketing seems futile to the casual observer, much of it is exceedingly effective, imposing considerable harm on the picketed enterprises. The assistance of the consuming public, union or non-union, is usually given without any inquiry into or knowledge of the merits of the immediate dispute involved and without any regard to such public's own personal economic interests. Any interest would-be patrons might have at stake is frequently to avoid trouble which they think might ensue from crossing the picket line. Certainly, union wage earners, in the capacity of patrons, feel this way as a matter of principle, even if success for the picketers means higher priced movies or merchandise, most of them feeling that they cannot afford to be branded as scabs for crossing a picket line. For obvious reasons, local merchants and professional men, all dependent on the patronage of the public for their economic welfare, as well as office holders out for the support of the electorate, frequently react the same way.

Naturally, this analysis is not intended as a condemnation of peaceful picketing as such. It is, rather, an attempt to make clear the issues involved in the use of economic pressures by organized groups and to show how many angles there are to the consistent administration of the only valid judicial principle of justification governing the use of harmful union pressures. Now there is nothing holy about picketing to warrant its approval whenever and however it occurs. If it is used to secure the same objectives sought by other forms of pressure and communication, then our courts ought to judge its use in accordance with the same standards employed to govern these other techniques.

Perhaps it would be more apt to say that our courts should look more at the substance than at the form of what unions and other types of pressure groups do. So far there is no reason to suppose that our courts have abandoned the practice of testing the legality of various economic pressures by inquiring into the interests of those exerting these pressures. Under this test they have professed to condone harmful economic coercion only when it is exerted in the pursuit of self-interest. In every case where courts have allowed business combinations to exert such economic coercion in pursuit of gain, all participating in its exercise have met this test. Of course, some participants have been unwilling actors but they have chosen to deal with dominant associations rather than with outsiders, in order to retain what they regarded as the best trade. Everyone involved was directly concerned with the economic conflict in question.

This is usually true of labor's organized pressures; but enough has appeared in this chapter to indicate that it is not always so. When it is not so, in clear-cut cases, our courts have not hesitated to declare sympathetic pressures unlawful. The real difficulty in applying this general principle arises in connection with peaceful picketing. Even here there is no trouble when unions use this device to notify an employer, his loyal employees and his would-be employees about the state of affairs at a plant under strike, as well as to apprise these same people of an economic situation harmful to organized labor's interests in a nonunion plant. Here everybody mentioned has a vital concern in what the unions are trying to do, whether or not they would admit it. If the present and would-be employees in any particular instance respond to the picketing by joining the union and participating in the economic coercion on the employer, then they are arguably serving their own interests as they see them and are not in any sense indulging in mere sympathetic pressure to help bring about a change in which they have no interest.

But courts seem to lose sight of the economic interest test when confronted by cases in which unions use picketing to muster and organize the sympathetic purchasing habits of ultimate consumers, many of whom are union adherents. Apparently they rationalize their position by claiming that they are merely permitting unions, by picketing, to publicize certain facts and to invite the consuming public to act as it sees fit. Any pressure exerted against nonunion enterprises and those in unity of interest with them is explained as being directly due to the whims of enlightened public opinion. Presumably they would say the same thing when they tolerate the sympathetic refusal of other unrelated craft unions to cross a picket line.

In this way the economic interest test is diluted and qualified in a manner which, unfortunately, promises to break down the only analytical technique enabling courts to recognize at common law a valid allowable area of economic conflict for organized labor—that is, an area stripped of all elements involving sympathy. Perhaps this would not be serious if our legislatures were still free to define this area strictly on the basis of economic interest. But quite recent constitutional developments in the Supreme Court have prevented this possibility in the picketing cases. And it threatens to do so in all instances of peaceful union undertakings to organize the sympathetic assistance of others to promote the aggressive union's own economic objectives.

CHAPTER VII

THE REMOVAL OF JUDICIAL CONTROLS OVER UNION EXPANSION BY ANTI–INJUNCTION ACTS

I am not speaking of conscious impartiality; but the habits you are trained in, the people with whom you mix, lead to your having a certain class of ideas of such a nature that, when you have to deal with other ideas, you do not give as sound and accurate judgments as you would wish. This is one of the great difficulties at present with Labour. Labour says: "Where are your impartial Judges? They all move in the same circle as the employers, and they are all educated and nursed in the same ideas as the employers. How can a labour man or a trade unionist get impartial justice?" It is very difficult sometimes to be sure that you have put yourself into a thoroughly impartial position between two disputants, one of your own class and one not of your class.—Lord Justice Scrutton, *Cambridge Law Journal*, 1921.

So FAR it is apparent that our courts are primarily concerned in labor cases with defining what Chief Judge Pound of the highest New York court so aptly called "the allowable area of economic conflict." They have conceded unions the right to fight with economic weapons of one sort or another for conditions thought advantageous by them. And considering the fairly conservative economic backgrounds of most judges, they have on the whole been tolerant in permitting unions to select and pursue their own values, which are so often at odds with the opinions of people brought up on classical economics. They have insisted that these disputes must be waged only between parties with conflicting interests—a position probably dictated by the principle of law that harm intentionlly imposed through the exercise of purely economic coercion is still actionable unless justified by the coincidental pursuit of gain.

Too often, however, our courts have taken exceedingly narrow views of what amounts to justification through the pursuit of gain. Thus, they have tended to outlaw the strike for the closed shop because they could see no direct economic end to be served by it. They have usually outlawed stranger picketing because they could see no connection between employmen⸀ conditions at the picketed plant and the economic interests of the picketers who were not employed there. And they have outlawed the secondary boycott, both labor and consumption, because they could not perceive the economic connection between those who activated the pressure and those on whom it was ultimately exerted.

THE SUPREME COURT AND THE CLAYTON ACT: 1914–1921

It was pointed out in Chapter IV that the adverse judicial restrictions imposed on these instances of union economic coercion were as a rule reflected in injunctions prohibiting their continuance. When during the first decade of this century the federal courts were beginning to exercise rather sweeping controls over unions under the Sherman Antitrust Act, and seemed to be using the injunction too freely against organized labor, considerable political pressure was focused on the passage of legislation to curtail the powers of courts over union self-help activities. The first systematic effort in this direction culminated in Section 20 of the Clayton Act, passed by Congress in 1914. Samuel Gompers, the president of the AF of L at that time, hailed this legislation as labor's Magna Charta. And several liberally inclined state legislatures quickly copied the anti-injunction section of the act in the belief that it would allay the abuses of judicial control over unions.

An analysis of this measure will shortly reveal how mistaken they all were. Anyone reading Section 20 of the Clayton Act would suppose that it achieves three objectives:

(1) Congress first tells the federal courts that they shall not issue restraining orders and injunctions "in any case between an employer and employees, or between employers and employees, or between employees, or between persons employed and persons seeking employment, involving, or growing out of, a dispute concerning terms or conditions of employment," unless it is necessary to do so in order to prevent injury to property rights of the complainant where no adequate remedy exists at law, and

(2) Congress then tells the federal courts that they shall not issue restraining orders and injunctions *under any circumstances* in order to prohibit persons acting in concert or otherwise

(*a*) "from terminating any relation of employment, or from ceasing to perform any work or labor, or from recommending, advising, or persuading others by peaceful means so to do"; or

(*b*) "from attending at any place where any such person or persons may lawfully be, for the purpose of peacefully obtaining or communicating information, or from peacefully persuading any person to work or to abstain from working"; or

(*c*) "from ceasing to patronize or to employ any party to such dispute, or from recommending, advising, or persuading others by peaceful and lawful means so to do"; or

(*d*) from paying or withholding from any person engaged in such dispute any strike benefits, money or things of value; or

(*e*) "from peaceably assembling in a lawful manner, and for lawful purposes"; or

(*f*) "from doing any act or thing which might lawfully be done in the absence of such dispute by any party thereto"; and

(3) Congress finally tells the federal courts that none of the acts or conduct described under (2) and its subsections shall "be considered or held to be violations of any law of the United States."

In other words, Congress declares that such acts and conduct shall not only be nonenjoinable before the federal courts but shall also be completely lawful, whether in criminal or tort proceedings under statutes or at common law.

Now all this seems clear enough. It does not require a legal education to read and understand this Section 20 of the Clayton Act. Sam Gompers was not a lawyer and he understood it plainly enough—or thought he did. But just to be sure, let us review the first part from a layman's point of view. What is "any case between an employer and employees"? It does not say "his" employees. Does it mean an employer and people who are employed, regardless of where they are employed or by whom? Incidentally, are people on strike or picketing, and thus temporarily unemployed anywhere, to be considered as employees at all in this phrase? Why did Congress include the phrase "between employers and employees" after it had mentioned the preceding phrase? What did it mean by the phrase "between employees"? And what is the significance of the phrase "between persons employed and persons seeking employment"? And what, of all things, is "a dispute concerning terms or conditions of employment"? Thus it suddenly becomes apparent that the meanings of these words are not so clear.

But Congress must have had something in mind. The second Circuit Court of Appeals thought that Sam Gompers' interpretation was correct. Two of these three judges believed that Congress, in this passage, had attempted under the first category to curtail the power of federal courts to issue injunctions in cases involving economic conflict between labor unions and business concerns, whenever the evidence showed that the particular union had some real economic interest at stake which was adversely affected by the employment practices followed by the company in question. They did not believe that this passage referred only to employers and their employees, whose employment was temporarily suspended by a strike. Rather, they thought that the word "employees" meant working people—"employables," if you will. The phrase "between employees" apparently seemed broad enough to them to include conflicts between union and nonunion "employables." The phrase "between persons employed and persons seeking employment" seemed to indicate a sufficiently broad category to include stranger picketing and other pressures by outsiders against nonunion employees at a plant. And "a dispute concerning terms or conditions of employment" they believed broad enough to reflect those actual developments in our broader common-law decisions which inclined toward the toleration of any concerted economic pressures aimed at promoting the interests of those exerting the pressure, as they saw such interests, whether or not any direct relationship of employment ever had or ever would exist between them and the employers affected.

Certainly there seems to be good reason to suppose that such was the intention of Congress, however ill-chosen the word "employees" might have been to describe the general class of wage earners and laborers. For people by 1914 were well aware of the fact that organized labor had just as much interest at stake in nonunion plants of a partially organized industry as they had in plants where unions were already established, because of the serious competitive problem between union and nonunion entrepreneurs and their respective employees, made possible by the differential between union and nonunion labor standards. To deny that the phrase "dispute concerning terms or conditions of employment" was broad enough to include organizational campaigns conducted by unions against nonunion units of partially organized industries was to shut one's eyes to the obvious facts of industrial life. Furthermore, such a denial ignored the full implications of the principle of common law allowing the imposition of harm through economic pressures in the pursuit of self-interest and gain, whether by business associations or labor unions, in strict contormance with the good old-fashioned rules of justification through competition, as they had been developed by the courts themselves.

But the Supreme Court disagreed with the lower federal court. In this case of *Duplex Printing Press Company v. Deer-*

ing, it seems that an international mechanics' union had undertaken to unionize a nonunion printing press company—the only unit, out of an industry consisting of four such companies, which was still not unionized. The union felt that organization of this fourth plant was imperative because of the adverse competitive effect otherwise brought to bear on the three unionized companies and their union employees, by the labor standard differential between the two sets of shops. Their way of exerting pressure against the company was not by strike so much as by the secondary labor boycott—members of the union refusing to repair or to work on this company's presses where they were installed or to work for anyone who used them.

This was harmful to the company. In a suit for injunction under the Sherman Act, it sought to prevent the continuance of this organized pressure. The union had relied on Section 20 of the Clayton Act as a defense, arguing that its terms covered this situation. But the Supreme Court held that Section 20 applied only in cases where the relationship of employment existed between the company and the union members involved. This seemed an exceedingly narrow interpretation of the first paragraph of Section 20, and many thought it an incorrect conception by the Court of what Congress had intended.

The second paragraph in Section 20 of the Clayton Act contains a description of the self-help economic activities which Congress declared should be available to organized labor in pursuing their objectives, free from the injunctive process and, indeed, lawful for all purposes in the federal arena. The first of these, (*a*), would seem to any ordinary intelligent person to include not only strikes by employees against their employer, to secure some advantage from him, but also *any* concerted cessation of work by *any* employees, whether or not they are employed by the company against which the ultimate pressure is focused. This, presumably, would cover organized refusals to work by employees of enterprisers using the nonunion company's product, in order to force such enterprisers to boycott the nonunion product—in other words, the secondary labor boycott. Furthermore, it includes recommending, advising and persuading others to do the same "by peaceful means," without placing any limitation whatsoever on who may so recommend, advise and persuade or how such recommending, advising and persuading can be done, as long as "peaceful means"—that is, free from violence and force—are employed.

The next provision which was marked (b), looks as if Congress had picketing in mind—peaceful picketing and patrolling, where persons have a lawful right to be, peacefully to get or give information and in a peaceful manner to persuade others to work or not to work. Anyway, if Congress didn't mean this, it is certainly hard to figure out what it *did* mean. The next provision, (c), reads as if Sam Gompers had at last persuaded Congress to nullify the Supreme Court's views in the AF of L nation-wide consumers' boycott case, involving the federation's "We don't patronize" list published to secure the economic support of all organized labor against the Bucks Stove and Range Company. For it seems to cover anybody's concerted refusals to patronize, without limitation, and then seems to allow recommending, advising, and persuading others to do the same thing, as long as such exhortation is "by peaceful and lawful means." The next two provisions, (d) and (e) above, are not sufficiently interesting in this connection to warrant discussion. But (f) is very broad, covering any conduct by labor unionists acting in concert, which any one of them alone might have done in the absence of a labor dispute—in other words, anything anybody has a civil right under the Constitution to do all by himself!

This is what Congress seemed to say—and it is hard to believe that it intended otherwise—in (2), which is the second paragraph of Section 20 in the Clayton Act. It is true that in (a) there appeared the qualifying phrase, "by peaceful means," in (b) the words "lawfully" and "peacefully," the latter word twice, in (c) the phrase "by peaceful and lawful means," in

(e) the words "peaceably" and "lawful," the latter appearing twice, and in (f) the word "lawfully." It seems quite plain that unless Congress was just playing with words in enacting this paragraph of Section 20—a dangerous thing to attribute even to our national legislature—it intended these significant words to be construed in terms of the old and established common-law categories of tort and crime, as well as in terms of statutory categories of illegality. Surely it must have had the normal self-help activities of labor unions in mind, since such activities were a matter of common knowledge and since it realized that of these activities there were two general types—those involving rough stuff, like actual and threatened violence, fraud and libel, and those consisting of purely economic pressures, like strikes, boycotts, and peaceful picketing.

It is hard to believe that Congress meant to have the words "peaceful," "peacefully," "peaceably," "lawful," and "lawfully" construed in accordance with the rationale of the same antiunion decisions which Section 20 was presumably designed to correct. Thus, just because the conduct described in (a), as it was practiced in some strikes and secondary labor boycotts, had been held unlawful, even though it involved only purely economic coercion and no vestige of illegality under traditional or statutory categories of tort or crime, was no reason to suppose that Congress was intending to perpetuate such judicial qualifications in a statute designed to curb more judicial intemperance in labor cases. Indeed, the natural supposition would be that Congress, the Supreme Court's superior in lawmaking, was ordering the federal courts, including the Supreme Court, to abandon these factitious judicial rules of illegality and to get back to their proper business of applying the real common law, as modified by this statute and by any other statute that happened to be on the books. The same observation is appropriate for the balance of the provisions.

It is true that several of our courts had declared that there could be no such thing as peaceful picketing—a ridiculous conclusion from presumably serious professional men. Why should the courts assume that Congress intended to perpetuate such folly, unless they were so vain as to believe that only they, the judges, could sensibly declare the meaning of such words as peaceful and peaceable? In (c) Congress apparently meant to imply that publishing a national union newspaper containing a plea to union folk not to purchase particular products was a program based on "peaceful and lawful means," and it seemed to be the Supreme Court's duty to recognize this. Just because that court had previously held this practice to be unlawful was beside the point. What Congress was trying to do, apparently, was to say that the court had gone too far and that it was now establishing the law as it thought it should be. It spelled out the conduct so carefully that any intelligent layman could understand it. But apparently the Supreme Court could not.

Perhaps subparagraph (f) presents the clearest item. Here Congress said, in such unmistakable terms that only a lawyer could misunderstand its statement, that *any* persons acting in concert might do *anything,* during the course of a labor dispute, which any party to it might *lawfully* have done in its absence. In other words, the concerted self-help practices of unions were to be adjudged by federal courts in accordance with what any individual interested in the dispute might have done with impunity all by himself. Why, the sky's the limit on such freedom of action, almost. For as long as he refrained from violence and other such overtly unlawful conduct, any such interested individual was free to refrain from work, to refrain from purchasing or patronizing, to persuade others to join him in doing these things, to go where he wished as long as he did not trespass, and to enjoy all of the ordinary civil rights any American accepts quite naturally as his birthright. These are the things, then, which Congress solemnly said in subparagraph (f) that organized labor might do.

When the Supreme Court decided the *Duplex* case in 1921, however, it seemed not to consist wholly of men who could grasp this novel but simple command of the lawmakers, for a majority of the Court there held that Congress had merely intended in this second paragraph to state the law as it already existed in judicial decisions—in other words, that in exercising its solemn legislative function it was doing nothing at all. The Court read this paragraph, with emphasis on the words peaceful and lawful and their variants, to reflect those very decisions which had aroused Congress, through political pres· sures on it, to pass Section 20 in the first place. And the strange part of all this was that a few of our state courts sympathetic to unionism had already held the common law to be that the conduct spelled out in the second paragraph of Section 20 was perfectly lawful.

Some of their decisions acknowledged its legality under any circumstances, as a matter of civil rights, and others only when those participating in this conduct had economic interests of their own at stake. Anyhow, the Supreme Court, by its reaction to Section 20, was perpetuating those same judicial errors described in detail in the first three chapters of this book. In short, it was forsaking its proper function of interpreting and applying the established principles of common law, which traditionally governed the exercise of coercion in situations involving business associations, and was superimposing on the real common law a set of factitious rules attributable to the social and economic predilections of the judiciary.

To recapitulate for clarity, and to add one item hitherto neglected, the Supreme Court refused to concede that Congress had made lawful any of organized labor's self-help techniques described in this portion of the Clayton Act, except as to such conduct as was already considered lawful, anyway, before this act was passed. Furthermore, it held that even if this second paragraph meant what the labor unions said it meant, it offered no protection to the union involved in the case before it because none of these defendants was or ever had been employed by the complaining printing press company.

The court based this conclusion, *first,* on its interpretation of the first paragraph of the section to mean that the statute applied only in cases of disputes over terms and conditions of employment between parties in the direct relationship of master and servant, so that only the employees of a particular employer, disputing with him their own personal terms and conditions of employment, were covered by the section. And *second,* it relied on the fact that the second paragraph of the section began with the words "And no *such* restraining order or injunction shall prohibit," et cetera, thus indicating through the use of the word "such" that everything said in the second paragraph was intended solely with reference to the "restraining order and injunction" covered in the first paragraph, that is, one in a case involving, as the court read it, a dispute between an employer and his own employees who were in direct master and servant relationship with him.

Justice Brandeis dissented vigorously in this case. As he read this section, Congress was attempting to enlarge the "allowable area of economic conflict" for labor unions by making it co-extensive with the pursuit and defense of union interests. For about the first time in the Anglo-American law reports, the real nature of union economic needs, as the unions saw them, was fairly analyzed and described in his opinion. He showed, as has already been related in previous chapters, how unions *do* have a vital interest in the terms and conditions of employment prevailing in the nonunion plants of industries in which they are already established. This interest is such as to compel them either to unionize these shops, regardless of the wishes of the existing employees in such shops, or to give up what they have already achieved elsewhere. He indicated how some state courts, particularly the highest court in the jurisdiction where most of the machinist union's coercive activities had been exerted, had recognized this interest and had permitted the exercise of systematic economic coercion from without to organize nonunion shops.

He insisted that this was what Congress had intended to permit in Section 20 of the Clayton Act. He suggested that if Congress were not intending to do just this, there was really no point in its having enacted this section, particularly as the presumption underlying any piece of legislation is that it is designed to change the existing state of affairs, and he pointed out this broadening of the area of economic conflict as the only possible change involved. Thus, he indicated, allowable economic conflict might occur either between an employer and his own existing employees, or between an employer and all employees economically affected by the working conditions in his shop, whether or not they were employed by him. If the former only was intended, no statute was necessary; but if the latter was to prevail, then the majority of the court was wrong in their interpretation of the first paragraph of Section 20. Naturally he gave the second paragraph of this section a liberal interpretation, for he believed that its provisions were intended for the benefit of all employees affected by the first paragraph, being all with any interest at stake, whether or not they were in the direct relationship of employment with the employer against whom their conduct was focused.

Justice Brandeis closed his opinion with a dignified reproof to a majority of the court, remarkable for its restraint under the circumstances. He said: "Because I have come to the conclusion that both the common law of a State and a statute of the United States declare the right of industrial combatants to push their struggle to the limits of the justification of self-interest, I do not wish to be understood as attaching any constitutional or moral sanction to that right. All rights are derived from the purposes of the society in which they exist; above all rights rises duty to the community. The conditions developed in industry may be such that those engaged in it cannot continue their struggle without danger to the community. But it is not for judges to determine whether such conditions exist, nor is it their function to set the limits of permissible contest and to declare the duties which the new situation demands. This is the function of the legislature which, while limiting individual and group rights of aggression and defense, may substitute processes of justice for the more primitive method of trial by combat."

It is hard to read this important chapter in the development of American labor policy without becoming disillusioned about two of our most important branches of government—Congress and the Supreme Court. Ever since this first interpretation of Section 20 of the Clayton Act, almost all educated opinion in this country has been that the Supreme Court sold organized labor down the river when it construed this section. But there is another angle to this. Several astute lawyers thought that Congress was the body which had betrayed the labor unions when it enacted Section 20. They believed that Congress deliberately made this section ambiguous, with the surface appearance of going very far indeed, but nevertheless using restrictive words like "employee" in close juxtaposition with the word "employer" and craftily inserting words like "lawful" and "peaceful," so that labor people would think, after a hasty reading, that they had achieved something substantial. These same lawyers thought that Congress had all the time actually hoped and believed that the Supreme Court would nullify by construction the liberal implications of the section.

If this suspicion were true, there would be revealed the worst kind of political chicanery. Evidence tending to support this belief was found in some of the Congressional committee reports on this section, indicating that Congress had no intention of going so far as to allow the secondary boycott. It is only fair to Congress, however, to remember that an understanding of concepts like the secondary boycott was even less clear in 1914 than it is today. Quite possibly none of the members of the committee knew what was being talked about when that group disclaimed all intention to legalize such a technique.

As Justice Pitney indicated, the spokesman for the House committee said that "the section as reported was carefully prepared with the settled purpose of excluding the secondary boycott and *confining boycotting to the parties to the dispute, allowing parties to cease to patronize and to ask others to cease to patronize a party to the dispute;* it was the opinion of the committee that it did not legalize the secondary boycott, it was not their purpose to authorize such a boycott, not a member of the committee would vote to do so." Now, if Congress had really intended to extend the provisions of Section 20 to union people not in the relationship of employment with the complaining employer—and it is very hard to see why it passed the section at all if it did not—then the italicized portion of the above quotation from Justice Pitney's opinion makes it fairly clear that Congress was legalizing exactly what the AF of L had done through its "We don't patronize" column in its federation newspaper and which the Supreme Court had previously thought to be an unlawful sympathetic consumption boycott. Hence, a rather broad interpretation of Section 20 might possibly still be consistent with Congress' denial of any intention to legalize the secondary boycott.

On the other hand, a factor to be thrown in the scales on the side of the Supreme Court is the extraordinary nature of Section 20 if it were to be accepted as most so-called liberals think it was intended. For under this broader construction, Congress went to extreme limits in allowing for union pressures. If such construction were accepted, then it must be deemed to have written into Section 20 the so-called civil rights theory of freedom of concerted economic conduct. This completely ignored that qualification of this theory based on a showing of some personal economic interest by those exerting the economic pressure, which the courts had carefully developed as justification under the common-law principle that harm intentionally imposed through purely economic coercion is actionable unless justified.

Of course, the civil rights theory had occasional support in state courts, and it had a tremendous political appeal. Furthermore it was much easier to set it forth in general statutory language than it was to draft a provision limiting the allowable area of economic conflict to those who had some actual economic interest at stake. Indeed, a reading of Justice Brandeis' dissent shows quite clearly that even he believed this allowable area should be defined in terms of economic interest rather than in terms of civil rights. He went on to declare that such a matter was entirely in the hands of Congress, as a matter of legislative policy, and was none of the Supreme Court's business. Nevertheless, it is possible that a majority of the Court was influenced toward the narrow interpretation by its fear of sanctioning the extreme latitude apparently allowed by Congress and by its refusal to believe that Congress could have intended to go so far.

During this same year, 1921, in a case involving picketing by outsiders, by a few actual strikers and by former employees who had been laid off but were hopeful of resuming their employment, the Supreme Court held Section 20 of the Clayton Act applicable. This was the case of *American Steel Foundries v. Tri-City Central Trades Council.* The opinion outlined a kind of peaceful picketing in which only the strikers and laid-off employees might indulge. This the labor folk promptly dubbed "pink tea picketing." No others were allowed to participate in this strictly limited and peaceful picketing. The reason for this was, said the Court, that they did not fall within the terms of Section 20, even if they did belong to a union whose standards in other organized shops were competitively affected by the nonunion conditions of employment in the picketed plant.

Shortly thereafter in *Truax v. Corrigan* the Supreme Court reviewed a decision of the Arizona Supreme Court interpreting that state's anti-injunction act which was modeled after Section 20 of the Clayton Act. The Arizona court had refused under this statute to enjoin picketing by strikers and others with placards containing defamatory and untrue statements about the employer in question, denying the picketed employer the relief he requested against its continuance. The Supreme Court took the case on appeal and held, under the due process clause of the Constitution, that the state act was unconstitutional as construed and applied by the Arizona court. Now it may seem odd that the Supreme Court could uphold the validity of a set of words in a federal statute and, at the same time, deny the constitutional validity of practically the same words in a state act. But this was not really what the Court did. In effect, it declared the state supreme court's *decision* unconstitutional in so far as it interpreted this act to prohibit injunctions against tortious and unlawful picketing. This left the Arizona anti-injunction act valid as long as it was properly construed and applied in the future.

The Supreme Court never passed on a state court decision in which a state anti-injunction act copied after Section 20 had been interpreted to mean that labor unionists might exercise coercive pressures against an employer with whom they had not been in the relationship of master and servant. Nevertheless, there is not much doubt that the Supreme Court's brusque reversal of the Arizona court in one limited respect generally influenced state courts to adopt completely the Supreme Court's narrow interpretation of their statutes patterned on Section 20 of the Clayton Act. It is true that a few state courts had, without the aid of any statute, already taken a position contrary to that of the Supreme Court concerning the area of allowable economic conflict by not requiring labor unionists to show a direct master and servant relationship between themselves and complaining employers before they were permitted to use economic pressure. These courts, of course, generally confined the area of permissible conduct to persons having some economic interest at stake. If they occasionally seemed to go farther and acknowledge the civil rights theory of complete freedom of conduct, even in the absence of an economic interest on the part of persons exerting pressures, such statements occurred in cases where an economic interest existed anyway.

The foregoing account shows the complete ineffectiveness of the first large-scale attempt to curb by legislation the abuse of judicial power against organized labor. By around 1910 organized labor's chief interest had primarily to do with extending organization. It seems fairly obvious that Congress in

Section 20 of the Clayton Act was trying to repair the defects in a judicial system which would not tolerate extended organization. All through the first three decades of the 1900's there were other manifestations of a judicial antipathy to freedom of union organization. It was not so much that our courts denied workingmen the right to organize into unions and to indulge in collective bargaining with their employers. On the contrary, if workers could form effective unions, our courts were by the early 1900's willing enough to let them bargain collectively. It was a timorous activity of this sort which the Supreme Court finally concluded Congress had provided for in the Clayton Act. All except a few state courts—and in those days the federal courts gave organized labor a very cold shoulder, indeed—used practically every feasible means to discourage extended union organization. Either they were unaware of the real economic interest unions had in organizing competitive nonunion plants, or they realized it and hoped that by thwarting the extension of unionism, the competition from nonunion plants would kill off what organization of labor had already taken place. One must remember that most of the judiciary of that day were men of the old school and that in their economics books, a labor union of any sort was virtual anathema.

THE ANTIUNION PROMISE OR THE "YELLOW DOG CONTRACT"

Perhaps the most effective judicial technique used to thwart extended organization was the so-called doctrine of *Lumley v. Gye*. This was the opera singer case which involved the tort based on inducing a breach of contract between others. Its use came about in this fashion. Many employers who were determined to stifle the spread of unionism in their own plants naturally took advantage of their relatively superior economic position in dealing with their individual workers. Anyone who believes that this attitude was wicked and unconscionable is entitled to his own opinion. But he must not feel upset if others consider him somewhat naïve. From management's point of view, what these employers did seemed most sensible, because unions were challenging their powers and interests as owners and operators of their own property. In pursuit of this end it became the custom in the 1890's and first decades of the 1900's to exact from each present employee a promise, conditioned on his remaining employed, that he would get out of any union he belonged to and would keep out as long as he retained his job. From each applicant for employment they exacted a similar promise as a condition of giving him employment.

This became known as the antiunion contract, which proponents of unionism endearingly labeled the "yellow dog contract." Both in Congress and in state legislatures labor unions then mustered sufficient political power to have this practice by employers made criminal under statute, only to have the Supreme Court declare such statutes unconstitutional under the 5th and 14th amendments in the federal Constitution. The reasoning was that this legislation invaded individual freedom of contract to sell labor and to offer employment upon such conditions as the workman and employer concerned were able to agree. In response to the argument that employers had an unfair economic advantage over individual wage earners because of their superior economic power, including the present control over the means of livelihood in an industrial system, and took advantage of such wage earners' absolute necessity to make a living on any terms available, the Supreme Court had a ready, if somewhat pontifical, answer.

Said the judges: "No doubt, wherever the right of private property exists, there must and will be inequalities of fortune; and thus it naturally happens that parties negotiating about a contract are not equally unhampered by circumstances. This applies to all contracts, and not merely to that between employer and employé. Indeed a little reflection will show that wherever the right of private property and the right of free contract co-exist, each party when contracting is inevitably more or less influenced by the question whether he has much property, or little, or none; for the contract is made to the very end that each may gain something that he needs or desires more urgently than that which he proposes to give in exchange. And, since it is self-evident that, unless all things are held in common, some persons must have more property than others, it is from the nature of things impossible to uphold freedom of contract and the right of private property without at the same time recognizing as legitimate those inequalities of fortune that are the necessary result of the exercise of those rights."

The court's logic is inescapable, granting its premises. But this passage nevertheless was troublesome doctrine. Organized labor has always been most keenly aware of just what the court said in this passage. That is why it has been so anxious to build up effective bargaining organizations to cope with the advantage which property and its control give to employers. This it could do only through organization. It was not anxious to extirpate the institution of private property. Rather, it wanted freedom of wage earners to form the organizations necessary to achieve economic equality. This freedom it believed to be a personal attribute of every worker, not to be interfered with by employers.

But if employers and the courts took the view that property in an industrial system implied the control by its owners over the personal affairs of nonpropertied people, and placed them as private citizens in a position to dictate to wage earners what organizations they could or could not belong to if they wanted access to the means of livelihood, then workers could hardly be blamed if they concluded that perhaps there was something vitally wrong with the institution of property as it had developed. What had happened in our society was, simply, that the control of the means of livelihood of vast masses of people had fallen into the hands of a relatively few. This, in the court's view, was the natural result (perhaps inevitable would be a more accurate word) of the industrial system, wherein small people had become divorced from their tools and personal home enterprise and completely dependent on the machines and factories of concentrated mass enterprise.

What many individual citizens seem unable to understand about this, however, is that others resent this concentration of power in private hands—a power over the lives of wage earners that they believe should be only in the government, if it is to exist at all. A few of the more resentful believe that the answer lies in kicking over the whole system of private property. But far and away the majority of them believe that the system is big enough to contain another kind of free enterprise—labor unionism—which will retain the social premise of private property and will leave power in private hands, yet on a more equitable basis of bargaining equality. But these more temperate wage earners believe—and there is absolutely no doubt that they are correct—that these matters are essentially political.

They find it hard to understand, assuming they can muster enough political power to procure statutes protecting from the economic aggression of employers their freedom to promote their own enterprise, why the Supreme Court should declare such results of the solemn legislative process to be invalid as contrary to due process. They eventually arrive at the conclusion that, while they were quite right in supposing this whole matter to be essentially political in its nature, including the function which the Supreme Court plays, the pinch occurred because the Supreme Court was not on their side politically. This troublesome flaw could be remedied, granting sufficient political power in the hands of organized labor, by seeing that the "right" personnel was appointed to the Court. This strategy is flawless, since it reflects a rational procedure designed to correct what the unions regard as an undesirable social balance. It is, nevertheless, very easy to understand why many thoughtful people of a conservative bent should become worried about what organized labor would do with this dominant political power, if achieved, and about what it is now doing with the strong political and bargaining power which it already has.

In any event, during the first three decades of the 1900's, employers were constitutionally guaranteed their freedom to impose any conditions on employment, as long as they remained within the law as the Supreme Court saw it. At the same time employees remained free under the same principles to accept employment on any terms it was offered. Consequently, antiunion agreements flourished and extended union organization was made more difficult. The unions, of course, did not hesitate to continue proselytizing in the face of such agreements.

Take the United Mine Workers of America, for instance. During the early part of this century they were in a most precarious position. They had successfully organized several of the big fields and had introduced fairly satisfactory working standards. But these employment conditions involved substantial overhead expense to the unionized employers. These operators sold coal in the same national markets supplied by nonunion operators, and the competition was tough. Nonunion operators enjoyed a very substantial competitive advantage over the unionized mines on the basis of the wage differential between union and nonunion rates. So desperate did this situation become that the unionized operators served notice on the UMWA that unless it went out and unionized all competing mines, they would either have to break with the union or shut down. This dilemma led to systematic organizational campaigns by the UMWA against the nonunion mines, needless to say with the unionized operators' blessings.

One of the union's organizers moved in on the Hitchman mine in West Virginia. The operator of this mine had previously been organized. But his experiences with the union had been so exasperating to him that after he had defeated a strike, he opened up again with the determination that he would never again have a union in his place. To insure this, he exacted from all of his employees, as a condition of giving them employment, agreements that so long as they remained in his employ, they would not join the union—the well-known "yellow dog contract." But the organizer, circulating deviously among the men and persuading them that they would suffer wage cuts if they did not join up, secretly enrolled enough of them as members so that he could finally call them out all at once on a strike and close down the mine.

Of course, the organizer knew about the antiunion agreements. His strategy had been dictated by the practical need of keeping the men at work until he had had enough of them signed up to call an effective strike. For if he called them out one by one, as they joined up, the operator might have taken successful defensive measures. When he did call the strike, and the mine was closed, the operator brought suit in the federal courts against the appropriate union officials to enjoin them from continuing these organizational activities. His theory was that the union's organizer had deliberately induced the workers to break their agreements with him and to remain at work after they had joined the union.

In *Hitchman Coal Company v. Mitchell* a majority of the Supreme Court accepted this theory, Justice Brandeis again speaking for the dissenters. Although the court did not mention by name the doctrine of *Lumley v. Gye,* the opera singer case already referred to, that was nevertheless the doctrine it applied in this decision. Here was a far cry, indeed, from the situation where an English court cracked down on a music-hall manager for persuading an opera singer to break her legally binding contract with a rival manager! It is true that American courts had long since adopted this doctrine to prevent inducing the breach of all kinds of legally binding contracts, whether or not they were merely for personal service. But in this coal mine case it was doubtful whether any real contract existed at all.

The coal miners were employed at will, and the employer was free to discharge them at any time, for any reason or for no reason at all, just as they were free to leave his employment on the same terms. It was a little hard to see how the antiunion promises of the miners were any more contracts than were their employment relationships to which those promises were incidental. The New York Court of Appeals, in a similar case some years later, thought that they were not. And in refusing to recognize, in the antiunion promise of an employee at will, a contract, for inducing the breach of which a tort action would lie, it clearly stated that it regarded the Supreme Court's decision in the *Hitchman* coal mine case unsound and not in accordance with the common law.

At any rate, the Supreme Court made new law to fit the occasion before it. This was not such a dreadful thing for a court to do, even though its professed function is to interpret and apply existing law and to leave lawmaking to the legislature. What seemed strange was that the court should go to such an extreme in protecting a mere promise, not enjoying the dignity of a contract, when that promise was wrested from the miners by economic compulsion and was of such dubious social validity that both Congress and some state legislatures had declared that exaction of it from workers, by withholding employment opportunities until it was given, should be regarded as a crime. After all, it was a well-settled part of the common law concerning inducement of breach of contract that no contract against public policy should be entitled to the protection of this common-law sanction. And all this, too, in a country in which neither state nor federal courts had hitherto allowed an action of this sort inducing the breach of anything but a mutually binding, dyed in the wool contract, except in a few labor cases of the same type.

This decision led to the increased use of the labor injunction. The antiunion promise became so popular among employers that one judge sarcastically referred to it as "the placement for equity's longest range injunction gun." The political bitterness occasioned by the use of this doctrine in labor cases appeared when President Hoover appointed Judge Parker of the federal Circuit Court of Appeals to the Supreme Court, and the Senate refused to confirm him because he had followed the *Hitchman* decision in a case before his court. This was one of the saddest pieces of injustice in senatorial annals, because Judge Parker, unlike the members of the New York Court of Appeals, *had* to honor the precedents of his superior court. Of course, it could be said that he didn't have to accept the *Hitchman* decision without question and could have shown his personal dislike of this precedent, even if he followed it. At any rate, although this incident seemed most unfair to Judge Parker, it served to tell the Supreme Court just what the Senate thought of its *Hitchman* decision, and for practical purposes discredited that case for all time as a precedent meriting nothing but contempt. Yet while this use of the doctrine of inducing breach of contract is probably defunct, there are other phases of its use.

Perhaps the most apt illustration of how this doctrine might be used judicially to prevent union self-help activities appeared in the Connecticut case of *R An W Hat Shop, Inc. v. Sculley*, involving the hatters' union. The felt hat industry is composed of two separate processes, frequently carried on in different plants. One process is the manufacture of blanks or roughs. From these the finished product is made in the second process. Although different manufacturers and employers carry on these two separate processes, the workers employed in both phases of manufacture are represented by the same hatters' union. It seems that a unionized manufacturer of blanks was under contract with a nonunion finisher to supply him with all of his output. For some reason, the blanks became difficult to procure, and the few unionized finishing plants were about to shut down for lack of them. In these circumstances leaders of the union suggested to this unionized blank manufacturer that he break his contract with the nonunion finisher and supply his product to the unionized finishing plants, thereby permitting the union employees of those plants to remain at work. They told him that if he did not do this, his union employees would strike. When, in order to avoid a strike, he complied with the union's request, the nonunion finisher concerned in this situation brought suit against the union.

The Connecticut Supreme Court, somewhat understandably,

declared that the union had unlawfully induced a breach of the contract. And yet this decision has shocking implications concerning the freedom of unions to further their economic welfare by concerted refusals to work. It opens up all sorts of speculations on the use of the injunction to prevent organizational pressures.

Obviously a labor union is entitled to no more privileges in promoting the economic welfare of its members than are businessmen who are out to achieve such ends. If a businessman secures advantage by inducing a breach of contract between his rival and one who was under agreement to furnish a scarce item of material to the latter, there is no question that he has behaved unlawfully, at least in jurisdictions where this tort has not been confined to binding contracts involving personal services. Hence, there was probably good reason why the Connecticut court should have penalized the union in this case. But the court would have to be most careful in setting up the actual facts as they occurred. Actually, the union appeared to have been concerned over the destination of the blanks, desiring them in union finishing shops for exactly the same reasons that the unionized employers wanted them.

Suppose, however, that there had been no shortage of blanks and that the union was simply anxious to organize the nonunion finisher and chose to do so by cutting him off from a supply of union-made blanks until he capitulated. Under these circumstances they would tell the unionized blank manufacturer that they would not work on any more blanks which were subsequently to be processed by nonunion labor. In order to avoid a strike, the unionized blank manufacturer would have to break his contract with the nonunion finisher—and the practical result would be much the same as it was in the actual case. Here, however, the court could hardly have regarded the union's move as unlawfully inducing the breach of a contract.

This would be a type of secondary labor boycott used as an organizational technique to compel the nonunion finisher to unionize his shop. The object of the union here would be to bring economic pressure on the finisher, through the blank manufacturer's refusal to deal with him unless he, in turn, dealt with the union. This is *not,* as it was in the decided case, an attempt to secure control of certain raw materials, at the expense of the nonunion finisher, so that unionized finishers and their union employees may continue to work. Reflection will indicate a very great difference between these two situations.

In the traditional case of inducing breach of contract which would involve liability for the tort of that name, it must always appear that the prospective wrongdoer is trying to secure for his advantage control of the item, be it personal service or supplies, which the person to whom the inducement is made is under contract to deliver to another. In ordinary union organizational campaigns the object sought is not control of a commercial commodity. It is extended unionization. Approached from another angle, it must appear in the tort of inducing breach of contract that the prospective wrongdoer specifically and intentionally has in mind the breach of the contract in question. On the other hand, in ordinary organizational drives the presence or absence of a contract between the person on whom direct pressure is exerted and the ultimate object of the union's undertaking, is purely incidental.

If this were not so, our law governing the self-help organizational and bargaining activities of unions would undergo a drastic modification. For instance, take a state like New York, where the courts have for almost half a century permitted unions to use the secondary labor boycott in extending their organization. Since its courts, in a case like this, would not interfere with the unionized blank makers' refusal to work on materials destined for completion in a nonunion shop—and vice versa— all the two manufacturers in question would have to do in order to thwart the union would be to enter into a contract with each other. Thus, by the indiscriminate judicial use of the doctrine of inducing breach of contract, the union and its blank workers would have their hands tied and would be denied recourse to a normal self-help organizational technique, just because the economic pressure involved would disrupt the performance of an existing contract.

It seems clear that if this union technique may lawfully be used to exert secondary economic pressure in the absence of such a contract, then the presence of the contract should make absolutely no difference in the lawful use of the same pressure—in the same way and for the same purpose. Any other result would place the union blank makers in a position of forced labor—collectively speaking at least—and would compel them to continue work under economic conditions which they are entitled to regard as disastrous to their economic program as a union comprising the workers in both phases of hat manufacture. Thus it would virtually put them in the position of having to continue work so that the nonunion finishing plant and its nonunion employees might remain at work, compelling them to support an enterprise which they believe to be undermining of and disastrous to their interests.

CONGRESS AND THE NORRIS-LAGUARDIA ACT: 1932

The judicial excesses in the use of injunctions were in no instances more keenly resented by organized labor than when their issuance rested, as they so frequently did, on the alleged commission by them of the tort of inducing breach of contract—chiefly of antiunion promises or "yellow dog contracts." Until the late 1920's, however, our unions did not fully appreciate the importance of co-ordinated political pressure to achieve their ends. They have become a factor of vital importance in American politics only since that time. For instance, the fiasco of the anti-injunction provisions in Section 20 of the Clayton Act showed how unimportant organized labor was politically before this period. That incident, as well as the spread of antiunion employment contracts and the closely allied judicial popularity of the doctrine of inducing breach of contract, spurred the proponents of organized labor's civil rights to draft and to have enacted a federal anti-injunction measure which might be truly effective in leaving labor unions free to carry on, unhindered by the courts, all purely economic self-help coercive activities necessary to their economic program.

Although the unions had experienced serious judicial setbacks in the early 1920's and before, they and their friends had learned much from these reverses. They realized that Section 20 of the Clayton Act had been too extreme in attempting to create an area of allowable economic conflict coextensive with individual civil rights and irrespective of fairly direct economic interests. They perceived that even if the Supreme Court had construed Section 20 to mean what those more sympathetic to unionism had thought it meant, its scope would have been too broad for general public convenience. And they concluded that a new law would have a better chance for survival before the courts if it were drawn to permit freedom of concerted economic action only by those having an interest at stake and not by those exerting purely sympathetic pressures. As for outlawing anti-union or "yellow dog contracts," it was clear that their chances were better if they abandoned the former tactic of making such promises criminal and tried merely to make them unenforceable as against public policy.

In any event, sponsors of organized labor's civil rights of free economic coercive activity backed an anti-injunction bill which was introduced by Senator Norris and Congressman LaGuardia. This bill, reputedly drafted by Professor Frankfurter, then at the Harvard Law School, became law in 1932. It was immediately copied by a dozen or more state legislatures, having been actually anticipated in 1931 by the Wisconsin legislators, who had had access to the bill then pending before Congress. The Norris-LaGuardia Anti-injunction Act is an exceedingly important piece of labor legislation. Its chief significance lies in the fact that it simply cancels out a small host of what might accurately be called judicial perversions.

What it accomplishes is a laissez-faire setup for organized labor's economic self-help activities, on both collective bargaining and organizational angles, by requiring the courts, in their injunction-issuing capacity, to keep their hands off such activities under prescribed circumstances. The point of this act is not what it does for organized labor but is what it permits organized labor to do for itself without judicial interference. Perhaps its most important contribution is to guarantee to labor unions freedom from injunctive interference when they undertake the same type of economic free enterprise which the courts at common law had always accorded to business associations, leaving them relatively free to promote their interests as they see them, in much the same general fashion that associated business enterprisers traditionally did. Naturally, Congress was aware that the particular self-help methods employed by unions were not exactly the same as those used by business associations. But it recognized the fact that these methods were much the same as a matter of general principle, consisting in either case mainly of concerted refusals to deal with others.

Enacted in 1932, this statute first of all prohibits the exercise of the injunctive power by federal courts in labor cases when the use of such power is contrary to its stated public policy. The reservation of the power to issue injunctions against labor at all remains only in carefully prescribed instances. The section on public policy acknowledges the state of business organization under prevailing economic conditions and the inability of individual workers to deal effectively with employers thereunder. There is then declared the necessity of permitting autonomous employee organization, choice of bargaining representatives and free use of their organizations in collective bargaining—all independent of employer domination. And the act also makes antiunion promises, or "yellow dog contracts," contrary to this public policy and unenforceable, thus rendering inducements of their breach by unions no longer unlawful or enjoinable.

The heart of the act is embodied in sections 4 and 13. The latter section by its broad definition of a labor dispute and by other pertinent definitional provisions gives the act a very broad scope. Section 4 deprives the federal courts of their powers to interfere by injunction with detailed types of union self-help "in any case involving or growing out of any labor dispute." The self-help techniques thus protected are:

(1) concerted refusals to work,

(2) joining or remaining in a union,

(3) supporting a union or strikers financially when the supporter is interested in the labor dispute involved,

(4) lawfully aiding anyone interested in a labor dispute, who is party to a law suit,

(5) publicizing a labor dispute and its details, "whether by advertising, speaking, patrolling, or by any other method not involving fraud or violence"—a fairly comprehensive cover-all for picketing,

(6) assembling peaceably to organize or promote labor disputes,

(7) stating an intention to do any of the above things, and

(8) "advising, urging, or otherwise causing or inducing without fraud or violence" the things detailed above, regardless of any antiunion promises.

This program of activities, on the whole, is made nonenjoinable when undertaken by those persons, acting singly or in concert, who are "participating or interested" in the labor dispute in connection with which such conduct occurs. Anyone reading this section over hurriedly must be impressed by its apparent mildness of content. Although it is reminiscent of the second paragraph of Section 20 of the Clayton Act, it seems on the surface to be much more restrained (which, of course, it is). A notable difference is that Congress did not, as it had done in 1914, make the conduct listed lawful for all purposes, but rendered it only nonenjoinable. This was deliberate, since the real evil to be laid by the act was the abuse of judicial equity power relating to injunctions.

The Wisconsin legislature, in the preceding year, had expressly made lawful for all purposes the conduct detailed in its counterpart of this section. But Congress clearly had no intention of going so far in 1932, regardless of its apparent openhandedness of 1914 in this respect. In addition to this, however, Wisconsin registered one quirk in its statute which affords no little amusement at this point. It specifically said that nothing in the act should be construed to make the secondary boycott lawful, although its legalization seemed implicit in the specific conduct actually allowed. The detailed provisions of Section 4, of course, say nothing at all about such boycotts. And that, perhaps, is why the language employed seems so mild when it is compared to the corresponding provisions in the Clayton Act —at least, as Section 20 of that act appears to the liberal eye. But the full implications of Section 4 do not become apparent until we understand the context in which the permitted conduct may occur—that is, until we appreciate the full extent of the term "labor dispute" in this new legislation.

Vitally important as are the provisions of the Norris-LaGuardia Act between Section 4 and Section 13, in which the term "labor dispute" is broadly defined, they are not particularly interesting in an account of this sort. These intervening sections forbid courts to enjoin concerted labor activities enumerated above on the theory that the participants "constitute or are engaged in an unlawful combination or conspiracy"—an obvious reference to the Sherman Act. Also they carefully hedge around the exercise of judicial equity power in those few situations arising out of "labor disputes" which Congress provides may still be controlled by the injunction.

Thus, for an injunction to issue it must appear that unlawful conduct is threatened or committed—that it implies substantial and irreparable damage greater to the complainant if it occurs than the damage the union would suffer if its conduct were prohibited, for which there is no adequate remedy in a suit at law—and that local peace officers are "unable or unwilling to furnish adequate protection." In any event, the hearing on the request for injunctive relief has to be after personal notice to all known persons against whom relief is sought, as well as to the local peace officials, allowance being made for temporary extraordinary preventive relief under carefully hedged circumstances for a brief five-day period, on condition that the complainant files a bond assuring payment of damages to the union if the temporary relief granted proves to have been unjustified and harms the union. No preventive relief at all is afforded any complainant who has "failed to comply with any obligation imposed by law which is involved in the labor dispute in question," or who does not reasonably try to settle the dispute by negotiation, through government mediation, or by voluntary arbitration. The court sitting in any case where relief is allowed must make a comprehensive finding of facts; appeals from relief granted are given precedence over other pending appeals; jury trial is allowed in contempt proceedings for violations of injunctive orders; and in contempt proceedings removal of the enjoining judge may be secured in that particular case if the alleged contempt involves a personal attack on him.

The very gist of the act—that which makes it really something—comes at the end in Section 13. Here Congress acknowledges, without any shadow of a doubt, all that Justice Brandeis and other like-minded judges on state and federal courts, had ever contended concerning the economic needs of organized labor. This section really did what many had thought Congress was trying to do in the first paragraph of Section 20 of the Clayton Act, in setting the stage for organized labor's self-help activities and in defining "the allowable area of economic conflict." Its scope majestically embraces whole industries, listing as legitimate participants in conflicts concerned with employment conditions therein "persons who are engaged in the same industry, trade, craft, or occupation; or have direct or indirect interests therein; or who are employees of the same employer; or who are members of the same or an affiliated organization of employers or employees." And this goes, whether the dispute in question arises (a) between one or more employers, including associations of employers, and one or more employees or labor unions, (b) between employers or associations of employers, or (c) "between one or more employees or associations of employees and one or more employees or associations of employees." It also goes when the situation involves "any conflicting or competing interests" in a "labor dispute." Now naturally persons or associations, including unions, are persons "participating or interested in a labor dispute" if they are "engaged in the same industry, trade, craft, or occupation in which such dispute occurs, or ha[ve] a direct or indirect interest therein," or are members, officials or agents of any such association or union. Finally, the definition of the term "labor dispute" must be quoted verbatim. It reads as follows:

"The term 'labor dispute' includes any controversy concerning terms or conditions of employment, or concerning the association or representation of persons in negotiating, fixing, maintaining, changing, or seeking to arrange terms or conditions of employment, regardless of whether or not the disputants stand in the proximate relation of employer and employee."

This is it, as the saying goes. In this definition of labor disputes and of cases arising out of labor disputes, Congress gave complete recognition to certain theretofore proscribed stranger activities of unions in fulfillment of their heartfelt need to organize entire industries so that, by standardizing employment conditions throughout such industries, they could eliminate the competitive hazard to already established standards in existing unionized units of such industries, presented by the undercutting effects of nonunion wage and labor standard differentials. But note, that in stating this "revolutionary" economic philosophy, Congress did not give organized labor a complete carte blanche as far as its economic activities were concerned. These activities, in such an economic context, it declared, should not be subject to the injunctive powers of federal courts. From this it may be implied that they were still subject to other legal procedures such as criminal proceedings and actions for damages, when appropriate. It may be assumed that all state legislatures copying this act, except Wisconsin, were addressing the same command to state courts. This qualification, however, did not detract much from organized labor's sweeping victory, for with the injunction out of the way, there remained no really effective control over union economic activities. And recently the Supreme Court has tinkered with the act in such a fashion that no legal controls at all remained over labor's nonenjoinable activities within the new area of economic conflict.

The important thing to appreciate here is just what Congress did in the Norris-LaGuardia Act and just why some people claim, with a good deal of justice, that it is the most revolutionary piece of labor legislation ever adopted by Congress, even including the later New Deal statutes. In effect, it erased the prevailing view of federal judges, both at common law and under Section 20 of the Clayton Act, that the commission of damage by labor unions indulging in economic self-help activity is unlawful unless the union people committing it were directly employed by the employer affected. It substituted for this narrow conception of possible union interest in employment conditions a much broader conception of interest, transcending the restrictive features of the immediate employment relationship. The displaced view had given scope only to such bargaining activities as strikes for what the judges thought legitimate ends, together with peaceful picketing and refusals to patronize only by such strikers to promote their strikes. And far from allowing any stranger organizational pressures, it did not acknowledge the legality of even organizational strikes by immediate employees against an employer, because the courts refused to concede that such strikes were labor disputes, concerned with direct objectives like wages and other terms of employment. As has been shown in previous chapters, this displaced view was completely out of gear with the common-law principles applied to the coercive economic activities of business organizations.

Really, the net effect of the Norris-LaGuardia Act was to establish the coercive techniques of labor unions on a par with those of business associations at common law. This was a great deal, in as much as it recognized the economic interest of associated laboring folk in the employment conditions prevailing in any nonunion unit of an industry, in the competing units of which members of the labor association were established. This interest, in turn, conceived and evaluated for all practical purposes in accordance with the union's own views of its importance and reality, operated as a complete justification for any harm imposed on such nonunion unit through economic coercion.

As far as the federal courts were concerned, this act was Congress' green light to nation-wide union organizational campaigns, both for the purpose of securing the closed shop in individual units where a union was already established, and for unionizing all units throughout an entire industry—the so-called "universal closed shop." It is as if Congress had said in this act:

"This you may do, using the techniques we have suggested, as long as you can show that your union economic program, conceived as *you* and not anyone else sees it, is affected by the existing employment conditions in the units of the industry with which you are concerned. We have instructed the judges to withhold the use of the injunction against your self-help coercive activities directed along these lines. From now on it is up to you union people to promote your own economic interests, as you see them, within the area of conflict we have defined."

Another way of looking at it is to suppose that Congress was creating laissez faire, or economic free enterprise, for organized labor as well as for big business. On the face of it, Congress left the federal courts free to use *legal* prohibitions against unions within the same area of economic conflict where it had forbidden them to exercise their equity powers of injunction. But as everyone knew that the injunction and its incidents were the only really effective controls over labor's self-help activities, this was letting the bars down almost completely.

There is one thing about the Norris-LaGuardia Act, however, that is extremely significant, particularly in comparison with the second paragraph of Section 20 of the Clayton Act, as read by the liberals. Under this liberal interpretation, Congress placed no apparent limit on the extent to which unions might have employed organized economic coercion. It made no attempt to confine the privilege of exerting pressure to those who had an economic interest at stake. Had this liberal interpretation prevailed, the stage would have been set for a veritable class war, with a union permitted to enlist any aid it could get, from any source, in putting the screws on any employer directly or through persons dealing with him, as long as such participants articulated their pressures by means of the conduct defined. This would have expanded the allowable area of economic conflict for organized labor far beyond what it was at common law for business combinations and even beyond what the most liberal state courts eventually came to think it should be for labor. In short, it would have been the exaltation of the civil rights philosophy, and the repudiation of the so-called economic interest philosophy, of organized labor's rights.

Congress made no such mistake in the Norris-LaGuardia Act. From where we now sit, it seems likely that those who drafted Section 20 of the Clayton Act, assuming that the liberal interpretation of it is correct, were obsessed by the conviction that labor unions should be allowed to do almost anything not violating traditional categories of tort and crime, such as assault and battery, trespass, fraud, and libel. The wonder is that Congress ever seriously considered sanctioning such a program, although in those days the choice between suppression and tolerance of union coercive activities revolved emotionally around issues of civil rights and not around the more sophisticated notion of pursuing economic interests. Hence, the political issue before Congress in 1914 probably was whether organized labor should or should not have the right to exert economic coercion as they saw fit, with no halfway measures even considered. Indeed, until Brandeis, in his *Duplex* dissent of 1921, took the pains to spell out a theory of justification along the lines of economic interest, it is doubtful if anyone within the legal profession had ever intelligibly expressed this economic theory in connection with labor unions.

It may appear odd to some that Congress did not provide for the secondary labor boycott in Section 4 of the Norris-LaGuardia Act. The short answer to this is that Congress did amply provide for just such a practice, although not under that name. Under Section 4 (*a*) of the act, "Ceasing or refusing to perform any work or to remain in any relation of employment" is not enjoinable if the person concerned, whether alone or in concert with others, is participating or interested in a labor dispute. Beyond any doubt whatsoever, this covers all secondary labor boycotts which any liberal state court has ever recognized as lawful. Naturally it does not include secondary sympathetic boycotts, because participants in a labor dispute must be able to show an economic interest at stake in order to invoke the protection of the act at all. The scope of the labor dispute in the act, while very broad indeed, is not that broad. It is interesting to note, however, that this section almost certainly affords protection to any labor group initiating a secondary boycott which effectively induces a breach of contract between the primary object of the union's pressure and the employer who is the ultimate object. This may not be apparent at first glance. But it would be exceedingly difficult for a federal court to explain away in this connection the word "any" as it is used twice in Section 4 (*a*).

To come back to the boycott situation, it is noteworthy that Section 4 of the Norris-LaGuardia Act says nothing about "ceasing to patronize" or "recommending, advising, or persuading others by peaceful and lawful means so to do"—which phraseology appeared in Section 20 of the Clayton Act. The explanation for this omission seems plain. It looks as if Congress did not intend to prevent the courts from enjoining secondary consumption boycotts, probably because such boycotts invariably depend on enlisting the organized aid of consumers who have no economic interest at stake and who, therefore, could not qualify as persons interested in the dispute or, indeed, even as participants of a dispute as defined in the act. Furthermore, it seems doubtful that the officials of a loose organization, like the AF of L, could qualify as participants of or persons interested in a dispute between, say, the stove workers' union and a nonunion stove company, when they organize such a consumption boycott through their federation newspaper. However, this is far from clear and will remain doubtful until the courts have clarified the act in this respect. On the other hand, had the liberal interpretation of Section 20 of the Clayton Act prevailed, it is likely that such secondary consumption boycotts would have become nonenjoinable at that time.

But Congress may have been a little subtle at this point. Section 4 (e) of the act makes nonenjoinable the following conduct of persons participating or interested in a labor dispute: "Giving publicity to the existence of, or the facts involved in, any labor dispute, whether by advertising, speaking, patrolling, or by any other method not involving fraud or violence." This is a pretty broad order, permitting publication of the facts involved in a dispute on a nation-wide scale, at least by those directly interested in the dispute. In view of the tendency of all union folk to stick together, a nation-wide consumption boycott might be effected inferentially in this way without fear of injunctive prohibition, merely by leaving out the exhortation not to patronize. Of course, no particular union has a paper which circulates generally among anyone but members of that union—all of whom are interested in the dispute and hence legitimate participants in an organized consumption boycott.

If the AF of L could carry an account of the dispute in its paper circulating among all members of all affiliated unions, the foundation of an overwhelming consumption boycott is apparent. The only thing lacking—and that might be con-

sidered something which would take care of itself—would be
the exhortation not to patronize. This idea would not be
difficult to get across. Now, under Section 13 of the act, it
seems pretty clear that the officials of the AF of L, aside from
its member unions, either have "indirect interests" in the disputes of its member unions, are "members of . . . an affiliated
organization of . . . employees," or qualify under the clause
which includes any "member, officer, or agent of any association composed in whole or in part of . . . employees engaged
in such industry, trade, craft, or occupation." At any rate, under
modern notions of constitutionally protected freedom of speech
it would be fantastic to think that a federal court would attempt to suppress a publication by anybody of the facts involved in a labor dispute.

Congress may have had all of this in mind when it omitted
from the act any mention of patronizing but, nevertheless, included Section 4 (e), quoted above. Hence it is impossible to
say just yet what the federal courts will do with secondary consumption boycotts which organize the sympathetic public
against a given nonunion employer and against all who continue commercial dealings with him. It is reasonable to suppose, however, that the courts will not extend the protection
of the act to organized consumption boycotts, either primary
or secondary, where the aid of the general union public is
enlisted directly and indirectly against nonunion employers
or against union employers having collective bargaining difficulties with their employees. Bad as such a device used to be
in organizational campaigns, the way out from under was always open to the nonunion employer. All he had to do was to
sign up with the union—an alternative which most employers
face philosophically enough these days. But now it would be
an ominous device to protect under the act. For since the National Labor Relations Act (NLRA) was passed in 1935, an
employer is no longer free to sign up with a union of his own
choosing. That is a matter on which his employees alone have
the first and last word.

Although the Norris-LaGuardia Act will require further consideration, one final observation about it is appropriate here. This act was passed in 1932, before the New Deal period. Hence, it belongs to that time bracket in which unions were expected to, and did, depend on their own economic resources to put their programs across. Thus the act is the last monument to the spirit of complete free enterprise for unions. This act is the very epitome of union self-help, which it fostered and protected to the utmost within the philosophy of economic interest as opposed to that of civil rights. It did not in any way commit the government to intervention on the side of the unions. Rather, it removed a judicial obstruction to union self-help and economic free enterprise. It did not provide for any administrative commission or board. Rather, it left the law to take its course in the usual way, merely depriving the courts which administered this law from using the injunction in the debonair fashion to which they had become accustomed. Naturally, the significance of this act has been drastically modified since the passage of the NLRA, under which government has stepped in with guaranties of autonomous organization for employees, providing a board for that purpose.

Nowadays a union's self-interest, as it sees such interest, is no longer the only test of whether or not the exercise of certain organizational pressures against employers are lawful. The opinions of the workers in a nonunion plant are now more important than those of their employer on this matter. If these workers are opposed to the organizational plans of the union, *they* are the economic enemy, and the union may focus its pressures against them at the plant—an undertaking which, of course, stands to hurt their employer in a situation where he can do nothing about it. And if his employees are already in a different union, either an independent or an affiliated union rival of the aggressor, the same situation holds true heightened in intensity, however, in a fashion not foreseen by Congress when it passed the Norris-LaGuardia Act.

These and other new issues will be discussed in subsequent

chapters. In the meantime, the career of the Norris-LaGuardia
Act before the courts may be of some interest. Curiously
enough, in spite of its clear wording, several federal district
courts and circuit courts of appeal tried to read Section 13 of
the act to include only disputes between an employer and his
employees who were in the immediate relationship of employment with him. Incredible as this may seem, it actually happened, betraying an inability on the part of the judges concerned to understand the elementary economic facts of a society
in which their own former concepts had been legislatively discarded. A more tenable position was that taken by the Old
Guard in the Supreme Court—to the effect that the act was unconstitutional in defining the area of allowable economic conflict broadly enough to protect stranger proceedings from the
injunction. At least they could read the act and comprehend
what Congress was driving at. But their position was equally
hopeless, since a majority of the Supreme Court could perceive nothing unconstitutional in Congress making the allowable area of economic conflict the same for labor unions as
for business combinations, in conformance with the principle
of common law that the infliction of harm on others through
economic means is lawful, if justified by the pursuit of self-
interest and gain.

Thus, in *Senn v. Tile Layers' Protective Union*, the Supreme
Court in 1937 upheld a judgment denying an injunction
against a tile layers' union which picketed a nonunion contractor at every job he got, because he worked on the job
himself. The union thought this practice harmful to journeymen tile layers because it deprived one of them of potential
employment. The contractor offered to unionize his two helpers, thus becoming a unionized employer, as long as he would
be permitted to continue working on the job. When the union
remained adamant, he refused to comply with its demands and
it picketed him out of work, nobody wishing to deal with a
tile layer if it meant having his premises picketed. This case
arose under the Wisconsin "little Norris-LaGuardia Act," but

it involved the very same constitutional issues which a test of the federal act would have raised. Hence, the constitutionality and meaning of the federal act were taken for granted after this decision. Indeed, the federal act itself was shortly thereafter construed in the same broad fashion by the Supreme Court in *New Negro Alliance v. Sanitary Grocery Company,* a case where a society to achieve social justice for Negroes sent agents to picket a grocery store in a Negro neighborhood in Washington, D. C., because the management would not employ Negroes in responsible positions.

CHAPTER VIII

FEDERAL CONTROL OVER EXPANDING UNION POWER—THE SHERMAN ACT I

> Organization and strikes may get a larger share for the members of an organization, but, if they do, they get it at the expense of the less organized and less powerful portion of the laboring mass. They do not create something out of nothing. It is only by divesting our minds of questions of ownership and other machinery of distribution, and by looking solely at the question of consumption,—asking ourselves what is the annual product, who consumes it, and what changes would or could we make,—that we keep in the world of realities.—Holmes, C. J., dissenting in *Plant v. Woods,* 1900.

ESSENTIAL to an understanding of organized labor in this country is some knowledge of the control over big unionism and union expansion exercised by the federal government under the Sherman Antitrust Act. Since this was the only important restrictive control of labor unions ever undertaken by the federal government, and because some analogous measure may again become vitally necessary in view of the increasing power of nationally federated unions, a fairly complete understanding of it is important. It is a matter on which whole books and hundreds of articles have been written. At times it has seemed much too complicated for professional understanding, let alone for the comprehension of laymen. Yet in retrospect—from the 1940's—much of what has appeared puzzling in the past has cleared up. It is now possible to give an account of this in fairly simple and clear terms so that almost anyone can appreciate what has happened and may yet happen in the way of federal control over labor unions.

The Sherman Act, passed in 1890, is exceedingly simple in statement. The gist of the act appears in its first two sections, which read, in part, as follows:

"Section 1. Every contract, combination in the form of trust or otherwise, or conspiracy, in restraint of trade or commerce among the several States, or with foreign nations, is hereby declared to be illegal. Every person who shall make any such contract or engage in any such combination or conspiracy, shall be deemed guilty of a misdemeanor, . . ."

"Section 2. Every person who shall monopolize, or attempt to monopolize, or combine or conspire with any other person or persons, to monopolize any part of the trade or commerce among the several States, or with foreign nations, shall be deemed guilty of a misdemeanor, . . ."

The federal courts are then given jurisdiction to enforce this act, and the attorney general is empowered to initiate criminal prosecutions or to secure injunctive relief against violations. All persons injured by violations of others are allowed to maintain civil suits for triple damages against those who violated the terms of the act.

From what has been quoted above, this act must seem to be fairly simple. In order to appreciate what Section 1 does, all you have to know is the meaning of the phrase "in restraint of trade or commerce." Unfortunately, this phrase has the delusive exactness of a good many other well-known words and phrases of general import current in our language. It is probably easier to understand the phrase, "to monopolize any part of the trade or commerce," appearing in Section 2 of the act, yet that phrase is not crystal clear itself. Justice Holmes is said to have thought these two sections so general in their coverage that they were almost meaningless, amounting to little, if anything, more than a fiat from Congress to the federal courts to do right by the consuming public in protecting it from the depredations of big enterprise. It set forth no economic program at all and took no position, implying at most what English and American courts had thought as a matter of common law to be the meaning of the phrase "restraint of trade." This invitation to the courts to exploit their own economic philosophy in controlling big enterprises of all sorts Holmes is said to have considered so vague and irresponsible as to merit being declared unconstitutional.

Everyone knew why the act was passed in 1890. It was in response to popular demand aroused by the fear of gigantic industrial and commercial enterprises which threatened to seize control of the manufacturing and marketing of consumer goods of all kinds. The public perceived safety of an economic nature only in what it called competition—that grand weasel word productive of so much confusion and misunderstanding. Sympathetic politicians, and economists who were sorely afraid of what was happening to our economic life, were convinced that national economic health and the security of consumers could be possible only if something called freedom of competition prevailed. This they apparently envisaged as a multiplicity of small productive and commercial enterprises continually vying with each other for the patronage of the public by shaving costs and prices, in order that each might make his merchandise more sought after than that of his competitors. Their philosophy was rather shortsighted—albeit it reflected a most commendable social ideal—in that it presupposed natural boundaries to the practices of competition.

The boldest of our big business leaders, on the other hand, recognized no such boundaries. Through collective action and high finance their aim was to eliminate un-co-operative competitors or buy them up, in order that thereafter they might govern particular commodity markets through strict control over the amounts of goods produced and over the pricing of such goods as were released to the public. These techniques they thought of as competition—a sort of commercial conflict with other enterprisers vying with them for the same markets. And since they themselves asked no quarter, they could not understand why they should be expected to pull their punches —especially since the aim of the act was to preserve the process of competition, in which they believed themselves to be busily engaged.

Competition, of course, is a question-begging term. A state of unlimited competition in a free enterprise society logically leads to the centralizing of control in the hands of the strongest, usually through combinations and mergers of formerly separated units which had carried on independently of each other. Thus, competition carried to its logical extreme paradoxically results in the antithesis of competition—or no competition. This result has led some of our leading economists to affirm that there is no such thing as real competition in the idealistic sense of a multiplicity of small units vying for the patronage of the consumer by offering the lowest possible prices for their goods. The legalistic definition of competition which appears in the court reports is this—it is a categorical justification for inflicting damage on others while in the pursuit of self-interest and gain, so far as the means employed do not constitute a violation of any settled category of tort or crime. If this definition is accepted, it might be thought that the proponents of the Sherman Act had in mind the preservation of something quite different from the idealistic competition discussed above. It seems certain, however, that the popular conception was that they were really trying to prevent much that our courts regarded as competition, and hoped to preserve an economy of relatively small units of production and distribution.

The courts at common law had traditionally maintained a prohibition against what they called restraint of trade. This was a negative control, in that it consisted merely of a refusal to enforce contracts in furtherance of restraints of trade and did not imply any punishment or liability in damages. Such restraints commonly occurred after combinations among enterprisers had seized control of markets through the exercise of ruthless competitive practices. For instance, a group of manufacturers of a particular commodity might combine to control the supply and price of this commodity in accordance with a contract among themselves, which provided a penalty against any one of them not observing the arrangement. This contract, and the combination supporting it, effected what is known as a restraint of trade—for it negatived the freedom of economic independence of enterprise that is the kind of competition epigrammatically spoken of as the life of trade.

As long as the combination in question remained mutually co-operative and retained the economic power to discourage independent enterprise in the same industrial field, its members could charge what they wished for the commodity involved. This arrangement the courts thought bad—but not bad enough to deserve the criminal and tort penalties of punishment, triple damages and injunction. It was bad because consumers suffered as a consequence of these production and marketing controls. But the courts, albeit there were historical precedents for punishments of a criminal nature, showed their displeasure only in refusing to enforce the contract holding the combination together when one of its members, in order to promote his own welfare, violated it. The courts considered this negative concession to the interests of consumers, together with the constant theoretical possibility of new enterprise entering the field, to be ample protection for the public.

Events preceding the Sherman Act indicated that this was not so. The public simply did not agree with this optimism. If the courts would not help out combinations and trusts to keep recalcitrant members in line, these organizations had other ways of enforcing their own arrangements through the exercise of economic pressures. As for the influx of new enterprise designed to compete with the combination, that was usually either eliminated or taken in, most handily. In view of all this, it seems fairly clear that what the proponents of the Sherman Act had in mind was merely by statute to supplant the traditional negative sanction against restraints of trade with the positive penalties of criminal punishment, liability in damages and the injunction, and to empower the federal courts to substitute these positive measures in dealing with restraints of trade formerly regarded as only nonenforceable in the courts. To be more explicit, it seems that what Congress did in the Sherman Act was to make expressly unlawful those undertakings which the courts, as a matter of common law and without legislation, had always tolerated as insufficiently evil to punish but only bad enough to ignore.

If this analysis is correct—and there is much evidence in that direction—it explains the ambiguity of sections 1 and 2 of the Sherman Act. Congress apparently presupposed a fairly definite body of common law, covering those types of situations involving monopolies and market controls through combinations, trusts, mergers and agreements, which the courts thought were undesirable. Instead of trying to define in fairly express legislative terms just what these situations were, it merely comprised them in the phrase restraint of trade or commerce and gave the federal courts three clubs to use against restrainers of trade, where before they had had available only the frown of disapproval. This discussion does not relate in detail what was comprised under common-law restraints of trade, as that is an undertaking not particularly necessary in this book. Suffice it to say that the phrase "restraint of trade" implied at common law the denial and suppression of freedom of independent and uncontrolled enterprise by contract and combination, and the control of supply and price of commodities through the same means. Hence it necessarily, or surely would seem to have, meant that violators of the act must have been engaged in the production or marketing of commodities. In any event, this observation is important, if it be true, when we come to deal with labor cases arising under the Sherman Act.

ARE UNIONS WITHIN THE SHERMAN ACT?

Now one of the most heated controversies of modern times was whether or not Congress intended the Sherman Act to cover the activities of organized labor. After all, the courts at one time had treated labor unions themselves, and their normal effects, as restraints of trade. If the purpose of the Sherman Act was to rejuvenate the principles of classical economics, then it might logically be used to prevent such restraints of trade as unionism was once thought to imply. The only trouble with this was that the courts themselves had by 1890 come to accept labor unionism in itself as an established social institution and had practically ceased to regard the purely bargaining functions of unions as restraints of trade.

During the first eighteen years of the act, the Supreme Court considered only business combinations as possible offenders under its terms. As to labor unions the lower federal courts were divided among themselves on this issue of whether or not the act was applicable. Even after the Supreme Court finally decided the matter in 1908, the argument has been carried on with more heat than light down to the present day. This issue still presents a most fascinating field of speculation; but extended argument on this question is a little like fighting the Civil War in retrospect—and about as profitable. Although many books and articles have been written on this matter alone, the Supreme Court gave the short answer settling the whole argument when it said that Congress did intend to have the act applied to organized labor. The Court then proceeded to do so, applying the act adversely to labor unions in a way that didn't seem sensible and thereafter refusing to apply it in many ways that would have made sense. An account of what the Supreme Court actually did do with organized labor under the Sherman Act will bear out this sweeping assertion.

The first case involving labor and the Sherman Act to reach the Supreme Court—the famous *Danbury Hatters'* case—was decided in 1908. A nationally affiliated union of hat workers was trying to organize all of the eighty or so large manufacturers of felt hats in this country. Most of them were already unionized. The few stragglers were sufficiently strong to resist the union and to offer it serious embarrassment, through competition with unionized units on the basis of lower labor standards, and chiefly the nonunion wage differential. The union had unsuccessfully attempted to organize one of these recalcitrants—Loewe's—by local strikes in Danbury, Connecticut. Thereafter it imposed on Loewe's hats a nation-wide secondary boycott, implemented through the refusal by AF of L folk all over the country either to buy his hats or to deal with merchants who sold them. An immediate effect of this boycott was a cessation of orders for Loewe's hats from merchants in other states. This involved Loewe in large losses. Taking advantage of the appropriate provision in the Sherman Act, he brought suit against the membership of the union for triple damages and secured a judgment of over a half million dollars!

One of the prerequisites of bringing a suit under the Sherman Act is to show that the federal courts have jurisdiction over your action. Loewe did this by showing that the effect of the union's boycott was to interfere with two kinds of interstate transactions—the influx of orders for new hats from merchants outside of Connecticut and the corresponding export of hats from Connecticut to merchants in other states. This was a clear showing that the federal courts had jurisdiction over the suit and that the application of the Sherman Act was proper, under the commerce clause of the federal Constitution, as far as the power of Congress to act at all was concerned.

Then it was up to Loewe to show that Congress had intended to use the act against organized labor and that the union in question had violated the act. To show a violation of the act, Loewe submitted evidence of the very same thing which he had already shown as the basis of federal jurisdiction in the first place—the stoppage of orders from without Connecticut and the interference with the fulfillment of orders from within. This, he claimed, was a "restraint of trade or commerce" within the meaning of Section 1 of the act. He was quite correct in claiming that it was a restraint in the sense that it was an interference—just as if the union people had derailed a carload of hats bound for Colorado and had burned them up or sent them back to Loewe's factory.

But, surely, this was not what the courts had meant at common law when they spoke of restraints of trade. In the first place, their usage of that term applied only to those who dealt in commodities as producers or marketers. The union dealt only in the services of working people, if it can be said they dealt in anything. Second, a restraint was in the nature of a control over supply and price—the sort of practice that hurt consumers. This phrase had never been used at common law to denote mere interferences with the transit of commodities.

The act nowhere used the term interfere or interference. Conceivably an interference of the sort involved in this case might have had embarrassing repercussions on consumers by keeping this one producer's contribution of the commodity in question from the market, thus lowering the supply appreciably enough to affect price. But no such theory was adopted in the *Danbury Hatters'* case. Even if it were, and assuming evidence had been adduced to support it, the fact remains that no such practice had ever been regarded as a restraint of trade at common law, except, perhaps, as an aggravation of a conventional restraint when practiced by a combination of dealers in a particular commodity. Thus, an association of retail lumber dealers, agreeing among themselves to boycott any manufacturer of lumber who sold over their heads directly to consumers, might well be regarded as having indulged in and having aggravated a restraint of trade in the conventional common-law sense of that term. But, clearly, no such thing was shown in this case.

It seems clear that in the *Danbury Hatters'* case, the Supreme Court accepted as proof of a violation of the act evidence merely tending to show, first, that Congress had jurisdiction under the commerce clause of the Constitution to do something to prevent what the union was up to, if it wished to do so, and, second, that the federal courts had jurisdiction in this particular case to carry out Congress' orders to prevent this, supposing such orders had been enacted at all. Naturally the Court had the *power* to say that in the Sherman Act Congress *had* given the federal courts orders to stop the sort of thing the union was doing in this case. After all, if former Chief Justice Hughes was right when he said that the Constitution means only what the Supreme Court says it means, then surely a mere Congressional statute can mean no more.

But in light of the history of the term "restraint of trade" at common law, it seems fairly obvious that the Supreme Court was in error in holding that Congress meant any interference with interstate commerce when it used those words of art in the Sherman Act. What this may be, then, is another instance of judicial interference with the development of national economic policy—a matter properly for the sole concern of Congress. Such a statement should not be construed as criticism of the Court for having decided that the act applied to organized labor at all, since the broad language of the statute seems to justify the Court in this respect. It is directed rather at the assumption of virtual legislative power by the Court in stretching the content of the phrase "restraint of trade" to include mere conduct which served only to give Congress and the federal courts jurisdiction to act at all under the commerce clause of the Constitution.

The next incident concerning the use of the Sherman Act against labor unions occurred when six years later, in 1914, Congress passed the Clayton Act. This new statute was intended to amend the Sherman Act and to make more clear the effect of certain specific practices under that act. As far as we are concerned, it was important in three respects. It allowed private parties to secure injunctions against continued violations of the Sherman Act, it purported in Section 20 to regulate the issuance of labor injunctions (as previously discussed), and it appeared in Section 6 to state the position of organized labor under the Sherman Act. Section 6 of the Clayton Act reads as follows:

"That the labor of a human being is not a commodity or article of commerce. Nothing contained in the antitrust laws shall be construed to forbid the existence and operation of labor, agricultural, or horticultural organizations, instituted for the purposes of mutual help, and not having capital stock or conducted for profit, or to forbid or restrain individual members of such organizations from lawfully carrying out the legitimate objects thereof; nor shall such organizations, or the members thereof, be held or construed to be illegal combinations or conspiracies in restraint of trade, under the antitrust laws."

This provision may appear on a casual reading to fix everything up for the unions as far as the Sherman Act was concerned. Actually it changed nothing for them and might just as well not have been passed. The Supreme Court readily conceded, when it construed the Clayton Act in the *Duplex* case, that the labor of a human being was not an article of commerce, implying, however, "So what!" The first part of the second sentence of this section the Court recognized as Congressional acknowledgment that labor unions, by the fact of their existence and operation, were not an offense under the Sherman Act any more than were countless manufacturing concerns— as long as they operated lawfully under that act and carried out their legitimate objects. The remainder of the second sentence was akin to this, in that it prevented the Court from regarding unions *as such* to be illegal combinations or conspiracies under the Sherman Act.

In this fashion the Supreme Court dismissed Section 6 as insignificant, because it changed nothing already conceded to be true. It is exceedingly difficult to see how the Court could have done anything else with this section. What the unions wanted the Court to read into Section 6 was a pronouncement that the Sherman Act would not apply to them at all. But Congress had very carefully refrained from saying just that, although it would have been so easy to say it if Congress had desired that result. Conceivably the tail end of Section 6 could be read by a sympathetic judge to mean that since unions should not be regarded as "illegal combinations or conspiracies," they could not play the role of convicted defendants under the Sherman Act. But this would hardly be the strict construction required in reading a modification of an already existing statute, especially when its ambiguity could be so easily resolved in the mode chosen by the Court.

Glimmerings of light began to appear when next the Supreme Court grappled with labor and the Sherman Act in 1922 in the so-called first *Coronado* case. It seems that the United Mine Workers of America (UMWA) were being sorely pressed by unionized operators to go out and organize competing non-union mines. In any event, District 21 of the UMWA struck a Coronado Coal Company mine, closing it up tighter than a drum, burning tipples and coal cars, dynamiting the mine, and behaving outrageously in general, to the company's great loss. The company might have brought suit for damages in the state courts, as the strikers had behaved in a highly illegal fashion. But apparently it preferred to proceed otherwise. The company brought suit for triple damages under the Sherman Act against District 21 of the UMWA and against the national union itself, assigning as the violation of the act the stoppage of those shipments of coal which would have been made to other states had the mine not been prevented by the strike from continuing operations.

Here again the Court was asked to construe an interference with the movement of goods in interstate commerce as a "restraint of trade or commerce" within the meaning of the act. But now the Court was on the spot! If it recognized the company's theory to be valid, then it was establishing once and for all the federal government's power and willingness to cancel out most of the tremendous gains organized labor had made during the preceding century. For if it held this stoppage of commerce to be a violation of the Sherman Act, then in the name of that act it would be declaring almost all important strikes and other union self-help bargaining devices unlawful. Reflection will show that this must be apparent, for by 1922 most of the significant units of industry in this country were producing for national markets and sent substantial portions of their output to other states. If a strike of *any* kind, for *any* purpose, were held to be a "restraint of trade or commerce" under the Sherman Act, simply because it shut down a unit of industry and thus kept its products from entering interstate markets, then in the name of that act the nationally affiliated unions established throughout American industry were finished as far as effective bargaining activity was concerned.

The Supreme Court just could not do a thing of this sort, so egregiously inept in both a political and a social sense. Chief Justice Taft realized this clearly. He said in his opinion, therefore, that the company had shown only an "indirect" restraint or interference with commerce—not the kind of direct restraint or interference which would constitute a violation of the act. He pointed out that the mining of coal was of purely local concern, showing that the union's interference was confined to production and did not touch on marketing or distribution, thus implying that the Court did not even have jurisdiction to pass on the merits of this case, whatever it might believe Congress had meant to prevent by the act. He distinguished this situation from the *Danbury Hatters'* case by showing that there the union involved had hit directly at commerce, as such. "The direct object of attack was interstate commerce." Thus he made it clear that whereas the act could be used to prevent interstate boycotts, it could not be used to stop strikes, even when they interfered with, or "indirectly" restrained interstate commerce.

In a way, this position was rather odd since the only difference between the strike and the boycott, as far as the unions were concerned, lay in their relative effectiveness in bringing pressure on stubborn employers. With either device the unions' objectives were to procure compliance with their demands through the exercise of economic pressure on the employers concerned. Practically, this meant closing employers down and keeping them closed down until they gave in. If a strike would be effective, so much the better. If it would not do the trick, as in the *Danbury Hatters'* situation, then the more cumbersome secondary boycott was necessary. The result would be the same in the long run—economic embarrassment of the employer concerned.

Certain incidental differences existed between these two techniques. If the strike was successful, the employer could not operate at all because he could not get the help to keep going. Naturally, if he could not operate, he could produce nothing to ship to customers or to markets, interstate or other. With the boycott, on the other hand, he could still operate and produce. For that matter, he could still send his goods anywhere he wished to send them. But since nobody wanted them, in view of the boycott, there was no point in sending them or even in continuing to operate and produce them. This was obviously a distinction without any practical difference.

Nonetheless, this distinction involved the Court in an admission that as long as the union technique employed in exerting pressure furnished jurisdictional grounds for federal intervention, which only the boycott did according to its views, then a violation of the act was proved. Perhaps it is expecting too much to suppose that anyone but lawyers can understand just what this means. It is legal double talk for saying that the Court was confusing on the one hand the Congressional power to act at all with having acted, on the other, in the particular statute in question to prevent the practice under scrutiny. By deliberately engaging here in this confusion— probably for the sake of maintaining the integrity of the precedents in the *Danbury Hatters'* and *Duplex* cases—the Court spoiled what was proving to be the first real economic insight displayed by judges in their application of the Sherman Act to labor.

Chief Justice Taft and his Court were skating on thin ice. They were undoubtedly glad to reaffirm any sanction against secondary boycotts, under the Sherman Act or otherwise. This was so because they regarded such boycotts as unlawful and thoroughly undesirable as bids for greater union power, since they were usually employed in organizational campaigns. But strikes were something else again. Of course, the Court thought organizational strikes, like those for union recognition and the closed shop, were just as bad as boycotts, and for much the same reasons. It was difficult, however, to use the Sherman Act as a device to suppress even such strikes, because their outward effects, such as would constitute an interference with interstate commerce, were identical to the effects of what might be called tolerated strikes—that is, strikes for higher wages, fewer hours and other immediate conditions of employment.

To understand this observation, one must realize that the Court had previously become accustomed to using the Sherman Act against unions on the basis of the outward effects of union activity, in so far as such effects might constitute restraints of trade or commerce in the sense of interferences therewith. Since these outward effects were identical in all successful strikes, calling such effects a violation in a strike thought "intolerable" from the point of view of its purpose would necessitate regarding even "tolerable" strikes to be violations of the act, because their outward effects on commerce and trade could not be distinguishable from those of intolerable strikes. But since this would be unthinkable from any practical or political point of view, the Court had to find a way to get at intolerable strikes under the act, at the same time leaving a green light for tolerable strikes. One might wonder why the Court didn't just take the position that the effects of intolerable strikes on commerce were direct, and therefore violations, while those of tolerable strikes were indirect, and thus not violations, and be done with it. But this recourse would have been too transparent, particularly when the Court saw another way of reaching the same result much more artistically.

Taft understood the purpose of most contemporary organizational campaigns of big national unions. This *Coronado* case itself indicated clearly what the union was driving at in its closed shop strike at this particular mine. It *had* to unionize all mines competing with already organized mines in national markets, in order to eliminate the hazard presented by the nonunion wage differential to unionized operators, and hence

to union standards, in the organized mines. Unionized operators simply could not continue indefinitely to compete with
nonunion operators who could produce coal for the same markets at a lower cost, because of their lower labor standards.
So, in his opinion in this first *Coronado* case, Taft dropped a
broad hint indicating that if, in a strike closing down a unit of
industry producing for interstate markets, it could be proved
that the actual subjective, that is, internal, intent of the
union's leaders was to keep the product of this unit from entering such markets as nonunion-produced coal, then a violation of the Sherman Act would be shown.

He knew, as a practical matter, that such intent did exist in
almost all organizational strikes and that it did not exist in
purely bargaining strikes for immediate objectives like wages
and hours, because in such instances the employees were usually
already organized. Apparently he believed that if counsel for
the employer could unearth evidence of such subjective intent
in strike cases, then the employer deserved to establish a violation of the act by the union in question. This was a little odd,
since the Court never worried about the subjective intent of
the unions in cases where the outward effects of their activities
constituted violations, as in the boycott cases. In such situations
it simply inferred the intent objectively from the fact of restraint. It introduced the subjective intent test in the strike
cases only to afford a line of demarcation between tolerable
and intolerable strikes under the act.

This approach was most ingenious and could have been
achieved only by a master craftsman in the law, such as Chief
Justice Taft. It was nevertheless irritating to have the Court
do this. It had already taken the general position that as far
as unions were concerned, the application of the act to their
activities should be determined on the basis of their outward
observable effects on commerce, as in the secondary boycott
cases. The Court did not worry about the unions' subjective
intent in such cases. Judged by this standard, *all* effective
strikes would either fall short of violation of the act or all such

strikes would constitute violations of the act, depending on which way the Court chose to jump. But the alchemy of the law, through the use of subjective or actual intent as a catalyst, could magically render an erstwhile innocent outward effect of a strike into a violation of the act, under Taft's expert manipulation. This seems unwholesome in our law, both because it is so difficult to understand and because it gives the average labor union official the notion that the Court is putting something over.

In any event, at a new trial, counsel for the Coronado Coal Company procured a disgruntled union official, who had been badly used by his fellows, to testify that, as a matter of subjective intent, District 21 had in mind the unionizing of the Coronado mine in order to keep its product, in its nonunion character, out of interstate markets, and that by the strike it sought to keep such coal out of such markets until the mine became unionized. The testimony indicated that this was intended in order to eliminate the competition in national markets between union-mined and nonunion-mined coal, pursuant to the economic program of the UMWA. Of course, everyone supposed that this was so, anyway, and believed that the same intent was fostered subjectively by the national union, but counsel for the company was unable to secure testimony from a national official to prove it. Thus, while District 21 alone lost before the Supreme Court in what is called the second *Coronado* case, it escaped reinstatement of an adverse judgment of over half a million dollars by a settlement out of court.

Now the exasperating feature of all this legal prestidigitation is that the Supreme Court was for the first time on the right track in applying the Sherman Act to labor unions. In the boycott cases it had made an egregious error by forgetting that the Congressional purpose behind the act was to prevent the suppression of competition. In the *Coronado* coal mining cases, however, the Court treated proof of the suppression of competition as the crux of the matter, even though its purpose in doing so was merely to provide a device under which it could discourage organizational or intolerable strikes under the act and, at the same time, avoid using the act to suppress bargaining or tolerable strikes.

WHAT THE *Coronado* CASES MEANT

At this point we must pause and consider just what the Court had done in the *Coronado* cases as far as long term union economic policy was concerned. By the 1920's, of course, all nationally affiliated unions were thoroughly committed to the necessity of the universal closed shop in every industry—that is, to the unionizing of all units in every industry in which a union was already established. The reason for this position was that no union could endure competition in any national market between its own union-made goods and nonunion-made goods produced more cheaply because of the lower nonunion labor standards, chiefly the wage differential. This economic program had become of such momentous importance to unions that it may be said to have become the very essence of American labor unionism itself. Certainly, this program went to the very heart of their organizational campaigns. They simply had to pursue it relentlessly if they were going to survive at all. Yet in one fell swoop the Supreme Court's *Coronado* decisions had condemned this economic program—or at least organized labor's only lawful means of pursuing it—as an offense under the Sherman Act.

Now, it is arguable that in the *Coronado* cases the Court had decided only that as long as a union, pursuant to its proved intent to prevent competition between union-made and nonunion-made goods in the same national markets, succeeds by a strike in keeping the products of a nonunion plant from entering such markets, then a violation of the act exists. In the case at hand, this view would emphasize the importance only of having kept out of national markets that particular coal which would have been mined, but for the strike. But this contention seems invalid.

If it were true, then it is apparent that the Court would have created a device under which any effective strike for any purpose, tolerable or intolerable, might be penalized under the act. The purpose of any simple bargaining strike is to impose economic embarrassment on the struck employer. One way of doing this, aside from preventing continued production, is to keep his goods from being sold, if possible. And the last thing the Court wanted to do was to create a means whereby the act might be used to suppress mere bargaining strikes. Still, there may be something to that argument, where strikers intend to, and do, prevent already mined coal from entering commerce to compete with union-mined coal. This possibility will be discussed later in connection with its subsequent consideration by the Court. At any rate, it seems much more plausible to suppose that the Court was awakening to the fact that organized labor's economic program of systematically eliminating all competition between union-made and non-union-made goods in national markets was, in itself, an undertaking in the direction of that kind of price standardization and market control against which Congress had really intended to legislate in the Sherman Act. For there can be little doubt that this union economic program smacked of the type of wholesale price standardization at which the act was originally aimed.

It seems fairly clear that in 1890, when the Sherman Act was passed, not even our economists, let alone Congress, had any clear-cut conceptions of this union economic program under discussion, for at that time it did not exist in any articulate form. Hence, if Congress did not have this sort of thing in mind, it could hardly be said to have legislated against it. Furthermore, as has been suggested, the act ought not to be applied to anyone not dealing in commodities of commerce. Now, unions normally deal only in the commodity of personal service or labor. Whatever else the Clayton Act did *not* do, it certainly stated clearly in Section 6 that labor is not a commodity of commerce as far as the Sherman Act is concerned.

Thus, would it not be a fair inference to conclude that the Court's position in the *Coronado* case was at fault, since the union was concerned only with the standardization of *labor* costs in all competing mines, and not with the standardization of *coal* prices? This question certainly presents food for reflection. The only possible drawback to this is that the union *did* concern itself with the commodity of coal in its attempt to keep a certain character of coal—that is, nonunion-mined coal—from competing with union-mined coal in national markets. In a limited sense, then, it might be said that the union was dealing in the commodity of coal and not just in the commodity of labor, although the standardization of wages was its long run objective, which would be only incidentally, albeit inevitably, reflected in the price of coal itself.

There is not a great deal more to say about the Sherman Act and labor before the New Deal era. Although during this interval of seven or eight years there were several decisions of the Supreme Court involving labor unions under the act, only two are of sufficient importance to require comment in the development of an understanding of labor policy as reflected in our law. One of these cases—the *Bedford Cut Stone* case, decided in 1927—was a reaffirmation of the boycott cases. In an attempt by the national stonecutters' union to organize the big Indiana limestone quarries, all union stonecutters working on buildings refused to handle nonunion Indiana limestone. This economic pressure put an end to the export of nonunion limestone from Indiana to building contractors in other states.

On the basis of the *Danbury Hatters'* and *Duplex* decisions, the Supreme Court recognized a violation of the act. Like the situation in the *Duplex* case, this was a secondary labor boycott, effected through organized refusals to work on nonunion stone, whereas the *Hatters'* case was a secondary consumption boycott, effected through organized refusals to purchase Loewe's

hats. But their effect as alleged restraints of trade and commerce were identical as far as the Sherman Act was concerned.
It is true that if Indiana cut limestone might be regarded as a
unique commodity in itself, then the effects of the labor boycott were sufficiently widespread to keep that commodity almost entirely off the market. Such a result might cause ab-
normal price increases for the particular commodity by
rendering it scarce.

This effect, in turn, might invite applications of the view,
later expressed by the Court, that a wholesale suppression of
the marketing of any commodity, sufficiently great to increase
its price through relative scarcity, would be contrary to the
policies of the act. But this theory was not adopted by the
Court in the *Bedford Cut Stone* case. It chose simply to rely
on the fact that the labor boycott had put an end to orders
and sales of the stone in question. Furthermore, the evidence
could hardly have shown any such market restriction, anyway,
since there was plenty of stone available for those who wanted
it and no restrictions at all on its physical transportation. The
only reason it remained off the market was the refusal of contractors to order it as long as union stone setters, in turn, refused to handle it.

Justice Brandeis tried hard in his *Bedford* dissent to persuade
the Court to adopt a more sensible position. First, he invoked
the "rule of reason" which had been developed by the Court
in connection with business structures like U.S. Steel and U.S.
Shoe Machinery, contending that the union was effecting a
reasonable restraint in view of the circumstances. As he said,
it was simply trying to prevent a powerful combination of
twenty-four corporations from breaking up the union. He
stressed the fact that only stonecutters and setters were involved—all with a common industrial interest—emphasizing
that the union's only weapon was the legitimate one of concerted refusal to work in order to advance their interests
through extended organization. He warned that in this case the
Court had held that Congress, in the antitrust law, had created

"an instrument for imposing restraints upon labor which reminds of involuntary servitude." After commenting on the overwhelming concentration of economic power and dominance the court had tolerated in the *U.S. Steel* and *U.S. Shoe Machinery* cases, he concluded:

"It would, indeed, be strange if Congress had by the same Act willed to deny to members of a small craft of workingmen the right to cooperate in simply refraining from work, when that course was the only means of self-protection against a combination of militant and powerful employers. I cannot believe that Congress did so."

But even Justice Brandeis concurred in the only remaining decision left for discussion in this chapter. In the *Brims* case, decided in 1926, the Court unanimously approved the use of the Sherman Act to condemn a three-cornered working agreement between the carpenters' union, the organized building contractors and the organized operators of woodwork mills in the Chicago area. Under this agreement the building contractors agreed to employ only union carpenters and to install only union-made trim. The woodwork operators agreed to employ only union carpenters. And the union, of course, agreed that its members would work for both sets of employers and that its building carpenters would install only union-made wood trim. This arrangement was disastrous to nonunion mills in Wisconsin, Indiana, and southern Illinois, which had formerly sent the bulk of their products to the Chicago market.

In view of this wholesale market control, obviously achieved at the expense of the Chicago public in their role of consumers of buildings, the Court sustained a conviction of the union leaders under the act for having helped to destroy competition from the out-of-state mills, whether or not they were unionized. The usually dissenting members of the Court approved of this decision, apparently because the union was in cahoots with the two sets of business enterprisers in an attempt absolutely to control a large market for their mutual advantage and was not engaged merely in an attempt to exert organizational pressures. Hence, completely lacking from this situation were any of those elements that Justice Brandeis thought to be legitimate union activities.

This case, as well as the others, will receive further consideration in an analysis of the Court's position on labor and the Sherman Act during the New Deal era. Perhaps it might be thought logical to proceed immediately with this analysis. But the drastic modifications in the Court's fundamental social philosophy under the political influences of the New Deal era make it necessary first to examine the intervening course of events, chiefly certain phases of the National Labor Relations Act.

This chapter has indicated the extent to which the federal government was willing prior to 1933 to restrict the organizational activities of labor unions. Later there will appear a detailed account of its relaxation of this control. And it may be stated now that in conclusion there will be a critical analysis of what might be done, either under the Sherman Act or through new legislation, to control some of the activities of organized labor which have become fully as harmful to the interests of consumers, and to our national economy in general, as were the practices of the great corporate structures that originally inspired the passage of the Sherman Act.

CHAPTER IX

THE NATIONAL LABOR RELATIONS ACT OF 1935

> The history of the rules governing contests between employer and employed in the several English-speaking countries illustrates both the susceptibility of such rules to change and the variety of contemporary opinion as to what rules will best serve the public interest. The divergence of opinion in this difficult field of governmental action should admonish us not to declare a rule arbitrary and unreasonable merely because we are convinced that it is fraught with danger to the public weal, and thus to close the door to experiment within the law.—Brandeis, J., dissenting in *Truax v. Corrigan,* 1921.

WITH THE passage in 1932 of the Norris-LaGuardia Act there was ushered in a period of almost complete freedom for union expansion through economic self-help. Yet, curiously enough, that act came within three years of marking the end of the epoch in which unions were completely free to expand, under their own power as they themselves alone saw fit. This was due to the changes in political philosophy and atmosphere expressed in early New Deal labor legislation. Beginning in Section 7 (*a*) of the Blue Eagle NRA in 1933, continuing in the amended Railway Labor Act of 1934, and culminating in the National Labor Relations Act of 1935, which is usually called the Wagner Act, these far-reaching changes partially eclipsed the full significance of this earlier anti-injunction legislation. And a subsequent organizational and psychological phenomenon of major importance—the creation of the CIO in 1936— profoundly affected the way in which the Norris-LaGuardia Act and the NLRA were no doubt designed to work together.

Taken at its face value alone, the National Labor Relations Act was fundamentally different from the Norris-LaGuardia Act because it pledged the government to aid employees in securing independent organization, free from employer interference. The anti-injunction statute, on the other hand, had simply removed the judicial restrictions on the freedom of organized labor to impose unionism on employers by means of coercive economic self-help. Until the NLRA became law, the federal government regarded union organizational campaigns as economic struggles between unions and employers, with practically no holds barred, except for violations of the Sherman Act. In the NLRA, however, Congress virtually ordered employers to stop resisting the spread of unionism, telling them that the desire of their employees to organize was none of their business and to keep their hands off. This, quite obviously, was an epoch-making step in itself, especially since the NLRA placed no restrictions on the freedom of unions to exercise economic pressures on these same employees, whenever they saw fit to do so.

It may be hard now to grasp the significance of a federal statute telling employers that they were no longer free to resist unionism in their plants. The employers had thought it was bad enough, under the Norris-LaGuardia Act, to have the federal courts forbidden to enjoin outside unions from moving in on open or nonunion shops. But at least they had been left free to fight it out with the unions, exchanging blow for blow in the economic tussle and frequently winning. After this Act they could not even defend themselves against what many of them sincerely regarded—and possibly still do—as a menace to our national economy. It was a bitter pill for rugged individualists brought up in the tradition of American economic free enterprise. Although most employers had always thought unionism itself an invasion of employer free enterprise—and certainly respectable economic doctrine supported them in this conviction—they could understand a statute like the Norris-La-Guardia Act, which left it up to unions to achieve what they could by their own economic strength. They had no doubt reasoned that that statute might possibly be described as insuring free enterprise to all—even to those organizations dedicated to pursuit of economic advancement and gain for wage earners!

The flaw in this concession, according to those employers, was the hopelessness of working people trying to better themselves by flying in the face of generally accepted economic truths. They just couldn't lift themselves by their economic bootstraps. But, the employers had reflected, if they insisted on trying to do so, let them try, as long as we remain free to fight them back with economic weapons. Possibly the Norris-LaGuardia Act might have been a concession in the hope of forestalling something thought to be far worse—like the NLRA itself—since stranger things have happened in American politics. But when the NLRA finally became law, what they must have regarded as a sort of shotgun wedding with the unions was too much for most employers.

The obvious distinction between the Norris-LaGuardia Act and the NLRA must, then, be apparent. The crux of this distinction is the fact of government intervention on the side of employees and, through them, of the unions. This intervention, no doubt, was as much the result of increasing union political power as the expansion of union self-help facilities had been three years previously under the Norris-LaGuardia Act. It is easy to suggest now that Mr. Roosevelt was using the NLRA to make a bid for the support of organized labor in 1936. But it is just as easy to reply that the Republicans may have been thinking about the 1932 election when they passed the Norris-LaGuardia Act. Such motives are merely realistic recognitions of organized labor's political strength. And it is possible also to explain the NLRA as a device in the New Deal's anti-depression program. The idea was to create purchasing power and a trend toward inflation through the expansion of labor unions with the collective bargaining strength to improve working conditions.

It should be kept in mind that all during this period or-

ganized labor meant the American Federation of Labor. Both
of these statutes were passed before the CIO appeared over the
horizon. This fact is very important to a complete understanding of what the NLRA came to mean in our national labor
scene as compared with what it probably was intended to mean
when it was drafted and enacted as law.

Prior to 1935 there were other unions besides those affiliated
with the AF of L. But it is common knowledge that they were
of relatively minor economic and political significance. Naturally the various unions under the AF of L roof had occasional
fights, chiefly craft jurisdictional disputes of the sort described
in previous chapters, but their mutual relations were cordial,
indeed, when compared to those that later existed between
AF of L and CIO unions competing for influence in the same
industrial fields. The feeble guaranties of independent unionism in the NRA days of 1933—possibly interpreted by industry
as the writing on the wall—had scared many employers into
forming ERP's, or employee representation plans. These constituted a type of "independent" union more or less under the
domination of management. These so-called company unions
had absolutely no economic or political significance of any sort
and were obviously fostered by management as a bulwark
against outside, really independent, unions.

Hence it is fairly clear that it was the political power of the .
AF of L that achieved the enactment of the NLRA. And in
retrospect it seems apparent that in passing the NLRA, Congress was doing its best to provide the AF of L with the means
to promote the unlimited expansion of its member unions,
free from the interference of employers. Later this reflection
would seem very odd, indeed. Yet if the CIO had not come
along, that is almost certainly what the NLRA, in effect, would
have been.

The inception and rise of the CIO drastically changed the
whole picture of American labor organization as it was probably foreseen by Congress in 1935. Whether or not anybody in
Washington had information to the contrary, not available to

Congress, we shall never know. The fact remains that the original plan of creating the NLRA for the sole convenience of the AF of L never materialized. It is possible, of course, that Congress anticipated the rise and growth of vigorous independent unions as the result of the guaranties in the NLRA—sufficiently numerous and strong to furnish real competition for the AF of L unions through adequate but lower labor standards. But the AF of L unions would have remained free under the NLRA to proselytize and persuade employees in plants all over the country to choose them as their bargaining representatives. As long as they could do this, while employers were compelled to refrain from interference, they would have had all they needed to become firmly established. The competition arising from the CIO, however, was more than Congress and the AF of L had bargained for. Inevitably it transformed the anticipated effect of the NLRA into something far different.

Before a discussion of the NLRA, its provisions and its effects, however, one last additional point is necessary. Not only were employers forbidden to bring pressure on their employees to keep them out of unions. They were also forbidden to tell their employees that they must join and be represented by any particular union. This was of the utmost practical importance. Until the passage of the NLRA, unions had customarily aimed their organizational pressures at employers and had counted on ultimate employer capitulation to win recognition and to secure collective agreements in their plants. Formerly an employer who could no longer hold out against the organizational pressures of a union seeking recognition in his plant would capitulate to the union and sign up with it. Naturally, it seldom occurred to him in those days to consult his employees' wishes on such a matter. Thus frequently large groups of employees found themselves represented by unions which they did not want.

As soon as the NLRA became law, however, an employer was no longer supposed to do this. He was told by law to keep his hands off of union organizational matters pertaining to his own employees, no matter what his personal notions in the premises might be. And a logical corollary of this change was that unions attempting to organize a plant would no longer bring pressure against an employer, but would exert their influence only on his employees. Now if there was only one strong union in the field seeking the right to represent a group of employees for bargaining purposes, this would be no serious disadvantage. Practically, under such circumstances, the AF of L unions would have been much better off than they had been before the NLRA became law, since the real opposition to their organizational drives had always come from employers. This was now canceled out by the new statute.

But when the CIO came into the field, competing almost everywhere with the AF of L unions for bargaining rights, and when healthy independent unions began to crop up, subtly encouraged by co-operative employers anxious to keep out either of the two big affiliated union systems, it appeared that the NLRA was something of a boomerang for the AF of L. The fact that its affiliated unions could no longer properly exert pressures directly against employers, with the hope of compelling their capitulation, became a matter of great practical importance. Henceforth these unions were supposed to confine their pressures to employees only. We shall see that they frequently did this by methods that were disastrous to the helpless employers. Thus, they initiated boycotts and other pressures, shutting down plants completely in the hope that the employees, who had selected CIO or independent unions, would shift their allegiance to the AF of L. And they also hoped, by exerting these pressures, that the employers concerned might frankly urge their men to reconsider their first choice in order to secure peace and industrial stability. Certainly, the importance of the employees' option was embarrassing to AF of L unions when employers were anxious to sign up with them simply to forestall the CIO—employers incidentally, who would no doubt have resisted the AF of L as much as they dared under the NLRA had that organization continued to be the only strong federation of nationally affiliated unions.

WHAT THE WAGNER ACT DID

Interesting as these speculations may be, it is high time to examine the original NLRA briefly and see just what it provided. Incidentally, a description of these provisions, with modifications to be noted later, will serve adequately to portray a large part of the existing provisions in the NLRA of 1947—Title I of the Taft-Hartley Act.

In the first place, the act set forth a series of findings and a statement of policy by way of an inducement to the subsequent detailed provisions. Thus it noted that "the denial by employers of the right of employees to organize and the refusal by employers to accept the procedure of collective bargaining lead to strikes and other forms of industrial strife or unrest." These in turn were stated to be a burden upon and to obstruct commerce, chiefly by interfering with the flow of raw materials and manufactured goods and by likewise diminishing employment and wages substantially enough to upset market demands for those same goods not otherwise directly affected by strikes and labor unrest.

It then went on to state that "the inequality of bargaining power between employees who do not possess full freedom of association or actual liberty of contract" and employers who did enjoy these privileges burdened and affected the "flow of commerce" and helped to bring about business depressions by lowering wages and the purchasing power of workers and "by preventing the stabilization of competitive wage rates and working conditions within and between industries." Finally, it asserted that "experience has proved that protection by law of the right of employees to organize and bargain collectively" protects commerce and promotes its flow by removing "certain recognized sources of industrial strife and unrest," by encouraging collective bargaining and its incidents, and by restoring equality of bargaining power between employers and employees. Aside from the empirical observations in general by members of Congress, this "experience" may have been based on the results of the Railway Labor Act of 1926 and 1934—a measure which in several ways anticipated for the railroads what the NLRA did for industry at large. And it cannot be gainsaid that whatever else the Railway Labor Act may have done for or to our national economy, it certainly seems to have put an end to the disruptive organizational strike.

In brief, Congress found that the strife over organizational activities of unions had caused so much harm to the national economy that the best way to secure relief to the body economic was to let employees organize as they saw fit, especially since the fruits of organization—collective bargaining by strong unions—was socially and economically desirable for the common good. And Congress added (for under the federal Constitution it *had* to justify all it enacted in this statute as a regulation of commerce among the states, usually spoken of as "interstate commerce"): If we guarantee to employees the right to organize and bargain collectively, this will do away with all the trouble that organizational activities have hitherto imposed on commerce, whatever additional effects it might have. Hence, Congress went on to say:

"It is hereby declared to be the policy of the United States to eliminate the causes of certain substantial obstructions to the free flow of commerce and to mitigate and eliminate these obstructions when they have occurred by encouraging the practice and procedure of collective bargaining and by protecting the exercise by workers of full freedom of association, self-organization, and designation of representatives of their own choosing, for the purpose of negotiating the terms and conditions of their employment or other mutual aid or protection."

To implement this policy Congress proceeded to enact the important substantive provisions of the NLRA. In Section 7 it declared:

"Employees shall have the right to self-organization, to form, join, or assist labor organizations, to bargain collectively through representatives of their own choosing, and to engage in concerted activities, for the purpose of collective bargaining or other mutual aid or protection."

This provision tended to summarize in declaratory form what Congress had been driving at in its statement of public policy. Next, in Section 8, there was the backbone of the act, in so far as it was designed to prevent employers from interfering with the desire of employees to organize. This section declared that "It shall be an unfair labor practice for an employer"

(1) to interfere with employees "in the exercise of the rights guaranteed in section 7"; and

(2) it made it an unfair labor practice for employers "to dominate or interfere with the formation or administration of any labor organization or contribute financial or other support to it."

This provision was intended to prevent the formation of company unions, such as the old ERP's in the post-NRA days after 1933, and to insure absolute independence of employee representation in true collective bargaining. It did have a proviso, however, to the effect that under certain conditions, an employer might permit employees to confer with him during working hours without loss of time or pay, apparently on union business.

The next subdivision, (3), of this section made it an unfair labor practice for an employer "by discrimination in regard to hire or tenure of employment or any term or condition of employment to encourage or discourage membership in any labor organization." This was designed to prevent employers from refusing to hire, or from refusing to retain in employment if already hired, any applicant for a job or presently employed worker because of his existing membership in any union or his desire to join one, or because of his refusal to join any particular union approved by the employer. It was also aimed squarely at the antiunion or "yellow dog contract."

But it did contain one exception to this—very necessary for union approval of the measure as a whole—permitting an employer, who had entered into a closed union shop agreement with a union duly representing his employees, to require membership in such union of any applicants for jobs, or of already hired employees who had refused to join the union when the agreement was made. And when an agreement condoned the hiring of nonunion employees, but denied the employer's right to retain them in his shop after a stated time unless they joined the union—the so-called union shop contract—this exception allowed the employer the same latitude.

The next provision, (4), made it an unfair labor practice for an employer "to discharge or otherwise discriminate against an employee because he has filed charges or given testimony under this Act." This subsection insured immunity from discriminatory treatment to employees who invoked the provisions of the act against employers, or who assisted fellow employees or a union in doing the same thing. It was broad enough not only to prevent discharge of an employee for such conduct but also to prevent the imposition on him of petty revenge such as demotions, layoffs, assignments to undesirable work and denial of promotion.

Finally, the last subdivision, (5), of this vitally important Section 8 made it an unfair labor practice for an employer "to refuse to bargain collectively with the representatives of his employees" duly chosen pursuant to other provisions in the act. This was an exceedingly important measure, and it gave rise to much bitter discussion. But its purport seems plain enough and quite consistent with the other strictures of Section 8. It was never intended to compel an employer to enter into an agreement with a union, and, if it had been so drafted in plain words, it is doubtful if any court in the land would have enforced it. Clearly it was intended to compel an employer merely to meet and negotiate with the representatives of his employees, chosen by them for collective bargaining purposes. Congress apparently believed that when the parties get that far, they usually come out with a contract and begin living together on a more or less rational basis.

This provision was never intended to subject employers to impossible conditions. They were left free to reject any union bargaining proposals as long as they themselves offered counter-proposals in good faith. Anyone familiar with practical labor relations can appreciate how necessary Section 8 (5) was, for he knows how easily an employer could set at naught his compliance with the rest of Section 8 merely by refusing to deal with the union his employees selected to represent them. Such stalling conduct quickly discouraged employee interest in union-ism, and frequently had done so, thus permitting an employer to achieve indirectly the very objectives denied him under the other provisions in Section 8.

Now these restrictions on employers were not self-executing. Indeed, Congress provided very elaborate machinery for their administration and enforcement. This consisted chiefly of a board of three men, the National Labor Relations Board, with all of the assistants such an agency might need, including counsel, field examiners, investigators, hearing officers, review officers, attorneys, and regional offices with similar types of assistants in them. Such administrative boards are commonplaces of the past, not much different in their operation from agencies like the Interstate Commerce Commission and the Federal Trade Commission.

Their function is to implement legislation of Congress in particular situations which Congress could not have anticipated in all their details and could not have provided for with sufficiently specific provisions if it had. The idea behind the administrative agency is the execution of the legislature's general will in a multitude of particular instances, far too numerous for the courts to handle directly. The legislature is supposed to establish standards of a general nature in a statute creating and empowering an administrative board, leaving discretion to the board in applying these standards to actual cases arising under the act. In theory, the legislature does not delegate any legis-

lative power to the administrative board, the functions of that
agency being merely to carry out the legislature's will. This, of
course, is perfectly good theory. And it would be impossible for
any government to concern itself with many aspects of a modern industrial society unless it could use administrative agencies
to get its work done.

The National Labor Relations Board and its staff thus came
into existence to see to it that employers refrained from the
"unfair labor practices" described in the act. Its intervention
was invoked either by one or more employees in a plant, who
complained that they had been the victims of unfair labor
practices on the part of their employer, or by a union either
seeking or already having bargaining rights in a plant and
complaining of the same offenses on its own behalf or for individual or collective employees in the plant. Naturally the
board and its agents had to conduct investigations and hearings
to be sure that the complaints were well-founded. Any other
course would be contrary to constitutional requirements of due
process of law. Formal action following these inquiries was
initiated, in appropriate cases, by the board's filing a complaint
against the employer charged with unfair labor practices.

The board had jurisdiction only over employers engaged in
what the Supreme Court calls interstate commerce. This is because Congress itself can act under the Constitution only pursuant to the powers there accorded to it. When it passed the
NLRA it purported to act under the commerce clause of the
Constitution in an attempt to regulate commerce and free it
from the troublesome effects of organizational strikes. Hence,
the strictures in the NLRA were addressed only to employers
concerned with national or interstate commerce. Now just
what that is depends upon what the Supreme Court says it is.
Some scholars believe the founding fathers had made it fairly
plain that commerce among the states covered practically all
gainful enterprise, whether or not such enterprise occurred
entirely within one state and was independent of all outside

markets, either for raw materials or for distribution of finished products. The Supreme Court, however, said it meant commerce *between* the states. For years it held enterprises to be engaged in such commerce only if they actually operated across state lines in carrying on their business. Thus, manufacture or coal mining wholly within one state was not thought to be the kind of commerce Congress could constitutionally regulate. This was the old transportational concept of commerce, and under it the NLRB would have had little enough to do. But nowadays, while it has not yet gone back to fundamental ideas of commerce among the states, the Supreme Court has considerably broadened its old transportational concept of commerce into a brand new one, the wheels of which may nevertheless still be heard clicking over the rails.

The Supreme Court now says that even if an employer is not himself engaged in transportational interstate commerce, yet if his products, or any substantial part of them, are destined for export to other states (and whether by him or his vendee is immaterial), or if his raw materials are brought in from other states (also whether by him or his vendor is immaterial), then he is sufficiently closely related to interstate commerce to make him subject to the NLRA and thus to bring him in under the board's jurisdiction. This is for the reason that a strike at his place of business caused by his interference with his employees' organizational desires would affect either the importation of raw materials or the export of finished goods, or both, to the extent that he would have consumed or produced them had his plant not been struck. A moment's reflection will indicate that in an interdependent industrial society, such as ours, it would be difficult to find an employer not covered by the NLRA, according to this test. At first the Supreme Court protected the board from being completely flooded with work by concluding that employers come under the act only when they are substantially concerned with interstate commerce, leaving the definition of that term conveniently (or inconveniently, depending on your point of view) up in the air for future reference; but with the expansion of the board's jurisdiction since 1947, the Supreme Court has not been so considerate.

HOW THE WAGNER ACT WORKED

The first thing the board did in unfair labor practice cases arising under Section 8 was to determine if the employer charged with violation was concerned with interstate commerce. If in the opinion of its agents it was not sufficiently concerned to sustain the board's jurisdiction before a court, then no complaint was issued. But when the board believed it had jurisdiction, and its preliminary investigation indicated a violation of this section by the employer, then the board pressed charges against him in complaint proceedings. At a hearing before one of the board's trial examiners, with the assistance of other board agents, a record of testimony was built up for the board's edification. The employer had ample opportunity to confront witnesses testifying against him and to offer evidence of his own. At these hearings the strict rules of evidence prevailing in ordinary law courts did not control, although the Supreme Court required the board to rest its findings and orders on substantial evidence. Nevertheless, as it does with most other administrative agencies, the Court allowed the board considerable leeway in drawing inferences from hearsay, self-serving testimony, and rather circumstantial evidence, the test being whether or not there was any testimony or evidence at all which might reasonably be construed to support the board's conclusion. A staff of review agents went carefully over the trial examiners' reports and presented the edited records, with proposed findings and rulings, to the board for final action. Occasionally the board allowed argument before itself if the parties requested such consideration. When important policy issues were involved, the board sometimes supplied the parties in advance with proposed findings and rulings and invited comments.

Now the board could not enforce its own orders at all. It could only issue those orders, and, if the employers against whom they were directed refused to obey them, it had to request the appropriate federal Circuit Court of Appeals to do the actual enforcing. At that time, the employer was enabled to secure a complete judicial review of the board's entire record, including the matter of jurisdiction in the first place. In addition, he had the privilege accorded in the act, under rather technical circumstances, of seeking a review of the board's order as a person aggrieved, even before the board had sought the court's aid in enforcing the order. These opportunities were supposed to, and did, furnish the employer with additional constitutional guaranties of due process. The judicial review also tested whether or not a fair hearing was had, whether the findings and rulings rested on substantial evidence, and whether the board's exercise of discretion and its interpretation of the act in applying its provisions were sound and accurate. If the reviewing court concluded that the board's order was in good shape, it entered judgment requiring the employer to obey it. Then it held its contempt power in readiness to compel compliance with its judgment. Otherwise it refused to enforce the order. In either event, the employer or the board, in accordance with the outcome, might ask to take the case on up to the Supreme Court. And the Supreme Court consented to hear the case if it believed, from a preliminary investigation, that the judgment below was incorrect.

The board's powers were rather extensive in issuing orders against employers who had violated Section 8, although they were somewhat vaguely outlined in the act. Its most obvious sanction was the "cease and desist" order, requiring the employer to abandon practices in violation of Section 8 of the act. Section 10 (c), establishing the board's complete remedial powers, read as follows: ". . . then the Board . . . shall issue and cause to be served on such person [the employer] an order requiring such person to cease and desist from such unfair labor practice, and to take such affirmative action, including reinstatement of employees with or without back pay, as will effectuate the policies of this Act." From this it is apparent that the cease and desist orders were only one part of the board's remedies. Its power to require employers to make whole any employees against whom they had discriminated was most important. Indeed, the board's remedial power was perhaps most frequently invoked in this direction, although that body always had to preface specific orders of reparation by findings of unfair labor practices that were subjected to cease and desist orders as a matter of course.

Now anyone reading the language quoted in the preceding paragraph will perceive that it is rather vague. What was required, in the board's opinion, to "effectuate the policies of this Act" depended a lot on what the board regarded such policies to be and how far it believed it ought to go in recommending their enforcement. Obviously it could not order the employer's "tail to be pulled out by its roots," even if in the exercise of its discretion it believed that such a course would be appropriate. No court would enforce any such decree of vengeance. Indeed, the Supreme Court made it amply clear that the board's function was only remedial and not punitive, and that the only force which could be directed at the employer was by a circuit court of appeals in contempt proceedings for his refusal to obey the court's judgment enforcing the board's order. What, then, was the proper conception of remedy for the board to entertain? Originally it was thought that the board, being composed of experts in the field of labor relations, should be left free to define its remedial scope as a matter of discretion. But a majority of the Supreme Court would have none of this, holding that the courts should define the area of the board's discretionary power by refusing to enforce orders which they believed went too far.

Here we begin to see some of the faults of the administrative process. Congress cannot think of everything in advance, so it sets forth general guides and standards, empowering an agency to fill in the gaps in accordance with those general standards.

Although theoretically this is not the delegation by Congress of its legislative powers, yet it looks somewhat like it. In any event, this particular board was presumably best equipped to deal with these matters. Now most people would dislike being subject to commission rule under the auspices of a busy Congress that might hesitate a long time before it specifically authorized some of the things done by the board under the general authority expressed in the act. This is where the Supreme Court comes in—that branch of our government which has the last word on most of our affairs. It readily conceded that the measures appropriate for effectuating the policies of the NLRA were matters of board discretion, but it insisted upon reviewing that exercise of discretion to see that it was reasonable. In other words, what Congress meant the board to do in the act, and what the board might do under it, depended upon what the Supreme Court might at any time believe to be reasonable. This, of course, probably worked out all right in the long run, although it depends entirely on where you sit economically and socially whether or not you agree that this observation is true.

At any rate, in exercising its remedial powers, the board frequently ordered the reinstatement with back pay of employees discharged as the result of discrimination. It also read into these words the power to instate, that is, order the hiring of applicants for employment who were denied jobs because of similar discrimination on account of their union interests—victims of so-called blacklists—with pay from the time they were denied employment to the time they were offered it pursuant to the board's order. This order to hire with back pay was sustained by a sharply divided Supreme Court, authority for this remedy being found in the act only by somewhat circumstantial implication. The board also read into its authorized remedial powers the right to order an employer to put in writing and sign any collective agreement reached with a union as the result of mutual negotiations. This position was unanimously sustained by the Supreme Court on the theory that such refusal was a violation by the employer of his obligation to bargain collectively. As Chief Justice Stone pointed out, any self-respecting businessman would be shocked if one of his fellow industrialists refused to conclude a bargain or contract already arrived at between them by reducing it to writing and would, no doubt, regard the whole transaction as spurious. He could see no difference when the party of the other part was a labor union.

Another important and entirely different aspect of the board's work was its handling of the so-called representation cases. It will be recalled that the NLRA guaranteed to employees the right "to bargain collectively through representatives of their own choosing." And Congress backed up this guaranty with an elaborate machinery to make sure that employees got the opportunity to assert their choice. In Section 9 it provided that a bargaining representative selected by a majority of the employees in an appropriate unit "shall be the exclusive representative of all the employees in such unit for the purposes of collective bargaining in respect to rates of pay, wages, hours of employment, or other conditions of employment." Thus, a union so selected by a majority of the employees to represent them in dealing with their employer had *exclusive* rights of bargaining out terms and conditions of employment for *all* of the employees in the unit, regardless of whether or not they belonged to the union. It is true, as the act went on to say, "that any individual employee or a group of employees shall have the right at any time to present grievances to their employer"; but this inscrutable proviso meant little, if anything, more than enabling minority employees to gripe. For if the employer bargained with them on their grievances, he was very likely to get into trouble with the certified union which under the act had the exclusive bargaining rights for all employees in the unit.

Now just what was meant by an appropriate bargaining unit? The act gave no ready answer, leaving that one for the board to decide in specific cases and instructing it to conclude whether, "in order to insure to employees the full benefit of their right to self-organization and to collective bargaining, and otherwise to effectuate the policies of this Act, the unit appropriate for the purposes of collective bargaining shall be the employer unit, craft unit, plant unit, or subdivision thereof." It would take a whole book to describe what these words have been and could be construed to mean.

Congress first told the board that when it fixed the appropriate bargaining unit to have in mind the fulfillment of the employees' best interests in getting all they could through collective bargaining. This was not to mean that the board should do all it could to create the most effective and formidable collective bargaining mechanism possible when it decided what the unit should be, but it certainly reads as if it did. If that is what it meant, then Congress had committed itself to the view that the creation of strong bargaining power in the hands of organized labor was definitely a social good. Such a position may well be valid, but it nevertheless carries in its wake about as much potential industrial conflict in bargaining for advantageous terms of employment as the act sought to avoid through obviating organizational strikes and boycotts. Yet it is hard to see what else Congress could have said in creating standards to guide the board in the performance of its duties. The board had to take charge of these organizational details. Congress could hardly have told it either to do what it wished or to see that weak bargaining power resulted from its designations of appropriate units. And when Congress told the board to effectuate the policies of the act generally in this connection, it probably wanted the board to guard against any possibilities of subtle unfair labor practices by employers.

Here are a few illustrations. Take an automobile plant with a variety of job classifications—some highly skilled, like tool and die makers, some less skilled like polishers, and the rest either semiskilled or virtually common labor. Suppose this plant was owned by a company having three similar plants in different localities. And we may also assume that in each of these plants there were foremen, supervisory and managerial employees, office workers, and a research and scientific staff. In representation proceedings the board had the task of deciding whether or not a majority of all of the employees mentioned above should have the opportunity to select an exclusive collective bargaining representative for all of them. The tool and die makers might prefer to choose their own bargaining representatives—a craft union. And if the choice was left to all of the employees, most of whom were either semiskilled or unskilled labor, it is certain that it would not be a craft union. The research and scientific staff would probably have preferred to keep out of the unit altogether, feeling that no union yet chartered could possibly appreciate their problems or do them justice, while at the same time handling the affairs of common laborers.

The managerial employees, of course, would no more want to be represented by a union than any craft or industrial union would wish to represent them together with the production workers. This was obviously because organized labor on the one hand, and management on the other, were in antagonistic positions, comprising the two groups ultimately destined to bargain with each other. The foremen and some other supervisory employees, while definitely on the side of management, were not so sure but what they would benefit from organization and collective bargaining. Yet they were reluctant to be represented by a union composed substantially of production workers, over whom they had direct daily supervision. Their mutual interests were far from common and these lower-down supervisory workers would be greatly outnumbered. On the other hand it was doubtful if the production workers as a whole would want company men like foremen in their ranks. The chances of company influence filtering through would be too great. For that matter, the company would not like to take a chance on having its foremen lined up in the same union with the production workers, because of the compromise of management prerogative which this might entail. And while office workers might need and desire the benefits of organization, their problems again were different, and it might be embarrassing to have them in the same union with the production workers because of their close contact with management.

Besides all of these issues, the board had to ponder the advisability of designating all four of the employer's plants in a single bargaining unit as against separating them into four different plant units. For all it could tell, the employer might plan to break up the union representing the employees in plant no. 1 by shutting down that plant for a while and distributing its allotted production temporarily among the other three plants. This technique was not new. If there were any evidence indicating that the particular employer had ever tried anything of the sort as a means of discouraging unionism, the board would probably decide that the employer unit—all four plants in a single bargaining unit—would be the most appropriate designation it could make. Under this designation, the union would be the same in all four plants and would bargain at the same time for the employees in all of the plants at once, leaving the employer no opportunity to play the workers of one plant off against those of the others. The employer might thus be deprived of a perfectly ethical collective bargaining recourse— the efficient use of his economic resources to counteract the pressure behind demands made by a union established at one of his plants. But, after all, the designation of the appropriate unit was not made with his interests in mind.

These illustrations become more helpful with an understanding of the problems involved in board-conducted elections. As part of the board's function in handling representation issues, Congress empowered it to investigate these controversies and to "certify to the parties, in writing, the name or names of the representatives that have been designated or selected" by the employees in an appropriate unit. In connection with this the board "shall provide for an appropriate hearing upon due notice . . . and may take a secret ballot of employees, or utilize any other suitable method to ascertain such representatives." Pursuant to this authority, the board ordinarily held elections so that the employees in the unit designated might choose their bargaining representative or even vote to have none at all. In these elections the majority choice governed, as it does in ordinary political elections. This did not mean, of course, that a bargaining representative, or union, could not be chosen unless it had the support of a majority of the employees in the particular unit. The board's conception of majority choice was the choice signified by a majority of the eligible voters in the unit who actually voted. Thus, in a unit of 1000 employees eligible to vote, 201 might elect the exclusive bargaining representative for all, if only 400 cast valid ballots.

At first blush some readers may think this unfair. But it is hard to see how else the board could have handled this matter, particularly as most political elections are run on the same basis. The point was that unscrupulous employers, in an attempt to circumvent the NLRA, would sometimes discourage employees from voting at these elections. And, judging from past experiences, they might be able to frighten away more than half of the eligible voters from the polls. If the board required the support of a majority of the eligible voters in a unit to elect a bargaining representative, an employer might in this fashion prevent any union from being selected by his employees. To obviate this possibility, which would be an unfair labor practice in itself, the board developed the conception of majority choice just outlined.

Board elections of this sort were usually held at the plants and were conducted by the board's agents. A list of eligible voters in the unit designated was previously compiled from the pay roll of a few weeks preceding the election. As the description of the unit designated by the board normally excluded supervisory workers, office help, and practically everyone but production and maintenance employees (and even the latter in some craft units), it was just as easy to ascertain in advance who might be privileged to vote as it is in ordinary political elections under modern methods of registration. The board provided official ballots, on which appeared the name or names of the bargaining representatives, or unions, up for election.

It is convenient to assume, for present purposes, that only one union was up for election. In such a case the question on the ballot was: "Do you wish to be represented by (name of union)?" The choices were "Yes" or "No." This enabled the employees to accept or reject the union that some of their fellows wanted enough to have the board hold the election. If a majority of the employees voted "No," then the whole business was over and collective bargaining did not occur in that unit—at least for the time being. But if a majority of the eligible employees voted for the union, then it was certified to the employer as the exclusive representative of all of the employees in that unit for the purposes of collective bargaining. Then the employer and the dissentient employees had to abide by this choice—the former to bargain with, and the latter to be bargained for by, the chosen union, whether they liked it or not. And again the similarity to ordinary political elections must be apparent.

The importance of the board's responsibility in designating the appropriate bargaining unit must now be clear. If, in the illustration that has been used, the board designated a plant-wide unit, the tool and die makers would inevitably be represented in collective bargaining by the union that the mass of the production workers wanted. On the other hand, if the board designated the tool and die room as a separate bargaining unit, they could select their own craft union to represent them. If the research and scientific staff were included in the plant-wide unit, they would inevitably be bargained for by the production workers' union, whether or not they wanted collective bargaining at all. And if the board established an employer unit, comprising all four plants, instead of designating separate plant units, the chances were very good that the production and maintenance employees in one of these plants—say, plant no. 3 —who either wanted no union at all or some independent or affiliated union of their own separate choice, would nevertheless be represented by the union appealing to the production workers in plants nos. 1, 2, and 4, simply because they were outnumbered at the ballot box.

Some very striking situations of this general type actually occurred, perhaps the most notable one being the West Coast stevedores' case. There the board at one time designated the whole West Coast as a single bargaining unit, thus transcending not only mere employer limitations on the appropriate unit, but also port and sectional limitations. In this way Harry Bridges' CIO union, numerically the largest on the coast but by no means the strongest in several of the ports, secured bargaining rights for the whole coast, although the competing AF of L union could easily have won several separate cities if the board had designated port or company units.

On the whole, the board handled this matter of designating appropriate bargaining units with great skill and understanding. Before making its decision it inquired patiently into the historical and economic factors involved, such as the background of unionism in the plant, company, or industry in question, and employer sentiment on unions in general. It did some odd things, however, in attempting to be perfectly fair in this matter. Yet it must be remembered that Congress gave the board no guides for its handling of representation issues and it had to make up its own rules and regulations for settling these controversies as it went along.

Thus, a question arose in the board as to how it would determine whether a small craft group in a large plant should be designated as a separate bargaining unit or should be included in a plant unit. Two members of the three-man board thought it fair to let the employees in the craft group decide that matter for themselves, thereby virtually deciding in favor of the craft unit. For if this issue had reached the controversy stage among the employees in the plant, it is apparent that the union competing for the plant unit, probably a CIO industrial union, and the union striving for bargaining rights in the craft group

—no doubt an AF of L craft union—would be at such logger-heads that the craft group, if given the choice, would inevitably elect to be a separate unit with a craft union as their representative. Actually, such a method of resolving this particular issue may have been sound. However, that would be true only on the assumption that the board had already decided for other reasons that the craft unit was appropriate under the circumstances and merely concluded that if the employees in the craft group really wanted to go in with the plant unit, they should be given the opportunity to say so in an election for that purpose.

This whole matter of representation proceedings was complicated by the rise of the CIO. When Congress enacted the NLRA, it anticipated recourse to the act chiefly by AF of L unions, although it probably foresaw some development of independent unions under it, as well. Naturally, there would have been some strife between AF of L and independent unions competing for bargaining rights in particular plants, and even a certain amount of such conflict was inevitable among AF of L affiliates. But the knock-down-and-drag-out scraps between AF of L and CIO unions, commonly spoken of as jurisdictional disputes (an unfortunate application of a term which, by usage, connotes disputes between craft unions competing for jurisdiction over work exclusively desired by each) made the board's work exceedingly difficult. The plight of employers in these interunion disputes was even less enviable than that of the board, since their places of business became the battlefields on which these conflicts raged. For they remained disinterested onlookers while their employees made up their minds in accordance with the board's parliamentary procedures.

According to theory, all of these situations could be adequately handled under the board's procedures. When only one union was seeking bargaining rights in a plant, a majority of the employees probably wanted it as their bargaining agency, and an election might be unnecessary on a show of membership cards. If it was necessary, however, an election was held in a ballot providing for "Yes" or "No" votes—that is, either for or against representation by a designated union. Then the employees could take it or leave it. If two unions were at the same time seeking bargaining rights in a plant, it usually meant that each had its supporters and members who were trying to establish their own union as the exclusive bargaining representative. Why, then, could not the board simply hold an election and have the matter decided immediately? The answer to this question is that the board was subjected to terrific pressures from either or both unions to defer the election pending campaigns for new members, neither union seeking the election until it felt sure it could win. Naturally, a state of confidence in one union was bound to imply a state of doubt and grim determination in the other. And while the first pushed for an early election, the second tried to defer it until it could shift the balance through more vigorous campaigning among the employees.

Originally, under the board's procedures, an employer in such a situation, although his business might be suffering from the tug of war going on in his plant, was compelled to sit by with his hands folded. Later the board adopted a rule permitting him to petition for an election. Although this enabled the employer and the board to bring matters to a head, it did not relieve the board from the pressures exerted on it by the unions. The employees themselves were protected under the act only from employer influence and were left completely exposed to almost any lawful pressures which the competing unions or fellow employees might wish to exert. For when Congress attempted to create an orderly procedure to govern these matters, it did not modify in any way the privilege of unions to use self-help techniques like picketing, or even boycotting—any activities declared nonenjoinable in the Norris-LaGuardia Act—to influence employees on issues concerning representation. Thus, while the effect of the NLRA had been to eliminate the need for recourse to these union pressures to persuade an employer, they were still available for use at his place of business in ways very harmful to him, in current efforts to persuade his employees. For instance, if the stronger of two competing unions could place an economic embargo on his plant and keep it shut down until the employees were willing to choose it as their bargaining representative, that union was at liberty to do so in strict accordance with federal law, as far as Congress and the NLRA were concerned.

But eventually elections were held in even these tough cases. The ballots were marked "X union," "Y union," and "No union," or "Neither." Sometimes a third union, perhaps an independent which had some following in the unit, also appeared on the ballot. If either of the unions secured a majority of the votes cast, it was certified as the exclusive bargaining agency, and there was an end to the matter. But if a majority were cast for "Neither," then both of the unions seeking bargaining rights were definitely out.

Suppose, however, that of 1000 votes cast, X union secured 425, Y union 350, and "Neither" 225. Under these circumstances the board conducted a "run-off" election, placing only X and Y unions on the ballot and dropping the category of "Neither." Now, unless there was a tie vote, one of the two unions was bound to be chosen. The fairness of this solution was rationalized by the argument that, since a majority of the employees had signified a desire to be represented by some union, there remained only the matter of determining which one. But suppose again that in the first election, X union had secured 375 votes, Y union only 300, and "Neither" 325. Then the board would conduct a run-off election between X union and no union at all, dropping Y union from the ballot. This seemed fair, since a majority of 700 of the employees had signified that while they did not want Y union, a majority of 675 of them had signified that they did want some union. Then if the employees who originally supported Y union still did not want X union, they could join forces with those originally voting for Neither and still keep X union out. Naturally, practical difficulties of all sorts arose in these run-off elections, and whatever the board decided to do in resolving these difficulties, it was invariably wrong from one side's point of view.

This skeleton outline of the National Labor Relations Act and of the board's duties under it, with the accompanying comments indicating the practical difficulties unforeseen when it was passed, should give an approximate idea of the act and how it worked. If the board members seemed to interpret the act broadly and appeared too ruthless in pressing charges against employers, it must be recalled that they were trying to do what Congress had ordered them to do, as they saw it. Any group of three men on such a board was inevitably bound to do questionable things, particularly when they were acting under a statute like the NLRA, so broad in its general policy directives and so meager in its specific directions. They were virtually put on their own to make practical sense of general instructions ordering them to guarantee to employees autonomous organization, representatives of their own choosing, and good faith collective bargaining, to boot. They were under constant fire and pressure from employers and competing unions, from politicians and from the press. Obviously they could not please everyone, and it is small wonder that some of the best of them, in their endeavor to achieve a balanced system of labor relations, ended up by pleasing nobody.

The enforcement activities of the board were confined to orders concerning unfair labor practices and restitution such as reinstatement of discriminatorily discharged employees, with or without back pay. The board had a staff of lawyers constantly engaged in pressing these orders before the courts. If the courts thought the board had gone too far in construing and applying the act, they would refuse to enforce its orders, concluding either that the board had no jurisdiction over the matter involved, or had incorrectly read and applied the act, or had taken an exaggerated view of its discretion in prosecuting the provisions of the act.

The board did not attempt to enforce its decisions in representation proceedings, as such, since these rulings concerning appropriate bargaining units, the details of elections, and certifications of exclusive bargaining representatives were not technically orders at all; and under the statute it had the power to seek enforcement only of its final orders. But if any employer refused to bargain with a duly certified union, he had presumably violated Section 8 (5) of the act. The board's only recourse to command respect for its certification in such a case was to issue a complaint against the employer, and, after the appropriate hearings and findings, to enter a cease and desist order directed at his unfair labor practice. If *this order* was not obeyed, the board then proceeded in a Circuit Court of Appeals for its enforcement, but this was the first opportunity that it had to secure observance of any ruling or decision on its part growing out of purely representation proceedings.

Likewise a union could not secure direct relief from adverse rulings in representation cases, since such rulings were not final orders. But sometimes it could obtain judicial review indirectly. Thus, the union would be allowed to appear and litigate these issues in court proceedings brought to enforce a board order requiring the employer to bargain with the certified union, the employer's refusal to comply with Section 8 (5) being based on disagreement with the representation ruling in question. Indeed, in this way employers occasionally enabled adversely affected unions to get before the courts simply by refusing to bargain with the certified union, thus forcing the board to issue a final order in complaint proceedings which raised the whole matter of representation. Of course, this was a somewhat roundabout way to achieve justice. And the foregoing account may sound as if the board were frequently rather highhanded. But Congress no doubt realized that the board had to dispose of representation issues expeditiously in some way, and that it would never get its work done if each of its rulings under Section 9 of the act was directly reviewable. Hence, although it could have provided for such direct review, its failure to do so was very likely deliberate. Nevertheless, though such review would be an exasperating and time-consuming recourse in most instances, in the long run much bitterness might be avoided and even some justice achieved by allowing it directly.

So much for an introduction to the scope of the Wagner Act and the activities of the board under it. In later chapters there will be discussed some of the decisions of the federal courts that deal with critical aspects of this act's development and its application in a variety of circumstances and with how the board should function in particular situations. Without such an account one's comprehension of this truly remarkable statute would be less than complete. And in addition there will appear an account of amendments to the NLRA. While these amendments modified slightly the nature of employer unfair labor practices and the representation procedure in Section 9, they changed the act drastically in other respects. This was particularly the case in connection with the economic activities of labor unions and the composition and organization of the administrative agency itself.

CHAPTER X

THE UNIONS AND THE SUPREME
COURT—THE SHERMAN ACT II

But it is not necessary to cite cases; it is plain from the slightest consideration of practical affairs, or the most superficial reading of industrial history, that free competition means combination, and that the organization of the world, now going on so fast, means an ever increasing might and scope of combination. It seems to me futile to set our faces against this tendency. Whether beneficial on the whole, as I think it, or detrimental, it is inevitable, unless the fundamental axioms of society, and even the fundamental conditions of life, are to be changed.—Holmes, J., dissenting in *Vegelahn v. Guntner*, 1896.

THE PRECEDING account of federal control exercised over organized labor under the Sherman Antitrust Act up to the 1930's indicated a pronounced bias against union expansion and the growth of nation-wide bargaining strength. With the passage of the Norris-LaGuardia Act in 1932, this policy began to crumble. For in that act Congress virtually invited unions to exert a variety of economic pressures in organizational campaigns and in collective bargaining. Of course, Congress made it clearly understood—or so most lawyers thought—that this act rendered the economic pressures described simply not enjoinable, leaving them subject to all other sanctions. In Congress' opinion, the courts had not abused their powers in actions at law or in criminal proceedings against unions, either at common law or under statutes like the Sherman Act. The abuse of power had been in issuing injunctions. And Congress was preventing a continuance of such abuse by virtually elimi·

nating the equity jurisdiction of federal judges over labor unions.

Since the injunction had long been the only effective control over union organizational and bargaining exuberance, most people regarded the Norris-LaGuardia Act as an official approval of organized labor's self-help techniques formerly subject to the injunction. Lawyers knew that the change was one of form and that all other sanctions, except the injunction, were still available. But the temper of the statute made many conservative members of our bar decidedly uneasy. This feeling was tremendously heightened by the passage of the National Labor Relations Act in 1935. Many lawyers thought this measure would be declared unconstitutional and so advised their clients, urging them to act on that assumption in dealing with their employees. Nevertheless, the political climate in which such statutes could become law was a strange one, indeed, for the continued existence of the doctrine developed by the Supreme Court against labor unions under the Sherman Act. The conservative bar, therefore, prepared for a last ditch stand to salvage what it could from the older law and to see to it that the Supreme Court cleared the air by declaring some of these new measures unconstitutional.

Up until late 1936 it looked as if these lawyers were going to have their way. The Supreme Court had declared several New Deal measures unconstitutional. In a New York minimum wage case, it maintained the traditional position that state legislatures could not invade freedom of contract, however much the economic and social conditions of sweated labor required standards of work below which no employer and his employees might lawfully agree to go. President Roosevelt had had no opportunity to make appointments to the Supreme Court during his first four years. While the popular approval of the New Deal philosophy registered by the election returns of 1936 practically insured—in the tradition of Mr. Dooley— the acceptance by the Supreme Court of the recently enacted social legislation, he decided to play it safe. Although the court packing bill eventually miscarried, it may well be that it had something to do with modifying judicial views toward such legislation. At any rate the Court declared a new minimum wage statute constitutional, overruling the classical precedent against legislation of this type. And in 1937 it upheld the validity of the National Labor Relations Act. Now the question arose: Could the same Court, entertaining this new attitude toward social legislation affecting labor, continue to honor its own institutional precedents regarding the use of the antitrust laws against unions? The answer was not long in coming.

THE *Apex* CASE

While the hosiery workers union was fairly well established, it was anxious to eliminate nonunion competition by organizing all open shops left in the industry. A union force, augmented by a small number of employees on strike, seized the Apex company's nonunion hosiery plant in Philadelphia. This sit-down strike and seizure was intended to force unionization on the employer, although it was a technique hardly in accordance with the NLRA or with the law of the land in general. Besides locking up the plant, and breaking windows and machines, the union people deliberately refused to let the employer ship 134,000 dozens of manufactured hosiery, approximately 80 per cent of which were destined to out-of-state customers.

All of this was highly illegal under Pennsylvania law, and theoretically local judges would have condemned it. But the company preferred recourse to the federal courts, possibly believing that it would thus obtain more important treatment, and it sought to have the union's conduct enjoined under the Sherman Antitrust Act. In this attempt the company was at first successful, but the Supreme Court later reversed the Circuit Court of Appeals. Thereupon the company sued the union's officers for triple damages under the Sherman Act, assigning the conduct described above as the violation of that

statute. The trial court gave the company a judgment for about
$750,000. This judgment the Circuit Court of Appeals re-
versed because interstate commerce had not been substantially
restrained—the company's product being only around 3 per cent
of the national output of silk stockings—and because there was
no evidence indicating an intent to restrain commerce.

When this case of *Apex Hosiery Company v. Leader* reached
the Supreme Court in 1940, the judgment in favor of the union
folk was affirmed. Justice Stone, speaking for a majority of the
Court, condemned the union's conduct as both tortious and
criminal under the laws of Pennsylvania. He pointed out that
the federal courts did not have general jurisdiction over the
case, since all of the parties involved were citizens of Pennsylvania, observing that they had only the limited jurisdiction tc
dispose of it under the Sherman Act. Whether or not a violation
of its terms could be shown depended upon what Congress had
intended when it passed that act. He conceded at once that
Congress had jurisdiction under the Constitution to pass legislation penalizing the union's sit-down strike and seizure, since
this conduct had effected an interference with interstate commerce, not only in preventing the shipment of already packed
stockings but also in stopping continued production by shutting down the plant. The question remained whether or not
Congress had actually exercised this power in the Sherman
Antitrust Act. A majority of the Court thought it had not
done so.

Certainly the union's interference with commerce in this
case would have justified Congressional legislation making
its repetition unlawful, quite as much as the unfair labor practices of employers had justified the passage of the NLRA—and
for the same reasons. Closer analogies perhaps would be statutes
aimed at train robbers and hijackers tampering with interstate
trains and trucks. These would in effect be policing statutes
and the alleged purpose of the NLRA was not much different,
since it was to maintain a free flow of commerce by outlawing
the causes of disruptive organizational strikes. Justice Stone

obviously thought it fantastic to suppose that Congress had ever passed the Sherman Act as a policing measure to insure the free flow of commerce or that the act could be used to prosecute or to sue for triple damages a band of robbers who had derailed an interstate train. He believed it was passed to prevent market restraints.

Hence, in spite of the evidence indicating the union's intention to keep the silk stockings from entering interstate commerce, he thought it clear that they were merely bringing pressure on the company to make it capitulate to the union and were not trying to exercise any kind of control over the silk stocking market. No doubt he meant to imply that there was no evidence of a specific intent on the part of the union people to exercise any control over the marketing of silk stockings. Even though their ultimate intent was to eliminate nonunion competition in national markets between union-made and nonunion-made silk stockings, and even if their interference with production and the shipment of already packed stockings was to further this intent, there was no such evidence in the record. The Court could hardly assume it.

Justice Stone curtly dismissed the union's argument that the Sherman Act was never intended by Congress to apply to organized labor. He went on to show that Congress had in mind "the prevention of restraints to free competition in business and commercial transactions which tended to restrict production, raise prices or otherwise control the market to the detriment of purchasers or consumers of goods and services, all of which had come to be regarded as a special form of public injury." According to him, Congress wanted to prevent restraints of trade, as they were known to the common law. It added the words "or commerce among the several States," not to denote another kind of forbidden restraint but merely as the means "to relate the prohibited restraint of trade to interstate commerce for constitutional purposes, so that Congress, through its commerce power, might suppress and penalize restraints on the competitive system which involved or affected interstate commerce." Such restraints the states could not prevent because of their interstate character.

This was all masterly analysis; but the opinion then verged into fiction. Justice Stone said he thought it was significant that the Supreme Court had never used the Sherman Act against anyone—capital or labor—unless it found "some form of restraint upon commercial competition in the marketing of goods or services." In this statement, he was plainly wrong, since there is not the slightest indication of any such restraint in any of the famous boycott cases—the *Danbury Hatters'* case, the *Duplex* case and the *Bedford Cut Stone* case. Then he went on to say that the Supreme Court had refused to apply the Sherman Act in cases of illegal local strikes, like this one, where the resulting shutdown had prevented substantial interstate shipments of products, "but in which it was not shown that the restrictions on shipments had operated to restrain commercial competition in some substantial way." This implies that if such an effect were shown, a violation of the act would be proved. No previous Supreme Court labor decisions support this implication that a local strike keeping from national markets an amount of the national total of any product large enough appreciably to upset the price and supply of that product would be a violation of the Sherman Act. Justice Stone's statement is on a par with the proposition that a court will not convict a man for the murder of someone whose money he has embezzled, unless it is shown that he took a large enough sum to cause the death by shock of anyone similarly situated. No such case as this has ever arisen, and the implication that the conviction for murder would stand, if it did arise and was proved, is completely speculative.

The opinion does return to more solid ground, however, when Justice Stone generalizes from the application of the Sherman Act to business combinations, although his observation that the only restraints prohibited by the act in such cases are those "which are so substantial as to affect market prices," becomes accurate only when he adds "or otherwise to deprive purchasers or consumers of the advantages which they derive from free competition." But he still fails to show that any such consideration was material in any of the Supreme Court's decisions against organized labor under the Sherman Act, especially in the three well-known boycott cases he discusses.

The opinion next comes back to the *Apex* situation and Justice Stone points out that it was not like the *Brims* case, previously discussed, where the union co-operated with two sets of employers to control the supply and price of wood trim in the Chicago area building industry. The object of the hosiery workers union was simply "to compel [Apex] to accede to the union demands"; and the resulting nonaccess of Apex hosiery to interstate markets "was not intended to have and had no effect on prices of hosiery in the market." Here he might well have added that even if such an effect were observable, there was no precedent of the Supreme Court in labor cases under the Sherman Act to indicate that it would have made the slightest difference.

The normal effect of labor unionism to restrain competition among union members in the sale of their services, he remarked, never has been regarded as unlawful under the Sherman Act and never can be, because of Section 6 of the Clayton Act, which states that "the labor of a human being is not a commodity or article of commerce" and that labor unions are not in themselves "illegal combinations or conspiracies in restraint of trade, under the antitrust laws." Then Justice Stone proceeds to make the most remarkable statement in his whole long opinion. After reciting that "successful union activity . . . may have some influence on price competition by eliminating that part of such competition which is based on differences in labor standards," he declared:

"Since, in order to render a labor combination effective it must eliminate the competition from non-union made goods, . . . an elimination of price competition based on differences in labor standards is the objective of any national labor organization. But this effect on competition has not been considered to be the kind of curtailment of price competition prohibited by the Sherman Act."

At this point we might ask Justice Stone: How about the second *Coronado* case? That was a local strike case, where the Supreme Court accepted evidence of the union's subjective intention to do this very thing—to eliminate in national markets the competition between union- and nonunion-mined coal, due to the wage or labor standard differential—as conclusive proof of a violation of the Sherman Act.

Justice Stone's answer to this question is a quotation from the Court's opinion in the second *Coronado* case, indicating that the "purpose of the destruction of the mines was to stop the production of non-union coal and prevent its shipment to markets of other states than Arkansas, where it would by competition tend to reduce the price of the commodity and affect injuriously the maintenance of wages for union labor in competing mines." This answer, in effect, is as if he had said: "When a union shuts down a nonunion mine by a strike so that it cannot operate and send nonunion coal into national markets to compete with union coal—and it can be proved that such was its intent—that is a violation of the Sherman Act. *But,* if a union shuts down a nonunion mine by a strike *in order to compel its unionization* so that, after unionization, its product can no longer compete with union-mined coal in its former nonunion character—even if its intent to do this can be proved —that is only a normal objective of unionism and is not a violation of the Sherman Act." His proposition that the second *Coronado* decision was still good law had the props kicked out from under it by his inconsistent statement quoted above in the separate paragraph.

If Justice Stone's distinction of the *Apex* case from the second *Coronado* case is sound, then all the Apex Company had to do to secure a judgment was to prove that the union shut down the factory and held up the already packed stockings in order to keep the company's product from competing with union-made stockings in national markets. But the elimination of such competition was exactly what the union was seeking in the *Apex* case, just as that was the objective in the *Coronado* case; and in each instance the union involved sought this end by unionization of the company. No big union is going to shut a plant down by a strike merely to keep its product permanently out of the market. That is utterly ridiculous, since the union's interest is equal to the employer's in having the plant operate. The employees have to eat and must earn wages to do so.

These two strikes were intended to achieve unionization of the enterprises involved. If the strikers at the Coronado mine kept already mined or potentially mined coal from reaching interstate markets, just as the strikers at the Apex plant kept the already packed and potentially manufactured silk stockings from reaching such markets, it was simply for the effect this might have in imposing economic embarrassment on the two employers. There is little doubt that the Supreme Court rested its decision against the union in the second *Coronado* case on proof of subjective intent that the union was trying to organize the Coronado mine so that its product would not henceforth compete with union-mined coal in its nonunion character. Yet this very purpose Justice Stone declared in his *Apex* opinion to be a perfectly lawful incident of labor unionism and, when carried into action, not an offense under the Sherman Act. It is a pity that he did not simply overrule the second *Coronado* case as outworn doctrine, instead of paying it lip service as a valid precedent and then undermining it, leaving it balanced on a distinction less palpable than that between Tweedledum and Tweedledee.

But this is not all. Justice Stone seemed very confused about the labor union boycott cases under the Sherman Act—the *Danbury Hatters'*, the *Duplex*, and the *Bedford Cut Stone* cases. He had neatly distinguished between the incidents of jurisdiction, such as interfering with interstate shipments, on the one hand, and actual violations of the Sherman Act through market restraints suppressing competition, on the other. Then he unfortunately overlooked this very distinction in his analysis of these boycott cases. This confusion became most apparent when he implied that the *Retail Lumber Dealers'* case and the *Danbury Hatters'* case were identical.

The retail lumber dealers' association throughout the eastern states had undertaken to prevent sales by lumber manufacturers directly to consumers. In order to obviate the loss of retail profits by such sales over their heads, the members of this association agreed to boycott any manufacturer who made such direct sales to consumers. The consequent forced elimination of such sales was the deliberate suppression of competition between manufacturers and retailers for the same market and, as the Supreme Court had held, a plain violation of the Sherman Act.

But the *Danbury Hatters'* case was not at all like that. The only common element in these two cases was keeping goods from crossing state lines. Thus, the retail lumber dealers' boycott prevented shipments from manufacturers either directly to consumers of lumber or to themselves, while the embargo of the hatters' union discouraged out-of-state orders for Loewe's hats. While the lumber dealers were interested in controlling the retail lumber market, the hatters' union had no interest at all in the marketing of hats but was only trying to cut Loewe off from his customers so that he would capitulate to the union's organizational overtures in order to escape the economic pinch placed on his business. And in the *Duplex* and *Bedford Cut Stone* cases the unions there concerned were likewise merely trying to bring organizational pressure to bear on the employers involved and were not trying to control the markets for printing presses and cut stone.

Justice Stone creates the impression in his *Apex* opinion that the vice in the *Retail Lumber Dealers'* case was the boycott which interfered with shipments of goods from one state to another. Then he seems to say that since this same effect is present in the three labor union boycott cases, they also involve violations of the Sherman Act, and for the same reason. Yet it is apparent that the *Retail Lumber Dealers'* case showed a real market restraint, whereas none was present in these other three cases. In other words, his conclusion that these four boycott cases involved violations of the act rests entirely on the fact that in each there was an interference with the mere passage of goods from one state to another.

This confusion is aggravated by his claim that these boycott cases are distinguishable from the *Apex* case, which involved only a local strike and sit-down seizure instead of a secondary boycott. If these three labor union boycott cases involve violations of the Sherman Act because of the interferences with interstate shipments present in them, then to exactly that extent the *Apex* case itself also reflects a violation of the act. And if we conclude that there is no violation of the act in the *Apex* case, then it is equally clear that there is none in the three boycott cases. For it makes no difference whether the interference with the passage of goods from one state to another occurs as a consequence of economic pressure created in the same state where the goods are produced, as by a strike, or in a different state—as by a secondary boycott. By the same token, it makes no difference whether the effect of the local strike is to prevent shipments of goods by denying the facilities for their production or by preventing already manufactured goods from being loaded on railroad cars and hauled away.

The fact remains that a secondary boycott is just a more complicated way of pursuing the same objective that a union seeks in organizational strikes. In so far as each device involves interferences with the shipments of goods across state lines, they are identical when viewed under the terms of the Sherman Act. And there is no more reason for using the subjective intent test of the *Coronado* cases in the strike situations than in the boycott cases. Hence there is every reason to suppose that the *Coronado* test no longer has any significance in our law. For if this test shows only that a particular union is attempting to eliminate nonunion competition, either by organizing a nonunion concern or by keeping specific already manufactured nonunion goods from entering commerce, that is a union objective which the Supreme Court now concedes not to be contrary to the Sherman Act.

In discussing these boycott cases Justice Stone made two other remarks which should be questioned. He said that in each of them "the activities affecting interstate commerce were directed at control of the market *and were so widespread as to substantially to affect it.*" This was not true, and there was nothing in the reports of these cases which made this element of substantial effect an operative factor in the decision of any of them. In each of these three labor union boycott cases the Supreme Court recognized a violation solely because of the fact that the union concerned had prevented the shipment of goods across state lines, irrespective of any effects of such interferences on any markets.

Then he went on to say: "That the objective of the restraint in the boycott cases was the strengthening of the bargaining position of the union and not the elimination of business competition—which was the end in the non-labor cases—was thought to be immaterial because the Court viewed *the restraint itself,* in contrast to the interference with shipments caused by a local factory strike, to be of a kind regarded as offensive at common law because of its effect in curtailing a free market *and it was held to offend against the Sherman Act because it effected and was aimed at suppression of competition with union made goods in the interstate market.*" Just what he meant by the phrase "the restraint itself," in the middle of this quotation, is hard to say, unless he meant the sort of interference with interstate commerce which would justify the assertion of power by Congress in the first place. If so, it is a frank admission that in the three labor union boycott cases the Supreme Court had confused the incidents of jurisdiction with violation of the Sherman Act. But the italicized portion at the end of this last quotation is more serious. There he attempts to justify the decisions in the three labor union boycott cases by reasoning that contradicts his main position earlier in the *Apex* opinion. He sets forth as the violation of the act in these cases the very thing he had just declared cannot any longer be construed as a violation of the act. That thing is the elimination of competition between union- and nonunion-made goods, which he had just said was a normal and lawful objective of any nationally organized labor union.

It is, of course, easy to sit back and criticize a Supreme Court justice's opinion. But when a member of the Court writes a long and involved opinion like that in the *Apex* case, trying to reconcile the irreconcilable and to make it look as if the Court's policy had always been consistent, he makes such criticism infinitely easier. This long account of the opinion is included to acquaint readers with the sort of thing our Supreme Court does when it tries to keep its output politically and socially up to date and at the same time consistent. Actually, it seems clear that in the three labor union boycott cases under discussion the Supreme Court had confused jurisdiction with substantive violation of the act, and had incorrectly decided against the unions on the former grounds.

Justice Stone would have made it easier for himself and for the bar in general, to say nothing of employers and unions, if he had simply declared that in the past the Supreme Court had fostered incorrect views about the application of the Sherman Act to labor unions and is now starting afresh with the correct view. Almost everything he says in his opinion about Congress' real intentions in the act seems extraordinarily lucid. He gets in hot water only when he tries to reconcile his views with previous decisions of the Court. If he had simply abandoned his regard for consistency by overruling the three boycott cases—the *Danbury Hatters'*, *Duplex* and *Bedford Cut Stone* cases—as well as the second *Coronado* case, the air would have been clearer, and he would have obviated much confusion.

Chief Justice Hughes, speaking for the three dissenting members of the Court in the *Apex* case, thought that Justice Stone's discourse about jurisdiction and the attempt to make the Sherman Act a policing measure was unsound. He felt that if employers could be prevented by the NLRA from provoking organizational strikes obstructive to interstate commerce, as the Court had held they could be, then combinations of employees could be prevented by the Sherman Act from initiating such obstructive organizational strikes, as well. Quite obviously, he might be right. But the fact remains that in the NLRA, Congress spelled out carefully just what it intended to do, and why, clearly creating a deterrent to prevent employers from provoking disruptive strikes by their unfair labor practices. Now Congress created no such stricture against labor in the Sherman Act, although it could have done so in that act or in a separate statute, by analogy to the NLRA.

Chief Justice Hughes contended that Congress had already done this in the broad and general terms of the Sherman Act. Thereby the chief justice seemed to confuse the incidents of jurisdiction with actual violations of the act as it was intended to apply. Could he possibly have thought that Congress had intended in the Sherman Act to exercise its complete constitutional powers to prohibit all conceivable interferences with interstate commerce by unions? Could he have been willing to use the Sherman Act to prevent all strikes and boycotts in plants purchasing raw materials through or sending their products into interstate commerce—in short, practically all strikes and boycotts in modern industry? Although his opinion seemed to indicate such possibilities, he finally disclaimed this position by drawing the line where unions conspire "directly and intentionally to prevent the shipment of goods in interstate commerce either by their illegal seizure for that purpose, or by the direct and intentional obstruction of their transportation or by blocking the highways of interstate intercourse."

Now the unusual thing about the *Apex* case is Justice Stone's remarkable statement to the effect that the organizational pressures of labor unions, intended to eliminate the competition between nonunion-made and union-made products of the same industry, are not unlawful under the Sherman Act. He repeatedly insists that the Sherman Act was intended to prevent market restraints and was designed to preserve free competition in national markets, emphasizing the enormity of any attempt to control prices. Yet in almost the plainest instance of conduct affecting prices and eliminating competition between commodities based upon price differentials, he refuses to recognize a violation of the act, dismissing this union economic program as "the objective of any national labor organization." Justice Stone thus side-stepped the unpleasant task of labeling virtually all of national unionism, in itself, as one gigantic and wholesale offense under the Sherman Act. But it was years too late for such a drastic step, anyway, if it ever was even theoretically possible after Section 6 of the Clayton Act had been passed in 1914.

His position is perhaps best supported by the argument that under this economic program, unions are interested in leveling off not so much the *prices* of commodities produced throughout a given industry as *wages* and other *working standards*. These are really the things they want to standardize. And it would be convenient for purposes of discussion to assume that a standard union *wage* level is the crux of the whole matter. The unions wish to eliminate the differentials existing between union and nonunion wages in all industries in which they are established. In so far as the competitive price differential between the union-made and nonunion-made products of a given industry reflect the wage differential between union and nonunion rates, *to that extent* the unions are trying to eliminate competition through restraints involving the control of commodity prices. Aside from this, unions exhibit no real interest in standardizing the prices of the products in any given industry, leaving employers relatively unhindered in making the most of other competitive factors like efficiency in management, advertising and incentive plans, as long as union employees' toes are not stepped on in the process. In effect, this is what the significant statement of Justice Stone fairly implies.

He also said that employees in combination, by securing

standard wage rates in a unionized shop, could not be assailed
under the Sherman Act for attempting to restrain competition
among themselves in the hiring out of their labor. None of
these propositions is obvious. Indeed, at one time such practices leading to the standardization of wages among the employees of a given shop or between all units in a given industry
were very definitely regarded as restraints of trade at common
law. The theory used to be that an employer was entitled to
get his labor at the lowest price he had to pay in the labor
market, just as he was entitled to get his raw materials in the
same competitive fashion. And the old judges maintained this
right of the employer in both situations as an incident of own-
ing property and of free enterprise in operating it productively.
As has been shown, early violations of this right were treated
not only as restraints of trade but as criminal conspiracies.

The only adequate explanation for a change in this view is
the passage of time with the consequent modification of political and social views concerning the rights of working men
to band together for self-protection and mutual advantage. For
this result the determined efforts of organized labor leaders and
outside sympathizers are no doubt responsible. At any rate,
these older views are now a part of ancient history in our
social culture. And it can hardly be wondered that our law,
including Supreme Court decisions, has reflected this change.
It would be impossible, politically and in every other way,
for our Supreme Court now to outlaw this principal plank
in organized labor's economic program, although it was possible for it to do so twenty years ago in Taft's time, in the
second *Coronado* case. And this is true, even if the idea of
competition is still exalted as desirable in our economy and
even if it is impossible to detect any analytical distinction between competition among businessmen, on the one hand, and
among laboring people on the other. But much water has gone
over the dam since 1925. By 1940, after the *Apex* decision,
speculative lawyers began to wonder if there were really *any*
normal labor union practices that might be regarded as viola-

tions of the Sherman Act. For they found it exceedingly difficult to take Justice Stone at his word, after reading the heart of his opinion, that the three labor union boycott cases and the second *Coronado* case were still valid precedents and good law.

THE *Hutcheson* CASE

It was not long before their misgivings were justified, although not many lawyers, if any at all, foresaw the extraordinary manner in which their premonitions would be fulfilled. It seems that in 1939 the carpenters' union had an old-fashioned jurisdictional dispute with the machinists' union over which of the two should get the work of dismantling certain machinery at the Anheuser-Busch plant in St. Louis. The company gave the work to the machinists' union. Thereupon its employees belonging to the carpenters' union went on strike and picketed the plant. In addition to this, the officials of the carpenters' union, through circulars and their union paper, requested all their friends and members to quit buying Anheuser-Busch beer.

This latter move was a secondary boycott, somewhat like that in the *Danbury Hatters'* case. And if that historical precedent was still good law, it looked as if the officials of the carpenters' union were caught, since the company sold its beer in interstate commerce and its interstate sales were drastically affected by the boycott. In any event, Hutcheson, the president of the carpenters' union, and his fellow officials actively promoting the boycott in question, were indicted and prosecuted criminally for having violated the Sherman Act. The federal district court held that no violation of the act was shown. Thereupon the prosecution appealed this judgment to the Supreme Court.

Justice Felix Frankfurter wrote the majority opinion for the Supreme Court in this case of *United States v. Hutcheson*. The judgment in favor of the union's leaders was affirmed. He observed that an indictment may be validly drawn under one statute and at the same time another statute, not referred to therein, "may draw the sting of criminality from the allegations." Thus, if an offense under the Sherman Act alone were found to have been absolved by the terms of Section 20 of the Clayton Act—the statute which was in some ways intended to amend and to modify the Sherman Act—then an indictment charging that offense could not stand up. He pointed out that a portion of Section 20 described certain conduct customarily engaged in by union people for purposes of extending organization and of collective bargaining and made it specifically non-enjoinable. He also reasoned that this paragraph "relieved such practices of all illegal taint by the catch-all provision, 'nor shall any of the acts specified in this paragraph be considered or held to be violations of any law of the United States.'" In short, if the actions of the four indicted union leaders in pursuing this secondary boycott amounted to conduct fairly described by this portion of the Clayton Act, then such conduct was not only not enjoinable but was not even illegal in any sense whatsoever. That is to say, it did not amount to a violation of any law of the United States, including the Sherman Act, under this concluding catch-all clause.

The only drawback about this theory of Justice Frankfurter's —indisputably correct as far as it went—was the Supreme Court's previous decision in the *Duplex* case, back in 1921. Then it was held that Section 20 of the Clayton Act did not apply to the sort of situation now before the Court. Hence, it seemed impossible to use the concluding catch-all clause for the purpose of deciding that Hutcheson's boycott was not a violation of the Sherman Act and was therefore not subject to any of its three adverse sanctions—particularly those of liability for triple damages and of criminality.

The Court knew very well that the *Duplex* case, not having been expressly overruled, was still an existing precedent. The effect of Section 20 under a standing decision of the Court was, first, to relax the antipathy of federal judges toward the self-help techniques of unions only when the laboring folk concerned were the immediate employees of the employer pressing charges against them and, second, that even then the self-help techniques to be tolerated were those already considered lawful. As one of the supporters of this section had explained when it was pending before Congress as a bill, this measure was not intended to make the secondary boycott either nonenjoinable or legal. And Justice Frankfurter must have known this.

He no doubt believed that his predecessors on the Court had been hopelessly wrong when they narrowly construed Section 20 of the Clayton Act. Nevertheless, he knew that as long as the *Duplex* case remained on the books, it settled once and for all the meaning of Section 20. Naturally, the Supreme Court itself could at any time overrule the *Duplex* decision and declare that its 1921 interpretation of Section 20 was incorrect. But this course would also indicate that the Supreme Court as an institution could with facility vary the meaning of certain words whenever it wished to do so. Such a course might be thought unwholesome, since it would advertise the fact that our law is unstable and unpredictable and can change with the shifting personnel of the Supreme Court. Obviously, the Court as an institution would stand to lose prestige if this fact became too generally known. It is therefore usually most reluctant to overrule its own precedents, no matter how little its new members like what former incumbents said and did some years ago.

The fact remains, then, that under the existing interpretations of the Sherman Act, Hutcheson and the other officials of the carpenters' union who had activated this boycott were guilty and were not eligible to invoke the protection of Section 20 of the Clayton Act. Justice Frankfurter's way around this impasse was through the provisions of the Norris-LaGuardia Anti-injunction Act. First he pointed out the similarity between the labor union conduct described in this second paragraph of Section 20 of the Clayton Act and that described in

Section 4 of the Norris-LaGuardia Act. He concluded that Congress in the Norris-LaGuardia Act was talking about the same sort of labor union conduct it had mentioned in the former act.

Next he pointed out that Congress, in Section 13 of the Norris-LaGuardia Act, had very clearly made the protection of that act available to labor unionists engaging in the conduct described in Section 4, whether or not they were or ever had been the immediate employees of the employer at whom such conduct was directed. Hence, he declared, one now reading the federal statute law should conclude that labor unionists engaging in nonviolent, nonfraudulent and nonlibelous economic pressures directed at an employer—as such pressures were comprehensively described in both Section 20 of the Clayton Act and Section 4 of the Norris-LaGuardia Act—are entitled to all of the protective features provided in both acts. This intermediate conclusion, of course, set the stage for the denouement. So far, at least according to Justice Frankfurter, it was Congress and not the Supreme Court that had introduced the change.

Now all of this circuitous effort was spent in trying to get at the concluding catch-all clause in Section 20 of the Clayton Act—"nor shall any of the acts specified in this paragraph be considered or held to be violations of any law of the United States." For the purposes of the *Hutcheson* case, Justice Frankfurter got at it by deciding that Congress itself had in the Norris-LaGuardia Act *redefined* the conduct set forth in the second paragraph of Section 20 of the Clayton Act, with reference to employees and nonemployees alike. In this way, he declared, Congress had given this catch-all clause a new vitality. This was virtually writing it into the Norris-LaGuardia Act, itself, as the concluding clause of Section 4 of that act. Naturally, if this clause had been so inserted by Congress, everything would have been exceedingly simple, indeed. But Congress had not done this, so Justice Frankfurter and a majority of the Court lent Congress a helping hand. With this clause read into the act, so to speak, all labor union conduct fairly described in Section 4 was not only nonenjoinable in federal courts but also became absolutely lawful for all purposes under federal law. Hence, as the boycott initiated by Hutcheson and his aids was clearly nonenjoinable under Section 4 of the act, it automatically became lawful even under the Sherman Act.

In all fairness to Justice Frankfurter and his associates, it should be stated clearly that they did not write the concluding catch-all clause of Section 20 into Section 4 of the Norris-LaGuardia Act. What they really did was to write sections 4 and 13 of the anti-injunction statute back into Section 20 of the Clayton Act! Many lawyers were profoundly shocked, regarding this as a sort of judicial legerdemain, to be explained only by the desire of the Court to free organized labor entirely from the inconvenience of the Sherman Act. Laymen may find it difficult to appreciate just what was objectionable about Justice Frankfurter's technique. Had his opinion been simply a straightforward disavowal of the *Duplex* decision, followed by a new interpretation of Section 20 of the Clayton Act to mean substantially what sections 4 and 13 of the Norris-LaGuardia Act quite clearly did mean, the American bar would probably have been disturbed but not shocked. Such a course would have suggested that the Court had dealt injustice to the labor unionists involved in both the *Duplex* and *Bedford Cut Stone* cases. How much neater if the Court could continue to honor its own precedents, implying that it was right all the time in the *Duplex* and *Bedford* cases, and then put the responsibility on Congress for having overruled these decisions in the Norris-LaGuardia Act. This would save everybody's face. The *Duplex* case would be dead for all time, yet it would have been Congress, and not the Court, which had done the killing.

Now we ought to pause here just to see what was going on. Everybody knew that the real abuse leading to both Section 20 of the Clayton Act and the Norris-LaGuardia Act was the intemperate use of the labor injunction. Shortly after Section 20 had been declared abortive in 1921, Justice Frankfurter—

then a professor in the Harvard Law School—led the fight to replace this measure with a thorough-going and honest anti-injunction act. The new bill, which became law in 1932, was sold to Congress on the representation that it was an anti-injunction act, and nothing more. It was intended to displace Section 20, as if that abortive measure were erased from the books, and was certainly not designed to overrule the *Duplex* decision in order to make that section an honest law after eleven years of shame.

When this new bill became the Norris-LaGuardia Act in 1932, it contained a section declaring that "all Acts and parts of Acts in conflict with the provisions of this Act are hereby repealed." Since Section 20 was the only law in conflict with this new statute, it is hard to see why this repealer clause didn't wipe it right off the books. If such a result was not intended by Congress, how can we possibly explain its desire to have two statutes covering the same matter—one in great detail but lacking a clause rendering nonenjoinable conduct generally lawful, and the other in highly ambiguous language, with no effective detail but including such a clause. The only conceivable explanation would be to keep alive the concluding catch-all clause in Section 20 in order to make the nonenjoinable conduct in the later statute generally lawful.

But if Congress had really wanted this result, all it had to do was to add a clause on the end of Section 4 of the 1932 statute, making the conduct there described lawful for all purposes. It knew that this had been done by a previous Congress in Section 20, and it knew that the Wisconsin legislature had done the same thing nine months previously in its state anti-injunction act. Its decision not to include such a clause in the Norris-LaGuardia Act was apparently deliberate. For the picture of Congress passing a law with the intention of overruling a Supreme Court decision merely to revitalize a clause of a former statute so that it, in turn, may be operative in the new statute is ludicrous. Look at it this way. When the new statute becomes law, instead of automatically repealing the old statute, it instantaneously overrules a previous Supreme Court decision and leaves the old statute no longer a conflicting act and, hence, not repealed—all to re-create a mere clause of the old act that Congress could easily have put into the new statute had it wished to do so. Such, unfortunately, is the stuff that law is sometimes made of; and it may be some consolation to laymen that lawyers themselves find it thoroughly mystifying. Justice Roberts, in his dissenting opinion in the *Hutcheson* case, thought it ". . . a process of construction never, as I think, heretofore indulged by this court." And he added: "I venture to say that no court has ever undertaken so radically to legislate where Congress has refused so to do."

Justice Frankfurter had other reasons for his conclusions in the *Hutcheson* case. "To be sure," he says in one part of his opinion, with reference to the Norris-LaGuardia Act, "Congress expressed this national policy and determined the bounds of a labor dispute in an act explicitly dealing with the further withdrawal of injunctions in labor controversies. But to argue, as it was urged before us, that the *Duplex* case still governs for purposes of a criminal prosecution is to say that that which on the equity side of the court is allowable conduct may in a criminal proceeding become the road to prison. It would be strange indeed that although neither the Government nor Anheuser-Busch could have sought an injunction against the acts here challenged, the elaborate efforts to permit such conduct failed to prevent criminal liability punishable with imprisonment and heavy fines. That is not the way to read the will of Congress, particularly when expressed by a statute which, as we have already indicated, is practically and historically one of a series of enactments touching one of the most sensitive national problems. Such legislation must not be read in a spirit of mutilating narrowness."

It would be rash to suggest that Justice Frankfurter was unfamiliar with the purpose of the Norris-LaGuardia Act, which he himself had helped to draft. But it is hard to understand how he could have forgotten that it was introduced and passed only as a measure to prevent the continued abuse by federal judges of their equity power in issuing labor injunctions. Apparently he did forget that the act on its face was never intended to deal with the *legality* of the union conduct which had traditionally been suppressed so summarily by these injunctions without all of the procedural guaranties afforded in actions at law and in criminal prosecutions. He spoke of "that which on the equity side of the court is allowable conduct" and of Congress' "elaborate efforts to permit such conduct." Now, in the Norris-LaGuardia Act, Congress did not set out to allow or permit any conduct, of any kind. It was not concerned with validating the activities of organized labor.

It was merely concerned with seeing that labor unionists were fairly tried by the federal courts for whatever they did do, lawful or unlawful. Of the three techniques available for calling labor unionists to account—actions for money damages, criminal prosecutions, and suits for injunctions—Congress believed that the first two were not misused by the federal courts, while the third was abused so badly by them that they could no longer be completely trusted with it. If unions indulged in certain specified conduct, even if it happened to be unlawful at common law or under a statute, the federal courts were no longer free to stop it by injunction but could deal with it only in criminal prosecutions or in actions for damages. And Congress felt so strongly about this that it included a separate section forbidding the use of the injunction even when labor unions were guilty of conspiracies, quite obviously having in mind violations of the Sherman Act. Thus while employers were deprived of their favorite weapon, the injunction, this does not mean that they were deprived of all of their recourses to the courts. Declaring illegal conduct nonenjoinable and no longer subject to the equity powers of judges does not make it lawful.

The conduct of Hutcheson and the other leaders of the carpenters in persuading the union members and its friends to quit buying Anheuser-Busch beer so that they might win in their jurisdictional struggle with the machinists was a secondary consumption boycott. This was a device considered lawful by few state courts and traditionally regarded as unlawful by the federal courts. Could a statute designed to make such conduct merely nonenjoinable make it allowable or permissible? The answer is no! For as far as these characteristics are concerned, a statute of this sort leaves such conduct exactly where it was, simply freeing it from the adverse effect of the injunction. You cannot properly say that as far as equity courts are concerned, the conduct has become allowable. All you can say is that equity courts are no longer permitted to pass on such conduct at all. Hence the additional reasons for the *Hutcheson* decision seem completely misleading.

In spite of all that has been said here, the *decision* itself in the *Hutcheson* case is consistent with the main position taken by the Court in the *Apex* case. This was not an attempt by the carpenters' union to gain control over the market for a particular brand of beer. It was, rather, an attempt to compel Anheuser-Busch to give certain work to the carpenters as against the machinists. The conduct of Hutcheson and his fellow unionists was certainly a violation of the Sherman Act according to the Supreme Court precedents in the *Danbury Hatters', Duplex,* and *Bedford Cut Stone* cases. But those precedents seem so plainly in error that the Court should have overruled them. Then it would have had before it the legality of the secondary boycott in question simply under the Sherman Act *and entirely aside from Section 20 of the Clayton Act.* The resulting opinion would then have resembled the better portions of Justice Stone's opinion in the *Apex* case, improved by the absence of lip service to these old boycott precedents. This would have left the Court free under the Sherman Act to deal with union practices designed to prevent actual market restraints, and it could have reached its decision by a sound and intelligible method.

In his opinion, however, Justice Frankfurter virtually took organized labor entirely out from under the Sherman Act. This, in effect, repealed that act as far as labor was concerned, on the strength of the Norris-LaGuardia Act. He did leave one loophole suggesting a further possible application of the Sherman Act to labor unions—in situations like the *Brims* case where the Chicago carpenters, building contractors and woodwork mills co-operated to control an entire local market. "So long as a union acts in its self-interest," he said, *"and does not combine with non-labor groups,* the licit and the illicit under § 20 are not to be distinguished by any judgment regarding the wisdom or unwisdom, the rightness or wrongness, the selfishness or unselfishness of the end of which the particular union activities are the means." In this passing hint he suggested that unions conspiring with employers to control the supply and price of commodities for their mutual benefit, thus departing from normal union bargaining and organizational activities, might still be regarded as offenders under the Sherman Act.

At this point it seems quite plain that he blundered, even conceding for argument the validity of his *Hutcheson* opinion as a whole. What the carpenters' union did in the *Brims* case with the connivance of the contractors and the mills, it could easily have done alone. Simply by refusing to allow its building carpenters to work on nonunion or out-of-town wood trim, the union alone could have achieved identically the same result as that actually reached in the *Brims* situation. Such conduct would fall squarely within the description of activities rendered nonenjoinable in Section 4 of the Norris-LaGuardia Act.

Then under Justice Frankfurter's rationale the union would be completely immune from attack under the Sherman Act. If its conduct created a market control over supply and price of commodities repugnant to the protective features of the Sherman Act, according to Justice Stone's views in the *Apex* case, that result would be most unfortunate. The ease with which unions could then circumvent Frankfurter's loophole, simply by effecting their market restraints through conduct described in Section 4 of the Norris-LaGuardia Act, makes his anchor to leeward seem attached to the sheerest gossamer. Certainly, implicit in this possibility of evasion, is this proposition. If the Court retains as gospel the doctrine of the *Hutcheson* case, then labor organizations can safely afford to forget the Sherman Act and may impose market restraints almost at will.

SOME CONSEQUENCES OF THE *Hutcheson* DOCTRINE

Subsequent events have indicated that the views of Justice Frankfurter are likely to endure and that unions sufficiently strong to control the marketing of goods in whole areas will be able to exclude competing goods and to promote unreasonably high noncompetitive prices, thus insuring their restricted memberships steady employment at attractively high wage rates. An instance of this sort actually occurred in *Allen Bradley Company v. Local No. 3, IBEW,* decided in 1945. This Local No. 3 of the International Brotherhood of Electrical Workers, AF of L, comprises practically all of the production and installation electricians employed in the New York area by local manufacturers of electrical equipment and by contractors and firms undertaking to install such equipment.

This local union was a close corporation, indeed. It had conquered the ravages of the depression and the terrific impact of the decline in building on the employment of its members, by imposing the closed shop on virtually all local employers of electricians. It would not permit anybody to do electrical work in this area unless he belonged to the union. And it would not accept new members unless there was more work available than the existing members could handle. By having its installation members refuse to handle any equipment manufactured by outside shops, thus discouraging its importation, the local insured a plentiful supply of production work for its members employed in New York shops. This practice eliminated from the New York area the competition previously afforded by out-of-state manufacturers, some of whom were organized by the same national union with which Local No. 3 was affiliated. The upshot of all this was that the unionized New York producers had the entire market to themselves. Thus they could, and they did, charge local consumers of their products far more than they charged outside consumers for the same articles. Local consumers were helplessly caught in this squeeze because union installation electricians refused to handle outside products, and there were few nonunion electricians available. Needless to say, the union was in a position to charge all that the traffic could bear for the services of its members.

In this *Allen Bradley* case several of the out-of-state electrical equipment manufacturers brought suit against the union and its officers under the Sherman Act to have this situation declared illegal and enjoined. Extensive hearings were held before a master appointed by the federal court. On the basis of his findings, these companies won the first round, securing an injunction against the continuance of this practice. Then the second Circuit Court of Appeals reversed this judgment and dismissed the complaint, holding that under the Supreme Court's statement of the law in the *Hutcheson* case, Local No. 3 had not violated the Sherman Act. Judge Clark, writing the majority opinion for the Circuit Court of Appeals, thought that the union was engaged in promoting its economic security through the exercise of conduct fairly described in sections 20 of the Clayton Act and 4 of the Norris-LaGuardia Act and therefore it remained immune from violation of the Sherman Act under the Supreme Court's doctrine of the *Hutcheson* case. He considered the possibility of sustaining the injunction, in part, on the basis of Justice Frankfurter's statement in the *Hutcheson* case that connivance between a union and several employers to control a commodities market would still constitute an offense under the Sherman Act. Certainly the evidence revealed a type of market control and elimination of competition that the Sherman Act was intended to discourage. But Judge Clark concluded that the findings in the case did not show any such connivance. Thus he did not see how he could sustain the injunction in any respect without derogating from the Supreme Court's position in the *Hutcheson* case.

Furthermore, he plainly doubted the significance of Frankfurter's alleged loophole, showing that it was the merest dictum, or side remark, which had been put in such a way as not necessarily to imply a violation of the act if connivance with employers were proved. And he obviously thought that taking this loophole seriously would only create trouble, because it would be so easy for the union to achieve exactly the same results without the connivance of employers. After all, the union had an interest in creating a monopolistic market control beneficial to the employers, since the security of its members depended entirely on their prosperity. If it could lawfully achieve and maintain this control with the employers' connivance (assuming it to have been present), so much the better; but if it could not, then it would achieve it without any help.

A majority of the Supreme Court, however, agreeing with Judge Swan's dissent in the Circuit Court of Appeals, held that the findings did show connivance and approved a limited injunction to prevent its effect. Justice Black, speaking for the Supreme Court, indicated clearly that the *Hutcheson* doctrine is here to stay and that a labor union is perfectly free under federal law to create and maintain any kind of market control, as long as it achieves this result without the connivance of employers and entirely through the exercise of conduct fairly described in sections 20 of the Clayton Act and 4 of the Norris-LaGuardia Act—including, of course, the secondary boycott. Now a fair reading of the findings of fact in this case makes it very doubtful, indeed, whether any connivance existed between the employers and the union. Any conclusion to that effect seems the sheerest inference which, of course, it was certainly the Court's privilege to draw.

Furthermore, as Judge Clark had pointed out, if the union continues its boycott with the same net result, carefully avoiding connivance with employers, then the district court would be powerless thereafter to enforce the injunction in contempt proceedings for the simple reason that it would not then have been disobeyed. Plainly he deprecated the ease with which a union might circumvent a judicial decree while appearing outwardly to ignore it. He must have felt sure that Local No. 3 would continue to boycott in order to maintain the prosperity to its members—forewarned, however, that it must meticulously avoid all connivance with employers. And he probably supposed that the employers would then batten on this market control so conveniently laid in their laps, although they would all be guilty under the Sherman Act if they themselves had helped to engineer it. He might have added that unions would become very coy about executing any collective agreements with employers which might be construed as connivance with them. This prospect of unions deliberately preferring to pursue the path of economic coercion as the safe and legal course, while eschewing the more pacific methods of negotiation and agreement as unsafe and unlawful, certainly emphasizes the paradox implicit in the Supreme Court's modern version of the Sherman Act.

A curious feature of this New York electricians' case is the Supreme Court's approval of an injunction against a labor union under the Sherman Act. According to Section 5 of the Norris-LaGuardia Act, such a course is forbidden against "persons participating or interested in a labor dispute" when their offense is assailed "because of the doing in concert of the acts enumerated in Section 4 of this Act," such as strikes, picketing, and boycotts. The issuance of the injunction in this case can only be explained under one or the other of two assumptions. The first is that the union was not engaged in a labor dispute when it exercised its boycott. And the second is, regardless of this, that it was enjoined from continuing to do things over and above the sort of conduct described in sections 20 of the Clayton Act and 4 of the anti-injunction act.

The phrase labor dispute is a complicated term of art, the scope of which is not limited in any way by the illegality of the means employed or the objective pursued. Roughly, a labor dispute occurs whenever a combination of working people or their representatives resort to self-help coercive economic pressures in order to achieve some objective which they conceive to be of advantage to themselves. On this point the district court thought that there was no labor dispute involved in this case. Judge Clark thought that Local No. 3 was engaged in a labor dispute. And the Supreme Court did not touch expressly on this matter at all. But it is hard to see how the Supreme Court could avoid conceding the existence of a labor dispute without also taking the rather absurd position that after Local No. 3 had consummated the results of an admitted dispute in an agreement with the employers, the dispute suddenly evaporated. Thus, while the union is striving for economic advantage through the use of the boycott, it remains immune from injunction. But after its nonenjoinable coercion has successfully terminated in an agreement—the normal objective of all labor disputes—it suddenly becomes subject to the injunction. If this were the rule, there would certainly be a considerable premium on dilatory union tactics—that is, the maintenance of economic coercion which is about to become a contract but which never results in one. The point is that the union's chief aim, and the one it would pursue to the exclusion of all others, would be to maintain the boycott.

Exactly the same observation is appropriate concerning the enjoinability of conduct on the union's part over and above that described in Section 4 of the Norris-LaGuardia Act. If the union by acting alone in the exercise of its secondary boycott remains immune from injunction and its activity becomes enjoinable only when it is merged in agreements or understandings with employers, then naturally it will be reluctant to reflect such otherwise successful and effective economic pressure in these agreements. Justice Black does not discuss this matter in his opinion. But he does indicate, without explaining why, that a collective agreement embodying the promise "not to buy goods manufactured by companies which did not employ the members of Local No. 3" would not, in itself, be unlawful under the Sherman Act. The actual offense in this New York electricians' case, he says, is the mutual effort of the union and the employers to police the agreed-to boycott and to see that it works smoothly. But since Judges Clark and A. Hand, as well as Justice Murphy of the Supreme Court, thought that there was no evidence establishing this offensive conduct, and since everybody apparently concedes the union's ability to get results without recourse to anything more than the conduct described in Section 4 of the Norris-LaGuardia Act, the whole matter seems somewhat up in the air. And it still appears odd to see an injunction popping up against the purely economic activities of a union in the year 1945, after all that Congress and the Supreme Court have said and done about that remedy in labor cases.

This is the confusion that the Supreme Court has created by its own excess of ingenuity in using the Norris-LaGuardia Act to resurrect the concluding catch-all clause of the repealed and out-moded Section 20 of the Clayton Act. As a result organized labor is now free to create and maintain the most flagrant of market controls—concededly in violation of the Sherman Act when construed according to the principles laid down by Justice Stone in the *Apex* case—as long as it relies on its own resources and does not connive with employers. And apparently it is now a matter of indifference to the Supreme Court that unions may effect market controls in an area with no intention of organizing the employees in outside plants, the normal objective of any nationally affiliated labor union.

In the case of *United States v. American Federation of Musicians,* which involved Petrillo's union comprising "virtually all musicians in the nation who make music for hire," the Supreme Court has said that the union might with impunity conspire to prevent the use of canned music by radio broadcasting stations, in tavern juke boxes, and even in the home, through coercion exercised on record-making companies by the refusal of union members to make musical recordings.

This, of course, was not an attempt to improve the working conditions of men employed by record manufacturers and radio stations but was, rather, an undertaking by the union to drive these enterprises out of business unless they would provide unnecessary employment for its members. This secondary boycott was enforced not in a local, but in a national, market. In another case—*United States v. International Hod Carriers', etc., Council*—the Supreme Court allowed a union to prevent the importation from a sister state of cement-mixing trucks, designed to lower the cost of building through the saving of labor, unless the contractors proposing to use these trucks hired just as many laborers as they had before, thus defeating the whole point of the technological improvement in question and depriving property owners of the normal benefits flowing therefrom. This is challenging, indeed, when one reflects how important technological progress can be as a factor in real competition.

Similarly, the Court has permitted a union to discourage the general use of cheaper prefabricated and improved building materials by condoning a building carpenters' secondary boycott focused against such materials produced in other states by employees organized in a rival union. There the Court acknowledged that rival union factions are free to fight out the new interunion dispute—a struggle between conflicting economic and political union ideologies—with the channels of interstate commerce as their battleground, quite regardless of the effect on consumers' markets. These are the cases of *United States v. Building and Construction Trades Council* and *United States v. United Brotherhood of Carpenters and Joiners,* both decided in 1941.

In a suit under the Sherman Act, the Court has even permitted a union to drive an employer completely out of interstate commerce, not because he refused to deal with the union on perfectly satisfactory terms but because the union cherished a long-standing grudge against him. This was the outstanding fact in *Hunt v. Crumboch,* decided in 1945. During a strike conducted by the truck drivers' union against this employer some years ago, one of the union members was killed. An officer of the company was tried for his murder and was acquitted. Later on the union succeeded in organizing all of the trucking companies in the area and secured an agreement from the large chain store using their services, and for which this same employer had trucked interstate for fourteen years, that it would patronize only carriers organized with the union. Then, although the employer in question earnestly sought an agreement with the union, the union refused to deal with him or to permit its members to work for him because, as it said, he was a murderer. Hence, under its agreement with the union, the chain store was compelled to cease patronizing this particular employer, Hunt. Then he had to look elsewhere for whatever uncontrolled business he could find. This is arresting, because it illustrates the use of union power completely to eliminate an interstate business and, in a slight degree, to lessen competition, on the basis of personal dislike and not in pursuit of organization or improved working conditions—the normal economic objectives of labor unions.

All of these restraints on markets and enterprises, assailed under the Sherman Act as such, were tolerated by the Supreme Court because they were imposed by unions through the exercise of coercive economic conduct fairly described in sections 20 of the Clayton Act and 4 of the Norris-LaGuardia Act. This state of affairs directly stems from the doctrine of the *Hutcheson* case. It is true that even Justice Frankfurter dissented in the truckers' case just discussed, apparently because he believed that the immunity implied in his *Hutcheson* opinion should be available to unions only when they are trying to promote what he seems to regard as legitimate interests, such as organization and improved employment conditions—in short, when they are engaging in legitimate labor disputes. Possibly he has forgotten that "the licit and the illicit under § 20 are not to be distinguished by any judgment regarding the wisdom or unwisdom, the rightness or wrongness, the selfishness or unselfishness of the end of which the particular union activities are the means," as he had so deftly put it in the *Hutcheson* case. But this intriguing suggestion of a belated illegal purpose doctrine has little appeal to the majority of the Court, which insists upon taking his *Hutcheson* opinion at its face value. Indeed, from Frankfurter's concurrence in the other cases following the *Hutcheson* decision it is hard to believe that he himself places much confidence in it. Anyway, four years earlier in the case of *Milk Wagon Drivers' Union v. Lake Valley Farm Products, Inc.*, the Court had committed itself to the view that a labor dispute is still a labor dispute, regardless of the disputants' motives or the illegality of their objectives.

What has happened here, as Justice Roberts indicates in his dissent, is the creation of an impossible situation. As he says, "This court, as a result of its past decisions, is in the predicament that whatever it decides must entail disastrous results." If this were not such a serious matter, it would be amusing. The Supreme Court is mired so deeply in its own complicated circuity of words that it cannot get out gracefully unless the infusion of new members enables a break from its present position or unless Congress saves the day with a statute, comparable in effect to the Sherman Act but directed at the market restraints of organized labor. The latter solution will be exceedingly difficult, because Congress will perforce have to maintain tolerance of certain types of union market restraints which the very existence of large, powerful, nationally affiliated unions itself implies. In any event, to quote from Justice Jackson's dissent in the *Hunt* case:

"With this decision, the labor movement has come full circle. The working man has struggled long, the fight has been filled with hatred, and conflict has been dangerous, but now workers may not be deprived of their livelihood merely because their employers oppose and they favor unions. Labor has won other rights as well, unemployment compensation, old age benefits and, what is most important and the basis of all its gains, the recognition that the opportunity to earn his support is not alone the concern of the individual but is the problem which all organized societies must contend with and conquer if they are to survive. This Court now sustains the claim of a union to the right to deny participation in the economic world to an employer simply because the union dislikes him. This Court permits to employees the same arbitrary dominance over the economic sphere which they control that labor so long, so bitterly and so rightly asserted should belong to no man.

"Strikes aimed at compelling the employer to yield to union demands are not within the Sherman Act. Here the employer has yielded, and the union has achieved the end to which all legitimate union pressure is directed and limited. The union cannot consistently with the Sherman Act refuse to enjoy the fruits of its victory and deny peace terms to an employer who has unconditionally surrendered."

There remains only the task of suggesting what should be done about this state of affairs. Briefly, if the Supreme Court abandoned its unfortunate doctrine established in the *Hutcheson* case and adhered faithfully to the best of what Justice Stone said in the *Apex* case, it could even yet achieve substantial justice under the Sherman Act. In the alternative, however, the next move seems to be up to Congress.

CHAPTER XI

THE RISE AND DECLINE OF THE *THORNHILL* DOCTRINE

> Because I have come to the conclusion that both the common law of a State and a statute of the United States declare the right of industrial combatants to push their struggle to the limits of the justification of self-interest, I do not wish to be understood as attaching any constitutional or moral sanction to that right. All rights are derived from the purposes of the society in which they exist; above all rights rises duty to the community. The conditions developed in industry may be such that those engaged in it cannot continue their struggle without danger to the community. But it is not for judges to determine whether such conditions exist, nor is it their function to set the limits of permissible contest and to declare the duties which the new situation demands. This is the function of the legislature which, while limiting individual and group rights of aggression and defense, may substitute processes of justice for the more primitive method of trial by combat.—Brandeis, J., dissenting in *Duplex Printing Press Company v. Deering,* 1921.

IN OUR society the regulation of economic activity is traditionally a matter of policy for state legislatures and Congress. Of course these legislative bodies are supposed to act within their respective jurisdictional spheres and otherwise to remain within the powers allowed them under the Constitution. At the same time the proper function of our courts is to interpret and apply the law in particular cases. And an additional important function of the federal Supreme Court is to determine whether Congress and state legislatures have exceeded the powers granted, or ignored the restrictions imposed upon them, by the federal Constitution. Hence it is generally agreed that our courts should not presume to shape or develop regulatory controls over purely economic activity that is not already covered by statute or is not illegal at common law. These observations are most pertinent in the law of labor relations and they acquire particular significance in connection with the regulation of peaceful picketing.

Prior to the 1930's, state legislatures and Congress frequently attempted to regulate or prohibit outright practices relating to the employment of workers and the organization of effective labor unions. Attempts to establish minimum wages and maximum work days were declared invalid as deprivations of property without due process of law. Legislation, both state and federal, aimed at antiunion or yellow dog contracts was consistently held to be an unconstitutional interference with liberty of contract. And in so far as Congress attempted to outlaw child labor and to regulate conditions of employment or employer interferences with unions, the Supreme Court repeatedly declared that such steps were not proper exercises of power under the commerce clause of the Constitution. Such matters, the Court declared, were purely local concerns, such as manufacturing and mining, over which Congress had no authority to act even if the circumstances seemed to justify exercise of its police power to deal with especially injurious practices.

From these judicial views of the limitations on the state and federal legislatures to enact regulatory laws, there resulted a uniform policy of freedom for employers to combat the rise of unions and to set whatever labor standards the mass of unorganized labor would continue to tolerate. In a sense, this policy could be said to be attributable to the Supreme Court, since in the name of the Constitution it had prevented legislative attempts to improve labor standards and to prohibit direct employer interference with the desire of employees to join unions. Actually, such a statement seems unfair, because the Supreme Court did not initiate such a policy. It had resulted simply from the Court's exercise of its proper function to pass on the constitutionality of legislation. At the same time many legal scholars and some judges in high place thought that the manner in which the Supreme Court applied the test of constitutionality to these legislative social experiments was hopelessly wrong, ill-conceived, and out-of-date. It was also apparent that the Court took for granted the constitutionality of scattered state laws and the Sherman Act under which certain union self-help techniques were made illegal. From the Court's point of view, the real question seemed to be, not whether legislatures could constitutionally deny to minority and underprivileged groups their alleged right through organization to help themselves out of their economic plight. Rather the question was whether or not legislatures had the constitutional power to give them a boost by creating previously nonexistent rights in their favor. The constitutional presumption was against the proponents of what might be called social legislation and in favor of those who opposed any change.

During the 1930's, however, the Supreme Court seemed to become aware of a dormant potentiality in the Constitution. After the 1936 election a majority of the Justices discovered a power within the Court to reverse the traditional attitude of that body toward legislation affecting labor relations and standards of employment. For many years, now, the Court has taken all manner of social legislation in its stride, reserving its constitutional strictures for legislatures that attempt to deny the assertion of rights by those referred to above as minorities and the underprivileged, including organized labor. By abandoning the old "substantive due process" notion, the Court has left legislatures free to deal with what are found to be injurious practices. Interestingly enough, after World War II this change was found to cut both ways so as to permit a reaction in the states and in Congress against the strong labor unions originally fostered by the latter. And, by adopting a generous view of federal power under the commerce clause of the Constitution, the Court left Congress free to deal with almost everything of importance it wished to regulate. In any event, during the years shortly after its personnel became reconstituted, beginning around 1940, the Court showed a tendency not only to foster legislation directed at improving the conditions of labor and strengthening unions, but also to invalidate legislation aimed in the opposite direction—all in its role as guardian and interpreter of the Constitution. While the ultimate goal of the Court was for some time a matter of speculation, a review of its decisions in the picketing cases will show that its institutional adaptability to changing conditions and the national temper is nothing short of remarkable.

THE *Senn* CASE

Not many years prior to the 1930's, picketing of any kind was generally held to be unlawful as a tort. Indeed, in 1909 the California Supreme Court in *Pierce v. Stablemen's Union* indicated this as the basis for holding illegal what it regarded as a perfectly proper secondary boycott, merely because an appeal to consumers had been communicated through a picket line. Apparently it made no difference to courts generally that the picketing was by strikers who were attempting to secure higher wages, or by strangers to an employer who were attempting to organize his plant—so-called stranger picketing. Nor did it seem to matter that the picketing was peaceful—that is, without violence, fraud, or libel. By the 1920's most courts perceived a difference between peaceful picketing by strikers, who were conceded to have some interest to serve, and by outsiders, who "had no legitimate interest" to serve because they were bent only on organization. The former was generally regarded as lawful and the latter, unlawful—a dichotomy suggestive of the way in which various courts had lined up on strikes for the closed shop as against strikes for higher wages. Toward the end of that decade, however, a few of our liberal courts had taken the position that all peaceful picketing was lawful, conceding that the same kind of interest was served by stranger picketing as by the strike for the closed shop—the elimination of competition between union and nonunion labor standards. The law reports published during this period reveal a picture of complete confusion on peaceful picketing. While some of our appellate courts were stoutly declaring that there was and could be no such thing as peaceful picketing and that inherent in all picketing lay a threat of force and violence, other courts were firmly maintaining that picketing could be and frequently was peaceful and free from all suggestion of violence and that, as such, it was merely a form of communication analogous to speech.

All through this period it was taken for granted by most people that picketing could be forbidden or restrained and that its toleration in any form was a matter of judicial or legislative grace. Certainly the manner in which the Supreme Court had grudgingly conceded in 1921 that there could be such a thing as a limited peaceful picketing on the part of strikers and, possibly, by laid-off former employees, fairly implied this to be true. Of course, there had been occasional intimations that peaceful picketing should be protected under the sheltering category of "freedom of speech." Yet it is doubtful whether many impartial people took this notion seriously or regarded it as more than rhetoric.

In 1937, Justice Brandeis made everyone give this matter serious thought by an assertion he made in *Senn v. Tile Layers' Protective Union,* a case arising under Wisconsin's "little Norris-LaGuardia Act." Senn was a nonunion tiling contractor who conducted from his home a two-bit enterprise with the aid of a couple of helpers. In 1935, for instance, his net earnings from this business were about $1500, half of which was attributable to work with his own hands. The tile layers' union proposed that he unionize his business. Senn was willing to co-operate with the union by signing up his helpers, but he himself could not join under its rules and still continue to work on his own jobs. Indeed, he was not even eligible for membership in the union as a journeyman worker because he had never served an apprenticeship under a master tiler. As his business was so small that he could not continue to operate it unless he himself were allowed to work on his own jobs, he refused to accept the union's proposal.

The union, on the other hand, took the position that he should not contract for jobs as an entrepreneur and at the same time work on them as a tiler, because he would then be depriving a union tiler of employment. Furthermore, continuance of his business as a nonunion tiler was in their opinion detrimental to their interests because it undermined the labor standards established by the union. Therefore the union picketed Senn's office-home and the various premises at which he had undertaken tiling jobs. As a result, he found himself virtually out of work and he brought a suit to secure an injunction against this peaceful stranger picketing. Under the state anti-injunction act the trial court denied Senn's request, and he appealed.

The Wisconsin Supreme Court affirmed the judgment below, holding that the picketing which ensued was not enjoinable under their anti-injunction act, a provision of which rendered all nonenjoinable conduct lawful for all purposes. Senn thereupon appealed this decision to the Supreme Court on the ground that the state anti-injunction act was unconstitutional. This appeal was doubly important, since on its outcome inferentially seemed to depend the constitutionality of the Norris-LaGuardia Act itself, upon which the Wisconsin statute had been modeled. In a five-four decision a majority of the Supreme Court held the state act constitutional, affirming the judgment in favor of the union.

When the Wisconsin court had upheld the validity of the state anti-injunction act in this case, it had also decided that the union's conduct was lawful for all purposes under the statute. The Supreme Court in affirming this decision merely declared that a state act having that effect in a stranger picketing case of this sort was not going too far as a matter of constitutionality. Justice Brandeis said, in part:

"Clearly the means which the statute authorizes—picketing and publicity—are not prohibited by the Fourteenth Amendment. Members of a union might, without special statutory authorization by a State, make known the facts of a labor dispute, for freedom of speech is guaranteed by the Federal Constitution. The State may, in the exercise of its police power, regulate the methods and means of publicity as well as the use of public streets. If the end sought by the unions is not forbidden by the Federal Constitution, the State may authorize working men to seek to attain it by combining as pickets, just as it permits capitalists and employers to combine in other ways to attain their desired economic ends . . . In declaring such picketing permissible Wisconsin has put this means of publicity on a par with advertisements in the press."

This statement, and particularly the second sentence, has been sadly misconstrued by most American lawyers. They read Brandeis as having said that picketing—at least, peaceful picketing—is freedom of speech entitled to the guaranties of the federal Constitution. But a re-reading of this quotation will show that he did not say that at all, or even imply it. He said simply that unions may make known the facts of a labor dispute, as a matter of free speech—a constitutional right they naturally enjoy with all other Americans—without saying *how* they may do this. He had just previously said that there is nothing so obviously wrong or inherently illegal about "picketing and publicity" that would prohibit the state under the federal Constitution from making it a nonenjoinable and lawful technique.

This statement he apparently believed necessary in view of the fact that a state law suddenly making libel or assault and battery lawful would almost certainly be declared unconstitutional. The most he did was to concede that peaceful picketing was not that bad and that it was sufficiently innocuous so that a state legislature, having the power to "regulate the methods and means of publicity as well as the use of public streets," was free under the federal Constitution to use this power to permit unions to communicate the facts of a labor dispute by picketing. In other words, granting that unions are entitled as a matter of right under the Constitution to enjoy freedom of speech in disseminating information, the state legislature is not going too far under the 14th amendment when it declares that one of the ways in which they may enjoy this privilege is by peaceful picketing. In a later case Justice Frankfurter pointed out that the last sentence in the passage quoted above must not be read as if Brandeis had interpolated after the word "Wisconsin," the additional words "recognized that the Fourteenth Amendment." For that, in his opinion, would entirely change the meaning of what "so careful a writer as Mr. Justice Brandeis" had intended to say.

What Justice Brandeis actually said, therefore, is a far cry, indeed, from the proposition that peaceful picketing is a form of constitutionally guaranteed freedom of speech. Actually, he intimated that this was a somewhat dubious proposition, but declared nevertheless that a majority of the Supreme Court would not deny a state's power to make picketing a permissible form of communication if that is the way that state wanted it as a matter of local policy. The minority of the court, however, thought that the state no more had the power to do this under the due process clause than it would have had to pass a law legalizing libel or assault and battery. At best, the actual issue in this case was close enough, since even peaceful picketing had always been under a cloud.

THE *Thornhill* CASE

It was somewhat astonishing, therefore, to see the Supreme Court in 1940 come out with a decision in *Thornhill v. Alabama* that peaceful picketing was a form of speech entitled to constitutional protection and that under the 14th amendment no state legislature could pass a valid law prohibiting it, because such a statute would be a denial of freedom of speech. Alabama had passed a statute putting picketing on a par with loitering and making it a misdemeanor. As a consequence of his activities on the picket line, one Byron Thornhill was sentenced either to three days' imprisonment or to pay a fine of

$100 and costs. After his conviction under this statute had been affirmed by the state supreme court, he appealed to the Supreme Court on constitutional grounds. Thereupon the Supreme Court told Alabama, and any other state interested, that they were not allowed to make peaceful picketing unlawful, even if they wanted to do so as a matter of local policy. Thus, within the brief span of three years peaceful picketing—a concept dismissed by many courts as a contradiction in terms and regarded as tortious in some or all of its contexts—suddenly became transformed not only into something that was proper and lawful but also something that was above the law.

The Court's general method of approach, while not exactly orthodox, was certainly reasonable enough. Justice Murphy noted that in the 1st amendment to the Constitution, Congress is forbidden to pass any law "abridging the freedom of speech, or of the press." While the 14th amendment—which operates as a constitutional control over states—says nothing about freedom of speech, it forbids any state to pass or enforce any law abridging the "privileges and immunities of citizens" and goes on to say that no state shall "deprive any person of life, liberty, or property, without due process of law." He then remarked that it was proper in defining the word "liberty" in the 14th amendment, to refer to the 1st amendment to see what such liberties are. In this way freedom of speech is read into the 14th amendment as one of the liberties of which a state may not arbitrarily deprive any person. So far, then, it is plain that no state may constitutionally pass a law denying freedom of speech. The question then becomes, does a state statute prohibiting even peaceful picketing deny this protected freedom of speech? Obviously, the answer to this question depends upon whether or not peaceful picketing is, in itself, merely speech and nothing more. The Supreme Court must be understood to have decided that it *is* speech—a pure matter of communicating ideas or information—and nothing more.

Of course, ordinary speech is a vehicle for committing some unlawful acts, such as libel and fraud. Thus it is apparent that quiet and orderly picketing may be a medium for committing the same torts, as when picketers carry libelous or fraudulent placards. Naturally, the Court concedes that some instances of picketing may be prohibited, as when it is accompanied by violence or threats of violence, fraud, libel, et cetera, just as a state may prohibit any "wrongs" committed through the medium of speech. But when truly conventional speech—and this includes platform and soap-box talks, placards and handbills, newspaper and periodical matter, skywriting and radio addresses, and books like this one—is devoted to the frank discussion of anything, regardless of how annoying or even harmful it may be to some people, it cannot constitutionally be suppressed or penalized as such if it does not contain any element which would place it within one of the settled categories of illegality, such as libel or fraud.

Does this necessarily mean that our courts and legislatures are forbidden to recognize or create any new categories of illegality under which otherwise lawful speech may be penalized? Apparently not, for speaking the truth may occasionally invite severe constitutional reprisals in times of war. Both courts and legislatures have successfully undertaken to make unlawful certain instances of speech containing true statements about the private affairs of others. And under some sort of category called unfair competition, certain branches of our state and federal governments are tending to prevent business enterprisers from adversely criticizing competitors' wares.

Aside from these exceptional situations, however, the constitutional presumption is against the creation of new categories of illegality covering the medium of speech. The reason for this is plain. We believe as a people that there is no irrevocably established method of running society and that our community, our social and our economic ways and customs are matters of value, about which opinions may differ. We believe that anyone has the right to be as critical as he wishes in expressing his opinions about these things, with any interpretations he pleases to put on them. For it is our conviction that in this way alone can we grow into a fully matured society and make it possible to embrace new and better principles of social life. We think it important to have publicized any shameful conduct which may affect some or all of us adversely. And we live in the constant hope that the resultant of competing ideas on these matters may produce a better world.

But the whole of our law is a practical compromise between complete freedom of action and expression, on the one hand, and the common convenience of all, on the other. Our arbiters of policy, called legislatures and courts, have stated for us in laws the rules by which we shall live together. Some of their rules seem foolish, and occasionally they are so repressive that we either have them changed through political action or our courts throw them out as unconstitutional. Nevertheless, we have to live by laws. In general the test of their validity is whether or not they have the support of the majority. This does not mean that valid laws may be freely enacted against minority groups, although it very definitely does mean that minority groups are obliged to recognize most of the ways of life deemed appropriate by the majority. If certain conduct amounting essentially to speech or communication is thought by the majority to be so undesirable that it had better be suppressed by legislation, then the burden of proving that such legislation is an unconstitutional interference with freedom of speech is clearly on a court undertaking to declare it invalid. This is especially true if behind the conduct in question there has been a considerable background and tradition indicating that it is tortious and wrongful, such as there is behind slander and libel as well as behind orderly and peaceful picketing.

Conceding for argument that peaceful picketing equals pure speech, this by itself need not necessarily involve the proposition that a legislature cannot regard it as a socially undesirable form of speech. Nor need it follow that our local legislatures should be denied the constitutional power either to suppress it entirely or, short of that, to regulate it. The real difficulty seems to lie in the Supreme Court's belief that peaceful picketing is merely speech—the dissemination of information and nothing else. It sees in legislation suppressing peaceful picketing a denial of the right of free speech, even if such legislation makes no attempt to prevent unions from publicizing information concerning their disputes through any of the customary channels of communication. Perhaps everyone should accept this as an authoritarian statement of the truth, because the Supreme Court has said it is so.

But it is confusing to keep up with the changing fashions of the Court. Only 29 years before, in 1911, it had told Sam Gompers that he should not use the AF of L newspaper to say that the Bucks Stove and Range Company was unfair to organized labor. In 1921, it had grudgingly conceded the legality of peaceful picketing by strikers, implying that peaceful stranger picketing was still unlawful at common law. And it was but three years before in the *Senn* case in 1937 that the Court had split wide open, five to four, on the proposition that a state legislature had the constitutional power under the 14th amendment to make peaceful stranger picketing lawful at all—four of the Justices believing that such picketing was so inherently illegal that, like libel, it could not constitutionally be made lawful even by legislation. Within three short years, however, the Court discovered that legislatures could not even make peaceful picketing of any sort *un*lawful, because it turned out that all the time it was just plain speech, the dissemination of information, and nothing else!

Not many people would agree to support legislation denying unions the freedom to publicize labor disputes altogether. Indeed, many states have perceived a sufficiently great need for publicity of this sort that they have even made peaceful picketing a nonenjoinable medium for that purpose. While no state has attempted completely to prevent unions from publicizing matters of interest to them, some have tried to stop them from doing so by picketing of all kinds in various situations, leaving them free to pursue the conventional channels of disseminating information. In response to this, the unions renewed their traditional objection that they did not have access to the controlled press or to other effective mediums of publicity. They claimed that if they were prevented from picketing—the only form of publicity within their reach—they would virtually be denied the right to communicate information at all. Now this has always been a strong practical argument in favor of allowing unions the privilege of peaceful picketing. Any court or legislature might well have heeded it before denying the right of all picketing.

But some legislatures and courts, as a matter of policy, nevertheless have taken the position that picketing in all forms— or short of that, all stranger picketing—should be forbidden, believing that the unions should be required to create some access to the other available forms of expression. In such situations the unions had the political task of breaking this position down, an undertaking not at all hopeless in view of the progress they made in many states during the 1930's. But whether or not the unions were politically successful in this venture, at least the matter remained a close issue for local action until the Supreme Court threw the 14th amendment into the scales on the side of organized labor.

It seems plain enough to many disinterested people that picketing, even peaceful picketing, is not at all just speech or the dissemination of information but is, rather, a species of pressure or coercion and is intended as such by its users. Most people who are either sympathetic to organized labor or are sufficiently open-minded to realize that unions have a perfect right to strive for advantage have learned to tolerate peaceful picketing. Many others, however, even disinterested persons, remain unable to see anything but a kind of coercive pressure which they find socially offensive. Almost all disinterested citizens, however, must wonder how people who are directly exposed to peaceful picketing react to it.

How does the loyal employee, who wants to stay at work during a strike, react to picketing, and why? If he finally decides to stay at home during the strike, rather than cross the picket

line, does that mean he has been convinced of the merits behind the union's cause? And how about an applicant for employment during a strike, who decides not to cross a picket line,
although he may need the work? How about prospective customers who decide not to enter a picketed store? Are they
persuaded to go elsewhere by the merits of the union's cause,
assuming that they even know what the cause is, let alone its
merits? And how about property owners who would give work
to nonunion jobbers but who prefer to deal with union contractors in order to avoid having their premises picketed? Are
they inclined to this decision because they are convinced of
the merits behind the union's cause? And when the members
of other unions, unrelated by any common economic interest to
the picketing union, refuse to enter picketed premises, are they
reacting to personal intellectual conviction concerning the
worth of the picketers' cause, or are they merely reacting to
some tacitly understood signal that their sympathy is expected
and must be given pursuant to established labor union policies?

It is hard to believe that the reactions here recounted are all
expressions of intellectual conviction as to the worth of the
picketing unions' several causes. In the first place, no real attempt is made on picket lines to describe what grudge the
union has against the employment or commercial policies of
the picketed employer. And there is usually no attempt to define what the picketers want, and why. What even peaceful
picketing usually boils down to is a simple process of proscription. The picketed person is bad because he is either not doing what we, the picketers, want him to do, or because he is
doing something which we don't want him to do, and such
information is thrust at passers-by, whether they want it or not.
Such a procedure is, indeed, a dubious venture into the world
of ideas and opinions, and hardly seems to be the sort of thing
contemplated by the constitutional guaranty of free speech.
Rather, it suggests a sort of psychological embargo around the
picketed premises, depending for its persuasiveness on the associations most people have in mind when they think about

picketing. Hence it is likely that people hesitate to cross picket lines more because they wish to avoid trouble and to escape any possible scorn that might be directed toward them for being antiunion, than because they are persuaded intellectually by the worth of the picketing unions' cause. And if it were possible to conduct a carefully prepared opinion poll on these various subjective reactions to picketing, it seems safe to conclude that this guess would be confirmed.

Of course, it must be pointed out that many of these people have not actually been coerced, since they made a perfectly free choice in deciding to pursue a course of action which was agreeable to the picketing union. But it is impossible to conclude that Senn, the nonunion tiling contractor, was not subjected to economic coercion when he was run out of business by the union's peaceful picketing. It is true that the actual coercive pressure was supplied by Senn's past and future customers who would rather pay more to have a unionized tiling contractor do their work than to have their premises picketed. Their choice, however, was influenced by the picketing, as it was intended to be. And their preference resulted in Senn's economic annihilation, since he never had the option to continue his business as a unionized contractor, due to the nature of his particular enterprise.

At any rate, granting that a state legislature or court may express local economic and social values by allowing peaceful picketing, should they not be left free under the Constitution to conclude that some or all of such picketing is of too dubious social merit to be tolerated? Is it so very clear that peaceful picketing is purely and simply speech—the dissemination of information, and nothing more—that a state legislature or court is forbidden to conclude otherwise and to regulate it for the purpose of preventing that part of it which is thought not to be simply speech but, rather, psychological coercion or the organization of disinterested sympathy? And is a state legislature so obviously behaving unconstitutionally if it persists in viewing even peaceful picketing as an unwarranted interference with the freedom of its citizens to make up their own minds, in any way they may see fit, about whom they will deal with, what they will sell, and why?

Because of the sentimentality about peaceful picketing that has prevailed in the past, any discussion of this subject is compromised if it seems to be defending antipicketing legislation. But, surely, it must be apparent that the issue at stake is much larger than whether or not unions should be allowed the privilege of peaceful picketing. The real issue is whether or not the Supreme Court has any defensible right, on the basis of an arbitrary assumption that peaceful picketing *is* simply speech, to forbid a state to reach a contrary conclusion on this very dubious proposition and to protect itself against something it does not like. The Supreme Court has always had an extraordinarily great power in its hands to control the affairs of states under the 14th amendment of the Constitution. In past years many believe that it abused this power in denying states the right to enact certain types of social legislation intended to benefit labor. The Court still has this power, and real liberals perceived its wise use in the Wisconsin tile layers' case. But in the *Thornhill* case it looks as if the Court had begun to abuse its extraordinary power, in this instance in the other direction. This provokes the unhappy reflection that the Court was swayed more by political pressures and its economic and social predilections than by dispassionate considerations of the correct use of political power within the states, regardless of what values local legislatures may entertain.

Naturally, it must be conceded that the Court's most sacred mission is to protect at all costs the right of every person to speak freely and to advance his social, economic, and political views whenever he wishes to do so. The Court enjoys its extraordinary power of judicial review under the 14th amendment chiefly to see that freedom of speech and other civil liberties are maintained. But this should not give the Court a free hand to slap the label of speech on social conduct as dubious in its nature as peaceful picketing is and, thereby, to deny to the states the power to regulate it on the basis of contrary notions about its nature. Here is a situation where true liberals might paraphrase Voltaire by saying that they hate what the Alabama legislature did but they will defend to the death its right to do it, leaving the ultimate outcome to local enlightenment and the political process.

To get on with our story, however, it shortly appeared that all was not so clear on the Potomac. In 1941 the Supreme Court handed down two picketing decisions on the same day, Justice Frankfurter speaking for the Court in both cases. In each one he reaffirmed the doctrine of the *Thornhill* case, but he gave it some slight twists which indicated that he had been thinking the matter over somewhat reflectively. As he succinctly put it in one of these cases: "A union of those engaged in what the record describes as *beauty work* unsuccessfully tried to unionize Swing's beauty parlor. Picketing of the shop followed." Swing secured an injunction against this peaceful stranger picketing by the "beauticians'" union and the Illinois Supreme Court upheld it as proper. Upon the union's appeal to the Supreme Court under the 14th amendment, however, this decision was set aside as unconstitutional on the basis of the *Thornhill* case. This was also an illustration of the fact that the Supreme Court may use the 14th amendment to set aside decisions of state courts as well as to invalidate the acts of state legislatures.

This decision in *American Federation of Labor v. Swing* was not surprising after the *Thornhill* case. Nevertheless, it changed the common law of many states which had long before conceded the legality of peaceful picketing by strikers but had always held that since strangers to the picketed employer had no direct interest in his employment policies, they could not therefore justify the harm caused by their picketing. Justice Frankfurter took the trouble in this case to point out something which might seem irrelevant under the absolutism of the *Thornhill* case. He observed that under the 14th amendment a state could not prevent workers from stranger picketing "by drawing the circle of economic competition between employers and workers so small as to contain only an employer and those directly employed by him," noting that the "interdependence of economic interest of all engaged in the same industry has become a commonplace." Thus, while the presence of interest on the part of peaceful picketers seemed unnecessary under the *Thornhill* doctrine, Justice Frankfurter suggested that at least it makes the application of that broad doctrine more palatable.

In the case of *Milk Wagon Drivers Union v. Meadowmoor Dairies, Inc.,* decided the same day, it appeared that a milk wagon drivers' union had combined a little bombing, hijacking, and hatchet work with the picketing of companies organized by a rival union. An Illinois court issued an injunction forbidding violent, but permitting continued peaceful, picketing, although a master in chancery who heard the case had recommended enjoining all picketing because of the union's behavior. The Illinois Supreme Court overruled the trial court and extended the injunction to forbid all picketing for the duration of the dispute in question, resting its decision on the master's findings that any picketing this union did was colored by the violence it had committed.

Upon the union's appeal, a majority of the Supreme Court voted to sustain the Illinois judgment, Justice Frankfurter stressing the importance of leaving to the local courts this matter of drawing inferences from the evidence. As he observed, the Illinois court had concluded that even peaceful picketing, undertaken as part of the same dispute in which extreme violence had occurred, would carry over with it a "momentum of fear from past violence" and might persuade others not so much by enlightenment but rather by caution. He thought that it would be an abuse of the Supreme Court's power to deny the Illinois court the right to draw this inference from the evidence and then to conclude that future so-called peaceful picketing by this union in this dispute would not really be peaceful, at all, and should be enjoined. The minority Justices of the Supreme Court were furious with this decision, claiming that the *Thornhill* case had collapsed on the first attack against it. They contended that the only proper way to avoid future objectionable picketing in this dispute was "in the maintenance of order, not in denial of free speech." It was this latter remark which prompted Frankfurter to rejoin that nothing in the 14th amendment "prevents a state if it so chooses from placing confidence in a chancellor's decree and compels it to rely exclusively on a policeman's club." Quite obviously, the picture of peaceful picketing as speech, simon-pure, was becoming a bit cloudy.

A little later, in 1942, the Supreme Court issued simultaneously two other picketing decisions suggesting drastic modifications in the *Thornhill* doctrine. One of them, *Bakery and Pastry Drivers Union v. Wohl,* involved a union of bakery wagon drivers. Many wholesale bakeries around New York City had become unwilling to retain drivers as employees because it was too expensive. They discovered that by setting their drivers up as independent contractors to deliver their product, they could sell them their trucks at nominal prices, thereby saving the New York workmen's compensation premiums and federal social security taxes, as well as the cost of liability insurance and the upkeep of the trucks. Moreover, they could also avoid having to deal with the union and could get their deliveries made by these independents for substantially less than they would have paid out as union wages. Justifiably fearing that this trend would destroy their high employment standards, ·the union began to picket some of these independents both where they picked up their product and where they delivered it. The New York courts enjoined this picketing, concluding that there was no labor dispute within the meaning of the state anti-injunction act that was almost identical with the federal act. Thereupon the union appealed to the Supreme Court.

Because it had to accept the interpretation the New York court placed on its own statutory definition of the term "labor dispute," the Supreme Court had before it the narrow issue of whether or not there had been a denial of the right of free speech under the 14th amendment. Whereupon it set aside the state court's judgment on the ground that there had been such denial of free speech. Speaking for the Court Justice Jackson said he could see "no substantive evil of such magnitude as to mark a limit to the right of free speech" that the unions sought to exercise. Although, as he remarked, "A state is not required to tolerate in all places and all circumstances even peaceful picketing by an individual," the independent peddlers' "mobility and their insulation from the public as middlemen made it practically impossible for [the union] to make known their legitimate grievances to the public whose patronage was sustaining the peddler system except by the means here employed and contemplated," concluding that "those means are such as to have slight, if any, repercussions upon the interests of strangers to the issue."

Justice Douglas, speaking for Justices Murphy, Black, and himself, wrote a somewhat biting concurrence. "If the opinion in this case means that a State can prohibit picketing when it is effective but may not prohibit it when it is ineffective," he said, "then I think we have made a basic departure from *Thornhill v. Alabama.*" His chief concern was the majority's implication that if, in its opinion, the New York court had correctly concluded that no labor dispute was really involved, then it would have been free to enjoin the picketing. He did not see how, under the *Thornhill* decision, a state could be allowed to draw this line. He went on to remark, with engaging candor, that "picketing might have a coercive effect" and that "picketing by an organized group is more than free speech, since it involves patrol of a particular locality and since the very presence of a picket line may induce action of one kind or another, quite irrespective of the nature of the ideas which are being disseminated."

This was a remarkable concession from the liberal wing of the Court. It narrowed the whole issue down to who might make the judgment of whether peaceful picketing only persuades on the merits of the union's contentions, or merely coerces because of its very existence—the state legislatures and courts or only the Supreme Court? Justice Douglas however apparently thought the majority of the Court was doing something else—that while it was conceding peaceful picketing to be at least free speech, it was making the constitutionality of the New York court's judgment depend on whether or not the union was engaged in what has come to be known as a labor dispute. He feared that what the majority of the Court had done was merely to take issue with the New York court's narrow definition of a labor dispute, thus escaping its constitutional obligation to uphold peaceful picketing whether or not the union had any economic interest to pursue in its conflict with the independent peddlers.

The other picketing case decided by the Supreme Court on the same day as the New York bakery drivers' case, showed clearly the direction in which the Court was headed. In *Carpenters and Joiners Union v. Ritter's Cafe,* a Texas restaurant operator named Ritter let a contract to a nonunion contractor for the erection of his dwelling house about a mile and a half away from the business section of town, where his restaurant was located. Since the carpenters' union resented this, regarding its interests in higher union standards to be endangered, it peacefully picketed Ritter where such pressure would do the most good—in front of his restaurant. As a consequence, Ritter's unionized restaurant employees refused to come to work, union truck drivers ceased deliveries of supplies, and union patrons stopped eating at his cafe—not because any of these folk had anything to gain from Ritter but because they would not cross a "sister" union's picket line.

Now it is hard to deny that any nonunion building operation threatens to undermine union standards in this industry. And in this case the carpenters' union had a real economic interest at stake, justifying their exertion of peaceful economic pressures against competing nonunion enterprisers. Indeed, all union interests in the building trades are represented by such high rates that many people cannot afford to build unless they can find nonunion contractors. But in spite of our prevailing ethics of free enterprise and competition, affording the carpenters' union a justification at common law for focusing economic pressure against Ritter and his nonunion contractor, the Texas courts thought that this pressure could not be exerted by picketing Ritter's restaurant. The highest state court affirmed an injunction forbidding the union to picket the restaurant. But it did not prohibit picketing at the building under construction or publicizing the situation in any way other than by picketing the restaurant. From this judgment the union appealed to the Supreme Court, claiming a denial of free speech under the 14th amendment.

In this case the Supreme Court decided that the Texas court had the constitutional power to enjoin the peaceful picketing in question. Through Justice Frankfurter a majority of the Court enunciated a most intriguing analysis of why it reached this conclusion. Fundamentally, the Court regarded the conflict as a personal fight between Ritter and the carpenters' union concerning Ritter's labor policies *as a house builder and not as a restaurant owner.* The union had no dispute with Ritter concerning his employment policies at his restaurant. Picketing of his restaurant, however, implied that it did.

As the opinion puts it, patrolling at that place led to the "conscription of neutrals"—that is, Ritter's Cafe, a restaurant enterprise. And, of course, Justice Frankfurter might have added in this connection, members of the public, both union and general, who might exhibit some concern over low employment standards in restaurants but who had no interest in the employment standards of carpenters. Justice Frankfurter thought that the Texas court should be allowed, under the 14th amendment of the Constitution, to insist that picketing should be confined to the undertaking with respect to which the dispute existed and that by injunction it could "insulate from the dispute an establishment which industrially has no connection with the dispute."

He urbanely conceded that "as a means of communicating the facts of a labor dispute, peaceful picketing may be a phase of the constitutional right of free utterance." And then he made a statement much too revealing not to quote in full.

"But," he declared, "recognition of peaceful picketing as an exercise of free speech does not imply that the states must be without power to confine the sphere of communication to that directly related to the dispute. Restriction of picketing to the area of the industry within which a labor dispute arises leaves open to the disputants other traditional modes of communication. To deny to the states the power to draw this line is to write into the Constitution the notion that every instance of peaceful picketing—anywhere and under any circumstances— is necessarily a phase of the controversy which provoked the picketing. Such a view of the Due Process Clause [in the 14th amendment] would compel the states to allow the disputants in a particular industrial episode to conscript neutrals having no relation to either the dispute or the industry in which it arose." Then out of abundant caution he observed that the New York bakery drivers' case was not inconsistent with this because there, "in picketing the retail establishments, the union members would only be following the subject-matter of their dispute."

The minority of the Court in this five-four decision—Justices Black, Douglas, Murphy, and Reed—now realized that in spite of the majority's protestations to the contrary, the cat was out of the bag. The *Thornhill* doctrine, as the Court had originally promulgated it, was gone. With some reason, they could not understand why peaceful picketing should be subjected to any regulation at all, if it were really speech—the dissemination of information—and nothing more. They could not perceive why the rest of the Court should concede that Texas had the power to prevent the union from conscripting neutrals— strangers to the grievance—by the device of peaceful picketing when they freely admitted that the union had an absolute con-

stitutional right to undertake the enlightenment of these very
same neutrals by pursuing "other traditional modes of communication."

To their way of thinking—and their logic appears faultless—
this position meant that the majority of the Court did not
really regard peaceful picketing as constitutionally protected
speech at all, but rather as some sort of economic coercive device depending on communication for its effect. The minority
realized that Ritter's Cafe and its owner were identified in a
very real way with Ritter the house builder, that the eating
public and house building public might be much the same, and
that workers and truck drivers were no more neutral at one
place than another as far as the communication of ideas is concerned. Union programs are addressed to all these members of
the public, and it is the public's influence that might persuade
either a nonunion contractor that he should employ only union
carpenters or Ritter that he should deal only with unionized
contractors. Thus if peaceful picketing *really* is only communication, why should not the union be constitutionally protected in communicating facts to people in general at any
public place and under any circumstances?

If this basic assumption of these four minority Justices was
valid—that peaceful picketing really is constitutionally guaranteed free speech—they are absolutely correct and the majority
of the Court is absolutely wrong in drawing any line at all
around the union's constitutional rights. But the real trouble
is that it is extremely difficult to treat this basic assumption as a
valid one. The fact is that picketing is simply a coercive economic device traveling under the guise of speech for the purpose of enjoying constitutional immunity from state regulation.
In all probability, any candid labor leader would confess this off
the record. In this *Ritter* case, the union's purpose was patent.
It wanted to put Ritter on an embarrassing spot by creating in
front of his restaurant what the Texas courts thought to be a
kind of nuisance. The union members knew full well that if
enough patrons and members of other unions refused to enter

his restaurant because of their reluctance to cross a picket line, he would eventually try to appease the union by calling off his nonunion contractor—that is, unless he could first stop the picketing.

It is quite apparent that a majority of the Justices felt this way. It is hard to understand the Court's position as anything but a retreat from the *Thornhill* case, and this can mean only that the majority no longer believed peaceful picketing to be speech—the dissemination of information—and nothing more. For if they did, then they had entered on the monstrous undertaking of denying this liberty constitutional protection whenever they saw fit to do so. As the minority complained, the majority could not have it both ways. Peaceful picketing either *was* or it *was not* an instance of free speech under the Constitution. If it was, then the union's right peacefully to picket Ritter's cafe should have been upheld. But if it was not? Here is the critical question. For if it was not, then what business had the Court dealing with such matters at all?

The Supreme Court had traditionally held that local labor policy is a state's own concern and that what went on within a state was none of the federal government's business (with the exception, naturally, of constitutional matters) unless Congress made it so by a valid exercise of its commerce powers. By 1942, it had been recognized that Congress had broad powers to inaugurate a uniform labor policy throughout practically all of American industry. Included within this power was the ability to declare lawful whatever peaceful picketing it wished to protect in connection with any industry involved in interstate commerce. Indeed, there has always been speculation as to whether Congress might not have asserted this power with respect to peaceful picketing in Section 7 of the NLRA where it guaranteed employees "the right to engage in concerted activities for the purpose of collective bargaining or other mutual aid or protection." However, it has never been the officially accepted view that it did. Nevertheless, Congress had this power and apparently had not seen fit to use it. Furthermore, the

Court realized that even if Congress had done so, a great deal of peaceful picketing went on in connection with enterprise not connected with interstate commerce—at that time, indeed, in the building industry which was not generally swept up in the federal net until after the passage of the Taft-Hartley Act in 1947.

It is tempting, therefore, to surmise that a majority of the Supreme Court in the *Ritter* case were determined to use the *Thornhill* doctrine as a means of laying out a reasonable area of protection for *all* peaceful picketing—whether or not it was connected in any way with interstate commerce—and that the boundaries of such area were to be drawn along the lines suggested by the definition of the term labor dispute in Section 13 of the Norris–LaGuardia Act. It may be recalled that in the *Swing* case, involving stranger picketing of the "beauticians'" union, Justice Frankfurter had declared that Illinois could not "exclude workers from peacefully exercising the right of free communication by drawing the circle of economic competition between employers and workers so small as to contain only an employer and those directly employed by him," adding that the "interdependence of economic interest of all engaged in the same industry has become a commonplace." But in the *Ritter* case here was Justice Frankfurter himself drawing a circle— not so narrow, to be sure, as the one Illinois had drawn around constitutionally protected free speech. But nevertheless it was an odd thing for one in his position to be doing at all. Indeed, a moment's reflection suggests the possibility that the seeds of *Ritter* were germinated in *Swing* itself.

If this speculation is correct, what is wrong with such a scheme? The answer must be carefully framed, since it could be understood to impute fairly serious charges against a majority of the Supreme Court. It is possible, of course, that while all of the Justices concurring in *Thornhill* really believed at the time in the equation of peaceful picketing and constitutionally protected free speech, several of them had since then changed their minds. Hence the decision in the *Ritter* case may amount to no more than an orderly retreat from the *Thornhill* doctrine, in which a majority of the Justices, reluctant to overrule that basic precedent, were nevertheless willing to circumvent it by what they regarded as a reasonable compromise. On the other hand in *Thornhill* all of the Justices may have concluded that the quickest way to give organized labor a leg up would be for the Court to assume a novel power in the name of the Constitution by equating peaceful picketing with constitutionally protected free speech, thus putting itself in a position of imposing with respect to this facet of labor law a uniform policy throughout the country.

If this were true, *Thornhill* may have been only the first step toward a broader ambition of universally protecting strikes and certain types of secondary boycotts from legislative and judicial regulation or suppression. For at that time it was not uncommonly thought that strikes and secondary boycotts were also fundamental personal freedoms of labor unionists, as reasonably falling within the term "liberty" in the 14th amendment as peaceful picketing. Indeed, some might have argued that such conduct fits even more easily within that term, since they could see workers concertedly refusing to work, when they did not want to, or refraining from patronizing any enterprise or commodity—all of which is purely passive conduct. At the same time, those same observers might have regarded even peaceful picketing as an unwarranted intrusion and aggression. And many boycotts, through the use of "unfair" and "we don't patronize" lists, seemed to be informational techniques quite as much as peaceful picketing was said to be. Indeed, it was not altogether unthinkable at that time that the Supreme Court might write Section 4, along with Section 13, of the Norris-LaGuardia Act into the Constitution by embracing all union activities there described within the meaning of the term "liberty" in the 14th amendment.

Today this seems fantastic. However the somewhat analogous tour de force in the *Hutcheson* case has survived. There Sections 4 and 13 of the Norris-LaGuardia Act were read into the arguably defunct Section 20 of the Clayton Act in order to take organized labor out from under the Sherman antitrust law. And, after all, the *Thornhill* case itself is still on the books, as yet not formally overruled. Be this as it may, a majority of the Court, having assumed the power under the 14th amendment to declare state legislative and judicial prohibition of peaceful picketing invalid, decided in the *Ritter* case to qualify that power of protection by using it only when the picketing occurred in the same industry out of which the original industrial dispute had arisen. Thus, when the basic dispute occurs in the building industry, the constitutional protection will be confined to peaceful picketing in connection with aspects of *that* industry. Consequently, the states will be left free to prohibit picketing by a building trades union beyond the limits of that industry—for instance, at a restaurant. Such a limitation on the constitutional protection was no doubt borrowed straight from Section 13 of the Norris-LaGuardia Act defining the nature and scope of a statutory labor dispute. Thus the influence of this Section 13 definition broadened the scope of constitutionally protected union organizational activity in the *Swing* case while at the same time in the *Ritter* case it furnished a strait jacket confining this scope of protection.

Now this process looks very much as if a majority of the Court were using an established economic policy to measure and limit the extent of a constitutional guaranty. Such a process implies a preference between the economic policy established in Section 13 and that which would have prevailed had the union in Ritter's case been protected in picketing elsewhere than at the building site or at the nonunion general contractor's premises. But this is most strange! As the minority of the Court in *Ritter* so keenly appreciated, you cannot be choosy about how the Constitution sheds its protection and under what circumstances the matter to be protected arises. Hence it looks as if a majority of the Court in Ritter's case, consciously or unconsciously, were using the Constitution to enable them to exert a power to establish in one particular a uniform policy throughout the country. The Court cannot actually promulgate universal protection for peaceful picketing. But under the *Thornhill* doctrine it can knock down legislation and court decisions prohibiting peaceful picketing within the context of a statutory labor dispute, leaving the states free to suppress all other peaceful picketing. In this area the Court abandoned its function as watchdog over free speech and, by using its watchdog power indirectly, had undertaken the role belonging exclusively to legislatures of determining the proper economic context of peaceful picketing. Two legal writers suggested that Ritter's case is tantamount to the Supreme Court's having written Section 13 of the Norris-LaGuardia Act into the Constitution.

In all fairness to the Court's majority in the *Ritter* case, however, what it seems to have done was to retain the power it assumed in *Thornhill* to reject the exercise of state authority to prohibit *all* peaceful picketing and then to use this power to reject only those manifestations of state authority it did not like. Such a course strangely resembles the old "illegal purpose doctrine." It is the more unwarranted, however, in that it was adopted in the name of the Court's duty under the Constitution to protect freedom of speech in communicating all sorts of ideas in any economic context. Perhaps it would have been better for the Court simply to cut its losses and conclude that its decision in the *Thornhill* case had been a serious blunder. But the momentum of the New Deal days still pushed the Court along in its career of carrying the torch for labor unions. And although a majority of it had grown cautious, it was going to have to learn the full weakness of the *Thornhill* doctrine the hard way after Congress had passed the Taft-Hartley Act in 1947.

Before that day came, however, the Supreme Court in 1943 once more went all out for *Thornhill* in a case called *Cafeteria Employees' Union v. Angelos*. There a cafeteria workers' union picketed two restaurants run by the proprietors without any employees at all. The proprietors sought and secured injunctions against this peaceful picketing. The New York Court of Appeals upheld these injunctions on the ground that no labor dispute existed between the union and the two proprietors. This was because there were no employees with respect to whom employment conditions could become an issue. On the union's appeal to the Supreme Court under the 14th amendment, the New York decision was reversed as a denial of free speech. The union had insisted that a labor dispute did exist, within the broad definition of such disputes in the New York anti-injunction act. What it was after was to force these proprietors to hire employees they did not want. Its first interest was that the very existence of cafeterias run without any employees created a competitive situation harmful to cafeterias who did hire union employees. This was for the reason that the absence of such employees lowered their overhead costs and enabled them to dispense food more cheaply than the union enterprises. Secondly, it wanted more jobs for its members.

Here was a situation almost identical with the Wisconsin tile layers' case in 1937. It is difficult to understand how the New York court failed to see that under its state anti-injunction act labor disputes were involved. Possibly the judges were influenced by the fact that the picketers carried banners which denounced the proprietors as "unfair" to organized labor and said that the cafeterias served "bad food," telling prospective customers that by patronizing them "they were aiding the cause of Fascism." After all, peaceful picketing is supposed to comprise only nonviolent picketing from which are absent the elements of libel and misrepresentation. But as Justice Frankfurter, after noting that the peaceful character of the picketing was unquestioned, said about these banners: "And to use loose language or undefined slogans that are part of the conventional give-and-take in our economic and political controversies—like 'unfair' or 'fascist'—is not to falsify facts."

This must have led the New York courts to wonder just what

Justice Reed had meant when he generously conceded in the *Ritter* case: "We do not doubt the right of the state to impose not only some but many restrictions upon peaceful picketing. Reasonable numbers, quietness, truthful placards, open ingress and egress, suitable hours or other proper limitations, not destructive of the right to tell of labor difficulties, may be required." At any rate, whatever moved the New York court to construe its anti-injunction act as it did in these cafeteria cases, the Supreme Court is supposed to be bound by the state court's construction of its own laws. However, it was perfectly clear to the Supreme Court that this picketing had occurred within the context of a labor dispute as defined by Section 13 of the Norris-LaGuardia Act—virtually identical with the statutory definition in New York. Hence, under its holding in the *Ritter* case the Court felt free to use its constitutional power under the 14th amendment to reverse the New York court's decision in spite of its narrow interpretation of its own statute.

Where was all this going to end? Six years were to pass before the Supreme Court was going to have to face the music and confess publicly that the *Thornhill* doctrine might have been a mistake. Probably because of World War II the Court was not troubled with any more important picketing cases for some years. In the meantime state courts and legislatures had become cautious about enjoining and prohibiting peaceful picketing. Then in 1947 Congress passed the Taft-Hartley Act. While that statute, oddly enough, did not even mention picketing, it clearly forbade labor union activities commonly articulated through picketing, such as certain secondary boycott pressures. In that same year the California Supreme Court had before it a case involving picketing in violation of its "hot cargo" act. This precluded a union from using secondary pressures to compel any employer to cease handling the goods of any other employer with whom the union had a labor dispute. The court held this statute unconstitutional, the majority quite obviously being influenced by the Supreme Court's picketing decisions.

But a dissenting judge pointed out that Congress in the Taft-

Hartley Act had just declared secondary boycott operations by concerted action to be an unfair labor practice "in language the same in substance and effect" as the California "hot cargo" act. And he was clearly of the opinion that the Supreme Court would think twice before it held any part of *that* legislation invalid, even though a logical application of the *Thornhill* doctrine would appear to make it impossible for Congress constitutionally to regulate peaceful picketing, whether or not it was used to implement secondary boycotts. From the very beginning *Thornhill* had threatened any legislative attempt whatsoever, by either the states or Congress, to regulate or prohibit peaceful picketing. And the Supreme Court had indicated that the states could not circumvent this constitutional guaranty simply by making unlawful the purpose or objective of the peaceful picketing within the context of a Norris-LaGuardia Act labor dispute.

Meanwhile, some of the state legislatures and courts were becoming reluctant to leave unions a free hand in peaceful picketing. Wisconsin had already pulled the wool over the eyes of the Supreme Court. Its legislature had replaced in its anti-injunction act the broad definition of labor dispute that had produced the *Senn* tile layer's case, with the narrow definition behind which the Supreme Court had refused shelter to the Illinois court in the *Swing* case. Moreover, it had enacted a labor relations act aimed at unfair union practices, with the same narrow definition of labor dispute. And then in a couple of close cases the Wisconsin court had successfully upheld prohibitions against peaceful picketing under these two statutes by relying on statements in its opinions that nothing contained in them was intended as denying freedom of speech to anyone. Now other state courts were beginning more openly to question the vitality of the *Thornhill* doctrine. Then an appeal to the Supreme Court from a decision of Missouri's highest court marked the first major step in the decline of *Thornhill*.

THE *Giboney* CASE

In *Giboney v. Empire Storage and Ice Company,* a union of ice
peddlers, many of whom drove their own trucks in door-to-door
deliveries, tried to induce all such peddlers in the Kansas City
area to join up. But most of the nonunion peddlers refused to
join. The union then sought agreements from all local manufacturers and wholesale distributors of ice not to sell ice to
these nonunion peddlers. All agreed except Empire Storage &
Ice Company. Thereupon the union picketed Empire with
the object of compelling agreement, and since 85 per cent of
Empire's sales had been to union peddlers, its business was
suddenly reduced to that extent. Had Empire signed and lived
up to the agreement not to sell ice to nonunion peddlers, it
would have been in violation of a state antimonopoly law imposing a large fine on anyone guilty of restraint of trade. Consequently Empire sought and secured in the state court an injunction against the union's peaceful picketing; and this was
affirmed by Missouri's highest court, from whose judgment the
appeal was made.

Here was peaceful picketing squarely within the context of
a labor dispute as defined in Section 13 of the Norris-LaGuardia
Act. If the Supreme Court followed its own precedents and set
aside Missouri's injunction under the *Thornhill* doctrine,
Empire would be forced either to lose 85 per cent of its business
or become criminally liable under the state antimonopoly law.
This one was a real poser for the Court. Previously there had
been no difficulty about declaring unconstitutional any attempts to circumvent *Thornhill* by state laws making the objective of union picketing illegal. Such a recourse was simply a
thinly-veiled method of declaring the picketing itself unlawful,
and this was not allowed under the *Thornhill* doctrine. But in
the *Giboney* case compliance by Empire with the union's picketing request would be a serious crime. And there was no doubt
that the state's antimonopoly law was a proper and constitu-

tional expression of local economic policy in so far as it applied directly to the undertakings of business enterprises.

In any event, in this *Giboney* case the Supreme Court was on the spot. In a unanimous decision it upheld the state court's injunction against the picketing. First of all, Justice Black stated that labor unions are not entirely immune from valid state laws against restraints of trade. As for the *Thornhill* doctrine, he said that the Constitution does not protect "speech or writing used as an integral part of conduct in violation of a valid criminal statute." And where, as here, it appeared that the union's object was to "compel" or "induce" Empire to violate the law, it would not be an abridgment of freedom of speech to enjoin the communication leading up to such objective. "And," he observed, "it is clear that [the union officials] were doing more than exercising a right of free speech or press. . . . They were exercising their economic power together with that of their allies to compel Empire to abide by union rather than by state regulation of trade." In conclusion he noted that the Missouri antimonopoly statute resembled other state acts of this type and that nothing in the Constitution prevented the state from imposing its economic policies in this way on "groups of workers, businessmen or others."

The point of overwhelming importance in the *Giboney* case is that if a valid state law makes it illegal for the picketed employer to do what the union's peaceful picketing seeks to have him do, then the picketing may be enjoined, *Thornhill* notwithstanding. Now the states had found a Northwest Passage around the *Thornhill* doctrine, and a series of cases decided by the Supreme Court in 1950 and 1951 showed that but little of it remained to require circumnavigation. In *Gazzam v. Building Service Employees Union,* a case arising in the state of Washington, where the plaintiff employed fifteen workers in his hotel, at a meeting between the union and eleven of these employees, nine voted against joining the union, one remained neutral, and the other, who was willing to join, the union did not want as a member. Since the plaintiff refused to use his influence to persuade his employees to join up, the union picketed the hotel with the object of inducing him to bring pressure on them to join. This hotel enterprise was not sufficiently connected with interstate commerce to bring its labor relations within the purview of the NLRA. Hence the hotel proprietor would have violated no law, federal or state, by recognizing the union as bargaining agent for his employees, regardless of their wishes. In this respect the situation was quite different from that in the *Giboney* case, since here the plaintiff could have complied with the union's picketing pressure with impunity. And, incidentally, the picketing was within the context of a federal statutory labor dispute. While the state of Washington had a "little Norris-LaGuardia Act" containing the same provisions as those appearing in the federal anti-injunction act, nothing in that statute made it illegal for this proprietor to comply with the union's picketing pressure by recognizing the union as bargaining representative for his employees in spite of their expressed desire to the contrary. Nevertheless the highest Washington court sustained an injunction against the union's picketing, and on appeal, the Supreme Court upheld this judgment.

In effect, this decision was based on the *Giboney* precedent. But the actual facts were quite different. Like the federal statute the state anti-injunction act contained a declaration of public policy to the effect that employees should be allowed to organize as they wished and to designate representatives of their own choosing and should "be free from interference, restraint, or coercion of employers of labor or their agents, in the designation of such representatives or in self-organization." As this declaration did not have the effect of a prohibition against employers, the hotel proprietor would not have been subject to any legal sanction if he had recognized the union and bargained with it. But the Supreme Court was unanimous in its agreement with the Washington court, Justice Minton declaring:

"Here, as in *Giboney*, the union was using its economic

power with that of its allies to compel [the hotel proprietor] to abide by union policy rather than by the declared policy of the State. That state policy guarantees workers free choice of representatives for bargaining purposes. If [the hotel proprietor] had complied with [the union's] demands and had signed one of the tendered contracts and had lived up to its terms, he would thereby have coerced his employees. The employees would have had no free choice as to whether they wished to organize or what union would be their representative."

If the *Giboney* decision was a strategic retirement from the *Thornhill* doctrine, virtually compelled by circumstances, then this *Gazzam* case became the first sign of a general retreat. For even if the union's peaceful picketing could not be construed as exposing the hotel proprietor to legal penalties if he complied with the union's wishes, still such compliance would have been in the teeth of Washington's statutory public policy— amounting to no more than what might be called official sentiments with no sanctions attached.

Then in another of the 1950 cases, *Hughes v. Superior Court of California,* the Supreme Court went even further. There an association of blacks requested Lucky Stores to hire the number of black employees that reflected the percentage of its black customers—about 50 per cent. While Lucky Stores had no objection to this, it refused to comply because it preferred to work out any system of proportional employment by collective bargaining with the union with which it had a contract. Consequently the black association began picketing—a step which the United States Supreme Court had previously held in a similar case was within the context of a Norris-LaGuardia Act labor dispute and therefore not enjoinable in a federal court. Nevertheless the highest California court upheld an injunction against this picketing. In its view Lucky Stores' compliance with it would result in discrimination against white people, including those of Mexican descent, and members of the yellow race! This conclusion of the California court was based on one of its common-law precedents that denial of membership in a union to blacks was illegal where employment could not be secured without membership in the union. In other words, the California court used its judicial sanction against "closed shop—closed union" as a means of suppressing peaceful picketing by blacks to combat the effects of racial discrimination in hiring.

The major significance of the *Hughes* case is that in upholding the California injunction the Supreme Court ruled that compliance by Lucky Stores with the blacks' peaceful picketing would have involved it in a violation of the state's public policy as expressed, not by statute as in the *Giboney* case, and even in *Gazzam*, but by its common law.

Surely the *Thornhill* doctrine had little vitality left when the Supreme Court complacently allowed the California judges, under the shelter of the *Giboney* exception, to invent state policy off the cuff, so to speak, in order to prohibit peaceful picketing. Other than the passage of nine years and a change in the political complexion of the country, what possible difference was there between the public policy of the Illinois court in the *Swing* beauty parlor case and of the California court in the *Hughes* case?

But the real *coup de grâce* was given to the *Thornhill* rationale in the remaining two 1950 decisions of the Supreme Court. *International Brotherhood of Teamsters v. Hanke* and *Automobile Drivers and Demonstrators Union v. Cline* were appeals to the Supreme Court from the state of Washington's highest tribunal. Hanke ran a family business, he and his sons operating a used car lot. Because the Hankes would not agree to observe the same hours of operation that organized dealers did, their business was picketed. Then Cline, another self-employed person like Hanke, and also in the used car business, was picketed because he would not close on Saturdays at 1 P.M. and also because he would not hire as a salesman a member of the union who was to be compensated at 7 per cent of all the gross sales made at Cline's place of business. The Washington court held injunctions to be proper, and the Supreme Court, consolidating the two cases, agreed. Justice Frankfurter recognized that the state court's decisions were based on its conclusion that at common law any attempt by a union to suppress self-employment was unlawful. The dissenting Justices quite reasonably observed that these cases were no different from the Wisconsin *Senn* tile layer's case and the New York *Angelos* cafeteria employees' case. But Justice Frankfurter thought there *was* a difference.

He pointed out that Washington's highest court had taken the trouble to "declare a policy in favor of self-employers and to make conduct restrictive of self-employment unlawful." This was more than the New York court had done in the *Angelos* cafeteria employees' and the *Wohl* bakery drivers' cases, than the Illinois court had done in the *Swing* "beauticians'" case and Wisconsin had done in the *Senn* tile layer's case. But it is perfectly obvious that in every one of these cases the peaceful picketing had occurred in the context of a Section 13 Norris-LaGuardia Act labor dispute, and this suggests that Justice Frankfurter had even abandoned the stand he had taken in the *Ritter* case. He admitted that "Unions obviously are concerned not to have union standards undermined by nonunion shops," and that "[t]his interest penetrates into self-employer shops." But he emphasized the fact that "some of our profoundest thinkers from Jefferson to Brandeis have stressed the importance to a democratic society of encouraging self-employer economic units as a counter-movement to what are deemed to be the dangers inherent in excessive concentration of economic power."

No doubt the Justice had become aware of a series of state court decisions, like *Bautista v. Jones* in California, where judges were openly expressing their belief that unions were going too far when they used economic coercion against small businessmen operating without any employees. There an almost sentimental concern was exhibited for the self-employed milkman, barber, plumber, service station operator, and, of course, the farmer, whom, it was feared, unchecked unionism might destroy. Indeed, the California court thought such people had a constitutional right to conduct their enterprises without interference from unions.

Properly to assess the full significance of these *Hanke* and *Cline* cases is a difficult task. Circumstances surrounding them suggest that they might have resulted from following the *Giboney* precedent. But that does not make sense, because it would not conceivably have been unlawful for *Hanke* and *Cline* to comply with the unions' peaceful picketing. The only other explanation is that the Supreme Court had finally come to acknowledge a state's power to enjoin peaceful picketing aimed at achieving an objective made illegal or contrary to public policy under state law. A later example of this was the Court's decision in *Plumbers' Union v. Graham* in 1953. There the Court allowed Virginia to enjoin picketing of a nonunion shop because that state's right-to-work statute made it unlawful to require membership in a union to secure or retain employment.

Thus, in order to side-step the *Thornhill* doctrine, all that a state would now have to do would be to declare the union's objective unlawful instead of making the picketing itself illegal. Furthermore, that objective would not have to be unlawful in the sense that the picketed person's compliance would make *him* a law breaker. Rather, the state would be free simply to make unlawful what the union was trying to accomplish and then to enjoin peaceful picketing directed at that objective. And if, in order to protect self-employed enterprisers, a state were thus left free under the Constitution to prohibit peaceful picketing within the context of a statutory labor dispute, then why would it not also be able to prohibit ordinary stranger picketing like that in the *Swing* case, involving the "beauticians'" union? For in many states public policy and law still regard stranger organizational picketing as beyond the pale. After all, once the Supreme Court had allowed states to declare illegal *some* objectives of peaceful picketing within the context of a Section 13 Norris-LaGuardia labor dispute, it is hard to see where the line could be drawn. Thus, the strategic retreat from *Thornhill*, foreshadowed in the *Ritter* case and tactically essential in *Giboney*, had in the *Hanke* and *Cline* cases become a complete rout. And finally there came the Court's 1957 decision in *Teamsters' Union v. Vogt, Inc.*, where it allowed Wisconsin to enjoin simple stranger picketing, thus fully acknowledging this and amounting, as the dissenters observed, to "formal surrender."

When in 1947 Congress passed the Taft-Hartley Act, introducing a series of unfair union labor practices, it had clearly intended to forbid certain secondary boycott pressures in the context of a statutory labor dispute, whether or not they were implemented by peaceful picketing. And when in 1951 the test cases arose before the Supreme Court, it became equally clear that the *Thornhill* doctrine was not going to prevent Congress from pursuing this course. Here again it is difficult to see how the Supreme Court's position can be explained on the basis of the *Giboney* case. Reflection on all of the Court's picketing decisions since and including that case indicates how very odd it is that a doctrine footed in the Constitution should be so consistently accommodated to the economic regulations of Congress and of state courts and legislatures. Perhaps the answer is that the *Thornhill* doctrine had finally become recognized by most members of the Court for the real aberration that it was. Undoubtedly it was one of the greatest pieces of folly the Supreme Court ever perpetrated.

But instead of scuttling the doctrine, why didn't the Court frankly confess error and overrule the *Thornhill* case? For if it was not apparent in 1940, by 1950 it had become only too clear that peaceful picketing by labor unions in any context was an integral part of a pattern of economic pressure that should be subject to regulation in accordance with prevailing legislative policies. The Supreme Court, however, does not easily acknowledge error. And although it is willing to get out from under by distinctions and qualifications that are palpably evasive, it will never risk the loss of face involved in admitting so soon that it had been wrong about the Constitution. Consequently the *Thornhill* doctrine still remains on the books. It remains as a monument to the Supreme Court's good intentions and, incidentally, as a warning to any state foolish enough to enact and enforce blanket legislation outlawing all peaceful picketing, regardless of the circumstances in which it occurs.

Thus after this tumultuous vagary epitomized by the brief life of the *Thornhill* doctrine, it is now clear that peaceful picketing by labor unions, for all practical purposes, is safely back within the reach of legislative regulation. This is where it belongs. There is only one remaining serious possibility. The Supreme Court may upset state prohibitions of peaceful picketing where unions employ that device in committing unfair labor practices under the amended NLRA. But this could only be upon the ground of maintaining the exclusive jurisdiction of the National Labor Relations Board pre-empted by Congress under the commerce clause.

RACIAL DISCRIMINATION

In 1944 the Supreme Court had occasion to use the 14th amendment of the Constitution for a different purpose, one closely allied to the protection of free speech. But apparently it preferred to side-step the constitutional issue in favor of a more technical and less explosive approach. This was a situation involving racial discrimination by unions in the administration of their internal affairs—a matter with which the California court had dealt squarely as a constitutional issue and which the Supreme Court could hardly avoid treating in that fashion much longer. It appeared that the locomotive firemen's brotherhood was bargaining with railroads to exclude black firemen from securing the advantages of seniority normally arising from the contracts between the railroads and the brotherhood.

It was clear that under the terms of the Railway Labor Act a majority of the firemen, who happened to be white, had lawfully selected the brotherhood as their bargaining representative in spite of the fact that this union excludes blacks from membership.

Under the present state of the law it is impossible to say that such discrimination on the part of the union is illegal. The act does require, however, that the bargaining representative selected in any unit must represent the interests of all workers in the unit. Since there was a substantial minority of black firemen, their interests were administered in the same collective agreements negotiated between the railroad and the union to govern the employment conditions of the membership. Now one of the most important items in railway labor agreements is that concerning seniority. Under previous agreements the black firemen enjoyed the advantages of seniority along with the white firemen. But the brotherhood made new agreements with the railroads advancing several white employees over the heads of blacks who had already established preferences, in many cases supplanting them with whites having less seniority. Two reasons apparently lay behind this step. One was that the union wished eventually to exclude blacks entirely from the unit in question. The other was that since blacks for some reason were not promotable to the job of engineer, it was thought appropriate to advance white firemen to seniority positions from which they could eventually be promoted to that job.

A black fireman named Steele brought suit in the Alabama courts requesting an injunction against the union and the railroad employing him, to prevent them from putting this new scheme into effect. When the Alabama court held that an injunction could not be issued, since all bargaining had been in strict compliance with the Railway Labor Act, the Supreme Court agreed to pass on the case as "one of importance in the administration of the Railway Labor Act." It then decided in *Steele v. Louisville and N. R. Company* that what the railroad and the union had agreed to do was an improper disregard of the black firemen's established seniority rights and could not lawfully be put into effect under the Railway Labor Act.

Chief Justice Stone, speaking for the Court, likened the bargaining power of the union to the lawmaking power of a state legislature, hinting obliquely that such power cannot constitutionally be used to prefer the rights of some over others on the basis of any arbitrary classification. But he made it plain that the Court had decided as it did because the union had violated the Congressional intention to have the chosen union represent without discrimination all employees in the unit for which it was bargaining representative, whether they were or were not members of the union.

While he conceded that unions might have rules of eligibility for membership, he could not conceive of Congress' placing complete bargaining power in the hands of a union selected by a majority of the employees in a unit, with the idea that such a union might then lawfully use its power to promote the advantage of union members at the expense of nonunion employees in the same unit. He made equally plain the Court's astonishment to find that any railroad would suppose it could enter into a collective agreement of this sort and expect it to be lawful. He thus implied that the railroad might have to compensate the black firemen who had in the meanwhile sustained losses under the new agreement. He did not broach the issue presented when a union enjoying exclusive bargaining rights secures a closed shop contract and then arbitrarily excludes certain employees in the unit from membership on the basis of race, creed, or economic belief. Yet on that very same day—December 18, 1944—the Court handed down *Wallace Corporation v. NLRB* wherein it upheld the Labor Relations Board's order designed to prevent precisely this sort of thing as an unfair labor practice on the part of an employer.

Justice Murphy apparently detected some circumlocution in the majority opinion, for while he concurred in the *Steele* decision, he came out boldly against "the cloak of racism surrounding the actions of the Brotherhood in refusing membership to blacks and in entering into and enforcing agreements discriminating against them." He thought that any construction of the Railway Labor Act allowing this practice would render the act unconstitutional—a sufficient reason in his mind for construing the act otherwise. He deprecated a decision "solely upon the basis of legal niceties" while the Court remained "mute and placid as to the obvious and oppressive deprivation of constitutional guarantees." He concluded: "Racism is far too virulent today to permit the slightest refusal, in the light of a Constitution that abhors it, to expose and condemn it wherever it appears in the course of a statutory interpretation."

He, no doubt, highly approved of a California decision appearing two weeks later in which the state supreme court, on square constitutional grounds, enjoined the operation of a closed shop contract secured by a union which would not admit Negroes to membership. In this case of *James v. Marinship Corporation,* a union of boilermakers and shipbuilding workers, chosen as bargaining representative in a large unit, had set up a "Jim Crow" union for black workers. They were refused admission to the brotherhood itself and were forced in its collective agreement with the employer, under pain of discharge if they did not comply, to join this auxiliary union and to pay dues. It is true that the California court approached this case somewhat conventionally. First, it stated the fundamental issue to be "whether a closed union coupled with a closed shop is a legitimate objective of organized labor." After this invocation of the illegal purpose doctrine, the court denied the legality of a monopoly which "affects the fundamental right to work for a living," observing that "the discriminatory practices involved in this case are, moreover, contrary to the public policy of the United States and this state," with specific reference to the 5th, 14th, and 15th amendments of the federal Constitution.

This might not seem a very sturdy avowal of constitutional guaranties against racism. But the court was not in a position to do much more than it did, since it could not exercise the same power of review over the private actions of the employer and the union which the Supreme Court can exercise over state legislative and judicial acts under the 14th amendment. In finding the illegitimacy of objective by recourse to the federal Constitution, however, the California court did all it thought possible to treat the practice in question as an offense under our fundamental law, making it plain that unions are too closely concerned with the control of opportunities for livelihood any longer to "claim the same freedom from legal restraint enjoyed by golf clubs or fraternal associations." And shortly thereafter the California court in *Williams v. International Brotherhood* reaffirmed this position even though it was not alleged that the labor union had a monopoly over all employment opportunities in the locality in question. In that case it was made clear that after the injunction issued, employers operating under a closed shop contract with a union would be free to deny employment to a black applicant whom the union had not "cleared," without first inquiring whether the union's discriminatory practice had ceased. For if it transpired that the black applicant had been denied membership because of his race, then the contempt sanctions of the court would be directed solely against the union. The recurrence of this distressing situation is no longer possible in plants falling under the federal jurisdiction, because of the Taft-Hartley proscription against the closed shop.

An even more acute situation has arisen with respect to the rights of blacks to join labor unions at all, even where their securing or retaining of employment does not depend on membership. New York has a civil rights law declaring that no labor organization shall deny a person membership or equal treatment by reason of race, color, or creed. In *Railway Mail Association v. Corsi*, a union of railway postal clerks limited its membership "to eligible postal clerks who are of the Caucasian race, or native American Indians." As the result of a test case the highest New York court held that the union was obliged to offer membership to otherwise eligible black applicants. The union appealed to the Supreme Court contending that the state law was unconstitutional under the 14th amendment. Its appeal was unanimously disallowed, Justice Reed implying that the union had a nerve to invoke one of the pro-black amendments to perpetuate discrimination against them. Thus the state could not be prevented under the Constitution from protecting workers from exclusion because of race "by an organization, functioning under the protection of the state, which holds itself out to represent the general business needs of employees." Here again the Supreme Court intimated that modern labor unions, existing under state or federal statutes and enjoying thereunder rights and privileges not accorded to private fraternal organizations and social clubs, must expect to be treated like public organizations.

This *Corsi* case was decided in 1945. In a 1946 case—*Betts v. Easley*—the Kansas Supreme Court went much farther in a situation of this type than any other court has yet gone. All of the Santa Fe Railway's employees in its Argentine shops in Kansas were eligible to vote in an election conducted under the Railway Labor Act to determine what labor organization should represent them in collective bargaining. As a result of the election, the Grand Lodge Brotherhood of Railway Carmen was chosen and designated as the bargaining agent. About 100 black employees in the Argentine shops then requested admission into the Lodge, but they were told by its officials that blacks could not become members and that a separate auxiliary lodge would be set up for them. They would pay their dues to this auxiliary lodge, the affairs of which would be conducted by the white lodge which in turn would represent all of the employees. The blacks were to have no right to attend meetings of the white lodge, to vote on its officers, or to have any voice in determining its policies. Thereupon the black employees sought to have the Grand Lodge enjoined from acting as bargaining representative until it abandoned its policy of excluding black employees from membership. The Grand Lodge contended that as a private organization it was free to admit to or exclude from membership anybody it saw fit and for any reason, noting correctly that this had always been the traditional view of labor unions. Furthermore, it argued that the blacks had had their day in court when they were allowed to vote in the election to determine whether the Grand Lodge would be selected as bargaining agent.

Now Kansas had a statute that declared that no labor union should be allowed to represent employees in that state if it "excludes from its membership any person because of his race or color." But this statute did not apply to any union representing railway employees and hence it did not control in this case. Nevertheless the Kansas court held squarely that the Grand Lodge's exclusion of black employees from membership was "repugnant to every American concept of equality under the law," "abhorrent both to the letter and the spirit" of the federal Constitution and "in violation of the Fifth Amendment." It reached this decision because "[t]he acts complained of are those of an organization acting as an agency created and functioning under provisions of Federal law," and it declared that the contention that such acts were "solely those of 'a private association of individuals' is wholly untenable."

Here the Kansas court came to grips with a far more fundamental issue than that involved in the *Steele* case previously discussed. There the black firemen were concerned only about the fact that the white union ignored seniority interests of colored employees to the advantage of junior white firemen. And the Supreme Court had merely insisted that even if the black workers were not members of the brotherhood, its duty as exclusive statutory representative of *all* the employees was to represent them fairly and impartially. Then in the *James* and *Williams* cases the California court was merely insisting that a labor union having a closed shop agreement with certain employers could not lawfully require black workers to join a

"Jim Crow" auxiliary, maintained solely to take the dues of colored employees, as a condition to their securing and retaining employment. But in *Betts v. Easley* the Kansas court faced up to the really basic problem in this area—whether a labor union exclusively representing under a statute all of the employees in a bargaining unit can lawfully refuse membership to any of those employees because of their race or religion.

There the black plaintiffs were insisting upon the right to participate in the affairs of the regular union. They had been met with the rejoinder that they had had their chance to vote at the election when the union was originally chosen as bargaining agent. But this answer was no good because in modern industrial relations the choice of a union is only the beginning. What the union does thereafter, and how it is run, are matters for continual membership participation. The selection of local officials, including the bargaining committee and shop stewards, is by voting within the local union. What the local union's position will be concerning policies to be pursued by the national union is a question for the members to determine by vote. All of these matters affect the interests of every employee in the bargaining unit, black or white. And the further argument that black employees in a bargaining unit could select their own union to bargain for them was also worthless, since the incumbent union chosen by a majority of the employees voting in a government-conducted election has *exclusive* bargaining rights for *all* of the employees in the unit, whatever their race or religion. There is no place under our modern labor laws for minority representation in collective bargaining. It is becoming increasingly plain that if labor unions are to serve a quasi-public function in affording collective representation to workers, and if they are to exercise powers and enjoy the protection conferred on them by legislation, then they must cease denying membership to applicants on the basis of race, religion, or national origin.

But whether labor unions must as a general rule admit otherwise eligible black applicants for membership will remain in doubt until the Supreme Court has spoken. So far it has said in the *Corsi* case that a state may constitutionally forbid such unions from denying applicants membership for arbitrary reasons. In *Terry v. Adams*—a 1953 case—it held that a southern state might not by default hand over the function of conducting political primaries to a private all-white organization called the Jaybird Club. And it had previously refused in *Rice v. Elmore* to review a federal appellate court's decision that the Democratic Party in South Carolina could not exclude blacks from voting in primary elections, even though that organization was not an official agency of the state. Practically, of course, the devices used in these two primary voting cases virtually disfranchised blacks.

The analogy between this situation in general politics and the black worker's exclusion from labor unions may be far-fetched, but the trend of the times seems to indicate otherwise. Certainly, to modern labor unions created or existing under legislation and endowed with great power and many privileges has been handed over the function of representing workers collectively. Indeed, they are sometimes said to be in effect quasi-public administrative agencies. When selected they have exclusive powers of representation in administering collectively all aspects of the employment relationship. Even when the black may secure employment, he is powerless to negotiate the terms of his employment if there is a union in the picture. Hence, it is apparent, in view of the terrific power and responsibilities conferred upon unions by statute, that there must be some way in which the black employee may have as much to say in making and guiding the policies of the union representing him as have his white fellow employees. The state of New York, says the Supreme Court, may accomplish this by compelling unions to admit otherwise eligible black applicants to membership. And the highest Kansas court takes the position that it is unconstitutional for unions to refuse membership to such workers. But what will happen when a state legislature has declared such conduct illegal or contrary to public policy and the highest court of that state does not share the Kansas court's views concerning the unconstitutionality of a union's acts in arbitrarily denying membership to blacks?

In 1957 this situation confronted the highest Wisconsin court, whereupon it upheld the right of a union to exclude blacks from membership. The circumstances behind this case make this Wisconsin decision seem very dubious. The bricklayers' and masons' union would not take otherwise eligible blacks as members. And these blacks, who were competent bricklayers and masons, were unable to secure employment on building projects unless they were members of the union. Of course, under the Taft-Hartley Act it is unlawful to make union membership a condition to securing employment; but practically it is almost impossible for nonmembers to secure work in the building trades where unionism prevails. The Wisconsin court recognized that the denial of membership to the black plaintiffs virtually excluded them from pursuing their trade. Now Wisconsin has a Fair Employment Code. But, unlike the one in New York, it has no teeth in it. In effect, all it says is that the "denial by some employers and labor unions of employment opportunities to [properly qualified] persons solely because of race, creed, color, national origin, or ancestry" causes "grave injury" to such workers. This statement of public policy was given no more legal effect than a resolution of the National League of Women Voters.

Nevertheless the black plaintiffs complained to the state Industrial Commission. This body "conducted an investigation, determined that the exclusion was solely on racial grounds, made a recommendation to the union that it admit plaintiffs to membership—which the union disregarded—and gave publicity to its findings." This, the court conceded, "is cold comfort to [the Negro plaintiffs] but it is all the legislature saw fit to provide." As for the effect of the 14th amendment, the court declared that it applied only to discrimination "by state action" and it relied on the Supreme Court's *Steele* case where Chief Justice Stone had said that the Railway Labor Act "does not deny to such a bargaining labor organization the right to determine eligibility to its membership." No reference was made to Justice Murphy's caustic observations concerning the constitutional implications of the *Steele* case under the 5th amendment; nor did the court so much as mention the Kansas decision in *Betts v. Easley.*

Here was retrogression with a vengeance. Surely the state legislature's expression of public policy in its Fair Employment Code meant something. And the Wisconsin Employment Peace Act established and maintained labor unions within the state, granting them considerable powers and affording them ample protection for the purposes of representing the interests of employees in organization and collective bargaining. Is it too great a strain to conclude, as did the Kansas court, that the discriminatory exercise of this delegated power by labor unions that have become quasi-public agencies is sufficiently a state act to be within the strictures of the 14th amendment? And even the Wisconsin court's decision itself might be such an objectionable state act. Indeed, it seems not implausible that on an appeal the United States Supreme Court might have answered these questions in favor of the black plaintiffs. Certainly the dissenting member of the Wisconsin court seemed to have no doubt of their rights under the Constitution.

These exclusionary practices of some of our modern labor unions seem glaringly out of joint with our times. They do not exist in any of the large industrial unions. Obviously our state and federal legislatures should deal directly with such discrimination precisely as they have done with similar monopolistic practices of business units under federal and state antitrust laws. In their dealings with employers, unions are unavoidably monopolistic in their controls over the available labor supply. But this should not mean that they should be free arbitrarily to prevent workers from securing employment or participating in the functioning of these government-fostered agencies now deemed essential to insure the full fruits of employment to workers in modern industry. Moreover, this policy of open membership should prevail, whether or not the securing of employment in any way depends on belonging to a union. Legislatures are the logical agencies of government to outlaw these anachronistic discriminatory practices. If they do not accept this responsibility, then it seems clear that our courts must do so. And if our state courts refuse to act in the absence of legislation prohibiting the arbitrary exclusion of workers from labor unions, then it seems clear that the Supreme Court has the power to force the unions to open their membership rolls in the name of the Constitution.

CHAPTER XII

THE ACT, THE BOARD, AND THE COURTS I

> No doubt an employer is as free as anyone else in general to broadcast any arguments he chooses against trades-unions; but it does not follow that he may do so to all audiences. The privilege of "free speech," like other privileges, is not absolute; it has its seasons; a democratic society has an acute interest in its protection and cannot indeed live without it; but it is an interest measured by its purpose. That purpose is to enable others to make an informed judgment as to what concerns them, and ends so far as the utterances do not contribute to the result. Language may serve to enlighten a hearer, though it also betrays the speaker's feelings and desires; but the light it sheds will be in some degree clouded, if the hearer is in his power. Arguments by an employer directed to his employees have such an ambivalent character; they are legitimate enough as such, and pro tanto the privilege of "free speech" protects them; but, so far as they also disclose his wishes, as they generally do, they have a force independent of persuasion. . . . What to an outsider will be no more than the vigorous presentation of a conviction, to an employee may be the manifestation of a determination which it is not safe to thwart. The Board must decide how far the second aspect obliterates the first.—Judge Learned Hand in *NLRB v. Federbush Co.*, 1941.

PRIOR TO ITS amendment in 1947, the NLRA of 1935, usually called the Wagner Act, was given fairly precise meaning in a multitude of cases by the National Labor Relations Board and in hundreds before the federal courts. An understanding of this Act is impossible without some familiarity with the high spots of this litigation. Hence the following account will indicate how the NLRB and the courts gave its provisions meaning, and it will describe in context the Taft-Hartley amendments.

Congress passed the Labor Management Relations Act over

President Truman's veto. This was the statute that is commonly known as the Taft-Hartley Act. It consisted of five main parts, or titles, and Title I was the new or amended NLRA. The other four titles were not a part of the NLRA and their significant provisions will be discussed separately in the subsequent chapters. While a great deal of the Wagner Act was left unchanged, some drastic innovations were added. First of all, the board was increased from three members to five. And the general counsel was made independent of the board, the power to issue complaints being lodged solely in his hands. No doubt this change was in response to charges that the board had been acting simultaneously as judge, prosecutor, and jury. As a result of this change the board's function became more judicial in nature. In view of the feeling of employers that the board had always leaned too far in the direction of organized labor's interests, it is possible that this change was also related to the introduction of a series of unfair union practices into the act. Thus perhaps an independent general counsel would be more likely to be objective about issuing complaints against unions than the board.

In Section 7 of the original act its whole spirit had been reduced to four lines of print. There it had guaranteed to employees the right to self-organization, to form, join or assist labor unions, to bargain collectively through representatives of their own choosing, and to engage in concerted activities for the purpose of collective bargaining or other mutual aid or protection. Into these words the board and the courts had read an extremely broad protection for all employees and for the organizational and bargaining activities of unions. Indeed, in their zeal they had gone so far that the organizational pressures of unions against workers as well as employers were virtually uninhibited. After all, the guts of the act—Section 8—was aimed exclusively at the prevention of employer interference with the autonomous organizational desires of workers. There was not a word about restraints upon unions.

The amended statute changed this. First of all, it narrowed the definition of employees, thus depriving certain categories of workers formerly protected under the Wagner Act of the benefits conferred by the NLRA. Then it expanded Section 7 by according to employees an additional right "to refrain from any or all such activities" as they had just been guaranteed the right to engage in. No longer would the unions be able to draw on this Section 7 to justify their exercise of economic coercion against employees to force them into organizations against their desire. Finally, specific sanctions against unions—a series of unfair labor practices of labor organizations—were included as Section 8 (*b*) of the act. A detailed description of these practices will accompany a discussion of the interpretation placed by the board and the courts on the unfair labor practices of employers, which remained substantially unchanged in the new act.

When the Wagner Act became law in 1935, there was a widespread feeling that it would be declared unconstitutional. In part this feeling rested on the conviction that Congress could not under the due process clause of the 5th amendment impose these drastic limitations on the traditional liberties of employers to manage their employment relations any way they saw fit. In part it was based on the belief that Congress could not validly delegate to an administrative agency the tremendous powers of making findings and issuing orders it had conferred on the NLRB. But the main case against its constitutionality was that Congress had exceeded its powers under the commerce clause. Ostensibly the act had been passed to do away with the interference caused by bitter organizational strikes with the movement of goods in interstate commerce. Perhaps the most obvious way to achieve this end would have been simply to forbid the strikes. But that would have frustrated the real purpose of Congress, which was to combat the deflationary effects of depression by encouraging the organization of strong unions with bargaining power sufficient to achieve better labor standards and high wages. According to the New Deal economists the consequent purchasing power would result in an inflationary spiral that would take us out of the depression. Therefore Congress chose to get rid of these bitter organizational strikes, so destructive to commerce, by eliminating their causes—the antiunion activities of employers. Thus the most serious obstacle to this plan was that the Supreme Court had traditionally taken a narrower view of Congress' power to regulate commerce, declaring that manufacturing and mining—the storm centers of union organizational drives—were local in their nature and not a part of interstate commerce.

But in April, 1937, the Supreme Court declared the Wagner Act constitutional when it decided *NLRB v. Jones & Laughlin Steel Corporation* and four companion cases by the close vote of 5-4. After these decisions, due process and freedom of contract took on a new look. And Congressional power, as well as the board's jurisdiction under the commerce clause, were ascertained in terms of whether or not labor strife at a particular plant or mine would have repercussions on the stream of commerce by adversely affecting the import of raw materials or the export of products between the states. Within a very few years it became apparent that practically all enterprise was under the board's jurisdiction, since our economy was now so interdependent that almost any strike resulted in the interruption of the influx or the export of materials or products between states. And the board, with the support of the courts, successfully claimed jurisdiction over employers whose businesses were very slightly connected with interstate commerce, as long as the need for assistance in organization was indicated. However, the Wagner Act board did not assert jurisdiction over the building industry. While one explanation of this could be that building was thought to be essentially local and not interstate in character, no doubt the building trades unions were more than able to take care of organization and collective bargaining without the intervention of the board. But right after the passage of the Taft-Hartley Act, the general counsel began to issue complaints charging the building trades unions with violations of the new unfair labor practices of unions. Because virtually all building depends upon materials shipped in from other states, there was never any doubt that the board had jurisdiction in these cases.

Nowadays it is taken for granted that the board may successfully assert jurisdiction over practically any enterprise, for it would be hard to name one that is not to some extent dependent on goods brought in from other states. Such comprehensive scope has proved to be a real embarrassment, since the board has neither the time, the personnel, nor the budgetary resources to handle the thousands of complaints and representation cases dumped in its lap. Moreover, coordinate with the growth of the board's power has been the development of what is called the doctrine of federal pre-emption by implication. What this means is that if Congress has acted with respect to the employment relations in a certain type of enterprise, either by guaranteeing the employees freedom of action to organize autonomously, by providing facilities for the handling of representation issues, or by forbidding certain unfair labor practices, then the states are precluded from intervening in such situations. Thus, a state may not by legislation or court action, or through an administrative agency such as a state labor relations board, do anything with respect to employment relations within its boundaries that the NLRB is empowered to do, or that the NLRA forbids or protects in Sections 7 and 8. For example, the employees of a small telephone company in Wisconsin split into factions over the issue of organization. The NLRB had never had occasion to consider this company's labor relations. Pursuant to a request, the state labor relations board assumed jurisdiction, held an election, and certified a union to the company. But the Supreme Court said that this Wisconsin action was void because the state board had unconstitutionally invaded federal territory. The same would have been true had the state board ordered the cessation of either employer or union conduct which was in violation of some provision in Section 8 of the NLRA.

The reason for this dog-in-the-manger attitude is the paramount importance of a consistent scheme of control with respect to matters over which Congress has asserted its authority. If the states were permitted to share with the NLRB control over subjects entrusted by Congress to the latter's jurisdiction, inconsistencies might occur. Insistence upon exclusive federal control is the only way to be sure this will not happen. The NLRA now provides in Section 10 (*a*) that the NLRB may cede to a state agency "jurisdiction over any cases in any industry (other than mining, manufacturing, communications, and transportation except where predominantly local in character)" as long as the state regulation is not "inconsistent with the corresponding provisions" of the NLRA or has not "received a construction inconsistent therewith." Moreover the NLRB announced that it would no longer take cases clearly within its jurisdiction unless the unit of industry involved is doing a certain amount of direct or indirect interstate business on a yearly basis, measured in dollar volume. To fill the resulting gaps several of the states proceeded to prohibit, either by local administrative or court action, or both, certain labor union activities involving violations of Section 8 (*b*) of the present NLRA. But in 1957 the Supreme Court declared that the states were powerless to deal with these cases falling within the NLRB's jurisdiction, unless their power to do so had been ceded to them under the provisions of Section 10 (*a*). And the same year, in unanimously holding that a teamster's local was an employer with respect to its own office employees under Section 8 (*a*), it went on to declare in a 5-4 decision that the board was powerless to decline jurisdiction over Section 8 (*a*) complaints filed against the union as employer.

The board took the position that it had the right to decline to assert jurisdiction over certain industries, such as hotels, private educational institutions, professional sports, private health care entities, symphony societies, law firms, and race tracks (all of which, at one time, the board did refuse to consider within its jurisdiction, and all of which, except for race tracks, it has now placed within its jurisdiction).

Congress has steadily increased appropriations to the board to enable it to discharge its representation functions more expeditiously; but unions have continued to complain of delays in the holding of elections, which delays allegedly enable employers to frustrate union organizing campaigns.

SUPERVISORY WORKERS

One of the hottest issues arising under the Wagner Act was whether or not supervisory workers were employees for the purposes of the act. Curiously enough, this was not finally settled by the Supreme Court until 1947, by which time it had become academic. All through the twelve years of the Wagner Act the board consistently held that foremen were employees for the purpose of sheltering them against unfair employer practices in Section 8; and early in its career supervisory workers were held to be entitled under Section 9 to organize and form unions for the purpose of collective bargaining. This decision aroused a storm of protest, the consensus being that foremen were essentially on the employer's side and that the board was dividing management against itself. A shift in the board's personnel then resulted in a change of policy on the reasoning that supervisory workers did not constitute a "unit appropriate for the purposes of collective bargaining" within the meaning of Section 9 (*b*). This was a complete misconception of that provision's purport. Then a further realignment of board membership again permitted foremen to organize and be certified under Section 9; and finally, in the *Packard* case of 1947, the Supreme Court held that this was proper. It is curious to note that during the period when the board was denying to foremen these Section 9 facilities, the New York state labor relations board certified a union of supervisory workers to one of Bethlehem Steel's plants in that state. Clearly that company was in interstate commerce and the New York board and courts justified their action by observing that since the NLRB had refused to consider the organization of foremen, they were merely filling the vacuum. But the Supreme Court said there was no vacuum and that the established federal policy during that period was that foremen's unions need not be recognized by any employer under the board's jurisdiction. Thus the state's action was inconsistent with this policy.

At any rate, foremen were employees in the conventional sense of being on the employer's payroll. But in a highly dubious decision the Supreme Court confirmed a board holding that Hearst Publications had to bargain with a union representing Los Angeles newsboys who were clearly not employed by Hearst in any conventional sense but were independent contractors. Then in the Taft-Hartley Act Congress obviated these embarrassing situations by declaring that individuals with the status of independent contractor were not employees under the act, and by specifically excluding supervisory workers. Thus while foremen remained free to organize and form unions, their employers were equally free to crush any such attempts by any of the retaliatory practices they were forbidden to use against ordinary unit workers. And even if the foremen did succeed in organizing, the employer was free to ignore their union, leaving them to strike if they wished to do so.

Oddly enough, throughout the Wagner Act days the board and courts uniformly regarded foremen as employers in another connection. That was where supervisors violated Section 8 in dealing with unit employees, even though management had specifically ordered them not to do so. Their unauthorized conduct was regarded as their employers' violations of Section 8. Indeed, the board and the courts occasionally pinned the anti-union conduct of local Chambers of Commerce on employers where speeches had been directed against the invasion of unions. On the other hand, under Section 6 of the Norris-LaGuardia Act, it was virtually impossible to hold a union responsible for any conduct of its national or local officials or members. Again Congress changed this in 1947 by applying the ordinary tests of the law of agency to determine responsibility of either employers or unions for the acts of others, declaring that "whether the specific acts performed were actually authorized or subsequently ratified shall not be controlling."

UNFAIR LABOR PRACTICES

The former Section 8 (1) of the Wagner Act, making it unfair for employers to interfere with, restrain or coerce employees in exercising the rights guaranteed in Section 7, remained unchanged in 1947. But it was now called Section 8 (a) (1). And this was to balance it with 8 (b) (1) which made it an unfair *union* practice to restrain or coerce employees in the exercise of Section 7 rights or to influence employers in their selection of *their* representatives for collective bargaining or handling grievances. Under the Wagner Act, Section 8 (1) had covered a terrific variety of situations before the board and courts. For the most part they were routine instances of espionage by employers against union adherents, threats against employees for engaging in union activities or blandishments for refraining therefrom, organizing municipal back-to-work movements, engaging professional strikebreakers, the systematic harassment of and interference with employees and outsiders who were attempting to start union organization, and allowing favors or facilities to a form of tolerated unionism while denying them to another not agreeable to the employer.

To recreate the atmosphere of the board's early work is impossible. It was faced with appallingly messy records. Its trial examiners took all sorts of conflicting testimony, highly emotional in content and much of it hearsay. Frequently the board's findings were not supported by a preponderance of the evidence. But under the act they did not have to be, the Supreme Court holding that as long as there was some substantial evidence sustaining them, they were acceptable. The board could not enforce its own cease and desist or other orders. That could be done only by a federal circuit court of appeals, whose judgment in turn was subject to review by the Supreme Court. Hence

judicial review was afforded to employers on such matters as
jurisdiction, due process as far as the fairness of the hearing was
concerned, the meaning of Section 8 (1), whether the board had
correctly apprehended a violation, and whether its findings and
orders were supported by evidence. If the board's order was
found to be proper, then the offending employer was compelled
to comply at the risk of being held in contempt of court. Perhaps it is too extreme to suggest that the federal courts of appeal
became, as one of their members once put it, "rubber stamps"
to approve what the board had ordered under Section 8 (1).
But in those early days there seemed little doubt that the Supreme Court was determined to give the board a free hand. The
board had been charged by Congress to allow labor to organize
throughout the country. It had a "hatchet job" to do, and the
Supreme Court was there to see that it was done!

A few of the outstanding cases will illustrate what occurred
under Section 8 (1). Interestingly enough, even before the Supreme Court was reconstituted in personnel by Roosevelt appointments the board suffered a temporary setback. A company
with 38,000 employees made a collective agreement with an
AF of L union on behalf of its members only, while board proceedings, initiated by a competing CIO union, were still pending. Before the board had completed its investigation, 30,000
of these employees had joined the AF of L union. The board
ordered the company to set aside this contract, apparently finding that it was arranged between the company and the AF of L
union, regardless of the employees' right to choose their own
bargaining representative. The board could not find that the
employer had dealt with a company-dominated union, since
AF of L unions are hardly in that category. But it did find that
the company had ignored the formalities of the act and had
made the contract without consulting its employees, thus influencing thousands of workers to sign up with the union which
had so rapidly succeeded in getting a good contract. In its opinion, the employer could not lawfully choose the union to represent any or all of his employees, regardless of their wishes ex-

pressed pursuant to the provisions of the act, thus setting at naught the policy that workers should be represented by unions of their own choosing. Apparently the company had done all this in order to side-step the CIO union, preferring to deal with the AF of L if it had to bargain collectively with either—a procedure quaintly called "sweethearting."

The Supreme Court, in *Consolidated Edison Company of N. Y. v. NLRB*, refused to enforce the board's order, chiefly because the AF of L union was not a party to the proceedings. Against the board's protest that this made no difference, the Court pointed out that in prior cases where contracts had been set aside under somewhat analogous circumstances, the unions had been found to be company dominated. This was not true here. Furthermore, the contract was advantageous to the employees covered—actual members of the AF of L union—and had achieved in the plant an industrial stability which would be completely disrupted if it were now set aside. Since the whole purpose of the act was to keep commerce on an even keel, this policy could best be served by letting things stay as they were, enforcement of the board's order inviting total disruption of the stability already established. For these reasons, the Court thought, its decision was imperative.

But none of these reasons answered the board's objection that the company had seriously interfered with independent and autonomous organization in the plant. The board remained unimpressed by the fact that so many employees had joined the AF of L union voluntarily, for it knew that they were naturally affected by the AF of L union's success in so promptly having achieved recognition and a desirable contract. All the board could see in the Court's decision was acquiescence in allowing an employer, through connivance with the union it preferred, to thwart the completely free choice by its employees of an exclusive bargaining representative. It knew that if the employees had been left to choose a representative under methods prescribed in the act, they still might have selected the AF of L union. But it also knew that they might have chosen otherwise, after having considered the merits of both competing unions. It simply objected to this opportunity for a completely free choice having been foreclosed by the employer's self-serving action, when matters pertaining to representation were none of his business under the act. And it wanted to afford an opportunity for a free choice by undoing the mischief and letting everyone really concerned—the employees and the two competing unions —start all over again pursuant to the proper procedure in the act.

From this account one might suppose that the board set too high a premium on the rights of the CIO union as an enterprise in itself, aside from the interests of the employees themselves. But many of the employees in the plant had preferred the CIO union; and, given equality of opportunity with the adherents of the AF of L union in the plant, they might have convinced a majority of their fellows to support their choice. They could not, however, compete with an accomplished fact. And the board's position that they should not have to do so may well imply greater emphasis on actual employee choice and less on the rights of competing unions, as such.

In any event, the Court subsequently modified its position in this type of case, upholding a board order that set aside a contract executed under similar circumstances. Eventually, Congress intervened during the war to deprive the board of its power to set aside contracts achieved in this fashion when it appeared that they had been in existence for a stated appreciable length of time and, because of the independent and un-dominated character of the contracting unions, there had been established stable collective bargaining in good faith. Possibly such a measure was justified to obviate the disruption of industry during a war. Yet it clearly remained so completely in conflict with the basic policy of the act as to invite employers openly to select the unions with which they preferred to do business.

The board also forbade under Section 8 (1) employer interference with solicitation by a union adherent among fellow employees on company property, although it acknowledged any employer's right to prevent such activity on company time. In these cases—*Republic Aviation Corporation v. NLRB* and a companion case decided in 1945—union employees had solicited memberships from fellow-workers on company premises during lunch time and in dressing rooms, as well as outside the buildings and in parking lots. The companies involved had rules against any solicitation whatsoever on their properties. Thereby they avoided the implication that they were discriminating against the unions in question. They argued that ordinary factories are different from lumber camps or company-owned mining towns, where contact with employees would be well-nigh impossible except on company land. They also contended that the board had no evidence indicating that the employees in question could not be solicited elsewhere and that it was substituting for such evidence its notions of convenience to the unions and its sophistication in dealing with union matters. But the Supreme Court concluded that the board's orders should be enforced. Reliance was placed on the board's judgment as to what was proper in view of the fact that after their shifts were over thousands of the employees peripherated for many miles in all directions in automobiles and they would have been hard for the union organizers to reach. But in 1956 the Court modified its position. It refused to enforce board orders that employers must cease denying access to company property by nonemployee union organizers soliciting memberships under otherwise similar circumstances. In this later group of cases, the Court recognized that while it might be difficult for the organizers to locate the employees after they had gone home, they were "in reasonable reach." At any rate, as long as the employer was not discriminatorily or coercively denying his employees the "exercise of their own rights," the Court said that the act "does not require that the employer permit the use of its facilities for organization when other means are readily available." Thus it is difficult to determine just how far the Court has backed away from the position it had taken in *Republic Aviation*.

In what appears to be a sharp contrast to this last utterance, the Court in between these two decisions upheld a board order that an employer should permit an outside union organizer to use a company hall for a meeting place in a company-owned southern town. This was *NLRB v. Stowe Spinning Company*, decided in 1949. The hall in question was the only local meeting place available. The company had loaned it to a lodge, whose leader was free to, and did allow other groups to use it. Indeed, he had given the union organizer permission to use it, but the company had countermanded this action because the union was trying to organize its employees. To the board this was discriminatory under Section 8 (1) and it ordered the company to undo its interference by letting the union use the hall. While the federal court of appeals thought the board could not even for a short time constitutionally give one person's property to another, the Supreme Court nevertheless enforced the board's order. In Justice Jackson's view the board's power was limited solely to ordering Stowe not to interfere with the lodge leader's personal disposition of the hall. Two other Justices dissented outright.

But a majority of the Court held that Stowe's action had been discriminatory and that it was essential to make the company let the union use the hall just as anyone else could. Otherwise it would be interfering with its employees' right to organize a union. Justice Murphy observed that "one of management's chief weapons, in attempting to stifle organization, is the denial of a place to meet," and he refused to "equate a company-dominated North Carolina mill town with the vast metropolitan centers where a number of halls are available within easy reach of prospective union members." In response to the company's argument that if it let the union use the hall it would be violating Section 8 (2), aimed at company-supported unions, this Justice answered that such could be the case only when the loan was a "facet in a pattern of domination found by the Board"; and if the NLRB found otherwise, the company's objection was disposed of. Far-reaching as this decision may seem, it does *not* mean that an employer is obliged to put his property at the disposition of union organizers. All it means is that in every respect touching his employment relations he must not discriminate against unions as such. Although he may lawfully shut his premises to all outsiders, if he nevertheless permits an independent union organizer to solicit members on company property and company time, then he must accord the same privilege to AF of L and CIO organizers. Perhaps the *Stowe* case goes even a little further, because there the evidence did not show that the company had ever permitted another labor union to use the hall. Indeed it seems doubtful if the Supreme Court would ever again go quite as far in enforcing a board order to permit the union use of company property.

FREEDOM OF SPEECH AND CAPTIVE AUDIENCES

One of the most interesting aspects of litigation under these Sections 8 (1) and 8 (a) (1) was the development of freedom of speech for employers in discussing unionism with their workmen. During the first years of the Wagner Act it was taken for granted that whatever an employer said to his men against unionism was a violation. However, in several cases before the board and the courts of appeal, employers kept maintaining that they should be allowed some latitude for discussing objectively the implications of unionism with their men, particularly in view of the complete freedom accorded union organizers to fill their heads with fantastic notions and to promise them the world with a fence around it if only they would join up. And when the Supreme Court handed down the *Thornhill* case, declaring that peaceful picketing was constitutionally protected free speech, consistency seemed to demand some scope for freedom of employers' expression of opinion. But if employers' interferences with their employees' right to organize were to remain statutory wrongs, then a strong argument could be made for maintaining that anything employers said against unionism constituted such an interference simply because of their relative economic position, and could therefore be prohibited. And just because interference of this sort is articulated through speech is no reason to lend it constitutional immunity, since violations of the antitrust laws by corporations and "We don't patronize" blacklists by unions—types of wrongs committed through communication—are clearly within the power of Congress to forbid. But the Supreme Court concluded that it must recognize some area of noncoercive discussion by employers, if for no other reason apparently than to compensate for the complete liberty of talking to employees that was enjoyed by the unions.

In *NLRB v. Virginia Electric & Power Company*, decided in 1941, the Supreme Court held that an employer's statements to his employees concerning unionism would not constitute a violation of Section 8 (1) unless on their face they showed evidence of coercion of the employees or unless, in accordance with findings of the board supported by evidence, they occurred in such close association with other acts of the employer violative of the act as to constitute a pattern of restraint and coercion. Later, the board found that this particular employer's statements had occurred in a context of coercion, and the Court then granted enforcement of the board's entire order.

But this case showed that there was an area within which an employer might talk frankly to his employees about what he regarded as the shortcomings of labor unionism, and employers were not slow in exploiting this possibility. To be sure, they were most interested in trying to dissuade their men from "going union" on the eve of board-conducted elections. And soon a rash of cases appeared where employers had read to their workers speeches carefully written by clever lawyers and had sent them mimeographed statements similarly conceived— communications designed to persuade them that unions were uneconomic, that they could not deliver what they promised, and, by a man-to-man discussion of practical economics including a casual disclosure of the firm's internal affairs, that everyone immediately concerned would fare better by voting "No union." In the same breath these communications assured the workers that the entire matter was in their hands, that they should all turn out and vote, that no penalty would be suffered by any employee however he voted, and that if a majority of those voting selected the union, the employer would abide by the result and do his best to live with it. In the meantime the employer had been particularly careful not to do anything that could be construed as interference, restraint, coercion, discrimination, or as being generally antiunion. Then, if the union lost the election and filed a charge based on the speech and letter, the board would issue a complaint and, after a hearing, would make findings and issue a cease and desist order based on a Section 8 (1) violation, incidentally setting aside the election and giving the union another try. But the circuit courts of appeal would not enforce these orders, pointing out that according to the Supreme Court the management statements, if not coercive on their face and not occurring in association with other conduct violative of the act, did not constitute evidence to sustain the board's findings.

As might have been expected, the employers began to push this new opportunity of defeating unionism to the limit. They did this by calling meetings of their employees on company time immediately prior to the election, thus depriving the union organizers of any opportunity to counteract any propaganda that might be spread. In *NLRB v. Clark Brothers Company*, where such a speech was made an hour before the board was to conduct an election between an independent and a CIO union, the company's vice-president delivered a speech against "outside unions," assuring the workers that they could vote as they pleased without fear of reprisal. Needless to say, the CIO lost and then filed charges under the act. The board found that the employer's use of a "compulsory audience" in itself constituted an independent unfair labor practice. And even though it conceded that "the speech itself may be privileged under the Constitution," it issued an order against the employer and set aside the election. In enforcement proceedings the board argued that Section 7 guaranteed employees the right "to determine whether or not to receive aid, advice and information concerning their self-organization," contending that "this right is violated whenever the employer utilizes his power to compel them to assemble and listen to speeches relative to matters of organization." Although the court of appeals thought this contention too broad, it enforced the order. Recognizing the employer's interest in presenting his views on unions to his employees, the court observed: "We should hesitate to hold that he may not do this on company time and pay, provided a similar opportunity to address them were accorded representatives of the union."

While there were other factors in the *Clark Brothers* case tending to support the board's order, the board regarded the decision as standing for the proposition that a "compulsory audience" was in itself a violation of Section 8 (1). Other federal courts of appeal rejected this notion, one judge declaring that "the First Amendment is concerned with the freedom of thought and expression of the speaker or writer, not with the conditions under which the auditor or listener receives the message." Then Congress used this *Clark Brothers* case, which had been handed down in 1947, as the basis for inserting Section 8 (*c*) into the NLRA when it passed the Taft-Hartley Act. Under that provision the expression "of any views, argument, or opinion, . . . whether in written, printed, graphic, or visual form, shall not constitute or be evidence of an unfair labor practice" under the NLRA, if it "contains no threat of reprisal or force or promise of benefit."

The effect of this Section 8 (*c*) was clearly to permit employers and unions to speak freely to employees about unionism under any circumstances, so long as there was no attempt in the communication by threat, coercion, or bribe to influence the audience. Of course the board and courts continued to recognize employer violations of Section 8 (*a*) (1) when employers interrogated workers about union membership, thus implying hidden reprisals, or otherwise made statements restraining or coercive in context. But by 1953 a majority of the board began to take a fairly broad view of what employers were permitted to say. Speeches were allowed that seemed to imply that if the employees elected a union, then certain promised benefits would not be forthcoming or the plant might have to shut down or move away. One president compared the "blight of unionism" to the chestnut blight, except that it had blighted New England industry instead of killing the chestnut trees. In answer to a question from the floor whether the company intended to close the plant if the union won the election, he responded: "Unfortunately if I made the proper answer to that thing—no, I'm sorry, I cannot make any comments on that particular question—it's against the law." Here the clear implication seemed to be that if the workers chose the union, the plant would shut down, since that is the only illegal answer the speaker could have made. Yet the board found no violation of the act.

After Section 8 (*c*) was adopted, the board's captive audience doctrine seemed doomed. Yet the board came up with a similar notion. This was to the effect that if an employer gave a noncoercive speech to a captive audience without affording the union the same facilities for replying, then while the speech itself was protected, denial of the union's chance to reply in the same manner constituted a violation of 8 (*a*) (1). While this conception was supported by one federal court of appeals, others denied its validity, declaring that the employer could not have his right to speak to his employees, in his own hall on his own time, conditioned by any obligation to provide a hall and speaking facilities to the union and possibly as well pay his employees for listening to the union's reply. In any event the board abandoned this new version of the captive audience doctrine.

Then it devised a new ·rule—that if either the employer

or the union spoke to the employees en masse within 24 hours
of the election, then the board would set aside the election
as invalid if its results were in favor of the party violating
this rule. In one case the application of this rule resulted in
setting aside an election that the union had lost and immediately allowing another election that the union won. The employer was furious. He refused to meet with the union after its
certification, claiming that the second election was a nullity
because it had been conducted within a year of the previous
one, contrary to a provision in the amended NLRA. But in
Section 8 (a) (5) proceedings the board held this a refusal to
bargain. Then the federal court of appeals enforced its order,
one judge dissenting because he thought this a circumvention
of Section 8 (c) and its guaranty of the employer's constitutional
right of free speech. The board had wisely not attempted to
regard this captive audience speech within 24 hours of the
election as a violation of Section 8 (a) (1), for it is doubtful
whether the Supreme Court would have upheld it. What it did
do was simply to establish rules in connection with its power
under Section 9 to hold elections and to declare the first election
invalid because the employer's meeting violated the 24-hour
rule. Thus, the statutory provision against a second election
within a year became inapplicable because the first election had
been held to be invalid.

COMPLAINTS AGAINST UNIONS

In 1947 the new board had to begin passing upon complaints
filed against unions under Section 8 (b) of the amended NLRA.
Most of the traditional union organizational techniques such
as direct contact with employees, promises of all sorts of benefits, and even peaceful picketing, would not be regarded as
8 (b) (1) (A) violations. That subsection forbids a union to restrain or coerce employees in their right to engage in or refrain
from self-organization. Consequently its sanctions are reserved
for cases where unions use physical force or threats thereof

against employees. They also apply in some instances where the coercion was economic pressure that was illegal because of another provision directed against requiring union membership as a condition to securing employment. Again this type of violation occurs where during a strike or otherwise the union coerces employees into engaging in conduct that is not protected by Section 7 against disciplinary penalties imposed by employers. All through these cases it became manifest that under the new agency test, unions could be found responsible for the acts of their agents quite as easily as employers. This was about as radical a change from the Wagner Act as the introduction of the unfair union practices themselves.

Naturally Section 8 (*b*) (1) contained no restriction of a union's right to strike during the course of bargaining. That is a normal union activity in which it may freely engage unless it has agreed not to do so. Moreover, part of the folklore of labor law has always been that the right of organized employees to strike and the employer's right to lock them out are co-ordinate and complementary aspects of the same basic freedom. But this is no longer so. For it has been held that an employer, by locking out his employees, may have unlawfully interfered with their organization or may have refused to bargain with a union in good faith. In 1956, the Supreme Court decided what is called the *Buffalo Linen Supply Company* case. There a truck drivers' union had been engaging in multi-employer bargaining with eight linen supply companies. The eight concerns bargained as a single unit with the union, and the resulting contract would be signed by all of them and by the union. During the negotiations for a new contract, the union called a strike at one of these eight plants, whereupon the other seven companies promptly shut down. The union filed charges insisting that the association members were behaving illegally. But the board held otherwise, saying that the nonstruck companies did not have to wait like sitting ducks to be picked off one at a time at the union's leisure. Against such "whipsawing" pressure the other members of the group might concertedly lock out the employees because this was not a premeditated interference with Section 7 rights. Rather it was legitimate economic self-defense in the collective bargaining process. And the Supreme Court agreed, apparently concluding that the pattern of multi-employer bargaining had been established for all purposes.

What would happen if the UAW called a bargaining strike at General Motors and all the other automobile companies that bargained with that union instantly locked out their employees? The strategy of such action is obvious. For if the union can force concessions from the struck employer, it can then use such concessions as the basic pattern of its demands against all of the other automobile companies. Obviously while these initial concessions at General Motors were being forged out in the heat of economic conflict, all UAW members except those striking GM would continue to work while their employers stood by waiting for the blow they knew was inevitable. By thus forcing the union's hand throughout the industry, the other automobile manufacturers could demand and secure participation in bargaining out the pattern of concessions. The only drawback to this possibility is that so far the automobile industry has not been set up on a multi-employer bargaining basis, and the analogy to the *Buffalo Linen* case thus fails. Consequently, even though the NLRA in express terms neither forbids nor permits lockouts, the chances are that the board, possibly with the Supreme Court's approval, would under such circumstances declare this technique to be a violation of Section 8 (*a*) (1) of the act.

Under Section 8 (2) of the Wagner Act, the original board had been ruthless in breaking up company-fostered and dominated unions. Of such were the old employee representation plans that were created throughout so many industries as the employers' answer to the growing popular demand for collective representation of workers. The board regarded any employer assistance to employees in forming independent unions as evidence of domination. It ordered that such assisted unions be disestablished, and it required the posting of notices that this had been done, coupled with statements that these independents would no longer be recognized. Nor would it let them appear on the ballot in a subsequent election. This was true even though an alleged independent union had not even been made a party to the Section 8 (2) proceedings. Sometimes the board seemed to make some awfully close calls, where the only "evidence" supporting its findings was that company assistance had been rendered in the past, and also, the fact that the alleged independent was affiliated with neither the AF of L nor the CIO. But as a rule, the Supreme Court in these cases upheld the board's disestablishment orders. It was perhaps natural that the old board never ordered the disestablishment of affiliated unions, even though there was evidence of company assistance or "sweethearting." It regarded such cases as Section 8 (1) violations and ordered the employer to cease recognizing the union pending an election to determine the choice of the employees as a whole. The *Consolidated Edison* case, described earlier in this chapter, was an instance of this. There, however, the Supreme Court refused to enforce the board's order.

However, under the amended NLRA the importance of 8 (*a*) (2) has declined. A provision in the new statute bars the board from treating unaffiliated unions any differently from those tied in with the AF of L, CIO, or any of the small chains of really independent unions affiliated with CUA or Confederated Unions of America. Consequently the board may not now disestablish any independent union on the basis of testimony that would be thought insufficient to order the disestablishment of an affiliated union. A curious consequence is that the board will now order disestablishment wherever it finds company domination, even of an affiliated union. However it is more likely only to forbid an employer to bargain with an assisted union until it is certified after an election.

Discrimination in hiring or "tenure of employment" or any "term or condition of employment" by an employer in order "to encourage or discourage membership in any labor organization" had been made an unfair labor practice by Section 8 (3) of the Wagner Act. But this subsection had a proviso, and this became one of the chief battlegrounds of the Wagner Act. For it was recognized that employers remained free under the act to enter into agreements with labor unions that were not "established, maintained or assisted" by any unfair labor practice, which required as one "condition of employment" membership in the union, so long as the union was duly qualified as bargaining representative under Section 9. In those days there was no federal bar against the closed shop. Thus a contractual condition of securing employment in the first place might lawfully be membership in a union.

Naturally the chief use of Section 8 (3) was to prevent discharges, demotions, or other reprisals against employees because of their union activities, and to put a stop to refusing employment of applicants because they had been active in unionism. Under its remedial power in Section 10 (c), the board ordered the reinstatement with back pay of employees who had been thus discharged. And if the employer's violation of Section 8 (3) were demotion or some other adverse action less than discharge, the board ordered the employer to rectify matters with any necessary monetary adjustment to make the employee whole. Needless to say the board also ordered the employer to cease and desist from such violations in the future.

A much closer case arose when an employer denied employment to applicants in the first instance because of their interest in unionism. Of course, it was generally acknowledged that this was a violation of Section 8 (3) and that a cease and desist order was appropriate. This was a variant on the old yellow dog contract and Congress had clearly intended to prevent its continuance in any form. Difficulty arose, however, in connection with the board's remedial power under Section 10 (c). In a case of this sort the board would issue not only a cease and desist order; it would also require the employer to undo his violation by hiring the applicant, with pay from the time he had been refused a job. Thereupon whether or not Congress had empowered the board to create the contract of employment where none had previously existed became a crucial constitutional issue, as well as a matter of considerable practical importance. The part of 10 (c) that was involved authorized the board "to take such affirmative action, including reinstatement of employees with or without back pay, as will effectuate the policies of this Act."

In 1941 the Supreme Court decided *Phelps Dodge Corporation v. NLRB,* and there it indicated that the board's powers were very broad indeed. While it was hiring men, this employer had turned down two otherwise eligible applicants for jobs simply because, as the board found on the evidence, they were active labor unionists. Thereupon it was ordered to cease and desist and to "instate" these two men into jobs, with reimbursement for the wages they had lost through denial of employment. And, as it usually did in reinstatement cases, the board made allowance in its "back pay" order for any money these men might have earned elsewhere in the meantime. A majority of the Supreme Court enforced this order.

Now reinstatement of discharged men was a basic modification of the employer's traditional freedom of contract. Nonetheless it was a step that Congress clearly thought essential to combating antiunionism. Nor was it so drastic an innovation when it appeared that these reinstated employees at all times had been acceptable in every way except for their interest in organization. But compelling the employer to hire applicants for jobs seemed revolutionary. For it imposed a contractual relationship where none had theretofore existed and under circumstances that suggested no terms or standards of employment to govern its inception. Furthermore, Congress had seemed to indicate the extreme limit of its authorization of power in providing even reinstatement with back pay by expressly mentioning this remedy. Thereby it was apparently implied that it wanted no misunderstanding as to how far it was empowering the board to go in taking affirmative action. It was widely believed to be very unlikely that Congress would expressly have authorized the board to impose the employment relationship where none had existed before if this power had been sought while the act was under consideration.

And it seemed extraordinary to suppose that Congress would have given this mere administrative agency a blank check of such proportions to be filled in according to the vague standard of what it might think necessary to "effectuate the policies of this Act."

On the other hand an astonishingly strong case can be made for the board's position—so strong, indeed, that in the Taft-Hartley amendments there was no attempt to change it. Admittedly the practice in question violated Section 8 (3) and hence was subject to a cease and desist order. But that sanction was not effective, as the following illustration will show. Suppose an employer in staffing his plant rigorously rejects all applicants with union records. He continues this policy while the board is processing a complaint against him. He continues it after the board has ordered him to stop, for the board's order is not self-executing. Indeed, he continues it while the board is seeking the enforcement of its order by a federal court. Not until the court's judgment enforcing the order comes down must this employer stop this practice. But by that time presumably he has his plant fully manned. He can then afford to promise that he will not do it again. However, the fact remains that he has perpetrated a massive violation of the act's basic policy and in effect has built up a barricade against unionism. How else could this employer be made to comply with this basic policy other than by compelling him to undo what he had done? The only way the board and the Supreme Court could see was to make him hire with back pay the applicants for employment whom he had rejected because of their union interests, even if in order to make room for them he had to let out other employees subsequently employed.

Counsel for Phelps Dodge had suggested to the Court that the clause in Section 10 (c), "including reinstatement of employees with or without back pay," marked the extreme limit set by Congress to the board's authority to order affirmative remedial action. But a majority of the Court were not disturbed by the fact that the rejected applicants had not been employees of the company when they were discriminated against. For they read the act's definition of employees to include virtually all workers. And noting that the act prescribed reinstatement as the appropriate correction for discriminatory discharges, Justice Frankfurter euphoniously observed that since experience had demonstrated "that discrimination in hiring is twin to discrimination in firing, it would indeed be surprising if Congress gave a remedy for the one which it denied for the other . . . a differentiation not only without substance but in defiance of that against which the prohibition of discrimination is directed." The company's counsel said this was exactly what Congress had done. It had not directed the board "to take such affirmative action as will effectuate the policies of this Act." Rather, it had empowered the board "to take such affirmative action, including reinstatement of employees with or without back pay, as will effectuate the policies of this Act," thereby carefully limiting its grant of authority by declaring in effect that the board might even reinstate discharged employees and make them whole. But Justice Frankfurter rejected this argument, declaring: "To attribute such a function to the participial phrase introduced by 'including' is to shrivel a versatile principle to an illustrative application." He found no justification for "such a casuistic withdrawal of the authority which, but for the illustration," Congress had clearly given the board, adding that the "word 'including' does not lend itself to such destructive significance."

No doubt Justice Frankfurter's rhetoric convinces all who agree with him anyway, and it is a persuasive argument for

the quasi-legislative action that the Court took to round out
Section 10 (c) with a symmetry it is hard to believe Congress
carelessly overlooked. Certainly Justice Stone, for the dissent,
could find no hint in the debates and committee reports that
Congress thought "it was giving the Board a remedial power
which few courts had ever assumed to exercise or had been
thought to possess." He remarked that authority for "so un-
precedented an exercise of power is not lightly to be inferred,"
adding that in view of the use of the participial phrase "as a
definition and enlargement" of the board's authority to take
affirmative action, "we cannot infer from it a Congressional
purpose to authorize the Board to order compulsory employment and wage payments not embraced in its terms."

Many lawyers thought that Justice Stone was inconsistent
because he had written the Court's opinion in the case enforcing
the board's order where an employer had reached a complete
collective agreement with a union and then refused to sign it,
holding that he must do so. That was held a violation of the
employer's duty to bargain in good faith under Section 8 (5),
and there also the board had acted on the authority granted it
in Section 10 (c). But the two cases are clearly distinguishable,
their only common element being that in each the board took
"such affirmative action" as would "effectuate the policies" of
the act. Nevertheless, it is Justice Frankfurter's reading of Section 10 (c) that has survived. For Congress made no attempt in
the Taft-Hartley amendments to qualify the board's assumption
of authority to "instate" rejected applicants for employment.
While this no doubt meant that the majority decision in the
Phelps Dodge case made good sense, perhaps it also implied
that our legal system can digest almost anything with the passage of time.

Still another significant aspect of the board's power under
Section 10 (c) arose in the *Phelps Dodge* case. The company had
also discharged several employees because of their union activity, most of whom had secured the same type of employment

elsewhere. Counsel contended that the board had no power to order their reinstatement because its power was confined to reinstating employees who, in Section 2 (3), were defined to include an individual whose work has ceased because of a current labor dispute or any unfair labor practice, "and who has not obtained any other regular and substantially equivalent employment." Here Justice Frankfurter observed that since the board's power under Section 10 (c) had already been shown not to depend on the participial reference to employees and their reinstatement, it had full authority to exercise its discretion in this situation. He refused however to concede that the definition in Section 2 (3) was definitive. He and a majority of the Court did disagree with the board on one item, holding that the board could not award back pay to a wrongfully discharged employee who had deliberately refused to secure work elsewhere. Since only actual losses should be made good, he said, "it seems fair that deductions in back pay should be made not only for actual earnings by the worker but also for losses which he wilfully incurred." And he dismissed as unjustifiable the board's plea that the administrative task placed on it by this ruling would be intolerably burdensome, arguing that in any event it would be offset not only by "the minimization of damages" but also by "the healthy policy of promoting production and employment,"—sentiments with which three of his brethren violently disagreed.

Occasionally situations arose where the board's resourcefulness was sorely tried and at the same time employers were innocently caught between the upper and the nether millstones. In *NLRB v. Star Publishing Company*, the employer had recognized the American Newspaper Guild, CIO, as the bargaining representative for all its employees in the circulation, business, and advertising departments of its newspaper. Dave Beck, then an international representative of the Teamsters Union, AF of L, claimed jurisdiction for his union over the circulation department employees. These twenty employees unanimously voted to remain in the Guild and their employer abided by their decision. Thereupon Beck's teamsters refused to transport the employer's newspapers to their distribution points.

Now strikes and other pressures by outside unions against employers who continued to bargain with recognized or even board-certified labor organizations had been held by the Supreme Court to be lawful labor disputes and not enjoinable under the Norris-LaGuardia Act. And of course nothing in the Wagner Act forbade such concerted activity. Thus in this particular case the publisher either had to capitulate to Beck and his teamsters or shut up shop, since his CIO circulation employees were unable to distribute the papers. At his wit's end he replaced them with Beck's teamsters and the papers were promptly distributed. But then of course, the Guild struck, and filed charges with the board under Section 8 (3). The board found a violation and ordered the employer to reinstate the discharged employees and to recognize the Guild as their representative. The federal appellate court reluctantly enforced this order, as it had to do, one of the judges pointing out that the employer had "endeavored to live up to the letter and spirit of the Wagner Act . . . and that its violation was solely because of the very serious dilemma" into which it had been thrust. Another judge observed that the employer's argument that he was "subjected to great hardship" should be submitted to Congress, but until the law was changed, the courts had no option but to enforce the board's orders in such cases.

That was in 1938. In the 1947 amendments Congress afforded relief by making it an unfair labor practice in Section 8 (b) (4) (C) for any union to force an employer to bargain with it if another labor union had been certified as the representative of the employees in question. Late as this change was in coming, it was even then incomplete and it would not have helped in the *Star Publishing* case; for it would not apply in any situation where an employer had recognized the incumbent union without having forced it to an election so that a board certification could be obtained.

But in another series of cases the board's ingenuity was more happily applied. In *NLRB v. Mackay Radio & Telegraph Company* a union of telegraphers called a strike for better terms of employment—what came to be called an economic strike. Acting within its rights the company replaced these strikers and continued business until the strike was broken. On their return to work, the company took back all but five of the strikers. These latter were informed that the replacements for their jobs during the strike had been promised permanent employment—the only condition upon which they would fill the jobs. So far the company was in the clear, since it had become established law that an employer may replace economic strikers permanently if he acts in good faith. However, in Section 8 (3) proceedings the board found it more than coincidence that the five permanently replaced strikers had been the most active union proponents. It concluded that Mackay's refusal to take them back was really because of their union activity, and it ordered their reinstatement with back pay from the time they sought to return to work after the strike. The Supreme Court recognized a violation of Section 8 (3) in this discriminatory refusal. It dismissed as irrelevant and inaccurate under the act the company's contention that they had ceased to be employees when they went on strike.

As a corollary to its consistent rule that an employer may permanently replace economic strikers if this is done without discrimination, the board has held that he must regard them virtually as applicants for re-employment on a preferred waiting list when jobs later open up. For if jobs do open up and in filling them he passes over such replaced strikers—assuming, of course, they have stated a desire to come back—the board is likely to conclude that his reason for such oversight was their union activity and to infer a violation of Section 8 (3). On the other hand the board does not recognize an employer's privilege permanently to replace employees who walk out on what is called an unfair labor practice strike. Thus, if an employer provokes a strike by substantial violations of Section 8, he may replace such strikers for the duration of the strike. But at its end he must take back the strikers, even if he has to fire the replacements to make room for them. Should he fail to do so, the board will find him guilty of violating Section 8 (*a*) (3). Thereupon it will reinstate the workers with appropriate back pay and no loss of seniority.

Still another in-between category occurs where employees go out on an economic strike during which the employer substantially violates Section 8, thus converting it to an unfair labor practice strike. Then the settled board practice, with judicial approval, is to permit the employer to retain such replacements as he had made after the strike began and before he violated Section 8. But any replacements he may have hired after he committed the unfair labor practice during the strike, he may not retain so as to bar the return of that many strikers. How the board determines under such circumstances which of the strikers are entitled to return to work is one of those matters of administrative expertise that is best left to the imagination.

PROTECTED VERSUS UNPROTECTED ACTIVITY

Perhaps the most colorful aspect of Section 8 (3) is that concerned with the two categories of protected and unprotected activity. Under Section 7 employees may engage freely in concerted action to promote organization and collective bargaining, and Section 13 guarantees the right to strike. The presumption is that all such conduct is protected against employer reprisal, and if it occurs in a plant under federal jurisdiction, against state prohibition. Originally the board assumed that it had complete discretion under Section 10 (*c*) to reinstate with back pay employees who were discharged for union activity even though they had engaged in outrageously offensive conduct which ordinarily would have justified their discharge. But in *NLRB v. Fansteel Metallurgical Corporation* the Supreme Court held otherwise. There the employer had engaged in a series of unfair labor practices, and his employees, anxious to organize with an affiliated union, began a sit-down strike in which they seized the plant buildings and excluded management. Such conduct was of course unlawful. And eventually many of these employees were punished by the state of Illinois. During the sit-down seizure counsel for the company discharged all those sitting in (trespassers) through a megaphone, neglecting at the time to address this formality at those equally guilty employees who were not inside, but who brought supplies to the garrison—the aiders and abettors, as they were called. When the strike was over the company refused to take back most of the trespassers and the aiders and abettors. Whereupon, in Section 8 (3) proceedings the board ordered their reinstatement with back pay. There was no question that the employer had violated Section 8 prior to the sit-down seizure and that in taking back a substantial number of the offending employees, it discriminated in denying re-employment to those who had been the most active union adherents.

The Supreme Court in 1939 denied enforcement of this order of reinstatement. And it denounced the sit-down seizure as "a high-handed proceeding without shadow of legal right." Thus was there summarily dismissed much of the then current defense of sit-down strikes that was issuing out of academic quarters, as a justifiable protection by the workers of their jobs. Obviously the Court feared placing a premium on resorts to force and the bypassing of the elaborate parliamentary recourses afforded the employees in the NLRA. Also it disagreed with the board's contention that within the meaning of the act the strikers remained employees, so that the board automatically had power to reinstate them. Chief Justice Hughes acknowledged that the NLRA protected the right of employees to engage in concerted activities in promoting self-organization and collective bargaining against employer reprisals. But, he said: "The conduct thus protected is lawful conduct." And when the employees resorted to an illegal seizure of the plant to force the employer's hand, "they took a position outside the protection of the statute and accepted the risk of the termination of their employment upon grounds aside from the exercise of the legal rights which the statute was designed to conserve." With specific reference to the board's remedial powers under Section 10 (*c*), he said: "The authority to require affirmative action to 'effectuate the policies' of the Act is broad but it is not unlimited." In response, the board contended that the question of whether reinstatement "would effectuate the policies of the Act [was] committed to the decision of the Board in the exercise of its discretion" as long as it was not "arbitrary, unreasonable or capricious." And to this Chief Justice Hughes replied: "We think that a clearer case could hardly be presented and that, whatever discretion may be deemed to be committed to the Board, its limits were transcended by the order under review."

Justice Stone disagreed with this limitation on the board's discretion. He took a distinction between the so-called "sitters-in" and those who had aided them. Believing that under Section 10 (*c*) the board's power of reinstatement was confined to employees, whether or not they were on strike, the discharge of the "sitters-in" for justifiable cause had placed them in his view beyond the board's power to help. But as to the "aiders and abettors," who had not been formally discharged for their lawless conduct, he thought that since they were still employees within the meaning of the act, the board had power to reinstate them. "Whether that power should be exercised," he declared, "was a matter committed to the Board's discretion, not ours." Justices Reed and Black dissented. The former expressed a fear that under the Court's ruling an employer who had good cause for discharging an employee might safely fire him for any cause whatsoever, thus acquiring immunity from violating the provisions of the act. And he gloomily predicted: "Friction easily engendered by labor strife may readily give rise to conduct, from nose-thumbing to sabotage, which will give fair occasion for discharge on grounds other than those prohibited by the Labor Act."

Here a considerable principle was at stake. On a few occasions the board itself had denied reinstatement in the face of unfair labor practices by employers because of violence it had considered inexcusable. But the board firmly believed that Congress had entrusted it with the discretion to judge and weigh each situation, regardless of the circumstances, in accordance with the basic policies of the act, and with the power to translate its discretion into the remedy it deemed most essential. Clearly the board members were not impressed by the argument that the unlawful strikers had engaged in conduct rendering future employment relations between them and Fansteel intolerable for the simple reason that that company had voluntarily taken many of them back. Hence they somewhat reasonably concluded that the company was using the illegal sit-down as an excuse to weed out the most pro-union employees, thus circumventing the act and getting away with it. No doubt the members earnestly believed that what appeared to them to be only an imposition on the employer was far less serious than his palpable defiance of the act's basic policies. As for the lawless employees themselves, any supposed condonement of their conduct by reinstatement would be more than outweighed by the punishment they had received from the state of Illinois for their illegal behavior.

In retrospect, however, it is impossible to deny that the *Fansteel* case exerted a salutary influence. Nevertheless it was occasionally carried to extremes. Thus, it is hard to understand why employees who went on strike because of disagreement with the employer over the meaning of a seniority provision in a collective agreement should be held to have engaged in unprotected activity. Certainly the board did not think so since it had ordered their reinstatement after they were discharged. But the Supreme Court denied enforcement of its order, with Justice Roberts observing: "The Act does not prohibit an effective discharge for repudiation by the employe of his agreement, any more than it prohibits such discharge for a tort committed against the employer." Nor was it altogether easy to perceive why the Supreme Court should disagree with the board's decision that a strike by sailors on a ship tied up at a wharf in Texas was protected activity, basing its disagreement simply on the fact that the ship's home port was in Philadelphia. To be sure, under a federal statute a concerted refusal of sailors to obey orders while their ship was absent from its home port was mutiny; but the board argued in vain that this was only technical mutiny and far less serious than a sit-down seizure. In a 5-4 decision the Supreme Court simply noted that the board must learn to accommodate the policies underlying the NLRA to those of other federal statutes; and if Congress saw fit to retain the mutiny act on the books, then sailors could not lawfully strike except when the ship was in its home port, no matter how orderly and otherwise lawful their conduct might be.

Perhaps more understandable was *C. G. Conn, Ltd. v. NLRB,* decided in 1939. There the employer had asked his employees to work overtime during the busy season so that he would not have to hire more men. A number of them concertedly refused to work after 6 P.M., although they were willing to continue on their own terms. Thereupon the employer laid off all those who would not agree to his terms. And although he subsequently took some of them back, to four he denied re-employment. When the board ordered their reinstatement in Section 8 (3) proceedings, a federal court denied enforcement because of their insubordination. The board had found that their concerted refusal to work after 6 P.M. was a strike and thus protected activity. But the court viewed this inference as a conclusion not binding upon it. Conceding that the employees had their choice of either continuing to work overtime while they negotiated, or to strike outright, either of which course would be protected activity, the court observed: "They did neither, or perhaps it would be more accurate to say they attempted to do both at the same time." Noting the "numerous variations of the recognized legitimate strike, such as the 'sit-down' and 'slow-down' strikes," the court observed: "It seems this might be properly designated as a strike on the installment plan." And it went on to say: "We are aware of no law or logic that gives the employee the right to work upon terms prescribed solely by him." Hence the court thought the employer was justified in discharging the employees for what amounted to insubordination.

However, during World War II the board itself inaugurated a stricter view of this protected activity. Thus in the *American News Company* case an employer and a union representing his employees agreed upon a wage increase which, under wartime stabilization regulations, could not be put into effect without War Labor Board approval. Becoming impatient at the WLB's delay in passing on the increase, the union membership went on strike to force the employer to grant it immediately. Thereupon the employer treated them as discharged and refused to reinstate them. Nor would the board order him to do so. It concluded that the employees' concerted misconduct in attempting to compel their employer to break the law was beyond the pale, even if it was intrinsically lawful and neither violent nor tortious. Likewise in the *Thompson Products* case the board denied reinstatement to a group of CIO employees who struck to compel their employer to recognize their union, when he was already obliged under the act to bargain with an independent union that had been certified to him by the board as exclusive representative of his employees. As a board member put it: "There would be neither moral, legal, nor practical justification for our requiring employees to respect our certifications if we were unwilling to respect them ourselves."

Perhaps the most important development in this direction occurred in the *Scullin Steel Company* case of 1946. There the board upheld an employer's refusal to reinstate strikers who had walked out in violation of a no-strike clause in a collective agreement. To be sure, this was a logical outgrowth of the Supreme Court's decision in the *Sands* case where employees had struck merely to impose their interpretation of a contract provision. But even here the board was careful to specify that the employer must also not have been in breach of the agreement, that the strike must not have been provoked by any unfair labor practices, and that the employees were not refused reinstatement because of their union membership. However, it was not until 1956 that the Supreme Court in *Mastro Plastics Corporation v. NLRB* held that engaging in a strike in violation of a "no-strike" clause is protected activity if the strike was provoked by substantial employer unfair labor practices. Nonetheless, three members of the Court dissented from enforcement of the board's reinstatement order because they thought that the strikers had ceased being employees in view of a noncompliance with the 60 day notice rule in Section 8 (*d*) (4). This will be discussed in Chapter XIII in connection with good faith bargaining.

The *Atlantic Towing Company* case shows how far the courts have invaded any discretion the board may have thought it still had in this area. At an AF of L union meeting, an employee declared that the company's general manager had urged the representative of a rival union to "beat" the AF of L to signing up the company's employees. This was a serious charge, for it imputed to a responsible company official a violation of the NLRA. Apparently it was also false. When he heard about this statement, the company's general manager fired the employee who made it, declaring that "he would not have a liar working for the company." There appears to have been some question whether the employee involved had been aware of the falsity of his charge when he made it. In any event, the board held that free discussion at a union meeting must be regarded as protected activity, and it ordered the employee's reinstatement with back pay. While the federal appellate court at first decided to enforce this order, it later changed its mind. On a rehearing it denied enforcement, and this whether or not the employee knew the statement to be false when he made it. Bearing in mind the lack of education and background that many union members have, coupled with the high feelings and emotional tension aroused at union meetings and bargaining sessions, this decision seems extraordinary. At this level surely the board could be trusted to decide whether or not strong language or even false statements uttered in hot temper could be regarded as protected conduct. Thus it reinstated a member of a union committee who was discharged because at a bargaining session he challenged the employer's honesty in keeping his books, asserting that he had had experience as a bookkeeper and knew that accounts could be juggled to show a loss. Of course, the board would presumably not afford this protection to an employee who was discharged for cursing or insulting a supervisor during the course of the day's work in a shop. It carefully reserves the protection of the act for such incidents when they occur during the course of legitimate concerted union activity. Indeed, it is doubtful if the new board would reinstate a striking employee who was discharged for obscenity or possibly even for strong language on the picket line.

Nice distinctions have constantly been drawn by the board in this area. An employee of a well-known chocolate manufacturer was discharged for having written and published a union resolution severely condemning his employer's actions in connection with a milk strike of dairy farmers. This statement was regarded by the employer as a grave injury to its business. Nevertheless the board ordered the employee's reinstatement; and a federal appellate court enforced its order. Judge Learned Hand declared that "so long as the 'activity' is not unlawful, we can see no justification for making it the occasion for a discharge. . . . [a union] may subsidize propaganda, distribute broadsides, support political movements and in any other way further its cause," even if such activities harm the employer, adding that "the statute forbids him by a discharge to rid himself of those who lay such burdens upon him," as long as nothing expressly illegal has been done.

On the other hand, enforcement was denied by the court when the board ordered reinstatement of employees who had been discharged because they had initiated a consumers' boycott against their employer's product in order to combat his antiunionism. This conduct was not illegal in itself and it followed a traditional pattern of union economic self-help. In this case, the board confessed that it was not free "to measure con-

certed activity in terms of whether the conduct is wise or fair, or
satisfies standards which we think desirable." Conceding that
the employer might be correct when he stigmatized the employees' conduct as "unjust and disloyal," just as a good deal
of labor union concerted activity no doubt is in the heat of
economic conflict, the board observed that in the absence of
proof that the boycott was not peaceful or its objectives improper, it could "find no authority to regard the concerted
activity involved herein as unprotected." Nevertheless, said the
Court, a wrong had been done the company when its employees,
"while being employed and paid wages," engaged in a boycott
to prevent the sale of "the very thing their employer is paying
them to produce." It added that the employer was not required
"to finance a boycott against himself." Those observations would
have been more to the point had the employees not been out
on strike when the boycott was maintained.

In the meantime the board was becoming more strict in its
scrutiny of protected activity, partly because of the changing
political scene and also, no doubt, because the federal courts
were refusing to enforce many of its orders of reinstatement.
The case of *Electrical Workers Union v. NLRB* introduced a
curious turnabout here. The employees of a television station
in North Carolina went out on strike and distributed handbills
on the picket line, talking down the station as an incompetent
producer of mediocre and poor transcriptions and implying
that the employer regarded the locale as a "second-class community," unworthy of anything better. In Section 8 (*a*) (*3*) proceedings the board decided that this was unprotected activity.
They did not find that the distribution of these handbills was
illegal but only that it was "hardly less 'indefensible'" than acts
of physical sabotage." However, it unrealistically rested its
conclusion on the fact that this attack on the TV station was
made independently of the labor dispute and was not a part of
the concerted activities envisioned by the act. Consequently it
dismissed the complaint as to these employees. Then the union
appealed and the court decided that the board had incorrectly

applied the law and had misconceived its authority to reinstate. The indication was that concerted union activity must be regarded as protected activity under the act unless it was actually unlawful. Certainly the court dismissed as untenable the board's criterion of "indefensible" as a criterion of determining loss of protection.

The Supreme Court, however, reversed this judgment and sent the case back to the board for proper disposal. It thought that "insubordination, disobedience or disloyalty" were plainly adequate grounds for discharge—certainly if they were dissociated from ordinary concerted union activity. And Justice Burton called attention to a 1947 amendment of Section 10 (*c*) —the grant of the board's remedial power—which read: "No order of the Board shall require the reinstatement of any individual as an employee who has been suspended or discharged, or the payment to him of any back pay, if such individual was suspended or discharged for cause." He plainly thought that the record in this case showed that the employees were discharged "for cause," because of their disloyalty. And he went on to declare that even if the attack by these employees on their employer's business were to be treated as a concerted activity "wholly or partly within the scope of those" protected in the NLRA, "the means used by the technicians in conducting the attack have deprived the attackers of the protection" of the act.

One novel feature of this television case was the appellate court's judgment that the board had not sufficiently exercised its power under Section 10 (*c*) to order the reinstatement of discharged employees. From the early days of the Wagner Act the effect of judicial review had been to put a brake on the board's tendency to find employer violations of the act whenever it could and to issue remedial orders on the basis of such findings. The assumption was that the board would always find a violation if it was possible to do so, no doubt because it read the statute as a command to promote unionism in every conceivable way. Hence it was also assumed that if the board dismissed a complaint filed under Section 8 against an employer, then that complaint must indeed have been groundless. In other words, the whole point of judicial review before enforcement was to provide insurance against too enthusiastic prosecution of complaints by the board against employers. Consequently it was surprising to see a federal court tell the board that it had not gone far enough in pressing a Section 8 (*a*) (3) complaint against an employer.

Perhaps the television case is unusual, merely because it was the first conspicuous instance when the board was slower than the reviewing court to recognize an employer's violation of Section 8. However, with the introduction of unfair union practices in the amended NLRA, reversals of board dismissals of complaints against unions have become routine. For in these cases the general apprehension was that an administrative board originally set up to promote the interests of labor unions might naturally be reluctant to lend itself easily to prosecuting complaints against them under the new Section 8 (*b*). And this proved to be the case after the Taft-Hartley amendments in 1947. In any event, in order that the authoritative meanings of the various provisions in Section 8 (*b*) might be established by the courts, it became essential that board dismissals of complaints filed against unions should be treated as final orders and thus be subject to judicial review. Hence the board had by now become reconciled to judicial orders requiring it to process previously dismissed complaints in accordance with the law as the judges had interpreted it.

Thus, since the early days of the Wagner Act the nature of protected activity in labor disputes and the board's power to reinstate with back pay have undergone drastic changes. As a result employers later enjoyed fairly broad powers, through the threat of discharge, to insist that their employees should remain within tolerably civilized limits when they are engaging in concerted activities or otherwise pressing union demands.

However there is one final observation to make concerning

protected and unprotected activity under the NLRA and this has nothing to do with the original Section 8 (3) or Section 8 (a) (3) of the new act. Throughout the country, state courts and labor boards had become impatient with what they regarded as the inadequate protection of employers against harassing labor union conduct. Hence they frequently attempted to prohibit such conduct, either by injunction or by enforcing local labor board cease and desist orders issued under state acts. As a result, they occasionally prohibited union conduct at plants under the federal jurisdiction, which the Supreme Court believed to be conduct protected under Section 7 of the NLRA or within the Section 13 guaranty of the right to strike. Under the doctrine of pre-emption, any state prohibition in the federal arena of conduct allowed by Congress is unconstitutional as an invasion of the national domain. An illustration from a leading case will show how nicely these lines have been drawn.

At the Briggs-Stratton plant in Wisconsin the members of an AF of L union invented a method both ingenious and effective of exerting economic bargaining pressure against their employer. They did not wish to strike, because that would mean that their wages would stop. Furthermore, it would enable the employer to close up and sit tight to see if he could outlast them. What they did was to call a series of 27 previously unannounced work stoppages over a period of five months in 1945 and 1946, their excuse being that the workers were to attend impromptu union meetings. While never very long, these stoppages were of sufficient duration and so timed that they threw production completely out of kilter. Instead of disciplining the employees, Briggs-Stratton filed a complaint with the Wisconsin Employment Relations Board under a state act making it an unfair labor practice for employees "to engage in any concerted effort to interfere with production except by leaving the premises in an orderly manner for the purpose of going on strike." The state board issued a cease and desist order which the highest Wisconsin court enforced. Thereupon the union appealed to the Supreme Court on constitutional grounds, since the plant was clearly operating in interstate commerce. Then, in *International Union, UAW, AF of L v. WERB*, decided in 1949, the Court in a 5-4 decision upheld Wisconsin's power to stop this practice.

The issue, as Justice Jackson put it, was simply "whether Congress has protected the union conduct which the state has forbidden." He noted that the employer, probably advisedly, had refrained from discharging any of the employees and thus exposing himself to a Section 8 (3) charge under the NLRA. Yet he concluded that the issue raised in this situation was similar to such cases and he used court precedents in cases denying enforcement of NLRB orders promulgated under Section 8 (3) to show that such concerted insistence by employees upon working on their own terms was unprotected activity. When the union contended that this was a type of strike and was therefore protected under the Section 13 guaranty of the right to strike, Justice Jackson disagreed. Obviously this was no more a strike than the "installment plan" program of the employees in the *C. G. Conn* case, where the employees concertedly refused to work overtime despite orders to do so. When Justice Jackson was taxed with the definition of a strike in Section 501 (2) of the Taft-Hartley Act, which included "any concerted slowdown or other concerted interruption of operations by employees," he stated that Congress had not intended by this language to broaden the protection of Section 13 guaranteeing the right to strike as protected activity. Rather, it was indicating the circumstances when a strike form of concerted refusal to work would be illegal in an attempt "to enforce what the Act calls unfair labor practices" of unions in Section 8 (b) of the new NLRA—"a definition plainly enough . . . designed to enable the Board to order a union to cease and desist from a strike so made illegal, whether it consisted of a strike in the usual or conventional meaning or consisted of some of the other practices mentioned in the definition." And so he went on to demonstrate that what the employees were doing in the Briggs-Stratton plant was not one of the unfair union labor practices forbidden in Section 8 (*b*) of the NLRA. Therefore, since this conduct was neither protected nor forbidden by Congress, it fell within the area that the states might legitimately regulate and prohibit.

From the foregoing account of the career of the National Labor Relations Act before the board and the courts, it is plain that government regulation of practical labor relations is no simple matter. After a stormy beginning, the application of the Wagner Act became fairly routine and the meanings of the statute's provisions ultimately evolved into workable rules. Perhaps the Taft-Hartley amendments were intended to clear the air and introduce a balance lacking in the original act. But their impact on the first part of the NLRA has not appeared to be drastic. However, a pursuit of their effect in the remaining sections of the act should indicate the nature of the change they wrought, and this is the aim of the ensuing chapter.

CHAPTER XIII

THE ACT, THE BOARD, AND THE COURTS II

> But it is urged that some employees may lose by the collective agreement, that an individual workman may sometimes have, or be capable of getting, better terms than those obtainable by the group and that his freedom of contract must be respected on that account. . . . The practice and philosophy of collective bargaining looks with suspicion on such individual advantages. . . . But . . . advantages to individuals may prove as disruptive of industrial peace as disadvantages. . . . Such discriminations not infrequently amount to unfair labor practices. The workman is free, if he values his own bargaining position more than that of the group, to vote against representation; but the majority rules, and if it collectivizes the employment bargain, individual advantages or favors will generally in practice go in as a contribution to the collective result.—Jackson, J., in *J. I. Case Co. v. NLRB,* 1944.

WHEN THE Wagner Act was passed in 1935, closed shop contracts between unions and employers were fairly common. Under such a contract the employer could hire only union members. And anyone in his plant at the time he signed the contract who thereafter refused to join, he was obliged at the request of the union to discharge. Indeed, it was quite possible that the union might deny membership to an individual already employed when the closed shop contract was signed and thus secure his discharge as a nonmember. More common perhaps were less rigorous contracts under which the employer remained free to hire whom he wished. But after a hiring the employee would be required, as a condition of retaining employment, to join the union within a prescribed period. This was the so-called union shop.

UNION SECURITY

In 1935 these union security or compulsory unionism arrangements were generally viewed as perfectly lawful, and Congress recognized this fact in the Wagner Act. As a proviso to Section 8 (3), which made it unfair to "encourage or discourage membership in any labor organization," it declared that nothing in the act or other federal laws should "preclude an employer from making an agreement with a labor organization" which was not "established, maintained, or assisted" by any Section 8 conduct, "to require as a condition of employment membership therein," as long as the union was a proper representative of employees within the meaning of Section 9. What this proviso did was to create an area of immunity for the employer so that he could live up to the commitments he had made in a valid closed or union-shop agreement. Thus, in the Wagner Act Congress did not declare such union security contracts to be generally lawful and permissible. That was clearly a matter of state law even then. All Congress had done was to make it quite clear that it was not going to allow an employer to be held in violation of Section 8 (3) simply for living up to the terms of any such contract.

Surely this seems uncomplicated. But like so many matters connected with law, it turned out not to be. Its first test before the Supreme Court was in *NLRB v. Electric Vacuum Cleaner Company*, in 1942. There the employer had a single written contract with several AF of L craft unions. An oral side agreement provided that all new employees hired would have to join the appropriate craft union. So far everything was in strict compliance with the NLRA, and, in effect, the parties had a union-shop arrangement for newly hired employees only. Then the CIO electrical workers' union—the old UE—began an organizational drive. In order to thwart this development, the employer and the AF of L representatives inaugurated a joint pressure movement to sign up *all* nonunion employees in the plant to prevent their defection to UE. Indeed, the employer shut down the plant to hinder further UE "proselyting" and to enable the AF of L unions to "get their lines in order." A few days later UE notified the employer that a majority of the employees had signed up with the CIO, and thereupon the employer reached a hurried oral agreement with the craft unions to reopen the plant on the following Monday, announcing publicly that "only those employees who are members of the crafts under contract with us will be employed." A month or so later the employer and the craft unions entered into a written closed-shop contract. On complaint of those employees who were not taken back because they did not belong to the AF of L, the board issued an order declaring the employer's refusal to reemploy them to be discriminatory under the act. This order the court refused to enforce because of what it regarded as the valid closed-shop contract with the AF of L.

On appeal the Supreme Court upheld the board and enforced its order, basing its decision on a curious line of reasoning. Justice Roberts was the sole dissenter. There could be little doubt that the employer vastly preferred to deal with the AF of L unions and that he had been "sweethearting" with them all during this period. Apparently, however, he was a little too coy for his own good, because he left the final clinch until after the rival suitor had appeared on the scene. Thus he made it possible for the Court to reason that the AF of L unions had been "assisted" unions, within the meaning of the words of exception in the Section 8 (3) proviso. And if that were true, then the closed-shop agreement was invalid and it did not furnish immunity to the employer from the penalty for his refusal to take back nonmembers of the AF of L. Hence such refusal was discriminatory under the act.

Now it seems fairly apparent that when Congress spoke of unions "established, maintained, or assisted" by acts amounting to Section 8 unfair practices, it referred to company created or dominated unions under Section 8 (2). Obviously no AF of L union is company created or dominated. Consequently it seems reasonable to suppose that the Supreme Court and the board had gotten off on their left feet and were just plain wrong in construing the Congressional intent. Nevertheless, the fact remains that this employer had finally done everything he could to cooperate with the AF of L and to help it keep out the UE. Such conduct arguably was a violation of Section 8 (1), just as all "sweethearting" is, although the Court had failed to acknowledge this in the "sweethearting" case discussed in the preceding chapter—*Consolidated Edison Company of N. Y. v. NLRB.*

But that was before the Court's personnel had been changed. Justices Reed and Black had dissented in that case, and now they had a majority of the Court behind them. Therefore, since the evidence seemed to show that the AF of L unions had been "assisted" by the employer to keep out the UE, and as this assistance was violative of Section 8 (1), then the closed-shop contract was invalid—and the employer lost his immunity under the Section 8 (3) proviso, even if the contract was with a union that clearly was not "established, maintained, or assisted" within the meaning of Section 8 (2) of the Act. Whether this result was a fulfilment or a denial of Congressional intent remains a matter of opinion. One thing, however, was clear. The Supreme Court had changed its direction with a vengeance.

On the whole, during the Wagner Act days few difficulties arose with respect to the employer's immunity from Section 8 (3) charges under the proviso. One situation, however, split the Supreme Court wide open. There an employer was beset by the rival claims of an independent and a CIO union, each claiming representational rights in his plant. Finally the CIO offered to withdraw Section 8 (1) and (2) charges against him, if he would consent to a board-conducted election on the understanding that the winning union would get a closed-shop contract. Eager to be taken off the spot, the employer agreed. Thereupon the CIO union withdrew its charges, the board held an election, and much to the CIO's surprise, the independent union won. It was promptly certified to the employer by the board as exclusive bargaining representative of his employees.

In compliance with the previous understanding the employer then entered into a closed-shop contract with the independent union which, in turn, refused membership to several staunch CIO supporters, and requested their discharge as nonmembers.

When the employer complied with this request, they filed Section 8 (3) charges. The case might never have become a *cause célèbre* if the board had simply ruled that there could not be a closed shop and a closed union at the same time and place under the act's policies, although even that would not have been easy to establish without compromising the employer's Section 8 (3) proviso immunity. But the board took the occasion to resurrect the old charges against the employer, to cancel its certification of the independent, to declare it a company-dominated union and disestablish it, and then to order the reinstatement of the discharged CIO employees with back pay. And in *Wallace Corporation v. NLRB,* the Supreme Court in 1944 upheld the board and enforced its order. The four dissenting members of the Court bitterly assailed what they plainly regarded as the board's perfidy in so lightly treating its own certification and they openly regarded their colleagues as equally guilty of sharp practice in approving what the board did.

For the majority, Justice Black explained that the board had allowed the consent election as a routine method of expediting its burdensome work, but in his view it would be bad policy to concede, as the dissenters argued, that an estoppel of this sort could stand between the board and the acquittal of its public duty to fulfil the policies of the act. Justice Jackson vociferously contended for the dissent that it was bad policy to deprive the employer of his immunity under the Section 8 (3) proviso after he had contracted with a certified union. The majority's decision depended on board findings that the employer knew ahead of time that the independent was going to deny membership to the CIO employees after the closed-shop contract was signed, and that the independent had really been company fostered all along. They agreed with the board that this was an unwholesome situation, which could be cured only by finding the employer guilty of unfair labor practices, since the Wagner Act contained no sanctions against unions. Of course, the weak spot in the board's position—and hence that of the majority of the Court—was that the board had actually certified the independent after the election. Certainly this case left a bad taste in the mouth. Also it seemed most unfortunately to place a premium on the employer's inquiries into internal union affairs in order to find out what they planned to do with union security if it were agreed to in the contract. And this was a development that was potentially more unwholesome than the situation the board was trying to cure.

A somewhat related situation turned up before the board in the *Rutland Court* case. There the employer and the union had signed a closed shop contract. A couple of months before it expired, two of the employees started a drive for a different union. Getting word of this defection, the contracting union deprived them of membership and then secured their discharge because they were no longer members. The board ordered reinstatement of these employees with back pay, finding that the employer knew that the union had deprived them of membership because of their activities in behalf of a rival union at a time when the current contract was drawing to a close. The board devised the *Rutland Court* doctrine to enable employees in a bargaining unit to use the democratic process among themselves as a means of securing different union representation when it was practicable and might be felt to be necessary. And several of the federal appellate courts gave it full approval, refusing to recognize the employer's immunity under the proviso in Section 8 (3) proceedings. Certainly the *Rutland Court* doctrine had the sympathetic support of almost all impartial observers in the labor relations field. But when it first came before the Supreme Court in 1949 it was summarily rejected as an attempt "to permit the board under the guise of administration to put limitations in the statute not placed there by Congress." That was in *Colgate-Palmolive-Peet Company v. NLRB*. Justices Reed and Burton dissented because, as they stated: "The use of the closed-shop privilege to interfere with the free exercise of the laborers' choice does not seem . . . to be within the purpose of the Labor Act." The whole point of the case was that the board had interpolated a modification of the Section 8 (3) proviso's immunity for employers under a union security agreement, which Congress had not put into the statute. Thus the board was diminishing the immunity as Congress had provided it for employers—a thing it had no power to do.

This decision of the Supreme Court was most astonishing. Yet it was academic in every respect except in so far as the company was saved from having to make a back-pay adjustment, and the contracting union was saved from losing face. This was because while the case was pending, the Taft-Hartley Act had made it an unfair labor practice for unions to secure the discharge of an employee under such circumstances. Hence a majority of the Court had no qualms about scuttling what was without doubt one of the most admirable devices the board had conceived.

It is curious, however, that Justice Black, who had written the opinion in the *Wallace Corporation* case and was a staunch supporter of the board's administrative ingenuity, should have voted with the majority to repudiate this *Rutland Court* doctrine. Indeed it was he who went to extreme lengths in the *Algoma Plywood* case, also decided in 1949, to assert that as a matter of the board's "settled administrative interpretation" the Wagner Act proviso of Section 8 (3) had legalized union security contracts so that a state law forbidding such contracts could be brushed aside under the doctrine of federal pre-emption as in conflict with the NLRA. As Justice Frankfurter, who spoke for a majority of the Court in that case, indicated, all Congress had obviously done in the 8 (3) proviso was to recognize that valid union security contracts existed and, he argued, it was a palpable error to imply that the board either had or could change the law by generally legalizing such contracts. The point of interest in these three cases is this—Justice Black's readiness to recognize the board's administrative ingenuity in modifying

Congress' intent when it would help certain unions, and his inability to appreciate this quality when the immediate consequences were not to his liking.

THE 1947 AMENDMENTS TOUCHING UNION SECURITY

In 1947 when Congress amended the NLRA, it drastically modified this Section 8 (a) (3) proviso. First of all, it withdrew completely the employer's immunity from liability under Section 8 (a) (3) for refusal to hire a nonmember of a union in accordance with the terms of a closed-shop contract. In effect, indeed, this outlawed the closed-shop contract. But it retained the immunity where the employer and the union had entered into a valid union shop contract requiring membership in the union as a condition of continued employment. That is, after the signing of a valid union contract, old employees who had not within 30 days tendered to the union the regular dues and initiation fee might be discharged. And where such a contract existed, upon the employment of a newly-hired worker, he or she had to tender such dues and initiation fee within the prescribed time or risk being fired.

At first Congress required that a majority of the employees actually in the bargaining unit should signify their approval in a board-conducted election before such a contract could lawfully be entered into. However, this requirement was soon dropped when it became obvious that practically all the elections went overwhelmingly in favor of the union shop. It had probably been expected that most employees would vote against union security and that the great expense of such elections would prove to be an investment against increased union strength. But when it transpired that most employees wanted the union shop, these elections proved to be an embarrassment to employers. For otherwise they might have refused to agree to something they could contend was contrary to their employees' wishes. Congress also stated that the employer's immunity under a union-shop contract would be lost if he had reason to believe that an employee discharged for failure to join the union had not been offered membership on the same terms generally applicable to others, or that membership had been denied or terminated by the union for reasons other than his failure to tender the periodic dues or initiation fee uniformly required from the rest of the employees.

And this was not all. In its amendment of Section 14 (*b*) Congress stated that nothing in the act should be construed as allowing the "execution or application" of union security agreements in any state in which such agreements were prohibited by law. Thus Congress was here deliberately recognizing the right of a state to forbid union-shop agreements in plants under federal jurisdiction, as long as such plants were within the physical boundaries of that state. Thus, suppose a corporation with plants in thirty states executed a master agreement with a union to cover the employees in all such plants, and some of these plants were in six states having so-called "right to work" statutes, which forbade union security agreements. In so far as the agreement applied to the plants in those six states, it would be illegal under the local laws. Certainly it would not furnish the employer immunity under the 8 (*a*) (3) proviso for discharging employees in the plants so located for refusal to join the union.

In a consolidation of three cases arising out of Arizona, Nebraska, and North Carolina, the constitutionality of these "right to work" statutes was assailed. The Supreme Court's decision, handed down in 1949, recognized the right of the states to pass such laws. Speaking for the Court Justice Black took notice of the retreat from the position that the social and regulatory legislation of states could be declared unconstitutional as a denial of due process of law. This had begun in 1934, and, continued Justice Black, the Court "has consciously returned closer and closer to the earlier constitutional principle that states have power to legislate against what are found to be injurious practices in their internal commercial and business affairs, so long as their laws do not run afoul of some specific federal constitutional prohibition, or of some valid federal law." Justice Rutledge questioned whether a state could go so far as to prohibit strikes by union employees who did not choose to work with nonunion people, but he did not challenge the states' right to prohibit union-shop contracts.

Undoubtedly these statutes, which now exist in about seventeen states, were really intended to govern the execution and application of collective agreements. But the highest Virginia court, in a decision of questionable wisdom, held that their statute governed an ordinary business contract between a council of trade unions and a printer. Wishing to have its magazine strictly "union made," the council asked the printer to undertake its publication, stipulating that he must employ only union workers on it. Eager to secure the job, the printer requested his one nonunion employee to join the typographical union, but he refused to do so. Consequently the printer fired him, hired a union replacement, and got the contract. The Virginia court held that both the printer and the trades union council had violated the statute and that they were jointly liable in damages to the discharged employee. One can argue that the council should not have been held liable unless it had insisted upon union membership as a condition of employment for a worker in one of its own constituent craft unions. For surely it had a right to spend its own money on a strictly "union made" product and to leave the responsibility of running an all-union shop to the printer!

Thus, an employer derives immunity against Section 8 (a) (3) charges from the new proviso, in the first instance, only under collective agreements conditioning the retention of employment on union membership 30 days after the employee is hired or, with old employees, after the contract is executed—and only then if his plant is not in a state making such an arrangement illegal—and, finally, he must not be aware of union discriminatory practices in admitting members.

In these amendments Congress also established in connection with these agreements some unfair practices for unions. Thus under Section 8 (b) (2) they could not exert pressure on an employer to make him discriminate against employees in violation of Section 8 (a) (3), or themselves discriminate against an employee by causing, or attempting to cause, the employer to fire the worker for some reason other than his refusal to pay the regular initiation fee or periodic dues. Moreover, in Section 8 (b) (5) it is an unfair practice for them to set an initiation fee that the board finds excessive or discriminatory under the circumstances. And Section 10 (c) was amended so that upon reinstatement of an employee, back payment might be "required of the employer *or labor organization,* as the case may be, responsible for the discrimination suffered by him." Under these amendments the board has been very alert in detecting various devices unions have contrived, sometimes with employers' connivance, to attach advantages to union membership or to penalize employees for having refused to join up before union security contracts have finally been executed. And it has been very strict in enforcing these amendments, either taxing back pay adjustments against both contracting parties or, quite often, entirely against the union.

A disturbing aspect of these amendments arose in the *Union Starch and Refining Company* case. After the company and the labor organization had executed a valid union security clause requiring membership as a condition of retaining employment, three workers tendered the required initiation fees and dues. But they refused to comply with two other requirements of membership: that they attend the next regular union meeting at which applicants were voted on, and that they take an oath of allegiance to the union. Somewhat reasonably construing this as a refusal to become members, the company on the union's request discharged the three men. Thereupon the board in complaint proceedings against both company and union ordered their reinstatement with back pay jointly assessed, deciding that their tender of accrued dues and initiation fees brought them within the protection of the 8 (a) (3) provisos and of 8 (b) (2). Two board members dissented. They stated correctly that "Congress specifically sanctioned contracts which require, under specified conditions, that employees obtain *membership* in labor organizations as a condition of employment." They insisted, "as the language of *both* 8 (*a*) (3) provisos clearly indicates . . . if a valid union-shop contract has been executed, employees must *seek membership* in the union in order to keep their jobs; and a union cannot be said to have denied membership to employees who have not sought membership." And they thought that "a desire to become a member of an organization imports much more than mere willingness to pay the organization's dues or fees, and certainly encompasses a willingness to comply with reasonable formalities in the process of joining." Nevertheless in 1951 the court enforced the board's order.

RIGHT-TO-WORK STATUTES

This matter of the union shop was perhaps the hottest issue in labor relations law in 1957. A generation ago unions had fought for the closed shop. If labor organizations were to exist at all, they believed it was necessary to get an absolute monopoly over jobs throughout each industry they were organizing. How else, they reasoned, could they compete with the lower standards of unorganized labor? The Wagner Act somewhat changed this picture when it provided that once a union was established in a plant, it became the exclusive bargaining representative for all the employees in the unit, whether or not they were members. At least this enabled a standardization of working conditions which relieved the pressure from lower nonunion terms of employment. But union members then became incensed at what they called "free riders"—fellow employees who benefited by union gains without contributing financially to the union. The only way they could see to remedy this was the closed shop. That, however, came to be generally regarded as too extreme, because it virtually placed the choice of newly-hired employees in the unions', rather than in the employers', hands.

The obvious compromise, in an industrial society committed to the organization of employees, it is said, is the union shop. And labor leaders, of course, have accepted this because it greatly strengthened unions and kept them in the saddle. For those very reasons, naturally, most employers were against any form of union security. Even if most of them had come to accept unions, they did not wish to let them get too strong. Moreover, there was probably a genuine feeling on the part of many people— shared by a substantial number of employees themselves—that it is somewhat immoral to deny human beings the opportunity of making a living, where they can get employment but cannot retain it without joining a union. In spite of what unionism claims to have done for the workingman, some of these people would apparently rather starve than be beholden to a labor union for their jobs and to let their means of livelihood fall under collective control.

These are the reasons why so many "right-to-work" statutes have been enacted by the states, why Congress has expressly given them precedence over its own provisions for union-shop contracts, and why the unions have fought so bitterly to prevent their spread and to knock out those on the books. There is a further possible compromise that is suggested by the *Union Starch and Refining* case. This is the so-called universal check-off of union dues. Under this plan, existing in some plants, employees not choosing to join the union pay the periodic equivalent of dues into the union treasury. By paying this type of service charge they cease being free riders, and have substantially conformed to the trend of collectivism in industry. At the same time they are able to keep out of the union organization, thus satisfying their inner spiritual or emotional needs to remain dissociated from direct involvement with collectivism. This compromise leaves the unions somewhat dissatisfied, because they cannot claim the loyalties of nonmembers. And it certainly leaves many employers and workers unhappy, because it strengthens the unions financially and, in effect, makes men pay unions for the privilege of working. What possible way out there may be from the dilemma surrounding this issue of union security or compulsory unionism is without doubt one of the gravest and most completely unanswered questions of our times.

In spite of the critical situation created by union security measures, and after it had given precedence in the Taft-Hartley Act to the local right-to-work statutes, in 1951 Congress reversed its former antipathy to union security among employees of interstate carriers and amended the Railway Labor Act to permit the union shop. What it said was that notwithstanding any other laws, federal or state, railroads and the railway unions or brotherhoods "shall be permitted to make agreements, requiring, as a condition of continued employment, that . . . all employees shall become members of the labor organization representing their craft or class." This requirement would not be effective until 60 days after hiring, or, in the case of old employees, 60 days after the effective date of the agreement. A proviso stated that the union shop agreement would not apply to any employees "to whom membership is not available upon the same terms and conditions as are generally applicable to any other member." To a large extent this would remove the pressure caused in some of the Negro cases, since auxiliary locals for colored employees of the railroads would now be meaningless. Also the proviso said that a union-shop agreement would not apply to employees denied or deprived of membership for any reason other than the failure to tender dues, initiation fees, and certain assessments uniformly required of members.

A good deal of litigation arose in connection with this statute. Many older railway employees did not wish to join a brotherhood. And when the railroads went ahead and executed union-shop agreements with their unions (as most of them felt forced by circumstances to do), some of these employees undertook to have the amendment to the act declared unconstitutional. It was argued by them that in so far as any of the local unions were in states having right-to-work statutes, the union shop agreements would be invalid. But all such hopes proved vain. The Supreme Court held that nothing in this new provision violated either the first or fifth amendments of the Constitution. In the first place, the union shop provision in the act was only permissive. The railroads did not have to agree with the brotherhoods to execute these agreements. On the other hand, Congress did clearly allow these agreements to be made. Therefore this unambiguous grant of permission took precedence over the state right-to-work statutes, particularly as Congress took the trouble to say notwithstanding any law "of any state," let alone its own contrary provisions for all other industries in Section 14 (*b*) of the 1947 NLRA. Hence the Court's decision in *Railway Employes' Department v. Hanson,* handed down in 1956, came as no surprise when it reversed the highest court of Nebraska which had enjoined the operation of a union-shop clause on a railroad under its right-to-work statute.

Why did Congress suddenly decide to permit union-shop contracts throughout the railroads where it had formerly prohibited union security or compulsory unionism? And why, of all things, did it brush aside the state right-to-work statutes in this area when it had given them precedence throughout all other industry? An answer to this last may be that if the railroad brotherhoods were to have union security at all, then it would be impracticable not to have it universally, due to the very interstate character of railroading as compared to the more local aspects of mining and manufacturing. Still, if the federal scheme as developed since 1947 in general industry was valid, this is not a very satisfactory answer.

But the nub of the matter is in the answer to the first question. It is possible that the railroad brotherhoods have been consistently enjoying preferential treatment over other unions. Evidence of this is the Congressional failure to adopt a workmen's compensation act for interstate carriers, while the Supreme Court lets virtually all actions by injured railroad employees go to juries which give very substantial damages, completely out of line with the limited schedules of awards afforded under state compensation acts. The inescapable inference here is that the brotherhoods have sufficient political power to preserve the present status under which they can have their cake and eat it, too. Perhaps the railway unions command more political sympathy in Congress than do labor organizations in general industry, although this seems hard to believe.

At present some of the older railroad employees are trying to effect a compromise under the amended Railway Labor Act. Disliking intensely to join unions, they are tendering their initiation fees and dues in order to buy their right to continue employment without having to declare allegiance to the brotherhoods. This is precisely what the board and one of the federal courts allowed as satisfying the terms of a union-shop agreement under the NLRA in the *Union Starch and Refining Company* case. Whether the Supreme Court will accept this modification remains debatable.

In the meantime, this battle over union security is still being fought. And the odds are with the labor unions to achieve at least equality with the railroad brotherhoods in removing the interposition of state right-to-work statutes. For despite the intense dislike harbored by many toward such a possibility, it is certainly consistent with the modern trend toward a complete collectivization of the employment relationship in American industry.

BARGAINING IN GOOD FAITH

The employer's duty to bargain collectively with the union representing his employees first appeared in Section 8 (5) of the Wagner Act. This was scrupulously ordered by the board and fairly rigidly enforced by the courts. From the outset it was recognized that compliance with this provision would be hard to secure because its breach would be difficult to detect. Indeed, it was thought by many to be impractical, if not impossible, to enforce. But the board knew that if an employer refused to take in earnest the bargaining demands of the newly-formed union which he had been compelled to recognize, such a "run around" would in many instances result in the folding of the fledgling organization because of the discouragement of its members and their unwillingness to strike. This Section 8 (5) gave the board all it needed to compel the employer to take a new union seriously. It required the employer to meet with the union and to bargain with it in good faith—that is, to make a bona fide attempt to reach an agreement.

The board and the courts acknowledged that employers could not be compelled to agree on anything. But they said that an employer could not meet with the union and simply say "No" to everything that was proposed. He must discuss matters concerning terms and conditions of employment with the union; and while he did not have to make counterproposals or suggest compromises, he had to keep an open mind and be ready to discuss all overtures seriously. One court observed: "As we view the statute, it is the obligation of the parties to participate actively in the deliberations so as to indicate a present intention to find a basis for agreement, and a sincere effort must be made to reach a common ground." The employer's representatives had to agree to meet with union committeemen at convenient times, and they had to come empowered to discuss terms of a contract and to reach agreement on them. Then they had to be ready to reduce to writing any term or contract to which they might agree. And the board was quick to recognize and to condemn employer tactics that were evasive and designed to frustrate negotiations.

One of the chief uses of this Section 8 (5) was to prevent employers from undercutting an already established union. In *Franks Bros. Company v. NLRB* the Supreme Court accepted the board's findings that 45 of 80 employees had designated a union as their bargaining representative, but that the employer had nevertheless refused to bargain on this showing. To bolster its position the union sought a board election and certification; but the employer's antiunion conduct so discouraged the employees that the union abandoned this course and then filed charges under Section 8 (1) and (5) of the Wagner Act. Thereupon the board ordered the employer to cease this conduct and to bargain with the union, although the evidence at the hearing showed that the union's majority had dwindled from 45 to 32 employees. Justice Black observed that on the basis of its experience the board had adopted "a form of remedy which requires that an employer bargain exclusively with the particular union which represented a majority of the employees at the time of the wrongful refusal to bargain despite the union's subsequent failure to retain its majority." He did not regard this as an injustice to other employees not in that majority, since the board's remedy was not intended "to fix a permanent bargaining relationship without regard to new situations that may develop." But he thought that "a bargaining relationship once rightfully established must be permitted to exist and function for a reasonable period in which it can be given a fair chance to succeed." Hence the Court approved the enforcement of the board's order, despite the intervening decline in the number of employees that had supported the union.

It is worth noting that in the *Franks Brothers* case the board and the Court had reached this result even though there had been no election with a formal certification of the union as the exclusive bargaining representative. For the union had demonstrated its majority by a card count, and pending an election to prove its majority beyond doubt, the employer had begun his antiunion campaign. In a number of other cases the board, with the approval of the courts, held that once a majority of the employees had effectively selected a union as their representative, they could not then turn around and reject it for another union, or repudiate collective representation altogether, until after the union had had a fair opportunity to show that it could operate successfully. Here the board was serving two policies.

First, it was trying to prevent capriciousness on the part of employees. Many employees had to be made to realize that their choice of a bargaining representative was a serious matter and not just a casual pick-up that they could discard at a moment's notice. Thus, if they had selected a union to represent them, they had to abide by their choice for at least a reasonable period. At first blush this looked as if the board were exalting unions, as such, above the employees whose interests the unions were intended to serve. While that was probably not true, still a good case could be made for the board's recognition that a national union would invest a good deal of time and money in organizing employees in a plant, so that for a reasonable period of time it deserved not only the loyalty of the employees but also a chance to establish itself, get some "return on its investment," and show that it could be effective.

And the second policy of the board was preventing an employer from easily persuading newly-organized employees to forsake their chosen union in return for immediate concessions which he appeared willing to give them directly, but not through a union. Too often in the board's experience an employer would promise his newly-organized employees substantial wage increases just to get rid of the union. After that was achieved, he would continue to keep out the union. And thus the purpose of the NLRA—to promote the organization of employees and collective bargaining—would be frustrated.

What occurred in *Medo Photo Supply Corporation v. NLRB* is a good illustration of this. There the employer recognized a union selected by a majority of his employees—18 out of 26 in the particular bargaining unit. After the employer had made a date to meet with the outside union representatives to bargain out a contract, a committee of his employees speaking for a majority approached him and suggested that if they could get certain wage concessions through their own efforts, they would abandon the union. At first the employer, apparently conscious of his statutory duty not to negotiate with the employees over the head of the union, refused to discuss the matter. But on reflection, he decided to accept the committee's offer, the wage increases were made, and he refused to meet with the union representatives, saying that the employees no longer wanted the union and there was nothing to discuss.

The board held that the employer had violated Section 8 (1) and (5) of the Wagner Act, finding that the employees had not revoked their designation of the union as their bargaining representative until after the employer had promised the wage increases. And the Supreme Court upheld the board. It declared that the employer's dealing with the employees under such circumstances was "subversive of the mode of collective bargaining which the statute has ordained." Justice Rutledge, dissenting, said he did not think that Congress had intended "to create rights in unions overriding those of the employees they represent." He declared that the employer's obligation to bargain with the union lasted only as long as it continued to be the choice of a majority of the employees, adding that it made little difference how the men cut the union loose as long as knowledge of the break was brought home to the employer. It is true that Chief Justice Stone, speaking for the majority, intimated that the employees had it in their power to revoke designation of the union as their representative as long as they did so before dealing with the employer. But that intimation was a dictum, possibly prompted by the fact that the union had not been formally certified by the board to the employer following an election. Certainly it was generally established that once a union had been certified after an election, some reasonable permanence of its representative status was required.

As Judge Learned Hand observed in such a case, "freedom to choose a representative does not imply freedom to turn him out of office with the next breath." And another federal judge pointed out that any other view would encourage an antiunion employer to delay good faith bargaining in the hope that the employees would discard the union, would discourage a lawabiding employer from spending time and effort in bargaining for fear that the union would suddenly be discarded, and would spur the union "to hasty and unconsidered action in order to anticipate the possibility that at some point during extended good-faith bargaining enough employees might waver in their support to reduce the union's majority, even momentarily, to a minority." At the present writing the board has a rule that once it has certified a union, the employer must bargain with it for one year after the certification, even though he can prove that *all* of the employees in the bargaining unit have rejected that union. And in *Brooks v. NLRB,* a 1954 case, the Supreme Court upheld this rule, acknowledging that the employer might ask for a new election after the year had expired.

In one important case decided under the Wagner Act, it appeared that the employer had made individual contracts with about 75 per cent of his employees. These contracts contained attractive terms and they were to last for a stated period of time. During that period a board-conducted election at the plant resulted in the majority choice of a CIO union that was certified to the employer. He would not bargain with the union over terms and conditions of work of the employees with whom he had made individual contracts. Thereupon the board in Section 8 (5) proceedings held him guilty of a refusal to bargain under the act. In *J. I. Case Company v. NLRB,* the Supreme Court upheld the board.

Speaking for the Court, Justice Jackson recognized that the individual contracts were lawful enough in themselves. But, he declared: "Wherever private contracts conflict with [the act's] functions, they obviously must yield or the Act would be reduced to a futility." Here a majority of the employees voting in the election had selected a union. And under the act a union chosen in this way was the exclusive bargaining representative for every employee in the unit. Regardless of the individual contracts, the policy of Congress required the employer to bargain with the union over the terms and conditions of employment for *all* of the workers. As Justice Jackson observed: "The workman is free, if he values his own bargaining position more than that of the group, to vote against representation; but the majority rules, and if it collectivises the employment bargain, individual advantages or favors will generally in practice go in as a contribution to the collective result." In any event, the individual contracts could not subtract from the collective ones. If the union achieved collective terms less advantageous than those in some of the individual ones, whether or not the employees in question could retain these advantages would be left to the general law of contracts.

In this *J. I. Case* decision the Court obviously perceived nothing illegal under the Wagner Act in the individual contracts when they were made. It was recognized that in the absence of a union they were perfectly proper. But it had previously upheld the board in condemning individual contracts that by their terms had been clearly intended to discourage employee organization. And to show how important the Court thought the collective majority rule concept to be, it held in *Order of Railroad Telegraphers v. Railway Express Agency* that any deal made by an employer directly with employees and over the head of a union was utterly invalid. This case did not arise under the NLRA, but the principle under the Railway Labor Act was the same. There the employer effected certain changes in routing carloads of produce so that the work of several of its dispatchers was drastically reduced per carload unit handled, and by the same effort previously expended, they cleared far more carload units than before. Had it continued to pay the dispatchers at the rate per unit provided in the collective agreement, their earnings would have been grossly excessive. Hence the company made deals directly with each of these dispatchers in which they agreed to accept substantially lowered unit rates. Later they sued for the difference between what they were actually paid and what they would have received under the terms of the collective agreement. The Supreme Court allowed recovery, approving an award of $40,000 to one dispatcher. Justice Jackson pointed out that the employer's duty was to bargain solely with the union as the exclusive contracting party and to refrain from bargaining with individual employees already represented by a union. Here, no doubt, the union would have been amenable to a reasonable adjustment of pay rates under the circumstances. But it had a right "to be consulted and to bargain about the exceptional as well as the routine rates, rules, and working conditions." And if the union and the dispatchers involved chose to hold the employer to its collective bargain as a lesson to discourage any future derogation from the majority rule principle, that was clearly their privilege under the modern philosophy of collective employment relations.

Closely related to the employer's duty under the Wagner Act to bargain solely with the union over collective terms of employment was his obligation to bargain out with it all grievances raised by employees under the contract. Section 9 (*a*) of the Wagner Act had a proviso permitting employees "to present grievances to their employer." This was construed to mean exactly what it said—to present grievances, and nothing more. For in the *Hughes Tool Company* case the NLRB decided that the employer violated Section 8 (5) by adjusting grievances raised under a collective agreement either directly with the aggrieved or, as they are called in the slang of the shop, the "grieving," employees, or through a union representing only those members who constituted a minority of the employees in the bargaining unit. The court upheld the board in this case, with some modifications. It declared that the employer might make an adjustment directly with the employee, on grievances concerned only with "some question of fact or conduct peculiar to the employee," presumably such as incorrectly adding up his wages due. Then it said that while the union had a right to be notified about all grievances filed, it could establish a violation of Section 8 (5) only when the union demanded a right to be heard on a proper grievance and was refused. The court agreed with the board that the employer was obligated to bargain with the union about all grievances involving an interpretation of the contract or dealing with matters affecting unit employees which had not been covered by the agreement. And while it said that minority unions had no place in these procedures at all, it reminded the contracting union that it was under a duty to process the grievances of nonmembers of the union without any discrimination against them.

Oddly enough, in *E. J. and E. Ry. v. Burley,* a bare majority of the Supreme Court in 1945 held that a contrary rule prevailed under the Railway Labor Act. That decision was unanimously assailed by employer and union organizations from all sides. It was immediately recognized that if employers had to deal with unions as bargaining representatives of employees, then in order to lend stability to their transactions, negotiations between them must be final. Thus, if an employer and a union reached a mutually satisfactory settlement over an employee's grievance, then the union must have the power to make a final disposition which would protect the employer from subsequent litigation by the dissatisfied employee. Here, again, the majority rule must prevail, exactly as it does in bargaining out the terms of a collective agreement with a union having exclusive representational powers.

Certainly this was the recognized rule under the NLRA until it was amended in 1947. At that time the Section 9 (*a*) proviso was amended to permit the final disposition of any grievance between an employer and an employee, as long as such disposition was "not inconsistent" with the terms of the collective agreement and also provided that a representative of the union had a right to be present when the adjustment of the grievance was made. Whatever this change was meant to accomplish, it was rather silly, since it afforded no way of determining whether or not any settlement made directly between an employer and an employee was consistent with the terms of the governing collective agreement. Furthermore, under this amended proviso, one of the federal courts held that an employee might have a minority union represent him in adjusting his grievance with the employer. This was a development that was certainly in derogation of the contracting union's exclusive bargaining prerogatives under the act.

During the early days of the Wagner Act it was generally assumed that an employer who refused to discuss a wage increase because of his professed inability to pay it was not bargaining in good faith if he also refused to open his books. But not until 1955 in *NLRB v. Truitt Manufacturing Company* did the Supreme Court support that view. There the employer had rejected the union's demand for an hourly increase of 10 cents, declaring that anything more than 2½ cents per hour would put him in bankruptcy. When the union asked that he substantiate his assertion either by opening his books or by permitting an impartial accountant to examine them and submit a report, the employer again said "No." Thus, such an attitude is a refusal to bargain in good faith in contravention of Section 8 (*a*) (5) of the act.

Justice Black remarked concerning this "asserted inability to pay an increase in wages" that good-faith bargaining claims "should be honest claims." He also observed: "If such an argument is important enough to present in the give and take of bargaining, it is important enough to require some sort of proof of its accuracy." And, he thought, "it would certainly not be farfetched for a trier of fact to reach the conclusion that bargaining lacks good faith when an employer mechanically repeats a claim of inability to pay without making the slightest effort to substantiate the claim." While it is not certain, it is a fair inference from this case that the employer does not have to open his books to the union so long as he permits an audit by an impartial accountant, whose report will be given to the union.

THE VANISHING PREROGATIVE OF MANAGEMENT

Perhaps the most crucial aspect of this duty to bargain in good faith concerns the subject matter of collective bargaining. When Congress passed the Wagner Act, did it in Section 8 (5) contemplate any more than that employers should take seriously union demands with respect to the conventional items of collective agreements such as wages, hours of work, seniority, grievance procedures, and, possibly, union security provisions, promotions, vacations, paid holidays, arbitration, and sickness and accident plans? During World War II the War Labor

Board refused to entertain union demands for some of these items, simply because they had not theretofore generally been included in collective agreements. But after the war it soon became apparent that there was no logical limit to the matters over which unions might bargain with employers. The only test was whether or not the demand concerned terms and conditions of employment. And this was broad enough to include almost anything. One of the first test cases arose over the union's right and the employer's duty to bargain about merit increases. Naturally the employer maintained that it was his sole function to determine and to reward merit. But the board and the courts held otherwise. Many employers were determined to make a last-ditch stand over pensions, particularly those employers who had unilaterally promulgated pension plans long before they had been unionized. But the board and the courts held that they must bargain over these items. And so it went with almost every conceivable union demand. For it is most difficult to imagine any aspect of the employment relationship or, indeed, of industry itself, which does not in some way affect the terms and conditions of labor.

An exceedingly important issue was at stake in this area covered by Section 8 (5) and 8 (a) (5). It was long a favorite dogma of employers that in spite of the new unionism, they had something left that they called management prerogative. This argument ran thus. There were certain matters which management alone should be left free to deal with. It assumed all responsibility for financing, production, and distribution, and it must be left free to make the decisions essential to efficiency and fiscal success. Thus, to take extreme instances, management alone could decide what to manufacture, how much to manufacture, what methods to use, how to market and price its product, and what managerial and supervisory personnel to hire and policies to pursue. Then why should it not also retain the exclusive right to govern promotions, to schedule production, to control merit increases, or, indeed, as part of its function of efficient management, unilaterally to deal with all items except those obviously and directly affecting the employment relation, such as wages, hours of work and, and—? and there was the rub. But at this writing it is only too obvious that the old dream of exclusive management prerogative has burst like a soap bubble. For the description of what affects the employment relationship—what are terms and conditions of labor—is as much in the hands of one side as it is of the other. And organized labor will quite naturally not recognize any limit to its wants and demands. In the beginning—before unions—the entire ball of wax was in management's hands. But such complete and utter control was lost when the first collective agreement was made. It has ever since been whittled down to the extent that unions have gained concessions in contracts. Employers still cling to the notion that there is a residue of management prerogative— all that they originally had minus what they have lost in concessions to unions through bargaining. But they seem to have overlooked their statutory obligation imposed on them by the NLRA to bargain with unions over almost anything that unions wish to make the subject matter of bargaining.

Here is the vital issue in a nutshell. Section 8 (5) was included in the Wagner Act to put incipient unionism on its feet—to *make* employers take fledgling local unions seriously. With the exception of certain areas in the south, unions no longer need artificial assistance from government to command respect and to have their bargaining requests taken seriously. They are free to make their demands and to strike for what they want if employers will not yield. For the strike and employer resistance to the strike are just as basic to the collective bargaining process as are conferences around tables in smoke-filled rooms. And it is plain common sense that the line between what should or should not be included in collective agreements will more adequately and satisfactorily be forged through collective bargaining, with or without strikes, than determined in the councils of the NLRB and by the courts.

However, under Section 8 (*a*) (5) unions have nothing to lose and everything to gain by pushing further and further with their demands on employers and securing government assistance to compel employers to meet them halfway on matters over which they might otherwise be most reluctant to strike. The board and the Supreme Court piously reiterate that Section 8 (a) (5) does not compel employers to agree to anything. But as a practical matter, employers find it almost impossible to avoid commitment to some extent over matters on which they are compelled to bargain under the statute. The difference between this and a direct statutory command from Congress that certain matters must be included in contracts is only one of degree. And yet the Supreme Court continues to insist that under the NLRA the board has no concern whatsoever with the subject matter of collective agreements or with the inclusion of provisions in contracts. A far more healthy bargaining climate would prevail in this country if Section 8 (a) (5) were stricken from the NLRA and the content of collective agreements were left to be worked out by direct dealings between employers and unions. Such a step would no doubt check the organization of employees and union success in parts of the south. But it is quite possible that the ingenuity of Congress could invent some special procedure to protect the interests of newly-formed local unions anywhere in the country.

In the meantime, a majority of the Supreme Court has inclined to check the general trend toward unlimited coverage of subject matter under Section 8 (a) (5)—at least in one respect. That was in *NLRB v. American National Insurance Company,* decided in 1952. There the certified union submitted to the company a proposed contract covering the conventional provisions, including promotions, as well as a grievance procedure with arbitration as the final step. But the employer insisted on a management clause which left in its hands the final responsibility for promotions, discipline, and the scheduling of work, with no recourse to arbitration on these matters. This the board held was a violation of Section 8 (a) (5) of the NLRA, because insistence upon the final say concerning any terms and conditions of employment was in its opinion tantamount to a refusal to bargain on such matters. A majority of the Court, however, thought such a view needlessly technical, particularly since "it is conceded that [the employer] would not be guilty of an unfair labor practice if, instead of proposing a clause that removed some matters from arbitration, it simply refused in good faith to agree to the Union proposal for unlimited arbitration." They declared that it was perfectly proper for the company to hold out for a management clause permitting it to control scheduling of work and promotions, since such a clause is as much the subject matter of bargaining as any other provision in a collective agreement.

Whether or not such a conclusion is sound under the statute as it is generally construed remains doubtful. If the Court was correct in this case, then why cannot an employer hold out for a management clause permitting it to assume the sole responsibility for every item ordinarily covered in a collective agreement? Presumably the answer to this question is that under the *American Insurance* case they may insist upon a management rights clause covering only such matters as call for the periodic exercise of judgment during the life of a contract, of which promotions and work scheduling are good examples. But such "standard" items as wages, hours of work, vacations, sickness and accident benefit plans, pensions, and guaranteed annual wages are presumably not matters which employers may refuse to bargain about with unions. Nevertheless, the *American Insurance* case does suggest a line, however vague it may be, at which employers may stand pat and simply refuse to consider concessions or compromises. But even here apparently they must conceal such refusals to bargain under the positive proposal of a management clause which recognizes their right to exercise final judgment on the matters in question.

Now how about the union's responsibility in this area? The Wagner Act of 1935 did not list any unfair labor practices of unions. Hence under it unions were not required to bargain in good faith. The presumption was that the bargaining overtures of the unions were always made in good faith, simply because they were proposed by labor organizations! In one case under the original act, however, a union submitted a complete contract to an employer and refused to discuss any modifications of the terms because it claimed that its constitution forbade any compromise. Naturally the employer declined any further discussion and the union initiated 8 (5) proceedings under the act. But the board held in the employer's favor. While it conceded that the NLRA imposed "no affirmative duty to bargain upon labor organizations, a union's refusal to bargain in good faith may remove the possibility of negotiation and thus preclude the existence of a situation in which the employer's own good faith can be tested." And that was the closest the board ever came under the original act to deciding that a union had not bargained in good faith.

In the amendments of 1947, however, Congress in Section 8 (b) (3) made it an unfair labor practice for a union "to refuse to bargain collectively with an employer" when it was the duly established representative of his employees. Although a part of the new act constituted a detailed description of collective bargaining in good faith applying to employer and union alike, this miserable passage was a palpable attempt to prevent unions from terminating or breaking their contracts even in the absence of a no-strike clause. No doubt Congress was right in requiring that the parties to collective agreements should abide by their terms and forsake the direct action of strikes for the parliamentary method of grievance procedure and arbitration whenever the contract provided it. In any event, a failure of both unions and employees to do so has been held by the board and the courts to be a departure from the statutory requirements of bargaining in good faith, as defined in Section 8 (d).

That provision flatly stated that any employee engaging in a strike called contrary to its terms should "lose his status as an employee" under the act, and might be discharged. In other words, such conduct was declared to be unprotected activity. In consequence the board and courts broadened the doctrine of the old *Sands* case—that the breach of any collective agreement by a strike was unprotected activity—by "equating a contract clause providing for arbitration of grievances to a no-strike clause." In 1957 the board held that it was a violation of Section 8 (*b*) (3) for a union either to attempt to impose its interpretation of contract provisions by striking instead of following the grievance procedure, or to strike against an arbitration award with which it disagreed. Previously the board had held that a series of harassing "quickie strikes" or brief unannounced walkouts, called by a union after the expiration of a contract and during negotiations for a new agreement, amounted to a violation of Section 8 (*b*) (3) as a failure to bargain in good faith.

But the court refused to enforce its order, declaring that nowhere in Section 8 (*b*) could it perceive a Congressional prohibition of such tactics, although concededly the employer might with impunity discharge the participants for having engaged in unprotected activity. Thus, Section 8 (*b*) (3), in light of the definition of bargaining in good faith in Section 8 (*d*), has developed into an effective sanction that the board can use to restrict direct union action during the life of a collective agreement, leaving employers to deal with harassing tactics after expiration of the contract by discharging the participants. However, in the *Mastro Plastics* case of 1956 the Supreme Court said that participants in a strike called in defiance of Section 8 (*d*) remained employees if the strike had been provoked by a substantial unfair labor practice of the employer.

Perhaps this is as close as Congress could be expected to come in any attempt to require bargaining in good faith by unions. What it adds up to is a restriction on union pressure techniques as well as an additional device for enforcing contract provisions. Certainly it has little to do with union motives, and they should be the crucial aspect of any inquiry into good faith bargaining. For it seems impossible to question the fact that the unions in all these instances pursued their objectives in genuine good faith. Unfortunately the Supreme Court has so far refused to hear these important cases on appeal, and this may or may not imply that it tacitly approves of interpretation placed at this writing on Section 8 (*b*) (3) of the act.

SECONDARY BOYCOTTS

The most drastic restrictions on union activity enacted by Congress in 1947 were contained in Section 8 (*b*) (4). This subsection contained four parts. And of them Section 8 (*b*) (4) (A) was by far the most important. For here Congress undertook to outlaw as a union pressure device the secondary boycott. Unfortunately this important provision is not clearly worded, and its interpretation by the board and the courts seems to have made it even more incomprehensible. Its main part makes it an unfair practice for a union "to engage in, or to induce or encourage the employees of any employer to engage in, a strike or a concerted refusal" to use, handle, transport, or work on any goods or materials, or to perform any services with the object of forcing any employer or other person "to cease using, selling, handling, transporting, or otherwise dealing in the products of any other producer, . . . or to cease doing business with any other person." Translated into plain English, this garbled provision says that unions shall not bring pressure against an employer, *through his employees,* designed to make him stop dealing with or handling the products of some other person. Although no word is said about secondary boycotts, the legislative history leaves no doubt that Congress wanted to stamp them out.

Now, just what does all this mean? Suppose a union wants to focus organizational or bargaining pressure on Zenith Corporation and is not in a position to do so directly. At the same time, however, since it is the bargaining representative for Atlas' employees, it *is* able to exert pressure against Atlas Company, which deals with Zenith. Therefore the union brings direct pressure against Atlas either by calling Atlas' employees out on strike if Atlas continues to deal with Zenith, or by ordering them to cease handling goods coming from or going to Zenith. If this step is effective, Atlas will cease all its dealings with Zenith. And thereby secondary economic pressure is generated against that company.

Atlas, with whom the union has no quarrel, is thus compelled against its will to assist the union in cutting Zenith off from its markets. Zenith can escape from this plight only by capitulating to the union. Atlas, the neutral, is called the secondary employer, although the direct or primary pressure is exerted against it. Since Zenith is the employer the union is really after, it is called the primary employer, albeit it is here made the victim of secondary pressure. And this whole gambit—the secondary boycott—is one of the most ruthless and effective methods conceivable of enforcing compliance with union demands.

Two years after these Taft-Hartley amendments were passed, the board's general counsel announced that it would not be a violation of 8 (b) (4) (A) for a union to persuade a neutral or secondary employer to agree not to deal any more with a primary employer or other person with whom the main dispute existed. This apparently correct observation was based on the fact that the statute prohibited only pressure exerted against the neutral employer through his employees—that is, by calling a strike of his employees or by ordering them concertedly to cease handling goods moving from or going to the primary employer. Theoretically a neutral employer may be perfectly willing to cooperate with a union and merely on request cease business relations with one of his customers or sources of supply. But it is hard to believe that he would do so except to keep the union off his own neck. He knows that if he does not comply, the union can force him to do so by calling out his employees. And that of course would be a violation. But it is apparently not a violation for the union business agent to threaten to do exactly that, as long as he speaks only to the neutral employer and does not actually coerce him through his employees. Naturally the practical result of the neutral employer's acquiescence *is* a secondary boycott. But it is still within the law!

Sometimes, an employer, as a part of a collective agreement, commits himself in advance not to deal with or to accept goods from nonunion employers during the life of the contract. This is known as a "hot cargo" clause in agreements between trucking companies and the Teamsters' union, under which a unionized connecting carrier will not deliver or receive shipments to or from a nonunion hauler. In *Carpenters Local 1976 v. NLRB* [*Sand Door*] (1958), the Supreme Court held that while Section 8 (*b*) (4) forbade union concerted action to force one employer to cease doing business with another, it did not forbid a union-employer agreement to secure the same result. In Section 8 (*c*) of the Labor-Management Reporting and Disclosure Act of 1959 (LMRDA), Congress sought to plug this loophole by making hot cargo agreements unlawful except in the construction and garment industries. In *National Woodwork Mfrs. Ass'n. v. NLRB* (1967), the Supreme Court held that under such exception, the Carpenters Union could legally secure an agreement from an employer which it could enforce through a product boycott, to protect or preserve work its members had traditionally performed.

One of the board's first decisions under 8 (*b*) (4) (A) was that picketing a struck employer which resulted in keeping the employees of another employer away from his premises was not a violation of the act. For instance, suppose a union calls a strike against A and pickets his premises. One natural effect of this picketing will be to persuade the employees of other employers doing business with A not to enter A's premises. In a sense, this results in the creation of a secondary pressure on A, effected through the employees of his customers.

But the board quite reasonably held that such primary picketing against A could hardly become unlawful merely because it also had a secondary effect against A by cutting him off from his customers. As the board said: "To hold otherwise might well outlaw virtually every effective strike, for a consequence of all strikes is some interference with business relationships between the struck employer and others." Actually in this case the union did not set out to put secondary pressure on A by exerting direct pressure on other employers through their employees to cease relations with A. What it did was to exert primary pressure directly on A. The secondary pressure was purely incidental, although the union no doubt counted on it. To prove a violation of 8 (*b*) (4) (A) by the union, it would have to be shown that the union had exerted *direct pressure on A's customers through their employees* with the object of compelling such customers to cease doing business with A. In short, A, the primary employer, would have to show that he was the victim of secondary pressure as the result of direct or primary pressure exercised by the union against the secondary or neutral employer! This little sample of verbal gymnastics in one of the simplest cases imaginable indicates what a complicated mess Congress brewed in Section 8 (*b*) (4) (A).

Another early case resulted in what has been called the "ally" doctrine. There the union representing A's employees calls a strike, whereupon A lets out most of its work to P company, an outfit which at the time is completely independent of A. During the course of the strike, however, P takes over virtually all of A's work, and A's supervisory staff moves into P's shop in order to supervise the work. As might be expected, the union finally pickets P's premises with the result that several of P's employees walk out. In connection with complaint proceedings against the union under Section 8 (*b*) (4) (A), the board sought an injunction against the union in a federal district court, as it was empowered to do under new provisions in Section 10 of the 1947 NLRA. But the court held that this was not a secondary boycott and that, in practical effect, A and P were not separate firms doing business with each other.

Rather, they were "allies." A sort of identity existed between them and, as the court said: "In every meaningful sense [P] had made itself party to the contest," and was no longer "neutral." The result "was precisely that which would flow from [A's] hiring strikebreakers to work on its own premises." Although the court did not put it this way, the upshot of its decision was that P could not qualify as a secondary employer and thus be forced through his employees to cease dealing with the primary employer, A. For under the circumstances they were virtually one and the same enterprise because of their "alliance" against the union. And picketing at P's plant was for all practical purposes the same as picketing at A's. Hence there was no violation of the act's prohibition of secondary boycotts.

In a somewhat similar case this application of the act was later confirmed by a federal appellate court and would no doubt be approved by the Supreme Court if it has occasion to pass on this matter. That was a case where the employees of Royal Typewriter Company were on strike so that Royal could not fulfil its repair contracts with customers. Royal farmed out this contract work to independent repair outfits and the union picketed these independents and persuaded many of their employees to walk out. Although the board held that this picketing of the independents was a violation of Section 8 (b) (4) (A), the federal court refused to enforce its order, calling the independent repair outfits "allies" of Royal. Thus they could not be considered as neutral or secondary employers with Royal as the primary employer.

Confident prediction as to what the board and courts will do in this area is unsafe, since the difference between employers who are "allies" and those who normally carry on business with each other must be kept carefully in mind. For an employer who merely continues to purchase and handle the products of a nonunion concern which the union is trying to organize does not thereby become its ally. Nor does the fact that the two are under contract with each other make any difference. And any attempt by the union to compel such employer *through his employees* to cease doing business with the nonunion company is clearly a secondary boycott under the act and a violation of

Section 8 (*b*) (4) (A). Only when he is virtually acting as a strike-breaker for the nonunion concern may the union go after him with impunity.

During the years since these Taft-Hartley amendments became law the Supreme Court has done a little, but not enough, to clear away the mists enshrouding Section 8 (*b*) (4) (A) of the act. In 1951 it handed down three decisions which are perhaps worth discussing, although in none of these cases is the Court's opinion enlightening. Indeed, the confusion among the board, the federal appellate courts, and within the Supreme Court itself over the meaning of Section 8 (*b*) (4) (A) prompts the reflection that the only real virtue in the highest Court's decisions is that they are the final word. For in no other sense are they helpful or authoritative. One of these cases—*NLRB v. Denver Building and Construction Trades Council*—involved picketing of a construction job because the employees of an electrical subcontractor did not belong to a union. The picketing unions represented the various crafts otherwise employed on the job. Here the board found a violation of Section 8 (*b*) (4) (A) because when the employees of the general contractor refused to work, he told the nonunion subcontractor to abandon his contract and ceased doing business with him. With some reason the federal appellate court refused to enforce the board's order, holding that "the action in the circumstances of this case is primary and not secondary." But a majority of the Supreme Court disagreed and upheld the board.

The situation was regarded as one where the unions had picketed the general contractor as the secondary or neutral employer, thus inducing his employees to force him to stop doing business with the nonunion subcontractor, the primary employer. Justice Burton conceded that if the subcontractor's nonunion employees had been hired directly by the general contractor, the picketing would not have been a violation of 8 (*b*) (4) (A), for there had to be two employers involved—a primary and a secondary. The Court did not think that the delegation of his work by subcontract to the nonunion employer made the latter any the less an independent businessman. Nor was the situation comparable to the "ally" cases previously discussed, since there the secondary or neutral employer was the ally—the "subcontractor," so to speak, who had taken over the struck employer's work somewhat in the role of strike-breaker—whereas here the nonunion subcontractor was the *primary* employer or person operating in the regular course of business. Nevertheless, this was indulging in some pretty hairsplitting distinctions.

Nor was it much different in another of these three cases— *International Brotherhood of Electrical Workers, Local 501 v. NLRB.* There the electrical workers' union picketed a construction job because a unionized general contractor let the electrical work by subcontract to a nonunion employer. Thereupon the union carpenters employed by the general contractor walked off the job, thus forcing him to cease doing business with the nonunion employer. Here again the Supreme Court upheld the board, agreeing with the federal appellate court that there was a violation of Section 8 (*b*) (4) (A).

While these two decisions conform technically to the wording of the statutory language, the reason they do not make much sense is that in each case the so-called primary and secondary employers were engaged in work at exactly the same situs—the building project. Everyone concedes that the building trades unions in the first case, and the electrical workers' unions, in the second, were free to picket the nonunion subcontractors for employing nonunion labor. Nothing in the Taft-Hartley Act was intended to prevent this. But the question is: Where may this picketing be done? Traditionally it would be on the job— at the place where they are performing work. That is all the unions were doing here, although there was evidence in the *Electrical Workers* case that the union still picketed the job while the nonunion subcontractor's men were absent from it. Justices Douglas, Jackson, and Reed dissented in these two cases. As Justice Douglas observed: "The employment of union and nonunion men on the same job is a basic protest in trade union history. That was the protest here. The union was not out to destroy the contractor because of his antiunion attitude. The union was not pursuing the contractor to other jobs. All the union asked was that union men not be compelled to work alongside nonunion men on the same job."

This picketing conformed to a traditionally fundamental privilege of unions in the building industry to work only with union workmen. And it is hard to believe that Congress ever intended to erase this privilege in Section 8 (*b*) (4) (A). That provision was aimed at secondary boycott pressures, and no part of this picketing even remotely resembled the customary pattern of secondary economic coercion. If the general contractor had directly employed the nonunion electricians, all concede that the picketing would have been proper. It was only coincidence that had brought the situation within the literal application of 8 (*b*) (4) (A). Hence it is possible that the Court was here using this provision to further the policy underlying the state "right to work" statutes—a most unfortunate development, if true.

The last of the Supreme Court's three cases—*NLRB v. International Rice Milling Company*—illustrates what fine lines are drawn in these situations. There a union picketed a rice mill in an attempt to secure recognition as bargaining agent for the mill's truck drivers. When a truck from one of the mill's customers approached the plant, the union pickets sought to induce the two employees on the neutral truck not to enter the mill property. In complaint proceedings under 8 (*b*) (4) (A) the board held that there was no violation; but a federal appellate court set this decision aside. Then the Supreme Court upheld the board. Justice Burton was willing to assume that the union's object was to compel the neutral employer, through his employees, to cease doing business with the mill. But he thought that Section 8 (*b*) (4) (A) forbade the inducing of the employees of the neutral employer only through "concerted activity" to force their employer to cease doing business with the mill, and that the picketing of the primary employer—the rice mill— appealed to the neutral employees only in their status as individuals. Here, he observed, there had been no attempt by the union to picket the neutral employer's premises and thus to influence his employees directly and collectively. The union's "primary" picketing he regarded merely as an attempt to persuade *anybody* who approached the premises not to enter, saying that "such conduct was no more than was traditional and permissible in a primary strike." And he added: "The union did not engage in a strike against the customer. It did not encourage concerted action by the customer's employees to force the customer to boycott the mill."

A remaining aspect of Section 8 (*b*) (4) (A) appears in what may be called the "situs" cases. Let us suppose that a union has a dispute with an employer and it wishes to picket him. But it happens that it cannot do so unless at the same time it pickets another employer with whom it has no quarrel, because both employers are operating at the same place. Both employers occupy the same premises and share a common entrance for their employees and customers. Apparently the union may picket its adversary if it makes it plain to the public that it is picketing only that employer and that its objective is not also to bring pressure against the other employer, through his employees, to cease any business relations he may have with the first employer.

Now let us suppose that the adversary conducts his business from a separate plant at which the union may picket him, but at the same time he constantly sends out workers to a situs which is shared in common with a neutral employer and his workers. May the union picket its adversary employer at the common situs without violating Section 8 (*b*) (4) (A)? Would it make any difference if the adversary employer maintained some of his employees full time at the common situs? If this were done under a subcontract with the neutral employer at the common situs, then what would be the difference between the picketing in such a case and that in the *Denver* and *Electrical Workers* cases, where the Supreme Court held that when the employees of the neutral general contractors refused to cross the picket lines there were violations?

In each of the last two cases the distinction seems to be that the Court found evidence supporting the board's finding that the objective of the union was to force the neutral employer to break off relations with the subcontractor. At any rate under the board's *Moore Dry Dock* ruling a union having a dispute with an employer may follow his employees when, in the performance of their work, they go to the premises of another employer, and it may picket them there as long as they remain, if the picketing is limited to places "reasonably close" to the operations of the primary employer's workers who are engaged in the company's normal business. And so, likewise, if the adversary employer's employees go to the common situs in trucks to deliver something, they may be picketed only while they are there. *But* the union placards must make it plain that only such employees, and not the neutral employer and *his* employees, are being picketed. At the same time, the federal courts have refused to sustain board decisions to the effect that the union may not picket their adversary employer's employees at a common situs whenever there is another place, such as their home plant, available for effective picketing. During a labor dispute a "struck" employer may establish at his plant a "reserved gate," through which gate neutral contractors, thus insulated from picketing by the striking union, may bring in supplies and *their* employees who are doing work within the plant area unrelated to the normal operations of the plant.

If this account of the 1947 NLRA's proscription of secondary boycotts does nothing more, it should indicate what a dreadful mess Congress created when it enacted Section 8 (*b*) (4) (A). Here is a provision which was aimed at secondary boycotts but which has been freely applied to all sorts of situations never before thought of as secondary boycotts. The authors of this measure, with a view to covering all instances of secondary pressures, were so cagey in drafting it that they produced something virtually unworkable. For if the lawyers and judges, including the members of the Supreme Court, become so involved in applying it that they constantly confuse "primary" and "secondary" employers and cannot decide exactly what the provision means anyway, then it should be scrapped. It should either be left out of the act entirely or replaced by a well-thought-out measure that can easily be understood by the legal profession.

This provision goes on to prohibit the use of concerted secondary pressure to force or require "any employer or self-employed person to join any labor or employer organization." But this part of the provision is self-explanatory. Did Congress enact this provision as a whole to protect neutral employers from being dragged in by unions as the instruments of economic pressure against other employers? That is commonly thought to have been the legislative intent. But the next provision—Section 8 (b) (4) (B)—indicates otherwise. There Congress forbade a union to force an employer, through appeals to his employees, to cease doing business with another employer in order to make that other employer recognize the union as bargaining representative of his employees "unless such labor organization has been certified as the representative of such employees under the provisions of Section 9."

This apparent willingness to let certified unions use neutral employers as clubs to hammer other employers into fulfilling their legal obligations suggests that Congress was going out of its way to permit self-help pressures for securing recognition of the board's certifications. Maybe it was a sort of direct sanction, supplementing the more formal administrative techniques of the act, to save the board the trouble of having to process Section 8 (a) (5) complaints. In any event, Section 8 (b) (4) (B) does not indicate the solicitude for neutral employers commonly read into the 8 (b) (4) (A) provision against secondary boycotts.

Indeed, the next provision, Section 8 (*b*) (4) (C) fits neatly into this line of reasoning. There unions were forbidden to use the secondary pressure technique through the employees of a neutral employer to compel recognition by another employer to whom the board had already certified a different union as bargaining representative of its employees. Certainly this sanction, completely lacking in the old Wagner Act, was a most welcome and necessary measure to support and command respect for board certifications.

The balance of Section 8 (*b*) (4) consists of a prohibition directed against the old-fashioned jurisdictional disputes between unions who were fighting over the assignment of certain kinds of work. Such disputes usually occur between craft unions in the building industry. The general contractor does not care who hangs metal doors—the carpenters or the metal workers. Subsection (D) takes him off the hook to the extent that a strike by union X against his assignment of the work to the employees in union Y may be prohibited as an unfair labor practice. The board at first tended to back up the employer in whatever assignment he may have made of the work. Now, however, this sort of dispute is handled by a privately set up board of jurisdictional awards maintained in Washington by the building industry and the craft unions. And if the NLRB were to be called in, it would be required to decide the dispute on its merits under *NLRB v. Radio and T.B.E.U., Local 1212, IBEW* (1961).

Tacked onto the end of this Section 8 (*b*) (4) is a proviso that nothing in subsection 8 (*b*) makes unlawful a refusal by anyone "to enter upon the premises of any employer . . . if the employees of such employer are engaged in a strike" called by the union representing his employees. What this was intended to mean besides declaring that it should not be unlawful for anybody to cross a picket line, it is hard to say. Yet this innocent-looking proviso split the Supreme Court wide open in *NLRB v. Rockaway News Company*, decided in 1953. There a unionized truck driver refused to deliver and pick up bundles of newspapers and magazines at the premises of one of his employer's customers because to do so required him to cross a picket line established by a different union representing the customer's striking employees. When he was told that persistence in such an attitude would be regarded as insubordination, he still refused, and was discharged. Thereupon the board declared this a violation of Section 8 (a) (3) by his employer and ordered him reinstated with back pay. A majority of the Supreme Court would not enforce this order. They regarded the employee's refusal to cross the picket line of another union in the performance of his duties as just cause for discharge. Speaking for the dissenters, Justice Black observed that even the Taft-Hartley Act, "designed to regulate and restrict the type of concerted activities in which employees could engage . . . did not attempt to deprive unions of the advantage of a policy that required union men to respect picket lines." He thought that the Section 8 (b) proviso "specifically declared that none of [the act's] union-restrictive provisions should be construed to make it unlawful for a man to refuse to cross a picket line thrown up to support a lawful strike." This, of course, was correct. Nobody claimed otherwise. This employee was not being prosecuted for an unfair labor act. He had been fired simply for refusing to do his work. Naturally it was his privilege to refuse to cross the picket line, just as it was to give up his job at any time. It is hard to see how Justice Black could torture from this immunity for employees against the provisions of Section 8 (b) an additional immunity from discharge for refusing to do their work when it meant crossing the picket line of another union. If he were correct in this conclusion, then union employees would be in a position to compel their employers by their actions to subsidize the strikes of other unions against other employers.

The most that Justice Jackson, speaking for a majority of the Court, could extract from this proviso was that it enabled a union and an employer "to embody in their contracts a provision against requiring an employee to cross a picket line if they so agree." Under such a contract, the persistent employee in the *Rockaway* case would have a right not to cross the picket line and nevertheless to retain his job. It is also likely that under this proviso the union representing the secondary employer's employees might order its members not to cross the picket lines of other unions engaged in valid strikes, without violating Section 8 (*b*) in any respect and without incurring liability for damages under Section 303 of the Taft-Hartley Act which makes union violations of 8 (*b*) (4) the basis for actions for money damages by injured employers.

FEATHERBEDDING

The only remaining union unfair labor practice is Section 8 (*b*) (6). Here Congress undertook to suppress what is commonly known as "featherbedding"—that is, where a union exerts pressure on an employer to pay money, "in the nature of an exaction, for services which are not performed or not to be performed." In other words these are union requirements through economic coercion that men be paid for work neither done nor wanted nor needed by the employer, although the union offers to have it performed. Previous attempts by Congress to deal with this sort of thing had proved futile. Before World War II the teamsters' union would stop the truck of each produce dealer entering New York City and compel the dealer to "hire" an unemployed union driver to take the truck to its destination, unload it, and bring it back—all for one day's pay. Of course, the dealer could drive his own truck and he did not want any part of the union driver. But the driver was ready to perform. And whether or not his services were accepted, the dealer shelled out a day's pay or his truck did not enter the city.

The Supreme Court in *United States v. Local 807*—a 1942 case—held that a conviction of the union under the antiracketeering act should be set aside because this was, within an exception of the statute, a good faith offer to work sponsored by a bona fide labor union and not part of a pattern of "terroristic activities of professional gangsters" at which the law had been aimed. Nevertheless Chief Justice Stone, dissenting, thought that the compulsion to hire such an extra driver to avoid trouble would, if not punished, "render common law robbery an innocent pastime."

Equally abortive was the Lea Act, occasionally called the "Anti-Petrillo Act," which was aimed at "stand-bys" or unnecessary musicians. Under this statute the criminal guilt of the offending union was determined in accordance with the employer's own statement as to what his personal needs were in the way of musicians—a tenuous standard, indeed, on which to convict people. Nevertheless the Supreme Court held it constitutional in *United States v. Petrillo*—a 1947 decision. But no conviction was secured because, as the federal district judge pointed out, it could not be shown that Petrillo had any basis for believing that the additional musicians were not needed and knowledge to that effect was an essential element of the offense. No doubt it was the futility of these two statutes that inspired Congress to try it again in Section 8 (*b*) (6) of the 1947 NLRA.

But the attempt to make featherbedding an unfair labor practice instead of a crime proved equally abortive. In *American Newspaper Publishers Association v. NLRB*, a 1953 decision of the Supreme Court, it appeared that the ITU—the typographical union—insisted upon resetting in type all advertising and other material already set up and submitted to the newspapers for printing. This was in conformity with a long-standing custom of the industry. Of course, it was wasteful, involved unnecessary duplication, and greatly increased costs; this bogus type, after being set, was proofread, reset for corrections, and then immediately chucked into the "hell box" as waste, where it was melted down and molded into lead pigs for re-use in the linotype machines. But the union insisted upon it to keep its members at full-time employment. Such duplicated effort was called "setting bogus," and it was fitted into the slack periods so as not to interfere with "live" work. The board nevertheless held this "setting bogus" to be work and that the pay given for doing it was not "in the nature of an exaction" for work not done. And the Supreme Court upheld the board.

On the same day the Court decided *NLRB v. Gamble Enterprises.* There a theatre chain had for years paid a local stand-by orchestra for doing nothing whenever it had a traveling orchestra appear at one of its theatres. This was required by Petrillo's musicians' union. After the passage of the Taft-Hartley Act, the employer discontinued this practice because of Section 8 (*b*) (6). The union then suggested that the local orchestra, which the theatre neither needed nor wanted, be allowed to play the opening overture, occasional bits between the acts, and "chasers,"—while the audience was leaving—all from the "pit," the traveling orchestra being on the stage. When the employer refused to do this, Petrillo had the traveling orchestra cancel its appearance. Again the board dismissed the Section 8 (*b*) (6) complaint, and again the Supreme Court upheld its decision, because here again the local orchestra was offering to perform "work" for the required pay, however unnecessary or unwanted such "work" might be.

Confusion was rife among the members of the Court. Justice Jackson voted with the majority in the "bogus" type case while Justice Douglas dissented, calling the " 'work' . . . not only unwanted" but "wholly useless"—in no conceivable sense "a 'service' to the employer." But then Justice Douglas voted with the majority in the stand-by orchestra case while Justice Jackson dissented. Chief Justice Vinson and Justice Clark, calling them "modern make-work gimmicks," thought that both were "boondoggles which the employer 'does not want, does not need, and is not even willing to accept.' " Nevertheless a majority of the Justices in each case were of the opinion that some work was actually done by the typesetters and was offered to be done by the stand-by musicians, in spite of Justice Jackson's caustic comment that "Congress surely did not enact a prohibition whose practical application would be restricted to those without sufficient imagination to invent some 'work'."

Thus Section 8 (*b*) (6) proved to be a futile gesture against featherbedding. Experience indicates that unless Congress is more specific in its prohibitions future efforts will be no more successful. And even then, as Senator Taft indicated in his report on this statute, while legislators may thoroughly disapprove of featherbedding, they may continue to feel it to be "impracticable to give a board or a court the power to say that so many men are all right, and so many men are too many." Until some standard is set, other than the ambiguous one of the employer's own wants or desires, or until some adjustments are made between employers and unions through collective bargaining, practices of this sort are bound to remain as a means of providing pay for the members of a few of our strong unions.

THE REPRESENTATION CASES

Did the union actually represent a majority of the employees? And what was the appropriate bargaining unit? The answers to these questions are contained in what are called the representation cases, and they constitute an important segment of the functioning of the National Labor Relations Board. Of the board's procedure in these cases under Section 9 of the Wagner Act there is a fairly detailed account in Chapter IX. This was not changed radically in the 1947 statute. However, the board was prohibited from conducting pre-hearing elections—a practice it had followed during 1946 and early 1947. Practice over the years has produced a complicated accumulation of rules and interpretations.

From the outset the courts acknowledged the board's power to establish appropriate bargaining units. While the determinations of the board under Section 9 were not directly subject to judicial review, an employer could force the board to issue a Section 8 (5) or 8 (a) (5) complaint by his refusal to bargain with the union certified to represent the employees in a specified unit. Then, in the proceedings to enforce the ensuing order he could raise the issue of the board's alleged incorrect ruling under Section 9. That is what happened in *NLRB v. Norfolk Southern Bus Corporation,* a 1946 case. The evidence showed that the company consisted of two divisions— the Virginia and North Carolina divisions. While it would have been most natural to treat the entire company as a single bargaining unit, it appeared that very few employees in the North Carolina division wanted a union, while the majority of those in the Virginia division did. Thus, if the board set up the entire company as a single bargaining unit, the chances were good that the votes of the Carolina employees would reject unionism in the ensuing election. Hence the board established the Virginia division as a separate bargaining unit, and in that unit a majority of the employees chose a union.

The board's chief reason for doing this was to achieve unionism where and to the extent it was wanted by the employees. However, it is quite obvious that it eliminated the Carolina division to prevent a probable rejection of a union altogether. And the board used as an excuse the fact that the two divisions had separate seniority lists and were in other minor respects distinguishable. Of course, the company was incensed over having half its employees represented by a union and the other half not; but the federal court accepted the board's contention that half a loaf was better than none when the policies of the act were so clearly to promote the organization of unions and collective bargaining.

During the early days of the Wagner Act many employers opposed the CIO industrial unions with a single bargaining unit for all employees in a plant. In later years, however, they usually preferred them since they found it easier to do business with one union than with several craft organizations. But after World War II there developed a steady desire among skilled workmen in industrial units to splinter off into craft groups, apparently to secure the more specialized collective representation of craft unions. This trend was opposed by the big employers as well as by the industrial unions, and in 1947 Congress amended the Section 9 (*b*) proviso to prevent the board from declaring craft units inappropriate on the basis of prior board determinations in the same plant, unless a majority of the craft employees voted against separate representation. The board has held that it could safely ignore this provision except in situations where it had actually made the previous unit determination in contested cases. In this way it might retain the industrial unit wherever it was originally recognized without contest between the parties or among the employees. Even so, there have been scores of cases before the board on this issue and as a result a good many craft unions have splintered off. Under the Taft-Hartley amendments, Congress made special rules about separate bargaining units for professional employees, plant guards, and the like.

In the interests of stability and to protect the board from overwork, Congress enacted the one year rule—that there could not be a representation election within one year of a previous valid election. At the same time the board created a complicated but effective practice to protect it from being overwhelmed with representation petitions by unions trying to horn in and replace established unions. First of all, a petition will not be entertained unless the petitioning union can show the support of at least 30 per cent of the employees in the proposed unit. Then, if there is an existing valid contract between the employer and another union, this operates as a bar against the petitioning union, except during the 60–90 day period prior to the expiration of the contract (up to three years of its duration). The board recognizes that it must maintain a balance between the stability of long contracts, on the one hand, and the possible needs and wishes of some of the employees for representation by a different union, on the other.

Board elections are conducted much as they always have been. Either a group of employees or a union, on the one hand, or an employer on the other, may file a petition for an election. "Employees on strike who are not entitled to reinstatement," says the 1947 act, "shall not be eligible to vote." This provision was included because under the Wagner Act the board at one time or another had said that such employees—admittedly still "employees" for certain purposes both under the Wagner Act and the amended statute—were and were not eligible to vote in elections. Indeed, at different times before 1947, three different rules were observed. Under one, striking employees were allowed to vote while those replacing them were not. Under another, the replacements were allowed to vote while striking employees were not. And under still another view, both strikers and their replacements were allowed to vote. The rule just quoted created a complication for the board, because theoretically it was required to try the right to reinstatement, if any, of each striker in order to determine his voting eligibility. Congress resolved this confusion with the adoption in 1959 of an amendment to Section 9 (c) (3) that limits the eligibility period of an economic striker to participation in "any election conducted within twelve months after the commencement of the strike."

The board still fixes the list of eligible voters as the payroll immediately preceding the election, and it tries to accommodate the date of election to surrounding circumstances in order to make it as fair as possible and not subject to the atmosphere of possible unfair labor practices. Where an election is between two unions, a heading for "Neither" still appears on the ballot, so that there are 3 possible choices. And if none of the three secures a majority vote, under the 1947 act a run-off election must be held between the two choices with the most votes, even if this should mean dropping one of the unions from the ballot. During the election either party may challenge the right of any employee to vote. The challenged vote is then placed in an envelope marked with the voter's name so that later, when the challenge is investigated and the voter's eligibility is determined one way or another, the ballot may either be dropped into the box or be rejected, as the case may be.

In *NLRB v. A. J. Tower Company,* decided in 1947, 230 valid votes were cast at a board conducted election, 116 in favor of the union and 114 against it, one other vote being challenged by the union. Although the vote of a Mrs. Kane was unchallenged, it was later determined that she was not an employee at the time of the election and had thus been ineligible to vote. In addition to the unopened challenged ballot, her vote might have affected the outcome of the election. But the board ruled that because he had failed to challenge her eligibility prior to her actual deposit of her ballot into the box, the employer had waived his right later to challenge Mrs. Kane's vote or to object to the election on this ground. A majority of the Supreme Court upheld the board. Justice Murphy, acknowledging that cutting off the right to challenge in this way might mean counting some ineligible votes, thought this possibility "to be far outweighed by the dangers attendant upon the allowance of indiscriminate challenges after the election." He declared that experience justified the rule "that once a ballot has been cast without challenge and its identity lost, its validity cannot later be challenged."

It is impossible even to suggest the multitude of details which the board has to handle in its administration of Section 9. Here in these representation cases the raw stuff of employees' autonomy to organize and bargain collectively is translated into action. Here the policy of Congress is articulated into labor unions of all kinds and on occasion even into a rejection of unionism altogether. The foregoing account is only a sample of the thousands of cases the board has processed under Section 9—as thankless and as unappreciated a task as has ever been performed. It has been done admirably by a board of administrators who have often been the objects of abuse, and who have seldom received the praise they so richly deserve for a necessary job well done.

CHAPTER XIV

THE ACT, THE BOARD, AND THE COURTS III

There is hardly a political question in the United States which does not sooner or later turn into a judicial one. Consequently the language of everyday party-political controversy has to be borrowed from legal phraseology and conceptions. As most public men are or have been lawyers, they apply their legal habits and turn of mind to the conduct of affairs. Juries make all classes familiar with this. So legal language is pretty well adopted into common speech; the spirit of the law, born within schools and courts, spreads little by little beyond them; it infiltrates through society right down to the lowest ranks, till finally the whole people have contracted some of the ways and tastes of a magistrate.—Alexis de Tocqueville, *Democracy in America,* Part I, 1840.

No matter whether th' constitution follows th' flag or not, th' supreme coort follows th' iliction returns. —Finley Peter Dunne, Mr. Dooley on the Supreme Court's decisions.

As THE nation celebrated its 200th anniversary in 1976, the National Labor Relations Board had entered its fifth decade. This New Deal agency of the Roosevelt era had now become an established part of the American government. While Congress deliberated over changing the laws that the board would administer, no one even suggested that the board be eliminated or that its powers be curtailed. Years earlier, there were those who declared that unfair labor practices should be prosecuted directly in the courts (some said in a specially created "labor court"), just as the criminal laws are enforced, thus eliminating the old NLRB's triple function of investigator, prosecutor, and judge. But the 1947 Taft-Hartley modifications, creating the

independent status of the general counsel to head up the
NLRB's investigative and prosecutorial functions, put a stop
to criticisms of the board's tripartite structure. The Labor
Board was here to stay.

The board's operations had grown enormously. In the fiscal
year ending September 30, 1977, the board processed 52,943
cases with a professional staff of 1,161. During that year, almost
a half million employees participated in 8,635 board elections—
46 per cent won by unions. There were 37,602 unfair labor
practice charges filed—an increase of 8.1 per cent over the prior
fiscal year; and merit was found in one-third of the unfair labor
practice cases filed. Two and one-half times as many charges
were filed against employers as against unions. About one-fifth
of the charges filed against unions involved allegations of secondary boycotts or picketing. And back pay totaling $17.4 mil-
lion was received by 7,552 workers.

DEFERRAL TO PRIVATE TRIBUNALS

Section 10 (a) of the act explicitly declares that the board's
power to prevent unfair labor practices "shall not be affected
by any other means of adjustment or prevention that has been
or may be established by agreement, law, or otherwise. . . ."
Because of the prevalence of arbitration clauses in collective
bargaining agreements, and in light of the provision in Section
302 (d) of the LMRA favoring arbitration as "the desirable
method for settlement of grievances," the board was frequently
asked by respondents to defer or discontinue processing charges
where arbitration is available or actual awards have apparently
resolved the issues against the charging parties. The first case
of this kind was *In re Spielberg Manufacturing Company*
(1955). There, the company was charged with discrimination
because it fired four strikers for alleged misconduct on a picket
line. These four employees had agreed to and actively participated in an arbitration proceeding where their grievances had
been denied. On the basis of this award, the board dismissed

charges of discrimination. The board stated that while it was not bound as a matter of law, as a matter of policy it would defer to the arbitration award and dismiss the complaint, since "the proceedings appear to have been fair and regular, all parties had agreed to be bound, and the decision of the arbitration panel is not clearly repugnant to the purposes and policies of the Act."

These elements became crucial in so-called deferral cases. In *Collyer Insulated Wire Company* (1971), the board dismissed a "refusal to bargain" charge growing out of the employer's alleged unilateral changes in working conditions, holding that the dispute should have been settled under the contract; but it retained jurisdiction to see that the arbitrator's disposition was fair and not repugnant to the act. Thereafter, the *Collyer* technique was increasingly used, especially in discrimination cases where the arbitrators had made findings with respect to the validity of and the reasons behind the discipline imposed. When the arbitration passed muster, the board applied *Spielberg*. During the thirty-month period between May, 1973 and December, 1975, 1,632 unfair labor practice cases were deferred or dismissed by the board—"*Collyer*-ized," as the practice came to be known. But the board was badly split on this issue. Betty Southard Murphy happened to be chairman of the board in 1977 when she became the swing vote in two decisions curtailing the use of the *Collyer* doctrine. The board decided henceforth to use it only in refusal-to-bargain cases involving contract interpretation issues, but not in situations involving alleged discriminatory denial of individual employees' Section 7 rights. In *General American Transportation Corp.* (1977), Chairman Murphy stated that the arbitration process was not "suited for resolving employee complaints of discrimination under Section 7." However, the board continues to apply *Dubo Manufacturing Co.* (1963), in cases where both parties voluntarily submit their dispute to arbitration. There, the board deferred the matter pending the award, indicating that it would apply *Spielberg* in all cases where both parties agreed to arbitrate the dispute, if the award was not repugnant to the act. Where arbitration is available but the parties have not voluntarily utilized it, which is the classic *Collyer* situation, the board under *General American* will defer cases before it not involving claimed violations of individual rights under the act, thus forcing the parties to pursue the private remedy. If the resulting arbitration decision is fair and regular and not clearly repugnant to the policies and purposes of the act, the board will then close its case.

This is the direction that the present board is expected to take, even under the helm of Chairman John H. Fanning, who has always opposed the extension of *Spielberg*. Courts have uniformly recognized this as an area for the board's exercise of administrative discretion, including a tacit approval of the board's use of *Spielberg* by the Supreme Court in 1974.

NEW RIGHTS ESTABLISHED—AND RELINQUISHED

An administrative agency like the NLRB breathes new life into the law as it decides new cases. "The responsibility to adapt the Act to changing patterns of industrial life is entrusted to the Board," said the Supreme Court in *NLRB v. J. Weingarten, Inc.* (1975). Justice Brennan quoted with approval the following language of the Court's in a prior case: " 'Cumulative experience' begets understanding and insight by which judgments . . . are validated or qualified or invalidated. The constant process of trial and error, on a wider and fuller scale than a single adversary litigation permits, differentiates perhaps more than anything else the administrative from the judicial process." Thus, in deciding *Weingarten* the board created a new Section 7 right for employees.

It began when J. Weingarten, Inc., the operator of some one hundred retail stores with lunch counters, received a report that a sales employee named Laura Collins was taking money from a cash register. Weingarten sent an undercover specialist named Hardy to investigate. The rumor turned out to be baseless; but while he was there, the store manager asked Hardy to investigate a report by a fellow employee that Collins had bought a box of chicken priced $2.98, but had put only $1.00 in the cash register. Collins was brought before the store manager and Hardy for questioning. Several times during the interview, Collins asked the store manager to call in a union steward, but he refused. Collins had a satisfactory explanation for what had occurred. It seems that they had run out of small boxes for the $1.00 orders. So when she bought a $1.00 order and made it up herself to take out, she simply had to put the chicken in the next largest box, one designed for the $2.98 chicken order. This explanation checked out. Hardy apologized and told her the matter was closed. Thereupon Collins burst into tears, blurting out that the only thing she had ever gotten from the store without paying was her free lunch. The store manager and specialist Hardy then began questioning her about the free lunches. In desperation, she again asked for a steward, but again her request was denied. On the basis of her answers to his questions, Hardy prepared a written statement showing that she owed the store $160 for the lunches. Collins refused to sign the statement. The store manager asked Collins not to discuss the whole episode with anyone, saying it was a private matter between her and the company. Collins, however, reported it to her union, which filed a charge against Weingarten, complaining that by repeatedly declining her request for union representation, the company had deprived Collins of her Section 7 rights. The board incidentally found that everyone, including the store manager, ate free lunches, since the home office had never said that they should not.

Section 7 protects the right of an employee "to engage in . . . concerted activities for . . . mutual aid or protection." According to the board, this includes an employee's right not to be interviewed without union representation when he reasonably suspects he may be disciplined. The employee must request representation. However, in balancing an employee's Section 7 rights with "legitimate employer prerogatives," the board de-

cided that the employer may conduct his inquiry without such
an interview; or he may take disciplinary action without any
interview. But if he does choose to proceed with an interview,
the employer has no duty to bargain with the union representative who attends.

In *Weingarten,* the Supreme Court enforced the board's order. Justice Powell, dissenting, noted that the Court spoke
"only of the right to insist on the presence of a union representative." He said that since Section 7 protects "concerted
activity" and not just "union activity," this right "also exists
in the absence of a recognized union." In other words, Justice
Powell suggests that a worker in an unorganized plant, whom
the employer interviews with discipline in mind, has a Section
7 right to have a fellow employee be with him during the
interview.

In *Amax, Inc.* (1977), the board extended *Weingarten.*
There, it held that the right to insist on the presence of a
union representative at an investigatory interview reasonably
believed to involve disciplinary action also includes the right
to consult a union representative prior to the interview. The
union, as well as the employee, may invoke this additional
right.

Another example of the board's ability to create rights and
responsibilities not spelled out in the statute is seen in the
Excelsior rule. In *Excelsior Underwear* (1966), the board laid
down the rule that within seven days after an election has been
agreed to by the parties or directed by the board, an employer
must make available for the other parties to the election a list
of the names and addresses of employees eligible to vote. Nothing can be quite as valuable to a union in an election campaign
as such a list. Indeed, an employer's failure to furnish an *Excelsior* list to the board may be a basis for setting aside an
election. One employer who declined voluntarily to furnish
such a list was subpoenaed by the board to produce the information. The Supreme Court in *NLRB v. Wyman-Gordon Co.*
(1969) enforced the subpoena and sustained the board's power

to require *Excelsior* lists from employers. The Court felt that Congress had "granted the Board a wide discretion to ensure the fair and free choice of bargaining representatives" and that the *Excelsior* rule furthered "this objective by encouraging an informed employee electorate and by allowing unions the right of access to employees that management already possesses."

The Supreme Court's endorsement of the *Excelsior Underwear* rule and the wide latitude it has given the board in representation matters certainly shows its approval of the board's conduct of elections under Section 9 of the act. In early 1977, the board announced that the 30 millionth voter in a board election had then voted. In some 300,000 elections, employee participation had averaged close to 90 per cent.

A vital question among board members under Section 9 is whether the board should be concerned with the truth or falsity of preelection campaign statements. This matter arises when a losing party files objections to an election and asks the board to set the vote aside because the other party's misrepresentation allegedly interfered with the fair conduct of the election. Under the board's *Ideal Electric* rule, the objectionable behavior must ordinarily have occurred after the union filed its petition with the board. Where the misconduct alleged involves threats, promises of benefit, as well as actual economic benefits conferred, or improprieties in the election process itself, the board has consistently set aside the election. However, there has been a persistent and difficult problem where the alleged misconduct consists of factual misrepresentations made in preelection campaign literature.

In *Hollywood Ceramics* (1972), the board held that a substantial misstatement of relevant and material facts, within the special knowledge of the campaigner, made to voters so shortly before the election that there is no effective time for reply, is grounds for setting aside the election results. Between 1971 and 1976, objections including charges of misrepresentations were filed in anywhere from three hundred to four hundred fifty cases per year; and second elections were directed in 7 per cent of such cases. However, in *Shopping Kart Food Market* (1977), the board, expressly overruling *Hollywood Ceramics*, announced that it would "no longer probe into the truth or falsity of the parties' campaign statements." The board stated its "unwillingness to embrace the completely unverified assumption that misleading campaign propaganda will interfere with employees' freedom of choice," choosing instead 'to view "employees as mature individuals who are capable of recognizing campaign propaganda for what it is and discounting it." The board saw the "ill effects of the rule" as including "extensive analysis [by the board] of campaign propaganda, restriction of free speech, variance in application as between the board and the courts, increasing litigation, and a resulting decrease in the finality of election results." However, the board indicated that it would continue to set aside elections where a party makes misrepresentations regarding the board's processes or where it uses forged documents that prevent the voter from recognizing the propaganda for what it is. Chairman Fanning and Member Jenkins took sharp exception to the move away from *Hollywood Ceramics,* declaring: "Were those standards to be relaxed —to the 'almost anything goes' standard proposed by our colleagues—one result can be fairly predicted. . . . As 'bad money drives out the good,' so misrepresentation, if allowed to take the field unchallengeable as to its impact, will tend to drive out the responsible statement." And they asked: "Are our colleagues now prepared to have these [*Excelsior*] eligibility lists used to grossly misinform the electorate?" Soon thereafter in another case, the majority refused to overturn an election where there was a wage misrepresentation of $1.90 per hour because it amounted to "no more than misleading campaign statements." Chairman Fanning, dissenting again, found it inconceivable "that a wage misrepresentation . . . of approximately $2.00 per hour made at a time when no reply was possible, would not have a significant impact on the election."

The critical importance of changes in the board's personnel appeared late in 1978 when the two dissenters in *Shopping Kart* picked up the decisive third vote they needed to reconvert their minority position into board law. This resulted from the intervening appointment by the President of John C. Truesdale, a career employee of the agency, to replace board member Peter D. Walther. In *General Knit of California, Inc.* (1978) the new majority overruled *Shopping Kart* and returned to the standards for investigating misleading campaign statements that were enunciated in *Hollywood Ceramics,* being "convinced that [such] rule better enhances employee free choice and the fairness of board elections. . . ."

The board's decision in *General Knit of California, Inc.*, reinstating the *Hollywood Ceramics* rule, was the subject of a critical discussion entitled "NLRB's Decisions as Changeable as Political Winds," which appeared in the *Wall Street Journal* of January 4, 1979. The writer there noted: "The NLRB tradition of flip-flops is so engrained that labor law text books refer to the changing positions of past boards by using the names of Presidents, such as the 'Eisenhower board' or the 'Kennedy board.' "

In *NLRB v. Iron Workers Local 103* (1978), the Supreme Court declared: "An administrative agency is not disqualified from changing its mind; and when it does, the courts still sit in review of the administrative decision and should not approach the statutory construction issue *de novo* and without regard to the administrative understanding of the statutes." The five-year term of office for board members is in contrast to the term of a federal judge, which is for life. But, as Mr. Dooley suggested, even judges themselves are not insensitive to political changes.

In *NLRB v. Savair Manufacturing Co.* (1973), the union prior to an election circulated "recognition slips" among employees. Employees were told by the union that if they signed the slip before the election, they would avoid having to pay an "initiation fee" if it prevailed. The Supreme Court in reversing the board said: "We do not believe that the statutory policy of fair elections prescribed in the *Tower* case permits endorsements, whether for or against the union, to be bought and sold in this fashion."

While a board-conducted election may be the best proof of a union's majority status, it is not the only method. If a union secures uncoerced signatures on authorization cards from a majority of the employees in an appropriate unit, where there is no claim by another union and where the employer has not assisted the union, the employer may validly recognize the union as the bargaining agent. However, the employer may also question the union's majority status in such a situation and not be legally obliged to recognize it. An exception was carved out in *NLRB v. Gissel Packing Co.* (1969). There, the Supreme Court upheld the board's ruling that the employer may lose his right to insist on a vote among his employees in order to ascertain their uncoerced preference where he commits serious unfair labor practices that tend to undermine the union's majority and impede the election process.

In *Handy Andy, Inc.* (1977), the board indicated that in representation cases, it would no longer allow an employer to litigate the issue of whether a union has engaged in race or sex discrimination in its own membership policies. It found that in such cases, "the Employer's purpose is to delay the onset of bargaining, rather than to protect the minority or female employees from actual discrimination by the bargaining representative." Moreover, it held that "issues involving alleged invidious discrimination by a labor organization should be considered in an adversary proceeding in which the accused union is accorded the full spectrum of due process, including particularly the right of judicial review." The board noted that a labor organization violated the duty of fair representation as well as Sections 8 (b) (1) (A) and 8 (b) (2) of the act when it rejected an employee's grievance because of race, when it entered into a collective agreement that allocates work on the basis of race, or when it called a walkout to protest an employer's attempt to remedy its past discriminatory conduct.

ACCOMMODATING PROPERTY RIGHTS TO SECTION 7

In Anglo-Saxon jurisprudence, the ownership of land carried with it a total control over its use and enjoyment—to the exclusion of all other persons. In the 5th amendment, our federal

Constitution declares that "No person shall . . . be deprived of life, liberty or property, without due process of law; nor shall private property be taken for public use, without just compensation." In *Republic Aviation* and *Stowe Spinning* (*supra,* pp. 353–54), we saw how the board, with the Supreme Court's approval, began the process of accommodating the property rights of employers to their employees' Section 7 organizational rights. In *NLRB v. Babcock & Wilcox* (1956), involving the distribution of union literature in company-owned parking lots, the Supreme Court emphasized that this accommodation "must be obtained with as little destruction of one as is consistent with the maintenance of the other." There the Court denied outside union organizers the same access to company parking lots for organizational activities that in *Republic Aviation* it had allowed to employees under Section 7. And in *NLRB v. Magnavox Co.* (1974) the Supreme Court held that the right of employees under Section 7 to distribute union literature on company property during nonworking time could not be validly waived in a collective bargaining agreement by a union representing them.

The advent of the shopping center recreated a situation reminiscent of the earlier *Thornhill* case—an attempt to protect peaceful picketing by the 1st and 14th amendments to the Constitution. This episode illustrates how constitutional doctrine emerges in the Supreme Court. It began with *Marsh v. Alabama* (1946), where Marsh, a Jehovah's Witness, distributed religious literature on the sidewalk of a company town owned lock-stock-and-barrel by the Gulf Shipbuilding Corporation. This violated a company rule; and Gulf put a stop to it. The Supreme Court held that Marsh's activity was protected by the 1st amendment, notwithstanding Gulf's private ownership of the sidewalk and his nonresidency in the town—even though the Bill of Rights in the Constitution ordinarily serves as a restraint only on governmental action. In *Amalgamated Food Employees v. Logan Valley* (1968), Supreme Court Justice Marshall, relying on *Marsh* and *Thornhill,* depicted the modern shopping center as the "functional equivalent of the business district . . . involved in *Marsh,*" declaring for the Court that the union had a 1st amendment right to picket Weis Markets, Inc., one of the stores within the privately owned plaza. But Justice Black, who had written the Court's opinion in *Marsh,* dissented vigorously. He commented caustically that "whether this Court likes it or not, the Constitution recognizes and supports the concept of private ownership of property." Justice Black distinguished the situation in *Marsh,* where the property had "taken on *all* the attributes of a town," from the shopping center, which has only one such feature present—a business district. "These pickets do have a constitutional right to speak about Weis' refusal to hire union labor," Justice Black concluded, "but they do not have a constitutional right to compel Weis to furnish them a place to do so on its property."

In a later Supreme Court case, *Hudgens v. NLRB* (1976), the owner of a shopping center threatened to arrest peaceful primary picketers of a retail store in the shopping center. The picketers were not employed at the store but were employees at the warehouse of the company operating the store; and their picketing of the store was to further a bargaining strike at the warehouse. The NLRB had entered a cease and desist order against Hudgens, the owner of the shopping center, finding that the warehouse employees enjoyed a 1st amendment right to picket on the shopping center property. Hence, it held that the owner's threat of arrest violated Section 8 (*a*) (1) of the act. The Court, however, quickly disposed of the constitutional argument. "We conclude, in short," the majority wrote, "that under the present state of the law the constitutional guarantee of free expression has no part to play in a case such as this." Thus, Justice Black, though no longer on the Court, had carried the day. Having thus discarded the doctrine that peaceful picketing in a shopping center was constitutionally protected, the Court thought that the question had to be resolved by a proper accommodation between Section 7 and property rights in accordance with its earlier decision in *Babcock & Wilcox,* and it remanded the case to the board for that purpose. But Justice

Marshall, joined by Justice Brennan, dissented. He thought that the "roadways, parking lots and walkways of the modern shopping center may be as essential for effective speech as the streets and sidewalks in the municipal or company-owned town," and that "the shopping center owner has assumed the traditional role of the state in its control of historical First Amendment forums."

Upon a re-referral of the case, the NLRB in 1977 unanimously affirmed its finding that the shopping center owner had violated Section 8 (*a*) (1) of the act by threatening the pickets in the shopping center with prosecution for violations of the criminal laws of trespass. This time around, the board rested its decision exclusively upon the violation of the employees' Section 7 rights. The Supreme Court had directed the NLRB's attention to three distinctions between the fact situation in *Hudgens* and in *Babcock & Wilcox* that became crucial to the board's decision on remand. First, the board concluded that economic picketing was entitled under Section 7 to "the same measure of protection afforded to organizational picketing." Second, the pickets as employees of the company's warehouse were entitled to "at least as much protection as would be afforded to nonemployee organizers." Since Section 7 "was intended to protect the rights of employees rather than those of nonemployees," neither access to mass media nor picketing in locations remote from the store were " 'reasonable' means of communication for employee pickets seeking to publicize their labor dispute with a single store in the Mall," according to the board. The fact that " 'the property interests impinged upon . . . were not those of the employer against whom the §7 activity was directed, but of another' "—the owner of the shopping center—does not exonerate Hudgens, the board said, adding that while he "is neutral in the sense that he is not the primary employer and is, therefore, not a party to the labor dispute, he is nonetheless financially interested in the success of each of the businesses in his Center inasmuch as he receives a percentage of their gross sales as part of his rental arrangement." The board concluded: "A contrary holding would enable employers to insulate themselves from Section 7 activities by simply moving their operations to leased locations on private malls, and would render Section 7 meaningless as to their employees."

It probably made no difference to Hudgens whether the right he transgressed was a Section 7 right created by Congress or a constitutional right. No doubt he was only sorry he could no longer prohibit union picketing in his shopping center. But the effect of resting the decision on a statutory rather than a constitutional ground is to make such picketing subject to Congressional control.

The board has recognized that the rights of employees to solicit membership and to distribute literature during nonworking time and in nonwork areas may be curtailed where the employer can show that the disputed activity would interfere with discipline or disrupt production. In that regard, the board has ruled that employees of restaurants and retail stores cannot solicit or distribute union material in customer areas. Similarly, the board allows health care institutions to prohibit union solicitation in the parts of the building that are designated strictly for patient care. "Solicitation at anytime in those areas might be unsettling to the patients—particularly those who are seriously ill and thus need quiet and peace of mind," the board said. However, in *Beth Israel Hospital v. NLRB* (1978), the Supreme Court upheld the board in ordering a hospital to rescind a rule barring solicitation and distribution of literature in any area to which patients or visitors have access, with specific reference to a hospital cafeteria and coffee shop used predominantly by employees and only incidentally by patients and visitors. The Court noted that while statements made by members of Congress, when it was enacting the 1974 Health Care Amendments to the NLRB, "addressed its concern for the unique problems presented by labor disputes in the health-care industry by adding specific strike notice and mediation provisions designed to avert interruption in the delivery of critical health care services; none expresses a policy in favor of curtailing self-organizational rights."

STRIKES AND LOCKOUTS

The Supreme Court case of *NLRB v. Erie Resistor Corp.* (1963) involved the legality of a highly effective technique to break a strike. The employer in that case offered superseniority to those of his employees who would come back to work while a strike was in progress, and notified the union of its strategy. Under this plan, the company offered to replacements, as well as to strikers who returned to work during the strike, twenty years additional seniority, to be available only for credit against future layoffs and not applicable for other benefits based on length of service. Within four days of the announcement, 34 new replacements, 47 employees recalled from layoff, and 23 strikers accepted production jobs in a plant with a normal complement of 450. This put the union under great pressure, so it offered to reduce its contract demands if the company would abandon superseniority or even go to arbitration on the question; but the company chose to stand pat. In the following week, 64 more strikers returned to work and 21 more replacements took jobs. When the number of returned strikers shortly thereafter reached 125, the union capitulated and the parties signed a new contract containing the superseniority provision. Thereupon, 173 members resigned from the union. At first there were no layoffs, as the employer was busy filling back orders. Within eight months, however, the work force dropped and a number of the last-back strikers were laid off because of their relatively low seniority due to the company's new superseniority policy.

In its charge filed with the NLRB, the union alleged that awarding superseniority during the strike was an unfair labor practice, and that the subsequent layoff of the last-back strikers pursuant to the new seniority provision was unlawful. The board's trial examiner (known as an administrative law judge) found that the employer had promulgated this policy for legitimate economic reasons, not for illegal or discriminatory purposes, and that there was insufficient evidence of a subjective intent to discriminate against the union. He therefore recommended that the complaint be dismissed. The board disagreed, holding that "super-seniority is a form of discrimination extending far beyond the employer's right of replacement sanctioned by *Mackay,* and is, moreover, in direct conflict with the express provisions of the Act prohibiting discrimination." The Supreme Court agreed with the board. It held that the company's conduct spoke for itself, saying "—it *is* discriminatory and it *does* discourage union membership," and "it carries with it unavoidable consequences which the employer not only foresaw but which he must have intended." The Court added that "super-seniority by its very terms operates to discriminate between strikers and non-strikers, both during and after a strike, and its destructive impact upon the strike and union activity cannot be doubted."

Following *Erie Resistor,* the Supreme Court, in *NLRB v. Great Dane Trailers, Inc.* (1967), held it was an unfair labor practice for an employer to pay accrued vacation benefits to strike replacements, returned strikers, and nonstrikers, while denying such benefits to striking employees "who are distinguishable only by their participation in protected concerted activity."

In *NLRB v. Insurance Agents' International Union* (1960), the Supreme Court criticized the board for "functioning as an arbiter of the sort of economic weapons the parties can use in seeking to gain acceptance of their bargaining demands." That was in a case involving union bargaining tactics—slowing down on the job pending completion of a collective agreement. Later the Court applied that very language to overturn board rulings in two 1965 cases where employers had been found guilty of Section 8 (*a*) (1) and (3) violations for lockouts that had occurred in labor disputes. In both instances, the employers were responding to the exigencies of tense bargaining pressures against them. After a bargaining impasse had been reached in *American Ship Building Co. v. NLRB* (1965), the employer temporarily shut down his plant and laid off his employees for the sole purpose of exerting economic pressure to support his bargaining position. And in *NLRB v. Brown* (1965), to offset a whipsaw strike against one member of a multiemployer bargaining unit, nonstruck members of the bargaining group locked out their regular employees, continuing to operate with temporary replacements. This was in accordance with advance notice to the union, which was told that such locked out employees would be recalled when the strike against the target employer ceased. The board had distinguished *Buffalo Linen* (*supra*, p. 361) because there, all the members of the employer group had shut down; here all the employers continued to operate with temporary replacements, the board conceding that only the struck employer could legitimately use replacements during the strike. The Supreme Court was not impressed with this distinction, observing: "While the use of temporary nonunion personnel in preference to the locked-out union members is discriminatory, we think that any resulting tendency to discourage union membership is comparatively remote, and that this use of temporary personnel constitutes a measure reasonably adapted to the effectuation of a legitimate business end." The Court reserved judgment on what it would do where the employers hired *permanent* replacements for their locked out employees; but its criticism of the board for stretching Section 8 (*a*) (1) and (3) to invalidate bargaining pressure devices simply because they give employers "too much power" suggests that the limit to the employer's use of the lockout defensively has not yet been fully realized.

THE ULTIMATE IN RETALIATION

Perhaps the most sweeping decision the Supreme Court ever made in an NLRB case is *Textile Workers Union of America v. Darlington Manufacturing Company* (1965). And it seems extraordinary in retrospect that not a single member of the Court dissented from its decision.

The facts were very simple. Darlington, a small South Carolina corporation operating a single textile mill, was controlled by Deering Milliken Company, a New York marketer of textiles which, in turn, was controlled by Roger Milliken, president of Darlington. Milliken and his family operated sixteen other textile "manufacturers," comprising in all twenty-seven different mills. When the Textile Workers' Union set out to organize the Darlington mill, the company embarked on a series of unfair labor practices, including threats to close down the mill if the union was successful. The union nevertheless persisted and won the labor board election. True to his threat, Roger Milliken called a meeting of the board of directors to consider closing the mill. With the shareholders' approval, the mill was shut down for good, and the plant machinery and equipment were sold piecemeal at auction. Of course, all of the employees were gradually discharged, group by group, as the closing of the Darlington plant was completed.

The union filed charges with the board, alleging that Darlington had discriminated against its employees in violation of Section 8 (a) (3), which makes it unlawful to "discourage membership in any labor organization," also complaining that it had unlawfully retaliated against them, in violation of Section 8 (a) (1), for having as employees exercised their Section 7 rights "to form, join, or assist labor organizations. . . ." The board held that under the circumstances of this case, closing the plant violated Section 8 (a) (3). It did not, however, order the plant to be reopened but did order back pay for all Darlington employees until they obtained substantially equivalent work elsewhere or were put on preferential hiring lists at the other Deering Milliken mills. The Supreme Court overruled the board, declaring that "an employer has the absolute right to terminate his entire business for any reason he pleases." To organized labor, this must have been as if robbery with a gun, arson, and kidnapping were treated as serious crimes while murder was not even regarded as a misdemeanor. Thus, an employer cannot discharge *one* of his employees because he votes for a union; but he can legally discharge *all* of them if he does it as part of a permanent shutdown of his entire business.

The Court said that an employer violates the act by closing down one of several plants he operates, but only "if motivated by a purpose to chill unionism in any of the remaining plants of the single employer and if the employer may reasonably have foreseen that such closing would likely have that effect." But as to the closing down of a one plant business, it said: "A proposition that a single businessman cannot choose to go out of business if he wants to would represent such a startling innovation that it should not be entertained without the clearest manifestation of legislative intent or unequivocal judicial precedent so construing the Labor Relations Act. We find neither." And the Court went on to say: "We hold here only that when an employer closes his entire business, even if the liquidation is motivated by vindictiveness toward the union, such action is not an unfair labor practice."

In a footnote, the Court pointed out that nothing in its opinion would justify an employer's interfering with his employees' organizational rights by threatening to close his plant, as distinguished from his announcing a decision already made by the board of directors to close down if they voted for union representation. The Court then conceded that its decision in the *Darlington* case "may result in some deterrent effect on organizational activities independent of that arising from the closing itself," because an employer may be encouraged by the *Darlington* case "to make a definitive decision to close on the theory that its mere announcement before a representation election will discourage the employees from voting for the union," thus taking him off the hook as far as implementing his contingent commitment to close down the plant. The Court goes on to console itself, however, that "[s]uch a possibility is not likely to occur" since "a solidly successful employer" is not apt to take the chance that "the employees will call his bluff by voting to organize." The footnote continues: "We see no practical way of eliminating this possible consequence of our holding short of allowing the Board to order an employer who chooses to gamble with his employees not to carry out his announced intention to close," concluding that the matter is not of "sufficient significance" to affect its decision in the *Darlington* case.

All this is very disturbing. In light of the NLRB's past history, including its career before the courts, the *Darlington* case remains a real puzzle, difficult to reconcile with many of the uncompromising judicial mileposts that made the board such an effective institution for establishing and maintaining employees' organizational rights.

In *Bruce Duncan Co.* (1977), an employer with a number of offices threatened to close its John F. Kennedy airport office if the employees there chose to be represented by a union. It then followed through on the threat, in the manner of Roger Milliken. The board concurred in the administrative law judge's finding that the employer had discharged these employees "in retaliation for (their) attempts to have a union." Relying on *Darlington,* however, it dismissed that part of the complaint alleging a violation of Section 8 (*a*) (3) in the discriminatory discharge of the JFK work force because there was "no evidence that would fairly support the inference that the Respondent, in closing the JFK office, was motivated by a desire to disparage the union interests of its other employees, or that Respondent would have reasonably foreseen such an effect. . . ." Moreover, the Section 8 (*a*) (5) allegations of the complaint were dismissed since there was nobody left at JFK to bargain for!

MANDATORY SUBJECTS OF BARGAINING

In its 1952 *American National Insurance Company* case (*supra,* pp. 413–14), the Supreme Court held that an employer lawfully refused to sign any contract unless it included a management rights clause that left in its hands the final say on promotions, discipline, and scheduling work, with no recourse to arbitration on any aspect of these matters, and did not thereby violate Section 8 (a) (5). In *NLRB v. Wooster Div. of Borg-Warner Corp.* (1958), the employer refused to sign any agreement not containing a clause requiring a vote among the employees on the employer's last offer before a strike could be called. Also, the employer insisted the contract would be only with the local union, and not with the International UAW, of which the local was an affiliate. It took this position in spite of the fact that under Section 9, the NLRB had certified the international union as bargaining representative for the employees involved. The union filed an 8 (a) (5) charge, and the NLRB eventually held that the employer had violated that section, ordering it to comply. The Supreme Court upheld the board, a majority declaring that the employer had refused to bargain in good faith over both the "recognition" and the "ballot" clauses. Incidentally, the parties had reached accord on all other terms and conditions of employment normally covered in collective agreements. Furthermore, it was found that both parties were acting in good faith. Concerning the recognition item there was no difficulty. Almost any line of reasoning would support the conclusion that the employer must recognize the certified union, international or other, and execute the agreement with that union in order to be in compliance with the good faith and other express requirements of Section 8 (d) of the 1947 act. But the "ballot" provision raised real difficulties.

Section 8 (a) (5) of the NLRA is very sketchy, merely making it unfair for an employer "to refuse to bargain collectively with the representatives of his employees. . . ." In Section 8 (d), however, Congress defines the term "bargain collectively" to mean a mutual obligation of the parties to meet and confer "in good faith" over "wages, hours, and other terms and conditions of employment, or the negotiation of an agreement, or any question arising thereunder," adding, however, that "such obligation does not compel either party to agree to a proposal or require the making of a concession. . . ." And this Section 8 (*d*) becomes crucial in the Court's new position on Section 8 (*a*) (5) violations. Take the "ballot" provision in this *Borg-Warner* case. Justice Burton observed that it was a perfectly lawful item to include in a collective agreement. However, if the union refused to agree to it, the employer could not insist on it. The reason is that it did not fall within the scope of those matters that were generally described in Section 8 (*d*). Hence, the employer was not permitted to insist upon the union's agreement with respect to a nonmandatory item of bargaining as a condition to his bargaining over the other items. For his refusal under those circumstances to sign the contract containing provisions covering such other items was, in effect, a refusal to bargain over them at all. Speaking for the dissent, Justice Harlan stated his inability "to grasp a concept of 'bargaining' which enables one to 'propose' a particular point, but not to 'insist' on it as a condition to agreement."

From *Borg-Warner,* it was only a short step to *Fibreboard Paper Products Co. v. NLRB* (1964). There, a few days before its collective agreement was to expire, Fibreboard decided for economic reasons to subcontract all of its plant maintenance work, which had been previously performed by its employees in the bargaining unit. The union representing its maintenance employees filed unfair labor practice charges with the NLRB. After some shilly-shallying, the board found that the employer's motive was economic and not antiunion, "but found nonetheless that the Company's 'failure to negotiate with . . . [the union] concerning its decision to subcontract its maintenance work constituted a violation of Section 8 (*a*) (5) of the Act.' " The board ordered the company to reinstitute the maintenance operation, reinstate its old employees with suitable back pay, and to fulfill its statutory obligation to bargain with the union over the subcontracting issue. The question for the Supreme Court then became: Is "contracting out," or subcontracting work performed by unit employees, a statutory subject of collective bargaining within Section 8 (*a*) (5), and is it covered by the phrase "terms and conditions of employment" within the meaning of Section 8 (*d*)? Put more simply: Is the contracting out or subcontracting of work a mandatory subject of collective bargaining? The Court, sustaining the board, held that it was. In doing so, however, it apparently limited its decision to "the facts of the present case." This implied a situation where the work in question was to be done by the subcontractor's employees on the same premises and in the same manner as the bargaining unit employees had previously performed it.

In *Fibreboard,* the employer told the union of its decision to subcontract its maintenance work to an independent contractor *after* the decision had been made. Since it was a mandatory subject for bargaining, the employer was under the duty to bargain with the union *before* it made a definite decision. Hence, the employer was found to have violated Section 8 (*a*) (5).

How did the Court determine that this subject was a mandatory subject of bargaining under the act? First, the Court said, because its inclusion as a mandatory subject "would promote the fundamental purpose of the act by bringing a problem of vital concern of labor and management within the framework established by Congress as most conducive to industrial peace." Second, in appraising the propriety of including a particular subject within the scope of mandatory bargaining, it is appropriate to look to industrial experience in the United States, which experience "illustrates that contracting out in one form or another has been brought, widely and successfully, within the collective bargaining framework. Provisions relating to contracting out exist in numerous collective bargaining agreements, and 'contracting out work is the basis of many grievances; and that type of claim is grist in the mills of the arbitrators.'" Thus, while interpreting a statute that gave no explicit guidance, the Court avoided a static view of the duty to bargain by seeking to determine what matters are "at the core of managerial control" from the objective judgment of unions and employers, as evidenced by collective bargaining agreements and practices.

The board has cautiously followed *Fibreboard,* avoiding a

blanket application of the doctrine to all subcontracting situations. Thus, it has more than once declined to apply *Fibreboard*
in a situation where the employer adhered to long established
practice in the plant when it refused to notify and bargain with
the union about each subcontract, but was willing to bargain on
the general subject, and where no economic detriment to unit
employees was shown.

"Our decisions in this area," the board has said in *Westinghouse Electric Corp.* (1965), "make it clear that *Fibreboard*
was not intended to lay down a hard and fast rule as to unilateral subcontracting and that even where a subject of mandatory bargaining is involved, there may be circumstances which
the Board would accept as justifying unilateral action," citing *Allied Chemical Corp.* (1965). Thus, the Supreme Court
and the board go in tandem—the Court lays down the major
legal principles and directions while the board refines and
delineates them to meet the varying situations that occur.

Borg-Warner was not the only case where the Supreme Court
refused to accept the board's views on mandatory subjects for
bargaining. In *Chemical Workers v. Pittsburgh Plate Glass Co.*
(1971), the employer made a midterm unilateral modification
that concerned not the benefits of active employees, but, rather,
the benefits of already retired former employees. The Supreme
Court, finding no violation of law, rejected the board's finding
that an employer is required by Section 8 (*a*) (5) to bargain
with the union over retirees' benefits. It declared flatly that already retired employees do not qualify as "employees," as they
are defined in the act. The fact that many employers and unions
have bargained over modifications of retirees' benefits, the
Court said, is not applicable here, in spite of what was said in
Fibreboard about past practice, because the retirees are not employees. "Common practice cannot change the law and make
into bargaining unit 'employees' those who are not." The
Court thought there was no real community of interest between
active employees and retired employees. In fact, it saw a risk
"that union representation on occasion might see fit to bargain

for improved wages or other conditions favoring active employees at the expense of retirees' benefits." Thus, bargaining over retiree benefits is merely permissive. In contrast, the Court held in *Ford Motor Co. v. NLRB* (1979) that where employers provide food or cafeteria facilities, the food prices and services are an aspect of the relationship and therefore are mandatory subjects of bargaining.

STRENGTHENING THE BARGAINING PROCESS

Several important decisions have further delineated the collective bargaining powers of unions. In *Emporium Capwell Co. v. Western Addition Community Organization* (1975), the Supreme Court, faced with a difficult choice, elected to side with collective bargaining as against civil rights activism. After investigating complaints that the company with whom it had a collective bargaining agreement was racially discriminating against employees, a union filed a grievance demanding that the joint union-management Adjustment Board be convened "to hear the entire case." Feeling that such procedure was inadequate, certain black employees refused to participate, and, against the union's advice, picketed the company's store. The company, after fairly warning these employees, fired them on their resumption of picketing. The local civil rights association to which the fired workers belonged filed charges with the NLRB alleging that such action by the company violated the employees' Section 7 rights to engage in concerted activity "for the purpose of collective bargaining or other mutual aid or protection."

The board dismissed the complaint, finding that the discharged employees' course of conduct "was no mere presentation of a grievance but nothing short of a demand that the [company] bargain with the picketing employees for the entire group of minority employees." The Court sustained the board's decision; and Justice Marshall, emphatically upholding the "majority rule" principle, declared; "The policy of industrial self-determination as expressed in §7 does not require fragmentation of the bargaining unit along racial or other lines in order to consist with the national labor policy against discrimination." In the United States (unlike the situation in some foreign countries), a single bargaining agent represents *all* of the employees in the unit for purposes of collective bargaining. A group organized along racial lines cannot usurp the functions of the certified union, and picketing for such a group does not constitute protected activity under Section 7. Accordingly, the Court held that Emporium Capwell could lawfully fire its employees who participated in such activities, however laudable the purposes they sought to promote.

Another important decision reinforced the powers of a bargaining agent. The employer in *NLRB v. Katz* (1962) unilaterally granted merit increases, announced changes in sick leave policy, and instituted a system of automatic wage increases during contract negotiations with the union representing his employees—all mandatory subjects of collective bargaining. Without any evidence that the employer was otherwise guilty of bad faith in bargaining, the board held that he had violated Section 8 (*a*) (5) of the act. The Supreme Court stated that even after an impasse in bargaining was reached, the employer could not grant wage increases to employees exceeding offers he had made to the union in bargaining sessions.

The Supreme Court in *NLRB v. Acme Industrial Co.* (1967) extended an employer's obligation to furnish a union with information as part of his duty to bargain in good faith. There the union requested information concerning shipments of machinery out of the plant for the purpose of determining whether it had a basis for a grievance under a subcontracting provision in the contract. In upholding the board, the Supreme Court rejected the notion that the availability of arbitration under the contract prevented the board from ordering the company to furnish this information to the union. It also emphasized that this obligation includes furnishing requested information *about* a grievance as well as *whether* there is a basis for filing and processing a grievance in the first place. The board showed that turnabout is fair play in *Oakland Press Co.* (1977), where it found that "a union's duty to furnish information relevant to the bargaining process is parallel to that of the employer." In *Detroit Edison Co. v. NLRB* (1979), the Supreme Court, on grounds of confidentiality, declined to order the employer to disclose to the union aptitude test scores of individual employees without the employee's consent.

In *H. K. Porter Co. v. NLRB* (1970), the Supreme Court nailed down the law that neither party is required to agree to a proposal or to make a concession in bargaining. An employer who engaged in dilatory and "hard bargaining" was ordered by the board to agree to a dues checkoff clause proposed by the union. The Court set aside this order because, it said, "it was never intended that the Government would in such cases step in, become a party to the negotiations and impose its own views of a desirable settlement." The Supreme Court's decision in *NLRB v. Insurance Agents' International Union* (1960) also limited the board's role. There the board had ordered a union to bargain in good faith solely because through its members it had put economic pressure on the employer to yield to its bargaining demands by harassing, on-the-job slowdowns designed to interfere with the carrying on of the employer's business. The board had found the union's tactics to be "the antithesis of reasoned discussion it was duty-bound to follow." In setting aside the order, the Court stated that the board's approach involved "an intrusion into the substantive aspects of the bargaining process" and observed "that at the present statutory stage of our national labor relations policy, the two factors—necessity for good-faith bargaining between parties, and the availability of economic pressure devices to each to make the other party incline to agree on one's terms—exist side by side."

UNION COERCION

The Taft-Hartley Act balanced the Wagner Act—the original NLRA—by establishing unfair labor practices of unions. Section 8 (*b*) (1) (A) of the 1947 act makes it an unfair labor practice for a union "to restrain or coerce employees in the exercise of the rights guaranteed in Section 7," going on to say: "*Provided,* That this paragraph shall not impair the right of a labor organization to prescribe its own rules with respect to the acquisition or retention of membership therein. . . ." And one of the critical provisions added by Taft-Hartley to Section 7 was language guaranteeing to each employee "the right to refrain from any or all such activities." In view of this, it was inevitable that conflicts would arise.

Where tenure of employment of a member was not affected, the Court has broadly construed the language of the 8 (*b*) (1) (A) proviso in favor of unions. Thus, it refused to find violations of Section 8 (*b*) (1) (A) when a union fined members for not complying with its rule against taking immediate —instead of deferred—piecework pay for work in excess of a production ceiling fixed by a union rule, when a union fined member-replacements who crossed the union's picket line during a strike, and also when a union brought suit in a state court to collect such fines, even where the fined member-transgressor happened to be a supervisor. Nor would the Court permit the board to inquire into the reasonableness of a fine by a union on a member who crossed the picket line to work, leaving such member's complaint to the tender mercies of a state court. Only when the union expelled a member on the ground that he had filed unfair labor practice charges against it with the NLRB before exhausting internal union remedies did the Court disallow the protective feature of the proviso, for "there should be as great a freedom to ask the Board for relief as there is to petition any other department of government for a redress of grievances. Any coercion used to discourage, retard or defeat that access is beyond the legitimate interests of a labor organization."

The following cases seem also to involve consideration of Section 8 (*b*) (2) of the LMRA as well as Section 8 (*b*) (1) (A). In *Radio Officers Union v. NLRB* (1954), the Supreme Court said that the policy of the act is "to insulate employees' jobs from their organizational rights" and "to allow employees to freely exercise their right to join unions, be good, bad or indifferent members, or abstain from joining any union, without imperilling their livelihood." The Court recognized, of course, that this was subject to the proviso to Section 8 (a) (3), which authorizes employers and unions to enter into certain union security contracts. The board has had to rule on the legality of clauses in collective bargaining agreements giving stewards preference over all other employees in securing job benefits. Since indifferent union members are unlikely to become stewards, such preferential provisions necessarily encourage union membership by discriminating in favor of the "enthusiastic unionist." In *Dairylea Cooperative* (1975), the board held that a clause in a collective bargaining agreement granting super-seniority to union officials is lawful, but only if limited to layoff and recall, since it "furthers the effective administration of bargaining agreements . . . by encouraging the continued presence of the steward on the job." But when a union negotiated a contract that afforded union stewards job-bidding preferences, the board held in *Allied Supermarkets* (1977) that this violated Section 8 (b) (1) (A), in addition to Section 8 (b) (2). In *Otis Elevator* (1977), the board extended *Dairylea* to include certain union officers, in addition to stewards, since "the representational activities carried out by union officials involved in the administration of the collective bargaining agreement . . . extend beyond the narrow confines of grievance processing. These encompass at the very least a functioning local to assert the presence of the union on the job."

In another case, *IAM Local 697* [*Canfield Rubber*] (1976), the board found a union to be in violation of Section 8 (b) (1) (A) when it refused to process a nonmember's grievances beyond the first step of the grievance procedure unless the nonmember first paid the costs of such processing. The board was not moved by the union's argument that it needed such payment to protect the dues paid by its members from being eroded by expenditures to protect nonmembers. "To discriminate against nonmembers by charging them for what is due them by right restrains them in the exercise of their statutory rights," the board said.

In *NLRB v. ILGWU* (1961), the Supreme Court sustained the board's position that it was a violation of Section 8 (*b*) (1) (A) for an employer and a minority union to enter into an agreement under which the employer recognized the union as exclusive bargaining representative of certain employees at a time when only a minority of those employees had authorized the union to represent them.

PERMISSIBLE SECONDARY CONSUMER ACTIVITY

Secondary pressure is permitted if it falls within the scope of the proviso to Section 8 (*b*) (4). That proviso states that nothing in the provisions shall be construed to prohibit a union from using publicity, other than picketing, for the purpose of truthfully advising the public, consumers, and members of unions that goods are produced by a struck employer and are distributed by the secondary employer. A proviso to the proviso adds the condition that the publicity must not interfere with pickup, deliveries, or other services at the secondary establishment. In *NLRB v. Servette, Inc.* (1964), the Supreme Court permitted a union having a primary dispute with a wholesale distributor to pass out handbills in front of retail stores and to urge managers, as well as customers, not to market or purchase items from that wholesaler that were being sold in the particular outlet. It did not seek to discourage any other purchases.

Another case involving union pressure at the retail outlet level against the products of the employer with whom it has its primary dispute was *NLRB v. Fruit and Vegetable Packers, Local 760* [*Tree Fruits*] (1964). There, however, the activity was picketing instead of "handbilling." In *Tree Fruits* the union called a strike against fruit packers who sold Washington state apples to Safeway stores in Seattle. The union supported the strike by stationing pickets at the entrances of forty-six

Seattle Safeway stores, who wore placards and distributed handbills that urged customers not to buy the apples. The hours of the picketing were arranged so that Safeway employees would not have to cross picket lines. There was no interference with the delivery of apples or the delivery or sale of any other product. The Supreme Court set aside the board's finding of a violation of Section 8 (b) (4), holding that Congress did not intend to bar all consumer picketing at secondary sites, but only that which would "threaten, coerce, or restrain" the secondary employer within the meaning of the statutory language in Section 8 (b) (4). Specifically, the Court held that the picketing here, "confined as it was to persuading customers to cease buying the product of the primary employer," did not violate the act. The Court considered it irrelevant that the volume of Safeway's sale of Washington state apples might be reduced or even stopped, since this was not an abuse at which the statute was directed, for customer response to the picketers' limited appeal in this case implied only persuasion and not a threat, coercion, or restraint. Only if the union intended to have Safeway customers stop doing business altogether with Safeway would there be a violation of Section 8 (b) (4)—when the secondary employer "stops buying the struck [picketed] product, not because of a falling demand, but in response to pressure designed to inflict injury on his business generally." In connection with both *Servette* and *Tree Fruits,* the case of *Goldfinger v. Feintuch* (1937) (*supra,* p. 147), is of interest in showing how history frequently repeats itself in the law.

LIMITS ON RECOGNITION PICKETING

Perhaps the most potent weapons added to the employer arsenal by the LMRDA were those permitting the board under Section 8 (b) (7) to act speedily and effectively against organizational and recognition picketing in certain situations. The provision makes it an unfair labor practice, enforceable by injunctive relief, for a union, unless it is currently certified as representative of the workers of the picketed employer, to engage in, or threaten to engage in, organizational or recognition picketing in three situations: (1) where the employer had lawfully recognized some other union and a question of representation could not therefore be raised under Section 9; (2) where the NLRB had conducted a valid election within the preceding twelve months; or (3) where the picketing had been conducted without a representation petition being filed within a reasonable period, not to exceed thirty days. A proviso to the third subparagraph permits picketing and other publicity for the purpose of truthfully advertising the nonunion status of the employer, unless an effect of such conduct would be to induce the employees of another employer not to pick up, deliver, or transport any goods or perform any services at the picketed employer's place of business. This section was designed to prevent unions from organizing from the top down, that is, organizing the employer rather than organizing his employees. It encourages resolution of representational questions by labor board elections that are expedited in this situation.

It should be noted that picketing or the threat of picketing does not become lawful under section 8 (b) (7) unless an object of the activity is to secure original recognition for the union. Thus, the proscription of Section 8 (b) (7) does not apply if the sole purpose of the picketing is to induce the employer to bring its substandard economic benefits up to "area standards" in order to avoid jeopardizing the level of benefits established in labor agreements with competing companies in the area. Similarly, if the picketing is aimed at securing the reinstatement of an employee who was discharged for union activity, it will not be held to violate these provisions. However, the board may find that the picketing, while ostensibly directed at securing area standards or reinstatement, is unlawful because recognition is in fact one of its objects.

"HARMONIZING" THE SHERMAN ACT WITH THE NLRB

The Supreme Court has in recent years decided three major antitrust actions involving labor unions (two against and one close to the line). In *UMW v. Pennington* (1965), the Court indicated its concern with "harmonizing the Sherman Act with the national policy expressed in the National Labor Relations Act of promoting 'the peaceful settlement of industrial disputes by subjecting labor-management controversies to the mediatory influence of negotiation.' " In *Pennington,* the Mine Workers' Welfare and Retirement Fund sued a small coal operator for unpaid royalty payments due under the union contract. The operator filed a counterclaim for actual money damages, alleging that in violation of the Sherman Act the union had conspired with certain large coal producers to drive marginal operators out of business by establishing a uniform industry-wide rate higher than the small producers could afford. The Court rested its decision squarely upon the union's agreement with the large coal producers that the smaller companies would be required to meet the same high standards as to wages and other labor costs by a provision in the major contract, often referred to as "a most favored nation" clause.

It is hardly surprising that employers, agreeing in negotiations to a higher pay scale, would want to be assured that they would not thereby be at a competitive disadvantage with any Johnny-come-lately who subsequently signed up. Yet Justice White declared for the Court that "a union forfeits its exemption from the antitrust laws when it is clearly shown that it has agreed with one set of employers to impose a certain wage scale on other bargaining units. . . . This is true even though the union's part in the scheme is an undertaking to secure the same wages, hours or other conditions of employment from the remaining employers in the industry." The Court had to acknowledge "that a legitimate aim of any national labor organization is to obtain uniformity of labor standards and that a consequence of such union activity may be to eliminate competition based on differences in such standards." However, the Court said, "The union's obligation to its members would seem best served if the union retained the ability to respond to each bargaining situation as the individual circumstances might warrant, without being strait-jacketed by some prior agreement with the favored employers." The Court recognized that the negotiations involved "a compulsory subject of bargaining," but, it said, "there are limits to what a union or an employer may offer or extract in the name of wages, and because they may bargain does not mean that the agreement reached may disregard other laws." Thus, under *Pennington,* if a jury finds that the union acted collusively with employers and that its purpose in insisting on the higher, uniform wage scale was to drive certain competitors out of business, then the antitrust act has been violated.

The case of *Amalgamated Meat Cutters Local Union No. 189 v. Jewel Tea Co.* (1965) was a civil antitrust suit involving a provision in a collective bargaining agreement resulting from negotiations over a mandatory subject of bargaining—this time, not wages but hours, and with a different result. The suit was filed not by a nonunion employer, but by an employer who had signed an agreement with the butchers' union. The employer, a grocery chain, charged that the union had compelled it to agree to a contract provision that limited the hours, from 9:00 A.M. to 6:00 P.M., when fresh meat could be sold at any of its stores. The Court, splitting three ways, held that this was lawful. Justice White, Chief Justice Warren, and Justice Brennan found that "the marketing-hours restriction" is "intimately related to wages, hours and working conditions." Therefore, the unions' successful attempt to obtain that provision through bona fide, arm's length bargaining in pursuit of their own labor union policies—and not at the behest of or in combination with nonlabor groups—falls within the protection of the national labor policy and is therefore exempt from the Sherman Act. Justices Goldberg, Harlan, and Stewart concurred for the same reasons that led them to dissent in *Pennington.* They accepted the union's argument that agreements dealing with mandatory subjects of bargaining are wholly outside the antitrust laws. Justices Douglas, Black, and Clark dissented on the ground that even absent evidence of a union-employer conspiracy against Jewel, "the contract of the unions with a large number of employers shows it was planned and designed not merely to control but entirely to prohibit 'the marketing of goods and services' from 6 P.M. until 9 A.M. the next day." This, they said, under *Allen Bradley* (*supra,* pp. 279–84) took the case out of the labor exemption to the antitrust laws.

In *Connell Construction Co. v. Plumbers Local 100* (1975), the local union, which represented workers in the plumbing and mechanical trades in Dallas, by strategically placing a picket on a major jobsite, forced a general contractor, Connell, to agree to subcontract mechanical work only to firms that had a bargaining agreement with the union. Connell brought this action to secure an injunction under the Sherman Act. The union lost in the Supreme Court on its claim of antitrust immunity. The Court held that the remedies available to Connell before the Labor Board do not preclude his resort to the federal antitrust laws. Moreover, it held, the "hot cargo" agreement the union signed with Connell was sufficient to divest the union of its antitrust exemption. And this despite the fact that the other party to the agreement was the one maintaining the suit and that the union's objective was a legitimate trade union objective—whether it was to protect wage standards of organized employees or to organize the unorganized. Despite this claim to legitimacy, Justice Powell, speaking for the Court, in a five-to-four decision, found the basis for a Sherman Act violation in the restrictive agreement with Connell to force nonunion contractors out of the market "even if their competitive advantages were not derived from substandard wages and working conditions but rather from more efficient operating methods."

It is too early yet to know whether *Pennington* and *Connell* presage a full-scale return to a period when the antitrust laws played a significant role in the regulation of collective bargaining and the control of labor unions in the United States. It is not, however, premature to observe the anomaly of a Supreme Court, so anxious in other situations to acknowledge and defer to the Congressional scheme for the control of labor relations under the labor laws of the United States, here so willing to see the water muddied by the intrusion of the antitrust laws into normal collective bargaining relationships.

Of particular interest is the way that the Supreme Court went out of its way in *Pennington* and in *Connell* to decide the two cases by expanding the Sherman Act to cover what are fundamentally traditional, unilateral, union practices. Thus, in *Pennington,* where the Court reached out to declare that the granting of a "most favored nation" clause to the coal producers' association was a Sherman Act violation, it could have reached the same result by resting its decision on the complaint's allegations of typical joint anticompetitive practices, such as collusive price cutting and joint agreements not to buy or sell coal to Pennington. Similarly, in *Connell,* the Court could simply have denied any remedy to the plaintiffs under the Sherman Act, while making clear that a remedy for the offending practices was available to them under Sections 8 (*b*) (4) and 8 (*e*) of the National Labor Relations Act.

The question that now remains is just how far will the Court pursue that tack? Or perhaps the Court will finally take to heart what it has so persuasively said to others in *Amalgamated Association v. Lockridge* (1971): "The rationale for preemption, then, rests in large measure upon our determination that when it set down a federal labor policy Congress plainly meant to do more than simply to alter the then-prevailing substantive law. It sought as well to restructure fundamentally the processes for effectuating that policy, deliberately placing the responsibility for applying and developing this comprehensive legal system in the hands of an expert administrative body rather than the federalized judicial system."

And it might bear in mind Justice Frankfurter's caveat to judges in *San Diego Building Trade Council v. Garmon* (1959): "But courts are not primarily tribunals to adjudicate such issues. It is essential to the administration of the Act that these determinations be left in the first instance to the National Labor Relations Board."

CHAPTER XV

COLLECTIVE AGREEMENTS AND ARBITRATION

An agreement upon wages and working conditions between the managers of an industry and its employees, whether made in an atmosphere of peace or under the stress of strike or lockout resembles in many ways a treaty. As a safeguard of social peace it ought to be construed not narrowly and technically but broadly and so as to accomplish its evident aims and ought on both sides to be kept faithfully and without subterfuge. In no other way can confidence and industrial harmony be sustained.—Sibley, J., in *Yazoo & M. V. R. Co. v. Webb,* 1933.

And therefore it is a law of nature, *That in every controversy, the parties thereto ought mutually to agree upon an arbitrator, whom they both trust; and mutually to covenant to stand to the sentence he shall give therein.* For where every man is his own judge, there properly is no judge at all; as where every man carveth out his own right, it hath the same effect, as if there were no right at all; and where is no judge, there is no end of controversy, and therefore the right of hostility remaineth.

An arbitrator therefore or judge is he that is trusted by the parties to any controversy, to determine the same by the declaration of his own judgment therein. Out of which followeth: first, that the judge ought not to be concerned in the controversy he endeth; for in that case he is party, and ought by the same reason to be judged by another; secondly, that he maketh no covenant with either of the parties, to pronounce for the one, more than for the other. Nor doth he covenant so much, as that his sentence shall be just; for that were to make the parties judges of the sentence, whereby the controversy would remain still undecided. Nevertheless for the trust reposed in him, and for the equality which the law of nature requireth him to consider in the parties, he violateth that law, if for favour, or hatred to either party, he give other sentence than he thinketh right. And thirdly, that no man ought to make himself judge in any controversy between others, unless they consent and agree thereto.—Thomas Hobbes, *The Elements of Law,* Chapter XVII, 6 and 7, 1640.

Since the passage of the Wagner Act in 1935, American labor relations and collective bargaining have undergone remarkable changes. Certainly the law with respect to the organization of employees into unions and as regards the use of their new bargaining strength to achieve collective agreements has matured and become extremely complex. An established adequate system of legal principles and rules governing the status of collective agreements and their enforceability has been at least two decades slower in development than effective regulation over collective bargaining.

This case of arrested development may not have been particularly serious prior to 1935. But thereafter it presented a real problem with the increase in the number of collective agreements facilitated by modern labor relations legislation.

Congress deliberately refrained from including in the Wagner Act any provision for the enforcement of collective agreements. According to tradition that was a matter for the states to take care of. All during the twelve years of the original NLRA the board and federal courts held to the view that the national government should not intrude in this field. Consequently this important practical aspect of labor relations was left to the haphazard controls of the common law. In effect this meant leaving the entire matter for the state courts to handle, although the federal courts occasionally applied the common-law rules in cases that arose under their diversity of citizenship jurisdiction. The courts in turn found it difficult to entertain suits by or against labor unions because these loose associations do not have legal personalities and hence could not appear as parties in litigation to sue or be sued. Several state legislatures, and a few courts without benefit of legislation, have recognized unions as legal entities. But even then, in most instances, the common-law rules governing the enforcement of collective agreements proved hopelessly inadequate.

AT THE COMMON LAW

This subject is so fraught with legal technicalities that it is extremely difficult to explain why this is so. But a glance at the law reports for the past half century or more indicates that most of our courts regarded these collective agreements as illegitimate hybrids, with no proper name or significance, legally speaking. Perhaps judges called on to enforce rights under them approached the task with too many preconceptions gathered from more traditional and established fields of law. No doubt they found it hard to see how an unincorporated aggregation of workers, even if it sported a full-time business agent, could act as a legal person for contractual purposes. Hence, they professed an inability to recognize a contract of any sort between an employer and a union, as such. Moreover, they tended to regard a collective agreement as a series of concessions from an employer to his organized employees, with no reciprocal concessions to him from the union. For the labor furnished to the employer was provided not by the union but by the individual employees. Thus the courts found neither the technical consideration from the union to make the instrument a contract enforceable at law nor the mutuality of obligation necessary to make it specifically enforceable by the decree of a court of equity. Furthermore, the courts were quick to find restrictive or monopolistic provisions in these agreements and these, according to the general law of contracts prevailing among merchants, rendered them unenforceable as against public policy.

This systematic tendency of lawyers and judges to think about these agreements in terms of conventional contract law has been chiefly responsible for the rudimentary stage of their development. In a sense, of course, they *are* contracts. But strictly speaking, they are not contracts at all in light of what that term traditionally signifies. As one court has well said, the collective agreement "resembles in many ways a treaty." The characterization is exceedingly apt. For the rigors of collective bargaining with strikes, boycotts, and picketing frequently suggest warring factions, each anxious to make peace with the other on a basis of selfish personal advantage. Indeed, the highest court in England has supported this analogy by declaring that collective agreements are mere "gentlemen's agreements" or moral obligations not enforceable in a court, but only by the union through the direct action of a strike. But this counsel of despair sacrifices most of the stabilizing advantages normally to be found in written agreements. For if these undertakings fail to keep the parties on a fairly businesslike basis of give and take, backed up by the orderly process of the law, then much of their contribution to civilized progress is lost. Fortunately our courts have never shared this helpless attitude of the House of Lords, although their attempts to provide redress under these contracts were for a long time unrealistic and inadequate.

The common-law tradition persisted that, even where collective agreements were enforceable under one theory or another, only individual employees, whose interests were at stake, would be able to enforce such agreements in actions brought directly by them. And even then it was not really the collective agreement that was being enforced. Rather, it was the individual contract of employment of the particular worker bringing suit, into which "contract" there had been incorporated by implication or reference the terms bargained out in the agreement between the employer and the union. This is neatly illustrated in a 1944 decision of the Supreme Court—*J. I. Case Company v. NLRB.* There Justice Jackson observed that the term "trade agreement" is more appropriate than "contract" to describe the formal arrangements ensuing from collective bargaining. In their practical effect at least, he likened them "to the tariffs established by a carrier, to standard provisions prescribed by supervising authorities for insurance policies, or to utility schedules of rates and rules for service, which do not of themselves establish any relationships but which do govern the terms of the shipper or insurer or customer relationship whenever and with whomever it may be established." His conception was that the individual contracts of employment, created between employer and employee, automatically incorporated the terms set forth in the controlling trade agreement. He also called attention to the fact that in some European countries a privately negotiated trade agreement of this sort, when approved by an appropriate government agency, becomes "a governmental regulation ruling employment in the unit."

However, Justice Jackson was suggesting only a rough analogy between collective agreements and tariffs, standard provisions and rate schedules. Unlike those arrangements, collective agreements are bargained out between private groups—unions and employers—who regard themselves as parties to these agreements, with rights and obligations apart from those of the individual employees. The final agreement is intended to reflect the mutual intentions of the parties, indicating what each was able to secure from the other in a series of horse-trading conferences that involved all sorts of concessions and compromises. The extent to which this might be true naturally depends on the relative bargaining strength of the parties—the willingness and ability of the union to strike, and the ease with which the employer might resist such pressure. And, to pursue Justice Jackson's analogy, the terms of a collective agreement are usually applied to all employees in a particular bargaining unit, whether or not they are members of the union.

In spite of these shortcomings, collective agreements need not be thought to have been completely meaningless in our common law. Unlike the corporation, the union as such was not a legal entity and could not sue or be sued at law. The courts, however, evolved three theories under which individual employees might sometimes be permitted to sue the employer for rights arising under a collective bargaining agreement: (1) that the terms became embodied in an individual contract of employment; (2) that the union was the agent of the employee; or (3) that the employee could sue as a third-party beneficiary of the contract.

Many of our courts recognized in collective agreements the crystallization of custom and usage prevailing in the plant or industry covered. Thus, where plants were covered by such agreements, the courts frequently held in an action by an individual employee that the conditions of labor provided for in the collective agreement operated to fix the terms of the individual contract of employment made by that worker with his employer. Certainly this was true if the employee could show that when he was hired, he knew about the terms set forth in the collective agreement and accepted employment with the intention that they should govern his own personal contract. While all courts following this custom and usage theory were not so strict in applying it, without exception they recognized that the union, as such, acquired no rights under the collective agreement and that the agreement was not in itself a contract in any sense of that word. Indeed, in many jurisdictions employers remained free to bargain out individually with applicants for employment whatever terms were mutually acceptable to them, despite the existence of the collective agreement.

Under a second category recognized by some courts—the so-called agency theory—the union bargaining out the collective agreement with the employer was regarded as having acted as the agent for the employees it represented. The terms and conditions of work appearing in the collective agreement were deemed to have been secured by this agent for its principals— the members of the union—to govern their individual contracts of hire with their employer. Here again the union, being a mere agent, was not regarded as a party to any contract and hence it could not in itself assert any rights under the collective agreement. Of course it was arguable that there was some sort of contract between each "principal" and the employer, over and above the individual contract of employment that came into being when he was hired; but this had no important legal significance. Thus, only the members of the union were in a position to secure from the courts by individual actions compliance with the terms of the collective agreement. Presumably, members employed after the agreement had been executed could not acquire rights under it until they had ratified its provisions.

And in the absence of the modern principle of majority rule, the union was helpless to negotiate modifications of the terms in the agreement without the approval of its "principals," the several members, since under this second theory it was merely acting as their agent.

To answer current needs the remaining common-law category for the judicial enforcement of collective agreements—the so-called third-party beneficiary theory—had little to offer. Yet it was a great advance over the other two theories. Under this development, which was copied directly from conventional contract law prevailing in some of our states, a union enters into an agreement with an employer for the benefit of all workers in the bargaining unit that is to be covered by its terms. This theory was borrowed from the law of contracts, where it had been developed in connection with mortgages. The idea was to allow a mortgagee to sue directly one who had bought the mortgaged premises from the mortgagor and had promised him, as part of the purchase price, to assume the balance of the secured debt still owing. The courts seized upon this analogy because it enabled them in the name of precedent to permit employees in the unit covered to sue the employer, even though they were not members of the union. Now, in its original setting, this theory contemplated a valid conventional contract between the promisor and promisee. Thus, when it was adapted to collective agreements, presumably it likewise contemplated a conventional contract between the employer and the union. But at common law a union could not enter into a contract because it had no separate legal personality such as a corporation has. In the first case where this theory was applied to a collective agreement, the union involved had been incorporated under New York law and hence *was* legally able to enter into contracts. Amusingly enough, when subsequent courts followed that theory in cases where unions were not incorporated, they overlooked the fact that the union there had had legal capacity to contract. But so much progress has been made in the direction of recognizing unions as capable of contracting in their unincorporated identities, both by statute and otherwise, that such recognition has come to be commonplace.

Courts no doubt adapted this third-party beneficiary theory to collective agreements in order to permit all of the employees in the bargaining units covered to sue employers directly in enforcing the contract terms, whether or not they were union members. They certainly did not have in mind giving any union independent standing as a party to a contract, with rights of its own to assert and enforce. Nevertheless this theory was an important factor in establishing unions as parties to collective agreements. And the step from that point to the judicial recognition of unions as parties with interests in labor contracts that they can enforce was not insurmountable. Some courts remained unwilling to treat collective agreements as contracts, or to regard the parties signing them as having any mutual rights or obligations under them. But others took a more realistic position that presaged a recognition of unions as contracting parties with enforceable rights of their own.

For some reason difficult to comprehend, most of our courts persisted in thinking that unions as such should not be allowed to have any rights under collective agreements over and above those secured for the benefit of the individual workers whom they represent. Apparently they believed that unions acted only in a sort of fiduciary capacity on behalf of employees. But this notion was obviously hopelessly out of date. Many modern labor unions are substantial enterprises with large property holdings and hundreds of employees. And every time they organize or agree to represent a new group of employees, they make very considerable investments of money and manpower. They did not wait for the law to pave the way for them in taking these steps. Rather they went ahead and created a situation that demanded legal recognition as a going concern. True, the courts evolved rules to govern the disposition of union property when these organizations were occasionally torn asunder by internal factional disputes. But they were extremely slow to recognize that a union as such, apart from the workers it represents, has interests and rights under collective agreements that it should be able to protect and enforce in the courts, just as any business corporation can. For example, a union shop provision or a dues check-off commitment are items of no beneficial concern to individual employees, but they are of vital importance to the union as an entity.

The foregoing account should indicate what an anachronistic institution the common law is when it is called upon to cope with a novel social development of such importance as the modern collective agreement. As Professor Witmer has observed: "If none of the analogies that have been adduced fits the picture completely, it would be strange if such an all-inclusive notion as that conjured up by the mere word 'contract' would do so automatically. That contract doctrine can be made to cover it, there is little doubt. It would be odd if a doctrine which already covers so great a variety of human transactions could not be revamped sufficiently to embrace still another. But it would be still more odd if a doctrine moulded in feudal society, adapted to commercial life, and only recently encountering industrial society, would give precisely the desired results immediately. It is this process of adaptation that we are going through today. Fifty years ago probably not one court in the country had heard of a collective bargain in its official ear. Twenty years ago the debate was whether collective bargains ought to be enforced. Today the question is how they shall be enforced, by whom they shall be enforced, to what effect they shall be enforced, and how far all the collateral doctrine that clusters about the abstract notion of an abstract contract between an abstract A and an abstract B shall be carried over and applied to the newest of the progeny." And his conclusion: that while "we have got beyond the stage of arguing whether collective agreements ought to be enforced at law . . . we have not got far beyond it."

This adequately described the situation as Witmer wrote in 1938. The United States was experiencing a virtual revolution in the labor relations field. With the passage of the Wagner Act

in 1935, closely followed by the Supreme Court's declaration
that the power of Congress to regulate interstate commerce
touched almost all economic activity of any importance in the
country, literally tens of thousands of collective bargaining
agreements sprang up where there had been merely hundreds
before. At the same time these new agreements came to cover
many more details of the employment relationship than they
had before World War II. As a result their enforcement became
critically important. It is commonly recognized that prior
to the parliamentary procedures of the Wagner Act most of our
bitterest strikes were called to further the organization of employees in opposition to the determined antiunionism of employers. The chief ostensible reason for the NLRA was to do
away with the causes of these strikes, which were considered so
harmful to commerce. Surely the community puts up with all
the industrial warfare it can fairly be expected to tolerate when
it allows direct action during the collective bargaining of the
controlling agreements in the first place. Self-help to secure the
enforcement of these agreements was certainly intolerable.

This was the fitting backdrop for Congress when it rolled up
its sleeves in 1947 and decided to do something about the situation in the Taft-Hartley Act. There was no opposition in the
Congress to passage of a law to make collective bargaining
agreements enforceable.

UNDER THE TAFT-HARTLEY ACT—SECTION 301

Prior to the 1947 legislation Congress had repeatedly made it
plain that the breach of a collective agreement should not be
treated as an unfair labor practice and that the NLRB should
have nothing whatsoever to do with the enforcement of labor
contracts. Then in 1947 it included Section 301 in the Taft-
Hartley Act, the first two subsections of which are the most
important. Section 301 (*a*) reads as follows: "Suits for violation
of contracts between an employer and a labor organization representing employees in an industry affecting commerce as de-

fined in this Act, or between any such labor organizations, may be brought in any district court of the United States having jurisdiction of the parties, without respect to the amount in controversy, or without regard to the citizenship of the parties." Without quoting Section 301 (*b*), it is worth noting that it says that any union or employer in commerce "shall be bound by the acts of its agents"; that any such union "may sue or be sued as an entity and in behalf of the employees whom it represents" in the United States courts; and that money judgments against a union shall be enforceable only against it as an organization and not against any individual member.

Now this language seems simple enough. When reading it the intelligent layman will no doubt say to himself: "What was all the fuss about in the preceding pages of this chapter, since Congress in 1947 so plainly declared that collective agreements within the federal jurisdiction are enforceable in the federal courts?" Indeed, it has required considerable restraint on our part to lay this foundation for a discussion of Section 301 and not to blurt out several pages back that all Congress had to do to solve the whole problem was simply to say that henceforth all collective agreements within its power to control should be enforceable in the federal courts! But nothing in the law is that simple; and the particular area of the law now under discussion is plagued with numerous perplexities and technicalities that render any easy solution almost impossible to reach. A full realization of this, however, was apparent only after the Supreme Court's 1955 decision in *Association of Westinghouse Salaried Employees v. Westinghouse Electric Corporation.* There a divided Court regarded Section 301 as a sort of passport merely enabling unincorporated unions to appear as litigants in cases involving breaches of collective agreements, without creating any substantive law pertaining to the nature and enforcement of such agreements. But another case was looming on the horizon that was completely to change all that.

IN THE SUPREME COURT—THE *Lincoln Mills* CASE

When we stop to consider what is actually being done in the industrial world to administer and enforce modern collective agreements, all this seems a good deal like tilting at windmills. Almost every one of these contracts contains a grievance procedure with arbitration as its last step. Under such an agreement unsettled grievances may generally be submitted to an arbitrator and a final and binding disposition be reached as a result. In this system the union has the last say as to what grievances shall be submitted to arbitration. Also it finances and conducts all grievances disposed of in this way, even using its judgment to settle them at any stage of the proceedings on the best terms thought possible. Indeed, under some agreements the employers themselves may raise grievances and have them carried to arbitration, although this is unusual.

In all this there is a clear illustration of unions and employers forging ahead of the law. They have been providing their own forums for the settlement of disputes arising out of their collective agreements. Here a close parallel exists with the old merchants' courts set up at the medieval fairs in England, where businessmen provided their own judges and their own law to settle their mutual differences on the spot rather than resort to the tedious, expensive, and technical processes of the king's courts. And while grievance arbitration in the labor field is as yet far from perfect, it is doing the job of enforcing collective agreements far better and far more cheaply than our courts can ever do it.

Most employers and unions seemed able to compose their differences satisfactorily by recourse to this voluntary grievance arbitration. Occasionally difficulties arose, largely because of the state of the law governing arbitration. Not many of the states had effective modern statutes in this field, and the federal arbitration act was probably not drafted with labor arbitration in mind. Consequently in most jurisdictions in the United States, the archaic common law governed in this field. Probably because they feared that arbitration tended to deprive them of business that would otherwise come their way, the old courts in England refused to enforce agreements to arbitrate future disputes of any kind. And this old English common law governing arbitration still prevailed in most parts of this country when Congress enacted Section 301.

According to these common-law rules, the courts will enforce an arbitrator's award, once it is given, if they find that an arbitrator did not exceed his jurisdiction under the submission. Even then they will not enforce it if they find that the arbitrator was dishonest, for instance, that he took a bribe from one party, or was arbitrary or capricious in making his award. If a dispute has arisen between two parties and thereafter they entered into an agreement, supported by consideration, to submit this dispute to arbitration, presumably this agreement was enforceable at common law and it will also be regarded by the judges as a bar to litigation of this dispute in the courts. Even here, however, the old common-law rule was that such an agreement was not specifically enforceable. The judges usually awarded only nominal damages for its breach and left the parties to their remedy on the merits through litigation in the courts. But on the other hand, if at a certain date the parties formally agree that they will arbitrate any disputes not then in existence but which may arise in the future, then such an agreement is not enforceable at the common law. Thus since in collective agreements the arbitration clauses have reference to future disputes, they are not enforceable at the common law in this country.

The *Westinghouse* decision in 1955 and Justice Frankfurter's opinion in that case had left the parties to collective agreements still without a viable alternative to the labyrinth of the common law. Then in June, 1957 came the Supreme Court's decision in *Textile Workers Union of America v. Lincoln Mills of Alabama*.

Justice Douglas wrote the majority opinion, speaking for five of the seven members of the Court who voted to enforce the agreement to arbitrate. He took a position that was refreshingly simple after the welter of technicalities that had been aired in the *Westinghouse* case and in the lower federal courts. He declared simply that Section 301 (*a*) in itself created a substantive right of enforcement of collective agreements, and that Section 301 (*b*) provided a complementary procedure. Thus he did not see that enforcement involved or depended in any way upon the federal arbitration act. Naturally he recognized that Section 301 (*a*) was a little general in its terms and other than to say that suits for the violation of contracts between employers and unions might be brought in the federal courts, it really did not provide any substantive law at all. "The question then is," said Justice Douglas, "what is the substantive law to be applied in suits under Section 301 (*a*)?" And he went on: "We conclude that the substantive law to apply in suits under Section 301 (*a*) is federal law, which the courts must fashion from the policy of our national labor laws." To some extent, he observed, the Taft-Hartley Act "expressly furnishes some substantive law" and it suggested other solutions. "Other problems will lie in the penumbra of express statutory mandates. Some will lack express statutory sanction but will be solved by looking at the policy of the legislation and fashioning a remedy that will effectuate that policy. The range of judicial inventiveness will be determined by the nature of the problem." He made it clear that federal law would govern throughout, adding that "state law, if compatible with the purpose of Section 301, may be resorted to in order to find the rule that will best effectuate the federal policy." But any such state law applied "will be absorbed as federal law and will not be an independent source of private rights."

This position is enough to make the legal profession hold onto their hats. What is amounts to is this: Congress in Section 301, in lieu of its power to write out a set of substantive rules to govern the enforcement of collective agreements and not wishing to have the matter covered by common law or state law, simply gave the federal courts carte blanche to make up a patchwork of law themselves, as long as it turned out to be consistent with the policies reflected in existing federal labor statutes. It is unlikely that so much has ever been read into so little before by the Supreme Court. It is reminiscent of the extraordinarily varied administrative powers turned over by Congress to the NLRB in the original Wagner Act, although there the grant of power was backed up by a fairly detailed statute and there was no question that Congress had intended to have the board do much the sort of things it did do.

THE *Steelworkers Trilogy*

In *Lincoln Mills*, the Supreme Court authorized the federal courts to develop a federal common law in cases arising under Section 301 of the Taft-Hartley Act. On June 20, 1960, the Supreme Court decided three cases that staked out a major sector of the developing common law. These cases—*United Steelworkers of America v. Warrior and Gulf Navigation Company, United Steelworkers of America v. American Manufacturing Company,* and *United Steelworkers of America v. Enterprise Wheel and Car Corp.*—were to become known as the *Steelworkers Trilogy*. These suits had been brought in the federal district court by the United Steelworkers of America against employers. Two of the suits sought to enforce agreements to arbitrate, and the third to enforce an arbitration award. In each instance, the Circuit Court of Appeals had decided against the union, which had then appealed to the Supreme Court. Each case involved a situation of vital and recurring importance with regard to the handling of grievances.

In *Warrior and Gulf* the grievance complained of the company's "contracting out" work, with a reduction in the size of the bargaining unit from forty-two to twenty-three employees. The collective agreement had a "no strike" clause; and it provided for arbitration, should "differences arise between the Company and the Union . . . as to the meaning and application of the provisions of the Agreement. . . ." The company refused to arbitrate the grievance. Its position was sustained by the courts below, a majority of the Circuit Court of Appeals "holding that the collective agreement had withdrawn from the grievance procedure 'matters which are strictly a function of management' and that contracting out fell in that exception." Speaking for a majority of the Supreme Court, in reversing the judgment below, Justice Douglas said: "An order to arbitrate the particular grievance should not be denied unless it may be said with positive assurance that the arbitration clause is not susceptible of an interpretation that covers the asserted dispute. Doubts should be resolved in favor of coverage." Douglas remarked that "the grievance machinery under a collective bargaining agreement is at the very heart of the system of industrial self-government," of which labor arbitration is an integral part. He continued: "The labor arbitrator's source of law is not confined to the express provisions of the contract, as the industrial common law—the practices of the industry and the shop—is equally a part of the collective bargaining agreement although not expressed in it." He admonished the courts to "view with suspicion an attempt to persuade [them] to become entangled in the construction of the substantive provisions of a labor agreement, even through the back door of interpreting the arbitration clause, when the alternative is to utilize the services of an arbitrator."

In *American Manufacturing* the union sued to compel the employer to arbitrate a grievance seeking reinstatement for an employee. The employer defended on the grounds that the employee had accepted a cash settlement of his workmen's compensation claim on the basis of being permanently partially disabled, that he was not physically able to work, and that the dispute was not arbitrable. The Circuit Court of Appeals, affirming the District Court, held the grievance to be "a frivolous, patently baseless one, not subject to arbitration under the collective bargaining agreement." The Supreme Court reversed, Justice Douglas observing: "The processing of even frivolous claims may have therapeutic values of which those who are not a part of the plant environment may be quite unaware." He noted: "The agreement is to submit all grievances to arbitration, not merely those that a court may deem to be meritorious.

There is no exception in the 'no strike' clause and none therefore should be read into the grievance clause, since one is the quid pro quo for the other." He added: "The moving party should not be deprived of the arbitrator's judgment, when it was his judgment and all that it connotes that was bargained for."

In *Enterprise Wheel* the union had won an arbitration award that ordered the employer to reinstate and give back pay to discharged employees for periods both before and after the expiration of the contract. The Circuit Court of Appeals held that the order reinstating the employees and the award of back pay for the period after the expiration of the agreement was not enforceable because the agreement had expired. Rejecting the employer's major argument that the arbitrator had failed to base his decision upon the contract because he had applied incorrect principles of law to the interpretation of the collective bargaining agreement, Justice Douglas commented: "This plenary review by a court of the merits would make meaningless the provisions that the arbitrator's decision is final, for in reality it would almost never be final. . . . It is the arbitrator's construction which was bargained for; and so far as the arbitrator's decision concerns construction of the contract, the courts have no business overruling him because their interpretation of the contract is different from his."

Despite the broad authority and the generous praise given labor arbitrators by Justice Douglas, he did back away from giving them completely unqualified powers. "Nevertheless, an arbitrator is confined to interpretation and application of the collective bargaining agreement; he does not sit to dispense his own brand of industrial justice," he cautioned, continuing to observe: "He may of course look for guidance from many sources, yet his award is legitimate only so long as it draws its essence from the collective bargaining agreement. When the arbitrator's words manifest an infidelity to this obligation, courts have no choice but to refuse enforcement of the award."

Following the decisions in the *Steelworkers Trilogy*, there have been relatively few cases in which courts have failed to enforce either agreements to arbitrate or awards by labor arbitrators. The observance of such obligations has now become usual and commonplace. Arbitrators themselves are highly respected; and their services are widely used in the resolution of grievances. "The ablest judge cannot be expected to bring the same experience and competence to bear upon the determination of a grievance, because he cannot be similarly informed," Justice Douglas observed in *Warrior and Gulf.* One discordant note in this respect has come from Judge Paul R. Hays of the Second Circuit Court of Appeals, himself a former arbitrator. In a book aptly entitled *Labor Arbitration: A Dissenting View* (1966), Judge Hays contended that many awards suffer from deficiencies such as (1) not being based on the evidence, on the contract, or on other proper considerations, but calculated to preserve the arbitrator's acceptability to both sides, such as rendering "compromise awards," (2) that they are made by arbitrators "who do not have the requisite knowledge, training, skill, intelligence and character" or who subvert the quick and inexpensive adjudication the system is supposed to provide by a variety of expensive practices such as fee padding and delay, and (3) that they are in some cases arranged, or agreed to in advance, without the knowledge of the grievant. As indicated by the title Judge Hays gave to his book, his views are at sharp variance with those generally heard. His conclusions and methodology have been criticized by some of the ablest scholars in the labor law field in the scattered reviews of his book that have appeared in the legal journals.

Judge Hays would have our courts carefully scrutinize awards instead of rubber-stamping them; and the views he expresses are totally at odds with Justice Douglas's sentiments in the *Steelworkers Trilogy.* But organized labor and management in the United States are solidly committed to arbitration as the preferred method of grievance settlement and would concur with Professor Theodore St. Antoine's observation: "Most arbitral aberrations are merely the product of fallible minds, not of overreaching power." And however the dispute is settled, the important thing from a public policy viewpoint seems to be that it *is* settled. Yet hovering in the background remain the words of Justices Brennan, Harlan, and Frankfurter, concurring with the majority in the *Steelworkers Trilogy*, where they suggested that "the parties were generally more concerned with having an arbitrator render decisions as to the meaning of the contract than they were in restricting the arbitrator's jurisdiction." However, if the parties were more interested in confining the arbitrator, this might be done, they said, by making "the arbitration clause very narrow, or the exclusion clause quite specific, for the inference might then be permissible that the parties had manifested a greater interest in confining the arbitrator; the presumption of arbitrability would then not have the same force and the Court would be somewhat freer to examine into the merits." Absent such a contract limitation, the courts hold, as Chief Judge Brown of the Fifth Circuit Court of Appeals put it in another case: "The arbiter was chosen to be the Judge. That Judge has spoken. There it ends."

In spite of these sentiments, the Burger Supreme Court in *Hines v. Anchor Motor Freight* (1976) seems to have threatened the finality of arbitration awards by encouraging judicial review of them on the merits. There, because of allegedly special circumstances, it permitted a lower federal court to disagree with an arbitration board's findings of fact and to allow a judgment for damages where the award had been to dismiss the grievance. It is difficult to predict how far the door will now be opened to judicial review of the merits of arbitration awards in view of the *Hines* decision.

THE EXPANDING SCOPE OF SECTION 301

In a series of cases and in a variety of ways, the Supreme Court has expanded the breadth of Section 301. This liberality in construction has been notable with respect to the types of contractual undertakings that will be enforced, the parties who may sue and be sued, and the courts in which such suits may be filed. The language of the statute, speaking of suits for "violation of contracts between an employer and a labor organization," made it appear that Section 301 actions had to be between an employer suing a union or a union suing an employer. This construction was rejected in *Smith v. Evening News* (1962) where the Supreme Court interpreted the section to permit an employee to sue an employer. However, in *Republic Steel Corp. v. Maddox* (1965) the Supreme Court made clear that an employee cannot pursue a Section 301 suit against the employer where the collective agreement on which he sues contains a grievance procedure culminating in arbitration. The employee's only recourse in such a situation is to file and pursue his grievance to arbitration. Moreover, in *Teamsters Union v. Lucas Flour Co.* (1962) the Supreme Court held that even in the absence of a specific no-strike clause, but where there is an arbitration clause in the agreement, a strike to settle a dispute over a discharge is unlawful and will enable the employer to recover damages against the union, although the "implied agreement" not to strike will be only as broad as the commitment to arbitrate. Although some had thought that Section 301 jurisdiction was limited to actions involving collective bargaining agreements, the Supreme Court in *Retail Clerks Int'l Ass'n v. Lion Dry Goods, Inc.* (1962) nevertheless permitted that section to be utilized for the enforcement of a strike settlement agreement. In *Charles Dowd Box Co. v. Courtney* (1962) the Supreme Court recognized the concurrent jurisdiction of state courts to entertain Section 301 (*a*) suits, since "the basic purpose of §301 (*a*) was not to limit, but to expand, the availability of forums for the enforcement of contracts made by labor organizations."

THE LABOR INJUNCTION AND EQUITABLE REMEDIES
UNDER SECTION 301

Previous chapters showed that the Norris-LaGuardia Act denied federal judges jurisdiction to issue injunctions against strikes, picketing, and boycotts by unions during the course of a labor dispute as defined in that act. Of course, by "labor dispute" Congress had in mind concerted union activities that occurred in connection with organization and collective bargaining. To replace the narrow conception of labor disputes in Section 20 of the Clayton Act, Congress went out of its way in the Norris-LaGuardia Act to make the new definition broad enough to cover all concerted union pressures in pursuit of economic objectives, whether or not the union people involved were directly employed by the enterprise in question. While curing some problems, the breadth of the language had prevented the courts from solving others.

During the decade following World War II, there occurred a number of cases in which unions asked the courts to compel employers to comply with undertakings they had made in collective agreements. These were situations where money damages would have been utterly inadequate. Only specific compliance with their promises by the employers in question would be the appropriate remedy. Most of these cases had arisen in the federal district courts or in the courts of those states that had enacted an anti-injunction statute modeled after the Norris-LaGuardia Act. Now, if the unions were successful in these actions, the courts' judgments ordering compliance by the employers with their undertakings would be in the nature of equitable decrees. While such decrees would not, strictly speaking, be injunctions of the type discussed earlier in this book, nevertheless their resemblance to injunctions is pretty close. Both would be equitable orders. At any rate, in most of these cases the courts decided that they were precluded by the controlling anti-injunction legislation, either state or federal, from granting the equitable relief asked for. Their reasoning was that the difference of opinion between a union and an employer over the meaning and application of their collective agreement was a labor dispute. And, under the Norris-LaGuardia type of anti-injunction act, the court no longer had the power to enjoin this labor dispute, regardless of who was asking for the relief—the employer or the union. For, as the saying goes, the Norris-LaGuardia Act was not a "one-way street" and a labor dispute was a labor dispute, whether started by the union or the employer.

This astonishing result, with which very few of the judges disagreed, seems to have been based on a series of misapprehensions. First of all, the Norris-LaGuardia type of statute was clearly concerned only with such labor disputes as strikes, boycotts, and picketing occurring in connection with the organization of employees and collective bargaining. Now, just because the parties to a difference of any kind happened to be a labor union and an employer, it would seem rash to conclude that the issue between them automatically became a labor dispute, regardless of its nature or source. Second, the anti-injunction legislation was aimed only at prohibitory injunctive orders issued against union economic activity on the theory that it was tortious conduct. A court decree ordering specific performance of a promise by a party to a contract is, of course, an equitable decree, just as an injunction is; but it is an order to *do* something—to comply with a solemn contractual undertaking—and it is not prohibitory in nature. Furthermore, it is a time-honored remedy for the enforcement of contracts where money damages for their breach would be inadequate. And it is inconceivable that the authors of the Norris-LaGuardia Act ever contemplated that its provisions would be used to abolish a remedy of any sort for the enforcement of a collective agreement. In such a case, denial of the appropriate remedy would only force the union to strike—surely the last thing legislators interested in stable labor relations would want to see happen.

Another aspect of the situation may seem to support the position taken by most of the judges in these cases. Suppose a union agrees to a no-strike provision for the life of the collective agreement in which that clause appears. Then suppose during the life of the agreement that the union calls a strike in violation of its contractual undertaking. Whatever else it might be, such an illegal strike is surely a labor dispute, simply because it is a strike. Then if the employer goes into court asking for an order requiring the union specifically to perform its no-strike undertaking, is he not also seeking to have a labor dispute enjoined contrary to the terms of the controlling anti-injunction act? But is this a sound view?

The correct answer would seem clearly to be that insofar as this strike involves a breach of the collective agreement, to that extent and in that respect, it is *not* a labor dispute within the meaning of that statute. Therefore, an equitable order requiring specific performance of the no-strike pledge could appropriately be issued against the union. A moment's reflection indicates that such a decision would in no way compromise the policies of the anti-injunction legislation. Those policies were designed to protect unions and employees using peaceful economic pressure to achieve organization or to secure some advantage or other through collective bargaining. While Congress no doubt contemplated that bargaining disputes would normally precede the signing of collective agreements, it surely was aware that collective bargaining continues between the parties to a contract even after its execution. Hence it must have realized that recourse by a union to direct action during the life of an agreement would still be a labor dispute within the protection of the anti-injunction act.

However, no union is required to execute a no-strike undertaking in a collective agreement. If it does so voluntarily, then it seems utterly absurd to let it evade this solemn undertaking by striking, just because the method of its breach happens also to qualify as a labor dispute. To be sure, the employer may still sue the union for money damages in such a case, but under the circumstances that remedy might be utterly inadequate. Certainly it is hard to believe that the policies underlying the anti-injunction statute would in any way be affected by the equitable enforcement of a no-strike pledge voluntarily entered into by a union. Yet the course of Section 301 litigation did not run smoothly.

In the *Lincoln Mills* case, the Supreme Court had begun the process of developing a federal common law under Section 301. There it had held that the Norris-LaGuardia Act did not prevent federal judges from ordering specific performance of a promise to arbitrate in a collective agreement. Yet the question still remained unanswered as to whether every refusal by either party—union or employer—to abide by the terms of a collective agreement is a labor dispute and hence not enjoinable under the Norris-LaGuardia Act. An outstanding instance was the breach by a union of a "no-strike" clause, where money damages would not afford adequate relief to the employer.

In early February, 1959, the Sinclair Refining Company at its East Chicago plant, docked three of its employees a total of $2.19. Under the prevailing collective agreement they could file grievances, which could be arbitrated if they remained unsettled. Instead there followed a series of nine work stoppages extending over a period of nineteen months. Sinclair sued the union and its officers in the federal district court under Section 301, requesting an injunction against the strikes as well as damages, relying on violation of a no-strike clause in the contract. Ultimately, in *Sinclair Refining Co. v. Atkinson* (1962), a divided Supreme Court, Justice Stewart voting with the majority, held that the lower federal court was forbidden by the Norris-LaGuardia Act to issue an injunction against the union because a strike under any conditions is a labor dispute. As Sinclair could not resort to the grievance procedure, as only employees and the union could file grievances under their contract, the Supreme Court allowed the action for damages against the union. However, as Section 301 (*b*) makes money judgments against a labor organization enforceable only against the organization as an entity and not against any individual member, the Court dismissed the action against the officers and agents of the union. This provision in 301 (*b*) was no doubt due to the *Danbury Hatters'* case discussed earlier in this book. There the employer secured a large triple damages judgment under the Sherman Antitrust Act against union members, many of whom consequently lost their homes. When it enacted Section 301, Congress made sure that this situation "was not to be permitted to recur."

Almost eight years later, *Boys Markets, Inc. v. Retail Clerks Union* (1970) was decided by the Supreme Court. That case also involved a strike in violation of a no-strike clause, where the collective agreement contained a provision for final arbitration, as well. Here the employer had been willing to arbitrate the dispute but was in the meantime suffering "irreparable injury" from the strike. This time Justice Stewart switched sides, taking refuge in an aphorism of Justice Frankfurter: "Wisdom too often never comes, and so one ought not to reject it merely because it comes late." Thus the minority position of the Supreme Court in *Sinclair* became the majority in *Boys Markets*. Henceforth the limitation on the power of a federal court to enjoin a strike in a "labor dispute" would presumably apply to all labor disputes *except* where the strikers are violating a no-strike clause in a collective agreement.

In a decade the Supreme Court had gone from the *Steelworkers Trilogy* to *Boys Markets*. The *Trilogy* had enormously boosted the agreement to arbitrate grievance disputes, which Justice Douglas termed the *quid pro quo* of a no-strike agreement. Through *Lincoln Mills* the Court "accommodated" Section 7 of the Norris-LaGuardia Act to permit specific enforcement under Section 301 of agreements to arbitrate. And having made such agreements enforceable, the Supreme Court was prompted to take the next step because, as it was quick to explain in *Boys Markets,* "employers will be wary of assuming obligations to arbitrate specifically enforceable against them when no similarly efficacious remedy is available to enforce the concomitant undertaking of the union to refrain from striking." Therefore the "accommodation" of Section 301 with Section 4 of the Norris-LaGuardia Act ("No court of the United States shall have jurisdiction to issue any restraining order . . . growing out of any labor dispute to prohibit any person . . . [from] refusing to perform any work. . . .") had been completed. And federal courts could now issue restraining orders—or, as it might well be put, equitable relief in the shape of specific performance—in one type of labor dispute, in spite of the sweeping prohibitory language of the anti-injunction act. Most people will no doubt applaud this result, since union strikes in violation of their contractual undertakings arouse little public sympathy or support. But the way in which this came about furnishes an extraordinary insight into the role of the Supreme Court as a policy-making body in our system of government.

Some may question the absence of record evidence in any of these cases upon which the Supreme Court based its notion that the arbitration clause and the no-strike clause each was in fact the *quid pro quo* for the other. Yet this leap of faith on the Court's part has established doctrine that will certainly promote maturity and responsibility in our industrial society.

If the arbitration clause and the no-strike clause are each the *quid pro quo* for the other, as the Court suggests, can an employer evade his obligation to arbitrate a dispute because the union at the same time violated the no-strike clause? No, said the Supreme Court in *Local Union No. 721 v. Needham Packing Co.* (1964). Indeed, Justice Brennan, concurring in the *Steelworkers Trilogy,* set forth his understanding that an agreement to arbitrate is specifically enforceable even if the contract fails to contain a no-strike clause. If, on the other hand, the suit is to secure a *Boys Markets* injunction to restrain a strike in violation of a no-strike clause, the Supreme Court made it clear in the 1976 *Buffalo Forge* case, involving a sympathy strike, that an injunction could not be issued where "the strike was not over any dispute between the union and the employer that was even remotely subject to the arbitration provisions of the contract." It would seem, however, that this decision could be circumvented by broadening the coverage of the arbitration clause to make all strike-producing disputes arbitrable under the agreement.

Without reference to the substance of Section 301, the process through which the Supreme Court went in resolving certain critical issues under that provision highlights the sharp philosophical differences concerning the proper role of the Supreme Court in our system of government. We all know about the constitutional doctrine of separation of powers under which the Legislature makes the laws, the Executive administers them, and the Judicial branch interprets them. Up to what point is it appropriate for a court, in interpreting a law passed by the legislative branch, to fill in blank spaces left by Congress, without doing violence to the doctrine of separation of powers? At one level, the disagreement among the members of the Court in *Sinclair* and *Boys Markets* was over the meaning of the Norris-LaGuardia Act as it applied to actions under Section 301 of the Taft-Hartley Act. But at another level, the Court was sharply split on the philosophical principle of whether or not it was appropriate for the Court to make a change in the Norris-LaGuardia Act that Congress had not made, even though it had been urged to do so. "When the repeal of a highly significant law is urged upon [Congress] and that repeal rejected after careful consideration and discussion, the normal expectation is that courts will be faithful to their trust and abide by that decision," Justice Black said for the majority in *Sinclair*. He went on to observe: "The question of what change, if any, should be made in the existing law is one of legislative policy properly within the exclusive domain of Congress—it is a question for lawmakers, not law interpreters." Eight years later, in *Boys Markets*, Justice Black was dissenting in a case involving the same issue as that in *Sinclair*. On top of the arguments he had marshalled in *Sinclair*, Black could now point to the principle of *stare decisis* under which the decisions of courts are guided by "precedent"—an issue once litigated and decided becomes "settled law." He pointed out that law review writers had praised the "judicial self-restraint" the Court had exercised in *Sinclair*. He noted the importance "of continuity and predictability in the law . . . in a field as delicate as labor relations" by quoting one of Justice Brandeis's classic dissents: *"Stare decisis* is usually the wise policy because in most matters it is more important that the applicable rule of law be settled than that it be settled right." Finally, Black concluded his *Boys Markets* dissent with some ringing words of John Adams: "The judicial [department] shall never exercise the legislative and executive powers, or either of them; to the end it may be a government of laws and not of men." But all to no avail. The tide had turned. "We fully recognize that important policy considerations militate in favor of continuity and predictability in the law," the majority said. "Nevertheless," it continued, "as Mr. Justice Frankfurter wrote for the Court [in an earlier case], '*Stare decisis* is a principle of policy and not a mechanical formula of adherence to the latest decision, however recent and questionable, when such adherence involves collision with a prior doctrine more embracing in its scope, intrinsically sounder, and verified by experience.' " It has "become clear," the Court wrote, "that the *Sinclair* decision does not further but rather frustrates realization of an important goal of our national labor policy," that is "the peaceful settlement of labor disputes through arbitration."

The irony of quoting Justice Frankfurter in support of the majority's position in *Boys Markets* was not lost on anyone. Frankfurter's name had become synonymous with "judicial self-restraint" and against what is called "judicial activism," that is, leaving to Congress the making of legislative policy. Indeed, it was Frankfurter who had first carried a majority of the Court with him in the 1955 *Westinghouse* case, when he found that Section 301 created no substantive law, only to have the Court turn full circle a scant two years later in *Lincoln Mills*. There, undeterred by *stare decisis* or anything else, the Court found that Section 301 directed the courts to create a body of federal common law in order to govern the enforcement of collective bargaining agreements. Thus Section 301 tells us a great deal about the judicial process in America!

SUCCESSORSHIP—THE *Wiley* CASE AND THEREAFTER

Because of the mobility of capital and the frequency of business mergers and acquisitions, our courts must occasionally consider the effect on the rights of unions and employees of such mergers or sales during the life of a collective bargaining agreement.

In *John Wiley & Sons, Inc. v. Livingston* (1964) the Supreme Court had to decide whether a successor company would be obliged to honor an agreement to arbitrate made by the predecessor employer. Wiley—a publishing firm—had a collective bargaining agreement with a union, which contained no express provision making it binding on a successor. Thereafter Wiley merged with another publishing firm, Interscience, and then went out of business. Interscience continued to employ almost all of Wiley's employees but refused to honor the collective bargaining agreement. The union filed suit asking that Interscience be required to arbitrate the issue of whether or not it was so obliged. The Supreme Court first decided the threshold question—that it was for the court, not the arbitrator, to determine whether the arbitration provisions of the agreement survived the merger at all. Then, concerning the main issue, the Court said: "The objectives of national labor policy . . . require that the rightful prerogative of owners independently to rearrange their businesses and even eliminate themselves as employers be balanced by some protection to the employees from a sudden change in the employment relationship. The transition from one corporate organization to another will in most cases be eased and industrial strife avoided if employees' claims continue to be resolved by arbitration rather than by 'the relative strength . . . of the contending forces.' . . . While the principles of law governing ordinary contracts would not bind to a contract an unconsenting successor to a contracting party, a collective bargaining agreement is not an ordinary contract." Apparently in view of the "substantial continuity of identity in the business enterprise," and "the impressive policy considerations favoring arbitration,"—especially as the union had clearly made known its claims both before and after the merger—the Court found Interscience obligated to arbitrate claims based on Wiley's agreement with the union.

Subsequently, in *Howard Johnson Company v. Detroit Local Joint Executive Board* (1974), the Supreme Court reached a different result. There Howard Johnson bought out Grissom's motor lodge and restaurant, hiring only nine of the seller's fifty-three employees and none of his four supervisors. The union, having a collective bargaining agreement with the seller, asked that Howard Johnson, the purchaser, be required to arbitrate certain matters, in accordance with an arbitration clause in the agreement. In denying this request, the Court said: "The primary purpose of the Union in seeking arbitration here with Howard Johnson is not to protect the rights of Howard Johnson's employees; rather, the Union seeks arbitration on behalf of the former Grissom employees who were *not* hired by Howard Johnson." The Court reasoned that there was no real "continuity of identity" since Howard Johnson hired less than 20 per cent of Grissom's employees. In dissenting, Justice Douglas criticized what he called the "bootstrap" argument accepted by the Court: "The effect [of which]," he said, "is to allow any new employer to determine for himself whether he will be bound, by the simple expedient of arranging for the termination of all of the prior employer's personnel." However, even where a new employer is not obligated to assume the existing bargaining agreement, he may be required to assume its obligation to bargain if during the certification year he hires a majority of the work force, the Supreme Court said in *Burns International Security Services, Inc. v. NLRB* (1972). And a successor who purchases with knowledge of the predecessor's unfair labor practice litigation may be bound by the NLRB back-pay order issued against the predecessor employer under *Golden State Bottling Company v. NLRB* (1973).

The questions of arbitrability raised in the *Steelworkers Trilogy* and the survival of contract rights under *Wiley* came together in the case of *Nolde Brothers v. Local 358, Bakery & Confectionery Workers Union, AFL-CIO* (1977). There a union and a bakery had been unable to agree on a new contract. The union terminated the contract that, under its original terms, had already run out but had been extended voluntarily by the parties, subject to the right of either party to cancel.

Bargaining continued; but when the union again rejected a contract offer, the company announced that it was closing down the bakery. Thereafter, the union filed a grievance demanding severance pay for its members under the expired contract. The employer rejected the severance pay claim; and it also refused to arbitrate the dispute on the ground that its contractual obligation to arbitrate disputes terminated with the collective bargaining agreement. The Supreme Court was not impressed with the company's defense to the arbitration demand, observing: "The dispute therefore, although arising *after* the expiration of the collective-bargaining contract clearly arises *under* that contract." The Court added that, "where the dispute is over a provision of the expired agreement, the presumptions favoring arbitrability must be negated expressly or by clear implication." In dissenting, Justices Stewart and Rehnquist found these assumptions "wholly inapplicable" because "the closing of the bakery . . . necessarily meant that there was no continuing relationship to protect or preserve." They would have afforded the union no arbitration remedy but only the right to seek enforcement of their contract claim in a court action under Section 301.

A LOOK AT GRIEVANCE ARBITRATION

Arbitration is a versatile concept that covers a wide range. Originally it was devised as an unofficial method of settling disputes over the meaning of contract provisions between businessmen, whether one of them had duly performed his obligations, and the like. And it has been widely used to settle boundary disputes and other differences between nations. In the labor field its use was at first probably confined to establishing terms and conditions of employment. In this connection, developments such as those in Australia created the impression that once it was adopted, its use became compulsory. That no doubt is why recourse to arbitration was so generally opposed prior to World War II. Neither employers nor unions relished a system under which some outsider would establish the terms and conditions under which they would have to live with each other. Compulsory arbitration had an odious connotation, and they preferred, even at the cost of strikes and lockouts, to bargain these things out between themselves.

Since World War II such misconceptions about arbitration have disappeared. It has become generally recognized to be a recourse entered into voluntarily. True enough, it took World War II to get it established as an institution prevailing throughout all organized industry. Even then it was under the compulsion of the unlimited emergency of a wartime economy. The War Labor Board saw to that by including arbitration as the final step in the grievance procedures that it placed in most collective agreements. Then after the war, the content of these arbitration clauses may have been changed by bargaining between the employers and unions, but in some form they remained in the contracts despite the parties' freedom then to dispense with them altogether.

Two categories of labor arbitration must be carefully distinguished. One is contract or interest arbitration. This is the less important, and concerns the submission by an employer and a union to an impartial outsider of some collective bargaining issue that they have been unable to settle themselves. Quite possibly the parties dread the consequences of a strike and they may prefer to accept the resolution of that issue by an impartial neutral rather than to attempt to achieve one more to their liking through recourse to industrial conflict with all its inconvenience and economic waste. Usually in these limited instances the disputed item arbitrated is wages, although that is not always the case. But whatever it is, the important thing to remember is that throughout all industry subject to the NLRA any such arbitration of contract issues is necessarily voluntarily undertaken between the parties. The Labor Board has held it to be an unfair labor practice for a party to insist upon a clause providing for interest arbitration. Unless Congress should provide for it—an inconceivable contingency—there can be no compulsion to settle bargaining disputes through arbitration and to abandon recourse to the strike and the lockout. And where some of the states have attempted to substitute compulsory arbitration for strikes in the public utility field, the Supreme Court has declared such statutes unconstitutional invasions of the exclusive federal domain.

In a sense, this submission of contract issues to an impartial outsider for final settlement is not arbitration at all. That is because the neutral person hearing the case has no recognized standards to guide his deliberations and influence his conclusions. Where the issue is a wage increase the parties may submit evidence of advances in the cost of living and how much it takes for an average family to live on under certain circumstances. They may also show what wage rates prevail in similar industries operating under similar conditions and what the trend of wage increases has been among the particular employer's competitors. Also testimony will no doubt be offered in connection with the employer's business prospects and his ability to pay what the union requests or to pay any increase at all. Regardless of how formally and scientifically all such evidence is prepared and submitted at the hearing, it is not really of much help to the arbitrator. It is almost as speculative as taking into account as a controlling factor what might have ensued had the union chosen to strike. Naturally this so-called economic evidence gives the arbitrator something to go on, but it furnishes only the roughest of guides.

The inherent fallacy in this type of arbitration is the assumption that a bargaining issue can satisfactorily be settled in any way other than by bargaining between the parties. In most instances when parties abrogate their right to bargain out the resolution of such issues, they deserve exactly what they get in the award. Whether they like it or not, this award in the long run is usually the best guess that the arbitrator can make on the basis of unsatisfactory evidence and a series of psychological considerations that in their nature must remain inarticulate. Hence recourse to the arbitration of bargaining issues

is generally avoided; but special circumstances may cause par
ties to undertake it.

However, there are times when the parties may be justified
in deciding that an arbitrator's award is preferable to a strike
and all its consequences. A deadlock may occur when each party
feels that retreat from its final offer will make it lose face. Each
of the parties may be secretly prepared either to accept the
other's final figure or to gamble on some intermediate award
from an arbitrator. And so in the urban trolley and bus line
industry, employers and unions frequently go to arbitration
over wage rates simply to avoid the troublesome consequences
of strikes. As long as the parties do this with their eyes open
and remain willing to put up with the award, there is no great
harm in such a course. But it is highly unlikely that it will ever
be acceptable in most American industries, except to dispose
of issues so relatively unimportant that their resolution one way
or the other is not significant.

The other type of arbitration—grievance arbitration—is far
and away the truly important feature of modern labor relations
in this connection. Here the arbitrator deals only with issues
pertaining to provisions in a contract and he follows the standards that the parties themselves have established by collective
bargaining. Indeed, each collective agreement is like a little
set of laws promulgated by the mutual effort of the parties.
They have agreed that their employment relations shall be
conducted for a given period in accordance with these laws
of their own. Most of the contract provisions pertain to the
terms and conditions of employment governing each of the
workers in the particular bargaining unit.

The usual provisions cover such matters as seniority, layoffs,
and recalls; the normal workday and workweek; extra pay for
overtime work; night shift bonuses; promotions and demotions;
the posting of vacant jobs for bidding; the equitable distribution among employees of overtime work opportunities; paid
holidays and paid vacations; leaves of absence; job descriptions
and work assignments; wage rates in general and what rates

govern temporary assignments of workers to jobs rated higher or lower than their regular work assignments; merit increases and cost-of-living increases, elaborate incentive plans with base rates and guarantees of earnings for normal incentive effort; arrangements for management to change work loads and equipment in response to production needs, with compensating provisions for arbitrating piecework or other incentive pay adjustments, if necessary; sickness and accident benefits and family hospitalization schemes; pension plans; guaranteed annual wage supplements to unemployment compensation benefits; plant rules governing the conduct of employees; and undertakings that workers will not be disciplined or discharged except for just cause. Other provisions of more direct interest to the union or the employer than to the individual employees cover such matters as union recognition; provisions against discrimination; union security clauses and union dues checkoff; no-strike pledges and agreements not to lock out workers; management rights clauses; automatic contract renewal provisions and contract expiration dates; and finally grievance procedures that lead up to arbitration as the final step.

This list of items no doubt seems long, and it suggests that the average industrial worker has all sorts of standardized arrangements incorporated by reference into his individual contract of employment. As a matter of fact the list is actually misleading in its simplicity and brevity. For it gives the impression that the terms and conditions of employment governing the rights of individual workers are so detailed and clearly stated as to be practically self-administering. Nothing could be further from the truth. While long and fairly complicated, most of these contract provisions differ from one agreement to another. Also, they are so vague and general that their application to the hundreds of varying situations arising under them becomes an extremely complex matter. Moreover the list is incomplete. It should, for example, include all of the manifold provisions that cover the various types of seniority and their application in a vast variety of contexts. And to one familiar with labor relations there would no doubt occur literally dozens of other matters that have not even received mention here.

These provisions in a collective agreement are ordinarily brought into play by the grievances that employees file. Thus an old employee will retire or move up into a higher rated job, and the employer posts the job he vacates for bids from workers who wish to fill it. From among those who bid, management selects an applicant and promotes him. Another of the employees who had made a bid for the position feels that he should have been promoted because he has greater seniority than the employee to whom it was given. Thereupon he files a grievance. He claims that under the controlling provision of the contract he should be given the job, with back pay amounting to the difference in rates between his present position and the one he aspires to. Now according to the contract, promotions are governed by three factors; length of service shall control only when the employees bidding for the vacant job are physically fit and equally qualified to perform the work required on that job.

Then comes the first step of the grievance procedure. This is handled by the aggrieved employee's shop steward and his foreman. If the foreman turns down this grievance because he thinks that the employee to whom the job was given is more qualified to perform the work required than the grievant, the grievance procedure thereupon goes into the next step. This time it is handled by a member of the union shop committee and the superintendent of the grievant's department. If no satisfactory settlement is reached at this stage, the grievance moves up another step or two until it is considered by an international representative of the union and top management. Assuming that the employer still insists that the correct man got the job, the grievant's only remaining recourse is to persuade the union to arbitrate. Whereupon if the union decides that this step is advisable, it files the necessary papers with management and the case is set for arbitration.

During the steps of the grievance procedure the company

and union are in a position to dispose of this grievance on any ground they see fit, provided the union is not motivated by hostility and acts fairly toward the grievant. Frequently the parties settle grievances after they have been scheduled for arbitration, but before they are heard. It should now be clear that this administration of the agreement by the parties continues to be a phase of collective bargaining all through the grievance procedure up to actual arbitration. During this period it is their proper function to settle as many grievances as possible on a mutually agreeable basis. But after a grievance has been submitted to arbitration, it is the neutral umpire's duty to render a clear-cut award on the merits of the case, and he should strictly avoid anything that smacks of compromise.

The parties to a collective agreement are entirely free agents when it comes to including any clause at all providing for the arbitration of unresolved grievances. Hence they are free by bargaining to limit the scope of the arbitration clause, the arbitrator's powers, and his jurisdiction. With rare exceptions these agreements specify that the arbitrator has power only to interpret and apply the provisions of the contract to grievances arising under it, and that he must neither add to nor subtract from the terms of such provisions. Occasionally a union will bring to arbitration a grievance that, in the employer's opinion, raises a bargaining issue. In this way unions may try to achieve before an arbitrator what they were unable to secure at the bargaining table. If the employer is correct, then the arbitrator has no jurisdiction to issue an award on the merits of the case. According to the best practice the initial determination of whether or not he has jurisdiction is up to the arbitrator. Should he agree with the employer that he lacks jurisdiction, he will dismiss the grievance for that reason. On the other hand, if he concludes that he *does* have jurisdiction and renders an award in favor of the union, then the employer can refuse to comply with the award, thus compelling the union or grievant to sue for its enforcement. And at that time the employer may persuade the court to deny enforcement on the ground that the arbitrator had exceeded his jurisdiction. But should the arbitrator dismiss the grievance because he concludes that he does *not* have jurisdiction, the union can do little about it in court. Even where an arbitrator clearly has jurisdiction over the grievance, a wise litigant will be careful to see to it that the issue stipulated for submission to him is so concisely stated as to prevent him from covering other matters in his award.

Most arbitrations are conducted on an *ad hoc* basis. That is, the parties select an arbitrator to hear only the one or more cases ready at the time for final disposition. On the other hand, it is fairly common for a large corporation and the union representing its employees to retain a permanent arbitrator for the duration of the contract to hear all grievances brought to arbitration thereunder. Still another device is a rotating panel of three or four arbitrators who hear batches of cases in turn as they arise during the life of the agreement under which they are acting. Most permanent arbitrators are selected directly by the parties; and this is frequently true of *ad hoc* arbitrators. More often, *ad hoc* arbitrators are furnished from the panels of the American Arbitration Association or the Federal Mediation and Conciliation Service. In any event, with rare exceptions, labor arbitrators are private citizens who have no official connection with either federal or state governments, and they are paid by each party for their services. A large number of them are full-time professional arbitrators. Many are university professors from departments of economics, law, and the social sciences generally, or are clergymen; with all of these arbitration is a side issue. While arbitrators are occasionally drawn from other sources, they are usually selected from groups that have no affiliation with either employers or unions. This system enables the parties to select whom they wish to hear and dispose of their cases.

It is conceivable that public arbitrators or special labor courts might be appointed and maintained as judges are, to perform this service. But as long as labor arbitration remains voluntary and entirely a creation of contract between employers and unions, the unofficial system of having arbitrators of the parties' own choosing seems vastly preferable. Many a collective agreement calls for a board of three or five arbitrators. Under such arrangements each side appoints one (or two) representatives to sit on the board as partisan arbitrators, and the neutral arbitrator sits in the middle. Of course, the decision always rests in his hands.

The presentation of a case before an arbitrator can be as formal or informal as the parties wish. Certainly the hearing is not conducted in accordance with the rules prevailing in courts. Usually the parties each make an opening statement to indicate to the arbitrator roughly what the case is about. The union traditionally leads off as the asking party, although it is customary for the employer to begin in discipline cases, since he imposed the penalty on the employee and should therefore explain why he did it. Next the parties put on witnesses to establish what happened, and each witness is subject to cross-examination by the representative of the other side. Little attention is paid to the technical rules of evidence, although objections are frequently made and occasionally sustained against attempts to push informality of presentation too far or to introduce testimony that has no relevance to the matter in hand. One reason why these hearings are not governed by the technical rules of evidence is that often neither the representatives for the parties nor the arbitrator is a lawyer or familiar with legal proceedings. Another is that experience shows the value of getting everything on the record and off the parties' chests. This makes for a more complete understanding and, possibly, it may reveal to the parties how good or how bad the points they are making seem to be.

In any event, after a record is built up and arguments made on the basis of pertinent contract provisions, the hearing is closed by the arbitrator. Then, unless the parties wish to file post-hearing briefs, the arbitrator has everything in his hands necessary to make his award. The parties often file exhibits relating to technical aspects of grievances, and quite frequently the arbitrator will go into the plant to examine at firsthand some process or machine involved in the case. Where there is a board of arbitrators, they usually meet sometime after the hearing, at which time the neutral arbitrator may informally reveal what he proposes to decide, and why. As a rule these arbitration boards are superfluous, and neutral arbitrators look at them as an attempt by the parties to get a second hearing under the guise of holding a sort of judicial conference. But they are exceedingly useful in cases requiring familiarity with technical matters such as machinery or work load changes. Nevertheless, single arbitrators constantly dispose of highly complicated situations without the aid of partisan arbitrators.

Grievance arbitration is not a process comparable to the common law in the courts, where decisions are referable to a more or less consistent body of principles and rules subject to the gloss of precedent. In grievance arbitration the controlling "law" is the particular contract under which the grievance in question arose. And the "legislators" were the two parties— the employer and the union—who bargained out and executed the agreement. While there is a tendency in some industries to adopt standard clauses, particularly where the same international union has virtually the entire industry organized, as in steel, at the same time there is likely to be a complete absence of uniformity in respect to items such as seniority, incentive systems, and the like. Hence arbitrators find it difficult to apply the precedents of other neutral umpires, for not only the contract terms, but also the facts, differ among the various cases.

To illustrate some of the difficulties confronting arbitrators, take the grievant who thought he should have been promoted on the basis of his greater seniority. No doubt many contracts provide for strict seniority. That is, the oldest man in point of service gets first whack at the vacant job. Of course, he must be qualified to perform it; and applicants are usually able to do so, having filled in on jobs ahead of them while the incumbents were sick or on vacation. Still, some contracts provide a brief learning period for the senior applicant, with a given amount of time to qualify. On the other hand, many agreements give priority to the applicant most able to perform the work in question; and relative ability among the applicants is determined on the basis of their past performance on other jobs, with respect to factors such as ability to learn, productive effort, punctuality and absenteeism, efficiency in the use of machines and materials, and the like. Judgments on relative abilities are usually made by the supervisory staff; and at the arbitration hearing the employer's case ordinarily rests on the testimony of foremen.

Since the basic issue is relative ability, the arbitrator under such circumstances is usually unable to tell whether the grievant actually is less able than the man who got the job or whether the foreman simply preferred the latter for some reason having nothing to do with his ability. Hence if he finds that the grievant can do the job in question at all, he is likely to allow the grievance on the basis of greater seniority. This is because an arbitrator can usually determine from oral testimony whether or not a man can do a job at all; but it is almost impossible for a neutral outsider to determine accurately the relative abilities of two or more applicants for a job. However, there is one exception. Where the testimony convinces the arbitrator that the junior applicant who got the job is head and shoulders above the grievant in ability, then he will probably dismiss the grievance. On the other hand, if management has established a systematic and carefully devised merit-rating plan, under which the various unit employees are periodically rated by all the supervisors on the basis of several factors, some arbitrators accept the results of such a plan and uphold the employer's promotions based on them. Others do not. Of course, these merit-rating plans are devised and operated unilaterally by management. But somebody has to make the determination of superior relative ability if the contract calls for it. And in the absence of contract language to the contrary, it would normally be a function of management to do this. Then, if the arbitrator is convinced that the merit-rating plan is scientifically conceived and impartially administered, it would seem that he has little choice but to accept and follow its results. However, this observation is by no means generally accepted.

From this account it may be apparent that construing the provisions of a collective agreement is no simple matter. Time and again it is extremely difficult to extract the meaning from contract language forged in the heat of intense feeling and badly tempered under bargaining pressure, by management representatives on the one hand determined to concede as little as possible and union negotiators on the other equally determined to get all they can. All too frequently contract provisions are not artistically drafted or are deliberately left ambiguous, each side hoping that the ambiguity will be resolved in its favor by an arbitrator. Difficult as the task may be of determining the mutual intention of the parties from a reading of their contract, it is frequently far more difficult for an arbitrator to make determinations of fact in his cases. Occasionally he finds it fairly safe to conclude that the witnesses on one side are lying. More frequently, however, when conflicting testimony is submitted on disputed issues of fact, he gets the impression that the witnesses on each side are convinced of the truth of their statements. Nevertheless, he must make up his mind as to what actually did happen, or, as the case may be, the actual amount of an alleged disparity in a wage adjustment after a work load change or the introduction of new equipment in grievances under incentive plans. Passing on issues of fact is quite as important as construing contracts.

Perhaps these quandaries over the facts underlying grievances occur most frequently in discipline cases. It is impossible briefly to relate the task with which management is faced in disciplining workers. Here is one problem that will always remain, even if every other aspect of employment relations becomes standardized and virtually self-administering, for the vagaries of human beings under modern industrial conditions are infinite. Before the spread of unionism employers could mete out discipline with a free hand, and in unorganized plants they may still do so, providing they do not discriminate against employees in violation of the prevailing labor laws. But the advent of unions has introduced a drastic check on their freedom to discharge workers, to give them penalty demotions, or to impose disciplinary layoffs.

Most collective agreements provide that management may not discharge or otherwise discipline employees save for just cause. Frequently there are plant rules, usually promulgated unilaterally by employers, since unions dislike being associated with restrictions upon employees' freedom of conduct. Occasionally, however, plant rules are drawn up jointly by employers and unions. Such rules furnish fairly specific criteria for acceptable conduct, and normally suggest the appropriate penalty for infraction. Even where there are plant rules, it does not follow that a breach is subject to discipline. For if the evidence shows that over a long period of time management has been aware that employees have systematically been violating a rule and supervision has done nothing about it, most arbitrators will refuse to sustain a penalty for a further breach unless the employees were fairly warned that henceforth the rule was going to be enforced. And if a plant rule is unilaterally promulgated by the employer, it will be strictly construed against him. Thus, a rule makes it a dischargeable offense to punch out another employee's card on the time clock. A foreman sees an employee in a line approaching the time clock with two cards in his hand, still several feet from the clock. He determines correctly that the employee intends to clock out one of his fellow workers who probably has skipped out some hours previously. So he orders the employee out of the line and discharges him for violation of the rule. Has the employee broken the rule? Obviously not. So the arbitrator has to reinstate him with back pay. Had the foreman waited until the employee had actually clocked out his fellow worker, the discharge would have been upheld. Whether or not the offending employee is subject to penalty for intending to clock out somebody else's card is beside the point, since that was not the reason given for his discharge.

In most cases the arbitrator does not have the benefit of plant rules to establish the standard of good conduct. Within the vague contours of the phrase "just cause" he must decide whether or not discharges were justified or disciplinary layoffs justly imposed. Offenses such as theft, sabotage, fighting, hitting a foreman, sexual immorality in the plant, being drunk on the job, and insubordination are obviously serious enough to warrant discharge. Still, there is the case where a foreman in the Missouri plant of a big automobile company called a unit worker a son of a bitch and the employee knocked him down. This looked like a clear case for the company. Nevertheless one of the country's topflight arbitrators reinstated the discharged employee because he thought the provocation, coming from a representative of management, excused the conduct. If this incident had occurred between two unit employees, the arbitrator would no doubt have upheld the discharge. How about impertinence, answering back, or charges of unjust treatment shouted at a foreman or plant superintendent under trying circumstances? How about negligence causing harm to company property or resulting in spoiled production? Or playing poker for money on plant property, either during work time or the lunch period? How about conduct outside the plant, such as fighting with a foreman, whether or not it is connected with internal plant affairs? How about inefficiency, tardiness, unexcused absenteeism, or unreported absences that turn out to be for good cause?

In one famous arbitration an employee of the Ford Motor Company was reprimanded and docked one-half hour because she wore red slacks in the factory. The objection was to the color, since women were required to wear slacks on the job. Some representative of management thought it tended to distract male workers in the vicinity. With admirable tact and no little humor the arbitrator, Harry Shulman, allowed the grievance. He noted that no formal safety rule had been issued on the basis of the alleged potential distraction, and that bright green slacks were tolerated. He observed that "what color was proper and what color was 'taboo' was apparently a matter depending entirely on the spot reactions of individual . . . Labor Relations officers to particular slacks as they appeared on the scene." Reminiscent of another famous case involving a "sweater girl" in a Bridgeport, Connecticut, plant, he noted that there had been no attempt here to specify "other articles of clothing, or the fit thereof, which might be equally seductive of employees' attention. Yet it is common knowledge that wolves, unlike bulls, may be attracted by colors other than red and by various other enticements in the art and fit of female attire." He thought that leaving the matter "largely to idiosyncracy of circumstance and of persons in authority" was no way "to prescribe or enforce rules of conduct."

The foregoing references merely suggest the myriads of disciplinary situations with which arbitrators have been faced. The offenses alleged vary from the very serious to the petty and frivolous; all of them, none the less, affect plant morale and are likely to disrupt plant operations. And difficult as it frequently is to determine whether or not the reason assigned for discipline is just, the arbitrator often has to determine on the basis of conflicting evidence whether or not the charges against the grievant are true in the first place. Then, even if he believes them to be established, he is occasionally faced with deciding whether there were especially extenuating circumstances sufficient to condone the offense.

Time after time an arbitrator is faced with this dilemma: the evidence will satisfy him that an employer's charges against an employee are established; but he believes the discipline imposed was too severe. This is particularly so in discharge cases. And the fact that so many interests such as seniority advantages, insurance, and pension rights are contingent upon continued employment, thus making discharge like capital punishment, makes this dilemma difficult to cope with. Some arbitrators view their role as determining whether the discipline was justified, not in second-guessing the particular penalty imposed. Hence such an arbitrator would not disturb the penalty imposed when he finds that the employee was in the wrong.

To avoid what they regard as overharsh penalties in such cases, some arbitrators simply conclude that no discipline at all was justified and allow the grievance in full. That, of course, is much worse than dismissing the grievance and upholding the penalty, regardless of how harsh it was. Some arbitrators, however, do not hesitate to take an intermediate position, and will modify the penalty—for instance, reinstate a discharged employee without any back pay at all or with a fraction thereof. One of the largest corporations in the country has agreed with the unions representing its employees to give arbitrators acting under their agreements the discretion to modify penalties when they find that discipline was warranted but that under the circumstances the punishment was too severe. This sophisticated position, taking account as it does of the realities of industrial society, works extremely well, affording to arbitrators the leeway that they should frequently have and sparingly use in a wise disposition of a case.

Whether or not an employee's grievance shall be taken to arbitration at all is a matter for the union to decide. This is consistent with the majority rule principle that governs the bargaining of contract rights in the first place. Offhand, such a rule may seem unfair to the employees; but it is obviously quite as fair to leave enforcement of the terms of the agreement to the union as it is to leave the making of the agreement itself to it. Now many grievances are filed by employees who feel that their rights under the agreement have been ignored when the union officials believe otherwise. Thus in many discipline cases the responsible union officers may after investigation conclude that the employer was justified in imposing a penalty, and that the employee's grievance does not merit pressing to arbitration. Then there are instances where union personnel must use their best judgment in deciding whether a grievance technically justified under the letter of the contract really should be arbitrated at all. Professor Cox of Harvard Law School has illustrated this neatly in a hypothetical case.

He assumes a contract providing (1) that the hours between

8 A.M. and 5 P.M. shall constitute the regularly scheduled workday; (2) that all work over eight hours a day and work outside the regularly scheduled workday shall be paid at time and one-half; (3) that maintenance men working above fifty feet shall be paid double time; and (4) that double time shall be paid for working on certain paid holidays, including Labor Day. A hurricane causes damage to the roof of the employer's plant, over fifty feet above ground, and Johnson, a maintenance employee whose regular hourly rate is $4, is asked to repair it on Labor Day. This he does working from 7 A.M. to 7 P.M. "If the company paid Johnson $8.00 an hour for this work, Johnson might contend that he should have been paid $16.00 for each hour between 8 A.M. and 5 P.M. and $32 for each hour between 7 and 8 A.M. and 5 and 7 P.M. The union might press the full claim, which is not an absurd interpretation of the words; or it might conclude that to demand a pyramiding of premium payments not contemplated during contract negotiations would exacerbate labor-management relations. Perhaps the union would take an intermediate position, claiming $16.00 an hour but not seeking to pyramid the overtime and before-and-after-regular-hours premiums."

Johnson might easily figure that the high work clause doubles his $4 rate to $8 per hour, and the holiday work doubles that to $16 per hour. On straight time for twelve hours, he thinks he should get $192. But four of these hours were in excess of eight hours a day, so he claims an additional $32 for overtime; and since three of them were worked outside the 8 A.M.–5 P.M. workday, he asks another $24. On his reading of the contract, this would put him up around $248 for one day's work. Should the union press this claim to arbitration and win for Johnson, the employer would be furious and many of Johnson's fellow employees would be most unhappy about his windfall in which they did not share. And when the union officials thereafter requested management to use common sense in handling other grievances, they would be met with bitter recriminations.

Thus, in the collective interest it is apparent that the union should retain full control over arbitration, and be free to use its judgment concerning what cases to prosecute and how they should be presented. After all, the union has more than the continuing relationship with the employer to worry about. Arbitration is costly and time-consuming, and most unions have limited resources with which to handle and pay for their share of the arbitrator's fee and expenses. Such control by the union over arbitration does not completely eliminate the grievant from the picture, since under Section 9 (*a*) of the NLRA he may present and process any grievances directly with management. However, under the statute any adjustment must be consistent with the bargaining agreement, and the union must be given the opportunity to be present.

A similar union control over the arbitration of grievances filed by unit employees who are not members of the union may be thought to be most unfair. But this is not true. It is the duty of the union to process those grievances exactly as it would those of union members, and some unions do so gladly in the hope of winning new adherents. In any event, the nonunion grievant can always present his grievance directly to management, taking advantage of the Section 9 (*a*) proviso. And if that is not satisfactory, he can insure the union's full-hearted support by joining it at any time.

One aspect of the majority rule principle in this field should always be kept in mind. Not only should the union have control over taking cases to arbitration—under modern collective agreements with grievance procedure and arbitration it should have exclusive control over all employee demands raised in connection with contract provisions. This means that a union must have the right to settle grievances on any basis it thinks best or to drop them entirely, subject to the limitations imposed by the doctrine of the duty of fair representation, which is discussed later. It also means that if an employee chooses to bring an action in court against an employer to enforce some provision of the collective agreement, the employer should be allowed to plead as a complete bar to this action the employee's failure to resort to the grievance procedure and arbitration provided for in the agreement. This development is a strictly logical consequence of the trend toward collectivism in industrial society, and it is essential to the protection of employers' convenience if they are obliged to recognize and deal with unions.

What about grievances filed by employers against unions? Some contracts provide for this, although it is only occasionally important. Thus, if an employer contemplates a change in equipment or layout that the union claims will violate the agreement, unless he can pursue the matter to arbitration and procure a declaratory award in advance, he will either have to give up his plan altogether or go ahead and make the change, with all the expense involved, at the risk of being told later that he was in violation of the contract. As a rule, however, the reason why the employer does not need to file grievances and bring them to arbitration is that he is already in the saddle. He may do about what he pleases in running the plant. The union is there to see that he does not violate the contract and to haul him up short before an arbitrator if he does. This is tied in with the fact that before unionism the whole ball of wax was under the control of management. Then when a union came in and bargaining ensued, the employer's complete control was limited to the extent that he made concessions in the agreement. Aside from this, the employer is left with the residual management prerogative not surrendered or modified by the terms of the agreement. This ball of wax theory is not popular among union leaders, although it is otherwise generally accepted. In any event, under it management is free to run its plant affairs as it chooses, at the risk only of being told by an arbitrator that it has deviated from some contract provision. Certainly under this theory most employers would agree that it is not absolutely essential for them to be able to file grievances and take cases to arbitration against unions. However, as the use of arbitration for the settlement of differences between employers and unions continues, it would seem desirable to provide an equal opportunity for both parties to have recourse to arbitration.

The culmination of the process of union organization and bargaining is the collective agreement. Prior to the Taft-Hartley Act the methods for securing compliance with obligations assumed in such agreements were clumsy and unpredictable. Section 301 has provided a simple and effective way to enforce the provisions of a bargaining agreement against an employer or a union who for one reason or another declines to respect obligations undertaken in the agreement. The Supreme Court has taken seriously its obligation under Section 301 to develop a federal common law for collective agreements. A central theme of this evolving body of law has been "to promote the arbitral process as a substitute for economic warfare." Notwithstanding the Norris-LaGuardia Act, the Court, to achieve this goal, has made available to judges the use of injunctive powers where appropriate. Where there is a continuity in the work force, a successor employer may be bound by the obligations of the predecessor. The Supreme Court continues apace to impose the rule of law over the obligations voluntarily undertaken by labor and by management. Meanwhile, as each year passes, our privately developed system of voluntary grievance arbitration in the labor field grows constantly more mature and more able to cope with the civilized administration and enforcement of collective agreements without any need for government intervention.

CHAPTER XVI

THE UNION AND INDIVIDUAL RIGHTS

Long ago we stated the reason for labor organizations. We said that they were organized out of the necessities of the situation; that a single employee was helpless in dealing with an employer; that he was dependent ordinarily on his daily wage for the maintenance of himself and family; that if the employer refused to pay him the wages that he thought fair, he was nevertheless unable to leave the employ and resist arbitrary and unfair treatment; that union was essential to give laborers opportunity to deal on an equality with their employer.—Hughes, C. J., in *NLRB v. Jones & Laughlin Steel Corp.*, 1937.

This and the other cases before us give ground for belief that the labor movement in the United States is passing into a new phase. The struggle of the unions for recognition and rights to bargain, and of workmen for the right to join without interference seems to be culminating in a victory for labor forces. We appear now to be entering the phase of struggle to reconcile the rights of individuals and minorities with the power of those who control collective bargaining groups.—Jackson, J., dissenting in *Wallace Corporation v. NLRB*, 1944.

MAJORITY rule is the central principle of American labor law. The union selected by the majority of employees in a bargaining unit speaks for all of the employees; and the employer is prohibited from bargaining with individual employees. The union and the employer fix the terms and conditions of employment in a collective bargaining agreement by which the individual employees are bound. And when employees file grievances under the contract, it is the union that ultimately decides whether to pursue, compromise or drop these grievances. With the concentration of such great power in the hands of unions, it is hardly surprising that the developing labor law moved toward the protection of the individual worker—particularly in a country that would not ratify its constitution until a bill of rights was added to it.

WITHIN THE BARGAINING UNIT: THE DUTY OF FAIR REPRESENTATION

In *Steele v. Louisville and N.R. Company* (1944) (*supra,* pp. 330–31), the Supreme Court declared that where Congress grants a union the powers of exclusive bargaining agent, then that union has an obligation to represent without discrimination all employees within the bargaining unit. Eighteen years later, in *Matter of Miranda Fuel Co.,* a union pressed an employer to penalize an employee, who had begun an extended leave of absence three days early, by dropping him to the bottom of the seniority list—a penalty not sanctioned by the agreement. The NLRB said the union's pressure against the interests of its member was an unfair labor practice. The board found the duty of fair representation to be an obligation arising from the union's status as an exclusive bargaining agent under Section 9 (*a*) of the LMRA. It held that arbitrary or invidious discrimination by the union against an employee in the bargaining unit was a violation of Section 8 (*b*) (1) (A) and Section 8 (*b*) (2) of the Labor Management Relations Act. However, it was in actions under Section 301 that the duty of fair representation was to become preeminent in modern labor law. But first, some brief background is in order.

Protected by the mantle of modern federal labor legislation, union organization grew in the United States. With this growth came many thousands of collective bargaining agreements. And with the boost from the Supreme Court in the *Steelworkers Trilogy,* arbitration as the final step in contract grievance procedures became widespread. A recent survey showed that there are over twenty thousand labor arbitration cases annually in the United States. At the same time, collective bargaining agreements have become increasingly sophisticated.

A look at the General Motors situation gives a startling illustration. The current master collective bargaining agreement between the United Automobile Workers and General Motors Corporation comprises 825 printed pages. This does not include the supplementary local agreements that are negotiated between plant management and the local union at each General Motors installation, with which local union officials must also be familiar. Of the 825 pages in the master agreement, 390 represent the basic agreement, 148 the insurance program, 149 the Supplementary Unemployment Compensation (S.U.B.) plan, and 138 the pension plan. The UAW represents some 400,000 General Motors employees. At the top level, the UAW has its General Motors department. Below this, at the plant level, there are hundreds of local union officers and committeemen who deal directly with the members and with the lower ranks of management. These officers and committeemen have only one absolutely essential qualification for office—that they receive the most votes in an election conducted among the local members. Educational requirements and experience are nonexistent, as in the case of persons seeking public office. The local officials represent employees in handling grievances with management, and also advise grieving employees with respect to their rights under the master agreement and the local supplement. This is a task that would severely test a Philadelphia lawyer, let alone an official with an eighth grade education who, when not acting as a union officer, operates a drill press! Of course, the union offers ambitious training programs and provides staff assistance. Yet one may rest assured that the problems with which the local union officials deal can be very complex. The legal situation for labor organizations could be perilous, indeed, were the lower echelon local officials, in performing their union tasks and advising grievants, held to prevailing professional standards of competency. Indeed, such requirements would undoubtedly change the character of local unions into far less democratic structures, with consequences never contemplated by Congress when it passed the Labor-Management Reporting and Disclosure Act and the

LMRA itself. For example, to lessen their legal liability, unions might impose educational qualifications for office that could turn them into elitist groups in which average workers might no longer be eligible to run.

In the following two cases, the Supreme Court fixed rules that will influence the future of processing grievances and the conducting of arbitrations in the United States. Justice White wrote the opinions for the Court in each case.

Unfair Representation Comes of Age • The first of these two cases was *Vaca v. Sipes* (1967). There, Benjamin Owens, a union member, alleged that he had been discharged in violation of the agreement between his union and Swift & Company's Kansas City meat packing plant. Owens, who had a long-time history of high blood pressure, became ill and entered the hospital on sick leave. He so improved with rest that his family physician certified him as fit to resume his heavy work in the packing plant. Swift's company doctor examined Owens upon his return, and denied him reinstatement because his blood pressure was too high. Owens then secured a second authorization from another outside doctor and returned to the plant, where, on January 6, 1960, a nurse permitted him to resume work. But when the plant physician discovered this on January 8, Owens was permanently discharged on the ground of poor health. Armed with his doctor's authorization of fitness, Owens then sought the union's help in securing reinstatement; and the union filed a grievance and processed it into the fourth step of the contract grievance procedure. Swift stuck to its position that Owens' poor health justified his discharge, rejecting the medical proof offered by Owens and by the union as not being based upon sufficiently thorough medical tests. The union then sent Owens to a new doctor at its expense "to see if we could get some better medical evidence so that we could go to arbitration with his case." This examination did not support Owens' position. The union's executive board then voted not to take Owens' grievance to arbitration because of insufficient medical evidence, and suggested that Owens accept Swift's offer of referral to a rehabilitation center. He declined to do so, and sued the union in a Missouri state court, claiming damages for its refusal to press his grievance to arbitration. The jury returned a verdict against the union, which the trial judge set aside on jurisdictional grounds. On appeal, the Missouri Supreme Court reversed, reinstating the verdict and granting judgment for damages. In the meantime, Owens died, and the administrator of his estate, Sipes, continued the suit. The U.S. Supreme Court agreed to hear the case.

First, the Supreme Court had to decide whether Owens' only remedy against the union was before the NLRB under the board's *Miranda Fuel* decision, as government attorneys had contended. The Court rejected this argument, contrasting an employee's open access to the courts in a Section 301 action, on the one hand, with recourse to the NLRB, on the other, where "the individual employee injured by arbitrary or discriminatory union conduct could no longer be assured of impartial review of his complaint, since the Board's General Counsel has unreviewable discretion to refuse to institute an unfair labor practice complaint" in his behalf. The Court further noted "the intricate relationship between the duty of fair representation and the enforcement of collective bargaining contracts," which makes the duty of fair representation "a critical issue" in a Section 301 action and militates against vesting the Labor Board with exclusive jurisdiction over such matters.

The Supreme Court figured that it would make more sense to let a federal court, clearly vested by Congress with authority to hear the breach of contract action, also consider and pass on any unfair representation contention that might be advanced, saying that to "leave the employee remediless in such circumstances would, in our opinions, be a great injustice." But having said that a federal court has jurisdiction to hear this kind of case, the Supreme Court then asked whether Owens' claim in fact did state a cause of action against the union. The Court thought not, observing: "Though we accept the proposition that a union may not arbitrarily ignore a meritorious grievance or process it in perfunctory fashion, we do not agree that the individual employee has an absolute right to have his grievance taken to arbitration regardless of the provisions of the applicable collective bargaining agreement." Good faith settlements winnow out costly, time-consuming, and frivolous grievances, assuring that "similar complaints will be treated consistently and major areas in the interpretation of the collective bargaining contract can be isolated and perhaps resolved." Moreover, "if the individual employee could compel arbitration of his grievance regardless of its merit, the settlement machinery provided by the contract would be substantially undermined," and the arbitration process so overburdened "as to prevent it from functioning successfully."

The Court then concluded that "as a matter of federal law the evidence does not support a verdict that the Union breached its duty of fair representation." Had it proceeded in a perfunctory manner "when Owens supplied the Union with medical evidence supporting his position, the Union might well have breached its duty," but here, the Court pointed out, "the Union processed the grievance into the fourth step, attempted to gather sufficient evidence to prove Owens' case, attempted to secure for Owens less vigorous work at the plant, and joined in the employer's efforts to have Owens rehabilitated. Only when these efforts all proved unsuccessful did the Union conclude both that arbitration would be fruitless and that the grievance should be dismissed." In addition, there "was no evidence that any Union officer was personally hostile to Owens or that the Union acted at any time other than in good faith." Since it was clear "that a breach of the duty of fair representation is not established merely by proof that the underlying grievance was meritorious," the Court concluded that the "duty was not breached here." Because the union did not violate the duty of fair representation, the employee could not hold the employer liable in court on an underlying grievance that the union declined to let go to arbitration.

The jury verdict was also in error, the Court held, because it included an award against the union for "damages attributable solely to the employer's breach of contract." The governing principle should be "to apportion liability between the employer and the union according to the damage caused by the fault of each. Thus, damages attributable solely to the employer's breach of contract should not be charged to the union, but increases if any in those damages caused by the union's refusal to process the grievance should not be charged to the employer."

Speaking for Chief Justice Warren, Justice Harlan, and himself, Justice Fortas in a separate, concurring opinion agreed that the jury verdict should be set aside, but took the position that jurisdiction over duty of fair representation cases ought to lie exclusively with the NLRB. Justice Black, dissenting, thought an employee ought to have an absolute right to have the merits of his grievance determined "by either a jury or an arbitrator." Justice Black ironically agreed with the Court's suggestion that its decision "furthers the interest of the union as statutory agent," but he thought the decision "entirely overlooks the interests of the injured employee," who will now be required "to take on both the employer and the union in every suit against the employer and to prove not only that the employer breached its contract, but that the union acted arbitrarily," converting "what would otherwise be a simple breach-of-contract action into a three-ring donnybrook." Justice Black wondered how the burden of proving that the union acted arbitrarily or in bad faith could be met. "Must the employee prove that the union in fact acted arbitrarily, or will it be sufficient to show that the employee's grievance was so meritorious that a reasonable union would not have refused to carry it to arbitration?"

Two major disagreements appear between the Court and Justice Black. The first arises from Justice Black's insistence that the individual employee ought to have an absolute right to arbitrate or litigate his grievance. When one considers the sheer volume of such grievances pending in some plants, and the ease with which they can be made to multiply, given a purpose to be served, persons experienced in industrial relations are certain to find Justice Black's suggestions to be wholly impractical.

For example, in the period of a three-year contract (1973–76) between the Fiat-Allis Construction Machinery, Inc., Springfield, Illinois, plant and the UAW, covering a unit of 2300 employees, there were 15,141 grievances filed. The cost to a union of arbitrating a single grievance frequently ranges from $1000 to $2500. Second, Justice Black would permit legal redress wherever the trier of fact (judge or jury) believes the grievance to be well-founded; the Court's position allows redress only upon proof that the union's conduct is "arbitrary, discriminatory or in bad faith."

The Court in *Vaca* relied upon a 1964 decision of the Supreme Court in *Humphrey v. Moore*. The employees of two trucking companies were combined in a single bargaining unit when one of the companies purchased the other. The same union had represented the employees of the two companies under separate contracts in which each group enjoyed separate seniority rights. In that case, the Supreme Court was "not ready to find a breach of the collective bargaining agent's duty of fair representation in taking a good faith position contrary to that of some individuals whom it represents nor in supporting the position of one group of employees against that of another."

Professor Ben Aaron has suggested that the *Vaca* decision and other developments in labor law have left nonunion or dissident union members in an unsatisfactory position. "The requirement of exhaustion of contract remedies, the narrow scope of judicial review of an arbitrator's award, the inability to sue an employer for breach of contract without first proving that the union has been guilty of a failure to represent them fairly, and the broad latitude of discretion customarily granted to the union by the courts all combine to leave such employees without adequate remedies," he writes. Yet courts have their way of leaving the door ajar in what they view as compelling situations.

*A Breach of Duty Without Malevolence • Hines v. Anchor Motor Freight*s (1976), decided a decade after *Vaca,* was to emphasize that the Supreme Court was not about to accept Justice Black's position; but neither would it turn a deaf ear to the complaints of employees whose rights to their jobs had been sacrificed by a union's slipshod grievance handling, however difficult it proved to articulate the applicable standard of care.

Anchor Motor Freight discharged a group of truck drivers for dishonesty. They were accused of seeking reimbursement for motel charges in excess of the actual expense incurred. Anchor's proof included motel receipts submitted by the drivers that exceeded the charges shown on the motel's registration cards, a notarized statement of the motel clerk asserting the accuracy of the registration cards, and an affidavit of the motel owner affirming that the registration cards were accurate and that the receipts presented to Anchor were inflated. When the drivers suggested that the motel be investigated, the union representatives assured the men that "there was nothing to worry about" and that they need not hire their own attorney. The joint area arbitration committee, consisting of an equal number of representatives of each party, heard the case; the truck drivers were afforded an ample opportunity to testify. No other evidence was offered. A provision of the contract made the joint committee's award final and binding. The committee denied the grievance and later refused to reopen the case when presented with a statement from the motel owner in which he said that he had no personal knowledge of the events and conceded that the clerk could have falsified the records and pocketed the difference.

Two years after the discharge the drivers filed suit in a federal district court against the employer and the union. They alleged that they had been fired on the basis of false charges of dishonesty by the employer in violation of contract and that the union, by failing to make any effort to ascertain the truth, had violated its duty of fair representation. Soon after the suit was filed the motel clerk admitted in a deposition that he had falsified the motel's records for his own profit.

The trial court dismissed the suit against Anchor and the union on the ground that while "the Union may not have met professional standards of competency, and while it might have been advisable for the Union to further investigate the charges against plaintiffs, the mere fact that the Union exercised bad judgment does not in and of itself constitute bad faith or personal hostility."

The Court of Appeals reversed the district court's summary judgment in favor of the local union but sustained the judgment for Anchor because there was no evidence of employer misconduct or conspiracy with the local union.

The Supreme Court reversed the district court's summary judgment in favor of both parties, holding that the drivers, "if they prove an erroneous discharge and the Union's breach of duty tainting the decision of the joint committee, are entitled to an appropriate remedy against the employer as well as the Union." Justice Stewart, concurring, urged that, in apportioning damages as "mandated" in *Vaca,* any wage loss incurred since the arbitral award "must fall not on the employer but on the Union." Justice Rehnquist dissented on the ground that "the Court has cast aside the policy of finality of arbitration decisions and established a new policy of encouraging challenges to arbitration decrees by the losing party on the ground that he was not properly represented."

Justice White, in the main opinion, emphasized that for an employee to prevail in this kind of suit "more than demonstrating mere errors in judgment will be required." The Court avoided saying just what the proper standard ought to be, however, except to suggest that erroneous arbitration decisions should not stand where "the employee's representation by the Union has been dishonest, in bad faith or discriminatory." It is interesting to speculate whether the result in *Hines* would have been any different had the award been by an impartial arbitrator rather than by a joint committee that included union officials who should have prepared the case better.

The *Hines* case fails to set down definitive standards on

which to judge whether in a particular fact situation a union has violated its duty of fair representation. This case's chief significance is that the Supreme Court found a violation in a situation where there was neither malevolent intent, double dealing, nor fraud shown on the part of the union; instead there was only what might be called inadequate investigation and presentation of a grievance by the union, with no evidence of bad faith or hostility toward the grieving employees. Henceforth it will be very difficult to draw a meaningful line between laxity and unfair representation. Each case will rest upon its own facts. In *Hines* we have entered the gray area beyond *Vaca*— if the reader will forgive us the pun, somewhere between White and Black. The Supreme Court seemed unable to abandon the drivers, once the room clerk had confessed. It just had to do something! Anyhow, the decision sent the following message to all shop stewards and union officials: "Be Careful!" At that, we still do not know which of the room clerk's statements to believe or why he changed his original story.

The Supreme Court may yet rue the day that it failed to heed its own words of wisdom in *Amalgamated Association v. Lockridge* (1971) where it emphasized that "the very distinction . . . between honest, mistaken conduct, on the one hand, and deliberate and severely hostile and irrational treatment, on the other, needs strictly to be maintained."

WITHIN THE UNION: THE LANDRUM-GRIFFIN ACT (LMRDA)

Investigations by the McClellan committee of the U.S. Senate during the late 1950's disclosed dishonesty and other maladministration within several of our large unions. Since the available law seemed unsuited for controlling this, Congress in 1959 passed the Labor-Management Reporting and Disclosure Act, commonly known as the Landrum-Griffin Act. The first six of the seven titles in this statute introduced drastic controls on the hitherto broad powers that union officials had exercised over the funds and the internal affairs of unions. They also established safeguards for the election of union officials and for other democratic procedures. Thus, in the first part of the act, Congress noted that breaches of fiduciary obligations, corruption, and utter disregard for the individual employee's rights made essential the passage of new laws to achieve responsibility on the part of unions in conducting their internal affairs. It specified procedures, including the secret ballot, for increasing dues, initiation fees, and assessments; and it established the right of individual members to bring suit against the union and its officers after certain internal procedures had been exhausted. While recognizing that unions ought to be able to cope with obstreperous members who interfere with the organization's processes and its legal or contractual obligations, Congress promulgated basic rules designed to assure due process in connection with the disciplining of members. In addition, it was required that every union must make sure that each member has a copy of the controlling collective agreement and is at least made acquainted with the provisions of the new statute.

Under the provisions of Title II of the act, every labor union must adopt a constitution and bylaws and must file copies of them with the Secretary of Labor, along with fiscal information concerning dues, fees, receipts, salaries, loans, participation in pension and insurance plans, etc. Also it must furnish information about all rules that prescribe or limit in any way member participation in union affairs, or that provide for discipline, such as fines or expulsion from the union. Employers were made to furnish information about payments and loans to union officers or their agents, to file statements concerning expenditures intended to restrain or coerce employees in connection with collective activities, and to make complete disclosures of any arrangements reached with labor consultants. Of course, this was not intended to apply to the retaining or employment of attorneys or others, including permanent employees, whose job it is to handle for employers the negotiation of collective agreements with unions as well as to process through arbitration the grievances arising thereunder and to handle cases before administrative boards and the courts. Presumably it was aimed at the "fixer" type of go-between shown up by the McClellan committee hearings. The act provided that all this information should be retained for a certain time and be made available to the general public. Title II also included criminal sanctions against those who violated its terms, and empowered the Secretary of Labor to secure compliance in civil proceedings.

Title III of the act established stringent controls over "trusteeships." This device was originally designed to permit a parent international union to assume control over the affairs of a local union that was insolvent or irresponsibly conducted. Trusteeships had eventually come to be used by unscrupulous international union officers to stifle local union democracy, to crush dissident movements, and to enable the plundering of local treasuries. In Title III Congress limited the purposes for which trusteeships may be imposed; and it established rules for their creation and operation, with appropriate sanctions to implement this title. Title IV provided for mandatory, frequent elections in all unions, with detailed regulations and standards for their fair, democratic conduct. The Secretary of Labor was empowered to investigate failures to comply with these measures, to have elections set aside by courts, to have wrongfully elected officers removed, and to have new elections conducted and their results certified.

The next part of the act—Title V—described at length the fiduciary relationship that exists between union officials and the membership in general. Moreover, it provided that when any member shows evidence that this fiduciary obligation has been violated and demands an accounting, he may secure an order for such an accounting from the courts if it is refused by the official concerned. In this suit the court may award a portion of the recovery against such official to the complaining member for legal fees. This title also has detailed and extensive provisions for bonding union officials, perhaps needlessly elaborate and arduous in many situations. Moreover, it prevents unions from lending any official more than $2000. And Communists and certain types of ex-convicts are prohibited from holding specified offices in unions or acting as labor consultants until after the passage of five years, there being criminal sanctions to enforce these provisions. And at this point Section 302 of the Taft-Hartley Act is strengthened in order more effectively to prevent payments of any kind by employers to union officials.

Title VI covers miscellaneous matters. Thus, it purports to outlaw extortionate picketing, and provides that criminal sanctions created in the statute do not interfere by pre-emption with the administration of state criminal law; it also makes it a crime for anybody to interfere with a member of a labor union, by the use of violence, threats, or any coercion while such member is trying to exercise any rights conferred on him by this statute.

The Bill of Rights: Freedom of Speech and Assembly • From the McClellan committee hearings, there emerged a vivid picture in which corruption and undemocratic practices went hand-in-hand. Congress thereupon acted to establish democracy in labor unions throughout the country. As Professor Meltzer put it, "The law, which had promoted freedom of association, was now to promote freedom within associations."

It was certainly no coincidence that Title I—the first title of the LMRDA—is labeled, "Bill of Rights of Members of Labor Organizations," since the protection of the rights of union members was the primary focus of the Landrum-Griffin Act. An early case arising under the LMRDA, *Salzhandler v. Caputo* (1963), is illuminating. Salzhandler, financial secretary in a New York local of the painter's union, discovered that certain other local union officials, including Webman, the president, were obtaining excessive "reimbursement" checks for attending a union convention. Salzhandler distributed a leaflet to the members accusing Webman of improper conduct with regard to union funds, attaching to the leaflet substantiating photostatic copies of the checks in question. In the leaflet, he also told the members that once the local's convention delegates received their mileage fare, they disappeared and missed the final day's session. Then he called Webman a "petty robber" for allegedly appropriating two $6.00 dues refund checks intended for the widows of two recently deceased members. Webman responded by filing charges against Salzhandler with the district council of the painter's union, accusing Salzhandler of "acts and conduct inconsistent with the duties, obligations and fealty of a member or officer of the Brotherhood" and of falsely charging him—the president of the local—with the crime of larceny. The officers of the district council sat as the trial board. They found merit in Webman's charges; and they prohibited Salzhandler for five years from participating in the affairs of the local, from having the floor at any union meeting, and from voting on any matter or being a candidate for office either in the local or district council. Having been physically prohibited by Webman from attending a union meeting on May 15, 1961, Salzhandler filed suit in the district court under the LMRDA bill of rights section requesting a nullification of the trial board's order, reinstatement as financial secretary, and damages.

Title I of that act reads in part: "Every member of any labor organization shall have the right to meet and assemble freely with other members; and to express any views, arguments, or opinions; and to express at meetings of the labor organization his views upon candidates in an election of the labor organization or upon any business properly before the meeting, subject to the organization's established and reasonable rules pertaining to the conduct of meetings. . . ." Judge Wham in the district court dismissed the complaint, holding that the trial board's declaring the leaflet to be libelous was supported by the evidence. He ruled: "The rights accorded members of labor unions under Title I . . . do not include the right of a union member to libel or slander officers of the union."

The Circuit Court of Appeals reversed. First, it found that Salzhandler's conduct did not fall within the proviso to the above quoted language from the act that permits the "labor organization to adopt and enforce reasonable rules as to the responsibility of every member toward the organization as an institution and to his refraining from conduct that would interfere with its performance of its legal or contractual obligations." Then the Court of Appeals rejected as "beside the point" Judge Wham's views on whether Salzhandler's statements were true or libelous, noting that Salzhandler's charges against Webman "related to the handling of union funds; they concerned the way the union was managed." The Court of Appeals continued: "The Congress has decided that it is in the public interest that unions be democratically governed and toward that end that discussion should be free and untrammeled and that reprisals within the union for the expression of views should be prohibited. It follows that although libelous statements may be made the basis of civil suit between those concerned, the union may not subject a member to any disciplinary action on a finding by its governing board that such statements are libelous."

Fifteen years after *Salzhandler,* that same court decided *Turner v. Machinists Lodge 1894, IAMAW* (1978). There a union had expelled a member, who was active in the Progressive Labor Party, for "advocating Communist ideas and incorporating those ideas with his campaign for Shop Steward." In overturning his expulsion the court said: "The free speech right guaranteed by LMRDA may not be infringed by expelling a member for advocating communist ideas." Some of the court's language, however, suggests the possibility of a different result had the person involved been a member of the Communist Party of the United States. For, as Judge Mulligan expressed it in a concurring opinion, "While criticism of union leadership or practices or policies is fully protected, the encouragement of activities or organizations which are fundamentally inimical to trade unionism is beyond the pale." Previously the Supreme Court in *United States v. Brown* (1963) had struck down a provision in the Landrum-Griffin Act that barred a member of the Communist Party from serving as a union official, because it violated the constitutional prohibition against bills of attainder.

Four justices dissented, asserting that Congress could rationally conclude that barring all communists from union office was an appropriate means for preventing political strikes in the United States. But the majority said that even if this be true concerning some communists, "it cannot automatically be inferred that all members shar[e] their evil purposes or participat[e] in their illegal activities." So adjudging their collective guilt, the Court held, would amount to a bill of attainder—in effect "trial by legislature"—which is proscribed by the constitution. In the *Brown* case the Court did not consider the question of the right of communists as union members under the LMRDA bill of rights.

In *Hall v. Cole* (1973) the Supreme Court put additional teeth in situations like *Salzhandler*. There it held that the plaintiff's attorney, in a successful action to vindicate a member's rights under Title I of the LMRDA, was entitled to recover legal fees from the union. For, "by vindicating his own right, the successful litigant dispels the 'chill' cast upon the rights of others." Thus, "to the extent that such lawsuits contribute to the preservation of union democracy," they frequently benefit the entire membership. Hence the legal fee of the litigant's attorney becomes a justifiable charge on the union's treasury.

Title I and Title IV: Equal Rights and Election Remedies • The *Salzhandler* case interprets and applies the "Freedom of Speech and Assembly" provision of Title I. A coordinate provision is labeled "Equal Rights" and declares: "Every member of a labor organization shall have equal rights and privileges within such organization to nominate candidates, to vote in elections or referendums of the labor organization, to attend membership meetings, and to participate in the deliberations and voting upon the business of such meetings, subject to reasonable rules and regulations in such organization's constitution and bylaws." In *Calhoon v. Harvey* (1964) the Supreme Court read the words "equal rights" literally in explaining that the section "is no more than a command that members and classes of members shall not be discriminated against in their right to nominate and vote." Thus, the violation of a union's bylaws gives rise to federal jurisdiction under Title I only if it is accompanied by disparate or discriminatory treatment among members. This is different from the "Freedom of Speech and Assembly" section featured in *Salzhandler*. For under the Equal Rights section, as long as all members of the union are treated alike in nominating candidates for office and in voting, there is no violation of the law. The Court also declared in *Calhoon v. Harvey* that individual union members complaining of alleged violations of their rights under Title IV, relating to elections and voting, may not as individuals bring suit against a union under Title I of the LMRDA but must, rather, complain to the Secretary of Labor, invoking his power under that title to investigate and, if he finds probable cause, to file suit against the union.

Such a suit occurred in *Local 3489, United Steelworkers of America v. Usery* (1977). There the Secretary of Labor, who is given the exclusive postelection remedy under Title IV to challenge an intraunion election, had sued for declaratory and injunctive relief on the ground of alleged impropriety in a union election. The Secretary took exception to a provision in the international union constitution limiting eligibility for local union office to members who had attended at least one-half of the regular meetings of the local for three years previous to the election, unless they were prevented from so doing by union activities or working hours. The Court's task was to construe the statutory language in Section 401 (*e*)—that "every member in good standing shall be eligible to be a candidate and to hold office"—which is made expressly "subject . . . to reasonable qualifications uniformly imposed."

The Court found that due to the effect of the challenged provision in the union's constitution, only 23 of 600 members in Local 3489 were eligible for union office. The meeting attendance requirement thus disqualified 96.5 per cent of the local members from seeking union office. It also had "a substantial antidemocratic effect" by "requiring potential insurgent candidates to plan their candidacies as early as 18 months in advance of the election when the reasons for their opposition might not have yet emerged. . . ." The Court, in sustaining the Secretary's position, noted: "The basic objective of Title IV of LMRDA is to guarantee 'free and democratic' union elections modeled on 'political elections in this country' where 'the assumption is that voters will exercise common sense and judgment in casting their ballots.' . . . Congress chose the goal of 'free and democratic' union elections as a preventive measure 'to curb the possibility of abuse by benevolent as well as malevolent entrenched leadership.' " Justices Powell, Stewart, and Rehnquist dissented because they thought the decision was "an unwarranted interference with the right of the union to manage its own internal affairs," observing that: "No member is precluded from establishing eligibility" under the union's constitution.

In *Wirtz v. Hotel, Motel and Club Employees Union, Local 6* (1968), the Supreme Court under Title IV struck down a provision in the union's bylaws limiting eligibility for major elective offices to union members who hold or have previously held elective office, when it found that the effect of this provision was to render 93 per cent of the union's members ineligible for office. Similarly, the Secretary has found unreasonable other conditions for nomination to office, such as a requirement that a candidate must file a declaration of candidacy prior to nomination, or pay a filing fee.

While recognizing that under Title IV only the Secretary of Labor can file a suit challenging an intraunion election that has already been held, the Supreme Court in *Trbovich v. United Mine Workers* (1972) still permitted the aggrieved member to intervene in the suit. This was because " 'the Secretary of Labor in effect becomes the union member's lawyer' for purposes of enforcing those rights given to individual union members under the statute," while at the same time "the Secretary has an obligation to protect the 'vital public interest in assuring free and democratic union elections that transcends the narrow interest of the complaining union member.' " In this situation, the Court acknowledged, "the union member may have a valid complaint about the performance of 'his lawyer,' " and may intervene to "present evidence and arguments in support of the Secretary's complaint."

To secure fair intraunion elections, the Landrum-Griffin Act mandates the following:

(1) Reasonable requests to distribute campaign literature at a candidate's expense must be honored by the union.

(2) No funds received from dues or similar levies may be used to promote any person's candidacy.

(3) No employer may contribute money or anything of value to the campaign of any candidate for union office.

(4) Any privileges extended to one candidate must be extended to all. For example, if literature is distributed at a reduced rate for one candidate, then all candidates must be treated equally; or if any candidate is allowed to copy membership lists, all candidates must be afforded the same opportunity.

A sharp contrast is presented between American and British law regarding legal requirements of democracy within unions. Americans assume the desirability of democratic procedures within labor organizations. On the other hand, British law makes no attempt to guarantee union democracy. The eminent British scholar, Sir Otto Kahn-Freund, has said that it "is impracticable, or at least inadvisable to lay down minimum rules of 'democracy' to be followed by all unions, irrespective of the constitutions they themselves have adopted." He then adds: "I am saying this not only because of the obvious need for protecting the autonomy of the unions, but also because I do not believe that union democracy is so clearly desirable that it should to any extent be imposed by the State."

Observers in America have noted some antisocietal effects of unrestrained union memberships who vote down contracts negotiated in good faith by their elected leaders with their employers and who on occasion tyrannize their own leaderships into irresponsible positions at the bargaining table—effects never contemplated by Congress in the enactment of the Landrum-Griffin Act. Others would say that this is a small price to pay for infusing into the governance of labor unions the same concerns for fairness and for individual rights that have become the hallmarks of our democratic society. The philosophical problem posed by Sir Otto remains:

"Is it possible to leave the control over their own membership to the unfettered discretion of the unions themselves without encroaching upon that freedom of the individual worker to be a member of a union which is, and must be, the foundation of any system of industrial relations in a democratic society? Is it, on the other hand, possible to restrict this control without depriving the unions of that autonomy without which they cannot perform their vital role in industrial relations?"

CHAPTER XVII

EMPLOYMENT DISCRIMINATION:
THE NATION'S CHALLENGE

The white race deems itself to be the dominant race in this country. . . . But in view of the Constitution, in the eye of the law, there is in this country no superior, dominant, ruling class of citizens. There is no caste here. Our Constitution is color-blind, and neither knows nor tolerates classes among citizens. In respect of civil rights, all citizens are equal before the law. . . . The law regards man as man, and takes no account of his surroundings or of his color when his civil rights as guaranteed by the supreme law of the land are involved.—Harlan, J., dissenting in *Plessy v. Ferguson*, 1896.

For us, however, American law has a much more important lesson: it is that the need for eliminating race discrimination overrides everything: union "autonomy," managerial "prerogatives" and whatever else you can think of. Here we are up against the fundamentals of civilisation.—Sir Otto Kahn-Freund, *Labour and the Law*, 1977.

DISCRIMINATION in employment on the basis of race, religion, or sex has deep roots in American history. Until the mid-twentieth century, minorities and women were generally restricted either by contract or custom, to menial, low-paying jobs. The professions and the skilled crafts were the domain of the white male.

It was only after World War II that a first tentative move at the federal level was taken toward ending employment discrimination. As a part of his "Fair Deal" President Truman proposed the Federal Fair Employment Practices Act, which would have banned racial discrimination by federal contractors. This proposal ignited a political explosion and was defeated ignominiously. Indeed, many of the bill's staunchest supporters were defeated when they ran for reelection. Federal "Fair Employment Practices" legislation had become known as a road to political suicide.

However, the civil rights movement continued to gain strength through the fifties and into the early sixties. The segregationists' bombings and violence, in Jackson and Birmingham in 1963, finally jolted the federal administration into action. Accordingly, President Kennedy proposed his civil rights bill on June 19, 1963. The central focus of the bill was the prohibition of racial discrimination in public accommodations (for example, in hotels, restaurants, public transportation) and the guarantee of voting rights. In light of the Truman administration's experience, Kennedy believed that any strong provision against employment discrimination would doom the entire bill. Therefore, he proposed legislation calling only for the creation of a "Commission on Equal Employment Opportunity," which was "to prevent discrimination against employees or applicants for employment because of race, color, religion, or national origin by government contractors and subcontractors. . . ." But the commission was to be given no powers to order compliance, and there were no penalties for continued discrimination.

Congressional liberals, led by Representative James Roosevelt of California, were outraged by the bill's toothless employment discrimination provisions. Roosevelt proposed an amendment that would create an administrative agency, resembling the NLRB, to police against employment discrimination. The agency would have broad powers to issue cease and desist orders against those employers who continued to discriminate. The liberals alone did not have sufficient votes to add the Roosevelt amendment to the civil rights bill. They needed to get the support of another bloc of votes with which they could combine to form a majority. They found those votes and created one of the most amazing political alliances in Congressional history. The group that voted with the liberals to add teeth to the bill was the southern conservatives—the very group most opposed to strong civil rights legislation.

The southerners' motive in voting for the Roosevelt amendment is not hard to discern. They felt that the administration bill, by prohibiting discrimination in public accommodation and the deprivation of voting rights, would have a major effect only in the south, where those practices were common. But since employment discrimination was a national practice, the southerners believed that including it in the civil rights bill would force many northerners to vote against the bill. In effect, the southerners voted for the Roosevelt amendment in an attempt to revive the coalition of northerners and southerners that had defeated the Truman bill.

President Kennedy recognized the threat that the southerners' strategy posed. He summoned legislative leaders to the White House and prevailed upon Representative Charles Halleck of Indiana, the House Republican leader, to accept a modified version of the Roosevelt amendment. Title VII of the Civil Rights Act would make employment discrimination illegal; but the provision was not to be enforced by an agency like the NLRB. Instead, under the compromise reached, a person who believed he was the victim of employment discrimination could file a charge with the Equal Employment Opportunity Commission (EEOC), which would seek to obtain relief by conciliation. Failing this, a victim of employment discrimination could sue the employer in a federal district court; not only for himself, but for all other members of his minority group. This made possible the use of the class action device, a potent weapon, indeed, as many an employer and union have ruefully attested. In placing the primary responsibility for the enforcement of Title VII in the federal district courts rather than in a quasi-judicial agency, Congress has vested the jurisdiction to implement it in tribunals having the power to enforce their own decisions. Moreover, it was a federal bench ready for the fray in the civil rights arena, with more than a decade of intensive litigation in education and voting rights cases.

But the southern congressmen had one more ploy in their strategy of "strengthening" the bill to death! This was an amendment offered on the House floor by Representative Howard Smith of Virginia, chairman of the Rules Committee and an implacable foe of civil rights legislation. His amendment, adopted by a majority, many of whom ultimately voted against the bill, added to Title VII a provision prohibiting employment discrimination based on sex. Thus, it is one of the great ironies of history that Judge Howard Smith, the leader of the anticivil rights forces in Congress, stands as the architect of that part of the Civil Rights Act of 1964 that many view as its most far-reaching and successful provision—the prohibition against sex discrimination in employment.

President Kennedy's assassination occurred midway through the legislative debate on the bill. Perhaps this is what finally insured passage of the bill, for many members of Congress thought its enactment into law would be a particularly fitting memorial to the fallen President. This, combined with the steady growth in power of the civil rights movement, resulted in the passage of the bill on July 2, 1964. Yet it remains one of history's great ironies that the strong employment discrimination provisions of Title VII were included primarily through the efforts of opponents of civil rights.

TITLE VII AS ENACTED

The current codification of Title VII (42 U.S.C. §2000e et seq.) covers all employers, including governmental agencies, who employ more than fifteen workers and who "affect commerce." The broad interpretation the courts have given the "affect commerce" clause means that virtually every employer having fifteen workers is covered by the act. However, the act specifically excludes "private membership clubs" from its compass.

To qualify for redress under Title VII, the discrimination must be based on race, color, religion, sex, or national origin. In *Espinoza v. Farah Mfg. Co.* (1973), the Supreme Court held that Title VII did not cover discrimination based on citizenship. Thus, a Mexican may lawfully be denied a job because he is not a citizen of the United States.

Under Title VII, it is an unlawful employment practice for

an employer to refuse to hire, to discharge, to segregate, or otherwise to discriminate on the basis of race, color, religion, sex, or national origin; for employment agencies to refuse to refer applicants for employment or otherwise discriminate; or for a union, on the basis of race, color, religion, sex, or national origin, to exclude anyone from its membership, to refuse to refer an applicant for employment, or to cause an employer to discriminate. It is also illegal to run a discriminatory training or apprenticeship program, to publish discriminatory employment notices, or to retaliate against anyone who makes charges or testifies in an unfair employment practice case.

Of course, a causal connection must be shown to exist between the race, sex, religion, or ethnic status of the employee and the action about which he or she complains. Clearly, if the employee can produce direct evidence of the employer's discriminatory intent, such as an admission that the reason he was not hired was because he is black, he has established a prima facie case, and he is entitled to relief. But such direct evidence is rare, for employers generally will not admit that they acted from discriminatory motives. Therefore, most plaintiffs, if they are to establish a case, must establish the causal connection by showing that the employer's hiring practices have the *effect* of excluding minorities. The statutory language of Title VII does not, on its face, indicate whether such a showing is sufficient to establish a prima facie case. The Supreme Court first addressed this issue in *Griggs v. Duke Power Company* (1971), a classic decision, which established a type of Title VII case known as disparate impact.

DISPARATE IMPACT

Griggs was a class action by black employees against an employer with a long history of preact employment discrimination where blacks had been frozen into the least desirable labor grade jobs. On July 2, 1965, the very day Title VII became effective, the employer inaugurated an additional requirement to qualify for a job outside of the plant's "labor department" by requiring applicants to have a high school education and satisfactory scores on two professionally prepared aptitude tests. This was to improve the overall quality of the work force, the company explained. The plaintiffs had no evidence to prove that the employer's purpose in initiating the requirements was discriminatory; but they did show that 34 per cent of North Carolina white males had completed high school, while only 12 per cent of North Carolina black males had, and that 58 per cent of whites could pass a battery of tests similar to those used by the company, while only 6 per cent of the blacks could. Thus, the effect of the company's requirements was to exclude proportionately more blacks than whites. The Supreme Court held that this statistical evidence alone was sufficient to establish the plaintiff's prima facie case, thereby shifting the burden to the employer to show that his requirements were a "business necessity" that bear "a demonstrable relationship to successful performance of the jobs for which it was used."

"The Act proscribes not only overt discrimination but also practices that are fair in form, but discriminatory in operation," the Court said. "The touchstone is business necessity. If an employment practice which operates to exclude [the protected group] cannot be shown to be related to job performance, the practice is prohibited."

But good intent or "absence of discriminatory intent does not redeem employment procedures or testing mechanisms that operate as 'built-in headwinds' for minority groups" the Court said, since "Congress has placed on the employer the burden of showing that any given requirement must have a manifest relationship to the employment in question." Then it summed it up for all to hear: "Far from disparaging job qualifications as such, Congress has made such qualifications the controlling factors, so that race, religion, nationality, and sex become irrelevant. What Congress has commanded is that any tests used must measure the person for the job and not the person in the abstract."

Therefore, the company had to show that a high school diploma and passing grades on its tests were necessary for successful performance of the jobs in order to rebut the plaintiff's case and establish a successful defense. The Court found that the company had failed to make this showing because the evidence "shows that the white employees hired before the company's requirements went into effect who have not completed high school or taken the tests have continued to perform satisfactorily and make progress in departments for which the high school and test criteria are now used."

The *Griggs* ruling continues to have a profound effect on employment practices. For if it can be shown that *any* criteria used in hiring or promotion exclude proportionately more members of a group protected by Title VII than members of the general population, an employer must justify such criteria as "job-related" or be held in violation of Title VII.

In *Albemarle Paper Co. v. Moody* (1975), the Supreme Court approved the use of the Equal Employment Opportunities Commission's 1970 guidelines on test validation as a standard for proof of "job relatedness." While a detailed explanation of these guidelines is beyond the scope of this work, their thrust is that a rather close correlation between the employer's hiring criteria and successful job performance must be shown, based on sophisticated statistical and psychological testing techniques.

These relatively early Title VII cases require that hiring criteria be validated only in relation to the actual job for which the criteria were being used. However, *Washington v. Davis* (1976), a suit brought under the Civil Rights Act of 1866, not Title VII, may signal a loosening of this approach. There, unsuccessful black applicants for employment as police officers in the District of Columbia sued, claiming that the recruiting procedures, including a written personnel test administered to determine the verbal skill of applicants, were discriminatory. That test, they showed, excluded a disproportionately high number of black applicants; and the District could not show the test was a valid predictor of success as a police officer. However, the District did show that the test score did correlate with successful completion of the course at the Police Academy, which all newly hired policemen must complete before they are assigned to their permanent jobs. The Supreme Court stated that that showing was sufficient to validate the test.

The authors of the standard reference work in this field (Schlei and Grossman, *Employment Discrimination Law*) state flatly: "For most employers validation in accordance with the EEOC guidelines is impossible." They caution that as adopted and applied in *Griggs* and *Moody*, these guidelines may have a perverse effect when employers, no longer able to use objective testing, will "rely more heavily on subjective criteria for employment decisions," a tendency that may not be "to the benefit of the groups supposedly protected by the Supreme Court decisions." They suggest "that employers will be led to make employment decisions primarily utilizing ratios of minority, female and Caucasian male employees." They see as the "only possible solution" some "relaxation of the requirements with respect to demonstrating job-relatedness" and they interpret *Washington v. Davis* as the Supreme Court "moving in this direction."

In the context of civil rights legislation, it is hard to disagree with the Supreme Court's skepticism toward generalized testing that has an adverse impact on blacks. This is particularly true in the face of what the Court said in *Griggs:* "Because they are Negroes, petitioners have long received inferior education in segregated schools. . . ." The Court is going to have to decide the extent to which society will require blacks to pull themselves up by their own bootstraps. The standard of job-relatedness adopted in *Griggs* appears to provide a desirable middle course between employment discrimination at the one extreme and quotas at the other.

Statistical data standing alone can establish a prima facie case of discrimination against an employer in a Title VII suit, thus shifting the burden to the defendant to prove that he did not discriminate. In *Griggs*, the disparate impact on blacks of certain required tests was demonstrated mathematically. In *Hazlewood School District v. U.S.* (1977), the Supreme Court emphasized the vital role that employment statistics in the labor market area can play in determining if the employer has been guilty of discriminatory hiring practices. As one judge said: "Figures speak; and when they do, Courts listen." "Statistics," the Supreme Court said in one case, "come in infinite variety," and "their usefulness depends on all of the surrounding facts and circumstances." To make the figures "speak" and to develop the significance of the "surrounding facts and circumstances," the expert testimony of actuaries and of statisticians has become commonplace in Title VII litigation, along with the testimony of industrial psychologists on issues relating to testing and validation.

The analysis of *Griggs* is applicable to all cases where an applicant, who cannot meet the qualifications set by the employer for hiring or promotion, seeks to overturn those criteria as discriminatory. But what happens when an applicant who *can* meet the employer's qualification is refused a job? In the case of *McDonnell Douglas Corporation v. Green* (1973), the Supreme Court considered just such a situation as another type of employment discrimination—individual discrimination.

INDIVIDUAL DISCRIMINATION

The leading case regarding all claims of individual discrimination or "disparate treatment" under Title VII is the Supreme Court's decision in *McDonnell Douglas Corporation v. Green* (1973). Green, a black civil rights activist, worked for eight years for McDonnell Douglas in St. Louis, where it employed over thirty thousand people in its aerospace and aircraft manufacturing business. He was laid off from his job as a mechanic soon after the Civil Rights Act was passed on July 2, 1964. He then participated in a series of protests against the hiring practices of McDonnell Douglas. One technique of protest was a "stall-in" plan, where teams of four cars would line up next to each other at intersections, thus blocking for one hour the five main access roads into the plant during the morning rush hour. Thereafter, the company advertised for qualified mechanics, which was Green's craft; and he applied for reemployment. The company turned Green down because of his participation in the allegedly unlawful demonstrations. Green sued under Title VII, claiming that he was the victim of racially discriminatory hiring practices. The Supreme Court overturned the district court's dismissal of the case; and in so doing it set forth the procedures under which claims of individual discrimination under Title VII were henceforth to be adjudicated. First, the complainant has the burden of establishing a prima facie case of discrimination. He may do this by showing: (1) that he belongs to a racial minority (or other protected group); (2) that he applied and was qualified for a job for which the employer was seeking applicants; (3) that, despite his qualifications, he was rejected; and (4) that, after his rejection, the position remained open and the employer continued to seek applicants from persons of the complainant's qualifications. Green met this four-point test, thus establishing a prima facie case. At this juncture, the Court said, the burden shifted to McDonnell Douglas to state some legitimate, nondiscriminatory reason for rejecting Green. This the employer did by stating that its refusal to rehire Green was due to his participation in the "stall-in" demonstration. "Nothing in Title VII," the Court said, "compels an employer to absolve and rehire one who has engaged in such deliberate, unlawful activity against it." However, "the inquiry must not end here," the Court went on, for Title VII does not permit McDonnell Douglas to use Green's conduct "as a pretext for the sort of discrimination prohibited" by Title VII. Green must be afforded "a full and fair opportunity to demonstrate by competent evidence that the presumptively valid reasons for his rejection were in fact a coverup for a racially discriminatory decision." McDonnell Douglas "may justifiably refuse to rehire one who has engaged in unlawful disruptive acts against it," the Court said, "but only if this criterion is applied alike to members of all races." Thus, if white workers had been involved in similar actions and yet had been rehired, the company's refusal to hire similarly situated blacks because of their "illegal activity" would amount to a pretext covering up the real reason —racial discrimination. In *McDonald v. Sante Fe Trail Transportation Company* (1976), the Supreme Court held that employment discrimination against whites based on race equally violated the law.

The four-point test for establishing a prima facie case under *McDonnell Douglas* has proven to be a satisfactory standard for use in the lower courts. Nevertheless, in *Furnco Construction Co. v. Waters* (1978) the Supreme Court found it necessary to caution federal district judges against taking remedial action solely on the basis of a prima facie showing under *McDonnell Douglas.* The Court reiterated that a *McDonnell Douglas* prima facie case raises only an *inference* of discriminatory intent; it does not prove discrimination. Thus, all the employer has to do to rebut the prima facie case is to prove "that he based his employment decision on a legitimate consideration, and not an illegitimate one such as race. To prove that, he need not prove that he pursued the course which would both enable him to achieve his own business goal *and* allow him to consider the *most* [minority] employment applications." The Court of Appeals ruling had required Furnco to revamp its hiring practices in specific ways so as to maximize the number of minority applications it would receive, simply on the basis of the prima facie showing. The Supreme Court said, "Courts are generally less competent than employers to restructure business practices, and unless mandated to do so by Congress they should not attempt it." Therefore, "courts may not impose such a remedy on an employer at least until a violation of Title VII has been proven. . . ." In *Board of Trustees of Keene State College v. Christine M. Sweeney* (1978), the Supreme Court rejected the notion that once a defendant has responded to plaintiff's prima facie case by articulating a legitimate, nondiscriminatory reason for its action under *Furnco,* it has any obligation to prove it has not discriminated. At that point the burden of proof of discrimination is upon the plaintiff, the Court reiterated.

The *McDonnell Douglas* case, as interpreted and applied in *Furnco,* has established the procedure for the trial of all Title VII litigation involving allegations of individual discrimination.

THE ECLIPSE OF STATE PROTECTIVE LAWS

Employers have sometimes sought to justify disparate treatment of females by pleading their obligation to comply with restrictions contained in state protective laws. Back in *Muller v. Oregon* (1908), the Supreme Court finally upheld as constitutional a state law prohibiting women from working in a factory more than ten hours a day. Agreeing with the famous Brandeis brief, the Court held that the Oregon law was a legitimate use of the police power since a woman "is properly placed in a class by herself, and legislation designed for her protection may be sustained, even when like legislation is not necessary for men, and could not be sustained. . . . Her physical structure and a proper discharge of her maternal functions . . . having in view not merely her own health but the well being of the race . . . justify legislation to protect her from the greed as well as the passion of men." There followed the general adoption of female protective legislation, state legislatures placing restrictions upon the occupations in which women could engage or upon their hours and working conditions, regulating such things as rest periods, weights, and premium pay for overtime.

Section 708 of Title VII invalidated state laws that required or permitted "the doing of any act which would be an unlawful employment practice under this title." Since disparate treatment in itself became unlawful, state protective legislation conferring benefits upon females had either to be invalidated or the same benefits be extended to males. The Supreme Court has yet to rule on whether Title VII requires "equalization upward"—that is, whether men should be held entitled to the benefits enjoyed by women or the benefit be taken away from the latter. In the absence of such a ruling either way.being read into Title VII by the Supreme Court, the pattern appears to have been one of wholesale invalidation of female protective legislation in the trend toward job equality. Provisions in collective bargaining agreements providing special benefits for women have faced the same attack—with the same result.

Thus social legislation once heralded as absolutely essential to the well-being of women, in time became anathema to the objects of its protection. It would appear that laws, like human beings, have their entrances and their exits; and a type of control that may make a positive contribution at one stage of societal development, at another becomes a deterrent to the new society.

STATUTORY EXEMPTIONS AND DEFENSES

While Title VII, as a general rule, bans all employment distinction based on race, religion, sex, or national origin, the statute provides that, in certain situations, such distinctions will not violate the act. The first of these situations is referred to as a "bona fide occupational qualification"; the second involves the application of a seniority system that tends to freeze certain groups into certain jobs.

Bona Fide Occupational Qualification • Section 703 (*e*) (1) of the act permits an employer to employ an individual "on the basis of his religion, sex or national origin in those certain instances where religion, sex or national origin is a bona fide occupational qualification [BFOQ] reasonably necessary to the normal operation of that particular business or enterprise. . . ." It is important to note that race can never be a BFOQ under the statute. The BFOQ was intended to support "the preference of a French restaurant for a French cook," "an Italian chef . . . for an Italian restaurant," and "male players for a professional baseball team." The EEOC has stated that the BFOQ exception is appropriate as a defense only where a particular sex "is necessary for the purpose of authenticity or genuineness . . . e.g., an actor or actress." The Supreme Court has said that EEOC guidelines are entitled to "great deference"; but it appears to accept or reject them, depending on how it wants to decide a particular case!

Dothard v. Rawlinson (1977) shows the use of the BFOQ defense. The plaintiff, Ms. Rawlinson, commenced her Title VII action against the Alabama Board of Corrections because the state had imposed minimum weight and height requirements of five feet two inches and 120 pounds in choosing its prison guards—a minimum standard that disqualified her from consideration for the job. (This was before Alabama prison officials adopted their final position, which was simply to bar females from "contact positions" in male security penitentiaries.) Ms. Rawlinson showed that Alabama's statutory standards would exclude over 40 per cent of the female population but less than 1 per cent of the male population. The Supreme Court said this made out a prima facie case of unlawful sex discrimination, which the state failed to rebut by a showing of job relatedness correlating the height and weight requirements with the amount of strength necessary for the position of prison guards.

However, the Court did accept Alabama's contention that maleness was a bona fide occupational qualification for being a prison guard. The Court indicated that the BFOQ defense was "meant to be an extremely narrow exception" to the prohibition against sex discrimination. But the Court stated that in Alabama, in maximum security prisons, "violence is the order of the day," and noted that inmate access to guards is facilitated by dormitory living arrangements, every institution is understaffed, and a substantial portion of the inmate population is composed of sex offenders who are mixed at random with other prisoners. "The likelihood that inmates would assault a woman because she was a woman would," the Court added, "pose a real threat not only to the victim of the assault but also to the basic control of the penitentiary and protection of its inmates and other security personnel." Justice Marshall, dissenting on this point, admonished the Court that its "error in statutory construction is less objectionable . . . than the attitude it displays towards women." The Court's "fundamental justification for the decision is that women as guards will generate sexual assaults," thus perpetuating "one of the most insidious of the old myths about women—that women, wittingly or not, are seductive sexual objects." Justice Marshall also noted that the presence of women guards had not led to a single incident amounting to a serious breach of security in any Alabama institution. Then he concluded: "To deprive women of job opportunities because of the threatened behavior of convicted criminals is to turn our social priorities upside down."

Bona Fide Seniority Systems • Although virtually no seniority systems are explicitly discriminatory, it is apparent that many have the effect of "freezing in" the effects of discriminatory hiring. Let us assume that, before Title VII became law and made such practice illegal, an employer engaged in discrimination by assigning all black workers to menial jobs in the laborer's department, while assigning only whites to jobs in better paying departments. The employer has accepted, in a collective bargaining agreement, a departmental seniority system whereby an employee's seniority is effective only so long as he remains in his original department. Should he transfer to a job in another department in the plant he will lose his accumulated seniority and all the advantages of it—protection against layoffs, a choice of jobs and shifts, and perhaps premium pay. These advantages are so great that few employees are willing to sacrifice them. Thus, the effect of a departmental seniority system is to lock employees into one department throughout their careers. And when this is combined with prior discrimination on the part of the employer, the result is to lock the victims of discrimination into the most menial department in the plant, thus preserving the effect of the discriminatory practices made illegal by Title VII.

The *Griggs* case stated that "practices . . . neutral on their face, and even neutral in terms of intent, cannot be maintained if they operate to 'freeze' the status quo of prior discriminatory practices." Were *Griggs* the only law on this matter, such a seniority system clearly would be illegal. However, Section 703 (*h*) of Title VII states:

"Notwithstanding any other provision of this title it shall not be an unlawful employment practice for an employer to apply different . . . privileges of employment pursuant to a bona fide seniority or merit system . . . provided that such differences are not the result of an intention to discriminate because of race, color, religion, sex, or national origin. . . ."

Thus, the question facing the courts is to what extent can a seniority system perpetuate past discrimination and still be considered a "bona fide seniority system"?

In *Quarles v. Philip Morris, Inc.* (1968) a federal district court early rejected the notion that a "facially neutral" (neutral on its face) seniority system was protected by Section 703 (*h*) where the system perpetuated the effects of prior discrimination, as long as the employer ceased all discriminatory employment practices. "Congress did not intend to freeze an entire generation of Negro employees into discriminatory patterns that existed before the Act," said the court. The remedy in *Quarles* allowed all blacks hired before a particular date who were locked into undesirable jobs, to transfer and fill vacancies in more desirable departments, taking with them full employment seniority, notwithstanding the fact of an already existing departmental seniority system. With unusual unanimity eight federal courts of appeal followed *Quarles*. But the Supreme Court had yet to be heard on this issue.

Meanwhile in *Franks v. Bowman Transportation Company* (1976), the Supreme Court heard the case of a black whose application for employment had been rejected years before the trucking company had begun to hire minority employees. "There is no indication in the legislative materials that §703 (*h*) was intended to modify or restrict relief otherwise appropriate once an illegal discriminatory practice occurring after the effective date of the Act is proved—as in the instant case, a discriminatory refusal to hire," the Court said. "Seniority principles are increasingly used to allocate entitlements to scarce benefits among competing employees," the Court noted. It is apparent, the Court went on to say, "that denial of seniority relief to identifiable victims of racial discrimination on the sole ground that such relief diminishes the expectations of other, arguably innocent, employees would if applied generally frustrate the central 'make-whole' objective of Title VII." Accordingly, the Court awarded Franks, an identifiable victim of racial discrimination, constructive seniority dating back to the first day he applied for the position. It did not, however, offer anything to those victims who had never actually applied for a position, even if the failure to apply was because they had heard about the employer's discriminatory hiring policies.

The use by the Court of the language—"such relief diminishes the expectations of other, arguably innocent, employees" —points up a significant fact about the nature of the seniority problem. Seniority is entirely relative—when one employee is given greater seniority, other employees move to a lower rung on the seniority ladder. These latter employees are both totally innocent and are the only ones hurt. The party responsible is the employer who discriminated against blacks; yet in a real sense it is immaterial to the company which employee occupies what seniority spot. It is this anomaly that caused Chief Justice Burger to opt for "front pay" in *Franks*—the payment to the victim by the guilty party of a monetary award rather than a grant of seniority, in order to compensate him for the harm done to him by the unlawful discrimination.

How can one undo the effects of past discrimination? In addition to "front pay," there are obviously several other approaches that might be taken where blacks have been frozen out of the good jobs by having been confined at an earlier date to a separate seniority unit. One approach has been called "freedom now," where the court simply eliminates the separate seniority systems and everyone, black and white, is dovetailed into a single ladder based on plant-wide or company-wide seniority. This can, of course, result in the displacement from their jobs of whites by blacks who have been in an historically separate seniority unit. So "freedom now" has not been favored as a remedy. Another approach has been termed the "rightful place" remedy—for purposes of bidding on vacancies only, the black can use plant-wide seniority even though the collective bargaining agreement recognizes only seniority acquired within a department or a classification. No one is displaced, but when openings occur high-seniority black employees have a superior position to whites with fewer years of plant service. Finally, the court can take a "status quo" approach, leaving everyone where they find them. Indeed, depending on how Section 703 (h) is interpreted, if preact discrimination is perpetuated by a "facially neutral" seniority system, there is nothing illegal; so the court is not called upon to supply a remedy.

In *International Brotherhood of Teamsters and T.I.M.E.— D.C., Inc. v. United States* (1977), the Supreme Court came squarely to grips with Section 703 (h). The prosecutor in this case challenged a "pattern-or-practice" of employment discrimination that prevented blacks and Spanish-surnamed persons from obtaining preferred positions as line-drivers. The evidence of discrimination presented in the form of statistics and testimony of witnesses was overwhelming. Members of minority groups were hired into positions other than line-drivers in a different bargaining unit with a different seniority system both before and after Title VII became effective. An employee who left one of these other positions to transfer to a line-driver job was required to forfeit all the competitive seniority he had accumulated. The practical effect was to lock minority workers into inferior jobs and perpetuate prior discrimination. The government—the prosecutor in "pattern-or-practice" cases—attacked the seniority system head-on as perpetuating pre- and postact discrimination, relying on *Quarles* and the many cases it spawned. The Court rejected *Quarles* and the government's argument. "Congress did not intend to make it illegal for employees with vested seniority rights to continue to exercise those rights even at the expense of pre-Act discriminatees," the Court said. It found the seniority system to be "entirely bona fide." To the extent that it locks minority employees into nonline-driver jobs, it does so for white employees, as well, the Court said. "Because the seniority system was protected by §703 (*h*), the union's conduct in agreeing to and maintaining the system did not violate Title VII," the Court concluded. It did broaden *Franks* somewhat so as to permit a recovery not only by identifiable victims of discriminatory hiring practices but by anyone who could prove "that he was deterred from applying for the job by the employer's discriminatory practices. . . ."

"SEX-PLUS"

The disparate treatment of a subclass within a protected group has been found to be a violation of Title VII. Disparate treatment of a male or female subclass has come to be known as a "sex-plus" case. A sex-plus situation arises whenever an employer adds a specification for one sex that is not added for the other sex. An example is *Phillips* v. *Martin Marietta Co.* (1971), where the employer's policy was not to accept job applications from women with preschool age children. It had no such policy with regard to men with preschool age children. The employer hired a higher percentage of women applicants than male applicants. Hence the policy against hiring women with preschool age children could not be shown to have resulted in discrimination against females as a group, but only against females with preschool age children. Nevertheless the Supreme Court found a violation of Title VII in the maintenance of "one hiring policy for women and another for men—each having preschool age children." Similarly, discriminatory policies directed only against married airline stewardesses as against unmarried have been found to violate Title VII, when the same policy is not applied to male airline personnel.

JUST WHAT IS SEX DISCRIMINATION?

As enacted, Title VII did not define what constituted "sex discrimination." The simple case of disparate treatment based on sex posed no problems different from any encountered in race discrimination cases; but the Supreme Court has followed a tortured course in finding its way around the periphery of the problem. For example, was it sex discrimination under Title VII for an employer to fail to cover pregnancy-related disabilities in an otherwise all-inclusive disability benefit plan? No, said the Court in *General Electric Co. v. Gilbert* (1976), for there was no "gender-based discrimination . . . simply because an employer's disability benefits plan is less than all inclusive." The Court found that General Electric's exclusion of pregnancy from coverage under its disability plan divided its workers into two classes—pregnant and nonpregnant workers. Although the class of pregnant workers obviously is composed entirely of women, the class of nonpregnant workers includes both men and women. Therefore, said the Court, this is not a sex-based distinction at all. Justice Stevens, in dissent, observed: "By definition such a rule discriminates on account of sex; for it is the capacity to become pregnant which primarily differentiates the female from the male." In *Gilbert,* the Supreme Court made clear that a pregnant woman can lawfully be denied disability benefits by her employer; yet in *Nashville Gas Co. v. Satty* (1977), the Court held that, in the absence of proof of business necessity, she cannot be denied the seniority she had accumulated prior to the pregnancy leave. Thus, the Court ended up in the somewhat inconsistent position that denial of insurance benefits for pregnancy was not "discrimination" based on sex, but that denial of seniority rights was.

Late in 1978 Congress overturned *Gilbert.* It amended Title

VII explicitly to prohibit discrimination against pregnant women. Employers are required to treat pregnancy and childbirth the same as other causes of disability under fringe benefit plans, but benefits are required to be paid only during the period when the woman is medically disabled from work. Abortion is not required to be covered "except where the life of the mother would be endangered if the fetus were carried to term" or "where medical complications have arisen from an abortion." The amendment strengthened the Supreme Court's decision in *Satty* by unequivocally protecting the reinstatement rights of women on pregnancy leaves, including credit for prior service and accrued retirement and seniority benefits. Employers are prohibited from terminating or refusing to hire or promote a woman because she is pregnant or forcing her to go on leave at a certain time during her pregnancy, when she is still able to work—the latter being practices the Supreme Court had earlier found to be constitutionally impermissible under the 14th amendment as applied to teachers in *Cleveland Board of Education v. Jo Carol LaFleur, et al.* (1974).

The Supreme Court found gender-based discrimination violating Title VII in *City of Los Angeles Department of Water and Power v. Marie Manhart* (1978). There, Ms. Manhart sued the Los Angeles Water Department on behalf of its two thousand female employees. The employer required females to make larger pension contributions than males because actuarially as a group they lived longer and would draw benefits longer. Even while conceding that "unless women as a class are assessed an extra charge, they will be subsidized, to some extent, by the class of male employees," the Court still held it invalid. This was because the question of discrimination was not to be determined by class characteristics but by individual characteristics. And the Court went on to observe that since some men outlive some women, even a "true generalization about the class is an insufficient reason for disqualifying an individual to whom the generalization does not apply." If we ignore the actuarial tables as regards pensions, where women as a group benefit, what will the Court do in the case of life insurance where women would be the distinct losers in requiring cost uniformity between the sexes? Is the use of gender-based actuarial tables by an employer in any event "discrimination" under Title VII? The Court shied away from prohibiting their usage by insurance companies; and employers approach them gingerly as a result of the *Manhart* decision. The fact that Justice Stevens, who dissented in *Gilbert,* spoke for the majority in *Manhart,* suggests that some internal gyrations have been going on within the Court as it gropes for the limits of permissible gender-based employment practices. The Court is not likely to find much help in the legislative history, remembering how it all began, with Judge Howard Smith of Virginia, on that extraordinary day when legislation against sex discrimination sprang full-blown upon the American scene! But the prod that Congress gave the Court in the 1978 amendment is not likely to be forgotten.

RELIGIOUS DISCRIMINATION

In *TWA v. Hardison* (1977) the Supreme Court again permitted a facially neutral seniority system to diminish the thrust of Title VII. The plaintiff, Hardison, was a member of Worldwide Church of God, who refused to work on Saturdays, even though he was required to do so under the terms of the collective bargaining agreement between TWA and the machinists' union. Hardison sued the airline under Section 703 (a) (1) of Title VII, which makes it an unlawful employment practice for an employer to discriminate against an employee or a prospective employee because of his or her religion. Hardison was employed as a clerk in the stores department of TWA at its Kansas City base, an operation required to be open 24 hours a day, 365 days a year. Under the terms of the union contract the most senior employees had job and shift preference while the junior employees had to work on Saturdays and Sundays in order to meet the employer's schedule needs.

Hardison's problems began when he used his seniority to transfer from building 1, where his relative length of service had enabled him to avoid Saturday work, to building 2 where he was second from the bottom on its seniority list. The union was unwilling to allow Hardison to circumvent the seniority provisions; and the airline, on the other hand, would not agree to solutions proposed by the union that would have permitted Hardison to work a permanent "short week" of four days. For leaving his job unfilled on Saturdays would impair supply shop functions; filling the vacancy with a supervisor or an employee from another area would underman another operation; and employing or assigning someone to work regularly just on Saturdays to fill the gap would involve the airline in overtime premium pay. A union steward canvassed senior employees, but they were unwilling to adjust their own schedules to relieve Hardison of his obligation to work on Saturdays. True to the tenets of his religion, Hardison refused to report for work on Saturdays. For this insubordination he was discharged.

The 1972 amendments to Title VII had defined "religion" as including "all aspects of religious observance and practice, as well as belief, unless an employer demonstrates that he is unable to reasonably accommodate to an employee's . . . religious observance or practice *without undue hardship on the conduct of the employer's business.*" (Italics added.)

The Court denied Hardison's claim under Title VII. It held that it "would be anomalous to conclude that by 'reasonable accommodation' Congress meant that an employer must deny the shift and job preference of some employees, as well as deprive them of their contractual rights, in order to accommodate or prefer the religious needs of others. . . ." The Court added: "To require TWA to bear more than a *de minimis* cost in order to give Hardison Saturdays off is an undue hardship. . . . In the absence of clear statutory language or legislative history to the contrary, we will not readily construe the statute to require an employer to discriminate against some employees in order to enable others to observe their Sabbath."

The employer is not required under Section 703 (*h*) to take any steps inconsistent with its collective bargaining agreement, the Court stated, going on to note that "absent a discriminatory purpose the operation of a seniority system cannot be an unlawful employment practice even if the system has some discriminatory consequences."

Justice Marshall, joined in his dissenting opinion by Justice Brennan, said flatly: "Today's decision deals a fatal blow to all efforts under Title VII to accommodate work requirements to religious practices." Marshall was quite prepared to do battle with the Court on the point made in the majority opinion that to accommodate Hardison would have required "unequal treatment," observing that "if an accommodation can be rejected simply because it involves preferential treatment, then the regulation and the statute, while brimming with 'sound and fury,' ultimately signif[y] nothing." Marshall found this result "deeply troubling, for," he said, "a society that truly values religious pluralism cannot compel adherents of minority religions to make the cruel choice of surrendering their religion or their job."

A familiar legal aphorism is that hard cases make bad law. Is it possible that the Court's decision in this case was influenced by Hardison's expectation that TWA and the union should accommodate their interests to his wishes when he chose to transfer to building 2, while he could more easily have accommodated himself to his employer and the union by remaining in building 1?

REMEDY

The successful plaintiff in a Title VII action in a federal district court is entitled to be "made whole" for any wage loss, under *Albemarle Paper Company v. Moody* (1975), and to recover attorney's fees and court costs from the defendant under the Supreme Court's decision in *Newman v. Piggie Park Enterprises* (1968). The employer can be enjoined from continuing to use discriminatory testing procedures or employment practices. In *Christianburg Garment Company v. EEOC* (1978) the Supreme Court decided that tit-for-tat does not apply with regard to the obligation of the losing side to pay the attorney's fees of the victor in Title VII litigation. Unlike the winning plaintiff, who always recovers fees, a successful defendant in a Title VII action is entitled to recover attorney's fees from the plaintiff only when the plaintiff's suit was "frivolous, unreasonable or without foundation."

The section of the act setting out remedies for discrimination vests broad equitable discretion in the federal courts to "order such *affirmative action* as may be appropriate, which may include, but is not limited to, reinstatement or hiring of employees, with or without backpay . . . or any other relief as the court deems appropriate." (Italics added.) From this language came the practice of terming plans to correct discriminatory practices as "affirmative action programs" (AAP's as they are sometimes called).

There is frequently found in collective bargaining agreements contract clauses that prohibit discrimination based on race, religion, or sex. This, of course, creates a prohibition against employment discrimination independent of Title VII. In *Westinghouse Electric Corp.* (1978) the NLRB held that where such a clause exists the employer must supply the bargaining agent with statistical data it requests concerning minority group and female employees within the bargaining unit, even if the union might use such information in connection with a Title VII suit against the employer. The board said that "the existence of Title VII should not restrict the Union's statutory right under the Act to relevant information concerning alleged discrimination" (*supra,* pp. 464–65). The union's request "was made in furtherance of its attempt to eliminate discrimination, which was plainly within its scope as bargaining representative," the board said.

A remedy for an act of employment discrimination claimed to be in violation of the collective bargaining agreement may

sometimes be sought through the contractual grievance procedure. In *Alexander v. Gardner-Denver Company* (1974) a
black employee pressed to arbitration a grievance complaining
of a discriminatory discharge, invoking a nondiscrimination
clause in a collective bargaining agreement; and the award went
against him. Although under the agreement, arbitration awards
were to be final and binding, the Supreme Court nevertheless
held that he was not precluded from pursuing his claim in a
Title VII action before a federal district court. The Supreme
Court deprecated the district court's inability to "accept a
philosophy which gives the employee two strings to his bow
when the employer has only one." It said that "the employee is
not seeking review of the arbitrator's decision" but is, rather
"asserting a statutory right independent of the arbitration process." The Court observed: "An employer does not have 'two
strings to his bow' with respect to an arbitral decision for the
simple reason that Title VII does not provide employers with a
cause of action against employees." And it went on to say that
"Congress intended federal courts to exercise final responsibility for enforcement of Title VII; deferral to arbitral decisions
would be inconsistent with that goal." However, it did direct
district courts to admit arbitral decisions into evidence in such
cases and to accord them "such weight as the court deems appropriate." Then it cautioned in the now famous footnote
twenty-one: "But courts should be ever mindful that Congress,
in enacting Title VII, thought it necessary to provide a judicial
forum for the ultimate resolution of discriminatory employment claims. It is the duty of courts to assure the full availability
of this forum."

Bakke AND "REVERSE DISCRIMINATION":
THE END OF A COLOR-BLIND CONSTITUTION?

In the past many courts have required employers to revamp
their hiring and promotional practices so that a specified number of minorities and women will be hired. They have done

this only as part of the remedy in cases where the employers were found to have committed previous acts of unlawful discrimination.

Some argue that such a remedy is a quota system favoring minorities or women and, in that respect, amounts to reverse discrimination against the rest of the work force who are no longer able to compete for the jobs thus reserved for members of the protected groups. They believe that the courts, in effect, have denied them the "equal protection of the laws" guaranteed by the 14th amendment.

The Supreme Court's celebrated case—*Regents of the University of California v. Bakke* (1978)—did not at all involve employment discrimination or Title VII. However, it was important to employment discrimination law. Bakke, a white applicant to medical school, alleged that a special admissions program at the University of California's Davis campus, reserving sixteen of the one hundred admissions to the entering class for minority applicants, violated his rights under the equal protection clause of the 14th amendment. (That was because, he pointed out, minority applicants less qualified than he were nevertheless admitted while his application was rejected.) Justice Powell's was the crucial swing fifth vote, as the rest of the Court divided four-four into two camps—Brennan, White, Marshall, and Blackmun in one and Burger, Stevens, Stewart, and Rehnquist in the other. Justice Powell, with the latter group, made up the majority, which held that allocating sixteen places to minority applicants was an impermissible quota in violation of Title VI of the Civil Rights Act of 1964 prohibiting discrimination in federally funded programs such as education. However, Justice Powell and the Brennan group held that a flexible admissions program including race and ethnic origin as factors to achieve ethnic diversity in the student body violates neither Title VI nor the 14th amendment.

The present chapter in this book began with a quotation from the classic dissent of Justice Harlan in *Plessy v. Ferguson* (1896), where Harlan expressed the view that the Constitution is color-blind. Now a majority of the Court in *Bakke* appears to hold that the equal protection clause of the 14th amendment does not require state action to be color-blind.

Justice Powell, writing the Court's opinion, bore down vigorously against "preferential classifications" (he avoided using the word *quotas*); but still seemed to justify such classification where there were "proven constitutional or statutory violations." It would appear that in such situations courts and administrative agencies will still be free to correct such violations by affirmative action programs, including the requirement of specific numbers or percentages in the hiring or promotion of groups who were victims of unlawful employment practices. The Court's ruling left open the possibility that a quota plan adopted voluntarily by an employer, however, might be held to be illegal reverse discrimination. The Brennan group made it clear that they would have gone much further in permitting, as they thought Congress had, "the consideration of race as part of a remedy for societal discrimination even where there is no showing that the institution extending the preference has been guilty of past discrimination, nor any judicial finding that the particular beneficiaries of the racial preference have been adversely affected by societal discrimination."

SECTION 1981 OF THE CIVIL RIGHTS ACT

In the stormy period following the Civil War, Congress in 1866 enacted the Civil Rights Act. Section 1981 provides that "All persons . . . shall have the same right in every State or Territory to make and enforce contracts . . . as is enjoyed by white citizens. . . ."

The 1866 Civil Rights Act had been passed by Congress after the adoption of the 13th amendment prohibiting slavery. And the 1870 act, which reenacted the 1866 act, was passed right after the intervening adoption of the 14th amendment, in hopes of bolstering the claim that it covered acts of private discrimination. This hope was dashed, however, in the *Civil*

Rights Cases (1883) when the Supreme Court narrowly construed Congressional power under the 13th amendment so as not to reach private acts of racial discrimination—a similarly narrow construction of Congressional power following later under the 14th amendment.

For more than a century after their enactment the 1866 and 1870 acts languished in total neglect, much as the equal protection clause of the 14th amendment slept until the Supreme Court in 1954 applied it to ban public school segregation in *Brown v. Board of Education.* The Supreme Court's decision in *Jones v. Alfred H. Mayer Co.* (1968), in the words of the *Harvard Law Review,* "exhumed the Civil Rights Act of 1866 from a century of desuetude" by finding for the first time that it prohibited racial discrimination, both public and private, in the sale of property. Then in 1976 in *McDonald v. Sante Fe Trail Transportation Company,* the Supreme Court was presented the question of whether white employees are entitled to the protection against race discrimination in employment set forth in Section 1981 of the Civil Rights Act. Two white employees were discharged for the theft of cargo. They brought suit against the employer and the union when they learned that Jackson, a black employee, who was accused of the same offense, had not been discharged. It seems appropriate that Justice Marshall, the only black member of the Court, decided for a unanimous bench that Section 1981 and Title VII prohibit "racial discrimination against the white petitioners in this case upon the same standards as would be applicable were they Negroes and Jackson white." Moreover, the Court said, while a union, in resolving grievances, may necessarily have to compromise by securing the retention of only some employees, in so doing it may not take into account the factor of race.

In *McDonald* the Court for the first time held that Section 1981 prohibited racial discrimination in private employment against whites. After recovering from the astonishment that it took the Supreme Court 112 years to reach this conclusion, one may well wonder what advantage there is in having *two* federal laws covering employment discrimination based on race. One advantage to plaintiffs is that by proceeding under Section 1981 they may avoid the jurisdictional requirement of all Title VII cases—that they must first have filed charges with the EEOC. Because of its close connection with the 13th and 14th amendments, Section 1981 appears to be inapplicable to cases of sex discrimination and perhaps to those involving claims of discrimination based on religion or national origin. Because the use of Section 1981 to ban acts of private racial discrimination is so recent, time alone can tell whether in practice the Court will find a significant difference between it and Title VII. The nation's policy against employment discrimination is also bolstered by the existence of many state fair employment practice acts. Congress has not preempted state law in the field of employment discrimination, as it has in labor relations.

AGE DISCRIMINATION:
THE *ADEA* WHOSE TIME HAS ARRIVED

The Age Discrimination in Employment Act of 1967 (ADEA) was spawned by a little-noticed provision in the Civil Rights Act of 1964 creating a council under the Secretary of Labor. The purpose of this council was to study equal employment opportunity legislation and make annual recommendations to the President and to Congress for such legislative or administrative changes as it concludes are desirable. One year later the council reported to Congress that pervasive age discrimination in employment existed in the United States, with debilitating effects on older workers. However, unlike the case with other discriminatory employment patterns, they found no evidence of prejudice based on intolerance or dislike for the older worker. Instead the discrimination resulted from seemingly erroneous assumptions by employers concerning the effects of age on job performance. As the Supreme Court said in *Massachusetts Board of Retirement v. Murgia* (1976), a case in which it rejected a constitutional challenge to a Massachusetts law requiring state police officers to retire at age fifty: "While the treatment of the aged in this Nation has not been wholly free of discrimination, such persons, unlike, say, those who have been discriminated against on the basis of race or national origin, have not experienced a 'history of purposeful unequal treatment' or been subjected to unique disabilities on the basis of stereotyped characteristics not truly indicative of their abilities."

Moreover, this discrimination differs from other types of employment discrimination because age *does*, at some point in the normal course of the aging process, inherently affect the ability to perform work efficiently. Moreover, the aging of employees results in other consequences to their employers. Thus, under the ADEA a company may lawfully reduce some fringe benefit levels for older workers, but only to the extent necessary to achieve parity in cost between older and younger workers. However, the employer is prohibited from reducing the wage rate of an employee for the alleged reason that he does so in order to comply with the ADEA. The employer may lawfully make a business decision to terminate the employee; but he may have to prove that such action was based on economics and not on age. For Congress declared its purpose was "to promote employment of older persons based on their ability rather than age; to prohibit arbitrary age discrimination in employment; to . . . find ways of meeting problems arising from the impact of age on employment."

While Congress might simply have added age to race, sex, religion, and national origin, as another protected class under Title VII, it chose instead to establish the ADEA as an independent statutory development, incorporating generally the enforcement procedures of the Fair Labor Standards Act (FLSA). The EEOC was overburdened with problems in the administration of Title VII. This no doubt led Congress to ask the Wage and Hour Division in the Department of Labor, already administering the FLSA, to take on the additional job of eliminating pernicious age discrimination. However, the President by executive order transferred, effective October 1, 1979, from the Department of Labor to the EEOC, jurisdiction to enforce the Age Discrimination in Employment Act (ADEA) as well as the Equal Pay Act of 1963 (EPA), which prohibits wage discrimination between the sexes. Under the ADEA Congress permitted either the agency, or the plaintiff himself, should the agency decline to act, to bring a private action in a federal or state court against the employer for the damages suffered, plus attorney's fees, as well as an additional equal amount, known as "liquidated damages," if the violation was "willful." In *Lorillard v. Pons* (1978) the Supreme Court held that, as in FLSA suits, a plaintiff may demand and get a jury trial. This is in contrast to Title VII actions where it is generally thought that no right to a jury trial exists because of the equitable nature of the proceeding.

The 1967 act protected persons between ages forty to sixty-five from discrimination based on age. The original bill had covered the age span of forty-five to sixty-five; but the threshold age was lowered in view of evidence that age discrimination in the United States begins at about age forty. The upper limit was set at sixty-five with almost no discussion. However, a recent Congressional report stated: "The upper age cutoff of 65 was originally selected because it was a customary retirement age and the age at which many public and private pension benefits became available—not for any scientific reason." In the decade after 1968, the year in which the ADEA became effective, some nine thousand employees received nearly $30 million in damages from their employers for age discrimination claims. The original act excluded from coverage any termination from employment under a retirement or pension plan, as the Supreme Court expressly held in *United Airlines v. McMann* (1977).

Congress in 1978 enacted far-reaching amendments to the ADEA that raised the maximum age limit in the private sector from sixty-five to seventy. The amendments forbade a seniority system or employee benefit plan to require or permit involuntary retirement of an employee under the age of seventy. A limited exemption was carved out that permitted the compulsory retirement at age sixty-five of a person in an executive or high policy-making position who is entitled to a pension of at least $27,000 a year, or of a tenured college faculty member (the latter exception expiring July 1, 1982). At the same time the amendments eliminated the mandatory retirement age of seventy, which presently applies to federal government employees.

One of the problems in connection with any employment discrimination legislation is the possible overkill effects of such prohibitions, which may tend to make employers lean over backwards in dealing with employees within the protected category. "Each time the employer makes a decision to hire or fire an older worker, he must consider the likelihood that suit will be brought, with the attendant expenses of litigation, and that he will be forced to legitimate his decision by a preponderance of the evidence," a leading law review study of the ADEA states. "As a practical matter, these considerations will probably dictate preferences toward older workers whenever there is some doubt that a judge or jury would accept his explanations, even if he is in fact deciding without reference to the individual's age," the writer adds.

While political leaders tread cautiously in the face of a growing and increasingly vocal geriatric segment of the population, privately even they must share the general concern over the possibly adverse effects of the ADEA amendments on an already troublesome national unemployment problem, particularly felt among the protected groups under Title VII. The Department of Labor projects that the changes will result in 200,000 older workers remaining in the labor force. This, it predicts, will cause an increase in the unemployment rate of only 0.2 per cent. Critics, however have called these figures "decidedly conservative." They point to a study made in late 1977 by Sears, Roebuck & Company, the nation's largest retailer, of its employees due to retire in 1978. Sears reported that among this group, 55 per cent chose to keep on working when they reached sixty-five. This would mean that this company, which employs

415,000 people, would have, it said, 7,790 fewer job openings and 33,240 fewer promotions and transfers during the next five years. In spite of all these considerations, the political posture of the age discrimination movement in the United States appears to make present trends irreversible. Age discrimination laws have spread rapidly in the nation. It was on July 10, 1974 that the first bill to outlaw mandatory retirement was filed in Congress by Representative Paul Findlay. By Labor Day, 1978, at the ceremony when he signed the 1978 amendment to the ADEA, President Carter implicitly endorsed extending the new federal law so that employees in the private sector, like federal employees under these amendments, would have *no* mandatory retirement age at all! Meanwhile, Congress has declined to preempt this field so that employers face sweeping state laws already adopted in states like Florida and California, which flatly prohibit mandatory retirement at any age and contain no exemption for highly paid executives and policy-makers. Yet a survey of forty-one top personnel officers of major United States firms, reported in December of 1978 by the Conference Board, an independent business research organization, found that ADEA would have only a slight impact on company-wide operations and promotional opportunities due to a widespread early retirement trend in American industry.

DISCRIMINATION AGAINST THE HANDICAPPED

Section 504 of the Rehabilitation Act of 1973 provides that "No otherwise qualified handicapped individual in the United States shall, solely by reason of his handicap . . . be subjected to discrimination, under any program or activity receiving federal financial assistance." Thus, by the terms of the statute it is aimed only at recipients of federal funding. Large numbers of educational institutions, from preschool to the college level, and any health, welfare, and other social service program receiving federal financial assistance, comprise employers affected by the sweep of this provision. Moreover, the many businesses that receive significant federal contracts are bound by similar restrictions under Section 503 of the same act.

Sparse statutory language has been expanded into extensive regulations adopted by the Department of Health, Education, and Welfare (HEW). Under these regulations, the like of which one can confidently predict will be adopted successively by each federal agency, employers who are recipients of federal funding in any form, or applicants for federal financial assistance, are prohibited from discriminating against "qualified handicapped persons." The handicap of the potential employee can be either a physical or a mental impairment that substantially limits one or more of his major life activities. The definition of handicapped persons included drug addicts and alcoholics; but in 1978 Congress expressly countermanded this interpretation by a specific change in the law. Discrimination "in any aspect of employment" is prohibited under the regulations. In addition, the recipient employer must make "reasonable accommodations" to qualified handicapped persons, unless the employer can establish that any such accommodation would impose an "undue hardship" on the operation of its program. The regulations further preclude the recipient employer from using tests and selection criteria that are not job related and would tend to screen out handicapped persons. Preemployment medical examinations may be used only if uniformly required of all applicants for employment. The handicapped may not be disparately treated. Under a 1978 amendment, these rights became enforceable by private suit in a federal district court, with attorney's fees allowable to a prevailing plaintiff.

HEW Secretary, Joseph Califano, was himself the target of militant protesters in wheelchairs at a critical point, when he appeared to be wavering on some of the regulations that had then been only tentatively promulgated. (A few of these "regs" specify accessibility requirements that will, for example, necessitate large capital outlays for construction and refitting of universities, lower schools, and health facilities.) With the HEW offices in San Francisco occupied by the protesters, and wheelchair pickets surrounding the HEW building in Washington, the Secretary finally signed the regulations as proposed. He said: "Section 504 established a mandate to end discrimination and to bring handicapped persons into the mainstream of American life. The Secretary intends vigorously to implement and enforce that mandate."

After the signing, a handicapped American, Michael Williams, uttered words that would have warmed the heart of that legendary union organizer Joe Hill, when he said from his wheelchair in Washington: "This was the key to everything. We never let Carter and Califano forget we were there. . . . On Sunday we demonstrated across the street from Carter's church. . . . Carter avoided facing us by entering the church by a side door and exiting by a rear door. It was at that moment I knew we were going to win the fight."

And win it they did—which is perhaps what this chapter was all about.

The second great confrontation between the bureaucracy and the "wheelchair lobby" occurred regarding the impact of Section 504 on the nation's major transit systems, all of which are recipients of substantial federal funding. In 1978 the Secretary of Transportation issued proposed regulations implementing Section 504. These proposed regulations required such transit systems to provide wheelchair users barrierfree access to all bus and subway services. The Chicago Transit System estimated that the cost of retrofitting its rail transit facilities to meet the proposed standards would be $910 million—more than all the capital invested in the system since 1890. Mayor Edward Koch estimated that the cost of retrospective application for New York City would be two billion dollars, which, the Mayor said, "would literally bankrupt us."

The difficult question of public policy is whether equal access by the handicapped to educational facilities and transportation ought to be considered an absolute civil right or only a relative one, to be balanced against attendant economic cost. Put another way, should economic hardship be a defense, offsetting the obligation to provide equal services to the handicapped? The issue is inescapable in a law of this kind; yet it is not touched upon in the statute, and there were neither committee hearings on it, nor any floor debate. Section 504 established an obligation in an imprecise law, a single sentence in length, and then left executive department officials to determine by regulation the extent of the obligation. There were more *pages* in the proposed regulations of the Department of Transportation alone than there were *words* in Section 504! In such a situation the decision by executive officials, with a multibillion dollar cost impact, cannot in reality be made on the basis of legislative intent, but only as a political judgment. The chief sponsor of Section 504, Rep. Charles A. Vanik of Ohio, questioned recently about how Congress came to mandate such unlimited obligations, said: "We never had any concept that it would involve such tremendous costs."

CHAPTER XVIII

COMPLETING THE PICTURE

The problem to be solved, either as a matter of theory or as a matter of practical necessity, is at bottom always and everywhere the same. How can the right of combined action be curtailed without depriving individual liberty of half its value; how can it be left unrestricted without destroying either the liberty of individual citizens, or the power of the Government? To see that this problem at the present day presents itself everywhere, and has nowhere received a quite satisfactory solution, is of importance.—Dicey, *Law and Public Opinion in England,* 1919.

"The older I get, the wiser I get," says a wry Mo Udall today. Although he still defends most of the changes, he talks of "Udall's Fourth Law," which is: "Every reform always carries consequences you don't like."—Congressman Morris K. (Mo) Udall of Arizona, quoted in the *Wall Street Journal,* May 3, 1979.

NEVER A dull moment is a constant characteristic of the ever-changing law of labor relations. While the latest word on it is being set in type, Congress and the Supreme Court, to say nothing of the lower federal and state judiciaries and the NLRB, are already grinding out new law. The trend toward stabilized labor relations in the United States is always unfolding, and it is marked from time to time by both retrogression and progress.

These final chapters demonstrate above all the enormous growth of federal regulation of labor law in the United States. After all, it was only in 1932 that Congress, in the Norris-LaGuardia Act, passed its first significant piece of federal labor legislation—and that was to keep federal officials *out* of union-management relations!

The first edition of this book, published in 1946, dealt with the Wagner Act, the federal anti-injunction and antitrust acts, and the common-law background. Now one faces a dazzling pattern of activities within the sweep of federal regulation, accompanied by new statutes never imagined even at the time the second edition of the book was published in 1958 and updated in 1961. Labor law did not then include employment discrimination law, much less federal control over factory inspection and retirement plans! The age of the acronym in labor law had not yet arrived.

The statutory material in this and the preceding chapter demonstrates the diversity and pervasiveness of the federal labor law under which we will live in the country's third century. Yet while Congress extends its regulatory powers into new fields of labor law, it finds itself still unable to deal effectively with the national emergency strike, as the coal strike of 1977–78 again demonstrated.

THE STRIKE AND THE COMMUNITY

The only mechanism for dealing with titanic disputes in the major industries, which periodically rock the nation's economy, is still the procedure established in the Taft-Hartley Act. Title II of that statute created the new Federal Mediation and Conciliation Service. Its purpose was to furnish assistance to the parties in settling labor disputes in any industry affecting commerce, except those covered by the Railway Labor Act. Then, in Section 206, Congress empowered the President to appoint a board of inquiry to investigate and report the facts and the parties' positions in any strike or lockout of such magnitude or in such a crucial industry in interstate commerce as possibly to "imperil the national health or safety." But this board's report, according to the act, should "not contain any recommendations." After receiving the report, the President may direct the Attorney General to ask a federal district court to enjoin such a strike or lockout. The court may grant the injunction if it finds that the dispute affects an entire industry or a substantial part of it in interstate commerce and that it may "imperil the national health or safety." Yet the coal strike of 1977–78 again served to demonstrate that the entering of such an injunction by a federal judge does not insure that the workers will return to the job.

On the issuance of the injunction the parties are under a duty to get together, using the facilities of the Mediation and Conciliation Service, to settle their differences. Meanwhile, the board of inquiry reconvenes, and, at the end of sixty days after the injunction was issued, it makes a progress report on how far the parties have proceeded in their negotiations. This report is made public by the President. Then within the next fifteen days the NLRB takes a secret ballot of the employees of each employer involved in the dispute to see "whether they wish to accept the final offer of settlement made by their employer as stated by him," certifying the results of the election to the Attorney General during the next five days. At that stage if the dispute is still unsettled, the Attorney General will nevertheless ask the court to dissolve the injunction and the court is required to do so. Then the President makes a full report of the whole matter, including the results of the ballot, to Congress, with any recommendations he may wish to make.

Thus, under this Title II, national emergency strikes may, if the members honor the injunction, be put on ice for eighty days, and during that period every effort is made to reach a settlement. But if no settlement is reached, then the union is free to go ahead and strike. So far, in the cases where this procedure has been invoked, the disputes have in one way or another been settled. Apparently Congress favored this method of handling emergency strikes over any form of compulsory arbitration because of the almost universal distrust of contract settlements imposed by government or any other outside agency. Title II is a gamble that some settlement will always be reached before the country is hurt by a harmful strike. This gamble is worth taking because the settlement terms are those ultimately agreed to by the parties themselves.

Why most employers and unions fear compulsory arbitration

or the outside settlement of bargaining disputes is not easy to state. But it all goes back to their belief that the essence of bargaining of any kind is the freedom of either party to haggle over each term, to compromise and balance out offers and counteroffers, and finally to reach a decision to accept or reject on the basis of their own values, with all of the circumstances in mind. Many intelligent people often wonder why the rational procedures of arbitration, or ones similar to those successfully used by the War Labor Board, cannot be substituted for recourse to the industrial warfare that is so embarrassing to the economy. And it is difficult to explain satisfactorily that the use of such devices, except during the crisis of an all-out war, is likely to end up in the fixing by the government of commodity prices and wages, as well as other working conditions. For the essence of collective bargaining remains the parties' privilege to fix their own terms in every respect—a process that no outsider can possibly be trusted by them to understand or accomplish.

Unions and employers figure that when they are compelled to abrogate this bargaining function—the weighing and balancing of values—then free enterprise has come to an end. This strongly held conviction is so fundamental that employers and unions will fight to the last political ditch to prevent a planned economy displacing their mutual right to make the final decision on the values under which they must live together. Labor unions certainly will never concede that any outside agency can possibly be allowed to decide what is or is not good for employees, or how much labor may insist upon.

When the nation is at war it is, perhaps, reasonable to conclude that collective bargaining should be confined to the conference room and not be extended to include strikes and lockouts, which are a luxury and an aspect of civil life that cannot be afforded during the crisis of such unlimited emergency. Furthermore, the unusual inflationary pressures inherent in such times apparently oblige modern government to place ceilings on all money items, such as prices and wages. With millions

in the armed services or government employ, and all other
civilians being in the same boat together, such arrangements
seem necessary. But even during World War II Congress did not
go so far as to outlaw strikes. Rather, the unions all entered into
voluntary no-strike pledges, which they observed with remarkable faithfulness. When during the war a few strikes did occur in
vital industries, Congress empowered the government to seize
the plants in question, with the usual result that the unions involved stopped their strikes. But the War Labor Disputes Act,
under which these seizures were made, did not provide for
the enjoining of strikes, even after government seizure. They
instead provided special criminal sanctions for interference with
production and special facilities for settling the disputes. All
through World War II the War Labor Board took over the collective bargaining process and it actually wrote contracts where
the parties could not agree. Of course, it worked. But then, it
had to work because of the emergency circumstances.

In 1959 the Supreme Court upheld the constitutionality of
Title II of the Taft-Hartley Act, dealing with national emergency strikes. The 1959 steel strike had shut down most of the
big steel plants and the parties seemed unable to reach an
agreement. As a consequence of this stalemate, the public became most disturbed. Pursuant to the terms of the statute, the
President appointed a board of inquiry to report on the matter. This board duly reported that the strike was of great
magnitude and that its continuance would imperil the national
health or safety. At the request of the President, who acted in
response to this report, the Attorney General secured an injunction from the federal district court stopping the strike.
Counsel for the union promptly appealed and the matter was
expedited before the Supreme Court, which handed down its
opinion affirming issuance of the injunction and upholding the
validity of Title II—all before the 80-day period had elapsed.
In a *per curiam* opinion the Court said that the district judge's
findings as to the magnitude of the strike and its threat to national safety through suspension of steel shipments to defense

plants were sufficiently supported by the evidence. Apparently a majority thought it immaterial that some arrangement might be made to open enough steel plants during the strike to supply defense needs. Moreover, in view of proof that the national safety was imperiled, it became unnecessary in this case to determine whether or not the threat to national health meant the physical or general economic health of the country.

There are precedents, of course, for the seizure of strike-bound industries by the federal government in time of war. President Wilson was authorized by Congress during World War I to seize the railroads in case of emergency, and he did so. However, they were run with such appalling inefficiency that the railroads did everything in their power during World War II to prevent a recurrence of government seizure and operation. Nevertheless this seizure power has been used sparingly to prevent strikes on the railroads; and the 1947 decision of the Supreme Court in *United States v. John L. Lewis and United Mine Workers of America* revealed what a weapon seizure could be in the hands of the federal government against fractious union leaders. Because the union and the operators could not agree on a new contract, the government had seized the coal mines under the War Labor Disputes Act and it was operating the mines—at least on paper—under a special contract with Lewis, which incorporated and extended the terms of the Bituminous Coal Wage Agreement of 1945. Taking advantage of a clause in this old agreement, Lewis, as head of the Mine Workers, served notice on the government that he was unilaterally terminating the agreement in five days. In spite of the government's protest that the old agreement was superseded by the special contract for "the period of Government possession," Lewis communicated his position to his various local unions, and pursuant to their traditional policy of "no contract, no work," the miners walked out.

At this point the government sought a declaratory judgment

to determine which version of the contract was correct, and an injunction to stop the walkout or strike. The district judge issued a temporary injunction against Lewis and his union, ordering a retraction of what he regarded as a virtual strike call. Lewis and his union ignored this order. In the contempt proceedings that ensued they were heavily fined for not complying with it. A majority of the Supreme Court upheld the contempt judgment, although they modified the amount of the fine—and the miners went back to work without anybody ever learning what the contract actually did mean.

The point of the case is that the government secured an order from a federal district court to stop a strike, in spite of the fact that the Norris-LaGuardia Act presumably deprived federal judges of their jurisdiction to issue injunctions to prevent the continuance of labor disputes. Four members of the Supreme Court thought that the judge had exceeded his jurisdiction and had issued an invalid decree, but five members of the Court held otherwise. Their reasoning was that no act of Congress can be read to deprive the government of its inherent rights unless that act specifically says so. Hence, they concluded, the Norris-LaGuardia Anti-injunction Act did not apply to the government as an employer—even in its capacity as an "employer on paper" through a mere technical seizure of the mines. The other four members of the Court quite reasonably pointed out that the anti-injunction law purported to deprive federal judges of the power to issue injunctions in labor disputes, regardless of who were the parties to such disputes. They also reminded the majority of the Court that the most flagrant abuses of the labor injunction, which had undoubtedly been largely responsible for the passage of the anti-injunction act, had occurred in cases where the government had come into court asking for injunctions. Those were the cases that gave rise to the slogan "government by injunction." And many feared a recurrence of this abuse in the *Lewis* case. But to this the majority countered with the retort that in those cases the government had not been suing in the capacity of employer, adding that the definition of labor dispute in the statute contemplated only private employers and not the government in that role.

So, while the legalistic honors appeared to be even, Lewis lost on a technicality, and the United States emerged with the assurance that in the future it *could* secure injunctions against strikes, without special permission from Congress, if it were the employer involved in the dispute. And all it needed to become the employer in otherwise private industry was the power to seize. But here was the rub. The seizure in the *Lewis* case was under the War Labor Disputes Act. That act, however, no longer exists; and the government has no practicable warrant for seizing any plant or utility except under such power as Congress may see fit to give it in times of war. And that is another story worth the telling.

In the spring of 1952 a long-standing dispute between the steelworkers' union and the steel companies over the terms of a new contract came to a head when the union announced a nation-wide strike in steel to begin on April 9. Fearing that a shutdown of this industry would harm the war effort in connection with the Korean crisis, President Truman ordered the Secretary of Commerce to "seize" the steel companies. This was done. Management in these companies then followed under protest the directions imposed from Washington, and at the same time they took immediate steps in court to challenge the validity of President Truman's seizure. After giving this case precedence over all others on the calendar, the Supreme Court decided on June 2, 1952, that the President did not have the constitutional power of seizure. It was amply clear from the evidence that this step had not been taken under either of the two statutes providing for seizures under certain very limited conditions, the government asserting that these statutory provisions were "much too cumbersome, involved, and time-consuming for the crisis which was at hand."

This was quite clearly a venture in the exercise of executive power. Not only had Congress expressly refused to set up a seizure technique to deal with situations of this kind, it had instead provided a procedure to be followed in Title II of the Taft-Hartley Act. The seizure technique had at one time been proposed as a part of that act, but had been rejected because Congress thought that this device, "like that of compulsory arbitration, would interfere with the process of collective bargaining." Any authority for the President to seize industrial plants would have to be found in the Constitution. And the Court unanimously declared that it did not appear in that basic document. "Even though 'theatre of war' be an expanding concept," said Justice Black, the Court still could not hold under the Constitution "that the Commander in Chief of the Armed Forces has the ultimate power as such to take possession of private property in order to keep labor disputes from stopping production." As he observed: "This is a job for the Nation's lawmakers, not for its military authorities." Nor could the Court perceive any such authority in the residual constitutional executive powers of the President. "The Constitution limits his functions in the lawmaking process to the recommending of laws he thinks wise and the vetoing of laws he thinks bad." The President's power was to execute. "And the Constitution is neither silent nor equivocal about who shall make laws which the President is to execute." The lawmaker was Congress; and it had enacted Title II of the Taft-Hartley Act to cover situations exactly like this one. Thus, as a technique for the control of labor disputes in enterprises falling under the federal jurisdiction, seizure may safely be counted out except perhaps, in time of an all-out war.

It is certainly advisable to consider the complexity of the industrial scene in which the disputes arise. Certain of our large industries are either already committed to industry-wide collective bargaining or are rapidly approaching that state in dealing with wages. Soft coal and railroads offer the conspicuous examples of established industry-wide bargaining; while the steel and automobile industries furnish instances of something closely akin, called pattern-setting and pattern-following. The difference between these two developments is easily described. Industry-wide bargaining implies a single overall agreement or treaty, bargained between and executed by one union and substantially all of the employers in the particular industry, usually represented by an association. Actually, there are two unions in the soft coal industry, but it is noticeable that the smaller of these unions and the employers with whom it deals usually wait until the United Mine Workers and the coal operators have completed their agreement and then tag along on the same terms.

This instance of employers and a union copying the terms of a previously executed agreement between others is somewhat like pattern-following, although the composite picture in the coal industry is really industry-wide bargaining. For true pattern-setting and following are apparent only in situations like that in steel and automobiles, where the main show is conducted by the United Steelworkers and the ten major steel companies or by the UAW and General Motors or Ford, in a central set of negotiations, while all of the Steelworkers' and UAW locals in other plants and companies wait around for the pattern to be set by the big boys. Then, when it is set, at least as far as wages and a few other money items are concerned, the international unions and their various locals demand that their respective patterns be followed in all the other plants where they have bargaining rights. This same thing, of course, is also going on in other industries, especially in agricultural implements, aerospace, and electrical equipment.

In several states laws have been passed prohibiting strikes in public utilities and substituting compulsory arbitration of bargaining disputes. But the Supreme Court has declared these statutes unconstitutional, at least in so far as they affect industries falling under the federal commerce power—which nowadays includes virtually all utilities—because they are inconsistent with the guarantees to engage in concerted activities and to strike, which appear in Sections 7 and 13 of the NLRA. It is perhaps unfortunate that experimentation is thus not allowed in this area, since it might reveal what could be done with compulsory arbitration in the labor field. A previous attempt of a similar kind in Kansas was declared unconstitutional by the Supreme Court in 1922 as a deprivation of property and liberty of contract under the due process clause of the 14th amendment. It is clear, however, that on those grounds a statute of this type would no longer be constitutionally objectionable. Under the more recent state acts applying to public utilities, in order to furnish standards governing their awards the arbitrators were to be guided by evidence concerning wages and working conditions in similar enterprises as well as throughout industry in general. Naturally the resulting wage rates and other terms of employment would not be freely bargained; but in the states enacting these statutes it was evidently thought that that was a minor consideration as against the inconvenience caused to the general public by a strike that might result in a stoppage of power, light, transportation, or communication. Furthermore, compulsory arbitration in this area could hardly be feared as leading to commodity price fixing, since utility rates already are regulated by public service commissions.

Even though compulsory arbitration, if given a chance, might conceivably work in the public utility field, its value throughout industry in general would be doubtful. It is true that bargaining strikes always cause inconvenience to somebody. Most of them, however, we take in our stride. This is so, if you stop to think of it, because as a community we are committed to the belief that if workers are unwilling to sell their services for less than they can secure through bargaining collectively across the table, then they have a right concertedly to withhold their services altogether until their employer comes to terms. They take the chance that the employer can outlast them, in which event they lose the strike and have nothing to show for the economic losses they have sustained. Of course, they may win the strike and get all they asked, although victory usually consists of some sort of compromise that helps the employer to save face and gives the union enough to make the strike more or less worth the trouble. While all strikes unquestionably cause economic loss and are wasteful, most of them do not have any perceptible effect on the general community. There is no difficulty concerning what to do about such strikes. In a federal community such as ours, which is both centrally and locally committed to labor unionism, the answer is to do nothing about them at all, except to provide the best conciliation and mediation facilities possible and, if they threaten the national health and safety, to apply the procedure set forth in Title II of the Taft-Hartley Act.

Theoretically we should do nothing more than this about any strike if we accept labor unions as established bargaining institutions—and, after all, we have little choice in that matter. But practically we are compelled to consider what can be done about strikes in particular areas of industry. Certainly this is true where they are sufficiently widespread to have an adverse effect on whole communities or substantial sections of the country, yet not sufficiently widespread to warrant application of the procedures in Title II of the Taft-Hartley Act. And even if those procedures are invoked in appropriate cases, signing an injunctive order does not guarantee that the members will return to work. Moreover, even if respected, it does not solve the problem of what would happen after the 80-day injunction expires, with the dispute unsettled, if the union members then go out on strike. For a few instances of embarrassing situations, take the strikes by government employees in city, state, or federal agencies; or strikes on our common carriers, such as railroads, steamships, air lines, bus systems, and local transit lines; or strikes in other public utilities, such as power and light companies, communication systems, and water and gas companies; or strikes in institutions such as hospitals, schools, and asylums; or strikes in businesses on which we all depend constantly for our daily needs, such as milk production and delivery, express carriage or trucking, and even stevedoring. The effects of strikes in these areas of activity are quickly and keenly felt by large numbers of people who have no immediate interest in the disputes and are impatient to have them settled as soon as possible, in any manner possible.

But this is not all; for the community can no more easily afford strikes in other areas such as the coal and oil industries. A nation-wide coal strike can tie this country up in knots almost overnight. It is true that few people will freeze during a coal strike; but the railroads are forced to cut down the number of trains they run, the steel mills presently have to shut down, and eventually plants dependent on steel for continued production begin shutting their doors. By that time, of course, everybody begins to feel the pinch, many through being laid off from their jobs. The whole national economy suffers in one way or another. Much the same thing would be true of a widespread strike in the oil industry. And a strike of large enough proportions even in the basic steel industry would soon begin to cripple the numerous businesses dependent on steel, the largest of which is the automobile industry.

How about strikes in the automobile, farm equipment, electrical equipment, chemical, textile, rubber, and meat-packing industries? While the effects of these strikes would certainly be noticeable, they would probably not be sufficiently disastrous seriously to inconvenience the entire community. It is probably safe to say that the community could "afford" strikes in those areas of industry, in the sense that they would not cripple the rest of the economy. After all, people can always get along a little while longer with the old car or truck, the old tires, the old plow, and the old suit. The 1977 auto strike in Ford was hardly felt by the public.

Nevertheless, when strikes do result in crippling the economy and in imposing general inconvenience, many people would no doubt say that the thing to do is simply to "outlaw" such strikes. But that sort of talk is ridiculous, since it is impossible just to repress strikes by making them illegal; and it would be a dangerous and foolish thing to do, even if it were possible. It is true that Congress has adopted a policy of repression, pure and simple, with respect to strikes of government employees—and in that restricted area the policy may work. However, a policy of repression—without more—is like sealing up a sore that has not healed. It will continue to fester until it causes far more harm in the long run than if it had been properly treated or even left entirely alone. Indeed, the general enactment of such a policy into law would result eventually in a process of nullification, which would exceed the disregard for law manifested during the prohibition era. Furthermore, the very desire simply to repress strikes, or the possibility of doing so, has most unwholesome political implications, for it signifies the kind of antidemocratic authoritarianism that would destroy all of our institutions based on freedom.

But these same people who would outlaw bargaining strikes sincerely believe, as do several of our leading economists, that big unions have become so powerful that there is not much real freedom left, anyway, as far as our economic system is concerned. What third alternative is there, they may ask, to complete license or complete repression in dealing with bargaining strikes of the sort under discussion? This, of course, is the great question—the one for which nobody has a sure answer and one which most of our outstanding labor relations experts feel hesitant about answering at all. For aside from the most effective and efficient mediation and conciliation facilities possible, these experts can think of no formula that does not at some point involve one or another aspect of compulsory arbitration—the decision of a government-sponsored board which gives a solution and establishes the prevailing terms of employment. That is the last thing they want—and it seems pretty certain that the employers and unions are in complete agreement with them on this score. These experts and their supporters know what they want in a general way. They want a method of settling

these socially inconvenient strikes whereby the parties themselves—the unions and employers involved—make their own
terms and agreements. In such a solution they apparently see
the retention of the American ideal of free enterprise and of an
economy not regulated and planned by the government. At this
point, however, they run up against the same question: How
can this agreement be achieved without the inconvenience of
strikes? Apparently they are seeking an answer in something
called "improved relations between management and unions"
and in "constantly increasing maturity and responsibility on the
part of union and management representatives," with the ability to "see each other's point of view," et cetera. And the various
industrial relations institutes throughout the country are working overtime trying to devise methods of bargaining out voluntary agreements without recourse to strikes and without legislative regulation of bargaining power.

Perhaps the most interesting attempt in the private sector
to resolve collective bargaining disputes, without recourse to the
strike, is found in what is called the Experimental Negotiating
Agreement (ENA). Under ENA, signed in the spring of 1973
by the United Steelworkers of America and by the ten major
steel companies, the parties eliminated the possibility of a
strike during collective bargaining negotiations by agreeing in
advance voluntarily to arbitrate unresolved contract issues. The
success of the plan is apparent not only because there has been
no industry strike in steel since the inception of ENA, but even
more so because the parties have been able successfully to
negotiate the terms of two successive contracts without having
to submit any issue to arbitration for resolution. A real advan-
age for the employees involved has been stability of employment. And the old days of stockpiling steel before the contract
negotiations, with the ensuing layoffs, have virtually disappeared
from the steel industry—to the immense gratification of all concerned, including the public. The 1977 round of contract negotiations in steel ended in agreement, although a few scattered strikes occurred subsequently over disagreements on local

conditions—one of the few items exempt from arbitration and the strike prohibition under ENA.

There is a general feeling that Title II of Taft-Hartley is inadequate to cope with the embarrassment caused by real national emergency strikes. A few observers who have had a wide experience in this field believe that there should be a˙permanent emergency disputes board to advise the President. They also say that he should be enabled to do what seems most appropriate in any particular situation: to appoint a special fact-finding board empowered to make recommendations; to set up a special board to arrange for voluntary arbitration, or, if that fails, to allocate the blame for such failure, such allocation to be included in a report to the public; to secure an injunction against the strike, possibly for as long as six months; and also, if deemed necessary, to seize the property affected by the dispute and to operate it. In addition, of course, he could always be given the power to order compulsory arbitration. The possibility that any one or more of these devices might be employed could very well result in reasonably quick private settlements between the disputing parties. For they could not possibly foresee which way the President would jump, and thus they would be completely unable to prepare their lines in advance for long resistance, as they may do at present.

Congress has been quite consistent in its reluctance to invade the sphere of collective bargaining and to interfere with the reaching of agreements by unions and employers themselves on their own terms. It is true, as has been indicated, that under the Railway Labor Act arbitration boards are occasionally set up to break bargaining deadlocks and hand down specific awards. Here also the President has power to defer strikes by insisting on cooling-off periods during which mediation, and, if necessary, arbitration can be used. But the unions are not bound by the awards of such arbitration boards. It is curious, therefore, to note the attitude of Congress toward possible labor disputes of regular governmental employees—not those of some plant that has been seized, where the government is employer only on paper, so to speak. Section 305 of Taft-Hartley makes it unlawful for "any individual employed by the United States or any agency thereof including wholly owned Government corporations to participate in any strike." Any violator of this provision "shall be discharged immediately from his employment, and shall forfeit his civil service status, if any, and shall not be eligible for reemployment for three years."

Thus the greatest "employer" of all, so sensitive to the needs of employees generally to organize into unions and engage in free collective bargaining for the maximization of their working standards, is shortsightedly unable to perceive that its own workers might regard similar procedures as necessary to their welfare. Of course, everybody (except, perhaps, public employees themselves) is aware that government employment is "different," and that you simply cannot run the country or its subdivisions when its agents are free to go out on strike. The concerted walkout of the police in Boston, which swept Calvin Coolidge from the state house to the White House, remains in the memories of some people. But in Section 305 Congress indulged in sheer suppression, without any safety valve at all. It seems surprising, indeed, that Congress, in its awareness of the needs of employees, should not at least have provided some form of arbitration mechanism through which government employees might collectively present bargaining demands for better terms and conditions of work.

THE PUBLIC EMPLOYEE

Government at all levels experienced a tremendous growth during the 1960's. The nation's attempts to solve old social problems with new programs not only increased the number of persons employed in existing agencies but also created new agencies with their many new jobs. By the mid-1970's more than one in five of the nation's work force was employed by federal, state, or local government.

This rapid increase in the number of government workers set

the stage for unionization and collective bargaining. And government employees responded enthusiastically to the idea. In 1960 virtually no government workers were organized, except for postal employees and some of New York's municipal employees. By 1969, however, about one-quarter of all government employees belonged to unions.

Much of this organizational effort occurred without the guidance of appropriate legislation. Indeed, in many situations it was unclear whether the right of government workers to bargain collectively would be legally recognized. There is no uniform federal labor law covering government employees; and the National Labor Relations Act specifically excludes them from its coverage. Organization of federal employees is to some extent regulated under Executive Orders 10988 and 11491, while that of state employees is regulated under local law. Although about thirty states give some legal recognition to unions of public employees, as a rule they do not grant the sort of comprehensive protection enjoyed by unions in private employment under the NLRA. In many states there is no obligation for the government to bargain with a union of its employees. Nor can such a union insist on discussing any particular subjects with the employer. The scope of bargaining is limited even in those few states that do provide for mandatory subjects of bargaining with their employees. That is because such "scope" clauses generally do not contain open-ended language that requires bargaining over "other terms and conditions of employment," as in the NLRA.

The most crucial difference between labor relations in the public and private sectors is that it is usually illegal for public employees to strike. While a few states bar strikes only by "public safety employees," such as policemen and firemen, in most states all striking public employees risk the imposition of legal sanctions, which may include fines and imprisonment.

Such laws, however, are steadily becoming less practical to enforce, since most public decision-makers have come to realize the futility of invoking them against striking public employees.

Public opinion often frowns on the use of criminal penalties against individual striking workers; and resort to such extreme sanctions is more likely to aggravate labor disputes than to end them. Thus, New York's Taylor Act, which prohibits strikes by public employees, has been "more honor'd in the breach than the observance." In November 1978, however, a rare contempt sentence was imposed on the leader of a bitter teachers' strike in Levittown, New York, for flagrant violation of a no-strike order issued by a court under the Taylor Act. In commuting this sentence, Governor Carey declared: "Teachers don't belong in jail. They belong in the classroom." The threat of legal sanctions did not prevent a New Orleans police strike in 1979, nor did it keep sanitation workers in that city from honoring picket lines established by the striking policemen. Both groups were represented by the Teamsters Union.

But few commentators believe that society can tolerate a prolonged strike by public workers such as policemen, firemen, or sanitation workers. The only effective way such strikes can be averted is to provide an alternate method of settling labor disputes, acceptable as legitimate by both public management and employees. The best and most popular method for achieving such settlements is "interest arbitration." Thus, when the parties fail to reach agreement on a contract through collecive bargaining, the unresolved issues are settled by resort to third party arbitration. Of course, reaching a contract through arbitration presents special problems. For example, the ready availability of arbitration may to some extent undermine good faith collective bargaining. Why should a union not get as much as it can at the bargaining table and *then* get a second bite through "interest arbitration"? Similarly, recognizing this, how can public employers be persuaded to make realistic settlement proposals? Many observers would confine prohibitions against strikes to critical categories of government workers, hoping that collective bargaining will work in the public sector as it does in private industry, where the threat of a strike remains the factor that checks unrealistic expectations by the parties.

Furthermore, determining what package of wages and benefits is equitable to the employees and at the same time to the public—the real employer—is a delicate and difficult task. There is no practical way to force such a determination upon unconsenting employees, nor to force a public agency to come up with money it does not have.

The practical problems are enormous. In private industry the management bargaining team can look to the business itself for the funds needed to back up its offer. In contrast, many public agencies can secure additional funding only from the state legislature or from tax increases that must be authorized by the consent of the voters.

In interest arbitration, where the employees do not enjoy the right to strike, it has been suggested that the arbitrator admit into evidence wage rates derived from settlements reached under free collective bargaining in private industry. There the right to strike virtually guarantees a just settlement, which can be used as a standard to provide parity between the public and private sectors.

The question of union security has been hotly debated in connection with public employee collective bargaining. Public employers may resist union shop and agency shop agreements, which require management to dismiss employees who refuse to pay union dues—basically for the same reason private business opposes them. That is, such clauses are thought to lock in the union as bargaining agent for the employees, in spite of the possibility that the membership may become fed up with the union and wish to get rid of it. Also, since such clauses provide for dues payments from *all* employees in the bargaining unit, they greatly increase the union's financial power in collective bargaining. And they may enable a union to raise money for political contributions and thus to influence the attitude of government officials toward public employee collective bargaining. In addition, some people see an inconsistency in government requiring membership in a private group as a condition of public employment. Unions respond to these objections by pointing out that if they are to negotiate for the benefit of all employees in the bargaining unit, and to process grievances for all of them, it is unfair to finance those services with the dues voluntarily paid by only some of the employees. In such a situation, the employees who refuse to pay dues get a "free ride" at the expense of the dues-paying union members.

When the parties in private employment agree to a union or agency shop, it is considered a matter of private contract law. While the courts will uphold the legality of such clauses, except in "right-to-work" states, it is the free act of the union and the employer—two private parties—that compels the workers either to join the union and/or pay dues, or their equivalent, or to lose their jobs. In such a situation the government is not forcing workers to pay union dues against their will. Hence it is not an instance of "state action." But with public employees, the government is the employer; and if government agrees to a union shop clause, state action in effect forces the workers to pay dues to the union.

Under the 1st amendment to the Constitution, a protected right of freedom of association forbids governmental interference with an individual's decision to join, or refrain from joining, any group. Thus, it is argued, by agreeing to a union or agency shop, a public employer abridges the public employee's freedom of association. Proponents of this view say that there is no practical difference between compelling the payment of union dues and compelling union membership, since for many members the payment of dues constitutes their entire involvement with the union, the argument goes.

The Supreme Court considered this question in *Abood v. Detroit Board of Education* (1977). There the Court held that an agency shop clause in the Detroit teachers' contract was constitutional, insofar as the dues were used to support collective bargaining activities. The Court reasoned that a "union-shop arrangement has been thought to distribute fairly the cost [of collective bargaining activities] among those who benefit, and it counteracts the incentive that employees might otherwise have to become 'free riders'—to refuse to contribute to the union while obtaining benefits of union representation that necessarily accrue to all employees. . . . To be required to help finance the union as a collective-bargaining agent might well be thought . . . to interfere in some way with an employee's freedom to associate for the advancement of ideas, or to refrain from doing so, as he sees fit. . . . But the judgment [in cited precedents] is that such interference as exists is constitutionally justified by the legislative assessment of the important contribution of the union shop to the [established] system of labor relations. . . ." However, the Court also held that the union may not use any portion of a member's dues to finance matters unrelated to collective bargaining, such as political action, if the member objects to such use.

In the same case the Court endorsed the observation of Professor Clyde Summers: "The uniqueness of public employment is *not in the employees* nor in the work performed; the uniqueness is in the special character of the employer." Thus in the *City of Madison, Joint School District No. 8 v. Wisconsin Employment Relations Commission* (1976), the Supreme Court again recognized a significant difference between private and public employment. There a teachers' organization filed a charge against a school board, alleging that it had committed an unfair labor practice by permitting a teacher in the bargaining unit named Holmquist to speak at a public school board meeting in opposition to an agency shop demand of the union. This, it was argued, undermined the union's role as the exclusive collective bargaining agent. The state board and the Wisconsin Supreme Court found for the union, but the U.S. Supreme Court reversed, stating: "Whatever its duties as an employer, when the board sits in public meeting to conduct public business and hear the views of citizens, it may not be required to discriminate between speakers on the basis of their employment or the content of their speech. . . . By prohibiting the school board from 'permitting employees to appear and speak at meetings of the Board of Education' the order constitutes an indirect, but effective, prohibition on persons such as Holmquist from communicating with their government."

The unique quality of public employment where the individual is in the dual role of an employee and a citizen was pointed up again by the Supreme Court in *Bessie B. Givhan v. Western Line Consolidated School District* (1979). There the school district discharged a teacher who in private conversations with the superintendent had harshly criticized the policies and practices of the system as racially discriminatory. "The First Amendment forbids abridgment of the 'freedom of speech,' " the Court said. "Neither the Amendment itself nor our decisions indicate that this freedom is lost to the public employee who arranges to communicate privately with his employer rather than to spread his views before the public." The Court had said in another case that in determining whether a government employee's speech is constitutionally protected, the interests of the employee, as a citizen, in commenting upon matters of public concern, must be balanced against "the interest of the State, as an employer, in promoting the efficiency of the public services it performs through its employees." And in *Mt. Healthy City Board of Education v. Doyle* (1977) the Supreme Court held that once the employee has shown that his constitutionally protected conduct played a "substantial" role in the employer's decision not to rehire him, the employer may avoid rehiring him only if it can show "by a preponderance of the evidence that it would have reached the same decision as to [the employee's] re-employment in the absence of the protected conduct."

While labor organization declines slightly in the private sector as a percentage of the total work force, it still continues to grow in the public sector.

THE POLITICAL ACTIVITY OF LABOR UNIONS

Labor unions have always been involved in politics. From early times, when they were regarded as criminal conspiracies, they have carried the burden of convincing the rest of society that they were not lawless aggregations of power bent on achieving illegal objectives by illegal means. And insofar as they have established themselves on a legal footing, it has been largely through ceaseless political pressure in Congress and in the state legislatures. Now they want to keep what they have won and to prevent what they look upon as regressive legislation, such as the spread of right-to-work statutes and the strengthening of those parts of the Taft-Hartley Act that are aimed at union practices. This means influencing voters to support candidates for office who will champion laws favoring union interests and will oppose antiunion measures. The first president of the American Federation of Labor, Samuel Gompers, urged union members to "reward your friends and punish your enemies," and labor created political arms like "COPE" and "CAP" to see that it was done. Now such programs cost money. For many years federal laws, culminating in the Hatch Act, have made it unlawful for corporations to contribute funds for the support of federal political candidates or to influence national elections. Presumably the real threats of political corruption of this sort were from corporate interests. And before World War II the unions did not present much of a problem, probably because of their relative lack of funds. But the growth of big unionism, with substantial treasuries, has changed the picture. And whether it has or not, employer interests in Washington in 1947 could not pass up the chance to keep the unions out of effective electioneering. At that time Congress, in Section 304 of the Taft-Hartley Act, amended the Hatch Act to cover union political contributions. Thus, it is now a crime for any labor organization "to make a contribution or expenditure in connection with any election at which Presidential and Vice Presidential electors or a Senator or Representative in . . . Congress are to be voted for," or in connection with any related primary or convention; and it is also unlawful for any candidate or political committee "to accept or receive" any such contribution.

The Federal Election Campaign Act of 1971, as amended,

and as interpreted by the Federal Election Commission, which Congress established in 1976 to administer the law, carved out three permissible areas where unions and corporations might use treasury money in connection with the election of federal candidates: (1) to send partisan political communications by unions to their members and by corporations to specified "in house" persons, including shareholders and management employees; (2) to participate in nonpartisan registration and get-out-the-vote campaigns directed to these groups; and (3) to be used as seed money to solicit contributions to a union or corporate political action committee (PAC) from these groups, but this may not be used as a subterfuge to exchange treasury funds for voluntary contributions, for, as one writer put it: "In today's complex regulatory framework, the password to the solicitation and use of political contributions by corporate and union sponsored political committees is 'voluntariness.'"

Clearly under Section 304 as thus amended, any direct contribution by labor unions to the election funds of federal political candidates is prohibited. The first big case under Section 304—*United States v. CIO*—was decided in 1948 by the Supreme Court. Philip Murray, the president of the CIO, authorized the expenditure of union funds to publish and disseminate a weekly union periodical, which carried an article by him urging CIO members to vote for a particular candidate in a forthcoming congressional election. Although the indictment charged that extra expenditures were made for additional copies of this periodical, it did not allege that such copies were distributed freely to nonsubscribers or to persons outside the union, not entitled to receive them. Without committing itself to what it would do where a union spent its funds on an extra edition for general free distribution, the Court made it plain that in this case the indictment did not state a violation of Section 304. A majority of the Court carefully refrained from expressing any opinion on the constitutionality of the act insofar as it might appear to be aimed at muzzling a labor union's organ of free expression among its members. Nevertheless, there is still a good deal of uneasiness about a union's using its funds for any purposes in connection with an election or the support of a political candidate. And just as part of the complaint against the use of corporate funds was that it constituted the use of stockholders' money without their consent, so the use of union funds meant spending dues received from workers, without their consent, and to support political candidates not necessarily to their liking.

In view of all this, were the expenditures made by a big CIO union to pay for poll-watchers in a Detroit area election illegal under this provision? This question is not easily answered. In the case of *United States v. UAW-CIO* (1957), a majority of the Supreme Court declared that under Section 304 the expenditure of union funds and dues to sponsor commercial television broadcasts intended to influence voters in electing candidates for Congress was illegal. Justice Frankfurter contrasted this case with the Court's earlier decision in 1948. Of that case, he said: "The organization merely distributed its house organ to its own people." Then he went on to observe: "The evil at which Congress has struck . . . is the use of corporation or union funds to influence the public at large to vote for a particular candidate or a particular party." Justice Douglas, speaking for himself and two colleagues on the Court, bitterly dissented from the majority's decision that the indictment in this case should be upheld. He regarded this particular application of Section 304 as a violation of the guaranty of free speech in the 1st amendment, decrying the majority's view that financing a speech in a political election is a part of the pattern of corrupt practices at which the statute was aimed. For henceforth, he declared, whenever a spokesman for a union makes a political speech, proof that he spoke in a hall or through a loudspeaker paid for by the union will make the speech a punishable crime. The majority, however, refrained from passing on the constitutional issue, merely deciding that under the statute as it read, the indictment stated a violation. In *Pipefitters Local Union No. 562 v. United States* (1972) the Supreme Court held that a union may make contributions to federal candidates from funds *voluntarily* contributed by members for that purpose—so-called free money as opposed to dues money.

The Supreme Court decided a series of cases in which it had to reconcile the rights of the union as the majority representative of the employees with each member's right of conscience and personal belief. Thus, in *Railway Employees' Department v. Hanson* (1965), under the Railway Labor Act authorizing union shop contracts, the Court found that such a provision in a collective agreement, requiring every member of the bargaining unit to pay dues to the exclusive bargaining agent, did not violate the 1st amendment. In *International Association of Machinists v. Street* (1961) the Court declared that a union could not use a member's dues against his wishes "to support candidates for public office, and advance political programs" that he opposes. And in *Brotherhood of Railway & Steamship Clerks v. Allen* (1963) the Court suggested that in such a situation a "practical decree" might provide the dissenting member with a refund of part of his dues in proportion to the percentage of the dues used for political purposes. It said it would be desirable for unions to adopt some sort of internal remedy for dissenters—a suggestion adopted by the UAW when it provided that members might allocate that portion of their dues, otherwise destined by the union for political purposes, to be used for the support of nonideological community groups. In *Abood v. Detroit Board of Education* (1977) the Court held that public employees had no greater rights than private sector employees to resist paying their share of the costs of collective bargaining and contract administration. The Court also declared that a union may use members' dues for lawful political expenditures and ideological causes unless a particular member objects to such use. And under *Abood* the burden is thus on the dissenting members to object, not upon the union to secure prior consent from the members. Only in the case where dues money is used for political or ideological purposes has the

Court recognized a member's right of conscience to prevent such usage.

In *Eastex Inc. v. NLRB* (1978), the Supreme Court concluded that a labor organization's Section 7 right to distribute union literature in nonworking areas of a plant during nonworking hours encompassed its right to distribute political matter as well (*supra,* pp. 449–50). There the union wanted to distribute in the plant its newsletter, a portion of which urged members to write their state legislators requesting them to oppose incorporation of a right-to-work provision in the Texas constitution. Another section of the leaflet criticized a Presidential veto of a bill increasing the federal minimum wage and insisted that employees should register as voters in order to "defeat our enemies and elect our friends." The employer argued that political literature was not relevant to the "immediate employment relationship" and should not be protected by Section 7. The Court rejected this argument, holding that the union distribution of the leaflet was protected by the language of Section 7—that "employees shall have the right . . . to engage in . . . concerted activities for the purpose of collective bargaining *or other mutual aid or protection. . . .*" The Court considered both the right-to-work and minimum wage issues to have some relationship to union bargaining objectives, and in a significant footnote observed: "As almost every issue can be viewed by some as political, the clear purpose of the 'mutual aid or protection' clause would be frustrated if the mere characterization of conduct or speech removed it from the protection of the act." And it added: "There may well be types of conduct or speech that are so purely political or so remotely connected to the concerns of employees as employees to be beyond the protection of the clause. But this is a determination that should be left for case-by-case consideration." Meanwhile, the opportunity under *Eastex* for a labor organization to utilize Section 7 rights to communicate with its members at the work location in this manner will significantly aid union political action programs. On the other hand, the *Wall Street Journal* has suggested that political contributions generated by corporate Political Action Committees are now decisively affecting the composition of the Congress and its legislative products in the labor-management field.

FEDERAL VERSUS STATE LABOR LAW

Much has heretofore been said about the doctrine of federal pre-emption. This concept has reference to the supremacy of our national government over the states in dealing with matters committed to its charge under the Constitution. Under the supremacy clause—Article VI, paragraph 2—and the commerce clause—Article I, Section 8 (3)—of the Constitution, Congress has the power to pre-empt an appropriate field from state regulation. With the greatly expanded coverage of its power under the commerce clause, which began roughly in 1937, Congress found itself in a position to regulate virtually all aspects of industry, including labor standards and labor relations. In a series of step-by-step decisions, the Supreme Court decided that Congress intended to do just that—and Congress has never indicated otherwise. With respect to any regulation that it enacted, to that extent, Congress "occupied the field." And hence states were disabled from enforcing any laws they might pass covering the same subject matter. This was irrespective of whether that state regulation was consistent with, or contrary to, the federal plan. Only in areas where Congress had not legislated at all were the states free to act. The importance of this concept cannot be overstated.

Certainly in the NLRA and in the Taft-Hartley Act Congress did provide a comprehensive federal plan for the regulation of labor relations. At the heart of this plan was the National Labor Relations Board. With so many enterprises doing business in so many states, a unitary system for regulating labor relations has certainly made it easier for major companies to operate efficiently and successfully. How could outfits like General Motors and General Electric efficiently do business if they were

constantly faced with different laws from state to state governing their relations with the unions representing their employees? After all, an International Harvester tractor is the end
result of a production process carried on in many states. A strike
at any one of its plants might cripple the entire operation.

Although several references to the supremacy of the federal
law are scattered throughout the previous chapters, perhaps a
few examples of its operation will more clearly indicate what
it is. *Hill v. Florida* was decided by the Supreme Court in
1945. It is the leading case in a long line of precedents concerning the domination of New Deal labor legislation over state
laws. Florida had made it a crime for anyone to act as a business
agent of a labor union without first obtaining a license from the
state. Also, persons of foreign birth could not obtain licenses
unless they had been citizens and been in residence for the
preceding ten years. Finally, any union operating in the state
had to file certain reports disclosing information about union
personnel. The Supreme Court held that insofar as this act
applied to unions representing employees in industries falling
within the federal jurisdiction, its provisions were invalid en-
croachments on a field already occupied by Congress. The reason was that they detracted from the guaranty in Section 7 of
the NLRA that employees were entitled to have unions of their
own choosing and not the choice of some state legislature. Somewhat akin was the Court's ruling in 1950 that the state of
Michigan could not require a union to take a strike vote or to
file information with the local mediation service before it called
a strike among employees whom it represented in a plant subject to federal jurisdiction. Again Congress had guaranteed recourse to concerted activities and the strike in Sections 7 and 13
of the NLRA, and thus no state could modify these rights. In a
similar vein was the Court's invalidation of state laws that
prohibited strikes and substituted compulsory arbitration in
public utilities.

Previously, in the *Allen-Bradley Local* case in 1942, the Supreme Court had declared that Wisconsin, by its employment

relations board, was free during a strike to forbid the continuance of mass picketing that threatened personal injury and property damage to employees wishing to work, obstructed entrance to and egress from the plant, blocked roads around the plant, and picketed employees' homes, even though the employer came within the ambit of the NLRA. The Court pointed out that "the federal Act does not govern employee or union activity of the type here enjoined," so it was hard to see how Wisconsin's prohibition of the conduct in question "impairs, dilutes, qualifies or in any respect subtracts from any of the rights guaranteed and protected" by the NLRA. Nor did the state board's order affect the status of the strikers as employees or cause a forfeiture of collective bargaining rights, thus indirectly compromising the federal policy. It resembled, rather, "the common situation where a State takes steps to prevent breaches of the peace in connection with labor disputes." The Court has never abandoned its decision to exempt from the pre-emption doctrine efforts by state or local authorities to deal with such breaches of the peace, even after Congress in 1948 made such conduct an unfair labor practice in Section 8 (b) (1) (A).

The pre-emption doctrine has been both modified and eventually strengthened, as indicated by the Court's handling of two cases from Wisconsin. In the 1949 *Briggs-Stratton* case a bare majority of the Supreme Court upheld Wisconsin's enforcement of its state labor board's order prohibiting the UAW-AFL's recourse to a series of "quickie" work stoppages sufficiently harassing to disrupt production in a large manufacturing plant. The union contended that these unannounced stoppages for brief periods were really strikes, or, at any rate, were concerted activity within the meaning of Section 7 of the NLRA. But the Court held otherwise. It declared that they were not strikes at all, and that they amounted to unprotected activity. Furthermore, it said that while this conduct was specifically called an unfair union labor practice in the state act, it was not one of the forbidden union activities described in

Section 8 (*b*) of the NLRA. Had it been, then its prevention would have been exclusive federal business, which the state could not constitutionally regulate. Here the union's conduct fell between two stools on exclusive state territory. This left the state of Wisconsin free to handle the situation in. its own way.

However, in the *Lodge 76, IAM* (1976) case the union used a somewhat different tactic to bring pressure on an employer during the course of negotiations—the members concertedly refused to work overtime. First the company filed a charge with the NLRB. The board dismissed it because a refusal to work overtime did not violate the NLRA. Then the company filed a charge with the state labor board, which ultimately entered a cease and desist order against the union. This order was set aside by the Supreme Court on the ground that the failure by Congress to make such activity unlawful manifests an intention to allow it. Thus, it is impermissible for Wisconsin to prohibit what Congress allows, since that would be an intrusion upon the federal scheme regulating labor relations and collective bargaining. Indeed, Justice Brennan, speaking for the Court, said "that the ruling of *Briggs-Stratton,* permitting state regulation of partial strike activities such as are involved in this case is . . . 'no longer of general application,' " and "*Briggs-Stratton* is expressly overruled."

The explanation for the differences between these two Wisconsin cases is not the distinction between "quickie" strikes and refusals to work overtime. It may rather be found in intervening decisions by the Supreme Court, most notably in the *Garner* and *Garmon* cases.

In *Garner v. Teamsters Union* (1953) the union picketed the employer's premises, apparently in an effort to compel him to bring pressure upon his employees for the purpose of getting them into the organization. While this conduct violated the Pennsylvania labor act, it was also a union unfair labor practice under the NLRA. As the employer was subject to federal jurisdiction, the highest state court held that it could not grant him a remedy, since in its opinion passing on the union's conduct was the sole affair of the NLRB. With this the Supreme Court agreed. In its view there could be no duplication of remedies for a violation of the federal labor act. However, the employer argued that in the NLRA Congress was concerned only with maintaining public rights and curtailing public wrongs, and that he had sustained a *private* wrong, which the state was free to prevent. In rejecting this ingenious theory, the Court said that even where conduct has dual characteristics so that at the same time it might be both a federal public and a local private wrong, nevertheless to the extent it was prohibited by the state as a private wrong, the federal remedy and policy has been circumvented. And this it would not allow, because it constituted an invasion of federal power.

In *San Diego Building Trades Council v. Garmon* (1959) a union peacefully picketed an employer. A California court enjoined any picketing by the union unless it was properly designated as a bargaining agent. The court also awarded $1,000 damages for losses sustained by the picketed employer. The California Supreme Court affirmed the judgment since the NLRB had declined to exercise jurisdiction. The U.S. Supreme Court reversed. When an activity is "arguably subject" to the NLRA, it said, that closes the matter for the states, whether or not the Labor Board will take the case. The employer contended that the board cannot issue an injunction or enter a judgment for damages. The Court had a ready answer for that one: To allow a state to grant a remedy that has been withheld from the NLRB "only accentuates the danger of conflict."

Based on *Garner* and *Garmon,* the Supreme Court drew the federal pre-emption noose tighter. The sum and substance was that the only areas of labor relations remaining for state regulation or individual legal action were suits for breach of contract under Section 301, suits for violation of the duty of fair representation, and recourse to traditional kinds of remedies such as actions for defamation or other common-law torts and for violence or mass picketing—be they for injunctions, damages, or state board orders. Indeed, it reinforced its position in *Farmer v. Carpenters Local 25* (1977). There the Supreme Court permitted a member to maintain in a state court a damage suit, grounded on the tort of intentional infliction of emotional distress, against a union that had subjected him to "outrageous conduct" after he complained of the organization's discriminatory operation of its hiring hall. An exception to *Garner* and *Garmon* of a different character emerged in the 1978 case of *Sears, Roebuck and Co. v. San Diego District Council of Carpenters.* Here the activity enjoined by the state court was peaceful picketing in connection with a labor dispute. No one could question that *this,* under *Garmon,* was "arguably subject" to the NLRB.

In this case the carpenters' union had learned that Sears was having carpentry work performed on its premises by nonunion men. The Sears manager failed to heed the union's demand that he meet union conditions established in the area. Two days later the union began peaceful and orderly picketing of the employer's store, which was located on private property with a large area for customer parking. The picketers patrolled on the parking area or on the adjacent privately owned walkways, the union refusing to withdraw the picketers on Sears's demand. Thereupon Sears requested and secured from a state court a temporary restraining order enjoining the union from picketing, on the ground that under California law it was a trespass on the store's private property. The state court of appeals affirmed this decree; but the Supreme Court of California reversed. It concluded that the picketing was both "arguably protected" by Section 7 and "arguably prohibited" by Section 8 (*b*), state jurisdiction therefore being pre-empted under the *Garmon* guidelines. It is immediately apparent that this peaceful picketing was "arguably"—indeed, demonstrably—subject to the NLRA, either as protected area standards picketing (*supra,* p. 470), as prohibited picketing to compel a reassignment of work (*supra,* p. 428), as recognitional picketing protected at the outset but prohibited if no petition for a representation election is filed within a reasonable time, not to exceed thirty days (*supra*, p. 469), or as primary concerted activity protected under *Hudgens* (*supra*, p. 451), even though it occurred on private property. Nevertheless, in a five-to-three decision the U.S. Supreme Court reversed, sustaining the state's jurisdiction to enforce its laws against trespass as "conduct traditionally subject to state regulation," even when used to prohibit peaceful picketing on private property in connection with a labor dispute.

A majority of the Supreme Court's participating members is required to reverse a judgment before it on appeal. The member designated by the Chief Justice to speak for the Court (that is, if the Chief Justice is on the majority side; otherwise the senior justice on the majority side designates the member to speak for the Court) must prepare an opinion that will be endorsed by a majority, even though each such member is permitted also to write a concurring opinion, adding his own views on the subject. In this case Justice Stevens wrote the majority opinion; and he based the Court's decision on the fact that the union had never filed an unfair labor practice charge against Sears with the Labor Board. Thus the Court created an exception to *Garmon* where "the party who could have presented the protection issue to the Board has not done so and the other party to the dispute has no acceptable means of doing so." This immediately raises the question whether the state court has jurisdiction to act in a case where the union *has* filed such a charge with the Labor Board. Justice Stevens fails to answer that critical question in the majority opinion. Two of the five members who comprised the majority wrote concurring opinions in which they expressed totally contradictory views on this question. Justice Blackmun asserted: "It should be made clear, however, that the logical corollary of the Court's reasoning is that if the union *does* file a charge upon being asked by the employer to leave the employer's property and continues to process the charge expeditiously, state court jurisdiction is pre-empted until such time as the General Counsel declines to issue a complaint or the Board, applying the stan-

dards of *NLRB v. Babcock & Wilcox Co.* [*supra*, p. 449], rules
against the union and holds the picketing to be unprotected.
. . . Once the no-man's land has been bridged, as it is once a
union files a charge, the importance of deferring to the Labor
Board's case-by-base accommodation of employers' property
rights and employees' rights mandates pre-emption of state
court jurisdiction."

On the other hand, Justice Powell sharply disagreed with
Blackmun on this point and flatly stated that he "would not join
in the Court's opinion if [he] thought it fairly could be read
to that effect." Justice Stevens maintained a discreet silence on
the issue since, if he lost the vote of either Blackmun or Powell,
he would no longer have a majority of the Court with him!
Of course, Justice Stevens could justify his failure to speak on
this matter because courts are supposed to rule only on the
issues necessarily raised by the facts presented in the cases before them. Such a resolution of an issue thus raised constitutes
the "holding" of a case, whereas any judicial comment on issues
not squarely presented for decision is ordinarily regarded as
mere *dictum* and is not binding on lower courts.

Justice Brennan, speaking for the three dissenters, argued in
vain against "the deleterious consequences" that would follow
from creating an exception to *Garner* and *Garmon* in trespass
cases since, as a result, courts, rather than the Labor Board, will
be called upon to accommodate property rights and Section 7
rights. "It simply cannot be seriously contended," he stated,
"that the thousands of judges, state and federal, throughout the
United States can be counted upon accurately to identify the
relevant considerations and give each the proper weight in accommodating the respective rights."

Of course, the states remain free to enact right-to-work statutes under Section 14 (*b*) of the LMRA, which the unions
have for years unsuccessfully tried to have repealed. However,
the Supreme Court in *Local No. 438 v. Curry* (1963) would
not let a court in a right-to-work state use Section 14 (*b*) as a
reason to enjoin peaceful picketing aimed at persuading an

employer to hire only union labor. For regulation of that conduct was a matter exclusively within the power of the NLRB; and state regulation was forbidden under the preemption doctrine. It seems odd that the Court made no attempt to square this with its 1953 decision in *Plumbers' Union v. Graham (supra,* p. 327). Perhaps the passage of ten years accounts for this oversight!

Congress may have cherished the thought that Section 10 (*a*) of the LMRA affords an adequate escape from this dilemma of federal-state conflict. Pursuant to Section 10 (*a*) any state may share with the NLRB control over labor relations matters falling within the federal domain. All it has to do is enact a statute setting up a state agency to administer local provisions so drawn that the determination of issues arising thereunder before such agency will not be inconsistent with the federal scheme in the LMRA. If it does that then the NLRB may cede a good deal of its work to the state board, save with respect to matters in the manufacturing, mining, communications, and transportation industries, "except where predominantly local in character." Albeit a few states have local labor relations boards, no cession agreement has yet been made between any of them and the NLRB. Perhaps this is because Section 10 (*a*) requires the states to follow the federal model too closely to suit their taste; and also because the states do not trust the federal board to achieve workable and understandable treaties with them along the vague lines set forth in the statute, especially as the NLRB would have the final say as to what it gave and what it kept back. Possibly the foreseeable litigation over what was or was not "predominantly local in character" might scare off the states. And then again, in view of our long tradition of states' rights, maybe some of them are just too proud to knuckle under in this way to get the leavings of the NLRB.

With the states everywhere operating under severe budgetary constraints, there is little incentive for a state to undertake regulation that is straitjacketed into following federal patterns.

WAGES AND HOURS (FLSA)

The Fair Labor Standards Act of 1938 (FLSA) had its genesis in a bill originally sponsored by Hugo L. Black, then a United States senator from Alabama, before his appointment that year to the Supreme Court by President Franklin D. Roosevelt, and by William P. Connery, a member of the House of Representatives from Massachusetts. The act established federal standards governing minimum wages, overtime pay, employer record keeping, and child labor in order to prevent "the channels and instrumentalities of commerce" from being "used to spread and perpetuate" among the several states "labor conditions detrimental to the maintenance of the minimum standard of living necessary for health, efficiency, and general well-being of workers." Twenty years previously the Supreme Court, over the powerful dissent of Justice Holmes, had in *Hammer v. Dagenhart* (1918) held that Congress was without power to exclude the products of child labor from interstate commerce. When the same issue was again presented in *United States v. Darby* (1941), the Court unanimously sustained the constitutionality of the FLSA, expressly overruling *Hammer*. "The motive and purpose of the present regulation are plainly to make effective the Congressional conception of public policy that interstate commerce should not be made the instrument of competition in the distribution of goods produced under substandard labor conditions, which competition is injurious to the commerce and to the states from and to which the commerce flows," Justice Stone said for the Court. And he went on to say: "The motive and purpose of a regulation of interstate commerce are matters for the legislative judgment upon the exercise of which the Constitution places no restriction and over which the courts are given no control."

Coverage is very broad under the act—the "broadest . . . ever . . . included in any one Act," the Court observed in *United States v. Rosenwasser* (1945). Originally the act covered every employee "who is engaged in commerce or in the production of goods for commerce," a provision which *Darby* sustained. In 1961 Congress adopted the "enterprise concept," under which coverage of the FLSA was extended to every employee who "is employed in any enterprise engaged in commerce or in the production of goods for commerce"—an extension the Supreme Court upheld in *Maryland v. Wirtz* (1961). Thus, the employee himself no longer had to be engaged in commerce or the production of goods for commerce to be covered by the act. It was enough if the enterprise in which he worked was so engaged. *Maryland* was the case where the Supreme Court, over the vigorous dissent of Justice Douglas, permitted the extension of the FLSA's coverage to include employees of the states—a step which, on federalism grounds, as Douglas had urged in his *Maryland* dissent, it reversed in *National League of Cities v. Usery* (1976).

The original act fixed the minimum wage in the United States at 40 cents per hour. In the 1977 amendments to the FLSA, the minimum wage, which was then $2.30 per hour, was scheduled as follows: $2.65 an hour beginning January 1, 1978; $2.90 an hour beginning January 1, 1979; $3.10 an hour beginning January 1, 1980; $3.35 an hour beginning January 1, 1981.

No doubt to encourage the employment of additional workers, the FLSA required that the payment of overtime, at not less than one and one-half times the employee's regular rate, be paid after forty hours of work in the workweek. Thus, a worker earning $4.00 per hour should be paid for any hours after forty in a workweek at the rate of $6.00 per hour. Pieceworkers should be paid a premium after forty hours of one-half of their average straight-time hourly earnings in addition to their full piecework earnings. An alternative method for computing overtime pay for pieceworkers, if agreed to in advance, is to pay one and one-half times the piece rate for each piece produced during the weekly overtime hours. Salaried employees covered under the act are required to be paid premium pay for the hours worked after forty. The overtime hourly rate is reached by dividing the weekly salary by forty and then multiplying by one and one-half. Overtime premium pay may not be required in two very limited situations: where there exists a guaranteed annual wage plan negotiated with a certified bargaining agent or where individual contracts have been signed between the employee and the employer under which the employee is to work at a rate prescribed in the contract that does not amount to time and a half but that meets the standards approved by the Supreme Court in *Walling v. A. H. Belo Corporation* (1942)—a so-called *Belo* contract.

The act does not require extra pay for Saturday, Sunday, or holiday work, as such, for vacation, holiday, or severance pay, or for rest periods; nor does it set any limit on the number of hours of work for persons sixteen years of age or over. According to the Wage and Hour Division of the U.S. Department of Labor, in which the authority to administer the act is vested: "These [items] are matters for agreement between the employer and the employees or their authorized representatives."

Any employee subject to the act must be paid for all hours worked during the workweek. This includes all the time an employee must be on duty, or on the employer's premises or at any other prescribed place of work, or any additional time the employee is permitted to work. Under the provisions of the Portal-to-Portal Act of 1947 the employer is not required to pay for "activities which are preliminary to or postliminary to said principal activity or activities," such as traveling to the actual place of performance of the work, unless made compensable by contract, custom, or practice.

An estimated fifty million full-time and part-time workers are covered by the act, of whom some three million are estimated to be employed at the minimum wage. The myriads of exemptions and exceptions from coverage under the various parts of the FLSA form a hodgepodge beyond the scope of this summary. The major category of workers exempt from coverage are executive, administrative, and professional employees and the employees of small retail or service establishments that make most of their sales within the state, as well as agricultural workers on small farms. Learners, apprentices, and handicapped workers may, under certain circumstances, be paid less than the minimum wage. This is also true of full-time students in retail and service establishments, agriculture, or institutions of higher education. An attempt by Congressman Paul Simon of Illinois during the consideration of the 1977 amendments to encourage the employment of youths by an amendment to establish a subminimum wage at 85 per cent of the applicable minimum for the first six months' employment was defeated by one vote in the House—212 to 211.

The FLSA child labor provisions seek to protect the educational opportunities of minors and prohibit their employment in jobs under conditions detrimental to their health or well-being.

To promote enforcement of the act, employers are required to keep records on wages, hours, and other relevant items. An employee may recover unpaid minimum or overtime wages by proceeding either through the Secretary of Labor or by retaining a private attorney who may file suit in a federal or state court to recover costs, attorney's fees, and back wages, plus an amount equal to lost wages as liquidated damages for losses that are "too obscure and difficult of proof for estimate other than by liquidated damages." Such employee is entitled to a jury trial if he wants one. Moreover, in an appropriate case, the Secretary of Labor may also secure an injunction to restrain any person from violating the law. No person may be discriminated against for filing a complaint or participating in a legal proceeding. Willful violators of the act are subject to criminal prosecution.

Finally, the act was amended by the Equal Pay Act of 1963 to prohibit sex discrimination and to afford a remedy under the FLSA where an employer pays an employee wages "less than the rate at which he pays wages to employees of the opposite sex in such establishment for equal work on jobs the performance of which requires equal skill, effort, and responsibility, and which are performed under similar working conditions. . . ." Jobs need only be substantially equal—not identical

—for comparison purposes. Where a violation is found, the employer may not reduce the wage rate of an employee in order to eliminate the unlawful wage differential. Usually this means increasing the wages of women to the level paid men—not reducing the men's rates to those paid to women. If based even in part on sex, a wage differential is illegal. However, the law does permit wage differences based on factors other than sex, such as seniority and merit systems or systems that reward productivity.

It must be constantly borne in mind that the foregoing account is a simplification of a very long and complicated statute, intended here only to suggest the barest elements of its essential provisions.

HEALTH AND SAFETY (OSHA)

Prior to the enactment by Congress of the Occupational Safety and Health Act of 1970 (OSHA), industrial safety had been the responsibility of state governments. The Senate Labor Committee reported in 1970 that "many times more" days were lost on the job from work-related disabilities than from strikes. The committee that year found that "14,500 persons were killed annually as a result of industrial accidents; accordingly, during the past four years more Americans have been killed where they work than in the Vietnam war." "Congress found the common law and other existing remedies for work injuries resulting from unsafe working conditions to be inadequate to protect the Nation's working men and women," the Supreme Court said in *Atlas Roofing Company v. Occupational Safety and Health Review Commission* (1977), going on to observe: "It created a new cause of action, and remedies therefor, unknown to the common law, and placed their enforcement in a tribunal supplying speedy and expert resolutions of the issues involved." That tribunal was the Occupational Safety and Health Review Commission, a quasi-judicial body consisting of three members appointed by the President. The new remedies provided by the act, in addition to any already provided under state law, were designed to guarantee a new federal right—that each employer "shall furnish to each of his employees employment and a place of employment which are free from recognized hazards. . . ." The statute permitted the federal government, in proceedings before the administrative agency, to obtain abatement orders intended to correct unsafe working conditions and to impose civil penalties upon employers.

In addition, the Secretary of Labor is given broad enforcement powers under the statute. His inspectors are authorized "to enter without delay and at reasonable times" any factory or work place and "to inspect and investigate . . . any such place of employment and all pertinent conditions" and to question privately any employer, agent, or employee connected therewith. Unions and employees are encouraged to bring any unsafe conditions to the attention of the Secretary of Labor; and the identity of persons making such reports in writing to the Secretary is protected from disclosure. Moreover, employees cannot be discharged or otherwise disciplined for having given testimony to, or otherwise cooperated with, the Secretary or his representative. A representative of the employer and of the union may accompany the inspector on his tour of the premises. In the absence of a union, the inspector "shall consult with a reasonable number of employees concerning matters of health and safety in the workplace." No advance notice of an inspection need be given to the employer.

If a violation is discovered, the inspector, on behalf of the Secretary of Labor, may issue a citation or notice to the employer fixing a reasonable time for its abatement, and, in his discretion, imposing a civil penalty, which may range from nothing for *de minimis* and nonserious violations, to not more than $1,000 for serious violations. Each citation "shall be prominently posted . . . at or near each place a violation . . . occurred." The employer may contest the proposed abatement order and penalties in an evidentiary hearing before an administrative law judge of the commission, at which hearing the burden of proof is on the

Secretary. Appeal from the decision of the administrative law judge is first to the Commission and from there to the federal circuit courts of appeals. In *Atlas Roofing* the Supreme Court held that it was not a violation of the 7th amendment to deny the employer a right to trial by jury in an OSHA proceeding, since Congress may "create new public rights and remedies by statute and commit their enforcement, if it chose, to a tribunal other than a court of law—such as an administrative agency—in which facts are not found by juries."

The Secretary of Labor is authorized to promulgate occupational safety or health standards that, when once adopted, have the force of law. Any party who may be adversely affected by a standard may seek a review in a circuit court of appeals within sixty days of its final issuance. However, the "determinations of the Secretary shall be conclusive if supported by substantial evidence in the record considered as a whole." These standards can thereafter be enforced by citations against "guilty" employers.

In *Marshall v. Barlow's, Inc.* (1978) the Supreme Court dealt with the question of whether Section 8 (*a*) of OSHA was constitutional under the 4th amendment. Without requiring a warrant, that section empowers the Secretary of Labor to enter and inspect the work area of any employment facility within the act's jurisdiction; and when Barlow was approached by an OSHA inspector, he claimed that Section 8 (*a*) was in conflict with the 4th amendment to the federal constitution, which prohibits "unreasonable searches and seizures."

This case was billed as a critical confrontation determining whether or not the Congressional scheme for securing factory safety in the United States would operate effectively. "If OSHA is required to obtain search warrants before inspecting work establishments," said the Assistant Secretary of Labor in a letter to Congress prior to the Court's decision, "its ability to ensure compliance with health and safety standards would be seriously curtailed, since many civil warrants could not be obtained and most procedures to obtain them would give employers advance warning." Noting that over 70 per cent of OSHA's random inspections "revealed occupational hazards which were significant enough to be ordered corrected, and which might be easily concealed if a plant manager knew an inspector was about to arrive," he concluded: "The resultant inspections would be virtually meaningless."

Lined up with the government, in support of Section 8 (*a*)'s constitutionality were, among others, the AFL-CIO and the Sierra Club as *amici curiae* (friends of the court), and arrayed against them, in support of Barlow, the heating and plumbing contractor who had refused to allow OSHA a warrantless access to his premises, was an unlikely combination consisting of the American Conservative Union and the American Civil Liberties Union!

In *Barlow's* the Court invalidated Section 8 (*a*) of OSHA insofar as it authorized warrantless factory inspections; but it did so in a way designed to minimize damage to effective federal factory inspection. The Court declared it to be "untenable that the ban on warrantless searches was not intended to shield places of business as well as of residence." However, it indicated that warrants may be issued *ex parte* (that is, in the absence of the owners of premises to be inspected), "thereby [as the Court put it] preserving the element of surprise." Moreover, to secure such a warrant, the Secretary need not demonstrate "probable cause to believe that conditions in violation of OSHA exist on the premises," but only that "a specific business has been chosen for an OSHA search on the basis of a general administrative plan for the enforcement of the Act." Thus construed, one may ask, what purpose is thereby served? The Court said that a warrant issued under such circumstances "would provide assurances from a neutral officer that the inspection is reasonable under the Constitution, is authorized by statute, and is pursuant to an administrative plan containing specific neutral criteria."

Justice Stevens, joined by Justices Blackmun and Rehnquist, dissented, concluding that the 4th amendment "has no application to routine, regulatory inspections of commercial premises." He further observed "that the inspection warrant adds little to the protection already afforded by the statute and pertinent regulations, and the slight additional benefit it might provide is insufficient to identify a constitutional violation or to justify overruling Congress' judgment that the power to conduct warrantless inspections is essential."

Thus the great constitutional challenge to the Secretary of Labor's authority to administer efficiently the federal factory safety program seemed to end up with the Secretary losing the battle but winning the war. At the end of 1978 the Secretary announced that since *Barlow's* the Labor Department had had to obtain a warrant in only one per cent of more than 80,000 inspections. Of greater concern was a sharp, unexplained rise in the nation's occupational death rate from what had been an encouraging four-year decline. Richard Bergman, the executive director of a presidential task force on workplace safety and health, said at the time he released the draft of a final report in December of 1978 that "OSHA knows little more about what works to prevent injuries today than it did in 1971." Then he added: "While factors out of OSHA's control contributed, the national rate of serious injuries has not declined since that time." Dr. Eula Bingham, OSHA director, commented: "These statistics reaffirm the fact that OSHA cannot do the job alone. We must have a commitment from every employer to eliminate these hazards."

It would appear that there is more to solving a problem than passing a law.

RETIREMENT SECURITY (ERISA)

On Labor Day, 1974, President Gerald Ford signed into law the Employee Retirement Income Security Act—ERISA, as it has come to be known. It represents the first comprehensive pension reform law passed by Congress.

In the four decades between the Wagner Act and ERISA, there

had developed in the United States a change of philosophy concerning pension and welfare plans. Historically, these plans had been viewed as a sort of "extra" or "fringe" benefit—a gift to employees in return for loyalty, long service, or for special contributions to the company. When employers became obligated under the NLRA to bargain with unions over such plans, and the plans became incorporated into collective bargaining agreements, employees came to view their rights under them not as matters of largesse but as something they were entitled to in return for their services. Since employers sought and obtained Internal Revenue Service tax-exempt status relieving them from paying taxes on contributions allocated to pension and welfare plans, and delaying until after retirement the taxability of the benefits to their employees, the federal government from the very beginning played a role advantageous both to the employer and the employed.

Pension plans fit in well with time-honored American virtues —thrift, planning for the future, and protecting one's self while able to earn against old age when one can no longer work. Imagine the shock felt by employees under pension plans that had been approved by the IRS when they discovered upon retirement that for one reason or another there was no pension. Unfortunately, this experience was not uncommon. Naturally, this sort of thing demanded reform. Like much modern legislation, pension reform began with a presidential commission. In 1962, President Kennedy appointed a group to study the problems associated with private pensions in the United States. The subject was then studied and restudied by various Congressional committees. In all, there were accumulated over ten thousand pages of formally recorded legislative history before the Employee Retirement Income Security Act of 1974 became law. The testimony was poignantly summed up by a Labor Department official who told Congress that the pension promise in the country had amounted to this: "If you remain in good health and stay with the same company until you are 65 years old, and if you haven't been laid off for too long a period, and if there is enough money in the fund, and if that money has been prudently managed, you will get a pension."

Increasingly in the 1960's and early 1970's, industrial pensions had become a major American institution "built on human disappointment." Sometimes the default was simply the result of poor economics—failure by the employer to make the contributions necessary to put the plan on an actuarially sound basis, poor financial management of the fund's assets, low rates of return on the investments, sudden business adversity of the employer—thus robbing the plan of that source from which the necessary funding was supposed to come. Again, the failure of some retired employees to receive benefits resulted from guile and chicanery or tainted judgment—double-dealing trustees who feathered their own nests at the expense of those they were legally bound to protect, or whose investment decisions were guided more by the interests of their friends or business acquaintances than by the needs of the fund's beneficiaries; from overly-technical eligibility requirements deliberately designed to disqualify trusting and uninformed employees from receiving benefits under the plan; or from conflicts of interest on the part of the trustees who "went along" with a floundering business's desperate need for cash, regardless of the risk to the pension plan's financial security and to the expectations of its beneficiaries.

When ERISA became law on September 2, 1974 there were an estimated 1.8 million pension and welfare plans operating in the United States. Of these, 350,000 were pension plans—that is, plans funded by employers to provide for retirement—the remainder being welfare plans, funded by employers to provide certain other types of employee benefits such as those for disability, death, and medical needs. About 35 million persons covered by private employee benefit plans were directly affected by the new law.

In ERISA, Congress declared that it was the act's policy to protect "the interests of participants in employee benefit plans and their beneficiaries" by requiring disclosure and reporting of financial and other information, by establishing "standards of conduct, responsibility, and obligation for fiduciaries of employees benefit plans"; by providing "remedies, sanctions and ready access to the Federal courts"; by "improving the equitable character and the soundness of such plans by requiring them to vest the accrued benefits with significant periods of service, to meet minimum standards of funding; and by requiring plan termination insurance." To effectuate this declaration of policy, Congress passed a statute whose text alone occupies 186 printed pages—now supplemented by tomes of regulations issued by the Treasury Department and the Department of Labor! Without question, it is the most technical and complex labor-related law ever passed in the United States.

The present section—that which you are about to read—is devoted to a simple account of what ERISA does and what it does not do, as well as what it has inadvertently brought about.

What ERISA Does • This section and the following ones indicate the broad outlines of ERISA.

(1) Administration. Whether the responsibility for administering the act would be in the Department of Labor, the traditional guardian of workers' interests, or in the Internal Revenue Service of the Treasury Department, long associated with private employee benefit plans through its authority to approve or disapprove them for tax purposes, became a bone of contention in Congress. True to the classic legislative tradition, Congressional partisans of each agency were placated by a political compromise, Congress placing the responsibilities for administering the law in *both*. It also created a new government corporation called the Pension Benefit Guaranty Corporation (PBGC) —chaired by the Secretary of Labor and established within the Department of Labor—to administer the termination of certain pension plans and to provide for plan termination insurance, thus guaranteeing payment to participants and beneficiaries of nonforfeitable benefits of the insured terminated plan, much as the Federal Deposit Insurance Corporation (FDIC) guarantees bank deposits.

This dual jurisdiction of the IRS and the Department of

Labor has been blamed for the mountain of paperwork required of employers and benefit plans. There are many complaints that the forms to be filed are duplicative and unnecessarily prolix. A business publication reports that employers seeking information on their obligations under the law "often get conflicting answers from the two bodies and are left in limbo until they resolve their differences,"—if they ever do!

Late in 1978 Congress approved a reorganization plan of the President to improve the administration of ERISA. The plan sought to reduce the "jurisdictional overlap and duplication" by the Departments of Labor and Treasury by more clearly delineating the responsibilities of the two agencies. It gave the Treasury Department primary jurisdiction over minimum pension standards while giving the Labor Department primary jurisdiction over the fiduciary responsibility and the prohibited transaction provisions of ERISA.

(2) Enforcement. The Department of Labor has the principal enforcement responsibilities in the area of reporting and disclosure and in setting standards with which fiduciaries must comply. The Internal Revenue Service has the main enforcement responsibilities with respect to the vesting, funding, and participation standards by fiduciaries, while the Secretary of Labor retains some responsibilities in these areas to protect employee pension rights.

In enacting ERISA, Congress had in mind protection for each individual participant in a pension plan. While participants retain the ultimate right, by legal action against the fiduciaries, to correct violations of ERISA or to vindicate their own personal rights as beneficiaries, Congress hoped that the plans themselves, through their fiduciaries, would achieve compliance with the law. Through the various sections of ERISA dealing with vesting, participation, reporting and disclosure, fiduciary standards, minimum funding, and the like, Congress sought to achieve a guarantee that each worker would receive the promised benefits, without recourse to lawsuits by the individual employees. However, where the act's policies are not effectuated through these channels, nor achieved administratively by the Internal Revenue Service or the Department of Labor, an adversely affected participant or beneficiary may sue directly; or in appropriate cases, the Secretary of Labor may sue in their behalf. The act bestows great power on the federal courts to implement its provisions and policies.

During the first four years after enactment of ERISA, approximately eighteen hundred private suits were brought under the act. The Department of Labor filed approximately twenty-six civil suits to enforce the provisions of the act and to establish new principles of fiduciary responsibility. The act gives the court discretionary power to allow attorney's fees and costs of litigation.

(3) Coverage. The law covers two different types of employee benefit plans—pension plans providing retirement benefits, and welfare plans, making available to participants and beneficiaries payments of money to cope with certain contingencies such as sickness, accident, and unemployment, as well as for apprenticeship-training programs and legal services. All of these plans must meet broad requirements for reporting and disclosure to the beneficiaries and to the government, as well as being subject to the fiduciary standards of the act. However, only the benefits provided by a certain type of pension plan, called a defined benefit plan, are insured by the PBGC, and only pension plans are subject to the participation, vesting, and funding provisions of the act.

(4) Participation. In the past, many employees were denied the opportunity to participate in a pension plan because of overly stringent participation rules. Now, an employee cannot ordinarily be denied participation in such a plan by reason of any minimum age or minimum service requirement after he has attained age twenty-five and completed one year of service, an exception being made for an employee who is within five years of attaining normal retirement age when first employed.

(5) Vesting. A notorious pension plan abuse has been failure to accord long-service employees any entitlement to benefits be-

fore they reach retirement age. For example, an employee might work for twenty-five years, then quit or be discharged, and discover that he had no pension rights when he reached retirement age. To meet this problem, ERISA established mandatory vesting requirements. The act permits plans to adopt any one of three vesting options. The most popular one declares that a member's rights are not vested until he earns at least ten years of service credit, at which time his benefits will be 100 per cent vested. (An employee who has at least one thousand compensated hours in a year must receive credit for one year of vesting.) Whatever happens to his employment after this ten years of service credit, his right to a pension at retirement age will remain unaffected. Of course, the amount of his pension may vary, depending on such things as total length of service under the plan and pension benefit increases. Nevertheless, the concept of vesting protects and preserves an employee's right to receive a benefit at retirement.

(6) Breaks-In-Service. ERISA places reasonable restrictions upon a plan's otherwise unlimited power to deprive a member of all unvested prior credited service. A celebrated case illustrates how this power has been abused. John Daniel was a truck driver and a member of the Teamsters Union for twenty-two years. During that time, he was involuntarily laid off for three months. When he retired because of illness, he learned for the first time that he was not entitled to a pension because his three-month break in employment prevented him from meeting the plan's requirement for twenty years of continuous service. Had ERISA been in effect, Daniel could not have been disqualified in this way.

(7) Funding. ERISA requires minimum funding standards to insure that there will be progress towards having sufficient money allocated for the payment of the benefits promised. These standards are designed to prevent a repetition of the kind of tragedy that occurred when the Studebaker automobile company closed down. The pension plan had not been adequately funded to provide retirement benefits. There was no

longer a weekly payroll available to supplement inadequate reserves, and when the company ceased to exist, so did the source of funds for the payment of retirement benefits.

(8) Plan Termination. Employers and their parent corporations face liability if a pension plan terminates without sufficient assets to pay benefits guaranteed by PBGC. When there is a funding deficiency, this employer liability, which could be up to 30 per cent of the net worth of the company, has introduced a whole new dimension into company decisions whether to close, liquidate, relocate, merge, or go into bankruptcy. If there is a pension plan, no sound decision to terminate it can be made without risking a possible substantial employer liability to the PBGC for the funding deficiency.

The PBGC is financed through its power to assess mandatory premiums upon pension trusts, as needed to finance its rescue operations, in addition to its authority to draw on the U.S. Treasury for up to $100 million. With such money-raising capabilities, it has not had to set up insurance reserves. Nevertheless, it faces some mammoth potential liabilities; and there are plans to escalate PBGC assessments.

(9) Allocation of Benefits. The act requires that benefit costs be allocated fairly among the various age groups. It prevents senior employees, who frequently control pension plans, from using their position of power to "load" a plan in favor of the older employees, to the corresponding detriment of the younger employees.

Another problem that the act covers is where a member beneficiary dies shortly before or after retirement with no provision having been made for his family's needs. The act does not require that survivor benefits be provided. However, it does require that the normal form of retirement benefit, which is paid to a married retiree, should be payable in the form of a joint and survivor annuity. But the retiree is free to reject this joint and survivor form of pension and may instead opt for the more traditional annuity for a single life. The fund is not restricted from making the employee pay (through lower monthly benefits for himself during his lifetime) for selecting the survivor option since that is necessary to protect the actuarial soundness of the plan. But the option must be made available to the employee, and the presumption favors the survivor annuity if the employee does nothing.

(10) Reporting and Disclosure. No longer can the operation of pension plans and welfare plans be a private prerogative. ERISA insists that a veritable deluge of documents, reports, and financial statements be filed with the government or be distributed or made available to plan participants. The philosophy is one of complete disclosure to all interested parties. Benefit data is even being fed into the Social Security computer so that every individual approaching retirement will receive a complete account of the pension benefits accrued during his or her lifetime. The amount of paperwork generated, however, has been a source of major criticism from employers and plan administrators.

The next section will treat a vital area covered by ERISA—fiduciary standards.

Fiduciary Standards—The Prudent Man and the Imprudent Expert • While ERISA covers many aspects of the law concerning benefit plans, the heart of the statute lies in the provisions directed at elevating the standards of those who manage the plans. "Notwithstanding ERISA's major provisions in the areas of vesting, funding, and termination insurance, from the liability viewpoint, the fiduciary responsibility provisions are the cornerstone of the act because they are the bases upon which employers, unions, pension funds, boards of directors and pension fund fiduciaries may be sued," one writer has said, going on to observe: "The prudent man rule is the centerpiece of the fiduciary standards mandated by the Act."

The prudent man rule has its origin in a famous case decided by the Massachusetts Supreme Judicial Court in 1830—*Harvard College v. Amory*—which illustrates the standards placed by Congress in 1974 upon those who handle other peoples' benefit plans—"fiduciaries," as they are known in the law. In the *Harvard College* case, a benefactor named John McQueen bequeathed $50,000 in a trust managed by Jonathan and Francis Amory. McQueen's wife, Ann, was to enjoy the income from the trust, but upon her death the trust was to be divided equally between Harvard College and the Massachusetts General Hospital. The trust instrument gave considerable latitude to the trustees in deciding how to invest the funds, empowering them "to invest in safe and productive stock, either in public funds, bank shares or other stock, according to their best judgment and discretion." After Ann McQueen's death, when Harvard and Massachusetts General became entitled to inherit, they sued the trustees, claiming that they had abused the trust by making risky and unsafe investments. The court ruled that the trustees had not abused their positions of trust, and set forth the particular language that was forever to be characterized as the prudent man rule:

"All that can be required of a trustee to invest, is, that he shall conduct himself faithfully and exercise sound discretion. He is to observe how men of prudence, discretion and intelligence *manage their own affairs,* not in regard to speculation, but in regard to permanent disposition of their funds, considering the probable safety of the capital to be invested. . . .

"These trustees are not to be made chargeable but for gross neglect and willful mismanagement."

The specific language Congress chose to use in ERISA went even beyond the prudent man rule because it required that the fiduciary use the "care, skill, prudence and diligence under the circumstances then prevailing, that *a prudent man acting in like capacity and familiar with such matters* would use in the conduct of an enterprise of like character and like aims. . . ." It would appear from the italicized words that the conduct of a pension trustee is to be measured by that of experienced pension trustees—the prudent expert standard, it has been called. If his actions fail to measure up to such a standard, he has violated his fiduciary responsibility to the beneficiaries and is personally liable to them for any resulting harm. Of course, the fiduciary may rely upon the judgment of actuaries, lawyers, and other professionals in discharging his responsibilities to the extent that "a prudent man acting in like capacity and familiar with such matters" would place reliance upon such advice.

In addition to the prudent man standard, the fiduciary must act for the exclusive benefit of the beneficiaries of the plan. To that end, the statute prohibits transactions where there might be actual or potential conflicts of interest between the fiduciaries and the beneficiaries. The fiduciary must never act in a situation where he profits personally; he must act only in the interests of the beneficiaries. Not only must the fiduciary meet this standard, but he may be liable if he knowingly participates in an improper act or omission of another fiduciary, or if he conceals an act or omission of another, or if he has knowledge of a breach of fiduciary responsibility and fails to take appropriate action.

Some Things ERISA Does Not Do • The major deficiency of ERISA is its failure to provide for the "portability" of pensions. The celebrated old Broadway play's title, "You Can't Take It With You," would apply well to private pensions in the United States. Pension plans have severely restricted the ability of workers to change employment. The price for mobility has usually been the loss of all unvested pension credits. Portability would allow a member's retirement service to follow the individual from one job to another, if each new employer has a pension plan. Since vesting may not be required until after ten years of continuous employment, it is possible for an employee to be constantly employed from age twenty to age sixty-five, be constantly participating in a retirement plan, have his employers constantly contributing, yet not be entitled to a single dollar of retirement benefit because he did not remain on any one job long enough to acquire a vested pension right. This is particularly unfortunate in view of the common practice of job changes in many industries, such as construction and engineering.

There are some other important things that the act does *not* do:

(1) ERISA does not require any employer to establish a retirement plan.

(2) It does not require the continuation of a plan.

(3) It does not require a minimum level of either benefits or contributions. However, when a level of benefits has been established, contributions must be sufficient to meet the minimum funding standards of ERISA or contractual levels, if higher.

(4) It does not require a plan to increase benefits or adjust for cost-of-living increases, nor does it ordinarily prohibit a reduction in benefit levels if deemed appropriate to the situation.

(5) With some exceptions, it does not prohibit the plan from establishing stricter eligibility or other requirements than those previously contained in the plan, provided that the minimum standards of ERISA are met by the new requirements.

(6) It does not cover the plans of governmental bodies.

(7) The PBGC does not provide termination insurance to guarantee payment of welfare plans, but only for some types of pension plans. It does not guarantee the benefits of a pension plan that is an individual account plan, where each participant has an individual account. It may guarantee the benefits under a defined benefit plan. This is the type of plan that is usually found in collectively bargained plans where the pension benefit is based upon a participant's years of service, multiplied by the dollar benefit per year of service.

The Price of Prudence and Financial Responsibility • The potential liability of employers to beneficiaries under the prudent man rule and the possible direct financial responsibility of an employer for inadequate funding have both contributed to a result never anticipated by the Congress when it enacted the pension reform law in 1974—a substantial slowdown in new pension plans and an enormous increase in the termination of existing plans by employers. The rate of new plans has been halved since 1974, while the termination rate of existing plans doubled the first year after ERISA and quadrupled the next year. In the years before ERISA, the ratio of new plans to terminated plans was 14.4 per cent; by 1976, this ratio had shrunk to 1.6 per cent. In 1976 and again in 1977 the number of plan terminations in these single years exceeded the aggregate number of plans terminated in the five-year period preceding the passage of the law. In the three-year period following enactment of ERISA, about 40,000 pension plans were terminated. A sample survey of those terminated plans by the House Small Business Committee showed over half of the companies reporting that ERISA was the major, or sole, reason for termination—an extraordinary result for a statute designed to promote the growth of private pension plans in the United States! A financial journal explained the concern of business about the new fiduciary standard imposed by Congress in this way: "Nobody is sure what these strictures mean," it said, "Yet a fiduciary who violates them is personally liable for any resulting losses to the plan and other such relief as a court may order."

ERISA has also had a significant effect on the American money market. Private pension funds in the United States have accumulated over 248 billion dollars in assets. The prudent man psychology produces significant investment consequences. "I am concerned about the impact that that type of investment strategy has on capital markets and on the willingness of fund management to venture at all into any kind of lesser securities, venture capital and so forth," the chairman of the Securities and Exchange Commission, Harold M. Williams, testified in October, 1977, when he urged Congress to clarify the prudent man rule. At the same time, unions have expressed their concern over the effect of the prudent man rule on diverting pension plan investment, as Melvin Glasser, the director of the social security department of the UAW, expressed it, from "such socially desirable areas as health maintenance organizations, day care centers and the like." For might not courts well ask whether an investment in a health maintenance organization, in order to benefit the health of union members, is a "prudent" investment when there are triple-A corporate bonds available that would yield higher interest rates? Glasser urged that the law be amended to allocate a certain portion of the fund to socially desirable investments without being subject to the full extent of the prudent man rule. Or consider the problem created by the "prohibited transactions" section of ERISA, as explained in testimony before the House Labor Standards Subcommittee. A benefit plan may have loaned money to the employer at a fair rate of interest. It may have been a good investment for the plan and also a good source of funds for the company. But now under ERISA it must cease doing this because of a potential conflict of interest. The problem is accentuated when the employer needs a loan to remain solvent and to continue providing employment to the members of the union.

In law, no less than in physics, for every action there is a reaction. Laws intended to solve one type of problem may create another. No one can fathom all of the consequences of sweeping legislation. That is why prudence, whatever its consequences in the investment field, is the mark of wisdom in the law-making process.

ERISA established federal standards for private pension plans. Public employees' pension plans at the state and local levels remain unregulated by federal legislation; but some wit has already coined the acronym PERISA as a nickname for anticipated regulation in this area. Noting that 20 per cent of the population receive benefits from public or private programs and that "no comprehensive, coordinated national pension policy has ever existed," President Carter, on July 12, 1978, created by executive order a presidential commission on pension policy to conduct a thoroughgoing review of all programs in the nature of pension plans. Significantly, this commission is charged with developing "national policies for retirement, survivor and disability programs that can be used as a guide by public and private programs."

The commission's executive director, Thomas C. Woodruff, stated that in 1978 total federal programs, including social security, reached about 27 per cent of the federal budget, exceeding that of the Defense Department. Further, one cannot overlook the significant cost implications of state and local government pension plans. In a statement accompanying the executive order that created the commission, the President noted an estimate of unfunded liabilities of public employee plans in the United States at over $500 billion—half a trillion dollars! Because commission reports of this kind are the frequent precursors of Congressional enactments, and as the number of Americans reaching retirement age is expected to continue increasing for the next half century, pension and retirement plans are certain to be an ever more important segment of labor law in the United States.

CHAPTER XIX

POSTSCRIPT

If you love the law and you love good sausage, don't watch either of them being made!—Old saying, quoted by Betty Talmadge in the *New York Times Magazine,* January 15, 1978.

As a power countervailing management the trade unions are much more effective than the law has ever been or can ever be.— Sir Otto Kahn-Freund, *Labour and the Law,* 1977.

In 1977, three decades after the passage of the Taft-Hartley Act, American unions massively sponsored the labor reform bill to correct what they believed had become inadequacies of the National Labor Relations Act. They offered considerable testimony before Congress, showing the extent to which anti-union employers had been systematically and successfully defeating employee organization by dilatory tactics and discriminatory acts. Despite strong administration support, this legislative attempt failed in June, 1978—the victim of a prolonged filibuster by a small group of senators who bitterly opposed the bill. Organized labor's best efforts fell short by two votes of securing the sixty required to invoke cloture, which, if achieved, would have closed off a nineteen day debate and would have brought about a roll call in the Senate on the labor reform bill. Earlier the bill had passed the House by a vote of 257 to 163.

The principal objectives of the labor reform bill were to eliminate the delays that interfered with the right of employees to form and join unions and to bargain collectively as well as to provide additional remedies that would deter antiunion employers from interfering with their employees' organizational rights. To accomplish these objectives the labor reform bill in its final version after recommittal to the Senate Committee on Human Resources contained the following proposals:

• Have the board give priority to representation petitions filed by a union showing authorization cards from a majority of the employees, also restoring to the board the right to conduct elections prior to formal hearings—a right that had been taken away by the Taft-Hartley Act;

• Permit the board, in discriminatory discharge cases growing out of union organizational campaigns, to award the employees concerned one and one-half times back pay for lost wages and as compensation for nonmonetary damage suffered;

• Authorize the board in such cases to seek immediate relief in a federal district court by securing a mandatory injunction reinstating an employee to his job pending the outcome of the usual proceedings before the NLRB;

• In refusal-to-bargain cases involving no apparent substantial issue, similarly allow the board to secure in a federal district court an interim order requiring the employer to bargain;

• Expedite the disposal of unfair labor practice cases by expanding the board from five to seven members, thus allowing for the creation of additional board panels; add a self-enforcing device by making board orders final unless the losing respondent, within thirty days, seeks a review in the federal circuit court of appeals; and permit either party, in an expedited proceeding before a board panel, to seek summary enforcement of an administrative law judge's decision;

• Empower the board to seek injunctive relief in a federal district court preventing stranger picketing of an organized plant or mine, not authorized by the bargaining agent; and recognize an international union's right to place in trusteeship a local union engaged in a wildcat strike;

• Add a conscience amendment permitting workers with religious objections against payment of union dues to remit an equivalent sum to a nonreligious charity.

In a "behind-the-scenes" compromise never reported out of the Senate committee, organized labor had apparently been prepared to back down from the following provisions in the labor reform bill that had drawn heavy fire from employer advocates in the Senate debate:

• A requirement that an employer holding a "captive audience" meeting of its employees during an organizational campaign, on company premises and company time, must allow the union equal access by letting it conduct a similar meeting of the employees on company premises;

• Authorize the board to order employers to compensate employees for wages lost through employer dilatory tactics in refusal-to-bargain cases (known as the *Excello* remedy);

• A debarment provision that the federal government, for a period of three years, may not award a contract to any employer where there has been a board finding that the company had engaged in a willful violation of a final board order. (The compromise proposed would have substituted a civil fine);

• Elections in representation cases should be held within specific periods ranging from fifteen to seventy-five days after a petition is filed, depending on the size of the unit and the complexity of the case.

The inability of organized labor to put across the labor reform bill in 1978, notwithstanding its willingness by compromise to meet objections raised during the Senate debates, resembles its earlier unsuccessful efforts seeking the amendment of Section 14 (*b*) of the NLRA in order to outlaw state right-to-work acts and to legalize common situs picketing. In much the same way, employers were unable to keep their Supreme Court victory in *General Electric Co. v. Gilbert* (1976) (*supra*, p. 565) from being overturned by the same Congress that failed to pass the labor reform bill. Moreover, management was unable to prevent Congress from enacting sweeping amendments to the age discrimination law; nor could it persuade the nation's lawmakers to restrict OSHA's jurisdiction or power.

As the 95th Congress ended in what organized labor called "the winter of our discontent," the AFL-CIO Executive Council late in 1978 declared that "the fight is not over . . . to restore balance to the nation's labor law to curb corporate abuse and violations of law where workers had sought representative elections or contract protection and had been denied these rights by employer delay, harassment, intimidation, discharge and discrimination, virtually without penalty." And it continued: "It is most ironic that throughout the Senate filibuster, while opponents of the bill proclaimed their undying concern for workers and the need for speedy resolution of their rights to organize and bargain collectively they adamantly refused to allow the Senate to work its will in a democratic forum. Their tactics were exactly those used by employers to thwart the legal rights of their workers—precisely what labor reform was all about." Then it added: "In the tradition of the historic drives for civil rights, human rights, minority rights, Medicare and Social Security rights, we will be back again, until justice on the job is achieved."

Thus, management and organized labor grapple in the nation's Congress as at the bargaining table, with uncertain success, each seeking to mold the law to its advantage.

EXCERPTS FROM THE CLAYTON ACT, OCTOBER 15, 1914, C. 323, SECS. 6 AND 20, 38 STAT. 731 AND 738

SECTION 6   That the labor of a human being is not a commodity or article of commerce. Nothing contained in the antitrust laws shall be construed to forbid the existence and operation of labor, agricultural, or horticultural organizations, instituted for the purposes of mutual help, and not having capital stock or conducted for profit, or to forbid or restrain individual members of such organizations from lawfully carrying out the legitimate objects thereof; nor shall such organizations, or the members thereof, be held or construed to be illegal combinations or conspiracies in restraint of trade, under the antitrust laws.

SECTION 20   That no restraining order or injunction shall be granted by any court of the United States, or a judge or the judges thereof, in any case between an employer and employees, or between employers and employees, or between employees, or between persons employed and persons seeking employment, involving, or growing out of, a dispute concerning terms or conditions of employment, unless necessary to prevent irreparable injury to property, or to a property right, of the party making the application, for which injury there is no adequate remedy at law, and such property or property right must be described with particularity in the application, which must be in writing and sworn to by the applicant or by his agent or attorney.

And no such restraining order or injunction shall prohibit any person or persons, whether singly or in concert, from terminating any relation of employment, or from ceasing to perform any work or labor, or from recommending, advising, or persuading others by peaceful means so to do; or from attending at any place where any such person or persons may lawfully be, for the purpose of peacefully obtaining or communicating information, or from peacefully persuading any person to work or to abstain from working; or from ceasing to patronize or to employ any party to such dispute, or from recommending, advising, or persuading others by peaceful and lawful means so to do; or from paying or giving to, or withholding from, any person engaged in such dispute, any strike benefits or other moneys or things of value; or from peaceably assembling in a lawful manner, and for lawful purposes; or from doing any act or thing which might lawfully be done in the absence of such dispute by any party thereto; nor shall any of the acts specified in this paragraph be considered or held to be violations of any law of the United States.

EXCERPTS FROM NORRIS–LAGUARDIA ACT, MARCH 23, 1932, C. 90, SECS. 4 AND 13, 47 STAT. 70 AND 73

SECTION 4 No court of the United States shall have jurisdiction to issue any restraining order or temporary or permanent injunction in any case involving or growing out of any labor dispute to prohibit any person or persons participating or interested in such dispute (as these terms are herein defined) from doing, whether singly or in concert, any of the following acts:

(a) Ceasing or refusing to perform any work or to remain in any relation of employment;

(b) Becoming or remaining a member of any labor organization or of any employer organization, regardless of any such undertaking or promise as is described in section 3 of this Act;

(c) Paying or giving to, or withholding from, any person participating or interested in such labor dispute, any strike or unemployment benefits or insurance, or other moneys or things of value;

(d) By all lawful means aiding any person participating or interested in any labor dispute who is being proceeded against in, or is prosecuting, any action or suit in any court of the United States or of any State;

(e) Giving publicity to the existence of, or the facts involved in, any labor dispute, whether by advertising, speaking, patrolling, or by any other method not involving fraud or violence;

(f) Assembling peaceably to act or to organize to act in promotion of their interests in a labor dispute;

(g) Advising or notifying any person of an intention to do any of the acts heretofore specified;

(h) Agreeing with other persons to do or not to do any of the acts heretofore specified; and

(i) Advising, urging, or otherwise causing or inducing without fraud or violence the acts heretofore specified, regardless of any such undertaking or promise as is described in section 3 of this Act.

SECTION 13   When used in this Act, and for the purposes of this Act—

(a) A case shall be held to involve or to grow out of a labor dispute when the case involves persons who are engaged in the same industry, trade, craft, or occupation; or have direct or indirect interests therein; or who are employees of the same employer; or who are members of the same or an affiliated organization of employers or employees; whether such dispute is (1) between one or more employers or associations of employers and one or more employees or associations of employees; (2) between one or more employers or associations of employers and one or more employers or associations of employers; or (3) between one or more employees or associations of employees and one or more employees or associations of employees; or when the case involves any conflicting or competing interests in a "labor dispute" (as hereinafter defined) of "persons participating or interested" therein (as hereinafter defined).

(b) A person or association shall be held to be a person participating or interested in a labor dispute if relief is sought against him or it, and if he or it is engaged in the same industry, trade, craft, or occupation in which such dispute occurs, or has a direct or indirect interest therein, or is a member, officer, or agent of any association composed in whole or in part of employers or employees engaged in such industry, trade, craft, or occupation.

(c) The term "labor dispute" includes any controversy concerning terms or conditions of employment, or concerning the association or representation of persons in negotiating, fixing, maintaining, changing, or seeking to arrange terms or conditions of employment, regardless of whether or not the disputants stand in the proximate relation of employer and employee.

APPENDIX C

SECTIONS 7 AND 8 OF THE NATIONAL LABOR RELATIONS ACT (WAGNER ACT), JULY 5, 1935, C. 372, 49 STAT. 452, AS AMENDED BY TITLE I OF THE LABOR MANAGEMENT RELATIONS ACT OF 1947 (TAFT-HARTLEY ACT), JUNE 23, 1947, C. 120, TITLE I, 61 STAT. 140 AND AS FURTHER AMENDED BY TITLE VII OF THE LABOR-MANAGEMENT REPORTING AND DISCLOSURE ACT OF 1959 (LANDRUM-GRIFFIN ACT), SEPTEMBER 14, 1959, PUBLIC LAW 86-257, 73 STAT. 519.

[Key to this appendix: Parts appearing in plain roman type were originally in the Wagner Act; parts in italics were added by the Taft-Hartley Act; parts in brackets were deleted by Congress in the Landrum-Griffin Act; and parts in heavy bold-faced type were added in the Landrum-Griffin Act. Thus everything except the bracketed portions constitutes the present text of Sections 7 and 8 of the current National Labor Relations Act.]

Section 7. Employees shall have the right to self-organization, to form, join, or assist labor organizations, to bargain collectively through representatives of their own choosing, and to engage in *other* concerted activities for the purpose of collective bargaining or other mutual aid or protection, *and shall also have the right to refrain from any or all of such activities except to the extent that such right may be affected by an agreement re-*

quiring membership in a labor organization as a condition of employment as authorized in section 8 (a) (3).

Section 8 (*a*) It shall be an unfair labor practice for an employer—

(1) to interfere with, restrain, or coerce employees in the exercise of the rights guaranteed in section 7;

(2) to dominate or interfere with the formation or administration of any labor organization or contribute financial or other support to it: Provided, That subject to rules and regulations made and published by the Board pursuant to section 6, an employer shall not be prohibited from permitting employees to confer with him during working hours without loss of time or pay;

(3) by discrimination in regard to hire or tenure of employment or any term or condition of employment to encourage or discourage membership in any labor organization: Provided, That nothing in this Act, or in any other statute of the United States, shall preclude an employer from making an agreement with a labor organization (not established, maintained, or assisted by any action defined in section 8 (a) of this Act as an unfair labor practice) to require as a condition of employment membership therein *on or after the thirtieth day following the beginning of such employment or the effective date of such agreement, whichever is the later,* (i) if such labor organization is the representative of the employees as provided in section 9 (a), in the appropriate collective-bargaining unit covered by such agreement when made . . . *and (ii) unless following an election held as provided in section 9 (e) within one year preceding the effective date of such agreement, the Board shall have certified that at least a majority of the employees eligible to vote in such election have voted to rescind the authority of such labor organization to make such an agreement: Provided further, That no employer shall justify any discrimination against an employee for non-membership in a labor organization (A) if he has reasonable grounds for believing that such membership was not available to the employee on the same*

terms and conditions generally applicable to other members, or (B) if he has reasonable grounds for believing that membership was denied or terminated for reasons other than the failure of the employee to tender the periodic dues and the initiation fees uniformly required as a condition of acquiring or retaining membership;

(4) to discharge or otherwise discriminate against an employee because he has filed charges or given testimony under this Act;

(5) to refuse to bargain collectively with the representatives of his employees, subject to the provisions of section 9 (a).

(b) *It shall be an unfair labor practice for a labor organization or its agents—*

(*1*) *to restrain or coerce (A) employees in the exercise of the rights guaranteed in section 7: Provided, That this paragraph shall not impair the right of a labor organization to prescribe its own rules with respect to the acquisition or retention of membership therein; or (B) an employer in the selection of his representatives for the purposes of collective bargaining or the adjustment of grievances;*

(2) *to cause or attempt to cause an employer to discriminate against an employee in violation of subsection (a) (3) or to discriminate against an employee with respect to whom membership in such organization has been denied or terminated on some ground other than his failure to tender the periodic dues and the initiation fees uniformly required as a condition of acquiring or retaining membership;*

(3) *to refuse to bargain collectively with an employer, provided it is the representative of his employees subject to the provisions of section 9 (a);*

(4) (i) *to engage in, or to induce or encourage [the employees of any employer]* **any individual employed by any person engaged in commerce or in an industry affecting commerce** *to engage in, a strike or a [concerted] refusal in the course of [their]* **his** *employment to use, manufacture, process, transport, or otherwise handle or work on any goods, articles, materials,*

or commodities or to perform any services [,]; or (ii) **to threaten, coerce, or restrain any person engaged in commerce or in an industry affecting commerce,** *where* **in either case** *an object thereof is:*

(A) forcing or requiring any employer or self-employed person to join any labor or employer organization or [*any employer or other person to cease using, selling, handling, transporting, or otherwise dealing in the products of any other producer, processor, or manufacturer, or to cease doing business with any other person*] **to enter into any agreement which is prohibited by section 8 (e);**

(B) **forcing or requiring any person to cease using, selling, handling, transporting, or otherwise dealing in the products of any other producer, processor, or manufacturer, or to cease doing business with any other person, or** *forcing or requiring any other employer to recognize or bargain with a labor organization as the representative of his employees unless such labor organization has been certified as the representative of such employees under the provisions of section 9* [;]*:* **Provided, That nothing contained in this clause (B) shall be construed to make unlawful, where not otherwise unlawful, any primary strike or primary picketing;**

(C) forcing or requiring any employer to recognize or bargain with a particular labor organization as the representative of his employees if another labor organization has been certified as the representative of such employees under the provisions of section 9;

(D) forcing or requiring any employer to assign particular work to employees in a particular labor organization or in a particular trade, craft, or class rather than to employees in another labor organization or in another trade, craft, or class, unless such employer is failing to conform to an order or certification of the Board determining the bargaining representative for employees performing such work:

Provided, That nothing contained in this subsection (b) shall be construed to make unlawful a refusal by any person to enter *upon the premises of any employer (other than his own em-* *ployer), if the employees of such employer are engaged in a strike* *ratified or approved by a representative of such employees whom* *such employer is required to recognize under this Act*[;]: **Provided further,** That for the purposes of this paragraph (4) only, nothing contained in such paragraph shall be construed to prohibit publicity, other than picketing, for the purpose of truthfully advising the public, including consumers and members of a labor organization, that a product or products are produced by an employer with whom the labor organization has a primary dispute and are distributed by another employer, as long as such publicity does not have an effect of inducing any individual employed by any person other than the primary employer in the course of his employment to refuse to pick up, deliver, or transport any goods, or not to perform any services, at the establishment of the employer engaged in such distribution;

(5) *to require of employees covered by an agreement au-* *thorized under subsection (a) (3) the payment, as a condition* *precedent to becoming a member of such organization, of a fee* *in an amount which the Board finds excessive or discriminatory* *under all the circumstances. In making such a finding, the* *Board shall consider, among other relevant factors, the practices* *and customs of labor organizations in the particular industry,* *and the wages currently paid to the employees affected;* [and]

(6) *to cause or attempt to cause an employer to pay or deliver* *or agree to pay or deliver any money or other thing of value,* *in the nature of an exaction, for services which are not per-* *formed or not to be performed* [.]; **and**

(7) **to picket or cause to be picketed, or threaten to picket** **or cause to be picketed, any employer where an object thereof** **is forcing or requiring an employer to recognize or bargain** **with a labor organization as the representative of his employees,** **or forcing or requiring the employees of an employer to accept**

or select such labor organization as their collective bargaining representative, unless such labor organization is currently certified as the representative of such employees:

(A) where the employer has lawfully recognized in accordance with this Act any other labor organization and a question concerning representation may not appropriately be raised under section 9 (c) of this Act,

(B) where within the preceding twelve months a valid election under section 9 (c) of this Act has been conducted, or

(C) where such picketing has been conducted without a petition under section 9 (c) being filed within a reasonable period of time not to exceed thirty days from the commencement of such picketing: Provided, That when such a petition has been filed the Board shall forthwith, without regard to the provisions of section 9 (c) (1) or the absence of a showing of a substantial interest on the part of the labor organization, direct an election in such unit as the Board finds to be appropriate and shall certify the results thereof: Provided further, That nothing in this subparagraph (C) shall be construed to prohibit any picketing or other publicity for the purpose of truthfully advising the public (including consumers) that an employer does not employ members of, or have a contract with, a labor organization, unless an effect of such picketing is to induce any individual employed by any other person in the course of his employment, not to pick up, deliver or transport any goods or not to perform any services.

Nothing in this paragraph (7) shall be construed to permit any act which would otherwise be an unfair labor practice under this section 8 (b).

(c) *The expressing of any views, argument, or opinion, or the dissemination thereof, whether in written, printed, graphic, or visual form, shall not constitute or be evidence of an unfair labor practice under any of the provisions of this Act, if such expression contains no threat of reprisal or force or promise of benefit.*

(d) *For the purpose of this section, to bargain collectively is the performance of the mutual obligation of the employer and the representative of the employees to meet at reasonable times and confer in good faith with respect to wages, hours, and other terms and conditions of employment, or the negotiation of an agreement, or any question arising thereunder, and the execution of a written contract incorporating any agreement reached if requested by either party, but such obligation does not compel either party to agree to a proposal or require the making of a concession: Provided, That where there is in effect a collective-bargaining contract covering employees in an industry affecting commerce, the duty to bargain collectively shall also mean that no party to such contract shall terminate or modify such contract, unless the party desiring such termination or modification—*

(1) serves a written notice upon the other party to the contract of the proposed termination or modification sixty days prior to the expiration date thereof, or in the event such contract contains no expiration date, sixty days prior to the time it is proposed to make such termination or modification;

(2) offers to meet and confer with the other party for the purpose of negotiating a new contract or a contract containing the proposed modifications;

(3) notifies the Federal Mediation and Conciliation Service within thirty days after such notice of the existence of a dispute, and simultaneously therewith notifies any State or Territorial agency established to mediate and conciliate disputes within the State or Territory where the dispute occurred, provided no agreement has been reached by that time; and

(4) continues in full force and effect, without resorting to strike or lockout, all the terms and conditions of the existing contract for a period of sixty days after such notice is given or until the expiration date of such contract, whichever occurs later:

The duties imposed upon employers, employees, and labor organizations by paragraphs (2), (3), and (4) shall become inapplicable upon an intervening certification of the Board, under which the labor organization or individual, which is a party to the contract, has been superseded as or ceased to be the representative of the employees subject to the provisions of section 9 (a), and the duties so imposed shall not be construed as requiring either party to discuss or agree to any modification of the terms and conditions contained in a contract for a fixed period, if such modification is to become effective before such terms and conditions can be reopened under the provisions of the contract. Any employee who engages in a strike within the sixty-day period specified in this subsection shall lose his status as an employee of the employer engaged in the particular labor dispute, for the purpose of sections 8, 9, and 10 of this Act, as amended, but such loss of status for such employee shall terminate if and when he is reemployed by such employer.

(e) It shall be an unfair labor practice for any labor organization and any employer to enter into any contract or agreement, express or implied, whereby such employer ceases or refrains or agrees to cease or refrain from handling, using, selling, transporting or otherwise dealing in any of the products of any other employer, or to cease doing business with any other person, and any contract or agreement entered into heretofore or hereafter containing such an agreement shall be to such extent unenforcible and void: Provided, That nothing in this subsection (e) shall apply to an agreement between a labor organization and an employer in the construction industry relating to the contracting or subcontracting of work to be done at the site of the construction, alteration, painting, or repair of a building, structure, or other work: Provided further, That for the purposes of this subsection (e) and section 8 (b) (4) (B) the terms "any employer," "any person engaged in commerce or an industry affecting commerce," and "any person" when used in relation to the terms "any other producer, processor, or manufacturer," "any other employer," or "any other person" shall not include persons in the relation of a jobber, manufacturer, contractor, or subcontractor working on the goods or premises of the jobber or manufacturer or performing parts of an integrated process of production in the apparel and clothing industry: Provided further, That nothing in this Act shall prohibit the enforcement of any agreement which is within the foregoing exception.

(f) It shall not be an unfair labor practice under subsections (a) and (b) of this section for an employer engaged primarily in the building and construction industry to make an agreement covering employees engaged (or who, upon their employment, will be engaged) in the building and construction industry with a labor organization of which building and construction employees are members (not established, maintained, or assisted by any action defined in section 8 (a) of this Act as an unfair labor practice) because (1) the majority status of such labor organization has not been established under the provisions of section 9 of this Act prior to the making of such agreement, or (2) such agreement requires as a condition of employment, membership in such labor organization after the seventh day following the beginning of such employment or the effective date of the agreement, whichever is later, or (3) such agreement requires the employer to notify such labor organization of opportunities for employment with such employer, or gives such labor organization an opportunity to refer qualified applicants for such employment, or (4) such agreement specifies minimum training or experience qualifications for employment or provides for priority in opportunities for employment based upon length of service with such employer, in the industry or in the particular geographical area: Provided, That nothing in this subsection shall set aside the final proviso to section 8 (a) (3) of this Act: Provided further, That any agreement which would be invalid, but for clause (1) of this subsection, shall not be a bar to a petition filed pursuant to section 9 (c) or 9 (e).

SECTION 703 OF TITLE VII OF THE CIVIL RIGHTS ACT OF 1964, JULY 2, 1964, 78 STAT. 253, AS AMENDED BY THE EQUAL EMPLOYMENT OPPORTUNITY ACT OF 1972, MARCH 24, 1972, PUBLIC LAW 19–261, 86 STAT. 104

[Key to this appendix: Parts in plain roman type were originally in the Civil Rights Act of 1964; parts in italics were added by the Equal Employment Opportunity Act of 1972.]

Section 703. (*a*) It shall be an unlawful employment practice for an employer—

(1) to fail or refuse to hire or to discharge any individual, or otherwise to discriminate against any individual with respect to his compensation, terms, conditions, or privileges of employment, because of such individual's race, color, religion, sex, or national origin; or

(2) to limit, segregate, or classify his employees *or applicants for employment* in any way which would deprive or tend to deprive any individual of employment opportunities or otherwise adversely affect his status as an employee, because of such individual's race, color, religion, sex, or national origin.

(*b*) It shall be an unlawful employment practice for an employment agency to fail or refuse to refer for employment, or otherwise to discriminate against, any individual because of his race, color, religion, sex, or national origin, or to classify or refer for employment any individual on the basis of his race, color, religion, sex, or national origin.

(c) It shall be an unlawful employment practice for a labor organization—

(1) to exclude or to expel from its membership, or otherwise to discriminate against, any individual because of his race, color, religion, sex, or national origin;

(2) to limit, segregate, or classify its membership *or applicants for membership,* or to classify or fail or refuse to refer for employment any individual, in any way which would deprive or tend to deprive any individual of employment opportunities, or would limit such employment opportunities or otherwise adversely affect his status as an employee or as an applicant for employment, because of such individual's race, color, religion, sex, or national origin; or

(3) to cause or attempt to cause an employer to discriminate against an individual in violation of this section.

(d) It shall be an unlawful employment practice for any employer, labor organization, or joint labor-management committee controlling apprenticeship or other training or retraining, including on-the-job training programs to discriminate against any individual because of his race, color, religion, sex, or national origin in admission to, or employment in, any program established to provide apprenticeship or other training.

(e) Notwithstanding any other provision of this title, (1) it shall not be an unlawful employment practice for an employer to hire and employ employees, for an employment agency to classify, or refer for employment any individual, for a labor organization to classify its membership or to classify or refer for employment any individual, or for an employer, labor organization, or joint labor-management committee controlling apprenticeship or other training or retraining programs to admit or employ any individual in any such program, on the basis of his religion, sex, or national origin in those certain instances where religion, sex, or national origin is a bona fide occupational qualification reasonably necessary to the normal operation of that particular business or enterprise, and (2) it shall not be an unlawful employment practice for a school, college, university, or other educational institution or institution of learning to hire and employ employees of a particular religion if such school, college, university, or other educational institution or institution of learning is, in whole or in substantial part, owned, supported, controlled, or managed by a particular religion or by a particular religious corporation, association, or society, or if the curriculum of such school, college, university, or other educational institution or institution of learning is directed toward the propagation of a particular religion.

(f) As used in this title, the phrase "unlawful employment practice" shall not be deemed to include any action or measure taken by an employer, labor organization, joint labor-management committee, or employment agency with respect to an individual who is a member of the Communist Party of the United States or of any other organization required to register as a Communist-action or Communist-front organization by final order of the Subversive Activities Control Board pursuant to the Subversive Activities Control Act of 1950.

(g) Notwithstanding any other provision of this title, it shall not be an unlawful employment practice for an employer to fail or refuse to hire and employ any individual for any position, for an employer to discharge any individual from any position, or for an employment agency to fail or refuse to refer any individual for employment in any position, or for a labor organization to fail or refuse to refer any individual for employment in any position, if—

(1) the occupancy of such position, or access to the premises in or upon which any part of the duties of such

position is performed or is to be performed, is subject to any requirement imposed in the interest of the national security of the United States under any security program in effect pursuant to or administered under any statute of the United States or any Executive order of the President; and

(2) such individual has not fulfilled or has ceased to fulfill that requirement.

(*h*) Notwithstanding any other provision of this title, it shall not be an unlawful employment practice for an employer to apply different standards of compensation, or different terms, conditions, or privileges of employment pursuant to a bona fide seniority or merit system, or a system which measures earnings by quantity or quality of production or to employees who work in different locations, provided that such differences are not the result of an intention to discriminate because of race, color, religion, sex, or national origin, nor shall it be an unlawful employment practice for an employer to give and to act upon the results of any professionally developed ability test provided that such test, its administration or action upon the results is not designed, intended or used to discriminate because of race, color, religion, sex or national origin. It shall not be an unlawful employment practice under this title for any employer to differentiate upon the basis of sex in determining the amount of the wages or compensation paid or to be paid to employees of such employer if such differentiation is authorized by the provisions of section 6(d) of the Fair Labor Standards Act of 1938, as amended (29 U.S.C. 206(d)).

(*i*) Nothing contained in this title shall apply to any business or enterprise on or near an Indian reservation with respect to any publicly announced employment practice of such business or enterprise under which a preferential treatment is given to any individual because he is an Indian living on or near a reservation.

(*j*) Nothing contained in this title shall be interpreted to require any employer, employment agency, labor organization, or joint labor-management committee subject to this title to grant preferential treatment to any individual or to any group because of the race, color, religion, sex, or national origin of such individual or group on account of an imbalance which may exist with respect to the total number or percentage of persons of any race, color, religion, sex, or national origin employed by any employer, referred or classified for employment by any employment agency or labor organization, admitted to membership or classified by any labor organization, or admitted to, or employed in, any apprenticeship or other training program, in comparison with the total number or percentage of persons of such race, color, religion, sex, or national origin in any community, State, section, or other area, or in the available work force in any community, State, section, or other area.

TEXT OF PREGNANCY DISABILITY AMENDMENT, OCTOBER 31, 1978, PUBLIC LAW 95–555, 92 STAT. 2096.

Section 701 of the Civil Rights Act of 1964 is amended by adding at the end thereof the following new subsection:

(*k*) The terms "because of sex" or "on the basis of sex" include, but are not limited to, because of or on the basis of pregnancy, childbirth or related medical conditions; and women affected by pregnancy, childbirth, or related medical conditions shall be treated the same for all employment-related purposes, including receipt of benefits under fringe benefit programs, as other persons not so affected but similar in their ability or inability to work, and nothing in section 703(h) of this title shall be interpreted to permit otherwise. This subsection shall not require an employer to pay for health insurance benefits for abortion, except where the life of the mother would be endangered if the fetus were carried to term, or except where medical complications have arisen from an abortion: Provided, That nothing herein shall preclude an employer from providing abortion benefits or otherwise affect bargaining agreements in regard to abortion.

The text of each of the labor statutes can be obtained at a nominal cost from the Superintendent of Documents, U.S. Government Printing Office, Washington, D.C. 20402, or from any GPO bookstore located in the principal cities of the United States. West Publishing Co., St. Paul, Minn. 55102, publishes *Federal Labor Laws* in paperback containing the texts of the various federal labor laws. The reader, however, may find confusing the fact that *Federal Labor Laws* utilizes the United States Code ("U.S.C.") citation system which does not coincide with the sections as designated in the acts of Congress and as used in this book generally.

AUTHORITIES

CHAPTER I

page 22, line 23, et seq. The *Philadelphia Cordwainers'* case, *Commonwealth v. Pullis* (1806), as reported in Commons and Gilmore, *Documentary History of American Industrial Society,* volume 3, pages 59–236.

page 26, line 2. Quoted from *People v. Melvin,* 2 Wheeler Crim. Cas. 262 (Ct. Gen'l Sessions, N. Y. C., 1810).

page 26, line 5. *Commonwealth ex rel. Chew v. Carlisle,* Brightly, 36 Pa. N. P. (1821).

page 26, line 34. *People v. Fisher,* 14 Wend. 10 (Sup. Ct. N. Y., 1835).

page 28, line 3, et seq. *Commonwealth v. Hunt,* 4 Metcalf, 111 (Mass. 1842).

page 30, line 1. Landis and Manoff, *Cases on Labor Law* (1942), Historical Introduction, 35.

CHAPTER II

page 31, line 13. *Mogul Steamship Co. v. McGregor, Gow & Co.,* C. A. [1889] L. R. 23 Q. B. D. 598; H. L. [1892] A. C. 25.

page 35, line 9. *Allen v. Flood,* H. L. [1898] A. C. 1.

page 40, line 17. *Quinn v. Leathem,* H. L. [1901] A. C. 495.

page 45, line 36. *Leathem v. Craig,* Irish Reports, Queen's Bench Division [1899] 667, 701 et seq.

CHAPTER III

page 53, line 17. *Bowen v. Matheson,* 96 Mass. 499 (1867).

page 55, line 26. *Carew v. Rutherford,* 106 Mass. 1 (1870).

page 58, line 26. *Thorne v. Motor Trade Association,* H. L. [1937] A. C. 797.

page 58, line 33. *Rex v. Denyer* [1926], 2 K. B. 258.

page 60, line 5. *Vegelahn v. Guntner,* 167 Mass. 92 (1896).

page 62, line 21. *Plant v. Woods,* 176 Mass. 492 (1900).

page 68, line 15. *Berry v. Donovan,* 188 Mass. 353 (1905).

page 69, line 18. *Pickett v. Walsh,* 192 Mass. 572 (1906).

page 76, line 23. *Curran v. Galen,* 152 N. Y. 33 (1897).

page 77, line 5. *National Protective Assn. v. Cumming*, 170 N. Y. 315 (1902).

page 80, line 25. *Jacobs v. Cohen*, 183 N. Y. 207 (1905).

CHAPTER IV

page 89, line 6. For instances, see *Letts v. Kessler*, 54 Ohio St. 73 (1896) and *Burke v. Smith*, 69 Mich. 380 (1888).

page 89, line 30. *Huber v. Merkel*, 117 Wis. 355 (1903).

page 90, line 11. Cf., *Tuttle v. Buck*, 107 Minn. 145 (1909).

page 90, line 20. *Dunshee v. Standard Oil Co.*, 152 Iowa, 618 (1911).

page 93, line 27. *Lumley v. Gye*, 2 E. & B. 216 (1853).

page 96, line 34. This somewhat fictionally graphic account is based on a reference in Frankfurter and Greene, *The Labor Injunction* (1930), 23, and authorities cited.

page 98, line 29. In *Truax v. Corrigan*, 257 U. S. 312 (1921).

page 99, line 23. Frankfurter and Greene, *The Labor Injunction* (1930).

page 101, line 8. *Taliaferro v. United States*, 290 Fed. 906 (C. C. A. 4th, 1923).

page 104, line 10. Section 20 of the Clayton Act, cited and quoted in Appendix A, pages 647–48.

page 104, line 16. The Norris-LaGuardia Act is cited and, in part, quoted in Appendix B, pages 649–51.

CHAPTER V

page 108, line 9. In *Dorchy v. Kansas*, 272 U. S. 306 (1926).

page 110, line 20. See *DeMinico v. Craig*, 207 Mass. 593 (1911).

page 119, line 20. See *Plant v. Woods*, 176 Mass. 353 (1900), and *Berry v. Donovan*, 188 Mass. 572 (1906), both discussed in Chapter III.

page 121, line 11. See *Bossert v. Dhuy*, 221 N. Y. 342 (1917).

page 125, line 18. *Iron Molders' Union v. Allis-Chalmers Co.*, 166 Fed. 45 (C. C. A. 7th, 1908).

CHAPTER VI

page 132, line 15. *Macauley Bros. v. Tierney*, 19 R. I. 255 (1895).

page 133, line 14. *Bohn Mfg. Co. v. Hollis*, 54 Minn. 223 (1893).

page 133, line 17. *Thorne v. Motor Trade Association*, H. L. [1937] A. C. 797.

page 134, line 26. *Auburn Draying Co. v. Wardell*, 227 N. Y. 1 (1919).

page 136, line 18. *Seattle Malting & Brewing Co. v. Hansen*, 144 Fed. 1011 (U. S. C. C., Calif., 1905).

page 138, line 3. *Gompers v. Bucks Stove & Range Co.*, 221 U. S. 418 (1911).

page 141, line 30. E.g., *A. T. & S. F. Ry. v. Gee*, 139 Fed. 582 (U. S. C. C., Iowa, 1905).

page 141, line 32. See *Gevas v. Greek Restaurant Workers' Club*, 99 N. J. Eq. 770 (1926).

page 145, line 22. *Exchange Bakery & Restaurant v. Rifkin*, 245 N. Y. 260 (1927).

page 147, line 30. *Goldfinger v. Feintuch*, 276 N. Y. 281 (1937).

page 153, line 26. *McKay v. Retail Automobile Salesmen's Union*, 16 Calif. (2d) 311 (1940).

CHAPTER VII

page 158, line 2. *Stillwell Theatre, Inc. v. Kaplan*, 259 N. Y. 405 (1932).

page 159, line 25. Section 20 of the Clayton Act is cited and quoted in Appendix A, pages 647–48.

page 161, line 24. *Duplex Printing Press Co. v. Deering*, 252 Fed. 722 (C. C. A. 2d, 1918).

page 162, line 36. *Duplex Printing Press Co. v. Deering*, 254 U. S. 443 (1921).

page 172, line 14. *American Steel Foundries v. Tri-City Central Trades Council*, 257 U. S. 184 (1921).

page 172, line 25. *Truax v. Corrigan*, 257 U. S. 312 (1921).

page 174, line 25. *Lumley v. Gye*, 2 E. & B. 216 (1853).

page 175, line 16. In *Adair v. United States,* 208 U. S. 161 (1908) and in *Coppage v. Kansas*, 236 U. S. 1 (1915).

page 175, line 28. In *Coppage v. Kansas*, 236 U. S. 1 (1915).

page 179, line 18. *Hitchman Coal Co. v. Mitchell*, 245 U. S. 229 (1917).

page 180, line 2. *Interborough Rapid Transit Co. v. Lavin*, 247 N. Y. 65 (1928), as to which see *Interborough Rapid Transit Co. v. Green*, 227 N. Y. Supp. 258, 264 (N. Y. Sup. Ct., 1928).

page 180, line 35. For a reference to sources on this incident, see Frankfurter and Greene, "Congressional Power over the Labor Injunction," 31 *Columbia Law Review*, 385, 387 (1931).

page 181, line 15. *R An W Hat Shop, Inc. v. Sculley*, 98 Conn. 1 (1922).

page 198, line 24. *Senn v. Tile Layers' Protective Union*, 301 U. S. 468 (1937).

page 199, line 6. *New Negro Alliance v. Sanitary Grocery Co.*, 303 U. S. 552, 304 U. S. 542 (1938).

CHAPTER VIII

page 201, line 1. 26 United States Statutes at Large, 209 (1890).

page 206, line 29. *Loewe v. Lawlor*, 208 U. S. 274 (1908), commonly known as the *Danbury Hatters'* case.

page 210, line 12. *Duplex Printing Press Co. v. Deering*, 254 U. S. 443 (1921).

page 211, line 6. *United Mine Workers of America v. Coronado Coal Co.*, 259 U. S. 344 (1922).

page 216, line 27. *Coronado Coal Co. v. United Mine Workers of America*, 268 U. S. 295 (1925).

page 219, line 23. *Bedford Cut Stone Co. v. Journeymen Stone Cutters' Association*, 274 U. S. 37 (1927).

page 221, line 13. *United States v. Brims*, 272 U. S. 549 (1926).

CHAPTER IX

page 238, line 20. *Republic Steel Corp. v. NLRB*, 311 U. S. 7 (1940).

page 238, line 29. *NLRB v. Fansteel Metallurgical Corp.*, 306 U. S. 270 (1939).

page 239, line 29. *Phelps Dodge Corp. v. NLRB*, 313 U. S. 177 (1941).

page 239, line 35. *H. J. Heinz Co. v. NLRB*, 311 U. S. 514 (1941).

page 246, line 7. See *AF of L v. NLRB*, 308 U. S. 401 (1940).

CHAPTER X

page 254, line 26. *Morehead v. New York, ex rel. Tipaldo*, 298 U. S. 587 (1936).

page 255, line 3. *West Coast Hotel Co. v. Parrish*, 300 U. S. 379 (1937).

page 255, line 4. *Adkins v. Childrens' Hospital*, 261 U. S. 525 (1923).

page 255, line 5. *NLRB v. Jones & Laughlin Steel Corp.*, 301 U. S. 1 (1937).

page 255, line 30. *Apex Hosiery Co. v. Leader*, 90 Fed. (2d) 155 (C. C. A. 3d, 1937).

page 256, line 2. *Leader v. Apex Hosiery Co.*, 108 Fed. (2d) 71 (C. C. A. 3d, 1939).

page 256, line 8. *Apex Hosiery Co. v. Leader*, 310 U. S. 469 (1940).

page 262, line 2. *Eastern States Retail Lumber Dealers' Association v. United States*, 234 U. S. 600 (1914).

page 269, line 39. *United States v. Hutcheson*, 32 F. Supp. 600 (D. C. Mo., 1940).

page 269, line 33. *United States v. Hutcheson*, 312 U. S. 219 (1941).

page 274, line 28. Wisconsin Laws of 1931, Chapter 376.

page 279, line 14. *Allen Bradley Co. v. Local Union No. 3, IBEW*, 325 U. S. 797 (1945).

page 280, line 18. *Allen Bradley Co. v. Local Union No. 3, IBEW*, 145 F. (2d) 215 (C. C. A. 2d, 1944).

page 284, line 29. *United States v. American Federation of Musicians*, 318 U. S. 741 (1943), affirming 47 F. Supp. 304 (D. C. Ill., 1942).

page 285, line 7. *United States v. International Hod Carriers' etc., Council,* 313 U. S. 539 (1941), affirming *United States v. Carrozzo,* 37 F. Supp. 191 (D. C. Ill., 1941).

page 285, lines 27 and 28. *United States v. Building & Construction Trades Council,* 313 U. S. 539 (1941) and *United States v. United Brotherhood of Carpenters & Joiners,* 313 U. S. 539 (1941), both affirming lower court decisions.

page 285, line 36. *Hunt v. Crumboch,* 325 U. S. 821 (1945).

page 287, line 8. *Milk Wagon Drivers' Union v. Lake Valley Farm Products, Inc.,* 311 U. S. 91 (1940).

CHAPTER XI

page 292, line 12. *Pierce v. Stablemen's Union,* 156 Calif. 70 (1909).

page 293, line 14. *American Steel Foundries v. Tri-City Central Trades Council,* 257 U. S. 184 (1921).

page 293, line 23. *Senn v. Tile Layers' Union,* 301 U. S. 468 (1937).

page 296, line 4. *Local Union 309 v. Hanke* and *Local Union 882 v. Cline,* 339 U. S. 470 (1950).

page 296, line 26. *Thornhill v. Alabama,* 310 U. S. 88 (1940).

page 300, line 10. *Gompers v. Bucks S. & R. Co.,* 221 U. S. 418 (1911).

page 300, line 13. *American Steel Foundries v. Tri-City Central Trades Council,* 257 U. S. 184 (1921).

page 300, line 16. *Senn v. Tile Layers' Union,* 301 U. S. 468 (1937).

page 305, line 25. *AF of L v. Swing,* 312 U. S. 321 (1941).

page 306, line 11. *Milk Wagon Drivers' Union v. Meadowmoor Dairies, Inc.,* 312 U. S. 287 (1941).

page 307, line 14. *Bakery & Pastry Drivers' Union v. Wohl,* 315 U. S. 769 (1942).

page 309, line 15. *Carpenters' & Joiners' Union v. Ritter's Cafe,* 315 U. S. 722 (1942).

page 315, line 35. *United States v. Hutcheson,* 312 U. S. 219 (1941).

page 317, line 10. Mozart G. Ratner and Norton J. Come, "The Norris-LaGuardia Act in the Constitution," 11 *George Washington Law Review,* 428 (1943).

page 317, line 33. *Cafeteria Employees' Union v. Angelos,* 320 U. S. 293 (1943).

page 319, line 29. *In re Blaney,* 30 Calif. 2d 643 (1947).

page 320, line 27. *Hotel & Restaurant Employees' Union v. WERB,* 315 U. S. 437 (1942), and *Allen-Bradley Local No. 1111 v. WERB,* 315 U. S. 740 (1942).

page 321, line 2. *Giboney v. Empire S. & I. Co.,* 336 U. S. 490 (1949).

page 322, line 30. *Building Service Employees' Union v. Gazzam*, 339 U. S. 532 (1950).

page 324, line 19. *Hughes v. Superior Court*, 339 U. S. 460 (1950).

page 325, lines 24 and 25. *International Brotherhood of Teamsters v. Hanke, and Automobile Drivers* and *Demonstrators Union v. Cline*, 339 U. S. 470 (1950).

page 326, line 32. *Bautista v. Jones*, 25 Calif. 2d 746 (1944).

page 327, line 16. *Plumbers' Union v. Graham*, 345 U. S. 192 (1953).

page 328, line 6. *Teamsters' Union v. Vogt, Inc.*, 354 U. S. 284 (1957). Perhaps the leading exponent of an interpretation of the *Thornhill* doctrine contrary to that set forth in the text of this book is Professor Edgar A. Jones, Jr. See his four vigorous and closely reasoned articles, in the first three of which he attacks the position maintained by the present author. These articles are: "Picketing and Coercion: A Jurisprudence of Epithets," 39 *Virginia Law Review*, 1023 and 1063 (1953); "The Right to Picket—Twilight Zone of the Constitution," 102 *University of Pennsylvania Law Review*, 995 (1954); "Picketing and the Communication of Ideas," 2 *U. C. L. A. Law Review*, 212 (1955); *"The Loder Letter—Have Union Picketers Finally Found the Formula?"* 4 *U. C. L. A. Law Review*, 370 (1957). For other support of the *Thornhill* doctrine, see E. Merrick Dodd, "Picketing and Free Speech: A Dissent," 56 *Harvard Law Review*, 513 (1943); and Francis E. Jones, Jr., "Free Speech: Pickets on the Grass, Alas! Amidst Confusion, A Consistent Principle," 29 *Southern California Law Review*, 137 (1956).

page 330, line 36. *Steele v. L & N. R. Co.*, 323 U. S. 192 (1944). And see the vigorous reaffirmance of this by the Supreme Court in *Conley v. Gibson* on November 18, 1957, 26 *U. S. Law Week*, 4013.

page 331, line 31. *Wallace Corp. v. NLRB*, 323 U. S. 248 (1944).

page 332, line 19. *James v. Marinship Corp.*, 25 Calif. 2d 721 (1944).

page 333, line 14. *Williams v. Brotherhood*, 27 Calif. 2d 586 (1946).

page 333, line 34. *Railway Mail Ass'n v. Corsi*, 326 U. S. 88 (1945).

page 334, line 18. *Betts v. Easley*, 161 Kan. 459 (1946).

page 337, line 4. *Terry v. Adams*, 345 U. S. 461 (1953).

page 337, line 7. *Rice v. Elmore*, 165 F. 2d 387 (C. C. A. 4, 1947); cert. denied 333 U. S. 875 (1948).

page 338, line 3. *Ross v. Ebert*, 275 Wis. 523 (1957). For the latest decision squarely dealing with this point at the time of this writing, see *Oliphant v. Brotherhood*, 40 LRRM 2696 (D. C. Ohio, September 27, 1957). There the court refused to recognize the right of Negro employees in the bargaining unit to be granted membership in the brotherhood representing them.

CHAPTER XII

page 344, line 11. *NLRB v. Jones & Laughlin Steel Corp.*, 301 U. S. 1 (1937).

page 345, line 30. *LaCrosse Telephone Corp. v. WERB*, 336 U. S. 18 (1949).

page 346, line 21. *Guss v. Utah LRB*, 353 U. S. 1 (1957).

page 346, line 26. *Office Employees Union v. NLRB*, 353 U. S. 313 (1957).

page 347, line 27. *Packard Motor Co. v. NLRB*, 330 U. S. 485 (1947).

page 348, line 2. *Bethlehem Steel Corp. v. NYSLRB*, 330 U. S. 767 (1947).

page 348, line 9. *NLRB v. Hearst Publications*, 322 U. S. 111 (1944).

page 351, line 7. *Consolidated Edison Co. v. NLRB*, 305 U. S. 197 (1938).

page 352, line 21. *International Association of Machinists v. NLRB*, 311 U. S. 72 (1940).

page 353, line 4. *Republic Aviation Corp. v. NLRB*, 324 U. S. 793 (1945).

page 353, line 25. *NLRB v. Babcock & Wilcox Co.*, 351 U. S. 105 (1956).

page 354, line 8. *NLRB v. Stowe Spinning Co.*, 336 U. S. 226 (1949).

page 356, line 15. *NLRB v. Virginia E. & P. Co.*, 314 U. S. 469 (1941).

page 357, line 28. *NLRB v. Clark Bros. Co.*, 163 F. 2d 373 (CCA 2, 1947).

page 359, line 9. *In re Lux Clock Mfg. Co.*, 113 NLRB 1194 (1955).

page 359, line 28. *Bonwit Teller, Inc. v. NLRB*, 197 F. 2d 640 (CCA 2, 1952).

page 359, line 29. *NLRB v. F. W. Woolworth Co.*, 214 F. 2d 78 (CCA 8, 1954).

page 359, line 36. *In re Peerless Plywood Co.*, 107 NLRB 427 (1953).

page 360, line 12. *NLRB v. Shirlington Supermarket, Inc.*, 224 F. 2d 649 (CCA 4, 1955).

page 360, line 31. But see *Alloy Mfg. Co.*, 119 NLRB No. 38 (Nov. 1957); *Curtis Bros., Inc.*, 119 NLRB No. 33 (Oct. 1957).

page 361, line 24. *NLRB v. Truck Drivers Local 449*, 353 U. S. 87 (1957), commonly called the *Buffalo Linen Supply Co.* case.

page 365, line 14. *Phelps Dodge Corp. v. NLRB*, 308 U. S. 401 (1940).

page 369, line 29. *NLRB v. Star Publishing Co.*, 97 F. 2d 465 (CCA 9, 1938).

page 371, line 3. *NLRB v. Mackay R. & T. Co.*, 304 U. S. 333 (1938).

page 372, line 32. *NLRB v. Fansteel Metallurgical Corp.*, 306 U. S. 270 (1939).

page 375, line 34. *NLRB v. Sands Mfg. Co.*, 306 U. S. 332 (1939).

page 376, line 12. *Southern S.S. Co. v. NLRB*, 316 U. S. 31 (1942).

page 376, line 13. *C. G. Conn, Ltd. v. NLRB*, 108 F. 2d 390 (CCA 7, 1939).

page 377, line 6. *In re American News Co.*, 55 NLRB 1302 (1944).

page 377, line 17. *In re Thompson Products, Inc.*, 70 NLRB 13 (1946) and 72 NLRB 886 (1947).

page 377, line 27. *In re Scullin Steel Co.*, 65 NLRB 1294 (1946).

page 378, line 3. *Mastro Plastics Corp. v. NLRB*, 350 U. S. 270 (1956).

page 378, line 12. *NLRB v. Atlantic Towing Co.*, 179 F. 2d 497 (CCA 5, 1950) and 180 F. 2d 727 (CCA 5, 1950).

page 379, line 5. *In re Bettcher Mfg. Corp.*, 76 NLRB 526 (1948).

page 379, line 21. *NLRB v. Peter Cailler Kohler S. C. Co.*, 130 F. 2d 503 (CCA 2, 1942).

page 379, line 37. *Hoover Co. v. NLRB*, 191 F. 2d 380 (CCA 6, 1951).

page 380, line 21. *Local 1229, IBEW (Electrical Workers) v. NLRB*, 202 F. 2d 186 (DCCA, 1952).

page 381, line 8. *NLRB v. Local 1229, IBEW*, 346 U. S. 464 (1953).

page 384, line 2. *International Union, UAW, AFL v. WERB*, 336 U. S. 245 (1949).

CHAPTER XIII

page 387, line 25. *NLRB v. Electric Vacuum Cleaner Co.*, 315 U. S. 685 (1942).

page 389, line 9. *Consolidated Edison Co. v. NLRB*, 305 U. S. 197 (1938).

page 390, line 16. *Wallace Corp. v. NLRB*, 323 U. S. 248 (1944).

page 391, line 13. *In re Rutland Court Owners, Inc.*, 44 NLRB 587 (1942) and 46 NLRB 1040 (1943).

page 391, line 35. *Colgate-Palmolive-Peet Co. v. NLRB*, 338 U. S. 355 (1949).

page 392, line 24. *Algoma Plywood & V. Co. v. WERB*, 336 U. S. 301 (1949).

page 394, line 26. *Lincoln Fed. Labor Union v. N. I. & M. Co.*, 335 U. S. 525 (1949).

page 395, line 9. *Finney v. Hawkins*, 189 Va. 878 (1949).

page 396, line 19. *In re Union Starch & Refining Co.*, 87 NLRB 779 (1949).

page 400, line 8. *Railway Employees Dep't v. Hanson*, 351 U. S. 225 (1956).

page 402, line 17. *NLRB v. Montgomery Ward & Co.*, 133 F. 2d 676 (CCA 9, 1943).

page 402, line 27. *Franks Bros. Co. v. NLRB*, 321 U.S. 702 (1944).

page 404, line 20. *Medo Photo S. Co. v. NLRB*, 321 U. S. 678 (1944).

page 405, line 25. *NLRB v. Century Oxford Mfg. Co.*, 140 F. 2d 244 (CCA 2, 1944).

page 405, line 35. *NLRB v. Appalachian E. P. Co.*, 140 F. 2d 215 (CCA 4, 1944).

page 406, line 3. *Brooks v. NLRB*, 348 U. S. 96 (1954).

page 406, line 16. *J. I. Case Co. v. NLRB*, 321 U. S. 332 (1944).

page 407, line 11. *Order of R. R. Telegraphers v. Railway Express Agency,* 321 U. S. 342 (1944).

page 408, line 12. *In re Hughes Tool Co.,* 56 NLRB 981 (1944).

page 409, line 1. *E. J. & E. Ry. v. Burley,* 325 U. S. 711 (1945).

page 409, line 30. *Douds v. Local 1250,* 173 F. 2d 764 (CCA 2, 1949).

page 410, line 1. *NLRB v. Truitt Mfg. Co.,* 351 U. S. 149 (1956).

page 413, line 27. *NLRB v. American National Ins. Co.,* 343 U. S. 395 (1952).

page 415, line 7. *In re Times Publishing Co.,* 72 NLRB 676 (1947).

page 416, line 2. *NLRB v. Sands Mfg. Co.,* 306 U. S. 332 (1939).

page 416, line 5. See, *W. L. Mead, Inc.,* 113 NLRB 1040 (1956).

page 416, line 9. *United Mine Workers Union,* 117 NLRB No. 154 (1957).

page 416, line 14. *In re Textile Workers of America,* and *Personal Products Corp.,* 108 NLRB 743 (1954).

page 416, line 19. *Textile Workers v. NLRB,* 227 F. 2d 409 (DCCA 1955).

page 416, line 25. *Mastro Plastics Corp. v. NLRB,* 350 U. S. 270 (1956).

page 419, line 26. *In re Pure Oil Co.,* 84 NLRB 315 (1949).

page 420, line 19. *Milk Drivers' Union v. NLRB,* 245 F. 2d 817 (CCA 2, 1957); *General Drivers' Union v. NLRB,* 247 F. 2d 71 (DCCA, 1957). But see *NLRB v. Local 1976, Carpenters' Union,* 241 F. 2d 147 (CCA 9, 1957). On October 14, 1957, the Supreme Court agreed to hear and pass on the two latter decisions.

page 420, line 21. *Douds v. Metropolitan Federation & Architects,* 75 F. Supp. 672 (D.C. 1948).

page 421, line 15. *NLRB v. Business Machine, etc. Board, IAM,* 228 F. 2d 553 (CCA 2, 1955); cert. denied, 351 U. S. 962 (1956).

page 422, line 15. *NLRB v. Denver Building & C. T. C.,* 341 U. S. 675 (1951).

page 423, line 14. *IBEW, Local 501 v. NLRB,* 341 U. S. 694 (1951).

page 424, line 23. *NLRB v. International Rice Milling Co.,* 341 U. S. 665 (1951).

page 428, line 34. *NLRB v. Rockaway News Supply Co.,* 345 U. S. 71 (1953).

page 430, line 29. *United States v. Local 807,* 315 U. S. 521 (1942).

page 431, line 12. *United States v. Petrillo,* 332 U. S. 1 (1947).

page 431, line 22. *American Newspaper Publishers Association v. NLRB,* 345 U. S. 100 (1953).

page 432, line 4. *NLRB v. Gamble Enterprises, Inc.,* 345 U. S. 117 (1953).

page 433, line 21. *NLRB v. Norfolk S. B. Co.,* 159 F. 2d 516 (CCA 4, 1946); cert. denied, 330 U. S. 844 (1947).

page 437, line 21. *NLRB v. A. J. Tower Co.,* 329 U. S. 324 (1947).

CHAPTER XIV

page 439, line 7. The courts have generally sustained the board's broad assertions of jurisdiction. A rare case to the contrary was the recent decision of the United States Supreme Court in *NLRB v. Catholic Bishop of Chicago*, 99 S.Ct. 1313 (1979). In that case, the Supreme Court set aside a board order that would have required the Catholic bishop of Chicago to bargain with a union for the lay teachers in parochial schools. This result enabled the Court to avoid "serious First Amendment questions" that might otherwise have arisen from governmental interference with a religious establishment.

page 440, line 16. In the fiscal year ending September 30, 1978, the number of filings with the board increased over the prior fiscal year by 4.7 per cent to a total of 53,300 cases—a new record. This resulted from a significant increase in unfair labor practice cases, offset somewhat by a decline in representation cases. Over 90 per cent of the 39,600 unfair labor practice cases filed with the board were disposed of in a median of 41 days without the necessity of formal litigation before the board. "Summary of Operations of NLRB Office of General Counsel in FY [Fiscal Year] 1978," Bureau of National Affairs (BNA), *Daily Labor Report*, February 6, 1979.

page 440, line 29. *Spielberg Manufacturing Company*, 112 NLRB 1080 (1955).

page 441, line 9. *Collyer Insulated Wire Company*, 192 NLRB 837 (1971).

page 441, line 29. *General American Transportation Corp.*, 228 NLRB 808 (1977).

page 441, line 32. *Dubo Manufacturing Co.*, 142 NLRB 431 (1963).

page 442, line 15. *William E. Arnold Co. v. Carpenters Dist. Council*, 417 U.S. 12 (1974).

page 442, line 21. *NLRB v. J. Weingarten, Inc.*, 416 U.S. 969 (1975).

page 444, line 16. *Amax, Inc.*, 227 NLRB 1189 (1977).

page 444, line 25. *Excelsior Underwear*, 156 NLRB 1236 (1966).

page 444, line 35. *NLRB v. Wyman-Gordon Co.*, 394 U.S. 759 (1969).

page 445, line 20. *Ideal Electric*, 134 NLRB 1275 (1961).

page 445, line 25. *NLRB v. Exchange Parts Co.*, 375 U.S. 405 (1964).

page 445, line 29. *Hollywood Ceramics*, 140 NLRB 221 (1962).

page 446, line 1. *Shopping Kart Food Market*, 228 NLRB 1311 (1977).

page 446, line 14. The intellectual underpinning of the shift to *Shopping Kart* was found in original research published by Julius G. Getman, Stephen B. Goldberg, and Jeanne B. Herman, *Union Representation Elections: Law and Reality* (New York: Russell Sage Foundation, 1976).

page 446, line 34. *Thomas E. Gates & Sons,* 229 NLRB 705 (1977).

page 447, line 4. *General Knit of California,* 239 NLRB No. 101 (1978).

page 447, line 13. *Wall Street Journal,* January 4, 1979.

page 447, line 18. *NLRB v. Iron Workers Local 103,* 97 LRRM 2333 (1978).

page 447, line 27. *NLRB v. Savair Manufacturing Co.,* 414 U.S. 270 (1973).

page 448, line 8. *NLRB v. Gissel Packing Co.,* 395 U.S. 575 (1969).

page 448, line 14. *Handy Andy, Inc.,* 228 NLRB 447 (1977).

page 449, line 8. *NLRB v. Babcock & Wilcox,* 351 U.S. 105 (1956).

page 449, line 16. *NLRB v. Magnavox Co.,* 415 U.S. 322 (1974).

page 449, line 25. *Marsh v. Alabama,* 326 U.S. 501 (1946).

page 449, line 35. *Amalgamated Food Employees v. Logan Valley,* 391 U.S. 308 (1968).

page 450, line 15. *Hudgens v. NLRB,* 424 U.S. 507 (1976).

page 452, line 25. *Beth Israel Hospital v. NLRB,* 98 S.Ct. 2463 (1978).

page 453, line 4. *NLRB v. Erie Resistor Corp.,* 373 U.S. 221 (1963).

page 454, line 20. *NLRB v. Great Dane Trailers, Inc.,* 388 U.S. 26 (1967).

page 454, line 25. In *Abilities & Goodwill, Inc.,* 241 NLRB No. 5 (1979), the board, overruling its 30-year-old policy of requiring discharged strikers to request reinstatement to trigger the employer's backpay liability, held that unlawfully discharged strikers are entitled to backpay from the date of their discharges, like all other employees who have been discriminated against.

page 454, line 26. *NLRB v. Insurance Agents' International Union,* 361 U.S. 477 (1960).

page 455, line 2. *American Ship Building Co. v. NLRB,* 380 U.S. 300 (1965).

page 455, line 5. *NLRB v. Brown,* 380 U.S. 278 (1965).

page 455, line 34. *Textile Workers Union of America v. Darlington Manufacturing Company,* 380 U.S. 263 (1965).

page 458, line 15. *Bruce Duncan Co.,* 233 NLRB No. 176 (1977).

page 459, line 5. *NLRB v. Wooster Div. of Borg-Warner Corp.,* 356 U.S. 342 (1958).

page 460, line 18. *Fibreboard Paper Products Co. v. NLRB,* 279 U.S. 203 (1964). An excellent discussion of *Fibreboard* and *Darlington* can be found in Clyde Summers, "Labor Law in the Supreme Court: 1964 Term," 75 *Yale Law Journal* 59 (1965).

page 462, line 14. *Allied Chemical Corp.,* 151 NLRB 718 (1965).

page 463, line 4. *Ford Motor Co. v. NLRB,* 44 *U.S. Law Week* 4498 (U.S. Sup. Ct., May 14, 1979).

page 463, line 11. *Emporium Capwell Co. v. Western Addition Community Organization,* 420 U.S. 50 (1975).

page 464, line 14. *NLRB v. Katz,* 369 U.S. 736 (1962).

page 464, line 25. *NLRB v. Acme Industrial Co.*, 385 U.S. 432 (1967).

page 465, line 1. *Oakland Press Co.*, 229 NLRB 476 (1977).

page 465, line 4. *Detroit Edison Co. v. NLRB,* 100 LRRM 2728 (1979).

page 466, line 17. *Scofield v. NLRB*, 394 U.S. 423 (1969).

page 466, line 19. *NLRB v. Allis-Chalmers Manufacturing Co.*, 388 U.S. 175 (1967).

page 466, line 21. *Florida Power & Light Co. v. IBEW*, 417 U.S. 790 (1974).

page 466, line 23. *NLRB v. Boeing Co.*, 412 U.S. 67 (1973).

page 466, line 33. *NLRB v. Industrial Union of Marine and Shipbuilding Workers of America*, 391 U.S. 413 (1968).

page 466, line 36. *Radio Officers Union v. NLRB*, 347 U.S. 17 (1954).

page 467, line 14. *Dairylea Cooperative*, 219 NLRB 656 (1975).

page 467, line 21. *Allied Supermarkets*, 223 NLRB 1233 (1977).

page 467, line 23. *Otis Elevator*, 231 NLRB 1128 (1977).

page 467, line 30. *IAM Local 697 [Canfield Rubber]*, 223 NLRB 832 (1976).

page 468, line 5. *NLRB v. ILGWU*, 366 U.S. 731 (1961).

page 468, line 22. *NLRB v. Servette, Inc.*, 377 U.S. 46 (1964).

page 468, line 31. *NLRB v. Fruit and Vegetable Packers, Local 760 [Tree Fruits]*, 377 U.S. 58 (1964).

page 471, line 1. *UMW v. Pennington*, 381 U.S. 657 (1965).

page 472, line 13. *Amalgamated Meat Cutters Local Union No. 189 v. Jewel Tea Co.*, 381 U.S. 676 (1965).

page 473, line 7. *Connell Construction Co. v. Plumbers Local 100*, 421 U.S. 616 (1975).

page 474, line 10. The board has held it to be a mandatory subject of bargaining for an employer to insist upon "a most favored nation clause" under which the union agrees to accord to the employer terms as favorable as those it accords to any other party. *Dolly Madison Industries, Inc.*, 187 NLRB 1037 (1970). Professor St. Antoine comments: "The NLRB distinguished *Pennington* on the ground that the clause sought by the employer in the case before the Board did not obligate the union to impose the same standards on the employer's competitors. . . . I should hope that the presence of a predatory purpose would be recognized as the critical factor, rather than the phraseology of the clause itself." Theodore J. St. Antoine, "*Connell*: Antitrust Law at the Expense of Labor Law," 62 *University of Virginia Law Review* 603, at 611 (1976).

page 474, line 22. *Amalgamated Ass'n of Motor Coach Employees v. Lockridge*, 403 U.S. 274 (1971).

page 474, line 32. *San Diego Building Trade Council v. Garmon*, 359 U.S. 236 (1959).

CHAPTER XV

page 477, line 33. *Young v. Canadian N. Ry. Co.,* 1931 A.C. 83.

page 479, line 26. The basic article in the field is Rice, "Collective Labor Agreements in American Law," 44 *Harvard Law Review* 572 (1931).

page 483, line 33. Witmer, "Collective Labor Agreements in the Courts," 48 *Yale Law Journal* 195 (1938).

page 485, line 29. *Association of Westinghouse Salaried Employees v. Westinghouse Electric Corporation,* 348 U.S. 437 (1955).

page 487, line 34. *Textile Workers Union of America v. Lincoln Mills of Alabama,* 353 U.S. 448 (1957).

page 489, line 18. *United Steelworkers of America v. Warrior and Gulf Navigation Company,* 363 U.S. 574 (1960); *United Steelworkers of America v. American Manufacturing Company,* 363 U.S. 564 (1960); *United Steelworkers of America v. Enterprise Wheel and Car Corp.,* 363 U.S. 593 (1960).

page 492, line 13. Paul R. Hays, *Labor Arbitration: A Dissenting View* (New Haven: Yale University Press, 1966).

page 492, line 29. Benjamin Aaron, 42 *Washington Law Review* 976 (1967); Bernard D. Meltzer, 34 *University of Chicago Law Review* 211 (1966); Julius G. Getman, 44 *Indiana Law Journal* 182 (1969).

page 493, line 1. Theodore J. St. Antoine, "Judicial Review of Labor Arbitration Awards: A Second Look at *Enterprise Wheel* and Its Progeny," 75 *Michigan Law Review* 1137, at 1153 (1977).

page 493, line 19. *Safeway Stores v. American Bakery and Con. W.I.U., Local 111,* 390 F.2d 79, at 84 (5th Cir. 1968).

page 493, line 23. See the article by Peter Adomeit, "*Hines v. Anchor Motor Freight:* Another Step in the Seemingly Inexorable March Toward Converting Federal Judges (and Juries) into Labor Arbitrators of Last Resort," 9 *Connecticut Law Review* 627 (1977).

page 494, line 5. *Smith v. Evening News,* 371 U.S. 195 (1962).

page 494, line 8. *Republic Steel Corp. v. Maddox,* 379 U.S. 650 (1965).

page 494, line 14. *Teamsters Union v. Lucas Flour Co.,* 369 U.S. 95 (1962).

page 494, line 23. *Retail Clerks Int'l Ass'n v. Lion Dry Goods,* 369 U.S. 17 (1962).

page 494, line 25. *Charles Dowd Box Co. v. Courtney,* 368 U.S. 502 (1962).

page 498, line 20. *Sinclair Refining Co. v. Atkinson,* 370 U.S. 195 (1962).

page 499, line 3. *Boys Markets, Inc. v. Retail Clerks Union,* 398 U.S. 235 (1970).

page 500, line 20. *Packinghouse Workers, Local Union No. 721 v. Needham Packing Co.,* 376 U.S. 247 (1964).

page 500, line 26. *Buffalo Forge Co. v. United Steelworkers*, 428 U.S. 397 (1976).

page 503, line 3. *John Wiley & Sons, Inc. v. Livingston*, 376 U.S. 543 (1964).

page 503, line 37. *Howard Johnson Company v. Detroit Local Joint Executive Board*, 417 U.S. 249 (1974).

page 504, line 24. *Burns International Security Services, Inc. v. NLRB*, 406 U.S. 272 (1972).

page 504, line 28. *Golden State Bottling Company v. NLRB*, 414 U.S. 168 (1973).

page 504, line 32. *Nolde Brothers v. Local 358, Bakery & Confectionery Workers Union, AFL-CIO*, 430 U.S. 243 (1977).

page 507, line 6. *Amalgamated Association v. WERB*, 340 U.S. 383 (1951).

page 519, line 3. *In re Ford Motor Co. & UAW*, Opinion A-117, "The Case of the Lady in Red Slacks" (1944).

page 521, line 21. Archibald Cox, "Rights under a Labor Agreement," 69 *Harvard Law Review* 601 (1956).

page 524, line 12. *Teamsters Union Local 174 v. Lucas Flour Co.*, 369 U.S. 95, at 108 (1962). This "reliance upon the arbitral process as a substitute for economic warfare" is part of a national labor policy which "contemplates that areas of common dispute between employers and employees be funneled into collective bargaining. The assumption is that this is preferable to allowing recurring disputes to fester outside the negotiation process until strikes or other forms of economic warfare occur." *Ford Motor Co. v. NLRB*, 47 *U.S. Law Week* 4498 (U.S. Sup. Ct. May 14, 1979).

CHAPTER XVI

page 526, line 12. *Miranda Fuel Co. v. NLRB*, 140 NLRB 181 (1962).

page 526, line 34. Report of 1979 Proceedings, Labor Relations Law Section, American Bar Association, page 105. An official of the American Arbitration Association (AAA) estimated in 1973 that the total annual number of labor arbitrations in the United States was "considerably higher" than 20,000. *Monthly Labor Review*, October 1976, p. 27. In the five year period between 1971 and 1976, the number of labor arbitrations conducted under the auspices of the American Arbitration Association more than doubled. 1977–1978 Annual Report, American Arbitration Association (AAA), p. 13.

page 527, line 26. In *Service Employees, Local 579 [Beverly Manor Convalescent Center]*, 229 NLRB 692 (1977), the board pointed out that "application of the strict standard of allegiance owed by an attorney to a client might well preclude representation by a union of more than one member because of the potential conflicts of interest." It rejected "any implication that, in the informal, investigative, or bargaining stage of a grievance, a collective bargaining representative's duty to an employee it represents is analagous to that owed by an attorney to a client." The board concluded: "The nature of the relationship between a labor organization and an individual employee is more nearly that of a legislator to a constituent."

page 528, line 10. *Vaca v. Sipes,* 386 U.S. 171 (1967).

page 532, line 6. The Federal Mediation and Conciliation Service (FMCS) found that the average cost per case of arbitrators' fees and expenses in 1975 was $621.31. The cost of the arbitrator was estimated to be 15 to 20 per cent of the union's total cost in arbitration cases with $2,290 as "the total cost to the union in a simple case." This included arbitrator's fees, legal fees, court reporting fees, and lost-time payments for union officials and witnesses. John Zalusky, "Arbitration: Updating a Vital Process," *AFL-CIO American Federationist,* November 1976, p. 2. The same author encourages more efficient handling of grievances and sets forth in tabular form examples of procedures for expedited arbitration in effect in the United States. *Id.* at p. 4.

page 532, line 10. In *Electrical Workers, IBEW v. Foust,* the plaintiff had lost the opportunity to appeal a claim against his employer because the union had missed a time deadline by two days. In a suit by the plaintiff-member against the union alleging a breach of the duty of fair representation, the Supreme Court affirmed that part of a judgment for damages that had been assessed against the union to compensate the plaintiff for actual damages suffered. However, the Court reversed a jury verdict of $75,000 against the union for punitive damages. It held that punitive damages are not recoverable in a suit for breach of the duty of fair representation. "Such awards could deplete union treasuries, thereby impairing the effectiveness of unions as collective-bargaining agents," the Court said, adding that otherwise unions might "feel compelled to process frivolous claims or resist fair settlements." Four members of the Court concurred in the result but said the Court went too far in holding that a union could never be liable for punitive damages "no matter how egregious its breach may be." (*New York Times,* May 30, 1979.)

page 532, line 12. *Humphrey v. Moore,* 375 U.S. 335 (1964).

page 532, line 31. Benjamin Aaron et al., *The Future of Labor Arbitration in America* (AAA, 1976), page 6.

page 532, line 36. *Hines v. Anchor Motor Freight,* 424 U.S. 554 (1976).

page 535, line 18. A sympathetic account of the Supreme Court's decisions in this area of the law can be found in Clyde W. Summers, "The Individual Employee's Rights Under the Collective Agreement: What Constitutes Fair Representation?" 126 *University of Pennsylvania Law Review* 251 (1977).

page 535, line 28. For a vivid and complete account of the findings of the McClellan committee, see Robert Kennedy, *The Enemy Within* (New York: Harper & Bros., 1960).

page 538, line 27. *Salzhandler v. Caputo,* 316 F.2d 445 (2d Cir. 1963), cert. denied, 375 U.S. 946 (1963).

page 540, line 19. *Turner v. Machinists Lodge 1894, IAMAW,* 590 F.2d 409 (2d Cir. 1978).

page 541, line 13. *Hall v. Cole,* 412 U.S. 1 (1973).

page 541, line 35. *Calhoon v. Harvey,* 379 U.S. 134 (1964).

page 542, line 19. *Local 3489, United Steelworkers of America v. Usery,* 429 U.S. 305 (1977).

page 543, line 19. *Wirtz v. Hotel, Motel and Club Employees Union, Local 6,* 391 U.S. 492 (1968).

page 543, line 32. *Trbovich v. United Mine Workers,* 404 U.S. 528 (1972).

page 544, line 26. Otto Kahn-Freund, *Labour and the Law* (London: Stevens & Sons, 1977), p. 217.

page 544, line 34. *Id.* at p. 212.

page 545, line 17. *Id.* at p. 181.

CHAPTER XVII

page 549, line 19. A personal account of these events is found in the foreword by Norbert A. Schlei to Barbara L. Schlei and Paul Grossman, *Employment Discrimination Law* (Bureau of National Affairs (BNA), Washington, D.C., 1976), pp. vii–xiii.

page 549, line 31. *Espinoza v. Farah Mfg. Co.,* 414 U.S. 86 (1973).

page 549, line 34. The 14th amendment may prevent a state from limiting the employment of aliens. Thus, an attorney was found by the Supreme Court to have a constitutional right to take a bar examination and practice law, despite his being a resident alien. *In re Griffiths,* 413 U.S 717 (1973). However, the Court subsequently held that the state of New York could exclude aliens from its police force and from positions as public school teachers because these occupations are so bound up with the operation of the state as a governmental entity. *Foley v. Connelie,* 435 U.S. 291 (1978) (police); *Ambach v. Norwick,* 47 U.S. Law Week 4387 (No. 76–808, U.S. Supreme Court, April 19, 1979) (teachers). Of course, the 14th amendment does not reach acts of discrimination by private employers. *Civil Rights Cases,* 109 U.S. 3 (1883). The Supreme Court has also invalidated a state law that provided employment preference in the private sector for Alaska residents. *Hicklin v. Orbeck,* 57 L.Ed.2d 397 (1978).

page 550, line 26. *Griggs v. Duke Power Company,* 401 U.S. 424 (1971).

page 552, line 17. *Albermarle Paper Co. v. Moody,* 422 U.S. 405 (1975).

page 552, line 28. *Washington v. Davis,* 426 U.S. 229 (1976).

page 553, line 10. Barbara L. Schlei and Paul Grossman, *Employment Discrimination Law* (1976), p. 181. On Sept. 24, 1978, new EEOC guidelines became effective. Ms. Schlei has by letter to the authors reaffirmed the continuing accuracy of the quoted comments under the new guidelines.

page 554, line 3. *Hazlewood School District v. U.S.,* 97 S.Ct. 2736 (1977).

page 554, line 7. *Brooks v. Beto,* 366 F.2d 1, at 9 (5th Cir. 1966).

page 554, line 10. *Teamsters v. United States,* 431 U.S. 324, at 340 (1977).

page 554, line 15. See William F. Gardner, "Expert Witnesses in Employment Discrimination Cases," 5 *Litigation* 18 (American Bar Association, 1979). The author also suggests, as useful expert witnesses in Title VII litigation, labor economists "to testify about labor and work force availability and qualifications," industrial engineers "whenever there is a dispute about the functions performed in the jobs," and labor arbitrators "to give 'neutral' opinion testimony that the employee selected for the promotion was better qualified than the plaintiff. . . ." *Id.* at 20–23.

page 554, line 21. *McDonnell Douglas Corporation v. Green,* 411 U.S. 792 (1973).

page 556, line 8. *McDonald v. Sante Fe Trail Transportation Company,* 427 U.S. 273 (1976).

page 556, line 14. *Furnco Construction Co. v. Waters,* 98 S.Ct. 2943 (1978).

page 556, line 35. *Board of Trustees of Keene State College v. Christine M. Sweeney,* 99 S.Ct. 295 (1978).

page 557, line 9. The decision of the Supreme Court in *New York City Transit Authority v. Beazer,* 99 S.Ct. 1355 (1979), illustrates the way the Court in a given case may utilize both the *Griggs* (*supra,* p. 550) and the *McDonnell Douglas* (*supra,* p. 554) tests to determine if there had been a violation of Title VII. The *Beazer* case was a class action brought on behalf of former and prospective Transit Authority employees who were in a methadone maintenance program. The Authority had a general policy against employing persons who used narcotic drugs, including methadone. The plaintiffs showed that 81 per cent of the employees who were referred to the medical director of the Authority for suspected violations of its narcotics rule were either black or Hispanic. The Supreme Court, applying *Griggs,* held that a prima-facie statistical case of discrimination was rebutted by the Authority's showing that its narcotics rule was job-related. The Court further found no supportable

McDonnell Douglas case since the district court's "express finding that the rule was not motivated by racial animus forecloses any claim in rebuttal that it was merely a pretext for intentional discrimination. . . . We conclude that respondents failed to prove a violation of Title VII." *Id.* at 1366.

page 557, line 14. *Muller v. Oregon,* 208 U.S. 412 (1908).

page 559, line 7. *Albemarle Paper Co. v. Moody,* 422 U.S. 405 at 431 (1975).

page 559, line 10. *Dothard v. Rawlinson,* 433 U.S. 321 (1977).

page 561, line 19. *Quarles v. Philip Morris, Inc.,* 279 F.Supp. 505 (E.D. Va. 1968).

page 561, line 34. *Franks v. Bowman Transportation Company,* 424 U.S. 747 (1976).

page 563, line 22. *International Brotherhood of Teamsters and T.I.M.E.-D.C., Inc. v. United States,* 431 U.S. 324 (1977).

page 564, line 23. *Phillips v. Martin Marietta Co.,* 400 U.S. 542 (1971).

page 565, line 13. *General Electric Co. v. Gilbert,* 429 U.S. 125 (1976).

page 565, line 27. *Nashville Gas Co. v. Satty,* 98 S.Ct. 347 (1977).

page 566, line 19. *Cleveland Board of Education v. Jo Carol LaFleur, et al.,* 414 U.S. 632 (1974).

page 566, line 22. *City of Los Angeles Department of Water and Power v. Marie Manhart,* 98 S.Ct. 1370 (1978).

page 567, line 19. *TWA v. Hardison,* 432 U.S. 63 (1977).

page 569, line 20. The subsequent decision of the Supreme Court in *Parker Seal Company v. Cummins,* 97 S.Ct. 2965 (1977), appears to justify Justice Marshall's concerns. In *Cummins,* the complainant was a supervisor, and no collective bargaining agreement nor bona fide seniority system was involved. Notwithstanding, the Court reversed a decision favorable to Cummins (516 F.2d 544) and remanded the case to the Sixth Circuit Court of Appeals for reconsideration in light of *Hardison.* Where fellow workers are unwilling voluntarily to accommodate to the religious practices of an employee, Title VII as interpreted by the Court appears to afford no relief to the person whose religious practices are impinged upon by the work schedule.

page 569, line 33. *Albemarle Paper Company v. Moody,* 422 U.S. 405 (1975).

page 569, line 36. *Newman v. Piggie Park Enterprises,* 390 U.S. 400 (1968).

page 570, line 2. *Christianburg Garment Company v. EEOC,* 98 S.Ct. 694 (1978).

page 570, line 15. 42 U.S.C. §2000e-5(g).

page 570, line 23. *Westinghouse Electric Corp.,* 239 NLRB No. 19 (1978).

page 571, line 2. *Alexander v. Gardner-Denver Company,* 415 U.S. 36 (1974).

page 572, line 12. *Regents of the University of California v. Bakke,* 98 S.Ct. 2733 (1978). Subsequently in *United Steelworkers of America AFL-CIO-CLC v. Brian F. Weber et al.,* 20 FEP Cases 1 (1979), the Supreme Court upheld an affirmative action plan voluntarily negotiated between the union and Kaiser Aluminum as part of a bargaining agreement. It sought to promote the employment of black skilled tradesmen until the number of Negro craftsmen equaled the percentage of blacks in the respective local labor forces. Plaintiff Brian Weber, a white employee, claimed racial discrimination under Title 7 because he was passed over for selection in an apprenticeship-training program in favor of two black employees with less seniority. There had been no prior finding that Kaiser had discriminated against blacks. The Court, in a five-to-two decision, held that Title 7 does not "condemn all private, voluntary, race-conscious affirmative action plans" designed "to abolish traditional patterns of racial segregation and hierarchy." Justice Rehnquist and the Chief Justice dissenting, said that Title 7 "outlawed *all* racial discrimination" and "that no action disadvantaging a person because of his color is affirmative."

page 574, line 1. *Civil Rights Cases,* 109 U.S. 3 (1883).

page 574, line 10. *Brown v. Board of Education,* 347 U.S. 483 (1954).

page 574, line 11. *Jones v. Alfred H. Mayer Co.,* 392 U.S. 409 (1968).

page 574, line 13. Note, "The Expanding Scope of Section 1981: Assault on Private Discrimination and a Cloud on Affirmative Action," 90 *Harvard Law Review* 412 (1976).

page 574, line 16. *McDonald v. Sante Fe Trail Transportation Company,* 427 U.S. 273 (1976).

page 576, line 7. *Massachusetts Board of Retirement v. Murgia,* 427 U.S. 307 (1976).

page 577, line 10. *Lorillard v. Pons,* 98 S.Ct. 866 (1978).

page 577, line 30. *United Airlines v. McMann,* 98 S.Ct. 444 (1977).

page 578, line 21. Note, "The Age Discrimination in Employment Act of 1967," 90 *Harvard Law Review* 380, at 396 (1976).

page 578, line 31. *N.Y. Times,* April 16, 1978.

page 579, line 3. Sears, Roebuck and Co., "Employment Impact Statement, Increasing the Mandatory Retirement Age to 70" (1978).

page 579, line 8. The first bill in a state legislative body to ban mandatory retirement was filed the same year by another Illinois legislator, State Representative Alan J. Greiman, in the Illinois House of Representatives.

page 579, line 13. *Washington Post,* April 7, 1978.

page 579, line 15. In *Oscar Mayer & Co. v. Evans* (1979), the Supreme Court held that in states having laws prohibiting age discrimination in employment and establishing agencies to provide relief from such discriminatory practices, a plaintiff must first pursue the remedies provided under the state law before pursuing the remedies provided under the ADEA. No. 78–275, U.S. Supreme Court (decided May 21, 1979).

page 579, line 17. Irwin Ross, "Retirement at Seventy: A New Trauma for Management," *Fortune* (May 8, 1978), at p. 112.

page 579, line 23. Bureau of National Affairs (BNA), *Daily Labor Report,* Dec. 11, 1978.

page 579, line 24. In connection with this general subject, see "Symposium on Employment Rights of the Handicapped," 27 *DePaul Law Review* (Summer 1978).

page 580, line 35. HEW officials estimated that $400 million in capital investments would be required to meet the regulations, mostly at educational institutions. Another $2 billion a year will be needed to provide additional services for the handicapped pursuant to the regulations. Timothy B. Clark, "Access for the Handicapped: A Regulatory Dilemma," *National Journal* (October 21, 1978) 1672, at 1673. The HEW was itself the recipient of a citation for maintaining illegal barriers in its own office building. *N.Y. Times,* May 5, 1979. The agency had declined to build a new passenger elevator, estimated to cost $200,000, to provide access to the gymnasium and TV studios "to overcome the slight inconvenience of [employees] using a freight elevator." *Ibid.*

page 581, line 15. Michael Williams, "Confronting the D.C. Power," *The Independent* (Summer, 1977), p. 13.

page 581, line 31. Timothy B. Clark, "Access for the Handicapped: A Regulatory Dilemma," *National Journal* (October 21, 1978) 1672, at 1674.

page 582, line 4. *Id.* at 1672.

page 582, line 12. The Department of Transportation, in the face of strong opposition, on April 3, 1979 modified its regulations so as to limit the access requirement to "key" subway and commuter stations and provided a thirty-year period for refitting. The estimated cost for New York City of the new regulations was pared from $2 billion to $700 million. *N.Y. Times,* April 4, 1979.

page 582, line 16. See Clark, *supra,* at 1673.

CHAPTER XVIII

page 587, line 20. *United Steelworkers of America v. United States of America,* 361 U.S. 39 (1959).

page 588, line 1. *Ibid.*

page 588, line 20. *United States v. John L. Lewis and United Mine Workers of America,* 330 U.S. 258 (1947).

page 590, line 27. *Youngstown Sheet & Tube Co. v. Sawyer,* 343 U.S. 579 (1952).

page 593, line 2. *Amalgamated Association v. WERB,* 340 U.S. 383 (1951).

page 593, line 9. *Wolff Packing Co. v. Kansas Court of Industrial Relations,* 262 U.S. 522 (1923).

page 595, line 16. A current study of the 1977–78 coal strike suggests that "the recent coal strike was not a national emergency warranting federal intervention. The dispute failed to embrace all or substantially all of the affected industry, and a surprisingly high level of production was maintained throughout the strike." John A. Ackermann, The Impact of the Coal Strike of 1977–1978, 32 *Industrial and Labor Relations Review* 175, at 187 (1979). The strike continued for 91 days before the President invoked the Emergency Disputes Provision of the Taft-Hartley Act. The author endorsed the following excerpt from an article in the *New York Times* of March 8, 1978: "Some officials of Mr. Carter's administration as well as industry experts have been saying that it is still unclear how much of an adverse impact the coal strike is having on the nation. How then can the President invoke the national emergency clause if he cannot prove there is a national emergency? The answer is that under the law he does not have to prove it. . . . The President has [only] to convince the court that there will be a threat to the national health or safety at some indeterminate time in the future if the strike continues, not necessarily that there is an emergency at the time the injunction is sought." The temporary restraining order was obtained, but on the 102nd day, a federal district judge took the unusual step of refusing the government's request for an extension of the order. A settlement was reached and a new pact ratified one week later.

page 601, line 11. *N.Y. Times,* November 17, 1978.

page 601, line 14. The union was fined $600,000 by the court upon the conclusion of an unsuccessful sixteen-day strike. *N.Y. Times,* March 7, 1979.

page 603, line 30. *Abood v. Detroit Board of Education,* 431 U.S. 209 (1977).

page 604, line 20. *City of Madison, Joint School District No. 8 v. Wisconsin Employment Relations Commission,* 429 U.S. 167 (1976).

page 605, line 6. *Bessie B. Givhan v. Western Line Consolidated School District,* 47 *U.S. Law Week* 4102 (U.S. Sup. Ct., Jan. 9, 1979).

page 605, line 21. *Mt. Healthy City Board of Education v. Doyle,* 97 S.Ct. 568 (1977).

page 607, line 16. Curtis C. Sproul, "A Primer for Corporate and Union Political Action Committees," 24 *The Practical Lawyer* 39 (1978).

page 607, line 20. *United States v. CIO,* 335 U.S. 106 (1948).

page 608, line 12. *United States v. UAW-CIO*, 352 U.S. 567 (1957).

page 608, line 36. *Pipefitters Local Union No. 562 v. United States*, 407 U.S. 385 (1972).

page 609, line 9. *Railway Employees' Department v. Hanson*, 351 U.S. 225 (1956).

page 609, line 14. *International Association of Machinists v. Street*, 367 U.S. 740 (1961).

page 609, line 18. *Brotherhood of Railway & Steamship Clerks v. Allen*, 373 U.S. 113 (1963).

page 609, line 27. *Abood v. Detroit Board of Education*, 431 U.S. 209 (1977).

page 610, line 3. *Eastex Inc. v. NLRB*, 98 S.Ct. 2505 (1978).

page 611, line 4. Robert W. Merry, "Firms' Action Groups Are Seen Transforming The Country's Politics," *Wall Street Journal*, September 11, 1978.

page 613, line 24. *United Auto Workers, International Union, AFL v. Wisconsin ERB* [*Briggs-Stratton*], 336 U.S. 245 (1949).

page 614, line 7. *Lodge 76, International Association of Machinists and Aerospace Workers, AFL-CIO v. Wisconsin Employment Relations Commission*, 427 U.S. 132 (1976).

page 614, line 30. *Garner v. Teamsters Union Local 776*, 346 U.S. 485 (1953).

page 615, line 15. *San Diego Building Trades Council v. Garmon*, 359 U.S. 236 (1959).

page 616, line 2. In *New York Telephone Co. v. New York State Dept. of Labor*, 99 S.Ct. 1328 (1979), the Supreme Court found that federal labor policy does not preempt a New York law providing for payment of unemployment compensation to strikers. This result is not surprising since unemployment compensation and workmen's compensation have generally not been viewed as being part of American labor law.

page 616, line 3. *Farmer v. Carpenters Local 25*, 430 U.S. 290 (1977).

page 616, line 11. *Sears, Roebuck and Co. v. San Diego District Council of Carpenters*, 98 S.Ct. 1745 (1978).

page 618, line 30. The board found a way to itself "identify the relevant considerations and give each the proper weight in accommodating the respective rights" in *Giant Food Markets*, 241 NLRB No. 105 (1979). There the board, carrying out its function to properly accommodate Section 7 and private property rights (*supra*, p. 450), held that area standards picketing by a union in a shopping center constituted protected concerted activity under Section 7 of the Act. Thus, "a demand made by an owner or leaseholder of the property that pickets remove themselves from that property is a sufficient interference with the exercise of protected activity to come within the ambit of Section 8(a)(1) of the Act." The *Giant Food* decision would appear to relegate a state's right under *Sears* to apply its trespass law to preclude peaceful picketing in a shopping center only to a shopping-center labor dispute not within the board's jurisdictional standards.

page 618, line 34. *Construction and General Laborers, Local No 438 v. Curry*, 371 U.S. 542 (1963).

page 620, line 16. *Hammer v. Dagenhart*, 247 U.S. 251 (1918).

page 620, line 18. *United States v. Darby*, 312 U.S. 100 (1941).

page 620, line 34. *United States v. Rosenwasser*, 323 U.S. 360 (1945).

page 621, line 6. *Maryland v. Wirtz*, 392 U.S. 183 (1961).

page 621, line 15. *National League of Cities v. Usery*, 426 U.S. 833 (1976).

page 624, line 17. See "Symposium: The Developing Law of Occupational Safety and Health," 9 *Gonzaga Law Review* (Winter 1974).

page 624, line 28. *Atlas Roofing Company v. Occupational Safety and Health Review Commission*, 430 U.S. 442 (1977).

page 626, line 19. *Marshall v. Barlow's, Inc.*, 429 U.S. 1347 (1978).

page 628, line 23. *Chicago Sun-Times*, December 19, 1978.

page 628, line 26. *Chicago Sun-Times*, November 11, 1978.

page 629, line 6. *Inland Steel Co. v. NLRB*, 170 F.2d 247 (7th Cir. 1948).

page 630, line 2. Employee Retirement Income Security Act, 1976 Report to Congress, p. 9.

page 630, line 5. See Ira M. Shepard, "A Compliance Guide to 'Prudence' Under ERISA," *Journal of Pension Planning and Compliance* (July 1977), p. 259.

page 633, line 11. Source: Letter from Carin Ann Clauss, Solicitor of Labor, to the authors, dated August 31, 1978.

page 634, line 29. Daniel, a truck driver, enlisted the aid of an imaginative attorney who sought to bridge this egregious pre-ERISA gap in the law by claiming that the antifraud provisions of Section 10(*b*) of the Securities and Exchange Act of 1934 required that he be paid a full pension based on fraudulent nondisclosure and withholding of material facts. In the ensuing case, *International Brotherhood of Teamsters, Chauffeurs, Warehousemen and Helpers of America, et al. v. Daniel*, 99 S.Ct. 790 (1979), the Supreme Court held that the Securities Acts do not apply to noncontributory, compulsory pension plans such as the one Daniel participated in.

page 636, line 34. *Harvard College v. Amory*, 9 Pick. 446 (1830).

page 638, line 18. See Michael J. Casey, "ERISA—The Exclusions and Limitations of Its Protection," 3 *Employee Benefits Journal* 8 (1978).

page 638, line 35. Job tenure of American workers declined from an average of 3.9 years in 1973 to 3.6 years in 1978, the U.S. Department of

Labor has reported. *Wall Street Journal,* May 1, 1979. Men averaged 4.5 years on the job, while women averaged about 2 years.

page 640, line 8. Ray Schmitt, "Private Pension Reform Issue Brief No. 1B77076," Library of Congress (June 22, 1978), p. 3.

page 640, line 18. Shirley Scheibla, "Revamping ERISA," *Barrons* (May 1, 1978), p. 4.

page 640, line 29. *Ibid.*

page 640, line 34. *Ibid.*

page 641, line 34. Bureau of National Affairs (BNA), *Daily Labor Report* (July 12, 1978), Executive Order 12701 and White House Statement.

page 642, line 2. *Christian Science Monitor,* December 18, 1978.

CHAPTER XIX

page 646, line 17. *AFL-CIO News,* Nov. 4, 1978.

TABLE OF CASES

FEDERAL LABOR-RELATED STATUTES
WITH POPULAR NAMES

YEAR OF PASSAGE	STATUTE	ALSO KNOWN AS	PAGES IN THIS VOLUME
1866	Civil Rights Act of 1866	Section 1981	573–75
1870	Civil Rights Act of 1870 [*42 U.S.C. §1981*]	Section 1981	
1890	Sherman Act	Antitrust Act	200–22, 253–
1914	Clayton Act [*15 U.S.C. §1*]	Antitrust Act	88, 470–74
1932	Norris-LaGuardia Act [*29 U.S.C. §101*]	Anti-Injunction Act	184–99, 494–502
1935	National Labor Relations Act [*29 U.S.C. §151*]	NLRA Wagner Act	341–442
1938	Fair Labor Standards Act of 1938 [*29 U.S.C. §201*]	FLSA Wage-Hour Act	620–24
1947	Labor Management Relations Act, 1947 [*29 U.S.C. §141*]	LMRA Taft-Hartley Act	409, 415–74 484–505
1959	Labor-Management Reporting and Disclosure Act of 1959 [*29 U.S.C. §153*]	LMRDA Landrum-Griffin Act	535–45
1964	Civil Rights Act of 1964 [*42 U.S.C. §2000e*]	Title VII	546–73
1967	Age Discrimination in Employment Act of 1967 [*29 U.S.C. §621*]	ADEA	575–79
1970	Occupational Safety and Health Act of 1970 [*29 U.S.C. §651*]	OSHA	624–28
1974	Employment Retirement Income Security Act of 1974 [*29 U.S.C. §441*]	Pension Reform Act ERISA	628–42

INDEX

(For specific cases see the Table of Cases, pp. 691–99.)